Readings in
Advertising, Society, and
Consumer Culture

Readings in Advertising, Society, and Consumer Culture

Roxanne Hovland
Joyce Wolburg
Eric Haley

Editors

Foreword by Ron Taylor

M.E.Sharpe
Armonk, New York
London, England

Library of Congress Cataloging-in-Publication Data

Readings in advertising, society, and consumer culture / edited by Roxanne Hovland, Joyce M. Wolburg, and
Eric Haley.
   p. cm.
   Includes bibliographical references and index.
   ISBN 978-0-7656-1544-2 (cloth : alk. paper)
   1. Advertising—Social aspects—United States. 2. Consumption (Economics)—Social aspects—United States.
I. Hovland, Roxanne. II. Wolburg, Joyce M. III. Haley, Eric.

HF5813.U6R36 2007
306.3′4--dc22   2006038940

Printed in the United States of America

The paper used in this publication meets the minimum requirements of
American National Standard for Information Sciences
Permanence of Paper for Printed Library Materials,
ANSI Z 39.48-1984.

∞

BM (c)   10   9   8   7   6   5   4   3   2   1

Dedication

To Ron Taylor. Teacher, scholar, friend.

Roxanne Hovland, Joyce Wolburg, and Eric Haley

The authors gratefully acknowledge the support (financial and otherwise) given to them by
The University of Tennessee School of Advertising and Public Relations,
The University of Tennessee EPPE fund, and
J. William and Mary Diederich College of Communication at Marquette University.

CONTENTS

FOREWORD

The United States is a world power in advertising. It accounts for more than half of worldwide advertising expenditures. American ideas about advertising often influence how people in other countries think about advertising as well as how it is planned and carried out. When students anywhere in the world want to study advertising, they set their sights on a university in the United States, one of the few countries where one can study advertising thought within the university setting.

One of the tremendous advantages of an American-style university education is that it affords the opportunity to learn the practice of advertising while questioning those very practices that one is learning. Therein exists the need for texts such as this one that introduce a wide range of thought and philosophy about the institution of advertising.

Why is the United States such a powerful force in the way in which people think about and do advertising worldwide? Part of the answer lies within the set of beliefs and values that formed our culture and provided a springboard for advertising more than 200 years ago. Becoming acquainted with these thoughts and values may not make you like advertising more, but it will help you to understand why present-day advertising is the way that it is. Understanding the past is prelude to understanding the present and the future. Examine the ideas presented in Part 1 and draw your own conclusions about the development of advertising.

Advertising interrupts our entertainment and intrudes into our daily lives. It is so ever-present that communication media without advertising have become the exception rather than the norm. Witness the recent upsurge in advertising delivered via Internet and by cell phone. Yet not everyone is a fan of advertising and certainly not everyone is a fan of American-style advertising.

Why do we allow advertising to run with such abandon in our culture? And despite its enormous size and ubiquitous nature, why is so little known about the effects of advertising on individuals as well as on the culture overall?

Advertising is ripe with controversy and contradiction. It enjoys relatively free rein in our culture; yet it is one of our most regulated forms of speech, and American advertising is among the most regulated in the world. A basic difference is that other countries often regulate for issues of taste and culture whereas the American system regulates almost solely on the issue of truthfulness.

I was having a conversation about the merits of regulation and prior restraint with an advertising practitioner in Paris several years ago when he commented, "Oh, yes, your First Amendment would get in the way." And so it does, but the First Amendment also gets in the way of many other cherished freedoms such as speech, religion, and assembly. Thus, advertising has to be considered and evaluated within the cultural context in which it appears and not as though it were an independent, free standing phenomenon.

Readings assembled in Parts 2 and 3 of this volume will take you on a journey to explore regulatory issues and others related to advertising such as the effects of advertising on consumer choice, on levels of competition, and on the media.

Advertising is very much a cultural product. What appears to work in one culture may not work at all in another. But even though advertising is a product of culture, does it also somehow contribute to the advancement of the very ideas that nurture it or even yet to the advancement of certain ideas and values at the expense of others? The readings in Part 4 invite you to consider the complex intertwining between advertising and consumer culture.

Part 5 provides a guide to many sources that will help you to locate additional information about advertising, about those who regulate it, about those who advocate for it, and about those who would temper its presence and influence.

Readers who aspire to a career in advertising will find little here that will help to find a job. You will, however, find a wealth of ideas and thought about advertising that will make you a much better advertising practitioner. Whether you seek to control, to practice, to weaken, to change, to criticize, or simply to understand why advertising is the way it is, the readings ahead will illuminate your path. Make what you will of advertising, and enjoy the intellectual journey.

Ron Taylor
Professor and Director, School of Advertising and Public Relations
University of Tennessee, Knoxville

INTRODUCTION

Several enduring controversies exist regarding the impact of advertising on individuals and society. Much has been written on the nature and effects of advertising, particularly related to specific audiences—children, women, minorities—and so-called vulnerable audiences, such as older consumers, the infirm, or people who are less educated. Collectively, these audiences might be referred to as the disenfranchised. However, to really understand these issues (and others), the study of advertising requires a broader context.

The study of advertising must be approached in the context of the historical, economic, and ideological factors that spawned the development of a consumer culture that, in turn, led to the growth of advertising. What, exactly, is consumer culture? While it might be defined in various ways, in this book it is defined as a society in which: (1) there is a surplus of goods typical of postindustrial economies; (2) society revolves around consumption; (3) commerce and culture are inseparable; (4) objects take on great significance beyond their original purpose; (5) continuous consumption is critical to the comfort and status of the individual and to the health of the economy; and (6) there is a tendency for everything (including intangibles) to be commodified.

Justification for this definition is plentiful. Kammen argues that consumer culture arrives when "commerce and culture [can] no longer be tidily compartmentalized" and it is widely believed to date from the 1920s.[1] Similarly, Jhally points to the existence of consumer culture when "consumption is the mode of living of modern culture."[2]

One of the most obvious prerequisites for consumer culture is a surplus of goods produced. Before a consumption-intensive society can develop, mass production and distribution must result in goods that exceed demand. This condition is unknown in preindustrial societies, where consumers only produce goods as they are needed.

Any book of readings is, by definition, incomplete. Presentation of an infinite number of articles is not possible. Those offered here are not intended to represent a comprehensive compendium of what has been written on advertising and consumer culture; nor is it even supposed to constitute a representative sample of this literature. Rather, it is intended as an interesting collection of work that, ideally, will stimulate the reader to seek more.

Notes

1. Michael G. Kammen, *American Culture, American Tastes: Social Change and the 20th Century* (New York: Alfred A. Knopf, 1999), p. 53.

2. Sut Jhally, *The Codes of Advertising: Fetishism and the Political Economy of Meaning* (New York: Routledge, 1990), p. 196.

PART 1

ADVERTISING AND CONSUMER CULTURE
Institutional and Historical Perspectives

Part 1 presents ideas that help readers examine the role of advertising within the larger context of the consumer culture that has allowed it to flourish. To appreciate the role of advertising in consumer culture at its broadest level, and the social and economic realities of consumer culture, many scholars have adopted an institutional perspective. This broad view places the focus on advertising in its most general sense. Attention falls not necessarily on individual ads or specific advertising campaigns or advertisers, but on general trends involving advertisers and consumers, as well as on the economic and historical events that led to their evolution.

The first reading in Part 1, by Hamilton, provides a general definition of an institution, followed by classic readings concerning the institution of advertising. These readings—by Rotzoll, Haefner, and Hall; Carey; Potter; and Norris—examine advertising in relation to the foundational principles of U.S. society, by showing how these foundational principles have been used to "defend" advertising from various criticisms. These articles also discuss that when advertising is criticized, it is often an indictment of the fundamental values (such as concerns about the rights of the individual versus the power of government) that provide the ideological basis for advertising. The last few articles in Part 1 discuss the history, formation, and implications of consumer culture. The hallmarks of consumer culture are traced to the beginnings of the industrial revolution through the present day in the article by Schudson. Based on Gerbner's theory of cultivation, the section closes with Harmon's astute look at the power of consumer culture and advertising to continue growing through cultivation and self-affirmation.

Ideally, the readings in Part 1 provide an intellectual and theoretical perspective through which issues in subsequent chapters can be interpreted. The classic and current articles in Part 1 should equip the reader to examine the numerous controversies presented in this book and the limitless issues constantly revolving around advertising and consumer culture.

CHAPTER 1

THE ENCYCLOPAEDIA OF
THE SOCIAL SCIENCES

WALTER H. HAMILTON

INSTITUTION is a verbal symbol which for want of a better describes a cluster of social usages. It connotes a way of thought or action of some prevalence and permanence, which is embedded in the habits of a group or the customs of a people. In ordinary speech it is another word for procedure, convention or arrangement; in the language of books it is the singular of which the mores or the folkways are the plural. Institutions fix the confines of and impose form upon the activities of human beings. The world of use and wont, to which imperfectly we accommodate our lives, is a tangled and unbroken web of institutions.

The range of institutions is as wide as the interests of mankind. Any simple thing we observe—a coin, a time table, a canceled check, a baseball score, a phonograph record—has little significance in itself; the meaning it imparts comes from the ideas, values and habits established about it. Any informal body of usage—the common law, athletics, the higher learning, literary criticism, the moral code—is an institution in that it lends sanctions, imposes tabus and lords it over some human concern. Any formal organization—the government, the church, the university, the corporation, the trade union—imposes commands, assesses penalties and exercises authority over its members. Arrangements as diverse as the money economy, classical education, the chain store, fundamentalism and democracy are institutions. They may be rigid or flexible in their structures, exacting or lenient in their demands; but alike they constitute standards of conformity from which an individual may depart only at his peril. About every urge of mankind an institution grows up; the expression of every taste and capacity is crowded into an institutional mold.

Our culture is a synthesis—or at least an aggregation—of institutions, each of which has its own domain and its distinctive office. The function of each is to set a pattern of behavior and to fix a zone of tolerance for an activity or a complement of activities. Etiquette decrees the rituals which must be observed in all polite intercourse. Education provides the civilizing exposures through which the potential capacities of individuals are developed into the abilities for performance, appreciation and enjoyment which are personality. Marriage gives propriety to the sex union, bestows regularity upon procreation, establishes the structure of the family and effects such a mediation as may be between personal ambition and social stability. A number of institutions may combine

---

From Edwin R.A. Seligman, editor-in-chief, *The Encyclopaedia of the Social Sciences,* 8 (New York, NY: The Macmillan Company, 1932): 84–89.

and compete to impress character upon and give direction to the mass of human endeavor. The state claims primary obedience and imposes a crude order upon the doings of mankind; the law by punishing offenses and settling disputes determines the outmost limits of acceptable actions; morality with neater distinctions and more meticulous standards distinguishes respectable from unconventional conduct. The community is made up of such overlapping provinces of social government. It is the institution in its role of organizer which makes of this a social and not a monadic world.

It is impossible to discover for such an organic complex of usages as an institution a legitimate origin. Its nucleus may lie in an accidental, an arbitrary or a conscious action. A man—savage or civilized—strikes a spark from flint, upturns the sod, makes an image of mud, brews a concoction, mumbles a rigmarole, decides a quarrel or helps himself to what he may require. The act is repeated, then multiplied; ideas, formulae, sanctions and habits from the impinging culture get attached; and gradually there develops a ritual of fire, a hoe and spade agronomy, a ceremonial for appeasing the gods, a cult of healing, a spell for casting out devils, a due process of law or a sound business policy. Even if it is deliberately established an institution has neither a definite beginning nor an uncompromised identity. A religious creed or a legislative statute is compounded of beliefs and ideas which bear the mark of age and of wear; a paper charter and a document engrossed upon parchment are not insulated against the novelties in usage which attend the going corporation and the living constitution. It is impossible even in the most rudimentary culture to find folkways which are simple and direct answers to social necessities. In all societies, however forward or backward, the roots of the most elementary of arrangements—barter, burial, worship, the dietary, the work life, the sex union—run far back into the unknown past and embody the knowledge and ignorance, the hopes and fears, of a people.

In fact as an aspect of a continuous social process an institution has no origin apart from its development. It emerges from the impact of novel circumstances upon ancient custom; it is transformed into a different group of usages by cultural change. In institutional growth the usual may give way to the unusual so gradually as to be almost unnoticed. At any moment the familiar seems the obvious; the unfamiliar appears but a little revealed—an implication in a convention which is itself taken for granted, a potentiality slowly quickening into life. So it is that the corporation is still a person, the work of the machine is manufacture, the labor contract concerns masters and servants and industrial accidents are personal wrongs. It often happens that new arrangements spring up under the cloak of an established organization. Thus the empire of the Caesars emerged behind the forms of the republic, the holy Catholic church is nominally the episcopal see of Rome and the British Commonwealth does its business in the name of His Majesty. In like manner in the domain of ideas the novelty in doctrine usually appears as a gloss upon the ancient text; systems of theology are commentaries upon the words of Scripture; Coke and Cooley set down their own understanding of the law upon the authority of Littleton and Blackstone. Thus too so intangible a thing as a social theory or a public policy may emerge from the practical commitments of the moment. A mere expediency, such as the abolition of the corn laws, is abstracted from cause and occasion and becomes a generalized policy of free trade; or a comprehensive scheme of railway regulation, such as obtains in the United States, appears as a by-product of the empirical elimination of specific abuses. In the course of events the fact arrives before the word and new wine must be put up in old bottles. Novelties win a tacit acceptance before their strangeness is noticed and compel before their actuality is appreciated. In institutional life current realities are usually to be found behind ancient forms.

As an institution develops within a culture it responds to changes in prevailing sense and reason. A history of the interpretation of Aristotle or St. Paul or Kant at various periods indicates how easily a document lends itself to successive systems of ideas. The public regulation of business has consistently even if belatedly reflected the prevailing winds of doctrine upon the relation of the state to industry. The pages of the law reports reveal the ingenuity with which, in spite of professions that the law remains the same, old rules and standards are remade to serve changing notions of social necessity. An institution which has enjoyed long life has managed to make itself at home in many systems of thought. The classic example is the Christian Gospel. The simple story of the man Jesus presently became a body of Pauline philosophy; the Middle Ages converted it into an intricate theological system and the rationalization of a powerful ecclesiastical empire; at the individualistic touch of the Reformation it became a doctrine of the personal relationship between man and his maker; it is today patching up a truce with Darwinism, the scientific attitude, relativity and even religious skepticism. In this continuous process of the adaptation of usage and arrangement to intellectual environment an active role is assumed by that body of ideas taken for granted which is called common sense. Because it determines the climate of opinion within which all others must live, it is the dominant institution in a society.

In an even broader way an institution is accommodated to the folkways of a culture. As circumstances impel and changing ideas permit, a usage in high esteem, like piracy, may fall from grace; while another under tabu, such as birth control, may first win tolerance and in time general acceptance. As one social system passes into another and the manner of living and the values of life are transformed, one institution gives way to another better adapted to the times. It required a number of changes in use and wont to convert the ordeal by combat into the trial by law; the prestige of the family tie, of blood vengeance, of the magical ritual and of might made right had to decline and a consciousness of the waste and injustice which attended legalized conflict had to become prevalent. An institution that survives, such as matrimony, responds surely even if stubbornly to cultural change. While the basis of Christian marriage is no more than the primitive custom of monogamy, the rigid lines of the institution bear the marks of the mediaeval order. It gave support to a caste system resting upon landed property, elevated the social values of family above the individual values of love, was blessed with the ascetic ideal of otherworldliness and became a sacrament. Companionate marriage is emerging from a different world of fact, appreciation, habit and belief. It reduces to usage an attempt to escape the rigors of matrimony without resort to casual relationships; it reflects the condition of an urban society where blood is no longer blue, life is impersonal, children are a luxury and women must earn their own livings. In a culture which develops slowly enough to allow a graceful accommodation folkways may be drawn together into rich and intricate institutional patterns. In the Middle Ages the usages of the church—the trinity, the creed, the litany, the ecclesiastical empire—were all fused into a single conventional whole, to which unity was given by the idea of the death of the god as a vicarious atonement. In the late eighteenth century politics, law, economics, ethics and theology in separate domains alike attempted to superimpose a symmetrical system of mechanical principles upon the mass of human behavior; the common element was an analogue borrowed from physical science. In the social process the life of an institution depends upon its capacity for adaptation. But always amid the whirl of change elements of disorder are present; and long before a harmony is achieved between unlike conventions disintegration has set in.

Nor is an institution introduced from an alien society immune to this process of development. The act of borrowing merely gives the opportunity for its transformation. The nucleus is liberated from its cultural matrix and takes on the character of the usages among which it is set down. In their native habitat the books of the Old Testament were the literature of a people; in the strange world of the mediaeval schoolmen they became a collection of verses inviting dialectical exposition.

In England "the higher law" was invoked to justify a popular revolution against an irresponsible monarchy; in America it has become the sanction for a judicial review of legislative acts. In appropriating the machine process Russia stripped away the enveloping business arrangements and made of it an instrument to serve a national social economy. The act of transplantation may at first retard but eventually is likely to promote growth. It introduces into a culture an unknown usage but allows it to emerge as an indigenous institution.

Its very flexibility makes an institution a creature of social stress and strain. In a stable or slowly changing society it fits rather neatly into the cultural pattern; amid the disorder which change brings its office may be compromised by the inflexibility of its structure. As necessity changes, tradition and inertia may stand in the way of the performance of new duties. A group of usages, for all the new demands upon it, may never quite escape slavery to its past. The shadow of ordeal by combat still hangs heavy over trial by law; the jury decides the contest, the judge is the umpire, the procedures are the rules of the game, the witnesses are clansmen armed with oaths and the attorneys are the champions; an appeal court orders a new trial not primarily for want of justice but because of error in the conduct of the ordeal. The United States Supreme Court has come to be the official interpreter of the constitution; yet by tradition its function is judicial, and it is only as an issue is germane to the disposition of a case that it can declare the meaning of the higher law. Almost every institution—from the superfluous buttons on the sleeve of a coat to the ceremonial electors in a presidential contest—bears the vestigial mark of a usage which is gone.

But its elements of stability may be powerless to prevent the conversion of an institution to a service for which it was never intended. Its existence and repute give it value; it may adventitiously or by design assume a new character and play a new role in the social order. Equity, once an informal method of doing justice, now possesses all the appurtenances of a system of law. The principle of "no liability without fault" was once the basis of an individualistic law of torts; in our times the rules of recovery are being socialized, as, for example, in workmen's compensation, by a mere extension of "fault" to acts involving no personal blame. An institution may even fall into the hands of the enemy and be used to defeat its reputed purpose. Thus a community of ascetics develops into a wealthy monastic establishment; a theory of social contract invented as a justification of monarchy is converted into a sanction for its overthrow; a party dedicated to personal freedom becomes the champion of vested wealth; and a philosophy contrived to liberate thought remains to enslave it. As time and chance present their problems, men meet them with expediencies as best they can; but those who contrive rules and formulae cannot control the uses to which they are put. The proneness of an institution, like a lost sheep, to go astray, has been caught in the sentence: "Saint Francis of Assisi set out to bring people to sweetness and light, and left in his wake a plague of gray friars." The folkways are marked by a disposition of event to belic intent.

In the course of time the function of an institution may be compromised by or perhaps even be lost in its establishment. The spirit may become the letter, and the vision may be lost in a ritual of conformity. In time a way of intellectual inquiry may become a mere keeping of the faith; a nice propriety in social relations may decay into a code of etiquette; or a morality intended to point the way toward the good life may come to impose the duty of doing right. Thus ceremonial replaces purposive action and claims a vicarious obedience. The existence of an informal institution gets buttressed about by prevailing opinion and by personal interest. In legislative "deliberation" statesmen cherish their stock in trade of time honored argument and resent the appearance of unfamiliar issues; scholars of repute defend the established ways of inquiry and the accepted verities; and social lights conserving the older proprieties against feminism "entrench themselves behind their tea-cups and defend their frontiers to the last calling-card." The persons immediately concerned have their stakes in arrangements as they are and do not wish to have personal position, comfort of mind or social prestige disturbed. As it crystallizes into reputable usages an institution creates in its defense vested interest, vested habit and vested ideas and claims allegiance in its own right.

If an institution becomes formal, an even greater hazard to its integrity is to be found in its organization and its personnel. A need for order finds expression in a government or the demand for justice in a legal system or the desire for worship in a church; and various groups become interested in its structure and offices, its procedures and emoluments, its ceremonials and consolations. A host of officials great and small comes into being, who are as solicitous about the maintenance of the establishment to which they are committed. They possess preferences and prejudices, are not immune to considerations of prestige and place and are able to rationalize their own interests. As the scheme of arrangements grows rigid, "the good of the nation"—or the church or the party or the lodge or whatever it is—tends to become dominant. The lines of activity may be frozen into rigidity and ecclesiasticism, legalism, constitutionalism and ritualism remain as fetishes to be served. An institution when once accepted represents the answer to a social problem. In the maze of advantage, accommodation, sense and reason which grows up about it lies a barrier to the consideration of alternatives. Its successor for better or for worse is likely to prevail only through revolution or by stealth.

In its ideal likeness an institution usually creates its apology. As long as it remains vital, men accommodate their actions to its detailed arrangements with little bother about its inherent nature or cosmic purpose. As it begins to give way or is seriously challenged, compelling arguments for its existence are set forth. The picture-as-it-is-painted is likely to be rather a work of art than a representation of fact, a product rather of rationalization than of reason; and, however adventitious its growth, disorderly its structure or confused its function, the lines of its defense lack nothing of trimness and purpose. The feudal regime was an empirical sort of an affair; men of iron lorded it over underlings as they could, yielded to their betters as they were compelled and maintained such law and order as the times allowed; but with its passing its sprawling arrangements and befuddled functions were turned into office and estate ordained of God. In the days of the Tudors kings were kings without any dialectical to-do about it; the overneat statement of the theory of divine right had to await the decadent monarchy of the Stuarts. The tangled thing called capitalism was never created by design or cut to a blue print; but now that it is here, contemporary schoolmen have intellectualized it into a purposive and self-regulating instrument of general welfare. If it is to be replaced by a "functional society," the new order will emerge blunderingly enough; but acquisition of a clean cut structure and clearly defined purpose will have to wait upon its rationalizers. An assumption of uniformity underlies all apologies; invariably they impose simple, abstract names, such as monarchy, democracy, competition and socialism, upon a mass of divergent arrangements.

In this endowment with neatness and purpose an institution is fitted out with the sanctions and trappings of ancient usage. Republican government harks back to Greece and Rome; the "liberties" for which seventeenth century Englishmen fought were the ancient rights of man. Magna Carta, a feudal document, was remade to serve the cause of Parliament against king; a primitive folk government was discovered in the dim twilight of the German forests to give to English democracy a fountainhead which was neither French nor American; and "the spirit of '76" grew up long after the event to serve the patriotism of another century. In the courts it is a poor rule which cannot find a good reason in former decisions and fit itself out with an ancient lineage. But law does not invoke the sanction of precedent more often than other institutions; the openness of its written records merely makes more evident the essential process. A succession of usages stretching from Aristotle to Calhoun has been justified as expressions of the natural order. Even—or above all—in the church the prevailing dogma is set down as interpretations of the creed of the apostles; and Christian marriage "was instituted by God in the time of man's innocency." As tradition leaves its impress upon fact, fact helps to remake tradition. The thing that is is the thing that always was.

It is only as stability gives way to change that the lines of an institution stand out in sharp relief. So long as a people is able to do as its fathers did it manifests little curiosity about the arrangements under which it lives and works; the folk of the South Sea Islands can administer justice after their ways, but they can neither give answers to hypothetical cases nor tell in abstract terms what they do. So long as the procedure of a group or a school is unquestioned it is little aware of the conventions and values which give character even to outstanding achievement: Scott had little conscious appreciation of the distinctive qualities of the English novel; Jowett could never have put in terms the peculiar features of Oxford education; and Kant might not have been able to place his own philosophy in time and opinion. But the break of usage from usage within a culture and the resulting maladjustment lead to a discovery of the detail which makes up an institution. A number of crises were required to reveal the customs which are the British constitution; it took a Civil War to make clear the nature of the union between the American states. The appearance of social unrest was essential to an appreciation of the difference between competition and laissez faire and between industry and business. An aesthetic revolt marked by a riding into almost all the winds that blow was requisite to a realization of the distinctive modes and values in classical music and in Gothic architecture and to an appreciation of the molds imposed by acceptable form upon creative effort. For such casual glimpses of the intricacies of social institutions as men are permitted to see they are indebted to the stress and strain of transition.

It follows almost of course that institutional development drives a fault line between current fact and prevailing opinion. Men see with their ideas as well as with their eyes and crowd the novel life about them into outmoded concepts. They meet events with the wisdom they already possess, and that wisdom belongs to the past and is a product of a by-gone experience. As new institutions gradually emerge from the old, men persist in dealing with the unfamiliar as if it were the familiar. A national legislature by the enactment of antitrust laws tries to superimpose the competitive pattern upon the turbulent forces of a rising industrialism; a trade union uses the traditional device of a strike to advance wages in an industry in which the unorganized plants can easily supply the total output; a group of elder statesmen approaches the problems of war debts and reparations with the old formula of protection versus free trade. At a time when a depression bears witness to economic disorder the institution of business is discussed in the outgrown vocabulary of private property, liberty of contract, equality of opportunity and free enterprise; and rugged American individualism is invoked as a way of order for a system which has somehow become an uncontrolled and unacknowledged collectivism. Even the Protestants as often as not turn belief into denial; and heresy shackled to an inherited ideology is merely a reverse orthodoxy. In the flux of modern life the various usages which with their conflicting values converge upon the individual create difficult problems that demand judgment; and in the course of very human events it is the fate alike of individual, group and society to have to meet emerging fact with obsolescing idea.

Thus an institution like the living thing it is has a tangled identity. It cannot be shown in perspective or revealed in detail by the logical method of inclusion and exclusion. It holds within its actuality the vestiges of design and accident, the stuff of idea and custom, from many ages, societies, civilizations and climates of opinion. In any important group of institutions, such as marriage, property, the market or the law, there are to be discovered as inseparable aspects of an organic whole notions, procedures, sanctions and values hailing from cultural points far apart. Each holds within its being elements in idea and in form drawn from the contemporary era of relativity, the rational universe of the eighteenth century, the mediaeval world of absolutes and verities and the folkways of some dim far off era. An institution is an aspect of all that it has met, a potential part of all that it will encounter. It holds many unknown possibilities which a suitable occasion may kindle into life. It may continue to hold sanctions which we think have departed; it may already have come to possess compulsions of which we are still unmindful. The discovery of its meaning demands an inquiry into its life history; but even the genetic method will tell much less than we should like to know of how a thing which cannot for long abide came to be.

Moreover the way of knowledge is itself an institution. The physical world, natural resources and human nature may be elementary things; but we can learn about them only in terms of and to the extent allowed by our prevailing methods of inquiry. The little we understand of the universe is a function of the size of the telescope, the sensitiveness of the photographic plate and the bundle of intellectual usages called astronomy. Our national resources are a product of technology, and their catalogues at different times reflect the contemporary states of the industrial arts. It was the steam engine and the machine which made of coal and iron potential wealth; it was not until Faraday and Edison had done their work that electricity became potential energy. The little we understand or think we understand about human nature is an institutional product. The inquiries called physiology, anatomy and neurology—each of them a bundle of intellectual usages—reveal no more than the raw material of personal character; the stuff has ripened into individuality within the matrix of the prevailing folkways. Man and woman are so much creatures of custom and belief that the word innate is most treacherously applied to masculine and feminine traits. In various societies the stages upon which peoples must play their parts are set so differently by social heritage that we can as yet speak with little certainty about racial characteristics. The physical world and the human nature we know are aspects of the prevailing state of culture. In matter and in the chromosome may lie limitless possibilities; the actualities which appear are creatures of social institutions.

Among the ways of knowing is "the institutional approach." Institutes as the ordained principles of a realm of learning or of life have long existed; they are known to theology, law, education and all subjects ruled over by dialectic. About the turn of the last century a genetic study of the folkways began to win academic respectability. It could make little headway so long as the Newtonian concept was dominant; inquirers went in search of laws and uniformities, explanations were set down in mechanical formulae and the end of the quest was an articulate and symmetrical body of truths. The institutional method had to wait until the idea of development was incorporated into academic thought and the mind of the inquirer became resigned to the inconsistency which attends growth. The analogy with a biological organism had to be renounced and a basis in ideology had to be discovered before it could become a fruitful method of study in economies, history, philosophy, law and politics. The practical impulse toward its use came with a change in public opinion; so long as laissez faire dominated our minds, dialectic served well enough to turn out explanatory apologies for the existing social arrangements; when we began to demand that order and direction be imposed upon an unruly society, a genetic study of how its constituent usages had grown up into an empirical organization seemed proper. An inquiry into institutions may supply the analytical knowledge essential to a program of social control or it may do no more than set adventures for idle curiosity. In either event the study of institutions rests itself upon an institution.

Accordingly an institution is an imperfect agent of order and of purpose in a developing culture. Intent and chance alike share in its creation; it imposes its pattern of conduct upon the activities of men and its compulsion upon the course of unanticipated events. Its identity through the impact of idea upon circumstance and the rebound of circumstance upon idea is forever being remade. It performs in the social economy a none too clearly defined office—a performance compromised by the maintenance of its own existence, by the interests of its personnel, by the diversion to alien purpose which the adventitious march of time brings. It may like any creation of man be taken into bondage by the power it was designed to control. It is a folkway, always new yet ever old, directive and responsive, a spur to and a check upon change, a creature of means and a master of ends. It is in social organization an instrument, a challenge and a hazard; in its wake come order and disorder, fulfilment, aimlessness and frustration. The arrangements of community life alike set the stage for and take up the shock of what man does and what he leaves undone. Institutions and human actions, complements and antitheses, are forever remaking each other in the endless drama of the social process.

CHAPTER 2

ADVERTISING AND CLASSICAL LIBERALISM

KIM B. ROTZOLL AND JAMES E. HAEFNER
WITH STEVEN R. HALL

In the first chapter [of our book], we suggested that it's important to keep in mind that advertising can be better understood by examining it in light of cultural expectations. And since the sets of assumptions that cultures hold are commonly expressed as institutions, it would seem appropriate to begin with an attempt to explore the relationship between ideas and institutions. For, as Carey contends:

> An understanding of advertising rests on an understanding of the nature of ideas and institutions in which advertising found a fertile seedbed to grow. Consequently, much of the modern controversy surrounding advertising is meaningless unless the listener is aware of the implicit assumptions carried by the protagonists about the nature of man, of society, of the economic and political order.[1]

Institutions, Hamilton informs us, "fix the confines of and impose form upon the activities of human beings,"[2] or, as Norris puts it, institutions "are the 'rules' according to which social life is carried on."[3] We will later explore in considerable depth why advertising in the United States can be considered one of these powerful phenomena. Let's begin, however, with the *ideas,* the "implicit assumptions" as Carey calls them, that are shared in some fundamental way by the members of a society; and, hence, shape its institutions.

THREE POWERFUL IDEA SYSTEMS

Any attempt to classify the incredible diversity of human societies risks ridicule. Yet a great deal can, we feel, be illuminated by asserting with Heilbroner[4] that at least three powerful idea systems (or "world views" or *Weltanschauungs*) have characterized many of our societies; and, consequently, have shaped the institutions that arise to deal with ongoing societal problems. They are: (1) Tradition, (2) Authority, and (3) Classical Liberalism. Some, as we shall see, are far more likely to produce Carey's "fertile seedbed" for advertising than others.

From Kim B. Rotzoll and James E. Haefner with Steven R. Hall, *Advertising in Contemporary Society: Perspectives Toward Understanding*, 2d edition (Urbana, IL: University of Illinois Press, 1990): 13–29. Copyright © 1990. Reprinted with permission of South-Western, a division of Thomson Learning: www.thomsonrights.com. Fax (800) 730-2215.

Tradition

Briefly, a society embracing ideas of tradition places a heavy investment in the status quo, often for religious reasons. Things are thought to be as they are for a reason, perhaps known only to God or the fates. It is frequently assumed that individuals are performing roles in a drama staged by a strong-willed deity or, at least, stern ancestors. Thus, economic tasks are handed down from father to son, mother to daughter, with "life chances" virtually set at birth. Any deviation would be considered an affront to those keepers of the tradition, both seen and unseen.

Now, *all* societies have traditional *elements* (e.g., our own family "traditions" about holidays, birthdays, etc.), and given the spread of worldwide communications, current examples of entire *societies* based solely on idea systems of tradition do not readily leap to mind. But we need to expand our vision; for, this idea system, along with authority, has dominated the activities of millions throughout history.

To get a better grasp of the trappings of a traditional society, remember the musical *Fiddler on the Roof.* From the opening song ("You ask me why we do these things, and I'll tell you . . . I don't know. It's *tradition!*") and throughout the play, Tevye, the milkman, confronts the pain of the shattering of tradition as his daughters break from the institution of the matchmaker and his village and its population are uprooted, along with the heavy investment in the past they embody. A recent example is found in the film *Witness* with actor Harrison Ford's detective character intervening in the subculture of the Amish and producing a predictable clash of values and actions ("It's not *our way!*"). On the grand scale of history, virtually every facet of life in the Middle Ages can be illuminated by understanding the implicit assumptions of the traditional world view, with the ensuing dominance of the medieval church.

Now, if Idea Systems → Institutions, would we expect advertising to arise as an institution under an idea system based on tradition? It would seem unlikely. Certainly, a compelling case can be made that one of advertising's primal messages is a call for *change.* Change your hair, your toothpaste, your life style. Aspire to be more. Indulge yourself. Be "all that you can be." These and other siren calls are familiar to us, but they would seem both alien and threatening when perceived from a world view of tradition.

This is not to say that the modern world cannot produce some striking accommodations of presumably conflicting idea systems. In a recent trip to Bahrain, a country of the Middle East, one of the authors led a seminar on advertising practices during which one of the participants used the coffee break to face Mecca and pray. At a nearby shopping center, Arabic women in traditional dress could be seen wearing fashionable footwear and shopping with apparent ease among a plethora of stores offering luxurious Western products.

Still, a society dominated by ideas of tradition generally would not seem likely to have advertising seen as a "natural" practice.

Authority

If the idea system of tradition relies on direction from the past, authority asserts it in the present and from the top. Basically, it contends that actions in a society are better determined by a few rather than the many. These few may be presumed to have special connections to God, be proven in combat, hold particular expertise, have been blessed with a high level of intelligence, or possess that elusive element, wisdom. They may be anointed, elected, or affirmed by raw power; and they may be one, a few, or a body. Whatever the rationale and structure for authority, it is assumed that some will direct while others will follow.

Throughout history more civilizations have shared this idea system than any other, with variations ranging from the iron rule of the dictator to the presumed enlightened leadership of a popular revolutionary leader or to the presumed representativeness of an elected legislature. Here, we find the seedbeds for institutions as diverse as planning boards, concentration camps, five-year plans, and "cultural revolutions."

And what of advertising's presence? On the surface, it would seem that a society choosing, to one degree or another, to have many decisions made from the top down would have no compelling reason to call on such a pervasive form of paid persuasion to attempt to influence the decision making of individuals. Certainly, Hitler had little need for advertising as we know it. Yet even in highly structured societies, there are apparently reasons to attempt to reinforce individual thinking and action, if not change it, and advertising has been called on to play a role. Thus, we have seen advertising in Russia—to serve to inspire in pursuit of national goals; to attempt to encourage particular consumption patterns (e.g., buy margarine rather than butter)—and are likely to see more with intents dealing with personal consumption as *Perestroika* becomes more evident in the day-to-day workings of Soviet life. For, as planning and decision making become more decentralized, advertising would predictably seem more compatible—e.g., advertising is a greater presence in Yugoslavia and Hungary than Russia and Poland, and it is becoming more important in China as the economic transformation to a more decentralized society continues in that enormous "people's republic." In the United States, the federal government is frequently listed among the country's top 25 advertisers, with the tasks ranging from attempts to sell in stiff competition (e.g., join the armed forces rather than take a traditional job) to the promotion of primary demand for primarily monopoly services (e.g., the post office, Amtrak).

Basically, then, societies relying heavily on an idea system of authority make many of the decisions *for* the citizens. Yet, advertising may still be a presence to reinforce decisions that have already been made—e.g., practice family planning in line with government policy—or, as decentralization of authority allows, to offer individuals real choices of alternatives—e.g., government brands competing against imported brands.

Now, as it becomes clear that advertising is more likely to flourish where decision making is decentralized rather than concentrated, we logically move to the most fertile of advertising seedbeds.

Classical Liberalism

Classical liberalism, Girvetz informs us, was crucial to the "epic transition of the Western world from an agrarian, handicraft society to the urban mechanized civilization of the present century."[5] (It is not, of course, liberalism as we think of it today; and, indeed, staunch believers in the tenets of *classical* liberalism today would tend to be labeled as arch conservatives.) Classical liberalism's ascendance in the seventeenth and eighteenth centuries was made possible, in part, by such enormous social convulsions as the Protestant Reformation, the Scientific Revolution, and the Renaissance. Based on these and other major societal forces, this startling idea system presented both an attack on the feudal order and an assertion of basic concepts about man and society that we still find engraved on public buildings, enshrined in the Constitution and Declaration of Independence, and falling easily off the tongues of politicians at many points on the political continuum. It is simply impossible to overstate the significance of this body of related ideas about human nature and the relationship of the individual to the whole in a quest for understanding virtually every facet of American society.

These ideas, breaking with the sway of tradition and authority that had dominated Europe for centuries, centered on the sovereign individual. The starting point was *EGOISM.* Apparently the ideas of Thomas Hobbes (psychological egoism) and Jeremy Bentham (psychological hedonism) found the time (roughly the seventeenth and eighteenth centuries) a fertile one. Basically, the egoistic interpretations of "human nature" held that the individual was, by nature, self-seeking. Thus, *all* of an individual's actions—even compassion—could be interpreted as being motivated by self-interest. It is important to realize that there was *no moral judgment* to be applied to the actions. In this context, Girvetz suggests an interpretation of particular relevance to activities of the economic system:

> Passion is no less noble than compassion. And, more significantly in the rough youth of capitalism, the callousness and venality of the most aggressive businessman are morally indistinguishable from the humanity and generosity of the dedicated idealist: each has exercised his preference and, while anyone may err in what best satisfies his preference, here error halts. (p. 10)

Even by today's decidedly selfish *zeitgeist,* these sentiments may seem shockingly stark. Yet, consider how frequently we ascribe the motives of others to naked self-interest—"She's (or he's) only out for number one." Or, how regrettably common it is to see the misdeeds of public officials attributed to unvarnished greed. Of course, somewhat closer to home, who would expect to find a text on advertising copywriting without the directive of appeal to the consumer's self-interest woven throughout its chapters?

Individuals, the classical liberals held, are self-interested animals. But there were other dimensions of the classical liberal idea system that served to lift us from the jungle.

The most important of these was *INTELLECTUALISM.* It held that the individual was "rational," to use that much abused word. Unlike the instinct-driven brutes of the animal world, an individual's behavior was thought to be deliberate and calculating.

> Reason looks to the consequences, carefully balances one promised pleasure or pain against another, and then, solely by reference to the quantity of pleasure or pain involved, delivers the verdict. The verdict having been rendered, conduct follows automatically. If the verdict should prove to be wrong, this will be because of imperfect education or inadequate information. (Girvetz, p. 15)

Herein, we find the skeletal structure of "economic man," the basic rationale for public education, and, lo, one of the more persistent arguments behind the consumerist's call for more "informative" advertising content, more functional package labeling, and so forth.

Dwell on this. After centuries of individuals being controlled by the cake of custom or the pressure of authority, the individual is now seen as capable of discovering the laws of his/her world (the Scientific Revolution), of communing directly with God (the Protestant Reformation), and of being celebrated in art, architecture, and literature (the Renaissance). As John Stuart Mill professed in his classic essay *On Liberty,* "Over himself, over his own mind and body, the individual is sovereign."[6] And lest you think this has little bearing on a subject like advertising in *contemporary* society, think of the defenses that cigarette advertisers are, *at this moment,* using to fend off proposed government regulation of their advertising activities. "Let the individual," they assert, "make up his or her own mind." Intellectualism—a powerful idea—was embraced, as we shall see, by both supporters and critics of advertising thought and practice.

It is the proposition of *QUIETISM* that adds a necessary dimension to the idea of a self-seeking, calculating individual. For if, as was assumed, effort is painful, it must follow that a person will expend energy only when there is some definite promise of reward, such that effort is worthwhile. The implication, then, is that an individual pursues various activities—backpacking, cooking, reading—not because the activity is desired for itself, but rather as a means to the end of pleasure. Thus, in the absence of an acceptable stimulus to self-interest, the individual will remain "quiet," apathetic, disinterested.

Certainly the recruiters who visit college campuses still operate—in addition to the more tentative flirtations with the "quality of the work experience"—under the assumption that work itself is not sufficiently appealing and that blandishments of salary, bonuses, and employee benefit programs are not required. The importance of the assumption of quietism to advertising is perhaps best captured in these oft-quoted lines from Winston Churchill:

> Advertising nourishes the consuming power of men. It creates wants for a better standard of living. It sets up before a man the goal of a better home, better clothing, better food for himself and his family. It spurs individual exertion and greater production. It brings together in fertile union those things which otherwise would never have met.[7]

Today, it is still an article of faith among many advertising practitioners that without the strong and continuing presence of advertising, the economy would falter. Thus, they express their implicit assumption that individuals are in need of constant stimulation to enter the market as buyers. Without that belief, one of the stronger rationales for the existence of advertising would be removed.

Now, thus far in the classical liberal vision we have self-seeking individuals pursuing their self-interests in deliberate and calculating manners after concluding that the reward is worth the effort. But what prevents this clash of self-interests from resulting in chaos? That is the province of *ATOMISM*.

Notice the root of the word. The classical liberals had drunk deeply of the elixir of "natural laws" as formulated by Newton and other giants of the time. And if, as the physical sciences suggested, the atom was the fundamental building block of all matter, then the individual could be assumed to be the essential element in society. The whole (society) was thus perceived as nothing more than the sum of its parts (sovereign individuals) in the same manner that a chair was nothing more than the sum of its individual atoms.

Now, from this perspective, it is simply absurd to believe that individuals can be "manipulated" by institutions of any form—e.g., government, the mass media, religion, advertising. For:

> . . . social institutions are created by the fiat of self-contained individuals, they are instruments, even expedients, which the individual can employ or discard without fundamentally altering his own nature. (Girvetz, p. 23)

So the picture completes itself. *The sovereign self-seeking individual is the key.* She or he acts in a calculating manner to obtain self-interest after it has been aroused by a sufficient promise of reward. He or she creates institutions to further reasoned self-interests and can discard them as they prove unproductive to achieving that end.

Egoism, Intellectualism, Quietism, Atomism—the Psychological Crucible of the Classical Liberal Idea System. One emerges with a pattern of ideas which, even though no individual nor generation has entertained in its entirety, has profoundly influenced the intellectual climate of this country (Girvetz, p. 27). It is, we believe, simply impossible to understand the American society and its institutions without first understanding the power of classical liberal thought. For, from this body of ideas emerges our institutions of religion, speech, press, justice, government, and countless others that touch the fabric of our daily lives. Commenting on one of these, *Time* magazine observed:

> . . . trial by jury realizes an essential democratic ideal: that the citizen's security is best protected not by any institutional or intellectual elite, but by the common sense of his fellow citizens; and that the jury system was quite properly designed, not to be efficient, but to be just.[8]

Thus, the institution of the jury system is a "natural" outgrowth of classical liberal roots. And it is in classical liberalism's dominant economic institution where we will find the most fertile of seedbeds for our subject. To understand advertising in contemporary society, we must first understand classical liberalism and then come to understand one of its most important institutional progeny: the remarkable market system.

THE CLASSICAL LIBERAL MARKET

Markets, as exchanges between buyers and sellers occurring at particular times in particular places, have existed through much of recorded history. (Think of today's farmer's market or flea market as an approximation.) But the *market system,* as a means of allocating resources of an entire society, is really quite new, a creature of classical liberalism scarcely more than 200 years old. The market system has been so much a part of this country that it is difficult to realize what a revolutionary idea it was. Ask the typical college student about the market system, and he or she will probably offer something about the interplay of supply and demand, but little more. Yet, here was a system that, as classical liberalism itself, "staked it all" on the *individual.* What an astounding contrast to the institutions based on tradition and authority that preceded it and that coexist to this day.

Consider that under an economic system whose institutions are creatures of an idea system based on *tradition,* economic roles established by custom are perpetuated from generation to generation. The goods of the society that are not provided within the self-sustaining household are usually distributed in accordance with status hierarchies—more for the feudal lord, less for the serfs, and so on.

Under *authority,* on the other hand, economic priorities and the life chances of the workers in the society can change dramatically, depending on the whim of the authority structure—planning board, dictator, etc. If the space program is considered more important than consumer goods, human and natural resources will be channeled accordingly.

But consider the *market.* As an institution arising from the classical liberal world view, it holds that the priorities of the society should be determined not by the cake of custom or the directives of the few, but rather by the aggregate of *individual decisions—all* individuals, not simply the elect or select.

The market emerged in part *inductively,* with pressures from the growing activities of the practitioners of commerce in seventeenth and eighteenth century Europe and England. These aspiring entrepreneurs sought change and agitated government to permit their profit-seeking activities to be carried on without undue restraint. And, as we have seen, the market as an articulated system also emerged *deductively;* with the supporting ideas of egoism, intellectualism, quietism, and atomism that culminated in the "world view" of classical liberalism.

If the writings of John Locke still influence our governmental system, there can be little doubt that Adam Smith and his masterpiece *An Inquiry into the Nature and Causes of the Wealth of Nations* (1776) still shape the ideology of much of our economic system. (There are no value judgments intended here—merely the observation that the rationale for the classical liberal market remains very much a part of the "conventional wisdom" of much of American economic life in spite of often glaring discrepancies between idea and reality.)

Smith, Heilbroner informs us,[9] was living in a time (the eighteenth century) and place (England) when the division of labor was becoming a dominant economic fact. Thus, the decline of self-sufficiency was a major current in his work, as, apparently, was the thinking of seventeenth and eighteenth century British clergymen, particularly the Puritans, with their belief in a rational, mechanistic universe.[10] But how was this supposed to relate to a system of resource allocation with the sovereign individual as its master?

First, Smith assumed that individuals were self-seeking by nature (egoism). "It is not from the benevolence of the butcher, the brewer or the baker that we expect our dinner," Smith reminded us, "but from their regard to their own interest."[11] Likewise, someone buying goods would attempt to acquire those that brought the greatest pleasure at the *lowest* price and, while in the labor market, would strive to perform as *little* work as possible for as *much* money as he or she could secure. The producer, of course, would attempt to sell the *lowest* quality merchandise at the *highest* possible price, and hire the *cheapest* labor to perform as *much* work as possible. It seemed a sure formula for chaos.

But, it was reasoned, the self-seeking individual would inevitably collide with others (atomism) seeking the same end. What then? Violence? Not if it is also assumed that the individual is by nature deliberate and calculating (intellectualism). For the self-seeking individual, stimulated from apathy (quietism) by an appeal to gain (egoism), will quickly realize that the reward for which he or she has exerted effort will not be achieved unless behavior is modified to some minimal degree. Thus, the producer who wishes to sell a poor quality good at a high price will have to face the realization that the deliberate and calculating individuals will not purchase the offerings if more "rational" choices are available. And the individual entering the labor market may shortly find herself/himself without work if she/he encounters others willing to toil slightly longer for the same wages.

But all of this hinges on the assumption that economic power will be fragmented among *many* buyers and sellers (atomism). With many suppliers, it is assumed that some will attempt to seek their self-interests by offering a better economic and/or qualitative value than their competitors. With many potential self-seeking laborers, it is certain that some will work longer hours for less money, and so on. If this fragmentation did not exist, it is easy to predict (according to the classical liberal world view) that those with some degree of power would pursue their self-interests by the exploitation of others.

Thus, in order for the market mechanism to perform its task of resource allocation with greatest efficiency, individuals *must* be stimulated to put forth effort in pursuit of self-interest, they *must* be deliberate and calculating in that pursuit, and there *must* be a sufficient number of buyers and sellers so that no one or few can influence the process.

And on whom does the market shower its favors? On the *efficient.* It is the efficient individual who stretches his/her earnings by buying the best quality at the lowest price. It is the efficient wage earner who expends appropriate effort to maximize his/her return. And it is the efficient producer who can offer the highest-quality goods at the lowest possible cost, and hence be rewarded with the patronage of the efficient consumer.

With this background, let us examine three pressing economic questions common to *all* societies, which, until the evolution of the market, had been answered only by tradition or authority.

What Will Be Produced?

What will be produced will, simply, be determined by what sovereign individuals, in their self-interests, wish to buy. Thus, as Heilbroner observes, the market "has no goal orientation, save to existing demand."[12] If there is a considerable demand for shoes, the fact that shoe supply lags behind existing demand means that shoe prices will rise, along with the profits of the current producers. But the abnormally high profits will soon attract producers from other fields (say, hats) who have fallen upon hard times with potential supply exceeding existing demand, thus leading to subnormal return. As hat producers become shoe producers, shoe supply increases until demand is met. Thus, in the long run, aggregate demand determines the types and qualities of what is to be produced. (To use a contemporary example, a demand for pornographic films, particularly for the home-video market, has led to a sizable allocation of human and material resources to meet that demand. It was not decreed by authority that this should be so, nor was it determined by custom—at least not in this country—but rather by a sufficient number of individuals willing to part with a certain portion of their earnings for the opportunity to view these epics. If demand slackens, many of the current participants will presumably seek other opportunities for profit and employment.)

To Whom Will It Be Distributed?

The output of the market system will be distributed to whomever has money to pay for its offerings. There is no welfare built into the pure ideology or its mechanism. Social Darwinism is a reasonable approximation of the humanitarian dimension of the market in its pure classical liberal form. Those having "marketable" skills who are willing to sell their services in the labor market will be compensated. They may then, in turn, partake of the output of the production sector that is theoretically responding to their demands and those of other sovereign individuals like them. Yet, if the lure of gain is not sufficient to overcome their quietistic nature, the market will offer no rewards. (Certainly the still heard call that disenfranchised individuals should "pull themselves up by their bootstraps" comes from this credo, as does the resistance some still express to the idea of "welfare.")

How Will the Work of Society Get Done?

Since the market visionaries assumed a geographically mobile labor force (a crucial condition), self-interested individuals will seek employment wherever wages are highest. As we have already seen, it is in production areas of high demand and short supply (to use our earlier example—shoes) where wages are likely to rise. Thus, workers are attracted to those areas of production that are currently high on the economy's list of priorities. Always assuming the lure of gain and the deliberate and calculating path to self-interest, it is assured that, at least in the long run, those tasks that society deems important will be undertaken. (Today, we see reference to "pockets of poverty," while other sections of the country are experiencing "boom times" with a presumably desirable market for labor. Classical market theorists would assume that rational individuals would go where the jobs are. Obviously, today, we consider the matter more complex.)

   Now, it is important to keep in mind that the market was seen as a system harmonious with the *natural laws* of society as articulated by the classical liberals. If supply should fall short of demand, the "laws" of the market would naturally be set into motion to correct the deficiency. Being in tune with "natural" order, it was, of course, self-correcting. It follows that the market, as a self-contained, self-repairing, complex mechanism, must be left alone (*lassiez-faire*) to follow its natural course. Its greatest enemy, then, was predictably, *any* concentration of power that could disrupt the atomistic nature of the market and hence the natural processes of the system. (It is often assumed that government was considered the greatest potential villain in the saga. Not so. Equally calamitous effects could be expected to result from concentration of undue—i.e., "unnatural"—power by big business, big labor or even consumer co-ops. *Any form of action that superceded individual decision making was considered a threat to the system.*)

The self-corrective powers of the market could thus be impaired by any deviation from its fundamental assumptions. For example, the development of a producer monopoly (affecting atomism) would enable the supplier to withhold output, leading to higher prices. Thus, wages and prices would be distorted, and the deliberating and calculating consumer would be thwarted.

"The great flaw in the market," one may hear from some sectors, "is that it provides no incentive for social responsibility on the part of the participants." Precisely. Under the assumption of the pure atomistic market, it was assumed that the participants would follow only one overriding law—do what is best for their own monetary interests. The atomistic force of competition (producers, laborers, buyers) would take care of the rest. For, in the process of "naturally" seeking his or her own self-interest, the individual contributes to the good of the whole (society) "as if by an invisible hand."[13] Indeed, always assuming that the other factors are operative, *the individual who did not seek monetarily selfish ends would be doing a disservice to himself or herself, and society.*

There is yet another point deserving of emphasis. The ghost of Adam Smith is far more likely to be called forth at a meeting of the Association of National Advertisers than the Consumer Federation of America. Yet, Smith must certainly be considered a "Consumerist," who regarded the end of all production as consumption and held no lofty illusions of the motives of businessmen. As he stated:

> People of the same trade seldom meet together, even for merriment and diversion, but the conversation ends in a conspiracy against the public, or in some contrivance to raise prices.[14]

To counter this, Smith looked to the fragmentation of power through competition and relied upon the individual's presumed deliberate and calculating nature.

So the *sovereign individual*—particularly the industrious and efficient—would be the beneficiary in the market. As production increased, so would the division of labor and the varieties of goods and services offered in response to aggregate demand. All who would diligently and intelligently participate would benefit. The lure of gain, the directive of reason, and the discipline of competition . . .

> The market thus determines how society shall invest its resources, human and material. It decrees when, where, and how men shall labor. It determines the disposition of capital. The market becomes the regulator of what shall be produced, its quality, quantity, and price. The market is truly called sovereign. (Girvetz, p. 117)

A remarkable vision and an essential reference point for understanding advertising in contemporary society.

A "FERTILE SEEDBED" FOR ADVERTISING

After examining the relationship between idea systems and institutions, it seems clear that the perspective of *tradition* provides the least compatible idea environment for advertising. The idea system centered around assumptions that *authority* could provide some promise, dependent upon the degree of individual decision making allowed. But it is clearly in the ideas of *classical liberalism* that we find the most promising basis for the emergence and proliferation of advertising as "world taken for granted."

Understanding Advertising's Classical Liberal Roots

In a 1987 statement on advertising and the Federal Trade Commission, newly appointed chairman Dan Oliver asserted:

> Advertising is one of the basic mechanisms through which the marketplace acts to ensure consumer sovereignty. It contributes to the achievement of an efficient allocation of resources and benefits consumers in several different ways. . . .
> First, advertising provides information about product characteristics and enables consumers to make informed choices among competing goods. . . .
> Second, economic theory and empirical studies indicate that advertising generally increases new entry and price competition and hence reduces market power and prices.[15]

Note the key symbols: "consumer sovereignty"; "efficient allocation of resources"; "informed choices"; "new entry"; and "price competition." The roots are clear. From "egoism" comes the assumption that advertisers can feel free to seek their self-interests through various forms of business activities, including advertising. So are potential buyers seeking *their* self-interests, assuming they are aroused from their natural "quietistic" state by appeal to their self-interests, perhaps through advertising messages. Advertisers can, of course, attempt to persuade as robustly as they wish, safe in the assumption that the "deliberate and calculating" individual will not be manipulated. Potential buyers can, of course, sort through the wealth of competing messages caused by the "atomism" of the competitive structure and arrive at a reasoned choice. And, who, presumably, is in charge of this directionless, self-correcting system? With this set of assumptions at least, the *individual* who can accept, reject, or ignore, directs the flow of societal resources through the full meaning of *consumer sovereignty.*

The seeds of conflict should also be apparent. As Leiss, Kline, and Ghally observe in their investigation of *Social Communication in Advertising,* the starting point of advertising supporters . . .

> is not the "bewildered" but the "rational" consumer who uses the goods of the capitalist marketplace and the information provided by advertising to satisfy his or her needs. This concept of how things *should* work, rooted in classical liberal economic theory, is something many defenders and critics of advertising share, but while the defenders claim that with the help of advertising, the market actually operates in this way to match peoples needs with suitable products, many of the critics think that advertising actually destroys the competitive and rational nature of the free market.[16]

An interesting insight into this clash of visions is provided by a series of print advertisements prepared by the American Association of Advertising Agencies to attempt to counter some of the common criticisms of advertising. They hoped to raise advertising's standing in public opinion polls, while attempting to make advertising's case among such key "publics" as government officials, academics, and so forth. Here are some of the headlines from the series:

- "Isn't It Funny How Stereo Ads Are Boring Until You Want a Stereo?" (Advertising as a guide to the rational consumer.)
- "Without Advertising Even the Best Ideas Take Ages to Catch On" (Advertising quickly joins the self-interest of sellers and buyers for the benefit of both.)
- "Is Advertising a Reflection of Society or is Society a Reflection of Advertising?" (Advertising is a mirror, not a shaper.)

You get the idea. As a particularly telling example of the ideas behind this defensive posture of advertising supporters, examine another ad in the series, shown in Figure 2.1. Notice the reasoning behind the refutation of each of the "lies":

- "Advertising makes you buy things you don't want." (No one, short of actual force, can do that. You're too smart, and there are too many other choices open to you.)
- "Advertising makes things cost more." (Competition, spurred by advertising, makes possible the efficiencies of mass production as advertising introduces individuals to products suited to their self-interests.)
- "Advertising helps bad products sell." (Once consumers have tried a product, they decide, in some self-interested manner, whether it is of value to them. If it isn't, future advertising efforts are wasted.)
- "Advertising is a waste of money." (Advertising is a friend of the market because it provides information and fosters competition. We *all* benefit.)

And finally the slogan for the entire campaign, encompassing strong classical liberal themes—"Advertising. Another word for freedom of choice."

(There are some interesting asides. Note, for example in Figure 2.1, that it is asserted that it is a "lie" that advertising *makes* you buy things you don't want. Yet advertising is given credit for "creating" a mass market for calculators. If it needed to be created, was it wanted in the first place? Etc. The tone of the entire message, however, is clearly set on a classical liberal foundation.)

In a similar mode, Professor Jerry Kirkpatrick provides a "Philosophical Defense of Advertising," relying heavily on the thinking of economist Ayn Rand. Confronting several of the common criticisms of advertising's social role (e.g., "Advertising Changes Tastes," "Advertising Offends Tastes") he asserts:

> The moral justification of advertising is that it represents the implementation of an ethics of egoism—the communication of one rational being to another rational being for the egoistic benefit of both.[17]

He summarizes, "The relationship between advertisers and consumers is strictly voluntary" (p. 48).

If we return to the working premise IDEAS SYSTEMS → INSTITUTIONS then, it seems apparent that advertising's roots (its "fertile seedbed"), as well as much of its current rationale and defense, can be found in the idea system of classical liberalism and its major economic institution, the market system.

To begin to understand advertising in contemporary society then, we must begin here. For, as suggested in [our] preceding chapter, much about the controversies of advertising can be illuminated by realizing "Who's looking and where." And those asserting advertising's case generally believe:

Figure 2.1

THIS AD IS FULL OF LIES.

LIE #1: ADVERTISING MAKES YOU BUY THINGS YOU DON'T WANT.

Advertising is often accused of inducing people to buy things against their will.

But when was the last time you returned home from the local shopping mall with a bag full of things you had absolutely no use for? The truth is, nothing short of a pointed gun can get *anybody* to spend money on something he or she doesn't want.

No matter how effective an ad is, you and millions of other American consumers make your own decisions. If you don't believe it, ask someone who knows firsthand about the limits of advertising. Like your local Edsel dealer.

LIE #2: ADVERTISING MAKES THINGS COST MORE. Since advertising costs money, it's natural to assume it costs *you* money. But the truth is that advertising often brings prices down.

Consider the electronic calculator, for example. In the late 1960s, advertising created a mass market for calculators. That meant more of them needed to be produced, which brought the price of producing each calculator down. Competition spurred by advertising brought the price down still further.

As a result, the same product that used to cost hundreds of dollars now costs as little as five dollars.

LIE #3: ADVERTISING HELPS BAD PRODUCTS SELL.

Some people worry that good advertising sometimes covers up for bad products.

But nothing can make you like a bad product. So, while advertising can help convince you to try something once, it can't make you buy it twice. If you don't like what you've bought, you won't buy it again. And if enough people feel the same way, the product dies on the shelf.

In other words, the only thing advertising can do for a bad product is help you find out it's a bad product. And you take it from there.

LIE #4: ADVERTISING IS A WASTE OF MONEY. Some people wonder why we don't just put all the money spent on advertising directly into our national economy.

The answer is, we already do.

Advertising helps products sell, which holds down prices, which helps sales even more. It creates jobs. It informs you about all the products available and helps you compare them. And it stimulates the competition that produces new and better products at reasonable prices.

If all that doesn't convince you that advertising is important to our economy, you might as well stop reading.

Because on top of everything else, advertising has paid for a large part of the magazine you're now holding.

And that's the truth.

ADVERTISING.
ANOTHER WORD FOR FREEDOM OF CHOICE.
American Association of Advertising Agencies

Source: Reprinted with permission of the American Association of Advertising Agencies.

Advertising is part and parcel of a highly industrialized, market-oriented society. Information and persuasion from uncounted sources swirl around all the individuals who live, work, and shop in this setting. Both informative and persuasive communications are vital and indeed necessary ingredients of decision-making processes in politics, in social relations, and in the marketplace. (Leiss, *et al.*, p. 42)

[. . .]

SUMMARY

In examining the relationship between fundamental societal idea systems and institutions, we began a search for the "fertile seedbed" of ideas that provides an appropriate growth medium for advertising as an institution.

It is clearly not in TRADITION, the set of assumptions placing heavy emphasis on the status quo, based on a well-understood societal plan provided by the Gods, ancestors, or both.

It may, in part, be in AUTHORITY, with its assumptions of the wisdom of the few directing the many. But much depends upon the degree of individual decision making allowed.

The fit seems tightest with CLASSICAL LIBERALISM, with its assumptions of self-interest (egoism), rationality (intellectualism), apathy (quietism), and the whole being no greater than the sum of the parts (atomism).

Still more understanding is added by examining the *market* as a resource allocation mechanism. Based on classical liberalism, it is assumed to be self-perpetuating and self-correcting, with the good of the whole ensuing from self-centered actions of individuals—"as if by an invisible hand."

Much assertion and defense of advertising's thought and action can be seen in these ideas. Shopworn and controversial as they may be in the last years of the twentieth century, they still provide much comfort for supporters of advertising in contemporary society, and useful analytic perspectives for those seeking to understand its dimensions.

NOTES

1. James W. Carey, "Advertising: An Institutional Approach," in C. H. Sandage and V. Fryburger, *The Role of Advertising* (Homewood, IL: Richard D. Irwin, Inc., 1960), p. 3.

2. Walton Hamilton, "Institution," *The Encyclopaedia of the Social Sciences,* vol. 8 (New York: Macmillan, 1932), p. 84.

3. Vincent P. Norris, "Toward the Institutional Study of Advertising," in *Occasional Papers in Advertising,* vol. 1, no. 1 (Urbana, IL: University of Illinois, Department of Advertising, January 1966), pp. 60–61.

4. See in general, Robert L. Heilbroner, "The Economic Revolution," in *The Worldly Philosophers* (New York: Time, Inc., 1961), chap. II.

5. Harry K. Girvetz, *From Wealth to Welfare* (Stanford, CA: Stanford University Press, 1950), chap. 1. Used by permission.

6. Quoted in Otto Friedrich, "The Individual is Sovereign," *Time,* July 21, 1986, p. 80.

7. Winston Churchill, quoted in S. Watson Dunn and Arnold M. Barban, *Advertising: Its Role in Modern Marketing* (Hinsdale, IL: The Dryden Press, 1974), p. 5.

8. "Idealism on Trial," promotional ad, *Time, Inc.,* 1982.

9. Heilbroner, *op. cit.* The authors acknowledge their debt to the ideas expressed throughout Chapters I–III in this excellent work.

10. Thoughts attributed to Sabin Rashid, Professor of Economics at the University of Illinois. See Tom Day, "Author of 'Wealth of Nations' 'borrowed' Many of His Ideas," *IlliniWeek,* April 19, 1984, p. 1.

11. Quoted in "Revolution of Self-Love," *Time,* April 21, 1980, p. 45.

12. Heilbroner, *The Economic Problem,* 2d ed. (Englewood Cliffs, NJ: Prentice-Hall, 1970), p. 547.

13. Quoted in Paul A. Samuelson, "Adam Smith," *Newsweek,* March 15, 1976, p. 86.

14. Heilbroner, *The Worldly Philosophers,* p. 65.

15. "The New FTC: Steady as She Goes," *American Advertising,* January 1987, p. 9.

16. William Leiss, Stephen Kline, and Sut Ghally, *Social Communication in Advertising* (New York: Methuen, 1986), p. 31.

17. Jerry Kirkpatrick, "A Philosophical Defense of Advertising," *Journal of Advertising,* vol. 15, no. 2, 1986, p. 44.

CHAPTER 3

ADVERTISING
An Institutional Approach

JAMES W. CAREY

Advertising is thought by many to be a peculiarly modern institution. This thought has some credibility as much of the spectacular growth of advertising has occurred since World War I concomitantly with the great expansion of American industry. But in reality advertising has a long prehistory. Its growth as an institution has been part and parcel of the growth of the Western industrial world. The last 200 years have seen the growth of the ideas and institutions which favor the development of an economic system in which advertising becomes a part of the very logic by which commerce is carried on.

An understanding of advertising rests on an understanding of the nature of the ideas and institutions in which advertising found a fertile seedbed to grow. Consequently, much of the modern controversy surrounding advertising is meaningless unless the listener is aware of the implicit assumptions carried by the protagonists about the nature of man, of society, of the economic and political order. These assumptions are not to be found in most modern writing on advertising; they are found in the intellectual history of society. Hence, much of the debate presented here has a historical orientation as it points out the transformation that take place over time in the way we think about the world and how this leads to frustration and a lack of communication in discussions of social issues.

But it points up something much more fundamental. It shows that history is a continuing process of revelation; that the past holds within it the reality of the present and the outlines of the future. It shows that the present and the future become more meaningful when viewed as part of the continuing process by which society reveals itself.[1]

And one of the powerful ways society reveals itself is through the institutions it creates for accomplishing tasks, for meeting problems, and through the values and beliefs that it actualizes in those institutions.

Advertising, as we know it, seems inextricably associated with industrial capitalism. Capitalism, like any system of economic organization, is designed to meet certain problems of human existence: basically those of sustaining life. Society creates other institutions—religious, political, military—to meet other and equally compelling problems of human existence.

Taking the broadest possible view, men have apparently found only three ways of meeting the

---

From *The Role of Advertising: A Book of Readings,* ed. Charles H. Sandage and Vernon Fryburger (Homewood, IL: Richard D. Irwin, 1960).

problems of existence and, hence, society has depended on Tradition, Authoritarian Control, and on the Market for insuring the performance of those functions necessary to human survival.[2]

When society decides how it shall govern itself, it creates institutions to implement these decisions. Institutions then are social creations which exist through space and time. They act as agencies of social control providing information and norms of conduct which protect society against chaos, and which lend stability to social life and viability to society.[3] In addition, institutions are the embodiment of ideas, for when society decides how it shall manage its activities—by tradition, the market, or authorization control—it bases this decision on some perspective or notion of the nature of man, of society, of the moral order, and of the meaning of life in general.

The thesis of this paper is that advertising is an institution; that is, it is a humanly designed method of handling certain problems of existence. It is an institution primarily designed to provide information on economic goods and services, but which now, under the impact of modern conditions, finds broader, noneconomic applications.

Different people see actualized in this institution different values, yes, even different ways of looking at man and society. But the importance of the institution is acknowledged by the amount of words written about it and the amount of study devoted to attempting to understand it; to understand what it represents, how it works, how it affects people exposed to it, how it contributes to the economic and political system—to society in general.

The object of this essay is to suggest a way of looking at advertising—a way that sees advertising as part of the world we live in, whose origins and growth are the result of certain historical forces. It hopes to show the nature, origin, and dominant value-belief system of a society in which advertising becomes a central part of the operation of the industrial order. It is hoped that the institutional function of advertising will become more clearly discernible when it is recognized how advertising is the inexorable result of certain fundamental assumptions on the nature of social life which leads to the organization of economic activity around a system of free markets.

THE TRANSITION TO THE MARKET SYSTEM

Industrial capitalism is a system of economic organization that arose out of the decaying feudalism of the Middle Ages. In part it was caused by and in part was the creator of a radically new value and belief system—Liberalism—which rose to dominance in the eighteenth century and literally conquered the world in the nineteenth.[4]

At the outset it would be well to see just what liberal ideas and capitalism were a reaction against. Medieval society insured the performance of economic tasks (as well as most other functions) by a complex web of *traditions*.[5] These traditions revolved around two interdependent institutions: the Medieval Church—the monolithic social and religious institution of the period; and Land—the economic foundation for an agricultural way of life.

There were two important consequences of these institutions: First, medieval society was a tradition-bound system of fixed status relationships between man and man—serf and noble, clergy and laity. Secondly, the dominant value and belief of the epoch was that the world of human life is and should be the scene of the great Christian drama of salvation.[6]

Men held almost exclusively by historical accident and heredity a fixed station in life from which they were prevented by tradition from rising. Medieval men were equal, but they were equal only in the eyes of God, for in the Aristotelian world view of the period human life consisted of an aristocratic graded hierarchy in which some men, by their nature, were fit to rule, whereas others were capable only of obeying.[7]

Men performed certain tasks not out of choice; nor were they compelled to perform them in any obvious way. They performed these tasks because they could conceive of doing nothing else. Father passed on to son not only his religion, his values and beliefs, but also his occupation and fixed station in life.

This then was a landlord society such as still exists today in many parts of the world where the power of the landlord elites is maintained over generations by the belief in a fixed status relationship, and by the fact that land, a factor of wealth which, unlike profits, cannot be destroyed, served as the productive base for the whole of society.

Life in the Middle Ages was largely conceived as a transitory period between the nothingness of pre-existence and glorious external life in the "heavenly city." Man, endowed with a soul, had as his purpose to serve God and to attain salvation, and life was to be devoted toward preparation of his human spirit for salvation. The universe was the scene of this great drama in which man attempted to realize his own essence and purpose.

The drama of salvation was supported by the astronomy of medieval science. Claudius Ptolemy, an Alexandrian mathematician and astronomer, systematized and projected a geocentric theory "holding that the earth is an immovable sphere fixed in the center of the universe."[8] The geocentric theory of the universe lent support to Christian theology; for if the highest purpose of the universe was the pleasing of God through the perfection of his children, then the earth must be the center of all the universe—the central focal point where the great drama was unfolding.

Society being motivated by the heavenly gains of salvation could not be easily accommodated to the pursuit of wealth or the drive for the material development of society. Further, the pursuit of wealth was immoral. In St. Augustine's Heavenly City there was no room available for the merchant. The economic ethic of the medieval period is summed up in the statement: *homo mercator vix aut numquam potest Deo placere* ("the merchant can never or hardly ever please God").[9]

Historians generally look upon the Reformation and the Renaissance as the periods and cluster of events which mark off the medieval world from the modern world. The Renaissance and the Reformation saw the decline of the Medieval Church and the enfeeblement of feudalism. In addition, it was a period that saw the development of nation states and nationalities, the invention and application of paper, the mariner's compass, gunpowder, printing, and the exploration of continents beyond the ocean. Although not exalting the individual, the Renaissance concept of the "Masterless Man" and the Reformation notion of "the priesthood of all believers" gave greater sway to individuality and individual judgment than was true of the Middle Ages.

The Renaissance and the Reformation saw more and more emphasis on all fields of human endeavor and on the growth and development of the potentialities of the individual. The new philosophy of individualism spread across Europe rising to dominance in the latter half of the eighteenth century, and it was accompanied by the burgeoning commerce which spread from the great commercial cities of northern Italy.

But it is important to recognize that the ideas of individualism were more than apologies for the growth of the commercial spirit and the rise of the bourgeois class. The leaders of the liberal revolt, including the classical economists, were developing the perspectives for a radically new set of human institutions that represented an entirely new way of looking at the world; a way which, to be sure, many times wore bourgeois blinkers, but which, more importantly, represented an entirely new conception of man and society based not on the whim and disposition of any class, but on the exercise of human reason.

This reformulation of medieval ideas is a long and interesting story and here we shall only hit a few of the high spots that are of direct pertinence to our understanding of the then new economic order.

After the Reformation a fundamental change took place in the way men viewed economic activity. No longer were the activities of the market-place shrouded in the same immorality which had characterized the Middle Ages. Puritanism had evolved an ethic that sanctioned the acquisitive ambitions of men and secularized Christian doctrine to the extent of making Christian duty more and more synonymous with economic virtue.[10] The road to salvation was increasingly seen as manifested in the zealous pursuit of one's worldly task as a "calling," a human service with divine encouragement. Further, material success in life served as evidence of God's approval of one's worldly activity.[11]

Although much of Christian teaching after the Reformation encouraged the pursuit of wealth, it also enforced some unpleasant responsibilities. The pursuit of wealth for the sake of sheer indulgence was decried and the goal of economic activity was seen as the practice of thrift.[12] And one of the remarkable coincidences of history (or is it a coincidence?) is that the practice of thrift, which results in a portion of the national output not being consumed during a given period, is the vital and necessary ingredient for the building of an industrial economy such as much of the Western world developed in the late eighteenth and nineteenth centuries.

Science, like religion, was not immune from the revolution then taking place in society, and it was the Polish astronomer Nicholas Copernicus (1473–1543) who attacked the geocentric theory of the universe. Working from observations of the movements of the planets, Copernicus projected an entirely new system of astronomy resulting in "a fundamental change in man's conception of the universe."[13] Copernicus felt that for any parsimonious explanation of the observations he had made the universe would have to be heliocentric with the planets, including the earth, revolving around the sun.

The work of Copernicus, and later Kepler and Galileo, which increasingly became a search for the "natural laws" governing the universe, culminated in the great synthesis of Isaac Newton (1642–1727).[14] His is one of those rare achievements in science that synthesizes the workings of the universe in a parsimonious way and provides the fundamental hypothesis on which the scientific activity of future generations is based. Newton synthesized the knowledge of science into that grand mechanical conception which has been called the Newtonian World Machine.

Working from the law of gravitation, Newton deduced that all objects must be made up of uniform particles—atoms; and that the physical laws in operation on the surface of the earth are equally in operation throughout the universe. Such a rational conception of the operation of the universe fostered the notion that the physical world is governed by the same Reason which is found in man, and hence can be understood by man. The universe of Newton was a uniform harmonious order governed by fundamental principles.[15] Hence, the goal of science became the search for these fundamental principles. These natural laws and the method of science became the rational deduction of Descartes.

What interests us here is that the fundamental ideas of Newton turn up over and over again during the next two centuries as arguments in every sphere of human study. The idea of mechanistic systems, of harmonious order in the universe, of natural laws governing the activity of phenomena, of the atomistic conception of matter, of the ability of Reason to apprehend Reality—these ideas infected the economic, political, and social thought of generations. And nowhere did they find more eloquent expression than in the ideas of John Locke, a friend and contemporary of Newton, who translated the discoveries of the physical science into the basis for a social physics, into the basic world outlook for the period.

Locke's philosophy aptly exemplifies the human penchant for translating revolutionary discoveries in the physical sciences into social and political ideas and programs. Man, to Locke, was like the Newtonian atom; that is, man was the basic unit of the social world in much the same way that the atom was the basic particle of the physical world. Society, then, was a collection of free and autonomous individuals and society existed only in lieu of its members. In Cartesian terms, the whole is the sum of its parts or the whole is caused by its parts and, consequently, man creates or causes society and the individual is the bedrock upon which all social life rests.[16]

In the same way that autonomous and freely interacting atoms make up the harmoniously co-ordinated mechanical universe, the actions of free and autonomous men will lead to a harmonious and rational social world. But how can war, discord, and antisocial behavior be explained? War and discord result in society because man imposes artificial institutions upon the natural order. But if man were truly left free, if he was allowed to use his rational faculties to create institutions which are in accord with the natural laws of society which reason reveals, then universal harmony and accord in social relations would result. It is when man is not guided by the dictates of reason and conscience that abberations result in society which destroy the fundamentally natural and harmonious relations which characterize man in a pure state of nature.

It was Locke's supreme faith that man possessed both reason and conscience which would allow him to live harmoniously within the natural order under the dictates of natural law. Men could develop society in accord with the natural order and thereby create an environment whereby the exercise of reason and conscience was encouraged and which included institutional safeguards to protect the individual against the exercise of wanton self-interest by those less reasonable and less conscience-stricken individuals—particularly the ogre of conscienceless government.

Central to Locke's thought is the view that the human mind is, at birth, a *tabula rasa,* a blank screen, onto which sense experience is projected and from which all our thoughts, sensations, and knowledge are derived. The notion of the *tabula rasa* was quickly transferred into a powerful argument for egalitarianism; for if men are all equal at birth they are by their nature equal, as equal as the atoms in Newton's system. The serf is as good as the noble insofar as innate worth is concerned. What differentiates them is environmental differences, particularly the fact that the noble has more opportunity for developing his faculties. The mass are every bit as worthy and capable as the upper class—only the upper class has been afforded opportunities which by the free and equal nature of man should be accorded to all men.[17]

It was but a short step from the idea of natural law and the equality of man at birth by virtue of common human nature to the doctrine of "natural rights." It was Locke's view that man originally lived in a state of nature possessing certain natural rights—life, liberty, and property—all of which were sacred and inalienable by the very construction of the natural order. In creating governments man surrenders certain rights he possessed in the free state of nature but he does not, because he cannot, surrender his natural rights.[18]

Locke's concept of natural rights became the keystone of the moral philosophy of the age of enlightenment.[19] The most interesting of these rights for our purposes was the natural right of property based on the self-evident principle that any person was entitled to any object with which he had mixed his labor.

Locke established an inseparable connection between individual freedom and property. In a perfectly natural state, land and the rest of nature are common property of all. However, the naturalness of private property comes from the principle that man has a "property" in his own person.[20] From this is deduced the conclusion that the individual is entitled to private ownership of whatever is comingled with the property man has in his person. Hence, the farmer who works the land takes such land out of the domain of common property by mixing his labor with the land, thereby turning the land into something distinct by virtue of the human labor it now contains. The land is now his because it contains a portion of his individuality—his labor.

One of the great and fascinating lessons that history teaches is that for any given historical epoch a certain core of ideas, of values and beliefs, rise to importance and infect and transform all areas of life. The eighteenth century was no exception to this proposition; in fact, it is an excellent example. The ideas of Newton and Locke and quite obviously many others turn up time and time again in all sorts of writings as the basis and justification for most of the institutions developed during this period.

The economic order and the market system were no exceptions. In fact, the values and beliefs which found expression in the market system were deduced with Euclidean-like precision from certain fundamental assumptions about the nature of man, society, and reality.[21] These assumptions, as we have seen, were forcefully articulated by Newton and Locke and their disciples, and in particular it should be noted that, as a result of these assumptions, the market system became a method of economic organization consistent with the temper of the time and the "climate of opinion" then prevailing among the intellectual classes. For our purposes the ideas that were of fundamental importance in justifying the new economic order were the notions that all was mechanistic, that natural law governed the physical and social world, that the world was characterized by fundamental harmony, that man possessed reason and conscience, that men were born equal and endowed with certain fundamental rights—life, liberty, and property. Let's see the form these ideas take in the economic order.

ADVERTISING AND THE MARKET SYSTEM

We have seen that society fundamentally is based on tradition, on authoritarian control, or on the market. The Middle Ages was characterized by static societies in which economic activities were governed by traditions surrounding the Church and the feudal manor. In the eighteenth century the Western world was poised on the brink of a revolution in economic life. From the end of the Middle Ages the life of individuals was being transformed as tradition-bound societies were being eroded by the quest for wealth, the use of money, and the development of markets.[22] In short, capitalistic forms of economic life were rising out of the decaying feudalism. At this point, it is our task to see how the ideas we have been discussing underlay the development of a free market system and how advertising was the logical analogue or an outgrowth of such a system.

Any system of economic organization ultimately answers the question as to where economic power is to be located.[23] The passionate individualism of the age of enlightenment above all wanted to avoid vesting this power in government, for it believed that the free and autonomous individual was the basic unit of social life and the "natural" economic order was the one which gave full sway to the individual in pursuing his own self-interest.[24] Social and economic life, like the universe itself, was felt to be governed by natural laws which the individual, exercising his reason, could discover and, further, because the individual was endowed with moral conscience he could live in accordance with these natural laws.[25]

Hence, the battle cry of economic liberalism became *laissez faire*—let the market alone—for if the market were allowed to obey the laws of its own motion it would, in the long run, produce a higher degree of efficiency and prosperity than it could if hamstrung by the regulation of government.[26] The problem of economic power is then settled under a free market system by fragmenting power among the many entrants in the market so that no one could exert any appreciable control over the laws which, in the absence of human intervention, govern the market.

The notion of a free market was reinforced by another powerful idea of Newton: the universal harmony of interests.[27] Free and autonomous individuals, like the atoms in Newton's system, were, in spite of the fact they pursued their own economic self-interest, linked to each other in fundamental harmony of purpose. This is a restatement of Adam Smith's proposition that the private interests and passions of men are guided by the "invisible hand" to the maximization of the social good. Men were bound together in such a way that the individual transcended himself by the exercise of his own self-interest resulting in the attainment of social as well as individual ends.[28]

Even though man was considered basically a self-interested animal pursuing what he considered would be to his gain and avoiding that which would incur him pain, he was nonetheless regulated in his activities by two powerful controls—one in the nature of man himself and the other in the nature of the market. First, man was, by his nature, felt to be a rational and moral individual. He would, in short, control his own selfish appetites rather than infringe on the natural rights of others. This does not mean that all men were perfectly scrupulous in their dealings, but it does hold that man, in the aggregate, was a moral creature. Second, the market had built into it a self-regulating mechanism that prevented the willful excess of self-interest. That mechanism was competition. Each individual pursuing his own self-interest ran into other individuals similarly inclined. These competing individuals forced each other to accept the decisions of the market and stifled any attempts to rig it to their own advantage.[29]

The beautiful and desirable thing about a free market situation is that it is self-regulating, controlling the actions of its members by its very mode of operation. And, further, it was felt to be a more beneficient system in creating the "wealth of nations" than any humanly contrived and necessarily artificial mode of economic organization.

The market as a central institution was likened to a *mechanism* that was governed by certain fundamental and discoverable laws, and its operation, when unfettered by artificial restrictions, could be predicted from the knowledge of its parts with the same certainty that characterized prediction of the physical universe.[30]

Economic liberalism found expression in the market and, like political liberalism, it stressed the individual. It made individual self-interest the motive force of economic life. It stressed freedom of trade (no tariffs or subsidies), freedom of contract between individuals, freedom from government interference or regulations, freedom of competition (no monopolies, especially no monopolies chartered by government).

The hallmark of a free market system is the concept of competition, and this notion that self-interest can be controlled through the natural conflict of opposing forces is basic to many of the institutions which arose in the eighteenth and nineteenth centuries. Democratic government, particularly the American federal system, reflects the faith that the free competition of interests in the legislative process will give rise to the most beneficient government and appropriate social legislation. What has been known as the "self-righting process" in the free market place of ideas is further evidence of the all-pervasive confidence in the notion of competition. The assumption here is that in the free market of ideas, where all ideas and opinions on any given social issue find expression, the truth will arise—the right idea will triumph because of the rational nature of man which allows him to discern truth from the clash of conflicting opinion.[31]

We then see that a fundamental attribute of the market—be it in ideas, in economic goods, or in the domain of government action—is that it is a device which operates through competition to protect and afford expression for man's natural rights. In particular, the market for goods and services is an institution for the expression of property rights controlled and protected by the forces of competition. The exercise of property rights thus became the vehicle for social action, or social action becomes the result of vigorous prosecution of property rights by free individuals, seeking their own self-interest and being controlled by their moral nature and the mechanism of competition operating in the free market. But the point must now be explicitly recognized that markets, the central institution of the prevailing economic order, must allow, in order to function efficiently, for the dissemination and absorption of relevant information.

One of the fundamental assumptions underlying theoretical analysis of competitive markets, and the whole concept of economic man, is that all entrants into the economic market shall have perfect knowledge; that is, each man should be aware of all prices resulting from supply and demand relationships and should have perfect knowledge of alternative forms of satisfying demand. *Caveat emptor*—let the buyer beware—simply means that every individual, being rational, is assumed to possess the ability to exercise correct judgment by basing his decisions on available market information.

The function of supplying information in purely competitive markets is generally assumed by the market as an institution. For example, publication of price and quantity information in the grain markets or the stock exchanges is handled by the market itself, not by any individual participant in the market. Property rights are expressed by individuals in face-to-face contact, and from the myriad interpersonal transactions information arises that represents generalizations as to price, quantity, and quality conditions existing in a given period. These generalizations represent the "true" value of goods and services. In other words, there is a self-righting process operating in the economic market whereby the interaction of the conflicting estimates by individuals on the value of goods gives rise to a price which is the true reflection of the worth of any particular product.

The point that needs to be reinforced here is that any and all markets demand for their operation adequate information. In fact, any marketing arrangement requires a highly developed system of communication as an essential prerequisite for co-ordinating the needs of producers and their intermediaries with those of consumers. It is *information* which gives the market cohesiveness and which allows for reductions in the cost of market operation.

The universality and spontaneity of this "informing function" is aptly demonstrated by anthropological studies of the rudimentary markets of primitive communities where the organization of markets in religious and economic goods creates the need and develops the facilities for the dissemination of market information.[32]

The institutional aspects of advertising are to be found in its performance of the function of supplying market information In fact, for the purposes of institutional analysis, which is the method taken here, the information provided in purely competitive markets and in primitive markets is *advertising*. We here define market information as advertising. In purely competitive markets we find information of a particular *type,* issued from a particular *source,* but it is nonetheless the data which brings buyer and seller together and which possesses utility in facilitating the exchange of property. This is not advertising as we generally use the word, but it does illustrate the institutional function of advertising.

One of the fundamental events of the nineteenth century was the rapid industrialization of the Western world, an industrialization which transformed the details of market organization but not the essence of the market system. As industrialization proceeded, a necessary requisite for efficiency and success was large-scale production. Technology created the means for low-cost production through the application of machines and mass-production methods. Mass production generally means centralized production and decentralized distribution, i.e., mass marketing. However, another concomitant requirement of mass production is mass communications.

As production became increasingly centralized, market power became more concentrated, branded merchandise developed, and the old interpersonal relationships in the market place became displaced by relationships mediated by mass communications facilities.

It is here we see advertising developed in its modern form because, as markets lost their formal organization, the function of supplying market information was placed more and more in the hands of fewer and fewer participants in the market. Markets still existed for the exercise of property rights except that advertising increasingly became the instrument by which these property rights were expressed.

Further, the "self-righting" process provided a basis for the overt use of persuasion by firms in the market. There is a sense in which the provision of information alone, i.e., data, is persuasion. But this is fundamentally different from the case in which the intent of the communicator is to cause a shift of attitudes or behavior in a specified direction. Under the assumption that man is rational and moral, attempts to persuade both in the economic and political arena become justifiable, for the moral nature of the communicator serves as a check on the willful abuse of his privilege to persuade. Man, being rational, was thought to be capable of ferreting out the truth from the varying claims of competitors and could discern the charlatan from the honest merchant.

However, as the number of firms in the market was whittled down due to the logic of technology and the demands of competition, the problem of market power reappeared, and the concentration of such power became a matter of concern as oligopolistic organization came to typify the market. This led quite naturally to a displacement of the principle of *caveat emptor,* and the substitution of a philosophy which recognizes that the individual can no longer receive from the market, as an institution, all the information necessary to the making of rational judgments. The institutional function of advertising is still the making available of information to facilitate judgment and free choice on the part of the consumer, but the information is no longer supplied by the market but by the firms in the market.

There is no longer any guarantee that the self-righting process operates to yield the "true value" of goods when individual firms possess a measure of control over the market. Because competition no longer provides the check on self-interest that it did under atomistic market organization, control in the market is increasingly being sought in human and corporate conscience—a conscience expressed through the notion of social responsibility.

As might be expected, the role of advertising in modern society has changed under the impact of modern thinking and in view of the changed nature of the market system. Over and above the supplying of information, advertising is seen by various writers to perform certain objective functions, that is, functions which any given advertiser may not realize he is performing as he goes about the day-to-day task of using advertising as an instrument of marketing activity. The suggestion here is that a fruitful approach to understanding advertising is through analysis of the functions, implicit and explicit, which advertising performs within the framework of a given market structure.

We here suggest two functions which advertising performs. First, advertising acts as an agency of social control providing norms of behavior appropriate to current economic conditions. Second, advertising still represents the expression of property rights held by firms in goods and services controlled, it is hoped, by social conscience.

The changed nature of markets and the changing conception of the consumer has modified the behavior of business in relation to markets and consumers. Man is increasingly defined, using Ernst Cassirer's terminology, not as *animal rationale,* but as *animal symbolicum.* This is not to say man has been totally divested of reason but, instead, that he is seen to operate in a psychological field wherein he reacts to his entire cultural environment rather than individual economic stimuli. Economic man, buying and selling, and equating cost and utility at the margin, has been replaced by psychological or symbolic man who makes economic decisions on the basis of economic and also noneconomic but equally potent psychological need-want stimuli.

Gone are the days when marketing was largely seen as a task of selling—the specialized effort that persuades an individual customer to buy whatever it is that business produces. Instead, the task of marketing is seen as the creation of markets and the creation of products and the mutual adaptation of the product for the customer and the market.[33] Or, to push the analysis further, marketing is increasingly being seen as the creation and development of demand and the performance of the dynamic economic task of distributing the gross national and international product of goods and services to individual units and groups of customers. And in this process advertising, as part of the "marketing mix," is daily playing a more dominant role.

The modern functions of advertising, when aligned with its ubiquity as national income rises, create the view that advertising is simply the appurtenance of a society with discretionary spending ability where production capacity tends to outrun consumption habits.

The danger in seeing advertising simply as a device that arises in a consumption-oriented society is that this view clouds the fact that advertising performs the historically given function of supplying the market with relevant information and, as such, is not to be thought of as a transitory concomitant of some particular form of competition, but as a logical corollary of a market system.

Consequently, the nub of the "advertising problem" really rests on a controversy over *who* shall supply the necessary market information, what *type* of information it shall be, and to what ends it should be directed. The reader might then reflect on the following two propositions: (1) That the source of advertising or market information is determined by the demands of technology and the location of economic power; and (2) that the specific form and nature of advertising messages is dependent on the particular economic problem which the society recognizes as most pressing and, more importantly, on the view that society takes toward the nature of man and to what it is that motivates "appropriate" market behavior.

This is only to say that the character of advertising is dependent upon the character of market structure and the values and beliefs which support that structure. As has been pointed out, advertising or the functions it performs and the way it performs them will change with changes in the structure and nature of the market. For example, the development of the doctrine of social responsibility, changes in technology, or changes in the location of economic power will affect what advertising is and does. If it is the choice of society that the economic system shall be guided by the choices and demands of individuals operating through a decentralized market system, then an institution must meet the function of supplying the information which allows the system to run efficiently and cohesively. The conclusion would then seem to follow that recommendations to change or modify the character of advertising, new legislation governing it, or new social policy relative to it, must consider the functions which advertising can and does perform and the total market structure and environment within which it operates.

NOTES

1. E. H. Carr, *The New Society* (Boston: Beacon Press, 1957), pp. 6–7.
2. Robert Heilbroner, *The Worldly Philosophers* (New York: Simon and Schuster, Inc., 1953), p. 10ff.
3. For a discussion of the nature of institutions see Francis E. Merrill and H. Wentworth Eldredge, *Culture and Society* (New York: Prentice-Hall, Inc., 1952), pp. 375–92.
4. See Harry K. Girvets, *From Wealth to Welfare* (Stanford, Calif.: Stanford University Press, 1950), pp. 3–6. Harold J. Laski, "The Rise of Liberalism" in *Encyclopaedia of the Social Sciences* (New York: Macmillan Co., 1930), pp. 103–24.
5. David Riesman, Nathan Glazer and Reuel Denney, *The Lonely Crowd* (Garden City, N.Y.: Doubleday and Co., 1953), pp. 26–28.
6. John Herman Randall, Jr., *The Making of the Modern Mind* (rev. ed.; Boston: Houghton Mifflin Co., 1940), pp. 17–36.
7. Pennington Haile, *The Eagle and the Bear* (New York: Ives Washburn, Inc., 1950), p. 20.
8. Louis Snyder, *The Age of Reason* (Princeton, N.J.: D. Van Nostrand Co., Inc., 1955), p. 17.
9. W. A. Weisskopf, *The Psychology of Economics* (Chicago: University of Chicago Press, 1955), p. 14.
10. Randall, *The Making of the Modern Mind,* pp. 159–61.

11. R. L. Heilbroner, *The Quest for Wealth* (New York: Simon and Schuster, Inc., 1956), pp. 138–39.

12. *Ibid.*, p. 141.

13. Snyder, *The Age of Reason*, p. 18.

14. Haile, *The Eagle and the Bear*, p. 27.

15. For an excellent discussion of the Newtonian World Machine see Randall, *The Making of the Modern Mind*, pp. 253–81.

16. Girvetz, *From Wealth to Welfare*, pp. 21–24.

17. For an excellent and extended discussion of the ideas of Locke, see F. S. C. Northup, *The Meeting of East and West* (New York: Macmillan Co., 1947) pp. 71ff.

18. Snyder, *The Age of Reason*, p. 65.

19. *Ibid.*

20. Weisskopf, *The Psychology of Economics*, p. 24.

21. See Girvetz, *From Wealth to Welfare*, pp. 3, 7–8.

22. Heilbroner, *The Quest for Wealth*, chaps. IV, V, and VI.

23. William W. Lucks and Weldon J. Hoot, *Comparative Economic System* (New York: Harper & Bros., 1952), p. 23.

24. Laski, *The Rise of Liberalism*, p. 123.

25. Carl Becker, *The Heavenly City of the Eighteenth-Century Philosophers* (New Haven: Yale University Press, 1932), p. 53.

26. O. H. Taylor, *Economics and Liberalism* (Cambridge, Mass.: Harvard University Press, 1955), pp. 165–66.

27. Girvetz, *From Wealth to Welfare*, pp. 113–14.

28. Glenn R. Morrow, *The Ethical and Economic Theories of Adam Smith* (New York: Longmans, Green & Co., 1921), pp. 83–84.

29. Taylor, *Economics and Liberalism*, p. 32. For a discussion of the relationship between philosophies, ideologies, and economic theory, see pp. 197–202.

30. *Ibid.*, pp. 34–35.

31. *Ibid.*, pp. 167–68.

32. In an economic study of a prisoner of war camp this same phenomenon—the universality and spontaneity of the "informing function"—was very much in evidence. In fact, almost immediately after markets developed in rations and Red Cross gifts, cigarettes became the currency of exchange, and an institution for disseminating information to control the activity of the market was developed. See R. A. Radford, "The Economic Organization of a P.O.W. Camp," *Economica* (London), New Series, Vol. XII, No. 48 (November, 1945), pp. 189–201.

33. Peter F. Drucker, *Landmarks of Tomorrow* (New York: Harper & Bros., 1959), pp. 26–27.

CHAPTER 4

THE INSTITUTION OF ABUNDANCE

DAVID M. POTTER

For millions of people throughout the world, during the last three centuries, America has symbolized plenty. This profusion of wealth, this abundance of goods, has borne a significance that far transcends the field of economics. American democracy, in the broad sense, was made possible to begin with by a condition of economic surplus, and the constant incidence of this abundance has differentiated American democracy from the democracy of other, less richly endowed countries.

Abundance, then, must be reckoned a major force in our history. But one may question whether any force can be regarded as possessing major historic importance unless it has developed its own characteristic institution. Democracy, for instance, produces the institution of popular government—the whole complex of parties, elections, representative bodies, constitutions, and the like. Religion manifests itself in the church, with a canon law, a clergy, and a whole ecclesiastical system. Science and learning find institutional embodiment in universities, with all their libraries, laboratories, faculties, and other apparatus of scholarship. If abundance can legitimately be regarded as a great historical force, what institution is especially identified with it? Does any such institution exist?

In *The Great Frontier*, Walter Prescott Webb contends that the four-hundred-year boom beginning with the age of discovery profoundly altered all the institutions of Western civilization, and especially that it led to the emergence of laissez faire capitalism. He maintains this view most ably and with great insight, and it would be hard to deny that, in the large sense in which he deals with the subject, laissez faire capitalism is an institution of abundance. It is, however, a modification, profound to be sure, of an earlier capitalism and is not a wholly new institution. If we seek an institution that was brought into being by abundance, without previous existence in any form, and, moreover, an institution which is peculiarly identified with American abundance rather than with abundance throughout Western civilization, we will find it, I believe, in modern American advertising.

Advertising as such is by no means a neglected subject. The excesses of advertising and of advertising men have been a favorite theme for a full quorum of modern satirists, cynics, and Jeremiahs. From the patent-medicine exposés in the early years of the century to the latest version of *The Hucksters*, advertising men have incurred fairly constant attack—their unscrupulous natures and their stomach ulcers being equally celebrated. Since advertising lends itself both to aesthetic criticism and to moral criticism and since humanity is ever ready with views in each of these areas, the flow of opinion has been copious.

But advertising as an institution has suffered almost total neglect. One might read fairly widely in the literature which treats of public opinion, popular culture, and the mass media in the United States without ever learning that advertising now compares with such long-standing institutions as the school and the church in the magnitude of its social influence. It dominates the media, it has vast power in the shaping of popular standards, and it is really one of the very limited group of institutions which exercise social control. Yet analysts of society have largely ignored it. Historians seldom do more than glance at it in their studies of social history, and, when they do, they usually focus attention upon some picturesque or titillating aspect, such as the way in which advertising has reflected or encouraged a new frankness about such previously tabooed subjects as ladies' underwear. Histories of American periodicals and even of the mass media deal with advertising as if it were a side issue. Students of the radio and of the mass-circulation magazines frequently condemn advertising for its conspicuous role, as if it were a mere interloper in a separate, pre-existing, self-contained aesthetic world of actors, musicians, authors, and script-writers; they hardly recognize that advertising created modern American radio and television, transformed the modern newspaper, evoked the modern slick periodical, and remains the vital essence of each of them at the present time. Marconi may have invented the wireless and Henry Luce may have invented the news magazine, but it is advertising that has made both wireless and news magazines what they are in America today. It is as impossible to understand a modern popular writer without understanding advertising as it would be to understand a medieval troubadour without understanding the cult of chivalry, or a nineteenth-century revivalist without understanding evangelical religion.

Before undertaking the consideration of advertising as an institution of social control—an instrument comparable to the school and the church in the extent of its influence upon society—perhaps it would be well to begin by observing something of the institution's growth to its present physical magnitude and financial strength.

A century ago advertising was a very minor form of economic activity, involving relatively small sums of money and playing only a negligible part in the distribution of goods or the formation of consumer habits. It was practiced principally by retail distributors who offered items without the mention of brands. Producers, who regarded the distributors as their market and who had as yet no concept of trying to reach the ultimate consumer, did not advertise at all and did not attempt to signalize their product by a distinctive name or label. Advertising ran heavily toward short prosaic notices like the want ads of today, in which the tone was didactic rather than hortatory or inspirational, and the content was factual. But patent medicines, even at that time, were a conspicuous exception.

Publishers usually assumed that advertisements ought to be of this nature, and, to protect the position of the small advertiser, some of them refused to accept notices using any type larger than agate. But, to apply the *New Yorker's* phrase historically, there has always been an ad man, and some of the ad men of the mid-century began to use great numbers of agate-sized letters, arranging them in the shape of large letters, just as the members of a college band are sometimes arranged in formation to spell out the initials of the alma mater. Publishers also correctly assumed that any considerable number of small, compact advertisements would lend a deadly monotony to the printed page, and some of them accordingly limited rather narrowly the amount of advertising that they would accept. In 1874, for instance, *The Youth's Companion* restricted the quantity of its advertising. As late as the 1870's, when the Howe Sewing Machine Company offered $18,000 for the back cover of *Harper's,* it was somewhat astonished to meet with a polite but firm refusal.

But those days are gone forever, and no other phenomenon of eighty years ago is now more remote. By 1880 advertising had increased threefold since the Civil War period. By 1900 it stood at $95,000,000 a year, which marked a tenfold increase over the amount in 1865. By 1919 it exceeded half a billion dollars, and by 1929 it reached $1,120,000,000. After 1929 it declined because of the Depression, but by 1951 it had again surpassed all previous levels and stood at $6,548,000,000 a year.

This immense financial growth reflects a number of vast and far-reaching changes. To begin with, the physical appearance of advertising underwent a complete transformation. The small box-insert ad gave way increasingly to larger spreads, and at last the full-page advertisement became the dominant form. Daniel Starch has shown, for instance, that in the 1860's and 1870's the average advertisement in the *Boston Evening Transcript* and the *New York Tribune* was about four column-inches, but by 1918 it was four times this size. In magazines, advertisers in the 1880's used half-page spaces two and a half times as often as they used full pages; by 1920 they did so only one-third as often. Before 1890 full-page entries constituted only a fifth of the advertising in magazines; but by 1920 they accounted for nearly half, and today the proportion must easily exceed half. Also, black and white gave way increasingly to color. As early as 1868 the *Galaxy* adopted the practice of using colored inserts, and, though this proved a little too far in advance of the times, it ultimately became standard practice among all large-circulation magazines.

Along with these changes in form went significant changes in the economic interests which advertised. For the first time producers began to perceive the possibilities in general advertising. At an earlier time they had addressed advertising by mail or on other limited bases to the distributors whom they hoped to induce to handle their goods, but they had left it to the distributor to deal with the ultimate consumer. As I have previously observed, they had apparently never conceived of the possibility of manufacturing their product under a distinctive brand name, or of using general advertising to create a consumer demand for their brand and thus of exerting pressure upon the distributor to keep their products in stock. But in the 1880's four pioneer producers began regularly to advertise their brands on a large scale. Significantly, perhaps, three of these were soaps: Sapolio, Pear's, and Ivory; the fourth was Royal Baking Powder. All of them achieved a large growth which was indisputably the result of advertising, and by doing so they demonstrated a truth which other producers were quick to grasp. As early as 1905, *Printer's Ink* proclaimed this new gospel when it declared: "This is a golden age in trade marks—a time when almost any maker of a worthy product can lay down the lines of a demand that will not only grow with years beyond anything that has ever been known before, but will become, in some degree, a monopoly. . . . Everywhere . . . there are opportunities to take the lead in advertising—to replace dozens of mongrel, unknown, unacknowledged makes of a fabric, a dress essential, a food, with a standard trade-marked brand, backed by the national advertising that in itself has come to be a guarantee of worth with the public."

As producers recognized the possibilities of this golden age, their advertising grew until it became primary: almost all so-called "national advertising" in magazines and over large networks is advertising by producers—while advertising by distributors, mostly in newspapers and over local broadcasting stations, has become secondary. The historian of the N. W. Ayer and Son Advertising Agency reports that "in the seventies and eighties, those who advertised through the Ayer firm were largely retailers and others who sold directly to the public. By 1890 most of these had ceased to use the Ayer agency, and its principal work was the advertising of manufacturers who sold through dealers and retailers but preferred to get control over their ultimate market."[1]

Concurrently, the nature of the appeal which advertising employed was transformed. Producers were no longer trying merely to use advertising as a coupling device between existing market demand

and their own supply; rather, they were trying to create a demand. Since the function of advertising had become one of exerting influence rather than one of providing information, the older factual, prosy notice which focused upon the specifications of the commodity now gave way to a more lyrical type of appeal which focused instead upon the desires of the consumer. This change was foreshadowed as early as 1903 by Walter Dill Scott, in an article on "The Psychology of Advertising," which formulated the basic law of the subject so clearly that he deserves to be regarded as the Archimedes, if not the Nostradamus, of the advertising world: "How many advertisers," he asked, "describe a piano so vividly that the reader can hear it? How many food products are so described that the reader can taste the food? . . . How many describe an undergarment so that the reader can feel the pleasant contact with his body? Many advertisers seem never to have thought of this, and make no attempt at such a description." That was in 1903. Today many advertisers seem to have thought of nothing else, and certainly all of them understand that advertising operates more to create wants in the minds of people than to capitalize on wants that are already active.[2]

Inevitably a question arises: Why did this immense growth of advertising take place? To this query each of us might offer responses of his own, but perhaps the most carefully considered answer, at least in terms of economics, is provided by Neil H. Borden in his extremely thorough study of *The Economic Effects of Advertising* (1942). Borden explains this growth partly in terms of the widening economic gap between producers and consumers and the consequently increased need for a medium of communication, and he attributes the growth of large-scale national advertising, with its color, large spreads, and other expensive features, to the growth of big corporations able to pay for such publicity. But in addition to these explanations he adds another very essential one: "The quest for product differentiation became intensified as the industrial system became more mature, and as manufacturers had capacity to produce far beyond existing demand."

In other words, advertising is not badly needed in an economy of scarcity, because total demand is usually equal to or in excess of total supply, and every producer can normally sell as much as he produces. It is when potential supply outstrips demand—that is, when abundance prevails—that advertising begins to fulfil a really essential economic function. In this situation the producer knows that the limitation upon his operations and upon his growth no longer lies, as it lay historically, in his productive capacity, for he can always produce as much as the market will absorb; the limitation has shifted to the market, and it is selling capacity which controls his growth. Moreover, every other producer of the same kind of article is also in position to expand output indefinitely, and this means that the advertiser must distinguish his product, if not on essential grounds, then on trivial ones, and that he must drive home this distinction by employing a brand name and by keeping this name always before the public. In a situation of limited supply the scarcity of his product will assure his place in the market, but in a situation of indefinitely expandable supply his brand is his only means of assuring himself of such a place.

Let us consider this, however, not merely from the standpoint of the enterpriser but in terms of society as a whole. At once the vital nature of the change will be apparent: the most critical point in the functioning of society shifts from production to consumption, and, as it does so, the culture must be reoriented to convert the producer's culture into a consumer's culture. In a society of scarcity, or even of moderate abundance, the productive capacity has barely sufficed to supply the goods which people already desire and which they regard as essential to an adequate standard of living. Hence the social imperative has fallen upon increases in production. But in a society of abundance, the productive capacity can supply new kinds of goods faster than society in the mass learns to crave these goods or to regard them as necessities. If this new capacity is to be used, the imperative must fall upon consumption, and the society must be adjusted to a new set of drives and values in which consumption is paramount.

The implications of the consumer orientation have received consideration from a number of writers, including David Riesman, who, in *The Lonely Crowd,* has described the consumer personality with notable insight. Among such writers, Percival and Paul Goodman, in their study *Communitas,* have, with brilliance and irony, pictured the life of a consumer society in the future. They begin by showing how, when unplanned production entered a phase of violent fluctuations in the 1920's, government responded with a New Deal which embodied a whole series of devices for the planning and stabilization of production. However, they observe, "there is no corresponding planning of consumption. . . . But hand in hand with a planned expanding production, there must be a planned expanding demand. . . . To leave the demand to the improvisations of advertisers is exactly on a par with the unplanned production of 1929." In order to plan an expansion of demand, they suggest, society requires an analysis of "Efficient Consumption," comparable to, though reversing, Veblen's concept of "Efficient Production." When Veblen set up laboriousness, interest in technique, and other productive virtues of the engineers in contradistinction to the restrictive qualities or practices of the capitalists, he was still thinking in terms of a need for more goods. "But," they continue, "the fact is that for at least two decades now it has been not scarcity of production which has kept men in political subjection (ironically enough, it has partly been the insecurity of so-called 'overproduction'); economically, it has been precisely the weakness, rather than the strength, of the consumption attitudes of emulation, ostentation, and sheer wastefulness which have depressed the productivity which is the economist's ideal. Only the instincts unleashed by war have sufficed, under modern conditions, to bring economic salvation.

"Then let us reverse the analysis and suggest how, even in peacetime, men can be as efficiently wasteful as possible. The city which we design on this principle is not only a theoretical solution for the economics which seem to have become official but also springs from the existent moral demands of the people who have crowded into such metropoles as New York."

In the society of consumption, as the Goodmans visualize it, production is only a means to the end of consumption, and therefore satisfaction in the work disappears. The workman accordingly focuses all his demands upon suitable working conditions, short hours, and high wages, so that he may hasten away with sufficient time, wealth, and energy to seek the goals of the consumer. This quest can be carried on "only in a great city. And the chief drive toward such goods is not individual but social. It is imitation and emulation which result in the lively demand. At first, perhaps, it is 'mass comforts' which satisfy cityfolk—these belong to the imitation of each other; but in the end it is luxuries; for these belong to emulation, to what Veblen used to call the 'imputation of superiority.' . . . All this can take place only in a great city. . . . The heart of the city of expanding effective demand is the department store. . . . Here all things are available according to desire—and are on display in order to suggest the desire. The streets are corridors of the department store; for the work of the people must not be quarantined from its cultural meaning."[3]

In their description of the department-store metropolis, the Goodmans have pictured an unlovely utopia, but the utopia, nonetheless, of a consumer society. I have quoted them at some length because of the clarity with which they show the intrinsic nature of a pure consumer culture. But consumer societies, like all other kinds, seem to fall short of their utopias, and we revert to the question how the citizen, in our mixed production-consumption society, can be educated to perform his role as a consumer, especially as a consumer of goods for which he feels no impulse of need. Clearly he must be educated, and the only institution which we have for instilling new needs, for training people to act as consumers, for altering men's values, and thus for hastening their adjustment to potential abundance is advertising. That is why it seems to me valid to regard advertising as distinctively the institution of abundance.

If it is correct to regard advertising in this way, we must recognize at once that we are dealing with a force that is not merely economic. We are dealing, as I have already suggested, with one of the very limited group of institutions which can properly be called "instruments of social control." These institutions guide the life of the individual by conceiving of him in a distinctive way and encouraging him to conform as far as possible to the concept. For instance, the church, representing the force of religion, conceives of man as an immortal soul; our schools and colleges, representing the force of learning, conceive of him as a being whose behavior is guided by reason; our business and industry, representing the force of the economic free-enterprise system, conceive of him as a productive agent who can create goods or render services that are useful to mankind. Advertising, of course, is committed to none of these views and entertains them only incidentally. Representing as it does the force of a vast productive mechanism seeking outlets for an overwhelming flow of goods, it conceives of man as a consumer. Each institution is distinctive, again, in the qualities to which it appeals and in the character of the reward which it offers: the church appeals to the spirit or conscience of the individual and offers the rewards of salvation and peace of mind; learning appeals to the reason of man and offers the hope of a perfected society from which evils have been eliminated by the application of wisdom; free enterprise appeals to the energies and the capacities of man and offers the rewards of property, personal attainment, and satisfaction in the job. Advertising appeals primarily to the desires, the wants—cultivated or natural—of the individual, and it sometimes offers as its goal a power to command the envy of others by outstripping them in the consumption of goods and services.

To pursue this parallel a step further, one may add that the traditional institutions have tried to improve man and to develop in him qualities of social value, though, of course, these values have not always been broadly conceived. The church has sought to inculcate virtue and consideration of others—the golden rule; the schools have made it their business to stimulate ability and to impart skills; the free-enterprise system has constantly stressed the importance of hard work and the sinfulness of unproductive occupations. And at least two of these institutions, the church and the school, have been very self-conscious about their roles as guardians of the social values and have conducted themselves with a considerable degree of social responsibility.

In contrast with these, advertising has in its dynamics no motivation to seek the improvement of the individual or to impart qualities of social usefulness, unless conformity to material values may be so characterized. And, though it wields an immense social influence, comparable to the influence of religion and learning, it has no social goals and no social responsibility for what it does with its influence, so long as it refrains from palpable violations of truth and decency. It is this lack of institutional responsibility, this lack of inherent social purpose to balance social power, which, I would argue, is a basic cause for concern about the role of advertising. Occasional deceptions, breaches of taste, and deviations from sound ethical conduct are in a sense superficial and are not necessarily intrinsic. Equally, the high-minded types of advertising which we see more regularly than we sometimes realize are also extraneous to an analysis of the basic nature of advertising. What is basic is that advertising, as such, with all its vast power to influence values and conduct, cannot ever lose sight of the fact that it ultimately regards man as a consumer and defines its own mission as one of stimulating him to consume or to desire to consume.

If one can justifiably say that advertising has joined the charmed circle of institutions which fix the values and standards of society and that it has done this without being linked to any of the socially defined objectives which usually guide such institutions in the use of their power, then it becomes necessary to consider with special care the extent and nature of its influence—how far it extends and in what way it makes itself felt.

To do this, it may be well to begin with the budget, for the activity of all major institutions—great churches, great governments, great universities—can be measured in part by what they spend, and, though such measurements are no substitute for qualitative evaluation, they are significant. In political history the importance of the power of the purse is proverbial. I have already said that the amount spent for advertising in the United States in 1951 was $6,548,000,000. Perhaps this may be a little more meaningful if I add that the amount is equivalent to $199 per year for every separate family in the United States. Compare this with what the nation paid for primary and secondary public education in 1949, which amounted to a total expenditure of $5,010,000,000. This means that, for every household, we paid $152. Our national outlay for the education of citizens, therefore, amounted to substantially less than our expenditure for the education of consumers. It would also be interesting to compare the financial strength of advertising and of religion, but, since the churches do not publicize records of their financial operations, I can only remark that there were 180,000 gainfully employed clergymen in the United States in 1950, and most of them were men of very modest incomes. For every clergyman supported by any church, advertising spent $36,000.

Perhaps more explicit comparisons may serve to reinforce this point of the relative magnitude of advertising activities. I will mention two: In 1949–50 the operating expenses of Yale University were $15,000,000; in 1948 the expenses, for newspaper advertising only, of two major distilleries, Schenley and National Distillers, were more than half of this amount, or $7,800,000. In 1944 the major political parties spent $23,000,000 to win the public to the support of Mr. Roosevelt or of Governor Dewey; in 1948, Procter and Gamble, Colgate-Palmolive-Peet, and Lever Brothers spent more than $23,000,000 to win the public to the support of one or another of their products.

With expenditures of this order of magnitude, advertising clearly thrusts with immense impact upon the mass media and, through them, upon the public. The obvious and direct impact is, of course, through the quantity of space it occupies in the newspapers and magazines and the amount of time it occupies in radio and television broadcasts. Either in space or in time the totals are impressive, and, if advertising had no influence upon the information in newspapers, the stories in magazines, and the programs in radio and television, it would still be a force worthy of major consideration because of the influence of the advertising matter itself. But it does have a profound influence upon the media, and for students of American opinion and American life it is important that this influence should be understood.

To appreciate this influence, let us consider the position of most magazines a century ago, as contrasted with their position today. At that time the only financial support which a magazine could expect was from its readers. This meant that, if a person did not care to read, the magazine had no means of appealing to him and no objective in doing so. If editors worried about circulation, it was because they needed more revenue from subscriptions, and if they had enough subscriptions to support them on a modest scale of operations, they could safely proceed on a basis of keeping their standards high and their circulation limited. They did not worry very much about advertising, for the reason that there was not much advertising to worry about. At the time of the Civil War, for instance, it is estimated that the total income from advertising received by all newspapers and periodicals averaged about 25 cents per capita yearly for the population at that time.

Today, of course, these conditions have ceased to apply. Newspapers and magazines no longer look to their subscribers as the major source of revenue. As long ago as 1935 the revenue of all newspapers in the country was $760,000,000, of which $500,000,000 came from advertising and $260,000,000 from subscriptions. At the same time, the magazines of the United States enjoyed a revenue of $144,000,000 from subscriptions and $186,000,000 from advertising. That is, approximately two out of every three newspaper dollars came from advertising, and more than one out of every two magazine dollars came from the same source. The subscriber had been reduced to a sad position: whereas at one time periodicals had fished for subscribers, they now fished for advertisers and used subscribers as bait. Since that time, newspaper advertising has increased more than threefold, to the total of $2,226,000,000, and magazine advertising has risen to $562,000,000, from which we may infer that the subscriber is now, more than ever before, a secondary figure. If I may express the same point in a different way, the situation is this: In 1935 American families paid an average of $6.60 a year to receive newspapers, but advertisers paid an average of $12.70 to have newspapers sent to each family, and in 1951 advertising was paying $56 a year to have newspapers delivered to each family. Clearly that was far more than the household itself could possibly be expected to pay. Similarly, with magazines, while subscribers in 1935 were paying $3.60 a year to receive them, advertisers were paying $4.70 to have them sent, and by 1951 American advertising had increased enough to pay $14 per family per year as its stake in the magazines on the living-room table of the American home. In many cases, as of magazines with large advertising sections, the real situation is that the advertiser buys the magazine for the "purchaser," and what the purchaser pays as the "price" of the magazine is really only a kind of qualifying fee to prove that he is a bona fide potential consumer and not a mere deadhead on whom this handsome advertising spread would be wasted.

If this were merely a matter of some magazines being published for consumers and other magazines being published for readers, with the public retaining a choice between the two, the result would not have been quite so sweeping; but the effect of this change has been to threaten with extinction the magazine that is published first and foremost for its readers.

The threat operates in this way: the magazine with large advertising revenue can afford to pay its contributors more, and therefore it can secure better contributors than the magazine which enjoys very little revenue of this kind. In a sense, the advertiser is prepared to buy better authors for the reader than the reader is prepared to buy for himself. But this means automatically that any magazine which wishes to secure or retain the best writers must get advertising. But to get advertising it must also get mass circulation. To get mass circulation it must publish material with a mass appeal. Also, it must keep its subscription costs low, which in turn makes it more dependent than ever upon advertising revenue. At this point a fixed cycle is virtually inescapable: millions of readers are essential to secure a large revenue from advertising, advertising is essential to enable the magazine to sell at a price that will secure millions of readers—therefore, the content of the magazine must be addressed to the millions. Thus the best writers, those who have proved able to write for the most discriminating readers, are put to work writing for consumers who may not be readers at all.

But it is even more significant to realize that other media are far more completely part of the institutional apparatus of advertising than are periodicals. Magazines and newspapers are still paid for in part by the consumer; but radio and television programs are paid for almost wholly by advertisers. In 1951 it was estimated that there were 100,000,000 radios in the United States, and radio advertising was estimated at $690,000,000. That is, advertisers were annually spending $6.90 to provide each set with programs, while the programs received by the 15,000,000 television sets were being subsidized at the rate of $32 a set.

What this means, in functional terms, it seems to me, is that the newspaper feature, the magazine article, the radio program, do not attain the dignity of being ends in themselves; they are rather means to an end: that end, of course, is to catch the reader's attention so that he will then read the advertisement or hear the commercial, and to hold his interest until these essential messages have been delivered. The program or the article becomes a kind of advertisement in itself—becomes the "pitch," in the telling language of the circus barker. Its function is to induce people to accept the commercial, just as the commercial's function is to induce them to accept the product.[4]

A year or two ago an English critic complained of American periodical writing that it "fixes the attention but does not engage the mind." If this is true, it is not because of any intrinsic vacuity on the part of American writers but because the most important financial supporters of such writing are paying for it to do exactly what is alleged. "To fix the attention but not to engage the mind" is a precise statement of the advertiser's formula.

In saying this, I do not mean at all to suggest that advertisers are personally hostile to thoughtful writing or that they consciously desire to encourage writing which has a low intellectual content. On the contrary, it should be recognized that some of the advertising associations have shown themselves soberly aware of the power they wield and acutely desirous of using it for the public good. But it is the nature of advertising that it must aim for a mass appeal, and it is the nature of the mass media that they must present any item—an idea or a fact or a point of view—in such a way that it will attract the maximum number of readers. To do this, of course, they must suppress any controversial or esoteric aspects of the item and must express it in terms of the least common denominator. But these terms are usually emotional ones rather than rational ones, for the emotional impulses of a large group of people are much more uniform throughout the group than are the mental processes of various individuals in the same group. Walter Lippmann expressed this idea very precisely a good many years ago, in his *The Phantom Public*. He was speaking of political action, but his words nevertheless apply to all communication which involves masses of people. "Since the general opinions of large numbers of persons," he said, "are almost certain to be a vague and confusing medley, action cannot be taken until these opinions have been factored down, canalized, compressed, and made uniform. The making of one general will out of a multitude of general wishes . . . consists essentially in the use of symbols which assemble emotions after they have been detached from their ideas. . . . The process, therefore, by which general opinions are brought to coöperation consists of an intensification of feeling and a degradation of significance."

Mr. Donald Slesinger, speaking at the University of Chicago some years ago, made a very similar observation in a context which included other matters besides politics. "Since common experience is essential to communication," he said, "the greater the number to be [simultaneously] reached, the simpler the communication must be."[5]

These factors of simplification, of intensifying the feeling while degrading the significance, and of fixing the attention of the mass audience are all related to one basic condition of the media, namely, that they are concerned not with finding an audience to hear their message but rather with finding a message to hold their audience. The prime requisite of the message is that it must not diminish the audience either by antagonizing or by leaving out anyone. Moreover, since the actual personnel and tastes of a vast, amorphous, and "invisible" audience cannot possibly be known, the result is, in effect, to set up an axiom that the message must not say anything that, in the opinion of a cautious proprietor, might *possibly* offend or leave out some of those who might *possibly* form part of the audience. For such an axiom there are several implicit corollaries of far-reaching importance. First, a message must not deal with subjects of special or out-of-the-way interest, since such subjects by definition have no appeal for the majority of the audience. Second, it must not deal with any subject at a high level of maturity, since many people are immature, chronologically or otherwise, and a mature level is one which, by definition, leaves such people out. Third, it must not deal with matters which are controversial or even unpleasant or distressing, since such matters may, by definition, antagonize or offend some members of the audience.

If I may examine each of these corollaries briefly, we are confronted first with the fact that many perfectly inoffensive and noncontroversial subjects are excluded from the media simply because these subjects appeal to only a limited number of people. Being directed to the millions, the media must necessarily avoid consideration of subjects which interest only the thousands or the hundreds. This implies a danger to freedom of expression, but not the precise danger against which the guardians of our liberties are usually warning us. They fear that large publishers and advertisers, wielding autocratic power, will ruthlessly suppress minority ideas. The dynamics of the mass market, however, would seem to indicate that freedom of expression has less to fear from the control which large advertisers exercise than from the control which these advertisers permit the mass market to exercise. In the mass media we have little evidence of censorship in the sense of deliberate, planned suppression imposed by moral edict but much evidence of censorship in the sense of operative suppression of a great range of subjects—a suppression imposed by public indifference or, more precisely, by the belief of those who control the media, that the public would be indifferent.[6]

For instance, as Slesinger remarked, motion pictures cannot concern themselves with topics that interest only a minority of people. To borrow his illustration, there is no group which would regard treatment of the themes of horticulture or antique-collecting as objectionable, yet, in fact, motion pictures are in effect barred from using these themes, because "the part of the audience that was interested in horticulture might very well be completely bored by the collection of antiques. But both the gardeners and the antique-collectors can readily get together on a kiss in the dark."

Closely related to the exclusion of special subjects is the avoidance of advanced or mature treatment of the subjects which are accepted. Paul F. Lazarsfeld has investigated this aspect of the matter as it manifests itself in connection with radio and has stated his conclusions very pointedly. He speaks of the appearance of a new type of "radio consumer" in many cultural areas. "Radio," he said, writing in 1941, "has helped to bring to the attention of the American people the important events in Europe and thus has contributed to the generally increased interest in news. However, it has been shown in special studies that this new type of news-consumer created by radio has a more hazy knowledge and a less acute interest in those events than the traditional and smaller groups of people with long-established news interests. A similar audience has been developed in the field of serious music. There is no doubt that the broadcasting of good music over hundreds of stations in this country has enlarged the number of those who like it. Still, a more detailed study of their tastes and attitudes has shown that the musical world of these new music lovers is different, if not inferior, to that of the musical elite of past decades and as judged by classical standards."[7]

In a democracy no one should disparage the value of any activity which serves to raise the level of popular taste, but it is still legitimate to count the cost of such a gain. Particularly in connection with news broadcasting and in connection with popular articles on public affairs, it seems to me that we can easily see the application of Walter Lippmann's formula, "the intensification of feeling and the degradation of significance."

Finally, there is the avoidance of the controversial or distressing. This manifests itself not only in connection with obvious matters such as labor unionization, race relations, or the like, but more fundamentally in the creation of a stereotype of society from which all questions of social significance are carefully screened out. Lazarsfeld has made this point, also, very strikingly with radio "soap operas" as his illustration. These programs, numbering nearly three hundred a day ten years ago, are eagerly awaited throughout the nation by millions of women who might certainly be expected "to pattern their own behavior upon the solutions for domestic problems that appear in the serials." But, in fact, Lazarsfeld found that the programs carefully refrained from exercising any such influence: "The settings are middle class—conforming to the environment of the listeners. In forty-five serials carefully followed up for three weeks, not one character was found who came from the laboring class. Inasmuch as they are upper-class characters, they are used to lend glamour to the middle-class settings rather than to play a role of their own. All problems are of an individualistic nature. It is not social forces but the virtues and vices of the central characters that move the events along. People lose jobs not for economic reasons but because their fellow-men lie or are envious. A simple black and white technique avoids any insoluble conflicts. Even the everyday activities of the characters are patterned according to what the listeners presumably do themselves; reading, for instance, is something which is rarely done in these plays. No other effect than the reinforcement of already existing attitudes can be expected from such programs."[8]

In a sense—a negative sense—the desire to offend no one involves an attitude of what may be called "tolerance." As David Riesman tellingly remarks, the writer or broadcaster, addressing himself to the amorphous audience, does not know how the virus of indignation may be received, and he must therefore "be preoccupied with the antibodies of tolerance." But, clearly, this tolerance is, as the phrase implies, one of mental asepsis rather than one of mental nourishment. It deals with ideas not by weighing them but by diluting them. Tolerance once implied that the advocates of an idea might be heard without prejudice and judged on their merits, but this toleration merely implies that, since society will refrain from exercising the power to judge them, it will relieve itself of responsibility to hear them. It involves not impartiality of judgment but simply default of judgment.

In the realm of politics, of course, antagonistic points of view do continue to receive a hearing, and the continued presence of vigorously partisan editorials and radio addresses by men in political life may seem to disprove all that I have just been saying; but the significant fact is that the political sector is the only one where the indulgence, or even the recognition, of vigorously maintained viewpoints is permitted. Many social questions, many of the profound problems of American life, lie beyond the pale.

In this discussion of the importance of advertising, the purpose has been to explore its effects upon the noneconomic phases of our culture. For that reason I have refrained from introducing some significant points in connection with the changes wrought by advertising in the economy. For instance, it is important that advertising tends less to provide the consumer with what he wants than to make him like what he gets. In this connection Richard B. Tennant, in his recent book on the American cigarette industry, shows that the American Tobacco Company, in the second decade of this century, produced at least eight different brands of cigarettes, designed to meet the diverse demands of varying smoking tastes and different purses; but after 1925 it began to concentrate its advertising upon Lucky Strikes and after 1927 began to dispose of its minor brands to other companies, though it did later develop Herbert Tareytons and Pall Malls.[9] Also, it is important that advertising tends to minimize information and maximize appeal, with the result that producers tend less to differentiate their products physically, in terms of quality, or economically, in terms of price, than to differentiate them psychologically in terms of slogan, package, or prestige. "How many advertisers," asked Walter Dill Scott in 1903, "describe an undergarment so that the reader can feel the pleasant contact with the body?" Surely this is one question to which time has given us a definite answer.

But the most important effects of this powerful institution are not upon the economics of our distributive system; they are upon the values of our society. If the economic effect is to make the purchaser like what he buys, the social effect is, in a parallel but broader sense, to make the individual like what he gets—to enforce already existing attitudes, to diminish the range and variety of choices, and, in terms of abundance, to exalt the materialistic virtues of consumption.

Certainly it marks a profound social change that this new institution for shaping human standards should be directed, not, as are the school and the church, to the inculcation of beliefs or attitudes that are held to be of social value, but rather to the stimulation or even the exploitation of materialistic drives and emulative anxieties and then to the validation, the sanctioning, and the standardization of these drives and anxieties as accepted criteria of social value. Such a transformation, brought about by the need to stimulate desire for the goods which an abundant economy has to offer and which a scarcity economy would never have produced, offers strong justification for the view that advertising should be recognized as an important social influence and as our newest major institution—an institution peculiarly identified with one of the most pervasive forces in American life, the force of economic abundance.

NOTES

1. Ralph M. Hower, *The History of an Advertising Agency: N. W. Ayer & Son at Work, 1869–1949* (Cambridge, Mass.: Harvard University Press, 1949), p. 207.

2. On the history of advertising in general see Frank S. Presbrey, *The History and Development of Advertising* (Garden City, N.Y.: Doubleday Doran & Co., 1929); Ralph M. Hower, *op. cit.* On advertising in periodicals see Frank Luther Mott, *A History of American Magazines* (3 vols.; Cambridge, Mass.: Harvard University Press, 1930–38). Presbrey's work contains the quotations from *Printer's Ink* and from Walter Dill Scott.

3. Percival and Paul Goodman, *Communitas* (Chicago: University of Chicago Press, 1947), pp. 60–64, 73.

4. *A Study of Four Media,* published by the Alfred Politz Research Company (1953), states that "the delivery of an audience for the advertiser is the fundamental function of any medium" (p. 5).

5. Donald Slesinger, "The Film and Public Opinion," in a symposium, *Print, Radio, and Film in a Democracy* (Chicago: University of Chicago Press, 1942), pp. 79, 88.

6. "In our society the captains of industry and princes of merchandise who, one would have thought, would be the great social initiators, are generally hamstrung in expressing the slightest overt public opinion, for it would be bound to be unpopular with at least a minority; and this would be fatal to sales" (Goodman and Goodman, *op. cit.,* p. 80).

7. Paul F. Lazarsfeld, "The Effects of Radio on Public Opinion," in *Print, Radio, and Film in a Democracy,* pp. 72–73.

8. *Ibid.,* pp. 67–68.

9. Richard Bremer Tennant, *The American Cigarette Industry* (New Haven: Yale University Press, 1950), pp. 81–84.

CHAPTER 5

ADVERTISING HISTORY
According to the Textbooks

VINCENT P. NORRIS

"Studying a subject without an appreciation of its antecedents is like seeing a picture in two dimensions—there is no depth. The study of history gives us this depth as well as an understanding of why things are as they are." (4) Thus Brink and Kelley introduce their discussion of the history of promotion.

Seventeen introductory advertising texts (4; 5; 8; 10; 12; 13; 16; 20; 21; 22; 24; 25; 30; 39; 50; 52; 53) published in the United States during the past 20 years were studied to discover whether their authors share Brink and Kelley's belief in the value of history. The 17 do not include all such texts now in print but they include all the leading texts as well as most of the others. Some were written by faculty members of schools of journalism and communications, some by faculty members of business schools and some by practitioners.

The research had its interesting moments but on the whole it was a depressing experience—especially if the texts are indicative of what advertising teachers in general know about the history of advertising, of what they think students should know, or even of what they conceive of as history itself.

Of the 17 texts, most of which run to more than 600 pages, six present no history at all. Three offer fewer than ten pages and five, from ten to twenty pages. Only three present more than 20 pages of history. The longest chapter, written by Brink and Kelley, runs 33 pages in a relatively short book of 490 pages.

There is even less history than those numbers suggest, since in the typical text from one-fourth to one-half of the space is given over to reproductions of old advertisements. These may amuse the students, but add little to their grasp of history.

More depressing than the small quantity of history is its poor quality. With only two exceptions (perhaps three, depending on how rigorous one wishes to be), the so-called history chapters are not history at all. They are collections of interesting tales of the deeds and sayings of such famous men as Dr. Johnson, Addison and Steele, Benjamin Franklin, Volney Palmer and P. T. Barnum, strung together in chronological order and liberally sprinkled with illustrations. Of the social, economic and political environments in which those men lived and in which the advertisements appeared, almost nothing can be found.

From *Journal of Advertising* 9, no. 3 (1980). Copyright © 1980 by the American Academy of Advertising. Reprinted with permission from M.E. Sharpe, Inc.

The lack of historical perspective in the texts results in a naive and indeed, incorrect view of how advertising developed and functions. The most important weaknesses, which I deal with below, are the failure to recognize the existence of premarket societies, the rise of capitalism, the Industrial Revolution's impact on society, the fundamental difference between retail and national advertising, and the nature of advertising as an economic institution.

ADVERTISING IN PREMARKET SOCIETIES

From most of the texts, students would infer that advertising is as old as mankind. In some cases, they are explicitly told that "advertisements in some shape or form have existed not only from time immemorial, but almost for all time," (38) that it "flourished" three thousand years ago (25) and "played an important role in the development of countless societies and cultures" (13, 20).

Inserted amidst such nonsense is "proof" in the form of examples. One encounters the same examples in one text after another. The repetition suggests a good deal of inbreeding or, perhaps, despite the statements to the contrary, the true paucity of advertisements in the ancient world. Further, many of the examples were not advertisements at all. Some were mere on-premise identifying signs. Others were personal selling. One text even claims that the wall inscriptions on Hammurabi's temple in Uruk were early examples of corporate billboard advertising and that the Rosetta Stone was an early poster (20, 5–8).

Of course, one of the best ways to legitimate anything is to say that it is as old as mankind—that, as Kleppner says of advertising, it is "human nature (21, 2)." An interesting variation on that theme is the inclusion of an out-of-context discussion of advertising in the Soviet Union—presumably to show that even communists can't get along without it (50, 44–47; 52, 56–57).

Only one text (39, 20–22) explains that advertising is associated with market activity and even more so with market economies, and that until very recently there was very little of the former and none of the latter. The explanation is far too brief, however, to enable the beginning student, who has never known anything but capitalism, to understand the fundamental differences.

Every society, even a group of castaways, must cope with the two basic economic problems: how to allocate scarce resources, and how to distribute output (wealth). By far, most of the "countless societies and cultures" man has developed during his time on this planet solved both of those problems according to principles of reciprocity, redistribution, and householding, types of economic organization in which there is no place for advertising (18; 27; 32; 37).

Reciprocity, simply, is gift-giving, according to traditional, well-defined patterns, so that every member of the society knows his assigned tasks and receives his rightful share of the wealth. Neither giver nor receiver has any reason to advertise.

Redistribution is based on central authority and functions much like the public sector of modern economies. The people, motivated by loyalty, respect, and ultimately by the threat of force, give some part of their produce to the leader as tribute or taxes. Some in turn is redistributed (hence the name) in the form of feasts, public works and so forth. There is no need for advertising in this system, either.

Householding is economic self-sufficiency by families or other small groups who produce for their own consumption, engaging in little or no exchange with others. The absence of need or opportunity to advertise is obvious.

THE COMING OF ECONOMIC SOCIETY

Since virtually all the texts fail to point out that the economies of the ancient world and medieval Europe were fundamentally different from modern free-enterprise capitalism, it is not surprising that little or nothing is said about the arrival of capitalism in the western world a few centuries ago, or about the historical forces associated with its birth, or even about how a capitalist economy is supposed to function.

Although two texts mention the guilds in passing, not one mentions the Commercial Revolution. Nothing is said of the Reformation or of the Protestant Ethic and how it differed from the Catholic Church's view of commercial activity. The word "mercantilism" is not mentioned in a single text, although one makes an oblique reference to the Trade and Navigation Acts. Not one text mentions the Scientific Revolution or the Enlightenment, and only one discusses (too briefly) the classical liberal *Weltanschauung* and its important role in the development of capitalism.

Neither do the texts explain that, even after the market assumed an important role in Western economies, householding remained the predominant feature of economic life for the majority of the population. Much is made of Benjamin Franklin (one text devotes an entire page to him) as though he exemplified the Americans of his day. But in Franklin's time it required many farmers to produce a sufficient surplus beyond their own needs to feed and clothe a single city dweller. Prior to the Industrial Revolution, more than 90 percent of the population lived on farms, householding (44). They sold their small surplus and bought the few things they could not produce, but money played a tiny part in their lives. They did not *earn* a living, they *made* a living. One New England farmer, far more typical of his contemporaries than was Franklin, wrote in his diary:

> My farm gave me and my whole family a good living on the produce of it and left me, one year with another, one hundred and fifty silver dollars, for I never spent more than ten dollars a year, which was for salt, nails and the like. Nothing to eat, drink or wear was bought as my farm produced it all (14).

So, while it is possible for authors to reproduce advertisements from early newspapers, their importance in the lives of the general population is exaggerated unless the reader is told how little advertising and commerce there were. Even among merchants, advertising was of little importance. As Max Weber said, "the advertisement as a notice by the merchant, directed toward finding a market, first becomes an established phenomenon at the end of the 18th century" (49). He was speaking, of course, of England, where the Industrial Revolution was well underway by that time.

THE INDUSTRIAL REVOLUTION AND NATIONAL ADVERTISING

The Industrial Revolution not only made possible the quantity and forms of advertising we have today, it transformed every aspect of the economy and of life in general. Most of the texts do not note these effects, characterizing the Industrial Revolution merely as a period of increased production. Neither do the texts show how the Revolution led to national advertising or even that national advertising is fundamentally different from retail advertising in both purpose and effects—a matter I will discuss later.

Dunn and Barban, for example, devote only three sentences to the Industrial Revolution:

> Immediately before and after the Civil War there began a great era of business expansion in the United States. Technological discoveries made it possible to expand production significantly and to replace hand labor with power driven machinery. This increased enormously the goods available for marketing (13, 27).

Those three sentences are true enough, but they do not begin to point out the sweeping economic and social changes that were, indeed, revolutionary. From a society in which more than nine out of ten families lived substantially like the New England farmer quoted above, America became in only two lifetimes a society in which only one family in 25 lives on a farm (45). And that family, like those in towns and cities, *earns* rather than *makes* its living, selling virtually all its produce and buying virtually everything it consumes. Householding is now so rare as to be a curiosity, practiced only by those who have "dropped out" of society.

Dunn and Barban do mention the population growth of a few cities but fail to explain the significance of urbanization. Only at the end of the chapter does one find any reference to the most important changes of the Industrial Revolution, but merely in the form of a disconnected list of "Forces Behind the Facts." Thus the growth of the middle class is brushed off in a one-sentence afterthought, while P. T. Barnum receives two paragraphs in the body of the chapter.

Most of the texts provide an even less satisfactory treatment of the Industrial Revolution. Norris says nothing about it except that as manufacturers' markets began to expand, some of them began to publish almanacs advertising their products. Weilbacher offers only one paragraph and Mandell a half-page about the expansion of markets. Wright, *et al.* offer one page containing several historical errors. Kleppner presents a bit more but has Henry Ford inventing mass production in 1913!

Only two of the texts offer satisfactory accounts of the Industrial Revolution and the growth of national advertising. The better of these is the tenth edition of *Advertising Theory and Practice* by Sandage, Fryburger and Rotzoll. Due to the newly added third author, this edition is a radical departure from the nine previous editions, all of which were essentially the same in structure and content (39). Rotzoll is senior author of *Advertising in Contemporary Society* (36) which deals with some of the same material. Since it is not intended as an introductory text, it is not a part of the sample under consideration here.

The other, somewhat broader in scope, is Brink and Kelley's *Management of Promotion*. Several pages are devoted to the Industrial Revolution and national advertising, the explanation of which is sound although somewhat less incisive than that in Sandage, *et al.*

Otherwise, if one finds any mention at all of the growth of national advertising, one finds the naive and incorrect explanation that as markets expanded, the increasing distance between manufacturer and consumer made it necessary for the former to tell the latter about his products. Here are three examples:

> A need arose to extend markets geographically, and the manufacturer had to find a way of communicating the value of his products to people who knew nothing of his reputation (52, 15–16).

> As manufacturers were separated from the ultimate consumer by wholesalers or franchisees, they looked to advertising to bridge this gap (13, 40).

> As manufacturers grew, they began to advertise to sell what they produced (25, 28).

That myth has become so firmly entrenched in the folklore of advertising that even an author who knows better slipped into the trap: "In essence, the distance between producers and consumers had grown too wide" (39, 33).

In the same text, however, one finds a reproduction of two pages of *The Pennsylvania Evening Post* of July 6, 1776, in which the Declaration of Independence is followed by several advertisements. In one of them, Isaac Hazelhurst offers the public "coffee of the best quality" (39, 27). Obviously that coffee was grown several thousands of miles from Pennsylvania, yet the farmer who grew it saw no need to advertise in the *Evening Post*. He simply sold it, at the market price, to a buyer. There is no reason to suppose the farmer was unable to sell all the coffee he could harvest. The coffee probably changed hands several times before arriving at Mr. Hazelhurst's store, but it is improbable that it was advertised by any previous seller.

The notion that physical distance between producer and consumer is the reason for, or makes necessary, national advertising is disproved not only by the example of Mr. Hazelhurst's coffee but also by the existence in the market of a great number of products, made or grown we know not where, but unadvertised by producer or even the retailer. All of us, including the authors of these texts, buy them regularly.

It is also disproved by the fact that manufacturers do not omit their own communities from their national advertising plans on grounds that people there already know them. If that were the case, General Motors would not advertise automobiles in Detroit and Procter and Gamble would not advertise soap in Cincinnati.

The correct explanation of the appearance and growth of national advertising is unmistakably clear in the writings of eyewitnesses to its birth: the manufacturers' motive was to achieve market power in their dealings with distributors.

One of the most successful advertising men of the time was Earnest Elmo Calkins (6). In 1905 he published in *Printers' Ink* an article tellingly entitled "Eliminating the Jobber" (34). He began by commenting on the widespread use of that expression in advertising circles, hastily adding that it did not refer to the jobber's extermination, but only to his subjugation.

Prior to national advertising, Calkins explained, the manufacturer was powerless. The jobber said to him, "You manufacture this, that, or the other. Make it so and so. Sell it to me for so much" (34). Naturally the jobber ordered from those manufacturers who could be depended upon to deliver goods of the desired quality, on schedule, at the lowest price. The manufacturer whose goods were defective or who could not meet the market price faded from the scene.

But the manufacturer who began to brand and advertise his goods could avoid the rigors of price competition. He could compel the distributor to buy *his* brand at *his* price:

> To the manufacturer who advertises it makes no difference what jobber or what commission man buys his goods. *All of them will have to buy them in the end.* Just as soon as a retailer finds that a certain line of goods is so strongly demanded that he must have it, he will go where he can get it. If a given jobber doesn't handle it, he will go to a new jobber (34, italics added).

In the trade, that is known as "forcing distribution."

The same issue of *Printer's Ink* carried an editorial making much the same point about the motives of manufacturers:

> They now realize that this is a golden age in trademarks—a time when almost any maker of a worthy product can lay down the lines of a demand that will not only grow with years (sic) beyond anything that has ever been known before, but will become in some degree a monopoly (26).

The editorial goes on to point out the value of national advertising in erecting barriers to potential competition:

In ten years at the farthest, perhaps in five or less, every commodity of large consumption will have its trademarked leader, firmly entrenched through advertising. The first will be that leader, and all that come after will necessarily take the leavings of demand. . . . To build up a demand for a rival of Sapolio today would take millions, if it could be done at all (26).

This preceded by 60 years David Ogilvy's estimate that a "warchest" of at least ten million dollars would now be needed to break into the detergent market (31). It also preceded Joe S. Bain's *Barriers to New Competition* by 50 years (1).

Calkins repeated his earlier explanation seven years later in *Modern Advertising,* which he wrote with Ralph Holden. Before the manufacturer began to advertise, "He had to manufacture to order what was wanted. He had to compete in price and in other conditions with the manufacturers" (7). After he began to advertise, however, "the commission man, the jobber and the traveling man became less and less necessary to him, until in some lines of business they have dropped out altogether" (7).

So, despite Calkins' earlier comment that "eliminating the jobber" did not mean exterminating him, many had been driven from the field.

Another eyewitness to the beginnings of national advertising and eminently successful practitioner was Claude Hopkins, who stated that "Most national advertisers are aiming largely to build effective barriers against competition" (11). In *My Life in Advertising* he told how, as advertising manager of Swift and Company, he used advertising to sell Swift's Conosuet shortening to bakers *at a higher price* than a rival's Cottolene, although "They knew Conosuet to be identical with Cottolene" (29).

Another practitioner, George Burton Hotchkiss, offered a similar explanation in 1933, adding that "National advertising by manufacturers was never looked upon with great favor by either wholesalers or large retailers," who realized its purpose was to enable manufacturers to dominate them (17).

Celebrating its fiftieth anniversary, *Printers' Ink* published a special supplement to its July 28, 1939 issue. Here, again, one finds the same explanation of the origins of national advertising. "The jobber told the manufacturer what he wanted made, how he wanted it made and what he would pay for it." After the manufacturer began to advertise, however, "he found that in a short time the jobber came to him and *asked him what he would charge for the goods*" (35).

In addition to all this eyewitness testimony, investigations conducted more recently by economists and government agencies provide a huge body of evidence consistent with the writings of the pioneers: the purpose of national advertising today, as it was originally, is to create product differentiation, a degree of monopoly, and barriers to entry. These enable the manufacturer to force distribution and engage in pricing discretion, pricing discrimination, and market domination (9; 28; 46; 48).

Although there are better and more recent studies than Neil Borden's *Economic Effects of Advertising,* the authors of these texts seem not to have heard of them—and the few who have, seem not to have read them. For that matter, they seem not to have read Borden either, despite an apparent rule that no one may write an advertising text without paying obeisance to him. For Borden makes it clear again and again that the purpose of national advertising is to enable manufacturers to gain market power so that they can raise prices and increase profits (3).

Despite all the foregoing evidence, however, or perhaps oblivious to it, most of the authors say that manufacturers advertise merely to make their products known to distant consumers so as to increase sales. That is economically unsound. Just as the South American coffee farmer could sell all the coffee he could harvest without advertising to distant consumers (or to anyone else, for that matter), provided he accepted the market price, American manufacturers could operate their plants at capacity and sell their products in the same manner—and indeed, thousands of them do exactly that to this day. Further, it is not to a manufacturer's advantage to attempt to increase his sales beyond capacity unless he can raise his price, for his production cost (never mind his newly incurred branding and advertising cost) would exceed his price.

A related error is the notion that advertising increased sales not only for individual manufacturers but cumulatively for all manufacturers, thus raising levels of employment and national income. In a magnificent non-sequitur, Mandell says, "Advertising has as its major objective persuading people to buy. Increased demand results in increased production and more jobs" (25, 50). He not only commits the fallacy of composition but incorrectly uses "demand" to mean quantity sold. Increased demand may simply mean the same quantity sold at a higher price, or even a smaller quantity at a still higher price.

This notion, that advertising increases aggregate consumption, is found in virtually every advertising text and is a common theme of advertising writers. It is an article of faith: in Presbrey's phrase, "beyond discussion" (33, v). Not one shred of scientifically acceptable evidence is offered to support it. The usual "proof" is "our rising standard of living." That is pure *post hoc* thinking, and backwards at that, since the evidence indicates that increases in consumption cause increases in advertising, rather than vice-versa (40, 54).

In a similar error, Wright, *et al.* says that national advertising "helped raise consumption so that the full use of machinery was possible, thus bringing about lower per-unit costs of manufacture" (52, 16). Any economics text, however, will demonstrate that it is the price competitor who makes full use of his machinery and minimizes per-unit costs, while the manufacturer of differentiated products almost invariably operates *below* capacity at *higher* per-unit costs.

What these authors overlook is that prices reflect both costs *and demand*—strictly speaking, marginal cost and marginal revenue. If advertising does increase demand (that is, shift the demand curve upward and to the right), the firm will probably find it more profitable to raise prices than to lower them. The lengthiest and most confused presentation of this and related fallacies is found in Dunn and Barban, in a four-page discussion of a hypothetical candy company (13, Chap. 4). Since the discussion contains more than a dozen errors, I will not even list them.

Another popular way of "proving" that advertising leads to lower prices is to present examples of products whose prices fell, presumably for the reasons stated by Wright, *et al.* This, too, is *post hoc* thinking which overlooks three important considerations. First, manufacturers who introduce new products know they can increase their profits by a technique known as "skimming." The introductory price is deliberately set high to "skim the cream off the market." Later a somewhat lower price skims off the next layer, and so on as the manufacturer "slides down his demand curve" until he reaches the point at which marginal cost equals marginal revenue, where the price is stabilized (41). The other overlooked factors are the technological improvements that invariably occur after the introduction of a new product, which lower production costs regardless of volume, and the increasing competition as new firms enter the field.

ADVERTISING AS AN ECONOMIC INSTITUTION

Given their propensity to see history as a chronology of old advertisements and famous admen (a variation of the "kings and battles" view of history), it is not surprising that with only four exceptions the authors do not even attempt to discuss advertising as an institution.

Two of those are only gestures. Kleppner merely labels the part of the book which deals with the regulation and the social and economic effects of advertising, "Advertising as an Institution."

The word is not seen again. Aside from a brief review of David Potter's well-known discussion (50, 50–51), Weilbacher mentions the word only once.

Wright, *et al.* do little more. They say they intend to "explore how advertising becomes an institution in our society" (52, 10), then promptly forget their task. Only once again is the word mentioned: "For advertising to become an institution, a need for it had to be recognized" (52, 17). Of course! The same may be said of slavery.

The only serious attempt to discuss advertising as an institution is found in Sandage, *et al.* Unfortunately it is not very incisive. It is not even stated why or how advertising has become an institution, or even what an institution is.

The discussion begins by repeating the hackneyed notion that advertising is a "tool." Advertising is thus beyond criticism since, like any tool, it can be used for good or evil.

But an institution is not a tool! Is private property a tool? A tool is an inanimate object, utterly at the disposal of its user. But we do not *use* institutions, we *participate* in them. They are not at our disposal; on the contrary, we are at theirs. "They may be rigid or flexible in their structures, exacting or lenient in their demands, but alike they constitute standards of conformity from which an individual may depart only at his peril" (19).

Apparently Sandage, *et al.* intend to say that advertising became an institution simply because its use increased until it became a ubiquitous feature of the American scene. That misses the point. It is true that ubiquity is a characteristic of institutions, but that must be properly understood. Wearing a watch on one's wrist instead of in one's pocket is ubiquitous behavior these days but it is by no stretch of the imagination an institution. Trial by a jury of one's peers, on the other hand, is a fundamental and cherished institution in our society, yet most of us live out our lives without ever once participating in a trial—and we are happy to avoid the experience. Competition is a fundamental capitalist institution, but despite all the government's attempts for nearly a century to preserve it, it has all but disappeared from the American economy.

Two characteristics of institutions are more important than mere ubiquity. First, institutions order human relationships into roles. For example, trial-by-jury orders the behavior of participants into roles such as defendant, prosecutor, defense counsel, juryman, judge. Slavery orders participants into roles of master and slave. The market orders participants into roles such as buyer, seller, retailer, broker; and in the factor markets, laborer (rather than slave), employer (rather than master), landlord, and so forth. These roles have no meaning or existence in market-free societies.

Second, an institution regulates (by means of human behavior, of course) the distribution of a society's desiderata to the advantage of some and the disadvantage of others. In general, we say that economic institutions—not just the market, but all of them—regulate the distribution of wealth while political institutions oversee the distribution of power. But in practice the distinction is not so clear, since power can be bought ("Money talks") and every significant political act redistributes wealth.

So it is not enough to say that advertising became an institution when it came into ubiquitous use. In fact, if that were the criterion, it would be difficult to make the case that advertising is an institution. Although most of our media are cluttered with advertisements and advertising is about the sixth largest single expenditure in the United States, it is by no means ubiquitous behavior. There are some 13 million business firms in the United States, but almost one-fourth of the total advertising expenditures are made by a mere 100 firms, mostly oligopolistic manufacturers of homogeneous packaged goods. Many other manufacturers do moderate or trivial amounts of advertising, and many do none at all. The same is true of wholesalers, retailers, plumbers, restauranteurs, architects, and television repairmen. The *Standard Directory of Advertisers* lists only some 17,000 advertisers, not all of them business firms or even located in the United States (42). No doubt that is an incomplete list but nevertheless it is a far cry from 13 million.

It is clear that advertising orders human relationships in the American economy. I refer not so much to the creation of new roles such as advertising agent, copywriter, space salesman, and so forth as to the *reordering* of the roles of participants in the market.

As Calkins pointed out, prior to national advertising, the manufacturer was powerless to set prices. But he failed to add that the wholesaler was equally powerless to set prices, either those paid to manufacturers or charged retailers. And he also failed to mention that every participant in the market *should* be powerless, for only then does the market function properly, with prices set by the "impersonal forces of supply and demand."

National advertising gives power to the manufacturer; his role changes from price *taker* to price *maker.* The wholesaler's role changes too; as manufacturers acquired the power to force distribution of their brands, wholesalers lost some freedom of enterprise, and so did retailers (51). In some lines, as Calkins said, the role of wholesaler disappeared entirely. To the extent that advertising creates barriers to entry, it limits the number of persons who may play the role of manufacturer.

Advertising has also reordered relationships in mass communications. Sandage, *et al.* mention this but do not pursue it. The role of publisher (except those who refuse to accept advertising) has changed from seller of a product to consumers to gatherer of consumers for advertisers. The roles of his employees have changed, too. A television "personality" is primarily a salesman, not a performer, and reporters learn that some stories are better left unreported. The role of the reader changes from sovereign consumer to advertiser bait (15).

Advertising also significantly affects both the allocation of resources and the distribution of wealth. Indeed, it could be argued that in the homogeneous packaged goods sector of the economy, advertising has largely supplanted the market as the institution performing those tasks.

A clear understanding of this matter and of the historical significance of the rise of national advertising requires some knowledge of the theory of capitalism. It is not found in any of the texts. A capitalist, free enterprise economy is based on certain premises about the nature of man and the world, and is expected to perform in a manner that, given those premises, is just and good. Specifically:

1. Since all men are rational and endowed with the inalienable right of property, since the world is a harmonious machine in which a self-righting process or "Invisible Hand" will function if given free rein, there should be freedom of enterprise.

2. Since all men are created equal, with the same right of property, every man deserves to enjoy the property he creates, less the smallest possible deduction to support a minimal government. In other words, every man's income should precisely equal the contribution to GNP of the productive factors he sells in the market. One should reap what he sows; no more, no less. His reward should equal his contribution.

3. Since all men are egoists (some would say hedonists) and a good society is one which provides the greatest happiness for the greatest number, output (wealth) should be maximized.

4. Since waste diminishes attainable output, given the scarcity of resources, production should take place as efficiently as possible. All resources should be attracted to their most productive use. All firms should operate at capacity, the point at which the various factors are combined in ideal proportions, minimizing per-unit cost. In the long run, all firms should operate at optimum scale as well as at capacity.

5. Since men are rational and egoistic, endowed with the right of property, the composition of output should be determined by consumer sovereignty. Using the dollars he receives from the sale of his productive factors, each man votes for the products he wants; these are the products which should be produced, in precisely the desired quantities.

How can all those goals be achieved? That is the marvelous thing: in a price-competitive economy, where men are free to do as they please and seek only their own selfish ends, the Invisible Hand will see to it that these goals are achieved.

The price a competitive manufacturer can obtain is set by supply and demand; it is the best available measure of how consumers are voting to have scarce resources allocated to satisfy their wants. This market price covers all costs including a normal profit, the necessary reward to the entrepreneur for his contribution, without which the good would not be produced.

The wholesaler, too, receives a price that just covers costs including his normal profit and the same is true of the retailer. Under these circumstances, every seller is compelled to be as efficient as possible if he wishes to receive his just reward, but no one can reap more than he sows.

It is incorrect, therefore, to discuss this situation in terms which imply that the manufacturer was the innocent victim of the "caprices and pressures" (21, 11) of the wholesaler who was in a "fortunate position" (39, 32) because he told the manufacturer what he wanted and what he was willing to pay for it. The wholesaler was behaving selfishly, of course, but he was nevertheless behaving precisely as the social good required. A capitalist economy will not function properly unless all the participants act as economic men, making rational, selfish decisions. As an institution, the market rewards appropriate behavior and punishes inappropriate behavior.

As the wholesaler behaved toward the manufacturer, so did the retailer toward the wholesaler, who had to respond to retailer's "caprices and pressures." And the retailer in his turn had to respond to the "caprices and pressures" exerted by sovereign consumers—for do we not attempt to buy precisely what we want at the lowest price we can find? (Except when, in our ignorance, we assume that a higher price is an index of great quality.) (41)

In a price-competitive market, the seller's demand curve will be highly elastic, and prices will tend to just cover costs, including a normal profit. From society's viewpoint that is the ideal situation. From the seller's viewpoint it is not: who among us does not wish to reap more than he sows? Some of the means to that end (e.g., price fixing) have been declared illegal. Among the means that have not are branding and advertising one's product. This creates a degree of monopoly, makes the demand curve much less elastic, and thus provides the opportunity to raise the price.

So the primary purpose of national advertising is not to enable the manufacturer to increase his sales. It is to enable him to *tell* the wholesaler, rather than *ask* him, the price of his goods. His new price will be higher than the old, competitive price—not only to cover his costs of branding and advertising, but beyond that to provide him with the greater profit he is seeking.

If he is rational, he will choose a price that maximizes his profit, the price that equates marginal cost with marginal revenue. That price will almost invariably result in a level of sales that is *less* than he would prefer to sell were he in a competitive market. Only under the most improbable set of circumstances will the national advertiser find that $MC = MR$ at his plant's capacity.

The consequence of all this is that the Invisible Hand is crippled. What is good for the manufacturer is no longer good for society. The firm, now operating at less than capacity, has higher average costs (even before branding and advertising costs are considered); it is wasting resources. But since price is even higher than average cost, the manufacturer is receiving a monopoly profit, a reward in excess of his contribution. As the practice spreads from firm to firm and from industry to industry, total output is diminished. To the extent that entry barriers are raised, freedom of enterprise is diminished. Thus four of the five goals of a capitalist economy, mentioned above, are lost. Some critics say that consumer sovereignty is also lost, since consumers are persuaded to like what they get rather than being able to get what they like. That question, however, goes beyond the scope of economic analysis.

And so it is that national advertising significantly affects both the allocation of resources and the distribution of wealth in a market economy. To the extent that consumers buy smaller quantities of products because their prices are higher, smaller quantities of resources are allocated to their production. This affects the incomes of the sellers of those resources. (Based on the elasticity of demand for automobiles, it has been estimated that several hundred thousand fewer automobiles are sold in the United States each year because of the manufacturers' emphasis on costly advertising and "fictitious style obsolescence" instead of competition through lower prices. Obviously this results in many fewer jobs for automobile workers and suppliers of other factors.) (47) In other cases, resources may be allocated to the production of products which might not be purchased at all if they were not advertised.

To the extent consumers are persuaded to spend their incomes for higher-priced advertised brands, wealth is redistributed from those consumers to the manufacturers. These "monopoly transfers" (as they are called because they can occur only when monopoly is present) are in the first instance a dramatic shift of wealth from consumers, who in the aggregate possess average amounts of wealth, to those few who possess great quantities. This is a kind of "private taxation" (which it is also called for obvious reasons) which, in violation of democratic principles, is highly regressive.

In the second instance, since a consumer's income is finite, his larger expenditure on the higher-priced brand leaves him with less to spend on other things; this reduces not only his own real income but that of the sellers of the other goods and services he can no longer afford to buy. They, in turn, must expend less on productive factors and on consumer goods. The ripples go on and on . . .

CONCLUSIONS

The first conclusion, in view of the fact that the authors of these 17 texts devote less than three percent of their pages to history, is that as a group they do not share Brink and Kelley's belief in the value of history. They seem rather to follow Daniel Starch, whose *Principles of Advertising* (1923) asserts that "it may not be of great value to devote a large amount of space to analyzing and discussing the history of a subject when we are primarily interested in the practical problems on the present day" (43). If that is the educational philosophy that guides advertising education, it is indeed deplorable.

The second conclusion is that, because of the number of egregious errors in these texts, most students receive a seriously distorted view of the history of advertising and its role in the economy. Since, as a rule, it is only in the introductory course that advertising students are exposed to any history at all, it is unlikely that this distorted view is ever corrected.

A possibility exists, of course, that individual teachers are better informed than the writers of these texts, and that they supplement the texts with lectures or additional readings from more scholarly sources. That is expressed more as a hope than as a probability. The "history" found in the texts is, after all, the conventional wisdom of the field. It is as much the received knowledge of the present generation of teachers as of the present generation of students. What was obvious to Calkins, Hopkins and their contemporaries has somehow been filtered out.

Why is that so? One possibility is that the authors have not been very painstaking in their research, and that does seem to have been the case. The footnotes, for example, suggest that the research was neither intensive nor extensive. As I mentioned before, the main source in economic matters, Borden, is not only inferior to more recent work but beyond that appears not to have been read. Most of the authors seem to be unaware of any of the more recent economic analyses of advertising. Those few who do seem to have heard of them and who even recommend them "for further reading" give no evidence of having read them.

Another possible explanation, not incompatible with the preceding one, is that the present day neo-liberal *Weltanschauung* (23) heavily emphasizes social responsibility and functionality. That it influences the writings of advertising practitioners is obvious. Their defenses of advertising are rarely if ever classical liberal in character. Instead, they focus on claims of social responsibility and functionality: advertising is said to lead to lower prices, higher quality, a higher standard of living, and so forth. Today's climate of opinion virtually dictates such an ideology. For advertising teachers to admit that advertising's purpose is not altruistic but solely to increase the wealth of the advertiser, even though it is an obvious truth, may strike them as indecent—almost like pointing out that the Emperor has no clothes.

NOTES

1. Bain, Joe S. *Barriers to New Competitions.* Cambridge, Massachusetts: Harvard University Press, 1956.

2. Blair, John M. *Economic Concentration.* New York: Harcourt Brace Jovanovich, 1972.

3. Borden, Neil. *The Economic Effects of Advertising.* Chicago: Irwin, 1942, pp. 34–43 and Parts II to IV, *passim.*

4. Brink, Edward and William Kelley. *The Management of Promotion.* Englewood Cliffs, New Jersey: Prentice-Hall, 1963.

5. Burton, Philip W. and J. R. Miller. *Advertising Fundamentals.* Columbus, Ohio: Grid, 1976.

6. Calkins, Earnest Elmo. *And Hearing Not . . .* New York: Charles Scribner's Sons, 1946.

7. Calkins, Earnest Elmo and Ralph Holden. *Modern Advertising.* New York: D. Appleton & Co., 1912, pp. 45–48.

8. Cohen, Dorothy. *Advertising.* New York: John Wiley & Sons, 1972.

9. Comanor, William S. and T. Wilson. *Advertising and Market Power.* Cambridge, Massachusetts: Harvard University Press, 1974.

10. Crawford, John. *Advertising* (2nd ed.). Boston: Allyn & Bacon, 1965.

11. "Dealing with Public Opinion," *Judicious Advertising and Advertising Experience,* Vol. 11 (December, 1912), pp. 45–47.

12. Dirksen, Charles, A. Kroeger and F. Nicosia. *Advertising: Principles and Problems* (5th ed.). Homewood, Illinois: Irwin, 1977.

13. Dunn, S. Watson and A. Barban. *Advertising: Its Role in Modern Marketing* (4th ed.). Hinsdale, Illinois: Dryden Press, 1978.

14. Frank, Lawrence K. "Social Change and the Family," *Annals of the American Academy of Political and Social Science,* Vol. 160 (March, 1932), p. 94.

15. Gossage, Howard L. "The Fictitious Freedom of the Press," *Ramparts,* Vol. 4 (August, 1965), pp. 31–36.

16. Hepner, Harry. *Advertising: Creative Communication with Consumers* (4th ed.). New York: McGraw-Hill, 1964.

17. Hotchkiss, George Burton. *An Outline of Advertising.* New York: Macmillan, 1933, p. 56.

18. Humphreys, S. C. "History, Economics and Anthropology: The Work of Karl Polanyi," *History and Theory,* Vol. 8 (1969), pp. 165–212.

19. "Institution," *Encyclopedia of the Social Sciences.* New York: Macmillan, 1935, Vol. 8, pp. 84–89.

20. Johnson, J. Douglas. *Advertising Today.* Chicago: Science Research Associates, 1978.

21. Kleppner, Otto. *Advertising Procedure* (7th ed.). Englewood Cliffs, New Jersey: Prentice-Hall, 1979.

22. Littlefield, James A. and C. A. Kirkpatrick. *Advertising: Mass Communication in Marketing* (3rd ed.). Boston: Houghton Mifflin, 1970.

23. Lodge, George Cabot. The *New American Ideology*. New York: Knopf, 1975.

24. Longman, Kenneth. *Advertising*. New York: Harcourt Brace Jovanovich, 1971.

25. Mandell, Maurice I. *Advertising* (2nd ed.). Englewood Cliffs: New Jersey: Prentice-Hall, 1974.

26. "Manufacturers Are Now Interested in Advertising," *Printers' Ink,* Vol. 51 (May 31, 1905), pp. 32–33.

27. Mauss, Marcel. *The Gift*. tr. Ian Cunnison, New York: Norton, 1967.

28. Mueller, Charles E. "Sources of Monopoly Power: A Phenomenon Called 'Product Differentiation,' 1" *Antitrust Law and Economic Review,* Vol. 2 (Summer, 1969), pp. 59–96.

29. Hopkins, Claude. *My Life in Advertising*. New York: Harper & Brothers, 1927, Ch. 6.

30. Norris, James S. *Advertising*. Reston, Virginia: Reston Publishing Co., 1977.

31. Ogilvy, David. *Confessions of an Advertising Man*. New York: Atheneum, 1963, p. 155.

32. Polanyi, Karl. *The Great Transformation*. New York: Rinehart and Co., 1944, Ch. 4.

33. Presbrey, Frank. *The History and Development of Advertising*. Garden City, N.Y.: Doubleday, Doran, 1929.

34. *Printers' Ink.* Vol. 51 (May 31, 1905), pp. 8–11.

35. "Rendezvous with the Consumer," *Printers' Ink,* Vol. 184 (July 28, 1938), Supplement, 12–4. (italics added)

36. Rotzoll, Kim B., James E. Haefner, and Charles H. Sandage. *Advertising in Contemporary Society: Perspectives Toward Understanding*. Columbus, Ohio: Grid, Inc., 1976.

37. Sahlins, Marshall. "On the Sociology of Primitive Exchange," *Stone Age Economics*. Chicago: Aldine-Atherton, 1972, Ch. 5.

38. Samson, Henry. *History of Advertising*. London: Chatto and Windus, 1875, pp. 19–20, quoted from (25).

39. Sandage, Charles H., V. Fryburger and K. Rotzoll. *Advertising Theory and Practice* (10th ed.). Homewood, Illinois: Irwin, 1979.

40. Schmalensee, Richard. *The Economics of Advertising*. Amsterdam: North-Holland, 1972, especially Ch. 3.

41. Scitovsky, Tibor. *Welfare and Competition* (rev. ed.). Homewood, Illinois: Irwin, 1971, Ch. 23.

42. *Standard Directory of Advertisers*. Skokie, Illinois: National Register Publishing Co., 1979.

43. Starch, Daniel. *Principles of Advertising*. Chicago: A. W. Shaw, 1923.

44. U.S. Bureau of the Census, *Historical Statistics of the United States,* Colonial Times to 1970, Bicentennial ed., Part 1, Washington, D.C., 1975, p. 12.

45. U.S. Bureau of the Census, *Statistical Abstract of the United States: 1978,* Washington, D.C., p. 687.

46. U.S. House, *Advertising and Small Business,* hearings, Subcommittee on Activities of Regulatory Agencies Relating to Small Business of the Select Committee on Small Business, 92nd Congress, First Session, Washington, D.C., 1971.

47. U.S. Senate, *Administered Prices: Automobiles, Report*. Subcommittee on Antitrust and Monopoly of the Committee on the Judiciary, 88th Congress, 2nd Session, Washington, D.C., 1958, p. 147.

48. U.S. Senate, *Competitive Problems in the Drug Industry, Hearings,* Subcommittee on Monopoly of the Select Committee on Small Business. Parts 1–31, *passim,* Washington, D.C., 1967 to 1976.

49. Weber, Max. *General Economic History,* tr. Frank Knight. New York: Collier Books, 1961, p. 220.

50. Weilbacher, William M. *Advertising*. New York: Macmillan, 1979.

51. "What Toy Retailers and Wholesalers are Saying," *Playthings,* March 1971; reprinted in (46), pp. 409–10.

52. Wright, John S., D. Warner, W. Winter, and S. Ziegler. *Advertising*. 4th ed. New York: McGraw-Hill, 1977.

53. Zacher, Robert V. *Advertising Techniques and Management* (rev. ed.). Homewood, Illinois: Irwin, 1967.

CHAPTER 6

HISTORICAL ROOTS OF CONSUMER CULTURE

MICHAEL SCHUDSON

In American society, people often satisfy or believe they can satisfy their socially constituted needs and desires by buying mass produced, standardized, nationally advertised consumer products. This was not always the case nor is it today a universal phenomenon. Why should it be so prominent a characteristic of contemporary American culture?

One approach to that question is to seek out the historical roots of consumer culture, and that is the task for this chapter. A set of clues may be found in one of the most famous American novels, Theodore Dreiser's *Sister Carrie*. In 1900, Dreiser published this book about Caroline Meeber, a small-town Midwestern girl who goes to the big city, Chicago, to seek her fortune and her future. The first few pages of the novel quickly identify the new social world Carrie walks into and Dreiser saw growing up around him, a social world that gave rise to consumer culture.

THE MEANING OF GOODS IN AN URBAN AND MOBILE SOCIETY

It is notable that the protagonist of *Sister Carrie* is a woman seeking her fortune, not a man. This upends the conventions of Western myths and fairy tales and opens a new tradition that Sinclair Lewis continued in *Main Street* and any number of feminist novels of the past decade have extended. Carrie is eighteen years old, she intends to find her pot of gold and to have adventures, and if "romance" holds any privileged place in her scheme of things, that is at least not clear in the beginning.

A woman seeking a fortune is not parallel to a man seeking his. While Sister Carrie is looking for work and therefore is concerned to find a place in the production side of the economy, she is very sensitive, more so than a man is likely to be, to signs of status and person displayed in items of consumption. She notices every detail of the dress of the man on the train who speaks to her. Dreiser comments:

> A woman should some day write the complete philosophy of clothes. No matter how young, it is one of the things she wholly comprehends. There is an indescribably faint line in the matter of a man's apparel which somehow divides for her those who are worth

glancing at and those who are not. Once an individual has passed this faint line on the way downward he will get no glance from her. There is another line at which the dress of a man will cause her to study her own. This line the individual at her elbow now marked for Carrie. She became conscious of an inequality. Her own plain blue dress, with its black cotton tape trimmings, now seemed to her shabby. She felt the worn state of her shoes.[1]

When a woman seeks her fortune, the group of independent, individualist, questing human beings has widened. It has also changed. Now success—and even the road to success—is not paved by work and career alone but by lifestyle and consumption.

It is notable that Carrie seeks her fortune, not by ship like Odysseus or raft like Huck Finn or foot like Tom Jones, but by train. Train travel, by the 1880s when the novel's action takes place, was a standard means of transportation, though only two generations old. Train travel differs from travel by foot or horse or wagon in a number of respects. It is, of course, faster. It is more comfortable. And it is socially distinctive. In train travel, one is a public person. One travels in the company of strangers where intimacy is a possibility—an opportunity or a danger—but where resources to avoid intimacy are also available. This made train travel unique as a form of transportation, but also made it a metaphor for the experience of the city dweller. If, as sociologists have argued, the modern world is a "world of strangers" and the city is a place of habitation where strangers are likely to meet, Carrie has become a city person from the moment she steps on the train.[2] And, indeed, she does meet a stranger, the sinister Charles Drouet.

Carrie arrives in Chicago and, after a night's sleep at her sister's, goes out looking for a job, walking through the wide streets and past the giant buildings. The scene, again, is a familiar one in literature, including nonfiction. Think of Benjamin Franklin, the young printer, walking alone through the streets of Philadelphia, looking for a job carrying two loaves of bread under his arm. By the end of the nineteenth century, it is an image of special importance. Dreiser himself delighted in walking through the streets of cities. As a newspaper reporter in the 1890s, he walked the streets both as vocation and as pastime:

> My favorite pastime when I was not out on an assignment or otherwise busy, was to walk the streets and view the lives and activities of others, not thinking so much how I might advantage myself and my affairs as how, for some, the lightning of chance was always striking in somewhere and disrupting plans, leaving destruction and death in its wake, for others luck or fortune.[3]

The scene of Carrie in the streets, then, is a forceful reminder that she is alone, anonymous, fresh and hopeful but nonetheless a reed in the gale of the city, unidentified, unsupported.

Carrie seeks a job at several department stores and Dreiser feels called upon to insert a small historical and sociological essay on department stores. Carrie is attracted to them because she has seen their ads in the *Daily News,* a Chicago paper she read in her hometown in Wisconsin. She walks into a department store and it is as if she has walked into fairyland:

> Carrie passed along the busy aisles, much affected by the remarkable display of trinkets, dress goods, stationery, and jewelry. Each separate counter was a show place of dazzling interest and attraction. She could not help feeling the claim of each trinket and valuable upon her personally, and yet she did not stop. There was nothing there which she could not have used—nothing which she did not long to own.[4]

The department store, like the city street, like the railroad coach or compartment, was a new kind of public place. It changed the entire act and art of shopping. One did not simply enter a shop and ask the storekeeper to go to his shelves or backroom for an item. In the department store, things were displayed, and the shopper had a range of things to observe. In Chicago in the 1890s, department stores were called "monsters," "inventions of the devil," "vultures," and "producers of crime, sorrow, and disgrace." These epithets were hurled not by communists or anarchists but by the North Side Businessmen's Association. Republicans in the state legislature introduced a law that would require a $20 license for any retail store carrying one line of merchandise, with the fee doubling for each additional line of goods. If a department store carried ten lines of merchandise, the fee would be $10,240. The measure did not pass but this legislative effort suggests the degree of business anxiety over the department stores.[5]

The department stores first, but then other retailers, began to change their business practices. *Speed* of sale became a factor it had never been before and the idea of "stock-turn" or, as we say today, turnover, became important. By the early 1900s, even dry goods and clothing stores in Emporia, Kansas, which had traditionally received carloads of goods twice a year, "began to get goods monthly in smaller packages; quick sales, quick turnovers in these stores were making more profits."[6] Customers became relatively more anonymous. They were less part of a buyer-seller relationship, more part of an audience for a spectacle of sales. With goods made visible before them, "eye-catching" appeal became a more vital attribute of a product, and merchandising for the retailer began to be less a matter of knowing the stock and more a matter of presenting it well.

Indeed, department stores made themselves great stages. The clerks acted as friendly, but elegant, hosts. People thought of the stores as social centers and dressed up to go shopping. Department stores displayed original paintings of new artists and claimed to do so better than museums. Department store owner John Wanamaker said: "In museums, most everything looks like junk even when it isn't because there is no care or thought in the display. If women would wear their fine clothes like galleries wear their pictures, they'd be laughed at."[7]

Daniel Boorstin has argued that the department stores democratized luxury by putting expensive goods on display before any customer who cared to peruse them.[8] It was not that simple. The department stores carried very high-priced goods and would sometimes provide an appropriately elegant, and forbidding, setting for them. Macy's introduced a ladies' waiting room in 1891 which, according to Macy's ads, was "the most luxurious and beautiful department devoted to the comfort of ladies to be found in a mercantile establishment in the city. The style of decoration is Louis XV and no expense has been spared in the adornment and furnishing of this room."[9] Luxury was not democratized so much as made markedly more visible, more public, and more often articulate—through advertising—than it had been before. The department stores did less to provide equality in consumption than to encourage a democracy of aspirations and desire. They contributed to the democratization of envy.

Carrie Meeber walked, but department stores could succeed at the end of the nineteenth century because at that time American cities became "riding" rather than "walking" habitations. Until the mid-nineteenth century, Eastern cities huddled close to their waterfronts. Travel was on foot or, if one was very wealthy, by carriage. In the 1820s hackney coaches began to appear. These were followed by the horse-drawn omnibuses that carried as many as forty people cheaply, comfortably, and quickly enough for persons of middling wealth to live beyond the walking distance of their employment and become omnibus commuters. One traveler in the 1850s marveled at New York's Broadway omnibus that brought together rich and poor, "men, women and children, in silks and rags—brokers and bankers, tinkers and tailors, laborers and lawyers."[10] But only later, when extensive intraurban rail lines developed and then cable lines and electric surface lines and then, by the turn of the century, elevated trains and subways, was a wider metropolitan area made available to large numbers of people at relatively little cost. This easy access to transportation changed the spatial possibilities of daily life. People did not any longer have to live within walking distance of their place of work; suburbs developed and the middle class especially began to move out and to become commuters to work. People did not have to shop in their own neighborhoods any more. They could take the train to some other part of town or to "downtown" to do their shopping. Thanks to newspaper advertising, they could learn what goods were available at what prices in all parts of the city if there were stores that sought a city-wide clientele for their wares.

The department stores were just such stores and there were crucial to subsidizing the growth of urban newspapers. In the 1880s, the ratio of editorial matter to advertising in daily metropolitan newspapers changed from about 70–30 to 50–50 or lower. Advertising revenue represented 44 percent of total newspaper income in 1880, 55 percent by 1900.[11] Of the expending use of advertising in the late nineteenth century, the most important by far was department store advertising. Charles Russell, a New York reporter and editor, remarked that at the end of the nineteenth century the newspaper became "an appendage of the department store."[12] In Robert and Helen Lynd's survey of Muncie, Indiana, newspapers of 1890, 23 percent of all advertising in the papers was department store advertising.[13] Department store ads were important not only in size but in style. Wanamaker's, for instance, sought self-consciously to "journalize" advertising, to make ads more newsy, informationally accurate and up-to-date with copy changing daily.[14]

Carrie Meeber, at home in a small Wisconsin town, was one person, but alone in Chicago was someone else. If she was attracted to the goods in the department stores, her attraction was closely connected to her new and uncertain social position. Where people live and die in the same small community, the people they associate with as adults are the same people they grew up with as children. When they look around for affirmation of their identity, when they seek, as Erik Erikson puts it, a sense of continuity in their own lives, the evidence is all around them.[15] People derive a sense of self as the self is reflected back in the opinions of other people. When "significant others" remain much the same throughout one's life, identity has a clear foundation. Indeed, it may never become problematic. Further, when a person's status in the community is established by birth or family, the consequences of one's own achievements or failures are not so far reaching. The ne'er-do-well son of the aristocrat is still an aristocrat. The peasant's son who learns to read and write and study the Bible is still a peasant and defers to the aristocrat. Status is no more problematic than identity.

No community was ever quite like the ideal I describe but many communities were more like it than almost any community has been since the industrial and democratic revolutions produced a highly mobile, urban, class society in which social mobility became a real possibility and a powerful ideology. Geographic and social mobility in modern society are especially potent forces for personal disruption. As Peter Berger and Thomas Luckmann have argued, mobility has severe psychological consequences.[16] Relations weaken with the people who socialized the mobile individual. The norms, rules, attitudes, and behaviors that to the child seemed natural, seem foreign to the adult who has moved away. What was internalized is now seen as external, arbitrary, even alien. The individual is separated from the past. This often is a great but wrenching liberation. One's roots are left behind and individuals thus become more and more dependent on people immediately around them to reaffirm their identities. Identity becomes less tightly connected to one's family of origin, more closely connected to one's associates, whoever they may be.

In contemporary society, geographic or social mobility does not just happen, people *expect* it to happen, so the family exercises a different kind of control than it once did. The family provides a socialization process for its children that anticipates their mobility. Children learn to pay attention not just to their parents but to their peer group and to the mass media. Their parents may encourage them to separate themselves from the family, to be independent. The battle in middle-class American households, when there is a battle, is not whether or not the child can go out with friends for the evening but *how long* the child will be allowed to stay out. From the parents' point of view, this is a struggle to retain authority but it is not intended to keep the child from friends. What the parents want the child to learn is that they must fight the battle, but the parents fully expect and intend to ultimately win a war only by losing each fight. The family remains crucial, but more and more, a common culture, that includes advertising and the mass media, plays its part. Berger and Luckmann argue that young people are encouraged to acquire "a prefabricated identity, advertised, marketed, and guaranteed by the identity-producing agencies."[17] This is too harsh. If the commercial and national forces for "prefabrication" through persuasion have grown, the local forces toward standard personalities through coercive religion, education, and family have weakened. This is worth remembering before condemning too quickly the new patterns of socialization.

Take, for instance, the evidence the Lynds' *Middletown* study provides on "anticipatory social-ization." The Lynds found that Muncie, Indiana, mothers of the 1890s generation valued "strict obedience" and "loyalty to the church" as the most important attitudes to instill in their children. Working-class mothers of the 1920s also found these to be the most important social values but "business-class" mothers of the 1920s thought "independence" to be just as important as obedi-ence and more important than loyalty to the church. They also cited "frankness" as being very important. In their new emphasis on independence and frankness, these mothers knew and planned for the fact that their children's world would differ from their own. They encouraged children to confront the new world and to be independent because their families could not teach them all they would need to know. At the same time, the parents feared the children would be lost to them unless frankness was also encouraged.[18]

With a more mobile society and, to some extent, a more open social fabric, realms in which choice rarely figured become open to individual decision making. Most important decisions—who to marry, what career to enter, what religion to adhere to—become matters of selection. As the early 1900s brought improved systems of transportation and communication and a vastly improved system for the distribution of goods to rural parts of the country, consumer "lifestyle" and indi-vidual expression and identity-formation through lifestyle became more widely available. William Leiss has ably argued that a society of high-intensity consumption is not so much one in which new needs are manufactured and foisted upon consumers as one in which citizens lose a secure understanding of what their needs are and to what extent commodities can satisfy them. Needs become "ambiguous" as individual choices multiply."[19]

The mass media help escort people into the wider world of choice, broadening horizons, blurring provincial demarcations. On the one hand, the media enlarge people's sense of their own and the world's possibilities; on the other hand, the media lead people to constantly compare themselves to others or to images of others. As Daniel Bell has suggested, "Mass consumption meant the acceptance, in the crucial area of lifestyle, of the idea of social change and personal transforma-tion."[20] But as well, it left people in flux, in uncertainty, full of anxiety about social standing and meaning, vulnerable to the turns of fashion more than playful with them, just as Carrie Meeber walking down Van Buren Street in Chicago was vulnerable to the social forces around her.

In this world, external signs hold great importance and people leap at anything that can be used to signify. As anthropologist Claude Lévi-Strauss suggested of primitive totems, and as Mary Douglas has more recently suggested of commercial commodities, they are "good to think."[21] In other words, they are symbols that people use as maps for charting a complex and uncertain world. People in the new mobile, urban world of the late nineteenth century required new symbol systems. They needed to locate and identify themselves and they sought what they believed would prove "good to think." People could, and did, recreate villages in cities and reestablish location rooted in family and neighborhood. At the same time, they could not ignore the presence of a wider world: the mass media would not let them be long insensitive to it. Most people needed to connect themselves to the wider world, the socially and geographically mobile, most of all.

There were various ways to find identity and placement in the larger world. Income was especially convenient because it provided a *ranked* identification, because it was subject to transformation, and because it tended to be a good, though by no means perfect, index of a variety of socially meaningful traits, including political power and social standing. It had the disadvantage of being, by itself, invisible. Increasingly, however, an index for income was visible and available in the status and quality ranking of consumer goods. Material goods became "visible symbols of inner worth" in worlds where few other symbols had permanence or continuity. As Berger and Luckmann put it, where there is high mobility "conspicuous patterns of consumption take the place of continuous interpersonal contacts within an individual's biography. . . . Material objects rather than human beings must be called upon to testify to the individual's worth."[22] Consumer goods begin to be an index and a language that place a person in society and relate the person in symbolically significant ways to the national culture.

During the nineteenth century, more and more goods manufactured in factories rather than in homes poured onto the market. More and more necessities of life were bought outside the home and outside the neighborhood, too. An excellent example is clothing. In 1790, 80 percent of all clothing was made in the home for family use. A century later, for men and boys, 90 percent was made outside the home.[23] As for women's clothing, while much was still made at home, it was made on a store-bought sewing machine according to patterns purchased from women's magazine companies like Butterick's. As late as 1910, newspaper advertisements for yard goods outnumbered those for ready-made dresses in the newspapers of Muncie, Indiana, but by the 1920s Middletown, too, responded primarily to ads for ready mades.[24]

The availability of store-bought, ready-made clothing helped extend and democratize fashion. While clothing or ornament is used universally to mark sex, age, and status, "fashion" is primarily a Western and modern phenomenon, at least on a mass scale. Fashion differs from dress in that it is not a traditional expression of social place but a rapidly changing statement of social aspiration. It emerged, as Anne Hollander writes, "as a form of presumption—the desire to imitate and resemble something better, more free, more beautiful and shining, which one could not actually aspire to be."[25] The early emergence of fashion was limited by the number of people able and willing to be fashionable and by the supply of fashionable things. In the nineteenth century, more people could participate in fashion as the development of machine-manufactured clothing made up-to-date goods more widely available. Fashion set a person in social space, linked to and differentiated from social groups. It also located a person in social time—in relation to others, being avant garde or *au courant* or behind-the-times, and in relation to one's own past, offering an index and symbol of the distance one had traveled from past experience and a readiness, or lack of readiness, to encounter something new.[26]

Fashion in dress, better than any other example of consumption, is a material, externalized symbol system that connects people to social worlds and individualizes them in those worlds. For more and more people in the late nineteenth century and after, clothing came to be expressive and signifying. But so, too, did other material objects. Where buying replaced making, then looking replaced doing as a key social action, reading signs replaced following orders as a crucial modern skill. Shorthands for expression and signification became more and more desirable and useful to urbanites; manufacturers exploited the desires of people for social location and identity with the production of "brand name" goods. Brand name goods *appeared* at the end of the nineteenth century for a number of reasons; they were *accepted* for the reasons discussed here. In a mobile society, commercial products with familiar names provide people with some sense of identity and continuity in their lives. And in a society with a high concern for social mobility, material possessions of known and ranked standing provide statements of social status and may provide entry into desired social worlds.

But it will not do to hang everything on this "identity" argument by itself. It explains too much, I think, and therefore too little. It is exactly the kind of argument by sociologists that rightly raises the hackles of historians. It is notoriously difficult to make such an argument historically specific. People have used a growing number of manufactured consumer goods for some time, beginning at least in the eighteenth century. Compared to the world of today, Carrie Meeber's notion of material variety looks anemic and the proliferation of brand names at the turn of the century paltry. At what point can it be said that people actively construct their identities from material things? If this is in some measure always true, when does it become predominantly true? And to what extent does it remain, even today, a rather modest truth, with people's surest sense of self and deepest foundation of social standing derived from family and occupation, not lifestyle?

That is one problem; there is another. People do not necessarily find whatever they may seek in the way of status and identity from consumer goods. Indeed as Marcus Felson has suggested, consumption today may do more to mask social standing than to express it. From the point of view of society, consumer lifestyles may confuse social ranking; from the point of view of the aspiring individual, however, this very confusion may serve personal ends.[27]

The growing importance of standard, identifiable products and brands may be conceived in a manner less dependent on psychological assumptions about identity. Some brand names, like "Yves St. Laurent," offer identity and status, but others, like McDonald's or Coca-Cola or Kentucky Fried Chicken, do not. Their promise is not identity but familiarity and reliability of product. Where consumers do not make their own goods and do not buy at neighborhood stores where they know and are known to the merchant, brand names become a form of consumer protection. The brand-name good, as economist George Akerlof argues, is "an institution which counteracts the effects of quality uncertainty."[28] Brand-name goods and other standard products such as the "convenience foods" that it is fashionable to complain about have this quality. Frozen concentrate rather than fresh orange juice has this advantage, as a waitress explained to writer John McPhee in his fruitless search for a Florida restaurant that served fresh orange juice: "Fresh is either too sour or too watery or too something. Frozen is the same every day. People want to know what they're getting."[29] A survey of five hundred housewives found that purchasing a major brand or a brand previously used is taken to be a better means of reducing risk in a purchasing situation than government reports or word-of-mouth information.[30] The housewives are not seeking status or identity when they opt for the brand name; they are minimizing risk to their families. In the late nineteenth century, they were doing the same thing. The world was changing so that available products were less often local and known and local retailers were more often large institutions serving a wider public than before. Further, the consumers themselves were less often local and known. Geographic mobility was high and immigration was at a peak. There was plenty of incentive, then, for shoppers to seek the guarantee of predictability that brand names would provide.

In Sister Carrie's world of the 1880s, all this was just beginning. Carrie Meeber was dazzled by goods, not by brand names. But in another generation, Sinclair Lewis's George Babbitt would be proud of his brand names. They connected his life in Zenith, Ohio, to the high and mighty of America. "These standard advertised wares—toothpastes, socks, tires, cameras, instantaneous

hot-water heaters—were his symbols and proofs of excellence; at first the signs, then the substitutes, for joy and passion and wisdom."[31] For historian Daniel Boorstin, the goods of mass
consumption are not to be denounced so glibly. He refers to the relations people establish with
one another through the insignia of mass consumption, through the sharing of Pierre Cardin shirts
or Harley-Davidson motorcycles as "consumption communities." This is a tendentious phrase; it
incorporates into a slogan the very question that needs to be addressed about a consumer society:
is there any community of consumption? And if there is, what kind of community is it? Does the
sharing of goods—not the sitting down at table and breaking bread together but the impersonal
sharing, the fact that John Smith from Buffalo and Jill Jones from Santa Barbara both wear Jor-
dache jeans—does that establish a sense of community between them?

The answer is no, it does not establish any kind of community a person could put much stock
in. Boorstin here is ideologue more than analyst. But may not Sinclair Lewis be an ideologue in
the other direction? Is there not something to the sharing of things and the names for things that
helps build a culture—at least a world of shared meanings if not shared ideals and relationships?
Goods themselves are not (only) the enemies of culture and not (only) the debasement of culture
and not (only) something foisted unwillingly upon defenseless consumers. Goods are constituents
of culture and the sharing of their names is a part of what it means to partake of culture.

Culture, anthropologist Mary Douglas asserts, *is* the sharing of names—and this includes
the sharing of names of material objects. When she looks at consumer goods in modern society, Douglas sees not a bundle of utilities, as the economist would, nor even a bundle of social
ties, as I have been suggesting, but a bundle of symbols, elements in cultural classification
schemes. For Douglas then, when people buy goods, they are not just trying to satisfy "needs"
in a narrow sense but are trying "to construct an intelligible universe" with the goods they
choose. She says:

> Enjoyment of physical consumption is only a part of the service yielded by goods; the other
> part is the enjoyment of sharing names . . . the anthropological argument insists that by far
> the greater part of utility is yielded . . . in sharing names that have been learned and graded.
> This is culture.[32]

Surely there is something to this. A personal name is sometimes called a "handle" in American slang and this is a revealing term. Through the name, we handle or come in contact with
and touch and hold people and things. Think of expatriates or travelers. Americans who travel
abroad and meet fellow Americans do not typically reach out to each other by discussing the
Declaration of Independence or the spirit of free enterprise. They talk about peanut butter and
playfully compare the merits of Peter Pan and Skippy and Jif, or they discuss chocolate chip
cookies, Frye boots, a 1957 Chevy, what they would give for a real milkshake, whether they
have been on Woodward Avenue in Detroit or Melrose in Los Angeles, or to the Broome Street
bar in Soho in New York. They take pleasure in the very saying of these names and in the familiarity the words establish.

But what kind of society is ours that produces the particular system of naming we have? What
is special about a system in which words like "Chevy," "polyester," and "Holiday Inn" take on
importance? Who does the naming in our society, who has the power of words, and how is that
power used? Douglas's position, by itself, does not get to these issues. Her views provide no room
for politics and no standards for judging the place of goods in society. For her, it seems, people
make good cultural use of goods in any society at any time, and the number or kind of goods they
use is beyond comment.[33]

The concepts of "identity" and "culture" and the changing needs of people in a mobile society do not suffice to explain the shift to a consumer society in the period 1850 to 1930. Nor do they explain "materialist" values. As Neil Harris points out, a consumer society is not the same thing as a materialist society; nineteenth-century Americans were regarded by most observers, including the trenchant Tocqueville, as archetypal materialists, even in 1830. But materialism was connected at that date to both consumption *and* production. People still made things at home and satisfied material longings that way. This became less true by the end of the nineteenth century. Industrialization displaced home industry and, in a rather short span of years, people found themselves unable "to match, in precision, variety, attractiveness, and especially cost, the provision of objects produced by American manufacturers, from clothing and furniture to food and drink." The changing nature and significance of consumption, then, grew not from autonomous changes in the life of the citizen or the family but from the intersection of such changes with the emergence of large-scale consumer goods industries. I turn, then, to a consideration of changes on the production side of the economy.[34]

CONSUMER GOODS AND THE PRODUCTION SIDE OF THE ECONOMY

Whether it was Brandreth's Vegetable Universal Pills or Radam's Microbe Killer or Lydia Pinkham's Compound, nineteenth-century newspapers were covered with patent medicine advertising. The Lynds found that 25 percent of all advertising in the Middletown papers of 1890 was patent medicine advertising, slightly ahead of department store advertising.[35] When *Press and Printer* of Boston tabulated advertisers who made regular use of advertising, they found that 425 of the 2,583 enterprises counted sold medicines and drugstore items, more than double the next leading category.[36] It is hard to exaggerate the importance of patent medicines in the history of advertising. "The back-bone of the typical advertising agency's business in the nineteenth century was patent medicine, and the Ayer firm was no exception to this rule," writes Ralph Hower, N. W. Ayer's historian. Patent medicine advertising made up a quarter of Ayer's total advertising volume in its first decade, the 1870s. It was "the mainstay of every agency of importance at the time." Some agencies even became part owners of the patent medicine companies—Rowell, Lord and Thomas of Chicago, and Pettengill and Company of Boston. Ayer did the same thing less deliberately, gaining an interest in exchange for unpaid bills.[37]

Ads for patent medicines intended two things. First, they sought to establish a clear, memorable *identification* for their product. This was more important than the particular "promise" about what the medicine would do. It was most important to establish a name people could remember, feel comfortable with, and believe to represent an important or well-established firm. The identification would often be with something exotic as in Hayne's Arabian Balsam, Hoofland's Greek Oil, Osgood's Indian Cholagogue, or Jayne's Spanish Alternative. Things remote, ancient, mystical were often used, relying where possible on established folk beliefs. Dr. Lin's Chinese Blood Pills suggested longevity. Turkish Wafers—for men only—suggested the romance and sex of veils and harems and hookahs.

Most patent medicine advertising was repetitious and dull. Many ads, all identical, would be placed in the same issue of the same newspaper. Dr. Donald Kennedy's Medical Discovery and Dr. T. Felix Gourard's complexion cure did not change copy during more than forty years of advertising. There was great weight placed on establishing and maintaining product identification, by the continuity and repetition of a name or trademarked image. Regarding the latter, James Harvey Young writes:

The trade-mark, indeed, was a fixed star in a universe of flux. The ownership of medicines might change again and again, and so might the formula. The diseases for which medicines were advertised might vary over time, and sometimes even names were altered. Trade-marks, however, protected first by common law and then by federal statute, endured forever.[38]

Secondary to product identification was product *identity*. By identification, I mean simply the association of a name or picture with a given product. Product identity, by contrast, associates the product with its function and, to some extent, with its intended market. So, for instance, some of the patent medicines promised to be especially potent for women's illnesses or for common colds or for general nervousness or depression or for baldness or for sexual disorders. But most often, it appears, the patent medicines were relatively weak in product identity. This has to do with the products themselves: they were not standardized, they were not reliable, and they did not do the things they claimed. Not surprisingly, their claims changed from time to time. Further, although the medicine ads invoked medical authority or testimonials from ministers or scientific terminology and Latin names, the advertisers were well aware that they faced a skeptical public. Some ads tried to make use of the skepticism. In booklets advertising his Microbe Killer, William Radam attacked other patent medicines. Gullible people, he explained, would buy these worthless products because "the public likes to be humbugged." He went on: "People should not be led away by every charlatan who jumps up before them and talks; but as long as the world lasts there will probably be fools in it, and fools are a godsend to rogues."[39] Similarly, the manufacturers of Vin Mariani used as advertising a pamphlet mailed to physicians entitled, "The Effrontery of Proprietary Medicine Advertisers." The competition among medicines, carried out largely through advertising, was severe, and it has been estimated that less than 2 percent of remedies launched in New York had even modest success.[40]

In the mid-nineteenth century, patent medicines were the most prominently advertised product. In the 1870s and 1880s, department store advertising came to match that of patent medicines. But, in retrospect, the development on the production and distribution side of the economy most important in creating an advertising-oriented consumer culture was the emergence of advertising for nationally branded goods. This was spawned by a relatively small group of new, technologically and organizationally innovative manufacturers. Nearly all of the first national advertisers were enterprises that used new continuous-process machinery to produce low-priced, packaged consumer goods. The massive increase in output made possible by the new machinery led manufacturers to build large marketing and purchasing networks and to engage in widespread advertising. These enterprises included many that remain to this day the leading advertisers in the country: Procter & Gamble, Colgate-Palmolive, H. J. Heinz, Borden, Eastman Kodak, Quaker Oats, Pillsbury, Campbell Soups, Carnation, Libby McNeil & Libby, and American Tobacco. They produced cigarettes, soap, canned foods, breakfast cereals, matches, and photographic film and equipment. These are, with a partial exception of photographic equipment, exclusively "experience" goods. Thus they are products whose advertising is likely to include very little direct information and is likely to focus on the reputability of the manufacturer. Probably the single largest newspaper advertiser in the 1890s was a firm of this sort, Royal Baking Powder.[41]

The Quaker Oats Co. may be taken as an example. Oats were raised in quantity in the late nineteenth century, especially in Iowa, Ohio, and Illinois. Ferdinand Schumacher, a German immigrant, was the first to develop a branded oat product for human consumption. When he began milling in Ravenna, Ohio, he used the same techniques millers had used since the fifteenth century. He believed his oatmeal to be a cheap and healthy substitute for the American breakfast that immigrants regarded as excessive. At first, then, his products circulated among German-American communities. But oatmeal and oat mush began to grow more popular and Schumacher soon had competitors. The competitors, too, operated on ancient milling techniques until Schumacher's innovation in 1875, a machine to convert hulled kernels into a coarse meal. About the same time, George Cormack at Rockford, Illinois, devised labor-saving systems for moving grain in and out of the mill. In 1877 Asmus J. Ehrrichsen, an employee of Schumacher's, developed the steel-cut process. Instead of crushing the grain through millstones, the hulled oats were cut into meal by fine knife blades, providing a uniform, flaky meal. A year later, Schumacher used porcelain rollers to manufacture rolled oats and converted his whole production to rolled oats which flaked rather than crushed grains.

In the meantime, one of Schumacher's competitors, Henry Parsons Crowell, was quickly adopting all the latest innovations. His mill, also at Ravenna, by 1882 became "the first in the world to maintain under one roof operations to grade, clean, hull, cut, package, and ship oatmeal to interstate markets in a continuous process that in some aspects anticipated the modern assembly line."[42] Crowell called his product "Quaker Oats." The development of highly efficient "continuous-process" methods was the first critical step in establishing a capacity for national advertising of cereals. The new technology expanded the industrial capacity of firms so that increasing production at little increased cost was no longer difficult. The main problem for the cereal manufacturers and others like them was "to move their goods quickly enough or to advertise them effectively enough to keep their high-volume production facilities operating steadily."[43]

Henry Crowell registered the trademark of a "figure of a man in Quaker garb" in 1877, the first registered trademark for a breakfast cereal. Crowell—and then Schumacher, too, when they joined forces with Robert Stuart of Cedar Rapids, Iowa, to create the American Cereal Company—pioneered in packaging, promotion, and advertising. Crowell introduced a folding carton for Quaker oats packaging, a method that had been patented only ten years before. Because the unfolded package lay flat, it could be easily printed on and so the Crowell carton displayed the Quaker emblem in four-color printing with recipes printed on the package. This was the beginning of the end of selling cereal to the retailers in bulk (although in health foods stores, the old methods of retailing have been revived).[44]

In 1886, for the first time, as the historian of Quaker Oats reports, a housewife could read a sales message on a food package: "We would call your special attention to the purity, rapidity of preparation, and the fact that they did not sacrifice sweetness and flavor for the sake of rapid cooking." This was followed by several recipes. It is curious that the message refers to the Quaker Oats company as "they" rather than "we." While the packaging was part of a continuous-process production, the company's copywriters clearly saw the package as something put around the product itself rather than as an integral part of the product and its identity.

The emphasis in advertising for nationally branded products, as for patent medicines, was more on identification than on identity. The advertising profession of the day "seemed to equate quality with quantity" and valued the ubiquity of a product name and trademark above all else.[45] For Quaker Oats, making the Quaker symbol well known was the all-important task. Claims for the specific merits of Quaker Oats varied and type of appeals changed. Ads at different times connected Quaker products to "love, pride, cosmetic satisfactions, sex, marriage, good health, cleanliness, safety, labor saving, and status seeking."[46] But the Quaker Oats symbol was permanent and visible everywhere, on billboards, streetcars, newspapers, calendars, magazines, blotters, cookbooks, Sunday church bulletins, metal signs on rural fences, company-sponsored cooking schools, free samples given away house-to-house, booths at county fairs and expositions.

Quaker Oats did not limit itself to advertising as a tool, nor did the other early national advertisers. Advertising was but one aspect of a national marketing effort. According to historian

Alfred Chandler, it was by no means the most important feature. More crucial than advertising was the development of national and sometimes global organizations of managers, buyers, and salesmen that the early mass marketing firms created. The new technology of continuous-process production made possible a new social invention—not advertising but the organization chart, a regular hierarchy of responsibility, an administrative structure responsible for marketing as well as the production of the manufactured good. In Chandler's view, the key innovation that made mass marketing possible was not advertising but corporate organization.

What happened with cereal happened with other products I have mentioned, too, and in the same era, between 1880 and 1900. These industries did not gradually drive out competitors to become slowly concentrated—they were oligopolistic almost from the beginning. Once established, it was very difficult for competitors to break into the market. Why? Chandler's answer is:

> The most imposing barrier to entry in these industries was the organization the pioneers had built to market and distribute their newly mass-produced products. A competitor who acquired the technology had to create a national and often global organization of managers, buyers, and salesmen if he was to get the business away from the one or two enterprises that already stood astride the major marketing channels.[47]

While advertising may be today a "barrier to entry" into markets, it was not a barrier in the late nineteenth century.[48] What was a barrier was the extensive marketing organization and the long-term ties between executives and managers and jobbers and retailers that constituted the human side of the organization. That was not easy for newcomers to duplicate. However, if advertising was not guaranteed market power in relation to competitors, it was certainly a form of market power in relation to retailers. Manufacturer advertising gives a firm direct communication to consumers and a way of forcing retailers into distributing their product without making price concessions to the retailer.[49]

By the turn of the century, advertising had become an important element in the American economy. Some of the reasons for the rise of advertising can be understood as "market driven": advertising provided information about what goods were available for sale in a society that no longer consisted of face-to-face economic relations. Some of the early informational advertising and the department store advertising was market driven, in this sense. So, too, was the development of warehouse catalog advertising, such as that of Sears and Roebuck. But some of the development of advertising is better thought of as "producer driven": for firms where technology had solved production problems, advertising arose as part of a marketing effort to sell goods whose supply could be increased easily at little additional production cost. In the case of the patent medicines, advertising was the main marketing tool. For nationally advertised, branded products that arose in continuous-process production industries after 1880, advertising was one important element in a marketing mix that included direct salesmanship, packaging, and the establishment of hierarchical, national marketing organizations.

The distinction between market-driven and producer-driven advertising bears on the controversy over whether advertising creates or simply responds to felt needs. To the extent that advertising arose in response to social and economic changes in a mobile market society, it is difficult to see it as an original or prime cause of consumer culture. To the extent, however, that technological developments in industrial manufacturing precipitated growing investment in distribution and sales and advertising, advertising can be seen as a somewhat independent, not solely reactive, force in American society. I do not think the historical record resolves the debate about advertising's role in creating "needs," but I do think it reveals some of the complexity of the issue and makes it hard for anyone to leap with unqualified certainty to one side ("advertising just responds to social trends") or the other ("advertising is the creator of consumer culture").

THE MEDIA AND THE AGENCIES AS PROMOTERS OF PROMOTION

Having considered, at least briefly, social changes that altered people's desires for goods and susceptibility to advertising and changes in manufacturing that led to markedly greater incentives for businesses to seek national distribution and the advertising that accompanies it, I have addressed the largest factors in the late nineteenth century that paved the way to a goods-intensive consumer culture. But a long footnote needs to be added on additional forces that institutionalized advertising itself as an element in the consumer complex. Advertising is a relationship between a producer (or distributor) who advertises, an agency that creates the ad, a medium that carries the ad, and an audience of consumers to whom the ad is directed. I have thus far considered market-driven forces that enabled the rise of advertising (changes in the lives of the people who represent the market for consumer goods) and producer-driven forces (changes in the technology of industry and the social organization of retailing). There were also changes in the mass media and the emergence of advertising agencies—together these can be taken as "self-generating" sources of advertising. The media live off advertising revenue and the advertising agencies' reason for existence is advertising. The presence of these institutions in the economy has been a force for the growth of advertising.

The first advertising agents were more the servants of the newspapers than of the firms that bought advertising space. Volney B. Palmer (1799–1864) is generally regarded as the first agent, having begun his business in Philadelphia in 1841. He was an agent for newspaper publishers around the country with authority to make contracts with advertisers on behalf of the publishers. Soon thereafter, the typical agent became a true middleman, a space jobber who sold newspaper space to advertisers and then bought the space to fill his orders. This was typical of agents in the 1850s.

As the agency system developed, agents moved from space jobbing to "space wholesaling." The leading agent of the 1860s and 1870s, George Rowell, initiated the practice of buying newspaper space in advance, in large lots, and reselling it in smaller lots to advertisers. In 1867, Carlton and Smith (and later J. Walter Thompson) began the "advertising concession agency" in which the agent made annual contracts with newspapers he served, taking over "most of the risk and management of the *entire* advertising space in the papers."[50] Competition among agents was based in part on the assurances of the agents to advertisers regarding circulation figures of the papers they represented. Rowell began in 1869 to publish a directory of newspaper circulation figures; as this directory became established, it was more and more difficult for newspapers to continue their decades-old habit of lying about circulation.

Nonetheless, the advertising agency remained for some time an institution of very limited scope. It bought and sold space. It did not produce ads. But its activities, however limited, provided businesses a real service, thanks to the growth of national markets and the developments in transportation and communication that made that growth possible. Merchants did not know much about the media for advertising outside their own town or region. Agents emerged to exploit business's ignorance of institutions that had become relevant for commercial success. The advertising agency's growth parallels the rise of credit agencies, which appeared about the same time. Both rated the worth of out-of-town businesses: the credit agency judged businesses one might sell or extend credit to, the advertising agency judged the value of newspapers as media for advertising. Both tried to standardize rating systems, the credit agency trying to make reliable judgments about net worth and the advertising agency trying to establish newspaper circulations reliably.[51]

This is not to say that businesses all quickly recognized that advertising agencies would be useful—or that advertising itself would be useful to them. From 1840 to 1870, according to advertising historian Ralph Hower, "the agency's chief service . . . was to promote the general use of advertising." In the 1870s and after, agencies actively propagandized for the idea of advertising. In 1876 N. W. Ayer & Son began publishing *The Advertiser's Guide,* a quarterly magazine with reprinted newspaper articles, jokes, and short news items "together with material urging the advantages of advertising." In 1886 Ayer developed its motto, "Keeping Everlastingly At It Brings Success," meant not so much to encourage its own employees as to remind businessmen of the advantages of advertising regularly.[52]

The first promotional work of the agencies, then, was to sell the idea of advertising to business. At N. W. Ayer and other agencies, this work continued into the twentieth century, indeed, to this day. Ayer's first efforts to be more than a space broker—to write copy, obtain illustrations, and plan whole campaigns—were designed as ways to promote the idea of advertising to Ayer's own potential clients. Between 1900 and 1910, Ayer advertised its own services in *Profitable Advertising* and *The Bill Poster* and for years thereafter in *Printer's Ink.* Between 1919 and 1932 Ayer regularly placed full-page ads in *Saturday Evening Post* and *Literary Digest,* speaking in general terms of the philosophy of advertising at Ayer.

The advertising agency began to shift from an institution serving the media to an agency serving the advertiser when George Rowell developed the "open contract" system in 1875. Rowell announced:

> One thing we clearly perceived . . . , that advertising agencies succeeded best when studying the interests of advertisers not newspapers . . . We have fully decided to announce as a rule for our future guidance (but which we have followed pretty closely for the past three years) that we will not hereafter be a party to any competition for advertising contracts.[53]

N. W. Ayer followed suit, taking Rowell's scheme a step further to a full "open contract" in which an advertiser agreed to an exclusive arrangement with an agent for a period of time. There would not be competition for the advertiser's business on each occasion for advertising. The agent would learn over time the best way to handle a given advertiser's account. The contract would be "open," meaning that specifications for where to buy advertising space would be flexible, the advertiser making final decisions.[54]

Only after this change did advertising art and copy become part of the responsibility of the agency. Between 1880 and 1900, agencies began to write copy for their clients. As the volume of advertising increased, skill in writing copy became more important. Buying more space or using heavier type or larger type sizes was not enough, and agencies that could offer services in writing more persuasive advertisements gained a competitive edge. As early as 1880, N. W. Ayer announced to businessmen that they had skills in the composition and illustration of newspaper ads. Only in 1900, though, did Ayer establish a separate Copy Department. The first systematically trained copywriting staff began at Lord and Thomas (later to become Foote, Cone & Belding) in 1904 under the guidance of Albert Lasker and John E. Kennedy.[55]

As agencies became established, they became an independent force promoting the idea of advertising, and so did their trade journals and trade associations. The early years of *Printer's Ink,* begun in 1888 as a promotional tool for George P. Rowell's agency, were dominated by its efforts at "interpreting and justifying the work of the general advertising agent to advertisers and potential advertisers." While the boosterism receded somewhat in the early twentieth century, *Printer's Ink* in the 1890s was full of homilies like "Advertising is the steam propeller of business success" and "United they stand, divided they fall—business and advertising."[56] When advertising clubs began to appear, they, too, became boosters for the idea of advertising in the business world. The first, the Sphinx Club, was organized in New York in 1896. A national association of clubs, the Associated Advertising Clubs of America, held its first meeting in 1905 and by 1916 had more than fifteen thousand members. *Printer's Ink* held in 1915 that the chief value of this club movement was "the education of businessmen generally to the importance of advertising as a business force."[57] The advertising agencies, however successful they may have been in stimulating the growth of advertising in general, were surely successful in promoting the use of agencies by businesses. In examining directories of advertisers, historian Daniel Pope found that 20 percent of firms listed as advertisers in New York in 1901 used advertising agencies, but that this increased to 35 percent in 1911. In Boston, similarly, the figure jumped from 20 percent in 1901 to nearly 50 percent in 1911.[58]

The media, too, increasingly dependent on advertising revenue, actively promoted the use of advertising. The media tried to convince businesses that it pays to advertise and that, in particular, it pays to advertise in one specific medium. Today, the pages of advertising trade journals are full of advertisements from radio stations, television stations and networks, magazines, and newspapers. Each extols its own ability to attract the largest consumer audience or the most affluent consumer audience or the largest audience per dollar spent on advertising. While the media today are particularly competitive, this is not a new development. The *San Diego Union,* for instance, in the 1890s, took pains to inform prospective and current advertisers that advertising was worthwhile. The front page "ears" in 1891 often included messages to advertisers. From June 18 to June 25, 1891, for example, the left-hand ears read: "The Brainiest Advertisers in this enterprising city use the daily and weekly Union right along. They wouldn't stay if it didn't pay them." If that was not encouragement enough, the right-hand ear said: "It pays to Advertise. In the Spring. In the Summer. In the Fall. In the Winter."

The advertising agencies, meanwhile, were growing not only larger and more important but more self-important. Agencies, especially the larger agencies with national advertisers as clients, sought to gain "professional" standing for advertising men. Thus they eagerly supported a move toward "scientific" advertising by sponsoring market research and by welcoming the language and literature of psychology into advertising work. Old-timers like George Rowell were not friendly to psychology, but others seemed to be obsessed with discovering what "human nature" is. American ad men were particularly taken with the work of Walter Dill Scott at Northwestern, an academic who became the earliest guru of scientific advertising.[59]

The psychology that entered market research and advertising was eclectic. Behaviorists, Freudians, and a host of others coexisted. One of the most eminent psychologists of his day, John Watson, when forced from his position at Johns Hopkins, left the academic world for a job at J. Walter Thompson where he quickly rose to a position as vice-president. Watson is representative of psychologists in market research in his fundamental assumption that all people are alike. As he wrote in 1935, "As a psychologist, I decry the fact that we are all trained so much alike—that there is so little individuality in the world. But, as an advertising man, I rejoice; my bread and butter depends on it."[60] But the first development of significance in market research was not to see the common elements in human nature but to see the obvious differences; especially to recognize that there are two sexes and that women, not men, are the primary consumers in American culture. "The proper study of mankind is MAN," said one ad in *Printer's Ink,* "but the proper study of markets is WOMAN."[61] It was a cliché among advertisers by the 1920s that women are the "purchasing agents" of their families; the trade journals cited the figure that 85 percent of all consumer spending is done by women. Even shaving cream and safety razors were advertised to wives. The view of the man as hapless, a bumbler—a figure who reappeared in comic strips like "Blondie" or television sitcoms like "Ozzie and Harriet," was well known in ads in the 1920s:

> What does a man know about complexion, the skin? Nothing. He rips and hacks away at his face and then washes it with strong soap, sprinkles on a little powder, and believes he is a beauty parlor wizard.
> You, the woman of the family, understand what the care of the skin means. You realize that a good lotion is invaluable. Protect that foolish husband of yours against himself; start that college-boy son of yours in the right path—put a bottle of Facefriend in the bathroom closet and see that they use it after shaving. They know no better—help them.[62]

Or, again:

> Jim always buys the same old ties, doesn't he? Year after year . . . dark blue with white dots is a standby. Men are unbelievably primitive in such matters. Here are ties, modern in pattern and stylish in fabric. Go to the nearest haberdashery and say: "I desire to select some neckties for my husband" (Sweetheart, Son or Father, or Brother). Dig Jim out of the dark-blue-and-white-dot habit. Make him stylish whether he wants to be or not. Help him in his utter helplessness.[63]

If the difference between men and women came to be seen as important, so did the difference between the affluent and people of moderate means. In Britain, advertising literature between the wars "strongly emphasized that the low-paid were able to buy only a limited range of products."[64] In the United States, this was also clear. The advertiser understood the difference between "quality" and "mass" audiences, as Walter Lippmann observed in 1922 in *Public Opinion:*

> In respect to most commodities sold by advertising, the customers are neither the small class of the very rich nor the very poor. They are the people with enough surplus over bare necessities to exercise discretion in their buying. The paper, therefore, which goes into the homes of the fairly prosperous is by and large the one which offers most to the advertiser. It may also go into the homes of the poor, but except for certain lines of goods, an analytical advertising agent does not rate that circulation as a great asset.[65]

While the language of psychology, in the 1920s and again in the 1950s, attracted the greatest interest and controversy in advertising, sophistication about basic sociological variables like class and gender has had a more pronounced impact on advertising practice.

The advertising agencies by the 1920s were becoming institutions of considerable resources and confidence. But advertising agents were not only men of confidence; they were confidence men. Their livelihood depended on selling to business the idea that advertising was an effective marketing tool. It would be naive to read their sales pitches to the business community as honest accounts of the power of advertising. Yet this is what Stuart Ewen has done in *Captains of Consciousness,* probably the best-known book among nonspecialists on the origins of American advertising. For Ewen, advertising is "a cultural apparatus aimed at defusing and neutralizing potential unrest."[66] It was part of a political attack on organized labor in the early decades of this century. What scientific management was to the workplace, advertising was to the cultural realm, an effort at control of the workers. Business sought to "invest the laborer with a financial power and a psychic desire to consume." Through advertising, classes engaged in production—and in politics—became masses, preoccupied with consumption and the passive enactment of corporate-manufactured dreams.[67]

Abstractly, Ewen's account makes sense—a view that sees the system of corporate capitalism as a highly rational and self-conscious juggernaut. Historically, however, it is without foundation. There are three problems with the construction of the argument. First, the evidence is, as I have suggested, inappropriate to the conclusions. Almost all the businessmen Ewen cites are not "captains of industry" showing their self-conscious understanding of the capitalist system but corporals of advertising and marketing, trying to make their case to the business world in terms they think will most delight it.[68]

Second, it does not make sense to imagine that capitalists who wanted to keep down "the workers" would try to do so by placing ads for consumer goods in magazines with an affluent, middle-class readership. Yet advertising was strongly directed toward the middle class and most of Ewen's examples of advertisements come from *Saturday Evening Post* and *Ladies Home Journal* and other magazines whose readership was affluent. And female. Capitalists may not all be mental giants but it seems unlikely that they would try to hold down working-class, largely male, rebellion by writing toothpaste and deodorant ads to a middle-class, largely female, readership.

Third, research reported after publication of Ewen's work suggests that despite growing affluence in the 1920s, the working class did not share very much in the prosperity. It is probable that the workers could not afford very many of the widely advertised goods. One's psychological hunches can then work either way—either this would lead the workers to work harder to be able, one day, to join in middle-class prosperity, or it would lead to frustration that might trigger political activity.[69]

Ewen recognizes, near the end of his book, that advertising in the 1920s was not *successful* in changing the habits of the working class, in part because the workers did not have money to consume and in part because advertising tended to be directed toward the affluent. He then restates his thesis more modestly, holding that business in the 1920s created in advertising a "model of social control."[70] That is a more cautious position, but it still assumes a self-consciousness in the business community that I do not believe can be demonstrated. That advertising is a form of social control can scarcely be denied, but that it was a calculated, classwide effort at social control is very doubtful. The development of advertising did not happen accidentally nor was it a self-conscious business scheme to turn workers into consumers.

The problem of advertising is more complex. Twentieth-century advertising and twentieth-century consumer culture have roots in the changing nature of the market in the late nineteenth century which developed along with changes in modes of transportation and communication, urban growth, and a cultural climate for and social fact of social and geographic mobility. In addition, changes in the manufacturing processes in various industries and the capacity to increase output without substantial increase in product costs encouraged a new emphasis in business on marketing and distribution; the growing independent influence on business of the media and advertising agencies also stimulated the development of advertising.

The social transformation that gave rise to advertising not only made mass-produced and advertised products more important to people but altered the criteria for consumption, the qualities in goods deemed desirable. The growth of a consumer society has been a qualitative as well as a quantitative change. I have now sketched in the general context for this position.

NOTES

1. Theodore Dreiser, *Sister Carrie* (New York: Bantam Books, 1958 [Doubleday, Page, 1900]), p. 4.

2. See Lyn Lofland, *World of Strangers* (New York: Basic Books, 1973), and Richard Sennett, *The Fall of Public Man* (New York: Alfred A. Knopf, 1976), p. 39.

3. Theodore Dreiser, *Newspaper Days* (New York: Horace Liveright, 1922), p. 139.

4. Dreiser, *Sister Carrie*, p. 17.

5. "The Department Store Question," editorial, *Chicago Tribune,* February 26, 1897, and "Big Stores Are in Scorn," *Chicago Tribune,* February 23, 1897. For a discussion of similar, and more successful efforts, in France, see Michael B. Miller, *The Bon Marché: Bourgeois Culture and the Department Store, 1869–1920* (Princeton: Princeton University Press, 1981), pp. 212–13. For a brief history of the American department store, see Daniel Boorstin, *The Americans: The Democratic Experience* (New York: Random House, 1973), pp. 101–18.

6. William Allen White, *The Autobiography of William Allen White* (New York: Macmillan, 1946), p. 400.

7. Quoted in Neil Harris, "Museums, Merchandising, and Popular Taste: The Struggle for Influence," in *Material Culture and the Study of American Life,* ed. Ian M. G. Quimby (New York: W. W. Norton, 1978), p. 152. Again, see Miller, *Bon Marché,* pp. 168–77, for a similar account of Bon Marché in Paris. As interesting and delightful as Miller's book is, his view that "it was the department store that was largely responsible for lowering prices and for creating overpowering urges to consume" (p. 184) cannot be accepted.

8. Boorstin, *Americans,* p. 107.

9. Quoted in Harris, "Museums," p. 152.

10. Joel H. Ross, M.D., *What I Saw in New York* (Auburn, N.Y.: Derby and Miller, 1851), p. 170.

11. See Michael Schudson, *Discovering the News* (New York: Basic Books, 1978), pp. 93, 206.

12. Charles Edward Russell, *These Shifting Scenes* (New York: George H. Doran, 1914), p. 309.

13. Robert Lynd and Helen Lynd, *Middletown* (New York: Harcourt, Brace and World, 1929), p. 532.

14. Joseph Appel, *Growing Up with Advertising* (New York: Business Bourse, 1940), pp. 25, 43, 92, 97. Appel was John Wanamaker's advertising manager.

15. Erik Erikson, *Childhood and Society* (New York: W. W. Norton, 1950), p. 261.

16. Peter Berger and Thomas Luckmann, "Social Mobility and Personal Identity," *Archives Européenne de Sociologies* 5 (1964): 331–43.

17. Ibid., p. 338.

18. Lynd and Lynd, *Middletown,* p. 144.

19. William Leiss, *The Limits to Satisfaction* (Toronto: University of Toronto Press, 1976), pp. 61–63 and elsewhere. Robert Lynd sensed this growing ambiguity of needs when he wrote of the proliferation of consumer goods in the 1920s, suggesting that "it is an open question whether factors making for consumer confusion in our rapidly changing culture are not actually outstripping the forces making for more effective consumption." Robert Lynd and Alice C. Hanson, "People as Consumers," in President's Research Commission on Social Trends, *Recent Social Trends in the United States* (New York: McGraw-Hill, 1933), p. 911.

20. Daniel Bell, *The Cultural Contradictions of Capitalism* (New York: Basic Books, 1976), p. 66.

21. Claude Lévi-Strauss, *Totemism* (Boston: Beacon Press, 1963), p. 89, and Mary Douglas and Baron Isherwood, *The World of Goods* (New York: Basic Books, 1979), p. 62.

22. Berger and Luckmann, "Social Mobility," p. 339.

23. Boorstin, *Americans,* pp. 97, 99.

24. Lynd and Lynd, *Middletown,* p. 165.

25. Anne Hollander, *Seeing Through Clothes* (New York: Viking Press, 1978), p. 362.

26. There is a large literature on fashion. America's premier analyst of clothing, Thorstein Veblen, saw dress in the late nineteenth century as primarily intended for the display of economic position. See Thorstein Veblen, "The Economic Theory of Women's Dress," in *Essays in Our Changing Order,* ed. Thorstein Veblen (New York: August M. Kelley, 1964 [1934]), p. 67. The essay appeared first in *Popular Science Monthly* 46 (November 1894). See also the rich and provocative book by Hollander, *Seeing Through Clothes;* Edward Sapir, "Fashion," *Encyclopedia of the Social Sciences* (New York: Macmillan, 1933), vol. 6, pp. 139–44; Georg Simmel, "Fashion," in *Georg Simmel: On Individuality and Social Forms,* ed. Donald N. Levine (Chicago: University of Chicago Press, 1971); and Herbert Blumer, "Fashion: From Class Differentiation to Collective Selection," *Sociological Quarterly* 10 (Summer 1969): 275–91. Also valuable is Neil McKendrick, "The Commercialization of Fashion," in *The Birth of Consumer Society: The Commercialization of Eighteenth*

Century England, ed. Neil McKendrick, John Brewer, and J. H. Plumb (Bloomington: Indiana University Press, 1982) on fashions in clothing and other consumer goods, from pottery to cut flowers.

27. Marcus Felson, "Invidious Distinctions among Cars, Clothes and Suburbs," *Public Opinion Quarterly* 42 (Spring 1978): 49–58, and Marcus Felson, "The Masking of Material Inequality in the Contemporary United States: Felson's Reply," *Public Opinion Quarterly* 43 (Spring 1979): 120–22.

28. George Akerlof, "The Market for 'Lemons': Quality Uncertainty and the Market Mechanism," *Quarterly Journal of Economics* 84 (August 1970): 499. For relevant comparative material on how the use of trademarks and advertising in the Soviet Union acts as a kind of quality control and consumer protection, see Marshall I. Goldman, "Product Differentiation and Advertising: Some Lessons from the Soviet Experience," *Journal of Political Economy* 68 (August 1960): 346–57, and M. Timothy O'Keefe and Kenneth G. Sheinkopf, "Advertising in the Soviet Union: Growth of a New Media Industry," *Journalism Quarterly* 53 (Spring 1976): 80–87.

29. John McPhee, *Oranges* (New York: Farrar, Straus & Giroux, 1967), p. 21.

30. Ted Roselius, "Consumer Ranking of Risk Reduction Methods," *Journal of Marketing* 35 (January 1971): 56–61.

31. Sinclair Lewis, *Babbit* (New York: Harcourt, Brace, 1922), p. 95.

32. Douglas and Isherwood, *The World of Goods*, pp. 75–76.

33. In American society, the names of products are not only culturally shared but privately owned. Brand names that become household words take from manufacturers the exclusive rights to the words. Bayer lost the right to "aspirin" and Abercrombie and Fitch lost the rights to "safari." The words cellophane, escalator, shredded wheat, ping-pong, yo-yo, thermos, and zipper all began as brand names. In recent litigation, the FTC challenged American Cyanamid's right to exclusive use of the word "formica." Xerox advertisements urge people to say "photocopy" rather than "xerox" as a verb to keep xerox in the public mind while keeping it from becoming a dictionary term. Similarly, commercials that stress "Sanka brand" decaffeinated coffee try to keep "Sanka" from being synonymous with decaffeinated coffee. The intention in these cases is to protect the name as a piece of property, to prevent its being part of a truly common culture. If culture is the sharing of names, it is also the structured absence of sharing, and this, too, requires examination. See Walter P. Margulies, "FTC vs. Formica Inc.: Trademarks Face Challenge of Their Lives," *Advertising Age,* August 13, 1979, pp. 53–54.

34. See Neil Harris, "The Drama of Consumer Desire," in *Yankee Enterprise,* ed. Otto Mayr and Robert C. Post (Washington, D.C.: Smithsonian Institution Press, 1981), pp. 196–211.

35. Lynd and Lynd, *Middletown,* p. 532.

36. Frank Presbrey, *The History and Development of Advertising* (Garden City, N.Y.: Doubleday, Doran, 1929), p. 362. See also an account of the predominance of patent medicine advertising in this period in Grace Margaret Busso, "A History of the *Des Moines Register*" (M.A. diss., University of Iowa, 1932), p. 134. For a detailed and interesting account of one key patent medicine, see Sarah Stage, *Female Complaints: Lydia Pinkham and the Business of Women's Medicine* (New York: W. W. Norton, 1979).

37. Ralph Hower, *The History of an Advertising Agency: N. W. Ayer & Son at Work, 1869–1949* (Cambridge: Harvard University Press, 1949), pp. 44, 91–92.

38. James Harvey Young, *Toadstool Millionaires* (Princeton: Princeton University Press, 1961), p. 167.

39. Ibid., p. 152.

40. Ibid., pp. 103, 169.

41. For the general analysis here, I rely on Alfred D. Chandler, *The Visible Hand: The Managerial Revolution in American Business* (Cambridge: Harvard University Press, 1977). On Royal Baking Powder, see Daniel Pope, *The Making of Modern Advertising* (New York: Basic Books, 1983), p. 148.

42. Arthur F. Marquette, *Brands, Trademarks and Good Will* (New York: McGraw-Hill, 1967), p. 33.

43. Chandler, *Visible Hand,* p. 287.

44. Marquette, *Brands,* p. 52.

45. Pope, *Modern Advertising,* p. 236.

46. Marquette, *Brands,* p. 51.

47. Chandler, *Visible Hand,* p. 299.

48. This is a much debated point. See, for instance, the account in Mark Albion and Paul Farris, *The Advertising Controversy: Evidence on the Economic Effects of Advertising* (Boston: Auburn House, 1981).

49. Vince Norris, "Advertising History—According to the Textbooks," *Journal of Advertising* 9 (1980): 3–11. Norris places too much emphasis on advertising as a weapon against retailers but he is right to call attention to the importance of this factor.

50. Hower, *Advertising Agency,* p. 16.

51. See Bertram Wyatt-Brown, "God and Dun & Bradstreet, 1841–1851," *Business History Review* 40 (Winter 1966): 432–50, and James H. Madison, "The Evolution of Commercial Credit Reporting Agencies in Nineteenth-Century America," *Business History Review* 48 (Summer 1974): 164–86.

52. Hower, *Advertising Agency,* p. 96.

53. Ibid., p. 56.

54. Ibid., p. 58.

55. See John Gunther, *Taken at the Flood: The Story of Albert D. Lasker* (New York: Harper, 1960), p. 62.

56. Daniel Pope, "The Development of National Advertising 1865–1920" (Ph.D. diss., Columbia University, 1973), p. 284.

57. Ibid., p. 309.

58. Ibid., p. 357.

59. Daniel Pope, *The Making of Modern Advertising,* pp. 239–42, and Quentin Schultze, "An Honorable Place: The Quest for Professional Advertising Education, 1900–1917," *Business History Review* 61 (Spring 1982): 16–32.

60. David Cohen, *J. B. Watson: The Founder of Behaviorism* (London: Routledge and Kegan Paul, 1979), p. 193. See also Kerry W. Buckley, "The Selling of a Psychologist: John Broadus Watson and the Application of Behavioral Techniques to Advertising," *Journal of the History of the Behavioral Sciences* 18 (July 1982): 207–21.

61. Roland Marchand, *Advertising the American Dream: Making Way for Modernity, 1920–1940* (Berkeley: University of California Press, forthcoming).

62. Quoted in Robert Wilber, "Men's Wear Stores for Women Only," *Printer's Ink,* September 15, 1917, p. 162.

63. Ibid., p. 164.

64. James Curran, Angus Douglas, and Barry Whannel, "The Political Economy of the Human-Interest Story," in *Newspapers and Democracy,* ed. Anthony Smith (Cambridge: MIT Press, 1980), pp. 288–347.

65. Walter Lippmann, *Public Opinion* (New York: Macmillan, 1922), p. 205.

66. Stuart Ewen, *Captains of Consciousness: Advertising and the Social Roots of the Consumer Culture* (New York: McGraw-Hill, 1976), p. 12.

67. Ibid., pp. 25, 33, 43, 109.

68. The one regularly cited person in Ewen's book who was not in advertising is Edward Filene, and even he was not an industrialist but a renegade department store owner. Filene supported independent unionism, helped establish the credit union movement, and, a life-long Democrat, supported Franklin Roosevelt in both 1932 and 1936, splitting openly in 1936 with the U.S. Chamber of Commerce that he had helped to found. Filene's insistence that employees at Filene's Department Store be represented in corporate decision making eventually led to his own ouster from management in 1928; he had hoped to transfer store management entirely to the employees. This is scarcely the representative voice of American capital. See Louis Filler's biographical sketch in *Dictionary of American Biography,* vol. 11, supplement 2 (New York: Charles Scribner's Sons, 1958), pp. 183–85, and also *National Cyclopedia of American Biography* 45 (1962): 17–19.

69. On the disposable income of workers in the 1920s, see Frank Stricker, "Affluence for Whom?—Another Look at Prosperity and the Working Classes in the 1920s," *Labor History* 24 (Winter 1983): 5–33. Stricker argues that "the masses were not affluent enough to worry about clean-smelling breath and fancy cars." The response to Ewen's book has varied from uncritical admiration—a reviewer in *Contemporary Sociology* called it a "masterwork"—to extremely hostile criticism, especially in the history journals. Probably the most balanced review is by Daniel Horowitz, "Consumption, Capitalism, and Culture," *Reviews in American History* 6 (September 1978): 388–93, which identifies the reason for the importance of the book: "It is the first major study by a radical historian that moves from analysis of capitalist control of production to that of corporate hegemony in consumption." See also Sue Curry Jansen's review of Stuart and Elizabeth Ewen, *Channels of Desire,* in *Contemporary Sociology* 12 (July 1983): 423 and the reviews of *Captains of Consciousness* by Otis A. Pease, *American Historical Review* 182 (October 1977): 1092–93, and Morton Keller, *Journal of American History* 64 (June 1977): 210. Ewen's work has had more influence in sociology than in history. See, for instance, Michael E. Sobel, *Lifestyle and Social Structure: Concepts, Definitions, Analyses* (New York: Academic Press, 1981), pp. 31–41, which closely follows Ewen's argument.

70. Ewen, *Captains of Consciousness,* p. 204.

CHAPTER 7

AFFLUENZA
Television Use and Cultivation of Materialism

MARK D. HARMON

The cultivation theory has been one of the more elaborately explained and meticulously explored approaches to mass communication effects. The idea grew in 1969 out of Gerbner's Cultural Indicators Project (Potter, 1993). "The basic hypothesis," wrote Signorelli and Morgan (1990), "is that heavy viewers will be more likely to perceive the real world in ways that reflect the most stable and recurrent patterns of portrayals in the television world" (pp. 9–10).

Thus, many researchers set out to test whether TV violence, for example, correlated with a view of the world as a dangerous place—the mean world hypothesis (Gerbner & Jhally, 1994). Other researchers have used the cultivation theory to explore such diverse hypothesized effects from heavy TV viewing as unrealistic female body expectations (Kilbourne & Jhally, 1995), adolescent drinking behavior (Laster, 1993), and even predisposition in the O. J. Simpson murder cases (Pearlstein, 1996).

Hirsch (1980) reanalyzed the National Opinion Research Center's General Social Survey data that Gerbner and his Annenberg School colleagues used to proclaim cultivation effects. Hirsch found that the relationship crumbles when one includes nonviewers and extreme viewers in the tally. Furthermore, any two of a multitude of control variables when applied can wipe out the cultivation effect.

Gerbner, Gross, Morgan, and Signorielli (1981) responded that cultivation sometimes creates a mainstreaming of views among disparate groups, but at other times, particular aspects of the TV view of life resonate more deeply with certain groups. Hirsch (1981) retorted that this created a theory so broad and flexible so as to be untestable and irrefutable, a hook on which to hang any set of responses.

Surprisingly, these claims and counterclaims did not get into the question of materialism as a better choice than fear, violence, or alienation as the central message of commercial television. Few researchers, in fact, have taken the path that the most consistent and significant message of commercial television is commercialism and that the place to look for long-term, subtle, and pervasive effects is in materialism among heavy viewers.

Twitchell (1999) asserted such a universal cultivation effect for materialism. He contended that any division between the commercials themselves and the surrounding programming is increasingly becoming an artificial, unnecessary, and contrived distinction. He wrote the following:

The impact of television on materialism is not via specific commercials. Along with commercial speech comes commercial context. We see on television how things fit together. Television illustrates a thousand times each hour how branded objects are dovetailed together to form a coherent pattern of selfhood, a lifestyle. If you are successful and happy you drive a new car, you wear designer clothes, you have a house full of branded appliances, you have an entertainment center, you travel a lot, you have a cell phone or whatever new gadget is making the rounds. We see . . . what a coherent pattern of consumable objects does in creating the stereotype of success and happiness. (p. 105)

Some of the predecessors, devotees, and advocates of the original cultivation theory have noted a materialism component. McLuhan (1947/2000), normally regarded as the antithesis of a message effects theorist, contended that the dramatic ad is a maker of "patterns of living." It sets up audiences, especially adolescents, for temporary emotional relief and popularity through goods. Postman (1988) wrote that commercial TV's foremost commandment is "thou shalt have no other gods than consumption" (p. 113).

Jhally (2000) argued that commercial culture, including TV, appeals to us as individuals motivated by selfish greed, rather than as compassionate, generous members of a society caring about collective issues. Jhally's observation neatly parallels the phenomenon of the Ronald Reagan question, "Are you better off today than you were 4 years ago?," which politically now holds sway, far ahead of the alternative question: Are we a better and more just society?

The cultivation of materialism approach complements several theoretical traditions. It most closely follows social comparison theory, the contention that people compare their lives with idealized images portrayed in advertising (Richins, 1995).

Cultivation of materialism also can be seen as a mass media extension of symbolic interactionism. Expressed in theories like identity theory and social identity theory, social interactionism postulates that people know or define who they are through interaction with others (LaRossa & Reitzes, 1993). Faules and Alexander (1978) and M. R. Solomon (1983) extended social interactionism to include one's mediated environment. The variation here is to replace "others" or "mediated environment" with the "central underlying message of commercial television."

LITERATURE REVIEW

Only a few studies have addressed materialism from a cultivation perspective. Reimer and Rosengren (1990) used Rokeach Value Surveys among Swedes to find cultivation connections. "The relationship between the values and media use is rather clear-cut," they concluded. "[Post-materialist value] 'inner harmony' and [materialist] 'a comfortable life' stand in two directly contrasting positions with the media. 'A comfortable life' is related to entertainment and other types of light media content; 'inner harmony' is related to high cultural media content and to news" (p. 195).

Potter (1994) observed that there has been a small amount of cultivation research on values, as opposed to feelings, perceptions, and attitudes. He mentions only Reimer and Rosengren (1990) and his own work (Potter, 1990) on TV program themes and adolescent values. The study of middle school and high school students found some cultivation effect for TV themes like good wins over evil, truth always wins out, honesty is the best policy, and hard work yields rewards. Consumer or materialist values, however, were not part of that analysis.

Sirgy et al. (1998) touched on cultivation when they set out to test a three-step link from television viewing to materialism to dissatisfaction with life. They sampled 1,226 respondents: 234 undergraduates at Northern Illinois University; 233 household respondents from Peoria, Illinois;

180 from Waterloo, Ontario; 249 from Wollongong, Australia; 139 from Istanbul, Turkey; and 191 from Beijing, China.

The respondents were asked about daily and weekly TV viewing as well as seven Likert-scaled questions taken from Richins's (1987) measure of materialism. The questions were as follows:

1. It is important for me to have really nice things.
2. I would like to be rich enough to buy anything I want.
3. I'd be happier if I could afford to buy more things.
4. It sometimes bothers me quite a bit that I cannot afford to buy all the things I would like.
5. People place too much emphasis on material things (reverse coded).
6. It's really true that money can buy happiness.
7. The things I own give me a great deal of pleasure.

The results were mixed. Regressions showed that materialism did correlate with TV viewing from the pooled Chinese, Australian, and U.S. panels, but not for the Turkish, Canadian, and U.S. student samples. The authors admitted that the samples used were not measured against populations for external validity. Furthermore, they noted at various points in the article that age, predisposition toward ad truthfulness, message content, and culture may all play roles in the strength of the connection. Thus, their work seems to qualify substantially the cultivation theory that, at least in its early incarnations, posited subtle but pervasive and near universal adoption of the TV themes.

Brand and Greenberg (1994) tried to measure some of the audience effects of Channel One, a 10-minute daily newscast with 2 minutes of ads. That newscast is aimed at middle and high school adolescents and is welcomed at some schools in exchange for the use of telecommunications equipment from Channel One's originator, Whittle Communications.

The researchers matched 373 students who regularly view with 454 not exposed to it. The experimental and control groups were from the same metropolitan area and had similar community characteristics such as standardized test scores, faculty-to-student ratios, per-pupil expenditures, family income, and cable TV channels available.

The hypothesis that Channel One viewers would report stronger consumer-oriented attitudes than nonviewers was tested using Likert-scaled questions. The researchers found statistical support for the hypothesis in the summed results of the five questions and strong support specifically for Channel One viewers reporting that they usually want what is shown in TV commercials and that designer clothing labels are important to them.

A follow-up survey administered to 383 students in Channel One schools and 437 in control schools (Greenberg & Brand, 1993) also reported a statistically significant increase in materialistic values among the Channel One viewers.

Easterlin and Crimmins (1991) conducted one of the largest analyses of materialism among teenagers and young adults. They conducted a secondary analysis of two major data sets, the Cooperative Institutional Research Program (CIRP) and the Monitoring the Future project. The researchers took CIRP data from 1966 to 1986. CIRP during that period was collecting data from approximately 200,000 entering freshmen per year from approximately 550 2-year and 4-year colleges and universities. The University of Michigan Survey Research Center conducted the Monitoring the Future surveys. Easterlin and Crimmins used 1976 to 1986 surveys from approximately 3,000 high school seniors per year.

Examining both data sets, the authors found a "substantial increase in private materialism as a life goal, a modest turning away from the public interest, and a sharp decline in emphasis on personal self-fulfillment" (Easterlin & Crimmins, 1991, p. 529). However, their TV viewing, as reported by the respondents, drifted modestly downward over the survey period. This surprising finding leaves several possibilities regarding a television–materialism link. The link is either not there, is much delayed, or is conditional on many other respondent or exposure variables. Any link could also run in the opposite direction; persons with strong materialistic values could be attracted to the materialistic content of commercial television.

Yoon (1995) conducted a small survey regarding materialism and advertising. Eighty-seven students from university classes and 79 community members intercepted in malls were surveyed using previously established questions and scales. Yoon found a positive and significant relationship between materialism and general advertising attitudes. Yoon also speculated that stronger correlations for African Americans were a consequence of higher levels of TV viewing. The two convenience samples present obvious problems. University students tend to watch relatively low levels of TV (Comstock & Paik, 1991). Mall shoppers, or at least mall regulars, might be predisposed to advertising or materialism.

Although only a few studies empirically address a cultivation effect of heavy TV exposure leading to materialistic values, many popular press articles, videos, lectures, and so on, have asserted such a connection. Anthropological tales certainly abound on how the arrival of television brought to isolated communities an unhealthy materialism and the destruction of culture. Typical is the case of the Gwich'in tribe of Arctic Village, Alaska. The first TV set, a 12-inch, black-and-white Zenith, arrived in January 1980. Even though only one distant signal could be received, people watched the novelty from sign on to sign off. It since has been followed by satellite dishes and video game systems (Lewan, 1999).

A Gwich'in artist, Sarah James, began a committee to preserve tribal customs, and she sees TV as a prime opponent. "The TV teaches greed," she told one reporter. "It shows our people a world that is not ours. It makes us wish we were something else" (Lewan, 1999, p. B1).

The Associated Press noted some of the TV materialistic effects on the Gwich'in tribe. Mothers stopped making ice cream from caribou bone powder and river slush; instead, they bought Ben & Jerry's. They also stopped making "tundra tea" with alpine spruce needles in favor of Folger's instant coffee. Kids chomped Bazooka bubble gum rather than dried caribou meat. They no longer waited for the elders to finish eating before starting a meal. Legends told around campfires were replaced with Bart Simpson lines. Nike sneakers soon replaced and outmoded beaded moccasins, just as the sled dog gave way to the gas-powered Ski-Doo Alpine and the wood stove to the microwave oven (Lewan, 1999).

Some popular press sources even have come up with a catchy term for the phenomenon, *affluenza.*

Recently, two public television programs, *Affluenza* and *Escape From Affluenza*, have drawn societal attention to the topic of materialism (H. Solomon, 1988). Gary Collins, the pastor of St. Mark Presbyterian Church in Newport Beach, California, used a tape of the program to stimulate discussion among his congregation. Collins said, "You see the glossy ads in magazines and on television, and that builds your expectations. You assume this is the way people who make it live, and if you don't get there, you feel disappointed" (Hong, 1998, p. B3).

One newspaper preview (Nye, 1997) of the initial show, *Affluenza*, asserted that most of us fall victim to advertising messages to "buy now, pay later" when it comes to the latest car or latest dress or latest whatever so we will be up-to-date, in step with the rest of society. "The advertising industry sets its sights on consumers at an early age," Nye wrote in his review (p. C5). "Clips are shown of a 'Kids Power Conference' held at Disney World where executives map out strategy on how to hook children on buying. It is estimated that by age 20, most Americans have been exposed to 1 million commercial messages" (p. C5).

One columnist chimed in that affluenza is a highly contagious disease spread by casual contact through TV and radio airwaves, shopping malls, and ad circulars and that the cure includes curtailed TV viewing (Borgman, 1996). Pediatrician Dr. Ralph Minear has taken up the term affluenza and the concern about it. He said, "Children are seduced by advertising and their peers into thinking possessions will bring them popularity and happiness" (d'Elgin, 1992, p. 6D). He recommended extensive firsthand training in how to handle money.

One striking similarity unites nearly all of these studies and popular press claims. Excepting Reimer and Rosengren (1990) and part of Yoon's (1995) sample, all of these attempts to link material values and amount of television viewing have concentrated on children. The time has come to get beyond looking at this possible television–materialism link as a new danger to youth. The vast majority of persons, at least in the United States, have had commercial television available for most, if not all, of their adult lives.

METHODS

Looking for indications of cultivation of materialism or affluenza, I conducted a secondary analysis of the electronic version of the Simmons Market Research Bureau (SMRB) Study of Media and Markets (SMM). The SMRB/SMM data set was made available on August 13, 1996, for educational uses and is generally analyzed using Choices II, SPSS, or Microsoft Excel (Li, 1998).

The data were collected from June 13, 1993, through March 22, 1994, using a four-stage module. The first stage was an initial hourlong personal interview on newspaper reading habits, plus individual and household demographics. The second stage was a self-administered questionnaire on psychographics, purchases, and some TV information. Approximately 11,000 respondents completed and returned the booklet (SMRB, 1994).

The third stage was a 35-minute personal interview covering changes since the first interview, plus additional questions on radio listening and magazine reading. A subsample also completed a telephone interview about radio listening. The fourth stage was a 2-week, mail-in diary of TV viewing. The diaries were staggered over a time period from April 13, 1994, through May 24, 1994 (SMRB, 1994).

The first-stage interviews were completed by 22,051 people (11,063 men and 10,988 women). The overall recovery rate, based on "total eligible designated respondents" was 69.7%. The follow-up interviews were conducted on 16,380 individuals, 74.3% of those completing the first interview, or slightly more than half the "total eligible designated respondents" (SMRB, 1994).

A total of 21,594 persons responded regarding TV viewing, although in crosstabs across a variety of questions, the number of valid cases slipped to approximately 20,000 regarding prime-time and daytime viewers, and approximately 14,500 regarding cable TV.

Regarding definition of materialism, this research goes slightly beyond the dictionary definition of "devotion to [physical/corporeal] rather than spiritual needs or interests; self interest" (Morehead & Morehead, 1995, p. 421). Materialism, furthermore, is the association of success or happiness with the acquisition or possession of goods or the means to obtain goods, wealth. Materialism also implies spending money freely, impulsively, and carelessly. Materialists, one can assume, are concerned not only about brand names and labels but also about what others think of them. This research also assumes that materialists are more likely than nonmaterialists to believe the claims of ads and to seek easy money solutions to life's problems.

I examined the data set and found 29 questions that could be regarded as either an embrace or rejection of materialistic values. These 29 questions came from the Attitudes, Buying Style, and Personal Views sections of the SMRB/SMM. The six questions in the Attitudes section were recorded in an agree–disagree format. The six questions from the Buying Style section and the 17 from the Personal Views section all were recorded in an "Agree a Lot, Agree a Little, Not Sure, Disagree a Little, Disagree a Lot" format.

These answers were compared with quintiles on level of prime-time, daytime, and cable TV viewing. The crosstabs thus yielded 2×5 tables for the six attitudes questions and 5×5 tables for the remaining 23 questions. The sheer size of the survey virtually guaranteed significance via chi-square. A Kendall's tau-b was chosen as a better measure of whether a correlation could be found moving in the projected directions—namely more viewing yielding more materialistic values and less viewing corresponding with antimaterialistic views.

Another secondary analysis was conducted of the 1972 to 1996 General Social Survey (GSS), as made available on the Computer Assisted Survey Methods Program, University of California, Berkeley, Web site.

The GSS typically conducted approximately 1,500 face-to-face interviews per year. The independently drawn sample is of English-speaking persons 18 years and older living in noninstitutional arrangements within the United States. GSS claims that this face-to-face method leaves in the pool being sampled 97.3% of the U.S. population. Each interview typically took approximately 1.5 hours to complete. Surveys were conducted in 1972–1975, 1977–1979, 1980, 1982–1983, 1985–1984, 1988–1991, and 1993–1994 during February, March, and April of those years. The total online GSS sample was 35,284 interviews, 4,218 columns per respondent (Davis & Smith, 1972–1994). I reviewed the online and published codebooks (Davis & Smith, 1994) and found seven variables related to materialism and one measure of TV viewing, self-reported daily viewing hours. The exact wording on TV use was "On the average day, about how many hours do you personally watch television?" Those other variables, expressed as statements or questions were as follows:

- Please tell me how important each thing is to you personally . . . having nice things.
- How important do you personally consider these job characteristics?
- Using the scale from 1 to 7 for your answers again . . . high income?
- You have to take care of yourself first, and if you have any energy left over, then help other people.
- People should be allowed to accumulate as much wealth as they can even if some make millions while others live in poverty.
- I would turn down another job for more pay in order to stay with this organization.
- How important to you is the opportunity to be promoted?
- How often would you say that you and your friends think about topics we've been discussing during the interview?
- Would you say that you and your friends think about . . . satisfaction with their present financial situation?

FINDINGS

The SMRB/SMM data yielded no strong (.5 or –.5) or even noteworthy (.2 or –.2) correlations on the Kendall tau-b analysis. Across all 29 questions analyzed by prime-time, daytime, and cable TV viewership, the measures ranged from a modest .074 to an even more modest –.053 (Table 7.1).

The GSS secondary analysis, however, showed some strong correlations in the expected direction. Respondents who regarded having nice things as important and who believed in taking care of yourself first before others also tended be heavier TV viewers (Table 7.2). Respondents who regarded a high income as important also had higher numbers for TV viewing; the pattern at the

Table 7.1

Viewing Quintiles and Materialism: Simmons Market Research Bureau Study of Media and Markets Statement Agreement: Prime-Time, Daytime and Cable TV (Kendall's tau-b Values)

Statement	Prime	Day	Cable
Very happy with my life as it is[a]	.007	−.010	−.044
Like other people to think I'm rich[a]	.007	−.007	−.035
Sacrifice time with my family to get ahead[a]	−.032	−.014	.004
Win lottery would never work ahead[a]	.024	.065	.055
Careful with my money[a]	−.001	−.014	.053
Money is the best measure of success[a]	−.019	.015	.031
Impulsive: Buy on spur of the moment	−.004	.019	.066
Experimenter: Change brands often	−.035	−.021	.025
Brand loyal: Always look for manufacturer name	−.014	.004	−.003
Conformist: Buy what neighbors approve	−.014	−.012	−.040
Ad believer: Advertising gives a true picture	−.018	.011	.020
Style conscious: Keep up with changes	−.001	.015	.022
Happy with my standard of living	−.020	−.017	−.037
Rather be bored at a job than not working	−.014	.003	.008
No good at saving money	−.022	.011	.054
Tend to spend money without thinking	−.025	.009	.048
Don't like idea of being in debt	−.003	.011	.025
Very good at managing money	.003	.001	−.033
Worth paying extra for quality goods	−.018	−.006	.007
Too much sponsorship in arts and sports	−.009	.010	.013
Important to me to look well dressed	−.033	−.007	.011
Not too concerned about my appearance	−.005	−.008	−.011
Like to keep up with the latest in fashion	−.021	−.009	.007
Really enjoy shopping for clothes	−.028	−.007	.024
Looking for new ideas to improve home	−.006	.013	.044
Decide what I want before shopping	.006	.015	.010
I look for the lowest price when I shop	−.007	.012	.033
Often enter contests and sweepstakes	.023	.057	.074

[a]Agree–disagree questions. The remainder were five-option (agree a lot, agree a little, not sure, disagree a little, disagree a lot) format.

opposite end of the spectrum is not as clear, but that may be an artifact of some small subsample sizes (Table 7.2).

Respondents did not vary significantly regarding TV viewing and the importance of being promoted, willingness to turn down another job with more pay, the acceptability of getting rich while others are poor, or how often they and their friends thought about their financial situation (Table 7.2).

These four variables, one should note, are the ones with the most tangential connections to materialism. One's desire for promotion may be more directly connected to a sense of appreciation. That same appreciation, plus family and community ties, may confound answers related to willingness to take another job with better pay. The acceptability of being rich while others are poor may be more of a political statement than a materialistic attitude. Finally, thinking about one's financial situation cuts both ways. Thinking about one's finances might be a direct materialistic concern with money. On the other hand, not thinking about one's finances may be a materialistic and carefree disdain for worrying about the cost of desired items. The question is further com-

Table 7.2

Hours Per Day Watching TV and General Social Survey Materialism Questions (1972–1996)

Question	TV Hours	N
Important to have nice things[a]		
One of most important	3.58	68
Very important	3.09	340
Somewhat important	2.78	731
Not too important	2.82	361
Not at all important	2.92	76
Total	2.90	1,576
Take care of self first, before others[b]		
Strongly agree	3.50	337
Agree	3.02	1,028
Neither agree nor disagree	2.67	281
Disagree	2.63	689
Strongly disagree	2.39	171
Total	2.90	2,556
Importance of high income[c]		
Unimportant (1)	2.94	16
(2)	2.50	14
(3)	4.44	16
(4)	2.65	65
(5)	2.91	201
(6)	3.09	193
Very important (7)	3.53	410
Total	3.23	915
How often think about finances[d]		
Very often	2.76	601
Sometimes	2.71	614
Almost never	3.03	301
Total	2.79	1,516
Importance of promotion opportunity[e]		
Very important	2.56	205
Important	2.64	122
Somewhat important	2.56	95
Not at all important	2.66	107
Does not apply (volunteered)	2.62	68
Total	2.60	597
Turn down another job for more pay[f]		
Strongly agree	2.28	75
Agree	2.76	138
Disagree	2.60	258
Strongly Disagree	2.53	100
Total	2.59	571
Okay to get rich, even if others poor[g]		
Strongly agree	2.73	181
Agree	2.81	722
Neither agree nor disagree	2.81	177
Disagree	3.07	379
Strongly disagree	3.16	91
Total	2.88	1,550

[a]Analysis of variance results: $F = 2.930$, $p = .0199$; asked in 1993. [b]Analysis of variance results: $F = 13.258$, $p = .0000$; asked in 1993 ($M = 2.53$ TV hours) and in 1996 ($M = 2.96$). [c]Analysis of variance results: $F = 2.764$, $p = .0114$, asked in 1982. [d]Analysis of variance results: $F = 2.378$, $p = .0930$; asked in 1978. [e]Analysis of variance results: $F = .087$, $p = .9866$; asked in 1991. [f]Analysis of variance results: $F = 1.147$, $p = .3294$; asked in 1991. [g]Analysis of variance results: $F = 1.539$, $p = .1885$; asked in 1993.

plicated by asking respondents to estimate not only how much they think about finances but also how much their friends think about the same.

DISCUSSION

This research project set out to determine whether, as suggested by cultivation theory, the central message of commercial television (materialism) is adopted by viewers who watch a lot of television. The researcher used two secondary analyses, one of a massive consumer marketing survey and the other of a long-term social survey. The first data set yielded no correlation across 29 different questions related to materialism. The second data set, however, showed a strong link across three fairly direct measures of materialistic attitudes (and no such link in four marginal measures of materialism).

The mixed results from this analysis fit nicely with the scant existing research on the TV viewing and materialism link. The link is tenuous at best, and other variables (culture, message, and viewer age) are likely to play key roles.

It may well be that a complicated interaction of effects or factors (socioeconomic status, age, education, gender, peer pressure, family interaction, psychological or cultural predisposition, birth order, disposable income, religiosity, past product experience, and multiple media sources, including content and program types, etc.) lead to materialistic values. The idea that television as the "central cultural arm" of U.S. society (Gerbner, Gross, Jackson-Beeck, Jeffries-Fox, & Signorielli, 1978) is wholly or largely responsible for materialism must be modified after this analysis.

Researchers should not become frustrated by these mixed findings or conclude that affluenza or materialistic values are not a problem worth exploring on quantitative and qualitative levels. Furthermore, these results should not be used to argue for minimal or no overall effects from television viewing. Instead, these findings should be viewed for what they are: two very large databases offering tantalizing clues about the role of commercial television in the cultivation of materialist values.

The lack of a consistently strong link should not be misinterpreted to mean that materialism is not, on an ethical level, a social problem. These findings also should not be used to claim that TV viewing does not play a role in the transmission of materialistic values. Cultivation theory, however, offers an overly simplistic and inexact formula for measuring, analyzing, and understanding these concerns.

It may be that some materialistic values are too subtle to be observed via quantitative survey methods. After all, a certain degree of socially acceptable answering may creep into the response set. Just as respondents may not want to admit to ill manners, criminal records, crude behavior, or not voting, respondents also may not want to admit to excessive TV viewing or to appear shallow and materialistic to questioners.

Secondary analyses such as this work with adults and that of Easterlin and Crimmins (1991) with young persons appear to rule out a simple TV exposure and materialism link, but secondary analyses probably cannot answer more detailed questions of the role of commercial television messages in materialism. Such future work should probably borrow from past efforts and include the Rokeach Value Survey as done by Reimer and Rosengren (1990), the TV themes as done by Potter (1990), and the Sirgy et al. (1998) and Richins (1995) questions.

Future researchers also may want to follow the example of Brand and Greenberg (1994) by seeking "moments of materialism" like Channel One in classrooms. These samples could include adult respondents drawn from frequent viewers of various home shopping networks, users of Internet shopping services, and persons suffering from excessive credit card debt. General adult populations also should be sampled as control groups. All groups will need multiple regression analyses to identify materialism factors. International and longitudinal studies could follow the groups similar to Gwich'in, remote communities newly exposed to a bombardment of commercial messages.

REFERENCES

Borgman, L. (1996, November 18). Is there no cure? Dreaded affluenza gives its young victims the snivels. *Pittsburgh Post-Gazette*, p. B3.

Brand, J. E., & Greenberg, B. S. (1994). Commercials in the classroom: The impact of Channel One advertising. *Journal of Advertising Research, 34,* 18.

Comstock, G., & Paik, H. (1991). *Television and the American child.* New York: Academic.

Davis, J. A., & Smith, T. W. (1972–1994). General Social Surveys [machine-readable data file]. Chicago: National Opinion Research Center, producer, 1996; Storrs, CT: The Roper Center for Public Opinion Research, University of Connecticut, distributor.

Davis, J. A., & Smith, T. W. (1994). *General social surveys, 1972–1994: Cumulative codebook* (National Data Program for the Social Sciences No. 14). Chicago: National Opinion Research Center.

d'Elgin, T. (1992, January 12). Teaching kids about money can cure their "affluenza." *Minneapolis Star Tribune*, p. 6D.

Easterlin, R. A., & Crimmins, E. M. (1991). Private materialism, personal self-fulfillment, family life, and public interest: The nature, effects, and causes of recent changes in the values of American youth. *Public Opinion Quarterly, 55,* 499–533.

Faules, D. F., & Alexander, D. C. (1978). *Communication and social behavior: A symbolic interaction perspective.* Reading, MA: Addison-Wesley.

Gerbner, G., Gross, L., Jackson-Beeck, M., Jeffries-Fox, S., & Signorielli, N. (1978). Cultural indicators: Violence profile no. 9. *Journal of Communication, 28,* 176–207.

Gerbner, G., Gross, L., Morgan, M., & Signorielli, N. (1981). A curious journey into the scary world of Paul Hirsch. *Communication Research, 8,* 39–72.

Gerbner, G. (Speaker) & Jhally, S. (Producer). (1994). *The killing screens: Media and the culture of violence* [Film/video recording]. Northampton, MA: Media Education Foundation.

Greenberg, B. S., & Brand, J. E. (1993). Television news and advertising in the schools: The Channel One controversy. *Journal of Communication, 43,* 143–151.

Hirsch, P. M. (1980). The "scary world" of the nonviewer and other anomalies: A reanalysis of Gerbner et al.'s findings on cultivation analysis. *Communication Research,* 7(4), 403–456.

Hirsch, P. M. (1981). On not learning from one's own mistakes, a reanalysis of Gerbner et al.'s findings on cultivation analysis, Part II. *Communication Research, 8,* 3–37.

Hong, R. (1998, December 12). Church near malls takes on "affluenza." *Los Angeles Times*, p. B3.

Jhally, S. (2000). Advertising at the edge of the apocalypse. In R. Andersen & L. Strate (Eds.), *Critical studies in media commercialism* (pp. 27–39). New York: Oxford University Press.

Kilbourne, J. (Speaker), & Jhally, S. (Producer). (1995). *Slim hopes: Advertising and the obsession with thinness* [Film/video recording]. Northampton, MA: Media Education Foundation.

LaRossa, R., & Reitzes, D. C. (1993). Symbolic interactionism and family studies. In P. G. Boss, W. J. Doherty, R. LaRossa, W. R. Schumm, & S. K. Steinmetz (Eds.), *Sourcebook of family theories and methods: A contextual approach* (pp. 135–163). New York: Plenum.

Laster, C. C. (1993). The influence of psychological factors and television exposure on the drinking behavior of adolescents: An examination of cultivation effects and the theory of reasoned action (Doctoral dissertation, Florida State University, 1993). *Dissertation Abstracts International, 54–12A,* 4296.

Lewan, T. (1999, May 23). Attack of the talking box: TV destroys culture of Alaskan tribe. *The Columbus Dispatch*, p. B1.

Li, H. (1998). A tutorial for Simmons Choices II [Online]. Retrieved September 7, 1998 from the World Wide Web: http://pilot.msu.edu/user/hairong/docs/choices2.html.

McLuhan, M. (2000). American advertising. In *Horizon.* (Original work published 1947)

Morehead, P. D., & Morehead, A. T. (1995). *The new American Webster handy college dictionary* (3rd ed.). New York: Penguin.

Nye, D. (1997, September 15). "Affluenza" in the U.S.: The "Haves" have it; PBS explores consumers' disease, cures. *The Arizona Republic*, p. C5.

Pearlstein, A. (1996). Television crime drama program viewing and O. J. Simpson bias: Applying the cultivation theory (Masters thesis, University of Nevada, Las Vegas, 1996). *Masters Abstracts International, 34–06*, 2108.

Postman, N. (1988). *Conscientious objections*. New York: Knopf.

Potter, W. J. (1990). Adolescent's perceptions of the primary values of television programming. *Journalism Quarterly, 67*, 843–851.

Potter, W. J. (1993). Cultivation theory and research: A conceptual critique. *Human Communication Research, 19*, 564.

Potter, W. J. (1994, October). Cultivation theory and research. *Journalism Monographs, 10* (Serial No. 147).

Reimer, B., & Rosengren, K. E. (1990). Cultivated viewers and readers: A life-style perspective. In N. Signorelli & M. Morgan (Eds.), *Cultivation analysis: New directions in media effects research* (pp. 181–206). Newbury Park, CA: Sage.

Richins, M. L. (1987). A multivariate analysis of responses to dissatisfaction. *Journal of the Academy of Marketing Science, 15*(3), 24–31.

Richins, M. L. (1995). Social comparison, advertising, and consumer discontent. *American Behavioral Scientist, 38*, 593–607.

Signorelli, N., & Morgan, M. (1990). Preface. In N. Signorelli & M. Morgan (Eds.). *Cultivation analysis: New directions in media effects research*. Newbury Park, CA: Sage.

Simmons Market Research Bureau. (1994). *Simmons Market Research Bureau study of media and markets* (Tech. Guide). New York: Author.

Sirgy, M. J., Lee, D., Kosenko, R., Meadow, H. L., Rantz, D., Cicic, M., Xi Jin, G., Yarsuvat, D., Blenkhorn, D. L., & Wright, N. (1998). Does television viewership play a role in the perception of quality of life? *Journal of Advertising, 27*(1), 125–142.

Solomon, H. (1998, July 7). "Affluenza" follow-up takes a shot at a cure. *The Boston Herald*, p. 34.

Solomon, M. R. (1983). The role of products as social stimuli: A symbolic interactionism perspective. *Journal of Consumer Research, 10*, 319–329.

Twitchell, J. B. (1999). Lead us into temptation: The triumph of American materialism. New York: Columbia University Press.

Yoon, K. (1995). Comparison of beliefs about advertising, attitude toward advertising, and materialism held by African Americans and Caucasians. *Psychological Reports, 77*, 455–466.

PART 2

ADVERTISING AND A CONSUMER ECONOMY

Part 2 addresses advertising and consumption in a consumer society, along with some of the abiding legal and economic consequences of life in a material culture. Not surprisingly, a pitched debate has emerged about the existence of a class-based culture driven largely by advertising versus the presence of a benign meritocracy in which advertising merely aids those blessed with the Darwinian good luck to know how to function within it. It is this issue that arises in the first article by Bagdikian. In other words, as one of George Orwell's characters in *Animal Farm* describes life on the farm, it is a place where some farm characters are "more equal than others" (George Orwell, 1946, 112).

Demand for a product or service requires consumers who are willing and able to purchase that product. In a consumer culture, advertising is an essential part of the demand formula that focuses on creating consumer willingness to purchase. Writers in Part 1, such as Potter, illustrate the importance of advertising in making consumption a high priority in a society that produces more than members can or are willing to use. However, most consumers have resource limitations that limit consumption—namely, they are not blessed with an abundance of money. However, society values economic growth, and in order to keep the economy growing, consumption must keep growing. That means either finding new markets for products and services or getting current consumers to buy more. Advertising can help by cultivating new markets, but unless consumers have the ability to buy, demand will not be created.

Consumer credit has become an essential part of consumer culture. Credit gives consumers the ability to act on the willingness to buy that advertising has created, thereby the demand formula is completed. But is this demand real? Or has hyperdemand been created? Do consumers really have greater ability to buy now with credit cards, or do they just feel that they do?

One of the "unsettling trends" addressed as a possible consequence of consumer culture, in the article by Medoff and Harless, is the widespread consumer dependency on credit cards and other forms of personal debt to ensure the relentless pursuit of the American Dream. Moreover, based on the broad fundamental financial issues inherent in a consumer culture, Part 2 broaches issues such as the consequent squandering of resources brought about by consumer culture in De Graaf, Wann and Naylor's article on "Resource Exhaustion."

When discussing the role of advertising in a consumer economy, issues arise over whether or not advertising leads to greater consumer choice. It may seem that advertising's ability to offer consumers information on product options leads to greater choices. These choices should lead to savvy consumers shopping for the best quality products at the lowest prices. Do consumers really act this way? Or by supporting product branding, does advertising merely encourage consumers to focus on psychological brand attributes rather than on a brand's physical attributes? The answer to both questions could be "yes." As a step toward understanding advertising's possible roles in product consumer choices, two articles have been included. Both the Abela and Farris and the Wolburg articles examine the potential impact of advertising on product competition, as well as the impact of advertising on media content and on media audiences. Along these lines, the role of advertising in the life cycle of brands is addressed.

The article by Richards and Murphy explores advertising's economic role as a possible form of free speech censorship. Do advertisers really have the right to withhold information from consumers? On the other hand, issues of individual significance, such as gender-based inequalities in magazine publishing are addressed in articles by Haley and Cunningham and by Steinem. Since advertisers provide the monetary support for media, advertisers have been tempted to use their money to influence media content. Do advertisers have a right to dictate media content? Is it ethical for them to do so?

The Haley and Cunningham article looks at the phenomenon of advertiser influence on media content by examining how consumers of media feel about the effects on media. Do consumers really care that advertisers are in some ways dictating media content? Given that women's media have had an especially hard time with advertiser assumptions and prejudices, the Haley and Cunningham article examines how women feel about two types of advertiser media content influence: complementary editorial matter and censorship. Here, as in subsequent sections, the fundamental issues involving advertising and gender, race, and class are explored based on the foundation laid in Part 1. Throughout the book, the indivisibility of economic, environmental, and social issues are inextricably linked in modern day consumer culture.

The influence of advertising on media content is further documented in women's media. The Steinem article is a first-person account of her efforts to publish *Ms. Magazine*, a progressive women's magazine, in light of the prejudices and assumptions advertisers had about women. Eventually, such obstacles led to the decision to publish *Ms.* without advertising. The article is an inside view into the culture of advertiser/media relations.

CHAPTER 8

ONLY THE AFFLUENT NEED APPLY

BENJAMIN H. BAGDIKIAN

> *We make no effort to sell to the mob.*
> Donald Nizen, senior vice-president,
> *New York Times*

NOTHING IN American publishing approaches the profitable heresies of *The New Yorker* magazine. In an era when magazine editors regard covers with eye-catching headlines and striking graphics as imperative for survival, *New Yorker* covers typically are subdued watercolors of idyllic scenes. While other magazines assume that modern Americans don't read, *New Yorker* articles are incredibly long and weighted with detail. The magazine's cartoons ridicule many of its readers, the fashionably affluent who are portrayed in their Upper East Side penthouses speaking Ivy League patois. Editorial doctrine on other leading magazines calls for short, punchy sentences, but *The New Yorker* is almost the last repository of the style and tone of Henry David Thoreau and Matthew Arnold, its chaste, old-fashioned columns breathing the quietude of nineteenth-century essays.

New Yorker advertisements are in a different world. They celebrate the ostentatious jet set. Christmas ads offer gold, diamond-encrusted wristwatches without prices, the implied message being that if you have to ask you have no business looking. A display of Jaeger–Le Coulture advises that the wristwatch "can be pivoted to reveal . . . your coat of arms." One ad for Audemars Piguet watches suggests giving three to impress a woman while another ad does suggest a price, murmuring in fine print, "From $10,500."

There are some homely products, like a Jeep station wagon. But it is displayed with a polo field in the background and is redeemed by other ads like the one that shows a couple in evening clothes embracing in the cockpit of an executive jet. Even in advertisements for products that cost less than $5,000 the characters seem to come from adjacent ads where cuff links are offered at $675, earrings at $3,500, a bracelet at $6,000, a brooch at $14,000. A Jean Patou perfume ad has no vulgar listing of price but says in bold letters what the spirit of all *New Yorker* ads seems to proclaim: "So rare . . . and available to so few."

Despite its violation of the most commanding conventions of what makes a magazine sell, *The New Yorker* for decades has been a leader in making money.

Over the years the magazine was the envy of the periodical industry in the standard measure of financial success—the number of advertising pages sold annually. Year after year, *The New Yorker* was first or second, so fixed in its reputation that other magazines promoting their effectiveness would tell prospective advertisers they were first or second "after *The New Yorker*," the implication being that, like 1950s baseball and the New York Yankees, first place was unassailable.

That was true until 1967. The year before was a record one for *The New Yorker*. Most people in the industry believe that in 1966 the magazine attained the largest number of ad pages sold in a year by any magazine of general circulation in the history of publishing. In 1966 *The New Yorker* sold 6,100 pages of ads. Its circulation was at its usual level, around 448,000.

In 1967 a strange disease struck. *The New Yorker*'s circulation remained the same but the number of ad pages dropped disastrously. In a few years 2,500 pages of ads disappeared, a loss of 40 percent. The magazine's net profits shrank from the 1966 level of $3 million to less than $1 million. Dividends per share, $10.93 in 1966, were down to $3.69 by 1970.

The disastrous loss of advertising occurred despite a continued high level of circulation which, to lay observers, would seem the only statistic needed for a magazine's success. The popular assumption is that if enough people care enough about a publication or a television program to buy it or to turn to it, advertisers will beat a path to their doorway. That clearly was not happening at *The New Yorker*.

The onset of *The New Yorker*'s malady can be traced to July 15, 1967. That issue of the magazine carried a typically long report under the typically ambiguous title "Reporter at Large." This is the standing head for *New Yorker* articles dealing in depth with subjects as diverse as the history of oranges, the socialization of rats, and the culture of an Irish saloon. This time the subject was a report from the village of Ben Suc in Vietnam.

The author was Jonathan Schell, a recent Harvard graduate who, after commencement, visited his brother, Orville, in Taiwan, where Orville was doing Chinese studies. Once in Taiwan, Jonathan decided to take a trip to Vietnam, where, according to the standard press, the American war against the Vietcong was going well. In Saigon, Schell was liked and "adopted" by the colonels, perhaps because he had proper establishment connections: He carried an expired *Harvard Crimson* press pass and his father was a successful Manhattan lawyer. The military gave him treatment ordinarily reserved for famous correspondents sympathetic to the war. In addition to attending the daily military briefing sessions in Saigon, the basis for most reports back to the United States, Schell was also taken on helicopter assaults and bombing and strafing missions and given ground transportation to battle scenes.

The assumption of his hosts was that the nice kid from Harvard would be impressed with the power and the purpose of the American mission. But Schell was appalled. The war, it seemed to him, was not the neat containment of Soviet-Chinese aggression that had been advertised at home or the attempt of humane Americans to save democracy-loving natives from the barbaric Vietcong. Like all wars, this one was mutually brutal. Americans shot, bombed, and uprooted civilians in massive campaigns that resulted in the disintegration of Vietnamese social structures. And the Americans were not winning the war.

Schell returned to the United States disturbed by his findings. He visited a family friend, William Shawn, the quiet, eccentric editor of *The New Yorker*, who had known the Schell children since childhood. Shawn listened to Schell's story and asked him to try writing about his experiences. Schell produced what Shawn called "a perfect piece of *New Yorker* reporting." The story, which ran in the July 15, 1967, issue, told in clear, quiet detail what the assault on one village meant to the villagers and to the American soldiers.

Shawn said he had serious doubts about the war before Schell appeared, "but certainly I saw it differently talking to him and reading what he wrote. That was when I became convinced that we shouldn't be there and the war was a mistake."

Thereafter *The New Yorker* in issue after issue spoke simply and clearly against the war. It was not the first publication to do so, but at the time most important media followed the general line that the war was needed to stop international communism and to save the Vietnamese and that the United States was on the verge of victory. Most newspapers, including the two most influential dailies in the country, the *New York Times* and the *Washington Post,* editorially supported the war. There were growing popular protests but the mass marches were yet to come. Neither the My Lai massacre nor the Tet offensive had occurred, and the exposure of the Pentagon Papers detailing a long history of government lying about Indochina was still four years away.

The New Yorker was the voice of the elite, the repository of advertisements for the hedonistic rich, of genteel essays on the first day of spring, of temperate profiles of aesthetes, of humor so sophisticated that it seemed designed solely for intelligent graduates of the best schools. The *Wall Street Journal* once labeled it "Urbanity, Inc." When the magazine spoke clearly against the war, it was a significant event in the course of public attitude toward the American enterprise in Vietnam. If this apolitical organ of the elite said the war was morally wrong, it was saying it to the country's establishment.

At the same time, the magazine was giving the message to a quite different constituency. A *New Yorker* staff member recalled that in 1967, "Our writers would come back from speaking on campuses and say that the kids are reading *The New Yorker* out loud in the dormitories."

Ordinarily this is a happy event in the life of a magazine. There is always a need for some younger readers so that when older subscribers die the magazine will not die with them. But advertisers live in the present. Throughout its crisis years after 1966, *The New Yorker* audience actually grew in numbers. But while the median age of readers in 1966 was 48.7—the age when executives would be at the peak of their spending power—by 1974 *New Yorker* subscribers' median age was 34, a number brought down by the infusion of college students in their late teens and early twenties. Many college students will form the affluent elite of the future, but at the moment they are not buying $10,500 wristwatches and $14,000 brooches. They were buying the magazine because of its clear and moral stand against the war and its quiet, detailed reporting from the scene.

It was then that ad pages began their drastic disappearance. An easy explanation would be that conservative corporations withdrew their ads in political protest. Some did. But the majority of the losses came from a more impersonal process, one of profound significance to the character of contemporary American mass media. *The New Yorker* had begun to attract "the wrong kind" of reader. Circulation remained the same, but the magazine had become the victim, as it had formerly been the beneficiary, of an iron rule of advertising-supported media: It is less important that people buy your publication (or listen to your program) than that they be "the right kind" of people.

The "right kind" usually means affluent consumers eighteen to forty-nine years of age, the heavy buying years, with above-median family income. Newspapers, magazines, and radio and television operators publicly boast of their audience size, which is a significant factor. But when they sit down at conferences with big advertisers, they do not present simple numbers but reams of computer printouts that show the characteristics of their audience in income, age, sex, marital status, ethnic background, social habits, residence, family structure, occupation, and buying patterns. These are the compelling components of that crucial element in modern media—demographics, the study of characteristics of the human population.

The standard cure for "bad demographics" in newspapers, magazines, radio, and television is simple: Change the content. Fill the publication or the programs with material that will attract the kind of people the advertisers want. The general manager of *Rolling Stone* expressed it when that magazine wanted to attract a higher level of advertiser: "We had to deliver a more high-quality reader. The only way to deliver a different kind of reader is to change editorial." If an editor refuses or fails to change, the editor is fired.

The New Yorker faced this problem but it did not fire the editor; nor did the editor "change editorial." It is almost certain that for conventional corporate ownership the "cure" would be quick and decisive. William Shawn would have "changed editorial," which would have meant dropping the insistent line on the war in Vietnam, or he would have been fired. In the place of the Vietnam reporting and commentary there would have been less controversial material that would adjust demographics back to the affluent population of buying age and assuage the anger of those corporations that disliked the magazine's position on the war.

But at the time, *The New Yorker* was not the property of a conglomerate. Later, in 1986, it would be sold to the Newhouse publishing group. The new owner altered advertising and promotion policies but left editorial content the same. After a year, however, the new owner replaced the editor, William Shawn.

Shawn, a Dickensian man, modest in manner and speech, reddens in indignation when asked whether, during the critical 1967–1974 period, the business leaders of the magazine informed him that his editorial content was attracting the wrong kind of reader.

> It would be unthinkable for the advertising and business people to tell me that . . . I didn't hear about it until the early 1970s . . . It gradually sank in on me that *The New Yorker* was being read by younger people. I didn't know it in any formal way. Who the readers are I really don't want to know. I don't want to know because we edit the magazine for ourselves and hope there will be people like ourselves and people like our writers who will find it interesting and worthwhile.

Shawn's words are standard rhetoric of publishers and editors when they are asked about separation of editorial independence and advertising. The rhetoric usually has little relation to reality. Increasingly, editorial content of publications and broadcasting is dictated by the computer printouts on advertising agency desks, not the other way around. When there is a conflict between the printouts and an independent editor, the printouts win. Were it not for the incontrovertible behavior of *The New Yorker* during the Vietnam War, it would be difficult not to regard Shawn's words as the standard mythic rhetoric.

"We never talk about 'the readers,'" Shawn said. "I won't permit that—if I may put it so arrogantly. I don't want to speak about our readers as a 'market.' I don't want them to feel that they are just consumers to us. I find that obnoxious."

The full-page ads of other newspapers, magazines, and broadcast networks in the *New York Times* and the *Wall Street Journal* are often puzzling to the lay reader. They do not urge people to read and listen. They seem to be filled with statistics of little interest to potential subscribers or viewers. They are intended to show the advertising industry that the demographics of the publication or station are "correct," that their audience is made up not of a cross-section of the population but of people in the "right" age and income brackets.

Eventually during the 1967–1974 period Shawn did hear what he called "murmurings":

> There were murmurings in the background about three things: The magazine was getting too serious, the magazine was getting too much into politics, and the pieces were getting too long. My reaction was that we should do nothing about it. Whatever change took place did so gradually and spontaneously as we saw the world . . . There's only one way to do it:

Did we think it was the right thing to do? Did we take the right editorial stand? . . . To be silent when something is going on that shouldn't be going on would be cowardly . . . We published information we believed the public should have and we said what we believed. If the magazine was serious it was no more serious than we were. If there was too much politics, it was because politics became more important and it was on our minds . . . I wish we could remain out of politics but we can't . . . I could enjoy life more if we could do nothing but be funny, which I love . . . but *The New Yorker* has gradually changed as the world changed.

Shawn noted that the Time-Life and Reader's Digest empires succeeded because they were started by men who expressed their own values regardless of the market and thereby established an identity that made for long-range success.

Now the whole idea is that you edit for a market and if possible design a magazine with that in mind. Now magazines aren't started with the desire for someone to express what he believes. I think the whole trend is so destructive and so unpromising so far as journalism is concerned that it is very worrisome. Younger editors and writers are growing up in that atmosphere. "We want to edit the magazine to give the audience what they want. What do we give them?"

There is a fallacy in that calculation . . . The fallacy is if you edit that way, to give back to the readers only what they think they want, you'll never give them something new they didn't know about. You stagnate. It's just this back-and-forth and you end up with the networks, TV and the movies. The whole thing begins to be circular. Creativity and originality and spontaneity goes out of it. The new tendency is to discourage this creative process and kill originality.

We sometimes publish a piece that I'm afraid not more than one hundred readers will want. Perhaps it's too difficult, too obscure. But it's important to have. That's how people learn and grow. This other way is bad for our entire society and we're suffering from it in almost all forms of communications.

I don't know if you tried to start up a *New Yorker* today if you could get anybody to back you.

A magazine industry executive was asked if a magazine owned by a conventional corporation would have supported Shawn during the lean years. He answered: "Are you kidding? One bad year like the one *New Yorker* had in 1967 and either the editorial formula would change or the editor would be out on his ear. It happens regularly."

By the 1980s *The New Yorker* was economically healthy again. Its circulation in 1980 was over 500,000, it was running 4,220 pages of ads a year, fourth among all American magazines, and its profits were back above $3 million. That seems to be a heartwarming morality lesson in the rewards of integrity. But a few years later, even *The New Yorker* would become another conglomerate property. Newspapers and magazines in the main do not want merely readers; they want affluent readers. Broadcasters do not want just any listeners; they want rich ones. Those who are not going to buy are not invited to read, hear, or watch.

Media executives don't tell the general public that only the affluent are wanted. But just as there is sometimes unguarded truth in wine, there is sometimes unguarded truth in the heat of competition. When individual media companies fight for business, or one medium tries to lure advertisers from another medium, the unvarnished truth escapes from behind high-sounding rhetoric. In 1978 the American Broadcasting Company emerged as the leading television network in size of audience; other networks fought to maintain their advertising revenues by deprecating the "quality" of ABC's audience. Paul Klein, then program director of NBC-TV, said ABC's audience might be the largest but it is "kids and dummies."

Reminded that ABC had large ratings "in homes making $20,000 and over," Klein said:

> Well, that is the kids watching in those homes, and sometimes the adults . . . We would like to pull away those adults, and leave ABC with the children . . . [ABC] may still have a very big audience but their audience will be worthless.

Broadcasting Magazine reported:

> More specifically, Mr. Klein defined as his target audience 18-to-49-year-old women who are in reasonably secure financial situations—"the women with some money to buy a product and the necessity to buy it." Since the cardinal rule of program demographics is that people like to watch people like themselves, Mr. Klein is pouring females into his prime-time programs . . . Sexually oriented plots also are becoming increasingly prominent.

In counterattack, ABC issued a booklet to impress potential advertisers. One section of the booklet was entitled "Some people are more valuable than others." When word of this title reached the nonadvertising world, ABC, not wishing to appear nonegalitarian in public, withdrew the booklet—but retained the demographic boast.

Broadcasters can safely be blunt in trade publications seen by advertising agencies. *Broadcasting Magazine,* for example, carries a great deal of corporate promotion aimed at advertisers. One ad announces in heavy type over a photograph of Mike Douglas, the talk show host:

> WOMEN 18–49: MIKE'S GOT YOUR NUMBER!
> The Mike Douglas Show today delivers more women in its audience 18–49 . . . a higher percentage of women 18–49 in its audience than the John Davidson Show.

Such advertising is also crucial for magazines in closed business circles. An issue of *Public Relations Journal* carried the following full-page ad:

> WANTED: 77,000,000 MOVERS AND SHAKERS
> Did they go to college? Are they professionals or managers? Are their household incomes $20,000 plus? Are their homes $40,000 plus? Are their corporate securities $20,000 plus? Have they played active roles in local civic issues? Have they written any elected officials or editors lately? Have they written any books or articles? Have they addressed any public meetings or worked for any political parties?
> Only 77,136,000 adults can answer yes to one or more of those questions . . . they're big on magazines and not so big on television . . . Make this your year to re-evaluate the balance of power between television and magazines in your media planning . . .

> MAGAZINES. THE BALANCE OF POWER.

The original mass medium, newspapers, in its early period carried ads that were marginal in the medium's economics. But in the late 1800s mass production of consumer goods expanded beyond normal consumption. At the time advertisers spent an average of $28.39 a year per household urging people to buy goods and services. By 1980 they were spending $691 per household, an increase far greater than the rate of inflation, with 29 percent of ad money going to newspapers,

21 percent to television, 7 percent to radio, and 6 percent to magazines. By now newspapers get 75 percent of their revenues from ads, general-circulation magazines 50 percent, and broadcasting almost 100 percent.

With more than $30 billion spent on those media each year, advertisers do not leave to chance who will see their ads. Surveys and computers make it possible now to describe with some precision the income, education, occupation, and spending habits of newspaper and magazine subscribers and broadcast audiences, though each medium tends to exaggerate the "quality" of its audience. Media operators fear "the wrong kind" of audience—too young or too old, or not affluent enough. The greater the pressure on newspapers, magazines, and broadcasters to increase their profits, the more they push not just for larger audiences but for higher-quality audiences, as each newspaper, each magazine, each broadcast station insists to the major advertisers that it has the highest-quality audience.

With billions in ads and more billions in product sales at stake, advertisers no longer leave the demographics of their ad carriers to rhetoric and speculation. They now insist on carefully audited subscription statistics and scientifically gathered audience data, with sophisticated computer analysis of exactly the kind of individual that is exposed to a particular kind of advertisement in a newspaper, magazine, or broadcast. And they are increasingly interested in the context of their ads in the medium—the surrounding articles in newspapers and magazines and the type of broadcast program in which their commercials are inserted. An ad for a sable fur coat next to an article on world starvation is not the most effective association for making a sale.

Thus, both the "quality" of an audience and the nonadvertising content around the ads have become dominant in the thinking of major advertisers. Not surprisingly, those factors have consequently become dominant in the thinking of owners of newspapers, magazines, and broadcast stations.

The president of Harte-Hanks Century Newspaper Group, owner of twenty-eight daily papers in the United States, said in 1980 that the company's editors are losing what he called their "prejudices" about separating news content from the desire to reach advertisers' model audience. "The traditional view has been for editors to focus only on the total circulation figures. Today we are seeing more editor emphasis on the quality of circulation."

The largest newspaper chain in the country, Gannett, owns ninety-three daily papers. A study of the Gannett chain by William B. Blankenburg of the University of Wisconsin concluded that the chain aims at fewer subscribers who are richer: "The lost subscribers, if less wealthy . . . may not have fitted into their marketing scheme."

Otis Chandler, head of the Times Mirror empire, owner of the *Los Angeles Times* and the fourth-largest newspaper chain, said, "The target audience of the *Times* is . . . in the middle class and . . . the upper class . . . We are not trying to get mass circulation, but quality circulation." On another occasion, he said, "We arbitrarily cut back some of our low-income circulation . . . The economics of American newspaper publishing is based on an advertising base, not a circulation base."

Years after the near-fatal disease struck *The New Yorker,* when recovery had set in, the magazine's Market Research Department commissioned a professional survey to analyze its subscribers. For the edification of prospective advertisers in *The New Yorker,* its salespeople could display 134 pages of statistical tables that showed that the magazine's readers were 58.5 percent male, 63.8 percent married (6.6 percent widowed, 8.1 percent separated or divorced); 94.0 percent had attended college or had degrees (21.8 percent had Ph.D.'s); 71.0 percent were in business, industry, or professions; 19.3 percent were in top management; 16.6 percent were members of corporate boards of directors; 40.1 percent collected original paintings and sculptures; 26.1 percent bought wine by the case; 59.3 percent owned corporate stock, which had an average value of $70,500 (though a scrupulous footnote to this datum says, "In order not to distort the average . . . one respondent reporting $25,000,000 was omitted from the calculation"); and the median age was 48.4. In other words, the elite audience was "the right kind" for advertising expensive merchandise.

By 1981 *The New Yorker* had recovered enough of its high-quality demographics to make it a desirable carrier for a full-page ad by the Magazine Publishers Association. The ad pursued the theme that magazines are superior for advertising because they don't want readers who aren't going to buy. The headline on the ad read: A MAGAZINE DOESN'T WASTE WORDS ON WINDOW SHOPPERS.

Neither does any newspaper or broadcast station that makes most of its money from advertising.

CHAPTER 9

UNSETTLING TRENDS

JAMES L. MEDOFF AND ANDREW HARLESS

What happened to the feeling that Americans were the most prosperous and blessed people in the world, with a future as brilliant and full of promise as a sunlit dawn? Perhaps some readers continue to experience that feeling. But the majority of readers more likely are plagued by nagging suspicions that America is about to awaken to a gray and uncertain morning. Evidence mounts to support the conclusion that a permanent cloud cover is forming over the American dream. No longer does the average American worker believe that lifetime employment with one company is possible. No longer does the average American believe that he or she can financially survive a serious illness. Parents worry about the safety of their children at school and about the quality of the education that their children receive. Mothers and fathers work long hours at jobs that barely allow them to make ends meet. Every worker is victim to the recurring nightmare that one day his or her employer will become one of the growing number of corporations in which workers are expendable.

The average American senses a rent in the fabric of society, not only at the personal level but also at the government level. Services that citizens once took for granted are being cut and eliminated. The supports that allowed families to prosper in the good times and survive in the bad are crumbling. The voices of ordinary Americans seem not to be heard over the din of downsizers, demagogues, and doomsayers. There is one notion, however, that the majority of Americans agree upon—that America is at a crossroads.

The political developments of the past ten years show that Americans are eager for a change, but uncertain of what that change should be or how it can be executed. A variety of interest groups vie for the reform platform, and modern-day medicine men hawking everything from cures for fiscal disaster to restoration of morality peer from the covers of magazines in corner markets and proselytize on the TV or talk-radio circuit. Some of the answers proffered by these contemporary prophets might be right. Some are surely wrong. One thing sorely lacking is a systematic examination of what is wrong and what can and should be done about it.

From James Medoff and Andrew Harless, *The Indebted Society: Anatomy of an Ongoing Disaster* (Boston, MA: Little, Brown, 1996). Copyright © 1997 by James Medoff and Andrew Harless. Reprinted with permission of Little, Brown and Company, Inc.

THE INSIDIOUS EFFECTS OF DEBT

Most Americans, when asked what is wrong with the country today, give answers that do not include the word "debt." More likely, they include words like "violence," "unemployment," "crime," "lack of family values"—the list goes on. The following chapters show, however, that the effects of debt bear a strong relationship to many of the problems plaguing America.

One easily understood example of this relationship is the case of the highly indebted firm seeking to service its debt by terminating workers. Often these workers are middle-aged men with families accustomed to a certain standard of living. This comfort is suddenly interrupted. In another time, such a worker might spend a short period of time unemployed and then be rehired or land another job with comparable wages and benefits. Today this is not the case. Temporarily unemployed workers are becoming rarer and rarer, and permanently displaced workers are becoming the norm. Even those lucky enough to obtain new employment must accept positions that pay much less and that often do not include such benefits as a pension plan or health insurance. Consequently, the family often evolves into a two-income household, with both parents working to make the same salary as one parent was previously able to earn. It is generally agreed that effective parenting is a full-time endeavor. With both parents working, full-time parenting becomes a physical and emotional impossibility.

In the late seventies and early eighties, latchkey children were considered a minority and worthy of society's sympathy and concern. In the nineties the child who comes home from school to milk and cookies, whether prepared by a mother or by a father, is the rarity. It is not a radical notion that adolescents with too much free time and too little guidance often find decidedly antisocial ways to spend their time. Some critics ask, "Where are the parents?" We answer, "At work."

This simple vignette could take other routes to its conclusion. For instance, the pressure of the husband's long-term unemployment might undermine the marriage and result in divorce. The children could then find themselves with less economic support and role-model guidance. In addition, the couple would become part of the growing statistics of broken marriages in America. It is not difficult to imagine that the problem which started with the husband's lost job could have some serious implications for the family unit and the children's future. We do not suggest that this relationship is causal in the same way that too much sun on the skin causes a burn. What we do argue is that certain groups have used debt to further their interests in opposition to those of ordinary Americans. Debt has played a leading role in the drama of declining real wages, diminishing job opportunities, and dwindling concern with the plight of America's poor. A climate has thus arisen in which high divorce rates, an explosion of juvenile crime, and plummeting self-esteem for Americans of all ages and financial status are fast becoming the norm. These phenomena, in turn, have broad and profound effects on the citizenry of this country, their pocketbooks, their lives, and their future.

A SHORT HISTORY OF OUR INDEBTEDNESS

It may come as a surprise that we do not believe debt to be, universally and forever, a bad thing. Under appropriate circumstances, and in proportion to the situation, debt can be very people-friendly. We would not suggest, for instance, that students forgo borrowing to pay tuition and drop out of college en masse. Nor would we counsel against borrowing to buy a house to live in, a car with which to conduct one's business, or the equipment needed to improve a firm's productivity. History has taught us that even an extreme level of debt can sometimes be better than the alternatives. Who would question the borrowing necessary for the United States and its allies to defeat Nazism?

The problem is not that all debt is bad, but rather that wherever debt exists, it has consequences.

Since the mid-1970s the United States—through its households, firms, and government—has borrowed inappropriately, incurring debt out of proportion with circumstances and without an informed understanding of the consequences. Somebody must pay and, as we shall see, somebody does.

What motivated this wholesale descent into fiscal irrationality? There are a number of factors, but in our view, the most important has been the dramatic slowing over the past twenty-five years of U.S. productivity growth. Productivity—the ability to make things—is what enables a nation to live well without borrowing. Between 1949 and 1973 American productivity more than doubled. The same number of workers could literally produce twice as much in 1973 as they could in 1949. Since the mid-1970s productivity has barely budged. As productivity stagnates, so do wages and profits. Consumption, unfortunately, has not stagnated, and consumption continues to feed private debt.

The private-debt nightmare epitomizes the opposite of the very positive American dream, in which economic well-being increases with successive generations. In 1958 John Kenneth Galbraith identified affluence as a quintessential characteristic of modern America. When Galbraith wrote *The Affluent Society,* the most critical question confronting society was what to produce. In our own time the most critical question is how much to consume.

History and human nature have combined to force government heavily into the red. Historically, actual or perceived overtaxation has led to wars and revolutions. In a democratic society, losing a reelection bid is the more common result. Nevertheless, the needs of the nation, many of which require public funding, have continued to rise. Spending more, but taxing less, has left the government with one alternative—borrow to cover the deficit. At times in the past, with a cooperative monetary policy, government borrowing has been extremely beneficial. In this respect, in fact, World War II was a blessing in disguise because it justified the deficit spending and the monetary accommodation necessary to lift the United States from the Great Depression. Right now, with an inhospitable monetary policy, government borrowing is at best an ineffective tool and at worst a disastrous drain on the nation's resources. Far from encouraging investment, low taxes on the rich have supported a buying binge that commandeered the very resources America might have used to invest in the future.

The lenders—those who live by creating debt—silently but forcefully echoed the slogan of the tax cutters. "No new taxes!" became "No new jobs!" If more people were working, America could produce more and perhaps satisfy both the desires of today and the needs of tomorrow without importing its needs and desires from abroad. The lenders, however, would not hear of it. More new jobs—more demand for labor—might mean rising wages, which might ultimately mean higher prices. To those who receive fixed interest payments, higher prices are the worst of all disasters. Even the slightest risk of inflation must be avoided. To America's now-powerful lender class, employment is the enemy.

Most consumers would probably point to the federal government as the cause of, or leader in, debt accumulation. The historical sequence of events shows otherwise. Throughout the 1960s and early 1970s, while consumer and business debt was rising rapidly, government debt was actually declining relative to what the nation produced. Only during the 1980s did government debt start to grow more quickly than the economy. It was the demand for tax relief by indebted citizens that led the government so deeply into debt. The Reagan revolution spilled no blood but shed gallons of red ink.

THE INDEBTED SOCIETY

Thirty years ago a family in America, enjoying growth in its real earnings, borrowed money to buy a house or a car, or to finance a college education. Firms borrowed dollars to invest and, in so doing, became more productive and increased their market shares. The government borrowed in time of crisis and when a broad consensus recognized the need for an economic stimulus.

Life in the Indebted Society is very different. Families borrow to maintain lifestyles eroded by falling wages. Firms under pressure to service their current debt forgo investments in future productivity. And the government borrows solely to meet interest payments. Today one can hardly imagine a world in which these three groups are not way over their heads in debt. Families now owe money for their children's education, the new TV, the refrigerator, the lawn mower, the very shirts on their backs. The corporation owes money for a newly acquired subsidiary (which it bought at twice the fair price) or because its new owner bought it with no money down. The government owes money for everything under the sun and finds itself caught in a downward spiral of borrowing more to service the current debt.

Thirty years ago, neither firms nor politicians used (or could use) massive indebtedness to justify their actions or inaction. Since 1980 firms, politicians, and others have regularly used debt to rationalize conduct that has been damaging to workers and to the poor. The country's lenders have been able to use their fear of inflation to justify the high real interest rates that strangle America's workers, block the creation of jobs, and stunt America's growth. Debt, directly or indirectly, has decayed the very soul of America.

The Indebted Society undertakes the tasks of identifying and explaining both the motivations and the underlying causes of the crisis now facing America. We start with a detailed examination of what is wrong and why, and then we move on to propose the steps that must be taken to solve these problems. Our argument is that debt—family debt, business debt, and government debt—is the underlying cause of the economic insecurity felt today by most Americans. Although debt is really only an abstract idea, it has taken on tremendous power. Later we outline the broad conditions of life in the Indebted Society—where it is and where it is going—and the steps that our nation must take in order to escape from these conditions. First, however, we must understand how America has stumbled into this dark and savage forest.

CHAPTER 10

RESOURCE EXHAUSTION

JOHN DE GRAAF, DAVID WANN, AND THOMAS H. NAYLOR

> We buy a wastebasket and take it home in a plastic bag. Then we take the
> wastebasket out of the bag, and put the bag in the wastebasket.
> —*LILY TOMLIN, comedian*

This just in:

WASHINGTON, D.C.—According to an EPA study conducted in conjunction with the U.N. Task Force on Global Developmental Impact, consumer-product diversity now exceeds biodiversity. According to the study, for the first time in history, the rich array of consumer products available in malls and supermarkets surpasses the number of living species populating the planet.

"Last year's introduction of Dentyne Ice Cinnamint gum, right on the heels of the extinction of the Carolina tufted hen, put product diversity on top for the first time," study chair Donald Hargrove said. "Today, the Procter & Gamble subphylum alone outnumbers insects two to one." The sharp rise in consumer-product diversity—with more than 200 million new purchasing options generated since 1993—comes as welcome news for those upset over the dwindling number of plant and animal species.

"Though flora and fauna are dwindling, the spectrum of goods available to consumers is wider than at any time in planetary history. And that's something we can all be happy about," Hargrove said. University of Chicago biologist Jonathan Grogan said, "Any complex system, whether we are talking the Amazon rainforest or the Mall of America, needs a rich array of species/products if it is to survive. That is why, in light of the crumbling global ecosystem, it is increasingly vital that we foster the diversification of the global marketplace by buying the widest range of consumer products possible."

Parody, yes. But this anonymous Internet joke is painfully close to the truth. The more we buy, the faster natural species disappear. And the damages accelerate every minute. As you read this chapter, at least thirty acres of farmland and open space are being bulldozed to meet a still-burning demand for suburban "starter castles." Each one of these homes typically requires an acre's worth of trees, as well as the equivalent of a house-sized hole to provide minerals for concrete, steel, and other construction materials.

Our demand for buildings, fuel, and consumer products sends huge draglines, combines, chainsaws, bulldozers, and oil rigs blindly into pristine wilderness.

"Industry moves, mines, extracts, shovels, burns, wastes, pumps, and disposes of *four million pounds* of material in order to provide one average middle-class family's needs for a year," write Paul Hawken and Amory and Hunter Lovins in *Natural Capitalism*.[1] According to the United Nations Environment Program, Americans spend more for trash bags than ninety of the world's 210 countries spend for everything! In an average lifetime, each American consumes a reservoir of water (forty-three million gallons, including personal, industrial, and agricultural uses)[2] and a small tanker full of oil (2,500 barrels).[3] Experts at the U.S. Geological Survey predict that world oil production will peak within ten to twenty years, then begin its final decline.

Depressed yet? Facts like these hit us like urgent, middle-of-the-night phone calls. Nature, our mother, is not looking well at all. Virtually unreported by the media, she's been admitted to the emergency room, with a critically elevated temperature and hemorrhaging chest wounds. Hours later, distant relatives of Nature (we typical Americans) wait in chilly air-conditioned rooms for news of her condition (or a *Married With Children* rerun, whichever comes first). Compulsively, we consume snacks, cigarettes, and electronic games as we wait, somehow oblivious that we are carriers of affluenza—the human disease that strikes Nature like a dozen ongoing hurricanes.

ON THE PAPER TRAIL

Most weeklong backpack trips eventually include a weight-comparison of the stuff in each pack. On a sixty-mile hike on Vancouver Island's West Coast Trail, Dave's sixteen-year-old son Colin insisted his pack was heavier than his father's, because it contained more of the shared food supplies. Dave maintained that anyone whose pack contained the tent, ground cloth, and cook stove was carrying the lion's share. When the sum total of your stuff weighs heavily on your back, you tend to perform cost/benefit analyses on each object. As they slowly made their way up the coast of Vancouver Island, across suspension bridges and moss-covered logs, the debate about the relative value of the stuff was a recurring topic of conversation. "You shouldn't have brought so many snacks," Colin needled. (Each carried their own energy bars, powdered drinks, and nuts.) Dave countered, "What if the Park provided a trailside scale so hikers could settle these differences of opinion? Then we'd find out who's doing the work."

"Next time pack a scale," Colin suggested, shrugging his shoulders.

That hike was a pivotal experience for both father and son. They "got" the value inherent in unmarketed, pristine nature—in their lungs, and in their senses—especially the sense of being alive. They reaffirmed a lesson that brought Dave to this book and Colin to a first stop as an Outward Bound instructor: *You don't need as much stuff when you genuinely appreciate the value of what's already here.* As their heads cleared out, other forms of wealth besides money came into focus: the biological abundance of the rainforest and ocean around them; the social and cultural wealth of indigenous inhabitants of Vancouver Island; and wellness, surely the most valuable wealth of all.

Originally constructed as a survival route for shipwrecked sailors, the West Coast Trail provides spectacular vistas of bright blue ocean and white, pounding surf, often through dark silhouettes of shady rainforest. Tide pools filled with starfish and crabs, families of bald eagles soaring silently overhead, and the breathing spouts of hundreds of humpback whales all speak of nature's abundance.

Yet the beaches were littered with the trunks of dead spruce and fir trees, riverborne escapees from a logging industry that has transformed much of the island's natural capital into barren terrain. One photograph from that trip shows Colin standing on a sawed-off trunk the size of a small stage. He and his father were graphically reminded that many of the products they consumed back home had their beginnings in this particular bioregion, where ten percent of the world's newsprint comes from.

If asked that week what Vancouver Island was good for, they probably would have said in exhilaration, "Wilderness. Let it regenerate." If the logger whose flatbed-semi transports three eighty-foot tree trunks had been asked the same question, he'd have said, "Timber. Let me harvest it." The issue isn't a simple one, especially since Americans consume a third of the world's wood. After returning home from their travels in Canada, Dave resumed his higher-than-average consumption of paper, being a writer, while the logger probably looked for a great, convenient place to take his kids, being also a father.

Although logging companies leave curtains of trees along the road to hide the damages, Dave and Colin caught glimpses of barren patches of land through the trees, spotlighted by afternoon sun. But less obvious was the fact that operations like these force society to work harder. Though hard to track directly, water utility bills go up when logging sediments pollute rivers that supply drinking water. Taxes go up when roads and bridges are washed out by floodwaters that run off clear-cut land. The price of lumber and paper goes up as companies feel compelled to advertise how "green" their practices are. In short, we each write checks and work extra hours to smooth over the *"out of sight, out of mind"* sloppiness.

OUT OF MIND

In the Middle Ages, people carried sticks of burning incense, hoping to ward off the plague, which they believed was caused by foul smells. Seven hundred years later, we still fail to make critical connections, for example, between what we consume and what's happening to the world. We buy plantation-grown coffee, not realizing that each cup of coffee exposes another migratory songbird to potentially lethal pesticides in coffee plantations. Like Rachel Carson, we no longer hear chirps in our own backyards, but we don't make the connection as we take another sip of coffee. The songbirds no longer fly thousands of miles each year from Central or South America to our backyards because they're dead. And if they do survive to return home, chances are good their northern habitats are covered with roads, houses, driving ranges, and parking lots.

When we buy a computer, it doesn't occur to us that 700 or more different materials went into it, converging from mines, oil derricks, and chemical factories all over the world. The sleek, colorful machine purring on each desktop generated 140 pounds of solid and hazardous waste in its manufacture, along with 7,000 gallons of wastewater, and about a fourth of its lifetime energy consumption. Every year, more than twelve million computers—amounting to more than 300,000 tons of electronic junk—are disposed of.[4] The point is, when we buy a computer, all the rest comes with it, even if it's *out of sight, out of mind.*

What about junk mail? Most of it comes as commercial advertising, but even the nonprofits are guilty on that one. According to Donella Meadows, it takes 150,000 direct-mail appeals to garner 1,500 memberships in a given organization. "That means 148,500 are just pollution. Made from trees, printed with inks by fuel-consuming machines, collated, labeled, sorted by other machines, loaded into pollution-spewing trucks, delivered to mailboxes, loaded into other vehicles headed for (twenty percent) recycling stations or (eighty percent) landfills."[5] When we toss a piece of junk mail without complaining, we encourage junk mailing.

Every time we eat a fast-food burger, an unseen 600-gallon tank of water comes with it, counting both what the cow and the feed crops drank.[6] And when we ceremoniously open the little jewelry boxes with the glittering gold wedding rings in them, six tons of very drab ore are invisibly connected to the rings—lying in a tailings heap back at the mine, often polluting a stream.[7]

REAL PRICE TAGS

The distinction of being the mother of unseen impacts and hidden costs goes to the automobile. Imagine your sticker shock if the price tag on your new SUV included not only the car's FOB price, but also the full environmental and social costs of the vehicle. The sticker would cover most of the vehicle's windows to list those hidden costs, but here's an executive summary:

THE REAL COST OF YOUR SHINY NEW LIGHT TRUCK

Congratulations! You've just purchased a vehicle that will cost $130,000 by the time it's paid for! (In fact, if you're in your 20's, financing new vehicles like this one every five years for the rest of your life, you'll spend more than a half a million dollars in interest and payments.) That's impressive. As an average American, you'll use your vehicle for eighty-two percent of your trips compared to forty-eight percent for Germans, forty-seven for the French, and forty-five for the British.

The cost of a thirty-mile round-trip commute in this vehicle will be about $15 a day, assuming gas prices remain at current levels. At that rate, you'll spend on average more than $3,500 annually to get to and from work. When insurance, car payments, maintenance, registration, fuel, and other costs are added together, you'll spend more than $8,000 a year to park this vehicle for 22 hours a day and drive it for two.

Your vehicle generated 700 pounds of air pollution in its manufacture, and four tons of carbon. It will burn at least 450 gallons of gas every year, requiring more than thirty-five gas station fill-ups. You'll spend three full days every year vacuuming, polishing, and cleaning the windows of the vehicle, and waiting anxiously for it at the auto shop. When you divide the miles driven by the time spent to buy and maintain your car, you'll be going about five miles an hour—even slower than rush hour in L.A.

Your new vehicle will contribute its fair share to the following national costs:

- 155 billion gallons of gasoline burned annually
- $60 billion spent annually to ensure Middle Eastern oil supply
- 40,000 fatal car crashes annually, and 6,000 pedestrian deaths
- 250 million people maimed or injured since the days of Charles Olds (1905), and more killed than all the wars in America's history
- 50 million animals killed annually, including at least a quarter million of "extended family": cats, dogs, and horses
- Noise and pollution that inhibit sleep and contribute to radical increases in asthma, emphysema, heart disease, and bronchial infections
- One-fourth of U.S. greenhouse gases, which increase drought, hurricanes, and crop failures
- 7 billion pounds of unrecycled scrap and waste annually

- More than $200 billion annually in taxes for road construction and maintenance, snow plowing, subsidized parking, public health expenditures, and other costs that come directly out of pocket
- A total of more than $1 trillion a year in social costs.[8]

Happy motoring!

THE COST OF HIGH LIVING

Alan Durning of Northwest Environment Watch observes, "Everything we use in our daily lives has an ecological wake that ripples out across the ecosystems of the planet." Durning and colleague John Ryan traced the impacts of everyday products in a book titled *Stuff: The Secret Lives of Everyday Things*. Their coffee, for example, came from the highlands of Columbia, where 100 beans were picked for each cup. The beans were packed in 130-pound sacks and shipped in a huge ocean freighter to roasting factory, warehouse, supermarket, and coffee cup. At each stage, energy and materials were expended to add value to their morning coffee. The beginning of the story is especially troubling:

> Colombia's forests make it a biological superpower. Though the country covers less than 1 percent of the Earth's land surface, it is home to eighteen percent of the world's plant species and more types of birds than any other nation. . . . In the late 1980s, farm owners sawed down most of the shade trees surrounding the coffee trees and planted high-yielding varieties, increasing their harvests, and also increasing soil erosion and bird fatalities. Biologists report finding just five percent as many bird species in these new, sunny coffee fields as in the traditional shaded coffee plantations. With the habitats of birds and other insect eaters removed, pests proliferated and the growers stepped up their pesticide use. Some of the chemicals they sprayed entered the farm-workers' lungs; others washed or wafted away, to be absorbed by plants and animals. . . . For each pound of beans, about two pounds of pulp was dumped into the river. As the pulp decomposed, it consumed oxygen needed by fish in the river . . . [9]

"When I first started looking at the real costs of stuff," said Durning, "a friend read my manuscript and said, 'Oh I get it, what you're talking about is guilt trips, not shopping trips.' But it's not really about guilt. It's about creating a lifestyle that doesn't require as much stuff to make us even happier than we are now. Simple things, like buying shade-grown coffee that reduces the use of pesticides. We need to be thinking about what we get, not what we give up."[10]

Because few of us supply our own materials for daily life, almost everything we consume, from potatoes to petroleum to pencils, comes from somewhere else. "The problem is that we're running out of 'somewhere elses,' especially if developing countries try to achieve a Western style of life," says engineer Mathis Wackernagel, a staffer at Redefining Progress.[11] Dividing Earth's biologically productive land and sea by the number of humans, Wackernagel and colleague William Rees come up with 5.5 acres per person. That's if we put *nothing* aside for all the other species on the planet. "In contrast," says Wackernagel, "the average world citizen used seven acres in 1996—what we call his or her "ecological footprint."

"That's over thirty percent more than what nature can regenerate. Or in other words, it would take 1.3 years to regenerate what humanity uses in one year." He continues, "If all people lived like the average American, with thirty-acre footprints, we'd need five more planets."

Exhibit 10.1

Endangered Species

Species	Observation
Plants	A quarter of the world's plants are threatened with extinction by the year 2010
Amphibians	More than 38% of US amphibians are endangered
Birds	Three-quarters of all bird species are declining; 11% are threatened with extinction
Carnivores	Almost all species of cats and bears are declining in numbers
Fish	One-third of North American freshwater fish are rare or endangered
Invertebrates	About 100 species are lost each day due to deforestation
Mammals	25% of species are threatened with extinction
Reptiles	Over 40% of reptile species are threatened, 20% with extinction

Source: Hutchinson Encyclopedia, Published by Helicon, 1999 www.helican.co.uk

Wackernagel observes, "We can't use all the planet's resources, because we're only one species out of ten million or more. Yet if we leave half of the biological capacity for other species (or if the human population doubles in size), human needs must come from less than three acres per capita, only about *one-tenth* of the capacity now used by Americans."

The solution? No sweat, we'll use the market. We'll just go out and buy another five planets.

DARWIN IN REVERSE

It's bad enough that resource supplies, along with recreational and aesthetic opportunities, are wearing thin as the affluenza-encouraged plundering of the planet continues. But even more distressing is the fact that life on Earth becomes far less diverse as habitats disappear. The loss of a key species from an ecosystem is like pulling out the wrong melon from a supermarket display. You create an avalanche of melons thunking to the floor, because each melon was supported by another. To give just one example, when sun heats up a mountain stream because clear-cutting has removed natural shade along the banks, it's a holocaust for the trout population because trout thrive in *cold* water. And when sediment washes off the naked land into that stream, it plugs up the cobbled spaces in rocks that are hiding places for the baby fish. In turn, mammals whose diet includes trout lose an important protein source, so ecological services provided by those mammals are diminished . . .

Eons of ecological work are instantly undone. The alarming truth is that hundreds of "melon avalanches" occur every day on the battlefields of resource extraction. Far from being just a rain-forest phenomenon, habitat destruction and accompanying extinction are happening right under our noses. "A silent mass extinction is occurring in America's lakes and rivers," says biologist Anthony Ricciardi.[12] His research indicates that freshwater species from snails to fish to amphibians are dying out five times faster than terrestrial species—as fast as rain-forest species, which are generally considered to be the most imperiled on Earth. Half of America's wetlands are gone, and ninety-nine percent of its tall-grass prairies. As these systems are being destroyed for development, agriculture, and other uses, 935 species in the United States (356 animals, 579 plants) are fighting for their lives.[13]

Before nature's health began to slide, we rarely thought about how a product got to us, and

Figure 10.1 **The Extinction Spike**

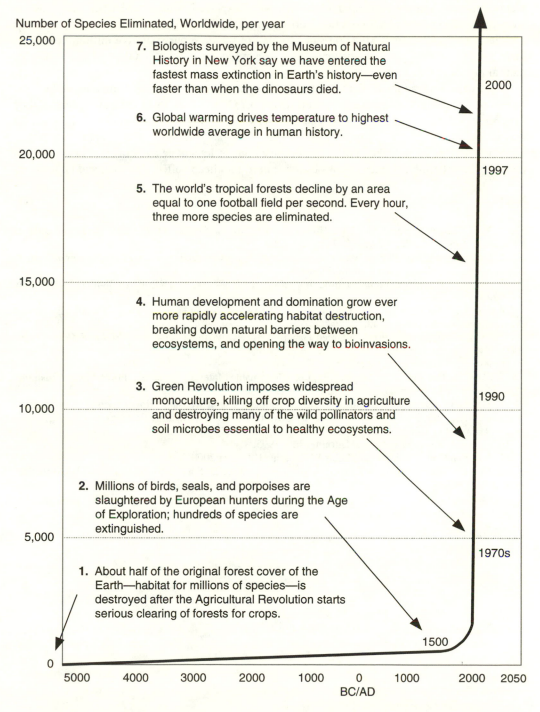

Number of Species Eliminated, Worldwide, per year

25,000

7. Biologists surveyed by the Museum of Natural History in New York say we have entered the fastest mass extinction in Earth's history—even faster than when the dinosaurs died.

6. Global warming drives temperature to highest worldwide average in human history.

2000

20,000

1997

5. The world's tropical forests decline by an area equal to one football field per second. Every hour, three more species are eliminated.

15,000

4. Human development and domination grow ever more rapidly accelerating habitat destruction, breaking down natural barriers between ecosystems, and opening the way to bioinvasions.

3. Green Revolution imposes widespread monoculture, killing off crop diversity in agriculture and destroying many of the wild pollinators and soil microbes essential to healthy ecosystems.

1990

10,000

2. Millions of birds, seals, and porpoises are slaughtered by European hunters during the Age of Exploration; hundreds of species are extinguished.

5,000

1970s

1. About half of the original forest cover of the Earth—habitat for millions of species—is destroyed after the Agricultural Revolution starts serious clearing of forests for crops.

1500

0

5000   4000   3000   2000   1000   0   1000   2000   2050

BC/AD

Source: Courtesy Ed Ayes, from the book *God's Last Offer* (NewYork/London: Four Worlds Eight Windows, 1999).

what came with it; we just consumed it and threw the leftovers away. We didn't think about the plants, animals, and even human cultures that were displaced or destroyed when the materials were mined. Now, when biologists like Norman Myers and E.O. Wilson tell us we may be in the middle of the most severe extinction since the fall of the dinosaur sixty-five million years ago, many people are finally moving beyond denial. We are losing species 1,000 times faster than the natural rate of extinction.

What will civilizations of the far future say about our era? Will they somehow deduce the causes of the calamitous decline in species diversity? Or will they shrug their shoulders (if they have shoulders to shrug) the way our scientists do when they ponder extinctions of the past? "It was global warming," the future scientists might conclude. "Inefficient use of land," others will hypothesize. But for the sake of our civilization's dignity, let's hope and pray that none of them uncovers humiliating evidence of our obsessive need for cheap coffee, gasoline, and underwear.

NOTES

1. Paul Hawken, Amory Lovins and Hunter Lovins, *Natural Capitalism: Creating the Next Industrial Revolution* (Boston: Little, Brown, 1999), pp. 51–52.

2. Sandra Postel, *Dividing the Waters: Food Security, Ecosystem Health, and the New Politics of Scarcity* (Washington, DC: Worldwatch Institute, 1996).

3. Energy Information Administration, *Annual Energy Review* 1997, DOE/EIA-0384(97) Washington, D.C., July 1998, Tables 5.1 and 1.5.

4. John C. Ryan and Alan Thein Durning, *Stuff: The Secret Lives of Everyday Things* (Seattle: Northwest Environment Watch, 1997), p. 43.

5. Donella Meadows, "How's a Green Group to Survive Without Junk Mail?" *Global Citizen,* June 2000.

6. Ryan and Durning, op. cit., p. 55.

7. Gary Gardner and Payal Sampat, "Forging a Sustainable Materials Economy," in Worldwatch Institute, *State of the World 1999,* p. 47.

8. Hawken, Lovins, and Lovins, op. cit.; Consumers Union website, "How Green Is Your Pleasure Machine?" 09/17/99; *The Roads Aren't Free,* by Clifford W. Cobb, Redefining Progress.

9. Ryan and Durning, op. cit., p. 8.

10. Personal Interview with Alan Durning, July 1995.

11. Personal Conversation with Mathis Wackernagel, August 2000.

12. Anthony Ricciardi, "Mass Extinction in American Waters," Society for Conservation Biology, September 30, 1999.

13. Ibid.

CHAPTER 11

ADVERTISING AND COMPETITION

ANDREW V. ABELA AND PAUL W. FARRIS

Does advertising increase or decrease competition? Our purpose in this chapter is to advance the understanding of this question, and particularly the impact of advertising on price, by critically reviewing recent research, adding some new insight, and identifying areas for future research. The main conclusions that we draw are that research should focus more on absolute price levels than on relative price differences (price dispersion) and that the significant impact of distribution policy on price needs to be examined more closely.

Accordingly, the chapter is divided into four sections. In the first section, we lay out the question, provide some initial assumptions and definitions, and set the scope for the discussion. In the second section, we summarize the opposing views that typically define debate around the question. In the third section, we provide a critical review of recent work on this question as well as some research that we think brings additional important perspective. In the final section, we present our own conclusions about the question and identify areas for future research.

QUESTION

Interest in the question of the impact of advertising on prices often starts with the observation that companies with relatively higher advertising budgets also usually charge higher prices. Consumers are willing to pay higher prices for a number of reasons that include advertising as well as superior product quality, better packaging, more favorable user experience, market position, and warranty and/or service. When these latter nonadvertising factors are assumed equal, we can ask why consumers can be expected to generally pay more for the advertised products. This is a question that invites all sorts of speculation—the implied confidence of manufacturers that are willing to advertise, mere familiarity or reminder effects, and even the psychic value of lifestyles associated with advertised brands. We claim no particular insight into these reasons, but we do find it difficult to believe that consumers would be willing to pay more for a product whose sole distinction is that it is *un*advertised. Therefore, the fact that advertised products tend to have higher prices is not very significant given that the opposite is highly unlikely (Farris and Reibstein 1979, 1997). On the other hand, what conclusions about levels of competition and of absolute retail prices in a market or category can we draw from the observation that prices of advertised brands usually are higher than those of nonadvertised, functionally equivalent products? And why might such differences exist?

In particular, we seek to expand the scope of the discussion to recognize that there are three important groups of actors: consumers, manufacturers, and retailers. We believe that understanding the effect of advertising on consumers' price sensitivity (although a significant challenge) would not be enough to definitely answer the question of whether advertising ultimately makes products more expensive. We need to integrate our knowledge of these effects with assumptions and models of manufacturer (seller) and retailer (middleman) behavior. As retailers, manufacturers, and consumers react to each other, there is no problem in running out of fresh material in this investigation. These interactions create new pricing and promotional strategies, such as yield management, that are more sophisticated methods for delivering targeted discounts. Technology is an enabler of these new strategies, as is the predicted rapid growth of the "friction-less" Internet economy (e.g., "bots" that search the Web for low prices), which adds further complication to the question.

We begin by providing three important assumptions and some definitions of price that will help to establish the scope of this discussion.

Assumptions

The impact of advertising on price competition and, hence, on price is part of the much larger network of effects that determine the degree to which commercial advertising is socially beneficial. We make three assumptions to simplify these effects for the purpose of our analysis.

Assumption 1: Products Are Only Imperfect Substitutes

When we speak of competition in this chapter, we do not have in mind the economic concept of "perfect" competition (an equilibrium condition under which marginal profits equal marginal costs and no manufacturer or supplier has the freedom to raise prices). Instead, we start from the assumption that products are only imperfect substitutes and that most manufacturers and retailers enjoy some limited product differentiation, market power, or other advantage that gives them realistic pricing options. In other words, there is some variation in prices that may result in higher or lower sales volume, but these variations are within the operating range of the company. The whole notion of price comparisons would be rendered invalid if we were to assume, however, that every product was so "different" as to justify whatever price differences were observed. We also need to recognize that each purchase is made at a unique point in time and space and that some different utility is associated with that timing and location. A cold soft drink is worth more on a hot day at a ballpark than on a cold day in a warehouse club store. Unlike classical markets, we accept that imperfect competition results in a certain amount of price dispersion for functionally equivalent products. We need to find ways in which to make sense of this level of dispersion.

Assumption 2: Resellers Play an Important Role in Stocking and Promoting the Product

Given this assumption, our focus is on analyzing advertising's influence on the marketer's ability to raise prices without losing appreciable percentages of sales volume (price inelastic) *or* to gain large increases in sales by only lowering price by a small amount (price elastic). Under different circumstances, either of these options would look good to marketers. Interestingly, the same product can provide both opportunities at different levels in the value chain at a particular point in time. As an example, take a leading product, such as Tylenol, that most retailers would agree absolutely had to be in stock. An increase in the price of this product to *all* retailers is not likely to cause much change in volume sold by all retailers in the short term. A temporary change in the *retail* price of the product by a single highly visible retailer, however, could lead to significant volume change for that particular retailer in the near term if brand switchers were drawn to it and loyal consumers stocked up (or vice versa). Tylenol then would be said to be price inelastic at the manufacturer level and price elastic at the retail level. If the price decrease were perceived by consumers to be permanent, however, then it is less likely that stocking up would occur. Thus, temporary price variations are part of the landscape as well. Indeed, retailers often resort to devices such as "clearance sales" and "going out of business sales" to communicate to consumers that the low prices are a temporary phenomenon and that consumers should "buy now."

Assumption 3: Quality Levels Already Are Established

The third assumption in our analysis of advertising-price relationships is that quality levels and product differences already have been established and, thus, are stable. We recognize that, in reality, these always are changing and that advertising has an essential role in communicating such changes. Over the long term, the incentive to invest in R&D activities that improve product quality and to invest in advertising and promotion programs that bring these innovations to market cannot be completely separated from the ability to use advertising to command higher prices and profit margins. The long-term role of advertising must include the ability of advertising to stimulate new product investments. It may do this by improving the new product introduction process and the diffusion of innovation as well as by providing margins and incentives to invest in marketing and R&D. If innovators could not capture the fruits of their new ideas and risk-taking activities, then the innovation process would suffer. Advertising, especially mass advertising, is helpful for introducing new products quickly and in a way that enables the innovator to capture value. Even if profit margins at any given time are "too high," we also must consider whether the market system that produced these margins is at the same time encouraging the development and introduction of innovative new products. Certain inefficiencies in finding the lowest price for a given quality level are arguably compensated for if the overall result is a productive process of replacing obsolete products.

Premium price strategies create margins that are available to invest in the risky activities of funding R&D projects and launching new products. These prices and margins compensate for the failed innovations as well. To ignore the uncertainties in this process would be to fundamentally misapprehend the management decision process concerning budgets for both. Although this is an essential part of the dynamic process that results in increased advertising and higher prices for certain products, the scope and focus of this chapter compels us to make the strong assumption that quality levels already have been established. Price comparisons are meaningful only when they are made among items of similar quality or among the same items sold at different times or in different markets.

Definitions

Measuring prices sounds simple enough but is complicated quickly by the need to distinguish among different types of prices. Therefore, we provide definitions of some of the different types of prices that we believe are important and yet often overlooked.

For the purpose of this discussion, *manufacturer price* is the manufacturer's selling price. Except in situations where there are intervening parties such as distributors, this price usually is the retailer's purchase price. *Retail price* is the retailer's selling price. As used here, it is synonymous with the consumer's purchase price. *Relative price* is the ratio between the price of the cheapest brand versus the price of the most expensive brand (measured in either retail or manufacturer prices) among functionally equivalent products. To distinguish from relative price, we use the term *absolute price,* which we use to denote the mean of the prices of all such brands (weighted by share of sales). Such an absolute price assumes that we are able to calculate the average price per statistical unit across different sizes, forms, and other product variations in a meaningful way. *Price range* is the difference between the highest and lowest prices available for the functionally equivalent products. There are other more developed measures of price dispersion (Brynjolfsson and Smith 1999), but for a nonempirical discussion, simple differences will suffice. Any empirical examination of these prices also has to deal with the problem of coupons, rebates, manufacturer allowances, and shipping/ transportation costs. These complications can confuse measurement. In the extreme, retailers might not be sure of their own selling prices (e.g., when retailers offer to triple the value of manufacturer coupons) or even purchase prices (e.g., when manufacturer rebates are grouped across product lines or are not available until the end of period and contingent on sales goals).

By *functionally equivalent* products, we mean products that are identical in their functional capabilities with regard to normal use and, hence, are substitutable in the eyes of the consumer who cares only about functional benefits (however difficult this type of equivalence might be to determine in practice). At the same time, however, we maintain that such a consumer is not necessarily the typical consumer and that benefits beyond purely functional product benefits can have a significant effect on consumer choice and, therefore, serve as a basis for differentiation. A recent survey of consumer purchasing habits for automobiles and cosmetics conducted for McKinsey & Company, for example, indicated that, in each case, a sizable segment of consumers valued benefits arising from the process of acquiring the product and from their relationship with the company *more than* the product's functional benefits. These segments represented 19% of the automotive buyers and 43% of the cosmetics buyers in the survey (Court et al. 1999).

Scope of Inquiry

We recognize that there are potential effects of advertising at the macro level, both positive and negative, such as driving the growth of new industries and creating a culture of consumption. We also note that the desirability of any given product always will be dependent on the existing technological, political, and cultural environment and that advertising seems to be firmly entrenched as part of our culture. Advertising practices always are evolving, and today there might be more concerns with the idea of how strong brands are priced than with advertising per se. There are other methods of building brands with nontraditional media such as sponsorships and point-of-purchase promotions. For example, limiting tobacco advertising does not seem to have hurt Marlboro. Indeed, some firms fear that the absence of advertising will increase the brand's dominance. The use of the Web to promote brands undoubtedly will become more important and probably more difficult to regulate.

Nevertheless, we limit our exploration to the micro level, and particularly to those situations in which there are no radical technological shifts or new competitors entering. We assume away all of these complications so as to sharpen our focus.

Within the scope of our inquiry, we are primarily interested in whether advertising results in consumers paying higher prices than they otherwise would pay (Figure 11.1). This is related to, but not exactly the same as, the notion of an efficient market as defined by Ratchford and col-

Figure 11.1 **Scope of Discussion**

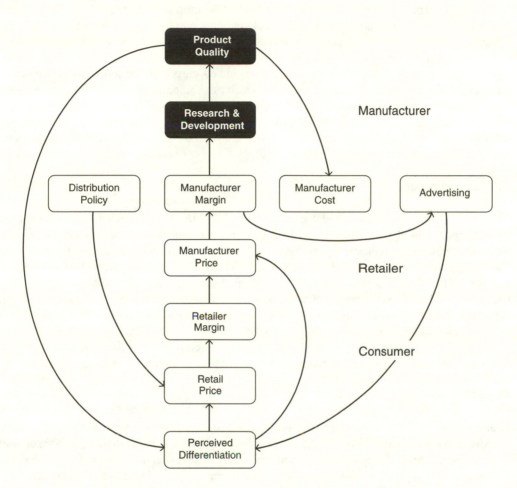

leagues (1996): a market in which "actual or potential losses to individual consumers, which result from imperfect information about alternatives . . . , are or can be large" (p. 168). The imperfect information is about prices and qualities of alternatives.

Economists have long used two principal models to describe the effects of advertising on price paid, the results of which appear to contradict one another. In the *advertising = market power* model, advertising is thought to influence consumer tastes, establish brand loyalty, and ultimately raise profits and consumer prices by decreasing price sensitivity and competition. In the *advertising = information* model, advertising is seen as providing information to consumers, resulting in increased price sensitivity, lower prices, and reduced monopoly power (Farris and Reibstein 1997). Both models have provided important contributions to the discussion, and both still have their followers.

Market Power Model

Proponents of the market power model argue that advertising too often creates the impression of higher quality where marginal or no product differences exist. There is little doubt that in many cases marketers attempt to justify price premiums and escape the intensity of price competition by using advertising to communicate marginal product benefits to consumers. Some brands, such as Absolut vodka, would not likely be able to charge their current prices without the support of advertising. Vodka is tasteless, colorless, and odorless, making it difficult to find characteristics on which to differentiate. (Thus, vodka manufacturers typically compete on "purity," e.g., asserting that their products are *more* tasteless, colorless, and odorless than the competition.) Perhaps a classic case is Extra Strength Tylenol, which was built on the claim, "You can't buy a more potent pain reliever without a prescription." Strictly speaking, the claim is only one of parity performance, asserting that no stronger product exists, and makes no comment as to whether there are any other products that are equally strong (and, in fact, there are several). Yet, the brand grew steadily with the help of this advertising claim (Strenio 1996).

Information Model

Proponents of the information model argue that our ability to determine whether there really are no differences among products is suspect and that we are better off allowing consumers to make their own decisions. This model argues that advertising makes consumers aware of alternatives and tries to highlight product quality differences that might not otherwise be apparent to the extent that this is possible. For example, to overcome the difficulties of advertising vodka just noted, Gray Goose vodka advertised the results of an "expert panel" that gave its product the highest marks in taste tests including Absolut and several other brands. By becoming more aware of viable alternatives—increasing their "evoked set"—consumers can become more price sensitive (Mitra and Lynch 1995). At the same time, by making real product differences more clear, manufacturers can lead consumers to pay more for certain products when they recognize their unique benefits.

Complications

In addition to the fact that the implications of the two models presented oppose each other, there are several other complications with the current understanding of the advertising and price debate. First, there are several somewhat contradictory ways of understanding the causal relationship between advertising and price. Second, there is significant difficulty in estimating the relationship between advertising and price premium. Third, brand loyalty has ambiguous implications. Fourth, the impact of the Internet promises to add significant complexity.

Causal Relationships

Two popular views see the direction of causality flowing from advertising to higher prices. The first view is that advertising is a "cost." As such, firms that advertise must charge higher prices to cover this cost. Furthermore, it is argued that if advertising were eliminated, then consumer prices could be reduced by the percentage of sales that advertising constitutes—about 2% to 3% for a wide variety of products, but as much as 30% to 40% for some others. Marketers themselves implicitly buy into this argument when they look at advertising and price promotion as competing for a share of marketing budgets instead of as complements. In the extreme, there is some truth in this view.

The second causal view also runs from advertising to prices. We assert that most marketers believe that increased advertising will enable them to charge higher prices (to some degree). Although some marketers might argue that it is higher quality that gives advertisers "something to say" in the advertising to justify higher prices, it need not always be the case that highly advertised products have superior quality. This is particularly true if the superior quality is not easily perceived or is easily believed (Borden 1942). Advertising, in this view, shifts the demand curve out (more volume sold at all possible prices) and may change the slope of the demand curve, making demand less responsive to price at higher prices. Firms with high advertising expenditures might have more options, but even these firms expect lower sales volumes for higher prices. Such firms also must find the combination of price and volume that maximizes (or "satisfies") total profits.

An alternative causal view presents the opposite direction of causality—that higher prices cause increased advertising by increasing the amount that marketers are willing to "pay" for incremental sales. The key intervening variable is gross profit margin. Empirically, it has been found that gross profit margins (before marketing and other fixed costs) are the single most important predictor of higher advertising-to-sales ratios among cross sections of firms and businesses (Buzzell and Farris 1977; Farris and Albion 1981; Farris and Buzzell 1979). Of course, higher gross profit margins also can result from lower costs of distribution or production. Therefore, we believe that, all else being equal, the firm with lower costs usually will advertise more as a percentage of sales. Clearly, the pricing and advertising decisions cannot be easily separated, even for functionally equivalent products. As joint decisions that affect each other, the causality is difficult to conceptualize and does not lend itself to simple empirical tests (Dorfman and Steiner 1954; Farris and Reibstein 1979, 1997).

Advertising and Price Premium Relationship

Even for specific brands, it often can be difficult to tell how advertising works on price premiums and sensitivity to price differences. For example, Quelch (1986) reported the results of a General Electric (GE) experiment on advertising for light bulbs. After GE aired advertising emphasizing the benefits of its soft white bulbs, the percentage of consumers who rated these bulbs as "very good value" increased by at least double the increase for competitive brands when the GE bulbs were priced at parity to competitors. When the GE bulbs were premium priced, their value rating still increased after this advertising, although only marginally. When the competitor bulbs were premium priced, their value ratings declined (p. 408). The implications of such a relationship between advertising and price premium are not clear-cut. Although the marketer could sell more at the higher price, the parity price is relatively more attractive after the advertising than before.

Brand Loyalty

Brand loyalty for the manufacturer also can result in higher or lower price sensitivity, depending on the time frame, on the types of prices, and on whether demand shifts are measured across or between retailers. A brand-loyal consumer is not necessarily less price sensitive. A distinction needs to be made between price differences among different brands and price differences in the same brand over time. Imagine the reaction of two consumers faced with a sale on a product. One is very brand loyal to the product, whereas the other is not. Which consumer is likely to buy more of this product when it is on sale (and, thereby, appear to be more price sensitive)? We assert that the brand-loyal consumer likely will buy more because the nonloyal one is happy to buy whatever goes on sale next week, whereas the loyal one will stock up while the brand is on sale. In this way, brand-loyal consumers can appear to be more price sensitive, at least to price differences for the same brands from week to week and from retailer to retailer. However, the same loyal consumer might continue to buy the brand if prices were increased relative to those for other brands. The reader should consider which price sensitivity is being measured with weekly or daily scanner data on sales and prices.

Impact of the Internet

The question of the impact of advertising on price developed and evolved through an era when the basic issues were defined in terms of the physical shipment of products and their promotion through periodic price reduction events. This question would appear to become more complicated and interesting with the growth of Internet commerce. The promise of frictionless transactions adds a new dimension to the problem while also providing the opportunity for new insights. No simple model explains all of the evidence.

CRITICAL REVIEW OF RECENT RESEARCH

Several recent empirical generalization studies, or meta-analyses, have summarized the findings from the substantial number of studies relevant to our question: Lodish and colleagues (1995) and Vakratsas and Ambler (1999) on advertising effectiveness; Ratchford and colleagues (1996) on market efficiency; Kaul and Wittink (1995) and Mitra and Lynch (1995) on advertising and price. We discuss each of these in turn along with selected individual studies.

Understanding the effect of advertising on price is complicated by the fact that, after 100 years of research, we still are not sure exactly how the effects of advertising occur. Beginning with the first formal advertising model in 1898, advertising has been primarily explained using "hierarchy of effects" models. However, these have been seriously questioned recently. Hierarchy of effects models propose that advertising works through a determined series of effects such as first gaining attention, then peaking interest, then creating desire, and finally motivating action. Yet, Vakratsas and Ambler's (1999) review of 250 journal articles on how advertising affects consumers con-cluded that there is little support for such hierarchy of effects models. Lodish and colleagues' (1995) meta-analysis of 389 split-cable television advertising experiments between 1982 and 1988 also emphasized how little we know about what makes advertising work. Although conventional wisdom holds that more advertising leads to more sales, Lodish and colleagues found "no obvious relationship between the magnitude of a weight increase [in advertising] and the significance of the impact on sales" (p. 128). They found that "the data explain less than half of the variance in sales changes associated with [television] advertising weight changes" (p. 138).

These two studies would seem to call for a major rethinking of our approaches to understand-ing the effects of advertising. This rethinking would include our approaches to understanding the impact of advertising on price competition.

Market Efficiency

Part of the difficulty with the debate on the effect of advertising on price has been that, until recently, there was no comprehensive theoretical framework to address consumer welfare aspects of pricing. Ratchford and colleagues (1996) made a significant contribution conceptualizing this problem by proposing a theoretical model to integrate existing findings. The focus is on determining measures of market efficiency, defined in terms of "actual or potential losses to individual consumers" (p. 168) resulting from imperfect information about alternatives. They reviewed the several different measures of market efficiency that have been used in previous studies: price-quality correlations, measures based on a frontier relation between prices and characteristics, and price dispersion.

They related each of these to a model of economic welfare and determined that, whereas the first two measures have serious limitations,[1] price dispersion does measure the variance in consumer surplus in this model when there is no variance in quality. Recognizing further limitations, they still concluded that

> the large order of magnitude of efficiency estimates observed in many markets across many studies makes it hard to avoid the conclusion that consumers are often presented with the opportunity to pay higher prices than they need to for a given quality and that many probably do so. (p. 177)

We would argue, however, that the use of price dispersion—relative price—rather than absolute price to measure the impact of prices on consumer welfare is problematic. Ratchford and colleagues (1996) allowed that measurements of market efficiency (including price dispersion) do not take into account the different types of value added offered by different retail outlets: "Retailer services can enhance utility and should be counted . . . , though they rarely are in published data such as the *Consumer Reports* data employed in many studies of market efficiency" (p. 172). We believe that extending the model proposed by Ratchford and colleagues to include space/time utility is a critical next step. Consumers typically are willing to pay a higher price for the identical item from a different retailer because of greater convenience in place or time, for example, or even because the shopping experience is more pleasant. Many varieties of products are available at different times and places where they might not otherwise be without the higher margins required to support them. Aspirin comes in various dosage sizes, coatings, forms (e.g., capsules, tablets, caplets, liquid), and package counts. These variations and their potential importance to different segments mean that we need to develop a theory of price dispersions that takes into account the opportunity that consumers have to purchase products at various prices. Assume, for example, that a small shop in an airport decides to add aspirin to its assortment of other products sold. Such a shop is likely to charge higher prices and margins than do most other retailers. Airport shops are able to do this, not because headaches are more severe in airports but rather because they have local monopolies. Higher income customers for whom time is a premium also are part of the equation. We do not believe that consumers, in the aggregate, are worse off because they now have this additional opportunity to purchase aspirin. Yet, both the average purchase price and the dispersion of prices likely will increase.

The Ratchford and colleagues (1996) studies measured price dispersion of "physically identical items across different outlets in a given retail market" (p. 168). "Physically identical" clearly means items that are physically *functionally* identical; this includes differentially branded and advertised products that nevertheless have the same functional performance. The problem is that highly advertised brands typically will have higher price dispersions because they are more widely distributed across a large number of retail formats with a great variety of margins. Private label products, on the other hand, typically are sold in only one chain and, therefore, have far less price dispersion.

Store Check Illustration

We illustrate our concern with a recent store check (which should not be interpreted as anything except an illustration of the point) and two hypothetical examples. We looked at extra-strength acetaminophen caplets across different distribution channel types, selected for the different levels of convenience they offer (i.e., drug store, warehouse, convenience store, gas station, airport

Exhibit 11.1

Variable	Price Dispersion (range)
Channel	1.3× to 2.5×
Brand	1.6× to 2.1×
Size	1.3× to 4.6×

shop). We noted the prices of a major national brand's caplets[2] (Tylenol) and those of store brand caplets in each channel type (where available). Across this sample, the price dispersion of the national brand only was 1.4× (highest to lowest price) for the 24-pack and 1.3× for the 250-pack of caplets (Exhibit 11.1). There was no dispersion across channel type for the store brand because each channel type carried a differentially labeled store brand. Dispersion of all the store brands together was 1.3× for the 50-pack and 2.5× for the 500-pack. Dispersion across the national and store brands combined was 1.7× for the 24-pack and 2.1× for the 250-pack. We also looked at price dispersion across *sizes* (in terms of cost per caplet). The national brand had dispersions of 1.3× (highest to lowest price per caplet) in the convenience store channel and 2.4× in the drug store channel. The store brand dispersion was as high as 4.6× in the warehouse channel. Comparing across brand, channel, *and* size, it is possible to buy extra-strength acetaminophen for as little as 0.8 cents a caplet (warehouse store brand, 500-pack) or as much as 37.5 cents a caplet (airport shop, 2-pack), representing a price dispersion of nearly 50×.

The central problem with price dispersion (relative price) rather than absolute price as a measure of market efficiency is that much of price dispersion could be explained by the legitimate increases in convenience offered by different distribution channels.

Hypothetical Illustration 1

Consider also the case in Exhibit 11.2. This illustrates a hypothetical but not unrealistic situation in which a higher relative price coincides with a lower absolute price. Recall that relative price is the ratio or difference between the price of the most and least expensive of a functionally equivalent product, measured in this case at retail; this is the same as price dispersion. Absolute price is the average price of the same set of products. Scenario A represents a situation in which the advertised brand (typically the national brand) goes on deal (i.e., is discounted by the retailer) frequently. In this case, it is off deal during Week 1 and on deal during Week 2 at a significant retail price discount. In Scenario B, the advertised brand does not go on sale; it is *every day low priced*. The unadvertised brand (typically the private label product) is assumed not to go on deal in either scenario. In addition, we make a simple and realistic assumption that when the advertised brand is on deal, its sales increase at the expense of the unadvertised brand sales as well as at the expense of its own nondeal sales. The resulting situation has Scenario A with a higher relative price but a lower absolute price, whereas the opposite occurs in Scenario B. Which scenario increases consumer welfare? We would argue that consumers are, in aggregate, clearly better off in Scenario A. Although the relative price (or price dispersion) is higher, the average amount paid is lower. Furthermore, the opportunity for consumers to find the product at lower prices is enhanced in Scenario A.

Hypothetical Illustration 2

For a twist on the preceding example, imagine a situation in which Scenario A offered a higher relative price (price dispersion) and a higher absolute price, whereas Scenario B offered a lower

Exhibit 11.2

	Scenario A: Advertised Brand Frequently On Deal		Scenario B: Advertised Brand Is Every Day Low Priced	
	Week 1	Week 2	Week 1	Week 2
Retail price				
Advertised brand	$5.00	$3.00	$4.00	$4.00
Unadvertised brand	$2.90	$2.90	$3.00	$3.00
Units sold				
Advertised brand	5	25	10	10
Unadvertised brand	10	5	10	10
Absolute price		$3.19		$3.50
Relative price		1.67×		1.33×

Note: In both scenarios, the unadvertised brand is every day low priced.

relative and absolute price. Would Scenario B be the more attractive one in every case? Not necessarily. The lowest price in Scenario A is lower than the lowest price in Scenario B; a very low price is available in Scenario A, for those who desire it, that is not available in Scenario B. We believe that whether the choice to buy at that lowest price is "informed" or "uninformed" cannot be determined merely from the existence of a wide dispersion of prices. Ratchford and colleagues (1996) argued—correctly, we believe—that consumer choice probabilities must be taken into account when evaluating the potential losses from an inefficient market, and this weighting of price by choice probabilities is very similar to our concept of an absolute *price*.

Increases in Welfare

We also should recall that a wide price dispersion on a particular product can even lead to *increases* in consumer welfare when it helps to serve market segments that could not afford the product if prices were closer to the mean (Schmalensee 1981). Although questions of the effect of price on distributive justice are outside the scope of this chapter, it would be interesting to explore to what extent greater price dispersion can actually benefit society. Such benefits might result from a transfer of wealth from segments that are willing to pay a premium for the same item for services (e.g., convenience) to segments that are willing to go through extra effort (e.g., clipping coupons) to get the cheapest possible price on that item. It seems to us that there is implicit recognition of this in discounts that typically are offered, for example, to seniors and students. Any serious inquiry along these lines must take into account the influences of mobility and education. For example, poorer consumers often have *less* ability to search for the best price (e.g., do not own cars, cannot afford to buy in bulk, cannot afford warehouse club membership fees). As stated earlier, these issues are interesting but outside the scope of this chapter.

The Internet and the Role of Price Dispersion

Recent work on Internet commerce also highlights the inadequacies of price dispersion as a measure of consumer welfare. A study of prices of books and music CDs sold through a number of Internet and traditional retailers found that the price dispersion of CDs sold on-line was approximately equal to that of CDs sold in traditional outlets, whereas the price dispersion of books actually was *higher* over the Internet. This is a surprising finding given the low search costs of the Internet. It led the authors to conjecture that something other than market inefficiency was at work (Brynjolfsson and Smith 1999). Because there probably is far less variation in the mobility, wealth, and education among those buying on-line than among the rest of the population, these findings are particularly interesting.

Overall, although we believe that Ratchford and colleagues (1996) made a significant contribution to the question of market efficiency measurement, we find that price dispersion is an inadequate and potentially misleading measure of impact on consumer welfare.

Reconciling the Market Power and Information Schools

There have been three attempts to reconcile the apparent contradictions between the market power and information schools. These attempts discussed the retailer-manufacturer dynamic, the importance of preference strength and consideration set size, and the difference between price and nonprice advertising. We briefly review each.

Retailer-Manufacturer Dynamic

Albion and Farris (1987) argued the importance of recognizing the retailer-manufacturer dynamic. They noted that manufacturers do not set consumer prices by giving a certain margin to retailers. In fact, the opposite usually is the case, with retail margins being a *result* of the retailers own pricing decisions. The authors argued that retail price decisions can be significantly affected by a manufacturer's advertising if such advertising increases the demand for a product and the amount of retailer competition on that product. Retailers might choose to accept a lower margin on a strongly advertised brand so as to drive traffic, build store image, and/or increase inventory turnover. When retailers take different profit margins on similar products, products with similar manufacturer prices can have significantly different retail prices. In some extreme cases, the manufacturer's price of one product can be higher than that for another, but because of the difference in retail margins, the retail price is *higher* for the product with the *lower* manufacturer's price. In all cases, the effects of promotion, such as coupons and rebates, must be included in the price paid (Ailawadi, Farris, and Shames 1999).

In the just-mentioned work, Albion and Farris (1987) showed that, by and large, the evidence on advertising and price elasticity is consistent with the notion that advertising decreases price elasticity for manufacturers and increases price elasticity for retailers. This earlier work was later buttressed by research showing lower retail gross margins for highly advertised national brands (Albion and Farris 1987). Together with analyses showing higher gross margins and higher relative prices for high-advertising manufacturers, there is support for the argument that advertising helps manufacturers differentiate their products (advertising = market power) but induces greater retail price sensitivity, more intense retail price competition, and lower retail margins (advertising = information).

The mitigating role of the existence of private label products in price also is significant. The best competition involves comparison between brands and between retailers, both interstore and intrastore competition. Private label products are not subject to interstore comparison, but they do provide price control through intrastore competition, offsetting the power of advertising to enable marketers to charge a higher price.

Preference Strength and Consideration Set Size

A second synthesis was provided by Mitra and Lynch (1995), who argued that whether advertising increases or decreases price sensitivity will depend on two mediating variables: relative strength of preference and consideration set size. Advertising provides information about product differences among products, and this can increase consumers' relative strength of preference and, therefore, decrease price elasticity. Advertising also provides information about the availability of substitutes, and this can increase consumers' consideration set and, therefore, increase price sensitivity. In addition

> beyond providing information on the existence of substitutes, advertising provides recall cues and, thereby, increases the number of effective substitutes considered at the time of choice. . . . For product markets in which consumers have to rely on memory to generate alternatives, the effects of increased advertising by brands may be to increase price elasticity, (p. 657)

If there are other stimuli increasing the consideration set (e.g., point-of-purchase material), then advertising will not have the same effect on the consideration set.

One concern with this attempted solution is that it is difficult to separate the two types of information (product difference and availability of substitutes). Although different ads were used in the study for reminding and differentiating, Mitra and Lynch (1995) recognized that "some amount of confounding is inevitable" (p. 657). The same advertising message can communicate product difference to one consumer segment and availability as a substitute to another segment. Consumers who already are aware of it as a credible substitute might perceive the ad as a differentiation message, whereas consumers who are not might receive it as an availability message.

A separate limitation in understanding the impact of advertising on price sensitivity is that research typically assumes that buyers know the prices of the products they consider for purchase. When research participants cannot recall the prices of the products being studied, the conclusion often is made that price information was not so relevant in their decisions (Dickson and Sawyer 1990). However, Monroe and Lee (1999) recently argued that what consumers remember explicitly is not necessarily a good indicator of what they know implicitly and that price information that is not remembered consciously still can exert an influence on buying decisions.

Price and Nonprice Advertising

The third attempt at reconciliation is Kaul and Wittink's (1995) empirical generalization of 18 studies. This research highlighted the difference between price and nonprice advertising. The authors found that empirical studies performed across many categories showed that an increase in price advertising leads to increased price sensitivity among consumers. They also found studies of the effect of local advertising on price. These studies concluded that the use of price advertising leads to actual lower prices. (These studies included categories where local advertising was prohibited in some regions and not in others [e.g., legal services, prescription medicines, eyeglasses, eye examinations], allowing for comparisons between regions with and without local advertising for the same products.)

In looking at nonprice advertising, Kaul and Wittink (1995) found several studies showing that an increase in nonprice advertising leads to lower price sensitivity among consumers. Their main argument explaining these results was that "non-price advertising is used for positioning purposes, thus making the brand more differentiated, which, if successful, may result in lower price sensitivity for the brand" (p. G156). However, their thesis was not universally supported by the data; several studies also showed nonprice advertising leading to increased price sensitivity.

Kaul and Wittink (1995) focused on the distinction between price and nonprice advertising.

Early on in their article, they recognized that price advertising generally is run by retailers and nonprice advertising is run by manufacturers (p. G153). We interpret their article as relying on the *content* of advertising to determine the difference between retail and manufacturer advertising. In drawing conclusions about the two types of advertising, they consistently assumed that it is the type of advertising (price or nonprice) and not the locus of it (retailer or manufacturer) that is causing the difference in price. Although we have a minor dispute with the notion that price advertising always increases price sensitivity, our major concern is with the question of what causes retailers to advertise price more than do manufacturers.

In the Kaul and Wittink (1995) work, we do not find a recognition of the key role of manufacturer distribution policies as the key intervening variable in the market mechanisms reversing the effects of advertising on price sensitivity for manufacturers and retailers (p. G154). Instead, Kaul and Wittink raised "three considerations that are relevant to the examination of the relationship between advertising and consumer price sensitivity" (p. G158). These considerations refer to the composition of the consumer sample set, the measure of price sensitivity, and the type of consumers. By ignoring the impact of vertical competition on the relationship between advertising and price, Kaul and Wittink—typical of the research in this area—ignored what probably is a key factor in the question of advertising's affect on price, that is, whether manufacturer market power (roughly, the ability to raise prices and margins) translates into more or less reseller (retailer) market power.

Importance of Distribution

We conclude our critical review of the literature by noting an important gap. The impact of advertising on retail prices is significantly moderated by the manufacturer's distribution policy, yet the importance of this vertical competition does not appear to be recognized in the literature. Intensive distribution of strongly advertised brands may lead to intensive price competition among retailers, causing lower retail prices either directly or indirectly as a result of retailers' price-focused advertising. With selective or exclusive distribution, however, such competition is mitigated and retailers are free to take higher margins.

The luxury automobile category provides an example of how exclusive distribution can even override the effects of price advertising on price sensitivity. Although we noted earlier that every case of price advertising identified by Kaul and Wittink (1995) led to increased price sensitivity, the case of Land Rover in North America provides a counterexample. Land Rover used print advertisements with the price of the vehicle clearly stated, yet no one could seriously argue that this increased price sensitivity. In fact, the purpose of price advertising in this case was to allow potential customers to self-select for willingness to pay the significant price premium for this car as well as to build the luxury appeal of the car by showing everyone how much it cost. In the words of the vice president at the agency in charge of the account, "The price drew the right audience. It was self-selecting. . . . It also saved the buyer the step of having to tell his friends how much he paid for this radically new vehicle" (quoted in Fournier 1995, p. 5).

Levi's is an example of the impact of selective distribution on price. Levi's refused to allow Wal-Mart to distribute its jeans for fear of the downward price pressure on the brand's retail price. Another example of selective distribution affecting price is the perfume industry in which premium brands maintain a price premium of 200% to 300% over midrange brands, despite similar product quality and similar product and marketing costs, primarily by limiting their distribution to department stores and staying away from mass merchandisers. Intel is another example of a strong brand that forces computer manufacturers to compete more intensely on price because no computer has an exclusive on the Pentium processor. If one manufacturer had such an exclusive, then prices of that computer certainly would increase (and Intel's prices might be forced down by the manufacturer power).

CONCLUSIONS

We draw two conclusions from the forgoing discussion. The first is that research efforts on the question of the impact of advertising on price should focus on absolute, not relative, prices. Price dispersion is not per se evidence of high absolute prices. The second conclusion is that the role of vertical competition needs to be recognized explicitly. Focusing on one stage in the value chain may yield misleading conclusions regarding the role of advertising, branding, and price levels.

Absolute, Not Relative, Prices

First, we believe that the preponderance of evidence and theory supports the notion that advertised products typically sell for higher prices and unadvertised products sell for lower prices, even (or especially) when differences in quality are taken into account. However, although it often is observed that strongly advertised brands tend to *charge more* (Kanetkar, Weinberg, and Weiss 1992), an equally compelling view is that *un*advertised brands *charge less*. In other words, advertised brands set the price ceiling for unadvertised brands. Is this ceiling a "lid" on prices that forces the unadvertised brands to offer consumers even lower prices than otherwise would be available? Or, is the ceiling a "pricing umbrella" under which the advertisers earn comfortable margins and are protected from the rigors of true price competition (Brown, Lee, and Spreen 1996)? We believe that advertised products that are widely available set the price ceiling under which competitors are forced to price their own products and services. In the short term, advertisers may raise or lower this ceiling with quite different effects on "competition."

At the ceiling, in the highest pricing location, sit highly advertised, high-quality, innovative products. Significantly below, in the lowest pricing positions, sit the private labels and "me too" brands. Between the two is a gap or band. Price dispersion measures the width of this band. We believe that such dispersion of prices is a given. We reject the notion that price dispersion is per se evidence of uninformed inefficient markets. Relative prices of brands in a particular set of functionally equivalent products might not tell us much about what the *absolute* (average) price level of the entire set would be without advertising. A variety of prices that offers consumers the opportunity to buy at many different places and at different times is something that few consumers would gladly sacrifice. Variation in price, even among similar products, is not prima facie evidence of reduced consumer welfare. It might even be a healthy indicator of dynamism and innovation in the category, signifying a breadth of retail availability and active price competition.

The more important question to us is the absolute height of this band itself, that is, the absolute price level. This is significantly more difficult to measure in a meaningful way. Measures of profits that capture risk and the cost of investments might provide better insight into the height of the band if they reflect the entire supply chain. It is dangerous to focus on a single link in the supply chain because profits often are inversely related among stages in the supply chain. We believe that a focus of further investigation should be on finding reliable methods for measuring and testing the effect of advertising on absolute prices given the expected variation in prices for different brands with equivalent functional quality and even different prices for the same brands at different retailers.

Role of Vertical Competition

The second conclusion that we draw in this chapter is that the role of middlemen (especially retailers) serves as a pivot point to reverse many conclusions about price sensitivity and monopoly power. We argue that the advertising and price research, with a notable exception of the substantial contributions of Steiner (1973, 1993), generally pays insufficient attention to vertical competition and the dynamics of the relationship between manufacturers and retailers. We believe that the field must move beyond the notion of merely recognizing that retailers and manufacturers are different. It is true that retailers advertise price more often than do manufacturers and that price generally is mentioned in advertising when it is low, not high. However, we believe that it is not just the fact that advertising mentions price or expands the consideration set that determines whether advertising is promoting (increasing) price sensitivity. The discussion needs to be put into the context of a causal explanation for why and how price and nonprice advertising come to dominate different markets.

In particular, it seems to us that the breadth of retailer availability is the primary determinant of the degree to which retailers focus on price or other marketing efforts. Having the same product available in many different retail outlets encourages price competition, especially when consumers regard the different outlets as similar. If a retailer were to enjoy a local monopoly on strong brands such as Heinz ketchup, Tide detergent, and Tylenol, then advertising that increased demand for these products likely would be reflected in higher prices (whether or not price were mentioned or competing brands were included in the consideration set). Of course, manufacturers do not have exclusive or selective distribution policies for these products, and as a result, these brands often are sold by retailers at very low or even negative margins. Many scholars fail to recognize the essential role of broad distribution in creating the conditions for price competition at the retail level. The key point is that the moderating effect of manufacturers' distribution policies determines whether retailers will be able to use increases in demand created by advertising to raise their own selling prices and margins. These distribution policies include promotional policies and allocation of production capacity. Even products with broad distribution but insufficient supply will result in retailers charging higher prices to exploit the shortage.

Directions for Further Research

Based on the forgoing discussion, we believe that several directions can be pursued to shed further light on the impact of advertising on price:

1. A key question that remains unresolved is whether the price of unadvertised brands is being forced down or, on the contrary, pulled up by the price ceiling of advertised brands.
2. Further development of approaches for measurement and comparison of absolute prices—the height of the price band—and lowest prices is required. As already noted, one possibility could be measures of profits that allow for the risk and cost of investments in new product development. Another possibility might be the change in absolute price over time, particularly before and after major changes in the marketing environment for the category such as deregulation and availability of a radical new technology. Comparisons of absolute or lowest prices across countries or large regions also might be useful (in effect, a meta-dispersion measure).
3. The forgoing arguments require the support of empirical study of both the effects of store format on relative prices and the effects of manufacturer distribution policy on relative and absolute prices.

4. Early on, we noted that we needed to limit the scope of this analysis. Extending the analysis to include the long-term impact of advertising in enabling new product development and diffusion also would be valuable.

5. As noted earlier, instead of studying the impact of advertising on price for consumer welfare in the aggregate, it would be interesting to study this and similar questions through the lens of distributive justice, with savings to the less well-off segments of the population valued more than the identical savings to the more well-off segments.

6. Finally, it would be valuable to revisit why this question is important in today's context of building strong global brands with means other than traditional advertising. Is it really advertising or strong brands that concern public policy and consume welfare issues?

We believe that if research efforts are focused on the impact of advertising on absolute price, and if due attention is paid to the impact of intermediaries, then a significant improvement can be made in our understanding of the relationship between advertising and competition.

NOTES

1. Price-quality correlation data need to be "augmented by data on the variance in price and quality," and "frontier measures of efficiency will measure the variance in consumer surplus only in the unlikely case of there being a perfect correspondence between the efficiency frontier and the consumer's valuation of each alternative" (Ratchford et al. 1996, p. 177).

2. In all cases, we compared only extra-strength acetaminophen caplets so as to maintain consistency. We did not include variations in strength (e.g., regular strength) or in delivery vehicle (e.g., "gelcaps," tablets).

REFERENCES

Ailawadi, K., P. W. Farris, and E. Shames (1999), "Trade Promotion: Essential to Selling through Resellers," *Sloan Management Review,* 41 (1), 83–92.

Albion, Mark S. and Paul W. Farris (1987), "Manufacturer Advertising and Retailer Gross Margins," in *Advances in Marketing and Public Policy,* P. Bloom, ed. Greenwich, CT: JAI.

Borden, Neil H. (1942), *The Economic Effects of Advertising.* Chicago: Irwin.

Brown, Mark G., Jonq-Ying Lee, and Thomas H. Spreen (1996). "The Impact of Generic Advertising and the Free Rider Problem: A Look at the U.S. Orange Juice Market and Imports," *Agribusiness,* 12 (4), 309–17.

Brynjolfsson, Erik and Michael D. Smith (1999), "Frictionless Commerce? A Comparison of Internet and Conventional Retailers," working paper, Sloan School of Management, Massachusetts Institute of Technology.

Buzzell, Robert D. and Paul W. Farris (1977), "Marketing Costs in Consumer Goods Industries," in *Strategy + Structure = Performance,* H. B. Thorelli, ed. Bloomington: Indiana University Press.

Court, David, Thomas D. French, Tim I. McGuire, and Michael Partington (1999), "Marketing in 3-D," *McKinsey Quarterly,* No. 4, 6–17.

Dickson, Peter R. and Alan G. Sawyer (1990), "The Price Knowledge and Search of Supermarket Shoppers," *Journal of Marketing,* 54 (3), 42–53.

Dorfman, Robert and Peter O. Steiner (1954), "Optimal Advertising and Optimal Quality," *American Economic Review,* 44, 826–36.

Farris, Paul W. and Mark Albion (1981), "Determinants of the Advertising-to-Sales Ratio," *Journal of Advertising Research,* 21 (1), 19–27.

———— and Robert D. Buzzell (1979), "Variations in Advertising Intensity: Some Cross-Sectional Analyses," *Journal of Marketing,* 43 (Fall), 112–22.

———— and David J. Reibstein (1979), "How Price, Expenditures, and Profits Are Linked," *Harvard Business Review,* 57 (November-December), 173–84.

———— and ———— (1997), "Consumer Prices and Advertising," in *Encyclopedic Dictionary of Business Ethics,* P. H. Werhane and R. E. Freeman, eds. Cambridge, MA: Blackwell, 139–41.

Fournier, Susan (1995), "Land Rover North America, Inc.," Case 9-596-036, Harvard Business School.

Kanetkar, V., C. Weinberg, and D. Weiss (1992), "Price Sensitivity and Television Advertising Exposures: Some Empirical Findings," *Marketing Science,* 11 (4), 359–72.

Kaul, A. and D. Wittink (1995). "Empirical Generalizations about the Impact of Advertising on Price Sensitivity and Price," *Marketing Science,* 14 (3), G151–61.

Lodish, Leonard M., Magid Abraham, Stuart Kalmenson, Jeanne Livelsberger, Beth Lubkin, Bruce Richardson, and Mary Ellen Stevens (1995), "How TV Advertising Works: A Meta-Analysis of 389 Real World Split Cable TV Advertising Experiments," *Journal of Marketing Research,* 32 (2), 125–40.

Mitra, A. and J. Lynch (1995), "Toward a Reconciliation of Market Power and Information Theories of Advertising Effects on Price Elasticity," *Journal of Consumer Research,* 21 (4), 644–60.

Monroe, K. and A. Lee (1999), "Remembering versus Knowing: Issues in Buyers' Processing of Price Information," *Academy of Marketing Science,* 27 (2), 207–25.

Quelch, John A. (1986), "General Electric Company: Consumer Incandescent Lighting," Case 2-587-014, Harvard Business School.

Ratchford, Brian, Jagdish Agrawal, Pamela E. Grimm, and Narasimhan Srinivasan (1996), "Toward Understanding the Measurement of Market Efficiency," *Journal of Public Policy and Marketing,* 15(2), 167–84.

Schmalensee, R. (1981), "Output and Welfare Implications of Monopolistic Third-Degree Price Discrimination," *American Economic Review,* 71 (1), 242–47.

Steiner, R. (1973), "Does Advertising Lower Consumer Prices?" *Journal of Marketing,* 37 (October), 19–26.

——— (1993), "The Inverse Association between Margins of Manufacturers and Retailers," *Review of Industrial Organization,* 8, 717–40.

Strenio, A. (1996). "The Aspirin Wars," *Journal of Public Policy & Marketing,* 15 (2), 319–21.

Vakratsas, D. and T. Ambler (1999), "How Advertising Works: What Do We Really Know?" *Journal of Marketing,* 63 (January), 26–43.

CHAPTER 12

DOUBLE-COLA AND ANTITRUST ISSUES
Staying Alive in the Soft Drink Wars

JOYCE M. WOLBURG

The Double-Cola Company is one of several small soft drink companies that compete fiercely for market share in the beverage industry. Headquartered in Chattanooga, Tennessee, it produces Double-Cola, its flagship brand; Ski, an orange-lemon drink; Cherry Ski; the Jumbo line of eight fruit flavors; Double-Dry Ginger Ale; and a variety of diet and caffeine-free versions of the original brands. Although Double-Cola Co. products were once distributed nationally, they currently have regional distribution primarily in the Southeast and Midwest with a strong following in rural areas. Unfortunately for small soft drink companies such as the Double-Cola Co., the prize of less than one percent market share is won only by fighting a daily battle for survival, especially against industry giants Coca-Cola and Pepsi-Cola.

The following investigation is a case study of the successes and failures of one small company in the soft drink wars. It is a testament to the meaning of brands and the lengths that loyal consumers go to keep Double-Cola as their favorite beverage. And it is an evaluation of how adequately the current regulatory environment serves the needs of these consumers as well as Double-Cola's owners and bottlers. It addresses criticisms that the regulatory environment permits an uneven playing field that is perceived as anti-competitive at best and illegal at worst. This is the story of the underdog in the soft drink industry.

To gain these insights we look at the competitors, the historical factors that have led to the growth of some—but not all—brands, the narratives that consumers provide, and the impact of potentially predatory business practices within the retail environment, such as shelf access fees and co-operative merchandising agreements.

COMPETITORS WITHIN THE CURRENT MARKET ENVIRONMENT

The total U.S. beverage market is both large and competitive. Brands of soft drinks compete not only against each other but also against other types of beverages including coffee, milk, alcoholic beverages, sports drinks, bottled water, and vegetable juices. The beverage industry produces annually close to 53 billion gallons, with soft drinks taking up the largest category at 15.3 billion gallons for a 29% share (Prince 2001). The typical American consumes about 55 gallons of soft

From *Journal of Consumer Affairs,* vol. 37, no. 2 (2003). Copyright © 2003 by The American Council on Consumer Interests. Reprinted with permission.

drinks annually (about 19 ounces per day), in comparison to 22 gallons of beer, 22 gallons of milk, and 17 gallons of coffee (Bentley 2002).

According to *Beverage Digest* (2002) data, Americans spend about $62 billion on soft drinks each year. Consumption is fairly stable, with the same companies and brands holding their rankings fairly consistently from year to year. Top-10 *Beverage Digest* figures for 2001 show that Coca-Cola brands dominate the soft drink market with 43.7% share and Pepsi brands follow with 31.6% share. The two companies thus create a duopoly, controlling a vast 75.3% of the soft drink market. The third ranked company, Cadbury Schweppes PLC, which owns 7-Up, Dr Pepper, and U.S. interests for Royal Crown Cola, has a market share of 15.6%, less than half that of Pepsi. The fourth-ranked, Toronto-based Cott Corporation, which produces a number of private label drinks including Wal-Mart's Sam's Choice, is even farther in the distance with a 3.8% share. All other companies and private labels, including the Double-Cola Co., are left to fight over the remaining 5.3% of the total market (see Table 12.1). Figures for 2000 place Double-Cola's share at 0.1% (*Beverage World* 2001).

Coca-Cola, Pepsi-Cola, and Cadbury Schweppes own all of the top-10 brands (*Beverage Digest* 2002), which are listed in Table 12.2. Double-Cola is noticeably absent, either as a company or a brand, from either of the most recent top-10 lists. In 1997, however, the Double-Cola Co. was ranked ninth (*Beverage Digest* 1998). After Coca-Cola, Pepsi-Cola, and Royal Crown Cola, Double-Cola has the distinction of being the fourth-largest cola brand in the U.S. (*Beverage World* 2001).

METHODOLOGY

This case study is guided by three basic research questions:

RQ1:   How does Double-Cola's historical evolution among other soft drink brands influence the company's ability to compete in the current competitive environment?

RQ2:   What is the meaning of Double-Cola brands to consumers, and what role do the brands play in their lives?

RQ3:   How adequately does the current regulatory environment serve the needs of consumers as well as those of bottlers and small manufacturers?

To find answers to these questions, a case study was conducted using standard qualitative procedures with attention to the following items: the historical background, the physical setting, the legal context, other cases, and informants whose stories illuminate the case (Stake 1994). In this study, the historical background was obtained through published works and interviews with former executives from the Double-Cola Co.; the physical setting was established through site visits to the Greensburg Bottling Co. (one of the largest bottlers of Double-Cola products, located in Greensburg, Kentucky) and to corporate headquarters in Chattanooga; the legal context was accessed by examining Federal Trade Commission reports and other documents available via government websites in addition to legal commentary in trade publications; other cases were studied through published articles on the soft-drink industry and its competitors; and key informants were the president of the Greensburg Bottling Co. and former Double-Cola Co. executives. All data was collected between 2001 and 2003, with the exception of some interviews with company executives and a site visit to the company headquarters in 1992 as part of an historical analysis of the company (Wolburg 1993).

Table 12.1

**Top-10 Carbonated Drink Companies for 2001 by Market Share
and Share Change from 2000**

Rank	Companies	Market Share	Share Change
1	Coca-Cola Co.	43.7	−0.4
2	Pepsi-Cola Co. (PepsiCo)	31.6	+0.2
3	Dr Pepper/7 Up (DPSU Cadbury Schweppes)	15.6	+0.9
4	Cott. Corp.	3.8	+0.5
5	National Beverage Corp. (Shasta/Faygo)	2.2	+0.1
6	Big Red	0.4	flat
7	Seagram	0.3	flat
8	Red Bull	0.1	+0.1
9	Monarch Co.	0.1	flat
10	Private Label/other	2.2	−1.4
Total		100	

Source: Beverage Digest 2002.

Table 12.2

**Top-10 Brands of Carbonated Drinks for 2001 by Market Share
and Share Change from 2000**

Rank	Brands	Market Share	Share Change
1	Coke Classic (Coca-Cola Co.)	19.9	−0.5
2	Pepsi-Cola (PepsiCo)	13.2	−0.4
3	Diet Coke (Coca-Cola Co.)	8.8	+0.1
4	Mt Dew (PepsiCo)	6.9	−0.3
5	Sprite (Coca-Cola Co.)	6.5	0.1
6	Dr Pepper (DPSU of Cadbury Schweppes)	6.2	−0.1
7	Diet Pepsi (PepsiCo)	5.3	flat
8	7 Up (DPSU of Cadbury Schweppes)	1.9	−0.1
9	Caffeine Free Diet Coke (Coca-Cola Co.)	1.7	flat
10	Barq's Root Beer (Coca-Cola Co.)	1.1	flat
Total		71.5	

Source: Beverage Digest 2002.

FINDINGS

The Evolution of Soft-drink Brands

To answer RQ1 concerning the influence of historical developments, it is necessary to examine the origins of Coca-Cola, Pepsi-Cola, and Double-Cola and to compare these companies' ability to compete in the current competitive environment.

Coca-Cola. The U.S. soft drink industry began in the late 1880s. John S. Pemberton, an Atlanta pharmacist, developed the Coca-Cola brand as a soda fountain drink in 1886 and positioned it as a "brain tonic and intellectual beverage" (Govan and Livingood 1977). Both the Coca-Cola brand and company took an early lead in the soft-drink industry, for the brand achieved national distribution early on and the company has consistently dominated the industry. For additional information pertaining to the history of the Coca-Cola Co., please see Irwin and Pearson (1987a; 1987b) and Heritage Report (2002).

Currently, Coca-Cola products are sold in about 200 countries with more than 230 different brands. Best-known beverage brands in the U.S. include Coke, Diet Coke, Mello Yellow, Fanta, Minute Maid, Mr. Pibb, Nestea, Sprite, Barq's Root Beer, Dasani Water, Fresca, Fruitopia, and Hi-C (www.coca-cola.com 2002).

Pepsi-Cola. Pepsi was one of several other brands that got their start in the late 1800s. A North Carolina pharmacist named Caleb Bradham invented "Brad's Drink" in 1893, which was later renamed Pepsi-Cola (Irwin and Pearson 1987b). Pepsi's early growth was less significant than that of Coke's, and its real strength as a competitor to Coke began after Alfred Steele became CEO in 1950, a time when Pepsi was nearly bankrupt. Steele was expected to liquidate the Pepsi-Cola Co. Instead, he made it his goal to "beat Coke." Through the introduction of new bottle sizes, increased supermarket sales, and new advertising campaigns, revenue increased more than 300% by 1958 (Irwin and Pearson 1987b). According to current corporate information, PepsiCo, the parent of Pepsi-Cola, also owns Frito-Lay snack foods, Tropicana Products, Quaker Oats, and Gatorade, in addition to having partnerships with Lipton Tea and Starbucks. Best-known Pepsi beverage brands in the U.S. include Pepsi, Diet Pepsi, Mountain Dew, Code Red, Sierra Mist, Mugs Root Beer, Slice, Lipton Brisk, Gatorade, Aquafina, SoBe, and Frappuccino (www.pepsico.com 2002).

Double-Cola. The late-19th-century beginnings of the Coke and Pepsi brands gave them a firm head start over new competitors that entered the market in the 1920s. Double-Cola's founder, Charles Little, first worked for the Cherco Cola Co. but left in 1922 to establish the Good Grape Company, named for its Good Grape soda brand. In 1924 he renamed the company the Seminole Flavor Co. and began developing a cola drink, which he finally perfected in 1933 (Wilson 1980). He named it Double-Cola to reflect its near double size of 12 oz. compared to Coke's 6½ oz. size, both of which sold for 5 cents. Using the slogan "Double Good, Double-Cola" in 1935, sales grew rapidly throughout the 1930s, according to former Vice-President of Marketing Karl Sooder (1992). Ironically, Pepsi used the same strategy but with greater success. In 1939 Pepsi launched a radio jingle—"Twice as much for a nickel, too. Pepsi-Cola is the one for you"—that was believed to be the "second-best-known song in America after the 'Star Spangled Banner'" (Irwin and Pearson 1987b, p. 2).

Sales for the Double-Cola brand were so strong that the Seminole Flavor Company was renamed the Double-Cola Company in 1953. Yet, Little was not a risk taker; he didn't want to compete head-to-head against Coke, for he intended his brand for a different market segment (Martin 1989). Former Double-Cola President L. Edward Shanks commented:

> There was a time when Double-Cola competed very well with Coca-Cola . . . But I don't think that he [Little] was willing to risk resources beyond a certain point. It wasn't that he was averse to risk. It's just that I don't think he had the long-term vision that Woodruff had—who was a real visionary (Shanks 1992). [Woodruff was CEO of Coca-Cola 1939–1942 and 1952–1954 (Butler 2000)].

Former Vice-President of Sales John Kirby agreed that Double-Cola had the chance to become a big player, but Little lacked the business acumen, the foresight, and the drive to expand the company and accumulate wealth (Kirby 1992).

Coca-Cola was such a formidable adversary by the 1930s that much of Double-Cola's rivalry was focused upon Pepsi-Cola. Shanks (1992) and Kirby (1992) believed that Double-Cola was as large a company as Pepsi-Cola and in many ways a superior one. Pepsi-Cola was believed to be near bankruptcy on several occasions by the mid 1940s, which gave Little the opportunity to buy the company and eliminate it as a competitor.

He [Little] had a chance to have bought enough stock in the Pepsi-Cola Co. to control it for about a quarter of a million dollars . . . but he told me "I've got a good cola. I don't need that." And that's the way he felt. I asked him, "Could you have done it without jeopardizing the backing you needed to continue to grow the brand as it was?" And he told me, "In 1946 I was ahead of everyone else" (Kirby 1992).

With the benefit of hindsight, it is easy to criticize Little's business philosophy as shortsighted; however, his decisions in the 1940s likely seemed valid to him. Many consumers find the taste of Double-Cola quite similar to Pepsi (more so than to Coke), and Little's decision was evidently based on his belief in the Double-Cola formula, which has never been changed (Kirby 1992). One can argue that Little's mistakes were not in his evaluation of the formulas, but instead in not foreseeing the advantages the Pepsi brand and company would eventually gain through distribution, mergers, acquisitions, and marketing strategy, or the overall growth of the soft drink industry. In 1946, sales were 514 million cases compared to 5.6 billion cases in 1989 (*Beverage Industry/Annual Manual* 1990/1991).

Though Little believed he was ahead of his competitors in 1946 and was optimistic about the future, Double-Cola's history is one of ups and downs. The company had not only passed up the opportunity to purchase Pepsi-Cola, but had made earlier mistakes that were later seen to have diminished its chance of becoming a big player in today's market, particularly Little's failure to capture the vending machine market in the 1930s. According to Shanks (1992), Little had a cabinet and refrigeration unit made by Westinghouse, but when the vending mechanism was added, it only worked under laboratory conditions—not in the humidity of the North Carolina textile mills, where Double-Cola sold well. Shanks believed that if Little had shown greater perseverance, Double-Cola could have been the market leader rather than a follower in the vending machine segment. Kirby (1992) added that Little's refusal to commit more money was based on the fear of jeopardizing what he'd accumulated. "He was comfortable. He had more money than he or his family really needed" (Kirby 1992).

Another challenge for the Double-Cola Co. was sugar shortages during World War II, which prevented everyone in the soft drink industry from producing sufficient quantities to meet demand (Shanks 1992). Many companies responded by downsizing their products, but both Double-Cola and Pepsi-Cola kept the 12 oz. bottles because size was key to their positioning strategy. Shanks felt that this strategy put Double-Cola at a great disadvantage because the downsizing allowed other brands, especially Coca-Cola, not only to meet consumer demand but also to expand distribution while Double-Cola struggled to meet its demand. Maintaining the 12 oz. bottle during WWII also contributed to Pepsi-Cola's financial difficulties (Dunagan 2001).

Despite these setbacks, the 1950s were prosperous years for the Double-Cola Co. A new beverage, Ski, was formulated and trademarked in the mid-1950s with phenomenal sales growth (*Beverage Industry* 1996). Double-Cola also became the first major soft drink company to use a 16 oz. returnable bottle (www.double-cola.com).

During the 1960s, Double-Cola faced a number of external problems affecting the entire industry including (1) an influx of store brands as private labels, (2) environmental concerns about recycling and packaging, and (3) increased taxes that raised the cost to consumers (Kelley 1994). A different set of problems emerged when Little sold the Double-Cola Co. to Fairmont Foods in 1962. According to Joe DeSpain, President of the Greensburg Bottling Co., Fairmont Foods bought the company for quick gains rather than for sustained growth. Without understanding the challenges of the soft-drink industry, the new owners depleted the available cash without adequately reinvesting money for the future (DeSpain 2003).

Table 12.3

Market Share of the Double-Cola Co. and the Top Five Companies in 1996 through 2001

Company	Market Share							
	1996	1970	1975	1980	1985	1990	1995	2001
Coca-Cola	33.4	34.7	35.3	35.9	38.6	40.2	42.3	43.7
Pepsi	20.4	19.8	21.1	27.7	29.7	31.5	30.9	31.6
7 Up	6.9	7.2	7.6	7.0	10.8	9.5	**	**
Royal Crown	6.9	6.0	5.4	4.3	3.1	2.8	2.0	***
Dr Pepper	2.6	3.8	5.5	6.0	4.9	5.4	**	**
Double-Cola	*	*	*	*	0.6	0.5	0.3	0.1

Source: Figures for 1966, 1970, and 1975 (Christensen 1977, citing *Beverage World*/John R. Maxwell, Jr. data); figures for 1980 (Irwin and Pearson 1987 citing *Beverage World*/John R. Maxwell, Jr. data); figures for 1985 and 1990 (*Beverage Industry/Annual Manual* 1990/91/John R. Maxwell Jr. data); figures for 1995 (*Beverage Digest* 1997/John C. Maxwell data): figures for 2001 (*Beverage Digest* 2002 /John C. Maxwell data).

*Market shares for the Double-Cola Co. were unavailable for 1966–1980 but were less than those of Dr Pepper and Royal Crown, who vied for 4th and 5th place.

**By 1995, Dr Pepper/7 Up were brands within the same company (DPSU) and the market share for all company brands combined was 15.3 in 1995 and 15.6 in 2001.

***By 2001, the Royal Crown Cola Co. was sold to Cadbury Schweppes.

Industry figures for the top five companies clearly demonstrate the distance between the companies at the time. In 1966, the Coca-Cola Co.'s market share was 33.4%, PepsiCo's was 20.4%, while Seven Up and Royal Crown tied for third and fourth place at 6.9% each (Christensen 1977). Dr Pepper took fifth place with a 2.6% share, which meant that Double-Cola's share was still smaller since it was not ranked. See Table 12.3 for industry estimates of market share from 1966 to 2001.

In the late 1970s, ownership issues continued to plague Double-Cola. Fairmont Foods sold the company to a group of private investors, who in turn sold the company to a Canadian firm, Pop Shoppes International. Shanks regretted the two-year ownership under Pop Shoppes because the Double-Cola brand became secondary to other company brands (Kelley 1994). DeSpain (2003) noted that by this time and in the years to follow, the distribution of Double-Cola products became far more regional. One by one, many distributors dropped Double-Cola in favor of other, more profitable brands that generated larger sales volume and had heavier advertising support from the manufacturer, including in-store promotions and calendar marketing agreements (discussed in a later section).

In 1981, current-owner K.J. International purchased the Double-Cola Co. and restored it to a more stable environment. However, the changes in ownership during the previous decades limited the company's ability to bounce back, especially during current, more fiercely competitive times. As Coke and Pepsi expanded their product lines during the 1980s, Double-Cola and other small soft-drink companies lost shelf space in grocery stores and were forced to devise strategies merely to stay alive (Ricks 1985). Two important strategies that characterize the later decades are keeping prices low and entering foreign markets. For example, during the 1980s and early 1990s, Double-Cola was able to offer greater value than the industry giants, just as it had in earlier decades. In 1991, Double-Cola sold a 20 oz. bottle for 49 cents compared to 16 oz. bottles for Coke and Pepsi, which both sold for 59 cents. In recent years, however, the price break has been lost as Coke and Pepsi products are frequently sold for $5.00 for two 12 packs of 12 oz. cans, which sets a nearly impossible standard for other brands. DeSpain (2003) explained that the industry giants can sell for such low prices because they use a volume versus profit strategy. They select certain markets as volume centers, where competition is tougher and market share is gained by aggressively lowering prices, and they select other markets as profit centers, where competition is low and prices can remain relatively high. Because industry giants can help support the low-price strategy with their resources and because certain markets can offer high profits, other markets can temporarily afford to sacrifice price. In contrast, the manufacturers, bottlers, and distributors of small brands, such as Double-Cola, cannot utilize this strategy. Selling at high prices for additional profits erodes sales, and selling at low prices results in little-to-no profit.

The low-price strategy among industry giants is believed to be a response to the growing concern over private labels (PLs). As early as 1990, when the PLs held only 7.6% market share, corporate executives of the Coca-Cola Co. and PepsiCo insisted that they were not a threat (Mitchell 1994a). However, by 1993, when PLs increased their share to 9.4% and began gaining prime shelf space in retail stores, the tide had turned (Mitchell 1994a). Coca-Cola's president, M. Douglas Ivester, referred to PL producers as "the parasites of the industry," and he called upon colleagues to stop being "sheep" by fighting PLs with innovation and creativity instead of price cutting (Mitchell 1994b, G1). Although PLs currently hold about 10.6% market share (Prince 2000), the Coca-Cola Co. and PepsiCo were able to maintain or increase market share throughout the 1990s. During this time, Double-Cola's share decreased from 0.6% in 1985 to 0.3% in 1995 (*Beverage Digest* 1997). See Table 12.3.

A second strategy has been to seek international markets with more level playing fields than in the U.S. However, the ability to compete internationally depends on the success a company can show prospective investors in the U.S. (Davis 1991). According to Kirby (1992), "not being that well known in the U.S. has kept us from growing as fast as we could have . . . sometimes you get shot down before they have a chance to see how good your product is." Although Coke and Pepsi have greater international success, the Double-Cola Co. currently does business in 17 countries in the Middle East, South Asia, and South America with the brands Double-Cola, orange-flavored Oranta, and lemon-lime Chaser. For a list of important events in Double-Cola's history, see Figure 12.1.

Over the years, the vast gap in market share, distribution, and resources between Double-Cola and the two industry giants has continued to widen. These differences limit competitive activities and require a more focused competitive style for the company that tries to be a niche player. Ten years ago Shanks recognized this.

> Coke and Pepsi have financial resources that we will not be able to match. If we go into any market, whether it be in the U.S. or international, and try to do it head to head with either of those companies . . . playing into their strengths, we will lose. We've got to be selective about the things that we do—be very focused, and show a high degree of flexibility (Shanks 1992).

DeSpain (2001) agreed. "Unlike Coke and Pepsi, we do not need to own the entire market to be profitable. We are just looking for a fair shot at store space and displays, a good campaign of awareness, and we believe the product will sell on its own. . . ."

The Meaning of Double-Cola to Consumers

When telling the story of the underdog and bringing to light the competitive environment that small brands inhabit, it is also essential to understand what these brands mean to consumers and

Figure 12.1

Important Events in Double-Cola's History

1916   Cherco Cola Co. was established.

1922   Charles D. Little left Cherco Cola Co. and with partner Joe. S. Forster estab-
       lished the Good Grape Co., which was named for their grape soda, Good
       Grape.

1924   After considerable growth, the company changed its name to the Seminole
       Flavor Co. and marketed the first cola, Marvel Cola. The formula improved
       and the name was changed to Jumbo Cola.

1933   The cola formula was perfected and given the name Double-Cola.

1934   Double-Dry Ginger Ale and Tonic Water became trademarked brands of
       Double-Cola.

1935   Double-Cola was marketed with the slogan "Double-Good, Double-Cola."

1953   The Seminole Flavor Co. was renamed the Double-Cola Co.

1956   Ski was formulated as an orange-lemon drink and trademarked in 1958.

1957   Double-Cola became the first major soft drink to use a 16 oz. returnable
       bottle.

1962   Charles Little sold the company to Fairmont Foods Co.

1964   Sugar Free Double-Cola was introduced after an earlier version in 1962.

1970s Fairmont Foods sold the Double-Cola Co. to private investors and later to
       Pop Shoppes International.

1980   London-based K. J. International purchased the Double-Cola Co., which
       became the Double-Cola Co.-USA.

1986   Diet Ski was introduced as a line extension.

1996   Cherry Ski was introduced as another line extension.

1998   Double-Cola Co.-USA sold the manufacturing facility in the business district
       and moved the corporate headquarters to downtown Chattanooga, TN.

2001   Caffeine Free Ski was launched.

Source: www.double-cola.com/history and company reports.

why consumers feel they lose something important—even irreplaceable—if these brands don't survive in the marketplace. The meaning and significance of the Double-Cola brands to consumers are the focus of RQ2, which is answered below.

Most Americans today easily recognize Coke and Pepsi products, although perhaps without knowing which parent company produces them. These drinks not only have national distribution, but they are heavily advertised. In fact, the advertising for the top 10 brands combined across 11 media was $604 million in 2000, up 24.5% over 1999 figures (Chura 2001). In comparison, many small, regional brands are popular in their local communities but are unfamiliar to consumers at a distance. A short but incomplete list of these brands includes Double-Cola, Ski, Ale-8-One, Big Chief, Caravan Ginger Ale, Cheerwine, Chocola, Chocolate Soldier, Dad's Root Beer, Kick-a-poo Joy Juice, Jumbo, Mason's Root Beer, Nehi, Nesbitt, NuGrape, Old Red Eye, Orange Crush, Tasty

Chocolate, and Sun Drop. Ale-8-One, for example, is similar to ginger ale and was named by tee-totaling workers asking at the day's end, "How about having *a late one?*'" (McGehee 2000).

Most small brands have limited distribution and are seldom supported with large advertising budgets. This means that their brand image is not really created through advertising, but instead is something that has evolved as people have found their own meaning for the brand.

Brand Image of Double-Cola and Ski. Double-Cola and Ski are the largest selling brands produced by the Double-Cola Co. Double-Cola's flavor is somewhat less sweet than other colas, while Ski is a fruit-based drink, sometimes compared to Mountain Dew (Hammond 2001). Despite the similarities in flavor to rival brands, Double-Cola and Ski mean something very different to consumers. The Double-Cola brand has connected well with people in rural communities, who are farther removed from corporate America than urban consumers. The brand belongs to a simpler, less-complicated life that some consumers have personally experienced and others long for. As a bottler of Double-Cola, DeSpain (2001) believes consumers feel they can "own" the brand as a product in a way they can't do with Coke or Pepsi because consumers perceive that Double-Cola is made by "real people in real work" rather than by anonymous employees of a large corporation.

Ski also has a grassroots following and was recognized in a 1990 Grammy-award-winning country song "Dumas Walker" by the Kentucky Headhunters (Schreiner 2001). Since the Headhunters grew up in an area where Ski has been the primary soft drink, it was a natural reference within the lyrics, unlike paid product placements. The lyrics say, "Come on down with my baby and me, have a slawburger, fries, and a bottle of Ski." For those who don't know that a slawburger is a hamburger topped with cole slaw and a favorite in rural Kentucky, or that Ski is a soft drink—not whiskey as some mistakenly believe—the lyrics may hold little meaning. But for those who understand the references, the song "created a tremendous amount of excitement" (Hammond 2001, quoting DeSpain). Like Double-Cola, Ski appeals to people who "psychologically tend to turn against slick products and slick advertising" (Sooder 1992).

Reverence and Nostalgia. Older consumers have strong nostalgic connections with Double-Cola and Ski, as well as many of the regional, hard-to-come-by brands. Some customers long for the days of drinking soda from glass bottles, which are still available from selected bottlers. Even more rare are bottlers who continue home-delivery of drinks in returnable bottles. Customers of the Greensburg Bottling Co. can leave their case of empties in the front yard and put the check in the mailbox. In return, the driver picks up the check and leaves a full case of drinks (Burdette 2001). One faithful 73-year-old customer has had Ski delivered to her home for 48 years (Schreiner, 2001).

Small brands often evoke such loyalty and devotion among their customers that their words take on a religious fervor. One writer spoke of his experience of pulling a drink out of an old-fashioned, ice cooler and said: "[It's like] plunging your arm deep in the icy water and pulling out heaven . . ." (Gulley 2001, p. 1). A newspaper reporter captured a similar feeling of reverence:

> Most people my age have fond memories of soft drinks savored on special occasions. I recall the '50s and the Double-Cola consumed each time I rode my bicycle through the woods and up a steep, rutty dirt road to Thomas Groceries in Macon. That was a simpler time . . . [and] . . . after a tiring trip on a hot summer day to fetch bread and a few basics for Mom, that Double-Cola always offered 16 ounces of pure liquid heaven (Bentley 2002, p. 2).

Transporting Favorite Brands to New Places. While nostalgia is a strong connection for older consumers, regional brands also have a loyal following among members of the younger demographic, who are the heaviest consumers of soft drinks. The connection is so strong that many young people who move outside the distribution area of their favorite beverage willingly transport it each time they go back home. Examples are numerous: a student from Mt. Sterling, Kentucky, fills his car's trunk with a cooler of Alc-8-Ones, which he takes with him to Wofford College in South Carolina (McGehee 2000); a Marquette University student from Breese, Illinois, stocks up on cases of Ski so she can drink them in Milwaukee (Bodinet 2001); and a hospital worker in North Carolina loads his car with cases of Double-Cola and Ski on visits back home to Kentucky to supply both himself and his friends, whom he has converted to the brands (Hammond 2001). The Greensburg Bottling Co. even sells Double-Cola concentrate regularly to a loyal California musician who has his own carbonator and makes his own in-home fountain drinks (DeSpain 2001).

Double-Cola Director of Marketing Beth Henderson recalls talking with one woman who drinks four cases of Ski a week and is so protective of her personal supply that she won't share it with family members. "My family cannot drink my Ski. It's in a separate refrigerator" (Russo 1998, p. 1).

Although some consumers don't care about the cost, the size and weight of soft drinks makes shipping expensive. While people outside the distribution area can order brands such as Double-Cola directly from bottlers or through web sites, the shipping costs are often prohibitive. For this reason, consumers usually try to find retail sources of the products close to home, though this is not always possible. Several consumers have shared their stories of having a relative ship Ski to them while in military service in Vietnam, Bosnia, or during Operation Desert Storm (Russo 1998).

The Lengths Consumers Go To. Some people have been steady consumers of a regional soft-drink brand for years, only to discover that the local bottler has discontinued it or that the bottler has closed. An estimated 80 small bottlers in Kentucky alone have closed in the last 40 years (Burdette 2001), which appears to reflect a national trend. When this happens, some consumers resign themselves to the loss and settle for a competitor's brand, but the most fiercely loyal consumers make it their mission to find other sources. The lengths that these consumers go to might be considered fanatical by some, but their actions speak loudly to the meaning of the brand. Ironically, industry giants cannot make similar claims because their products are ubiquitous. It is difficult to imagine a grocery store or convenience mart that does not carry either Coke or Pepsi; thus, legendary stories of how far people would go for a Coke or Pepsi don't seem to exist to the same degree as, say, stories about Double-Cola do.

For example, DeSpain tells the following story about an attorney in Paducah, Kentucky, who made it his mission to buy Double-Cola despite the difficulty locating it.

> Of course we come nowhere near Paducah, but I told him he could buy them in Henderson, or we might be able to work something out with . . . a Dr Pepper bottler/distributor in Madisonville who also buys some Ski from us from time to time . . . Recently the attorney's son had been attending the University of Kentucky, and he and his wife would go to Lexington to visit. Once on a trip they stopped in a "hole-in-the-wall" gas station along the way. His wife . . . came out and said, "Guess what I found," and she showed him a Double-Cola. He bought every one they had. From that time on when they went that route, they would stop there and buy Double-Cola (DeSpain 2001).

The story doesn't end there. DeSpain went on to explain that when the son finished college, the couple no longer drove that route regularly and lost their link to Double-Cola. In search of a new source, the attorney first asked a client who traveled to Evansville, Indiana (130 miles away), to bring back some Double-Cola, but the trips were too infrequent. In search of new sources, he asked DeSpain the proximity of Double-Cola retail outlets to Crossville, Tennessee, and Tupelo, Mississippi, because he visits those places regularly. Several phone calls later DeSpain found that the distributor in West Point, Mississippi, services Tupelo, and that the attorney could buy it there—about 220 miles from home in Paducah.

According to DeSpain, it is a common occurrence for bottlers of regional brands to get frantic calls or email messages from loyal customers in search of a particular drink. One such request came from a man in Cookeville, Tennessee, when the local bottler discontinued NuGrape. He had bought all he could find and was looking for a new source. He located NuGrape through a Texas bottler, but the shipping fee from Texas was prohibitive. After an Internet search led him to Greensburg, Kentucky, DeSpain arranged to have an employee who lives in Cookeville take him two cases of NuGrape from Greensburg, 100 miles away. Since then the bottler has helped the customer find closer, more convenient sources.

People who have lost touch with a brand sometimes rediscover it unexpectedly. An April 2001 article about the Greensburg Bottling Co. in the Louisville *Courier-Journal* was picked up by the AP. Soon afterward, DeSpain received numerous calls from people desperately in search of Double-Cola.

> About midmorning a couple arrived at the plant with the plant's story clipped from a Florida newspaper. They had been vacationing in Florida, saw the article, and decided to visit the plant on their way home to Ohio. If you look at your map, you will see that they had to make a significant detour to come to Greensburg on a trip from Florida to Ohio. I took them around the plant, and gave them a sample of the product . . . They bought a case of drinks . . . and it made their trip (DeSpain 2001).

Bottlers have also found that people driving through towns see delivery trucks with a brand's logo and ask the driver where they can buy it. This has been such a successful source of business for Prescott Bottling of Tullahoma, Tennessee, with the Sun-Drop brand that the bottling company considers their trucks to be part of the marketing strategy as "rolling bill-boards" (*Beverage Industry* 1998). Many people simply didn't know where to buy brands they have lost track of or do not know whether a brand they seek is still available.

Perhaps the best Double-Cola story revolves around the efforts to get the beverage to a high-school reunion in the coal mining town of Bluefield, West Virginia. DeSpain recounts that he was asked if he could supply seven cases of Double-Cola for the three-day event, since the brand was no longer sold in the area. The local bottling plant in Falls Mills, Virginia, had closed with the death of the owner; thus, the drinks had to be sent from Greensburg 315 miles away. The goal was for each person to receive a bottle of Double-Cola with a bag of peanuts tied around it to pour into the drink, reflecting an old tradition. The organizers wanted "a nice gift to help everyone remember," and Double-Cola evidently succeeded since several attendees wanted to save their bottle rather than drink it. Comments made to the bottler included "I don't believe this" and "I'll never drink this. It's a trophy" (DeSpain, 2001).

Additional comments given to DeSpain from the attendees reiterate the sense of loss that consumers experience:

> I am telling everyone about it . . . [but] they don't know what I am talking about. How sad that is. Double-Cola deserves its place in the drink market and should have never been shoved aside. It happened before I knew it and [now] there is none to be found. Try to keep Double-Cola alive. You don't know the feeling when you think it is gone.

Survival in the Retail Environment

Given the uncertainty of survival when small manufacturers compete against giants, it is important to consider the hopes consumers have that small soft-drink manufacturers and bottlers can keep their brands alive. This section addresses RQ3 to determine how adequately the current regulatory environment serves the needs of these groups.

Traditionally, the retail outlets for soft drinks have included food stores (both grocery and convenience stores), fountain-drink outlets, and vending machines (Irwin and Pearson 1987a). Of the three, a small soft-drink manufacturer's best chance for success has been in food stores because the fountain drink and vending machine segments allow little room for competitors. For example, fountain channels represent 23% of the entire carbonated soft drink business by volume (McKay 2000), and Coca-Cola and Pepsi-Cola products control 65% and 24%, respectively, of the $15 billion fountain-drink market (Steinriede 1998). Vending machines represent 12% of the soft drink market and are also dominated by Coca-Cola and Pepsi-Cola products (McKay 2000).

To avoid entering either the vending or fountain-drink fray, manufacturers and bottlers of smaller brands have searched for a more level playing field in food stores. Yet, a number of business practices have endangered competition in this environment, particularly shelf-access payments and calendar marketing agreements (CMAs). Both are discussed below.

Shelf-access Payments. Because the average supermarket stocks about 30,000 of the available 100,000 products, manufacturers and retailers bargain over the availability of shelf space by way of a variety of payments including (1) slotting fees (lump-sum, up-front payments), (2) pay-to-stay fees, and (3) payments to exclude rivals or to give them disadvantageous shelf space (FTC 2001). Willard K. Tom, Deputy Director of the Federal Trade Commission's Bureau of Competition, notes that slotting fees cover an extremely broad range of conduct—some of it clearly unlawful, such as commercial bribery; some clearly lawful, such as ordinary price discounts; and a great deal in the gray area in between (Tom 1999).

Two conflicting schools of thought dominate the debate on slotting fees. Defenders say they improve distribution efficiency and *stimulate* competition by compensating the retailer for the costs and risks of stocking new, unproven products (Bloom, Gundlach, and Cannon 2000, p. 93). Retailers have traditionally been strong supporters of slotting fees because they help offset the costs of restocking shelves, changing labels, and reprogramming scanner equipment, in addition to offsetting the potential costs of product failure.

Critics charge that slotting fees enhance market power and *damage* competition (Bloom, Gundlach, and Cannon 2000, 93). Manufacturers have traditionally supported this view in the belief that slotting fees damage channel relationships, hurt competition between manufacturers and retailers, create less product variety, and increase consumer prices. Senator Christopher "Kit" Bond (Republican, Missouri) regards slotting and related fees as "a brutal game of high-stakes poker for small manufacturers that threatens competition, jobs and likely drives up the cost of putting food on the table for millions of American families" (Senate Committee on Small Business 1999, p. 1). Retailers in the grocery industry receive an estimated $9 billion per year for slotting fees, with per-item costs of approximately $5,000 to $25,000, and there are growing concerns that slotting fees are spreading to other industries, such as computer software, compact discs, books, magazines, apparel, over-the-counter drugs, and tobacco (Bloom, Gundlach, and Cannon 2000).

More problematic are "pay-to-stay" fees that manufacturers of established brands pay to ensure their continued presence on retailers' shelves (FTC 2001). Because these fees are for existing products rather than new ones, the FTC regards them as a greater risk to competition but allows them nonetheless, despite manufacturers' complaints that they must pay up to hundreds of thousands of dollars annually or risk "being squeezed off the shelves'" (FTC 2001, p. 29).

Perhaps the most problematic are payments to limit or disadvantage rivals' shelf space. Some agreements negotiate outright exclusivity while others are for partial exclusivity or preferential shelf space. For example,

> ... a small supplier of canned tomatoes, tomato products, and sauerkraut stated that national brands of canned vegetables pay high slotting fees "just to keep us off the shelf"; an air freshener producer claimed that the dominant producers of automotive air fresheners "will pay large amounts of money to keep everybody else out"; and a small tortilla manufacturer claimed that a dominant supplier had paid to have the smaller firm's product placed in a disadvantageous shelf location, eventually taking all the shelf space except for "three feet in a corner" (FTC 2001, p. 31).

Much of the information acquired by the FTC was obtained at a two-day workshop on May 31 and June 1, 2000, at the behest of Senator Bond, who chairs the U.S. Senate Committee on Small Business. Bond's committee earmarked the sum of $900,000 to be used by the FTC to investigate slotting fee practices (Weir 1999; 2001), which are potential violations of the Sherman Act, the Robinson-Patman Act, and the Clayton Act (Levin 1991). The FTC's workshop produced a detailed report that highlighted issues but offered few clear outcomes. When three industries (the Independent Bakers Association, the Tortilla Industry Association, and the National Association of Chewing Gum Manufacturers) filed a petition asking the FTC to issue guidelines governing the use of slotting allowances, the commissioners denied the request. In a June 19, 2002 letter to the attorneys of the petitioning organizations, the FTC said:

> Development of guidelines often is highly resource-intensive, and the Commission believes, in this instance, that other steps better serve the public interest (Federal Trade Commission 2002, p. 2).

From this action, one can conclude that the FTC is aware of these questionable retail practices but is unlikely to come to the rescue of small businesses and consumers at this time. The FTC upholds the principle that antitrust laws are intended to protect "competition" in the abstract rather than "competitors" (Federal Trade Commission 2001, p. 35). Following this line of reasoning, as long as Coke and Pepsi remain healthy rivals in the soft drink market rather than co-conspirators, competition is preserved despite the loss of small manufacturers, bottlers, and brands.

CMAs. Another business practice that has received criticism for its impact on competition in the retail environment is the calendar marketing agreement or CMA. (The term CMA also refers to cooperative merchandising agreement, another name for the same business practice.) Many variations exist, although the usual agreement requires a food store to advertise a particular brand for a specific number of weeks per year in return for promotional allowances (Levin 1991). In recent years, though, CMAs have also included exclusive rights to advertising, display space, cold-drink equipment, and signage (Hays 2000). Lawrence R. Levin, an attorney who specializes in corporate law, observes that for smaller, less affluent soft-drink bottlers the term might as well mean "catastrophic methods of aggression" since CMAs have often squeezed small bottlers out of all available promotional activity for 52 weeks of the year (Levin 1991, p. 49).

Levin further observes that as more and more of the smaller bottlers have lost market share, a greater number of antitrust suits have been filed, which have typically argued that CMAs are "unreasonable contracts, combinations or conspiracies" that either attempt to "monopolize the soft drink market in specific geographical areas" or "require exclusive dealing in some way" (1991, 49). Despite the negative impact on competitors, Levin notes that the U.S. courts have usually upheld the validity of CMAs as "ordinary marketing methods." Prior to the 1990s, antitrust laws assumed that such tactics resulted in competitive injury. (Levin 1994, p. 129). Yet, during the 1990s the courts shifted their focus away from the nature of the conduct and concentrated instead on the injury to competition in the abstract. Thus,

> The beginning point of the Supreme Court's reasoning is that the antitrust laws protect competition, not competitors, and that all of the antitrust laws must "be construed consistently" with the "broader" policy. The issue was not whether the marketing method under review was part of "a predatory pricing scheme designed to purge competition from the . . . market" but, rather, did it in fact threaten to injure competition rather than competitors (Levin 1994, p. 129).

Despite the odds, it is sometimes possible for smaller brands to win a judgment against industry giants if they have the resources to finance a long-term court battle. For example, in 2000 nine bottlers and distributors of Royal Crown Cola (the third-ranked cola brand at the time with a 1.1% share according to *Beverage Digest* 2002 figures) won a judgment against Coca-Cola and its largest bottler, Coca-Cola Enterprises (CCE), though the decision came six years after the suit was filed (Hays 2000). The plaintiffs contended that Coke and CCE had unfairly tried to keep them out of supermarkets and convenience stores since the early 1990s by demanding exclusive advertising, displays, signs, and vending machines through CMAs. After a six-week trial, a jury found Coke and CCE guilty of breaking Texas antitrust laws and ordered them to pay a total of $15.6 million. PepsiCo and its local bottler were also named as co-defendants and paid an undisclosed amount to settle out of court (Hays 2000). Unfortunately, the victory for Royal Crown bottlers and distributors came too late; several of the plaintiffs had filed bankruptcy and were out of business by the time that the court rendered its decision (DeSpain 2001). Royal Crown Cola was sold to Cadbury Schweppes in 2000 (*Beverage Digest* 2002).

CMAs have taken their toll on Double-Cola as well. Alnoor Dhanani, current president of Double-Cola, agrees that CMAs and shelf space are the most serious issues facing the company (*Beverage World* 2001). DeSpain said that in one community, where Double-Cola was performing well in a convenience chain,

> Company A went in, offered big bucks through a CMA to move Double-Cola out of the store. Double-Cola asked the chain if they could go back in with their own visi-coolers [*refrigerated units usually placed near the check-out lanes for impulse purchases*] to which the chain agreed. After all, Company A had only asked for doors in the cooler. However, after Double-Cola put their visi-coolers in the stores, Company A went back and told the chain they would give the chain $2,000 for each visi-cooler they would take out. Fortunately, in that round Double-Cola stayed. However, Company B has now given the chain $1 million in upfront money for the coming year, and Double-Cola is reduced to a shelf or less on the bottom of a cooler door (DeSpain 2001).

The ultimate questions regarding questionable business practices include not only what happens to small businesses and the people they employ—a highly significant question in itself—but what effect these practices have on consumers. The problem is that the brands that ultimately gain the right to shelf space in the grocery store are not chosen based on consumer demand, past sales volume, or product quality, but instead are the result of "highly secretive bidding wars" between retailers and manufacturers (Aalberts and Jennings 1999, p. 213). Most consumers recognize that not all brands can survive in the marketplace, and they will quickly reject the undeserving ones. Yet, the current system doesn't give them that opportunity, for it is not the consumers who decide which products live or die on the shelf, but the manufacturer with the deepest pockets.

Industry sources agree that the real losers are consumers. When retailers ask companies to buy shelf space and when one or two brands dominate ad buying through CMAs, their actions leave consumers out of the mix and are in direct opposition to basic merchandising concepts. These practices:

> ... are not selling a customer, they're buying a customer. This damages our entire ability to sell product based on profitability, volume, attractiveness, consumer acceptance and basic merchandising realism (Phillips 2000, p. 163).

CONCLUSIONS

This case study posed three research questions and concluded that despite the desire among consumers and employees to keep the Double-Cola products alive, the company must wage a fiercely competitive war in a harsh, anti-competitive environment. Double-Cola's plight is not unique, for the story of the underdog plays out again and again, each time with fewer competitors remaining.

Part of the current soft drink war has roots in the past. History shows that two different visions arose for competing against market leader Coca-Cola. As owner of Double-Cola, Charles Little took the path of least resistance: he trusted that the formula itself would guarantee success, he refused to risk assets, and he believed that he could carve out a small niche that would keep the company profitable and manageable. As CEO of Pepsi in 1950, Alfred Steele took the path of greatest resistance: he believed the company could compete against and even "beat" Coke, he took risks, and he committed the company to a position of sustained growth through innovative campaigns.

During the last half of the 20th century, Coca-Cola and Pepsi-Cola each stood on firm foundations that allowed them to extend their product lines, acquire new products, enter into exclusive arrangements with organizations, widely expand their markets internationally, and develop successful marketing campaigns. Double-Cola (and other soft drink companies with small market shares) made tactical errors along the way, which put them too far behind the two giants to compete at their level and forced them to be niche players. Unfortunately, by the 1980s small companies faced an unforgiving retail environment, where slotting fees and calendar marketing agreements were the game pieces in the soft drink wars. Industry experts commented that not only is the little guy "getting littler" but he is going "out of business" (Ricks 1985).

Given the legal protection—or lack thereof—to small manufacturers by the FTC and the courts, Pepsi's path has proven the only effective one in the current competitive environment against market-leader Coca-Cola. Of all competitors, Pepsi is perhaps the only one that can afford to wage time-consuming legal battles and has deep enough pockets to meet Coke's ability to pay for CMAs and shelf access fees. In fact, Coke and Pepsi have learned to make the antitrust laws work in their favor so that shelf access fees and CMAs actually benefit them against small manufacturers. In particular, the lack of shelf space available to small manufacturers disables the effectiveness of other marketing tools such as advertising, for it would be a wasted effort to advertise a product that is locked out of the retail environment.

Though it is possible for small companies to win an antitrust suit, they must have the resources to wage a long battle with no guarantee of success. If winning comes too late to save a company, it is a Pyrrhic victory. Though the anti-competitive environment disadvantages small companies, new competitors face even more overwhelming odds. In the event that a new brand of beverage becomes successful, the best that a company could hope for is that the price tag will be large when purchased by Coke or Pepsi, such as the $370 million that PepsiCo paid to acquire the SoBe line of beverages in 2000, just five years after the South Beach Beverage Co. began with $2 million (Tannenbaum 2001). SoBe entered the market as a unique, non-carbonated, "New Age" brand that distributors could carry alongside their brands of soft drinks without the beverages being in direct competition with each other.

Ironically, it is Pepsi's success in competing against Coca-Cola that makes the playing field appear level to regulators. Because there are two rivals to do battle, competition is preserved, at least in theory. However, small manufacturers and bottlers have little protection, and consumers have even less. As long as prices are kept low, regulators believe that consumers' needs are met. The "result" of competition between industry giants, which can ultimately mean the death of a brand, is not an issue that receives legal protection, despite the loss to small businesses and consumers.

When one more town loses its regional brand to the two industry giants, more is lost than a brand. We have lost part of the American dream that it is possible for everyone to compete and even succeed in corporate America. Unless new laws are adopted that protect small businesses, or unless the interpretation of antitrust laws shifts its emphasis to competitors rather than competition, consumers should expect to be left with only Coke and Pepsi as the two real choices in the soft-drink industry.

REFERENCES

Aalberts, Robert J. and Marianne M. Jennings. 1999. The Ethics of Slotting: Is This Bribery, Facilitation Marketing or Just Plain Competition? *Journal of Business Ethics,* 20 (3): 207–215.

Bentley, Cecil. 2002. Bentley: You Have One Less Hour Today for Your Favorite Drink. *Athens Banner-Herald,* April 7. www.onlineathens.com, accessed July 22, 2002.

Beverage Digest. 2002. Top-10 U.S. Soft Drink Companies and Brands for 2001. Special Issue, February 18. www.beverage-digest.com/editorial/010215, accessed July 18, 2002.

———. 1998. 1997 Top-10 Soft Drink Companies and Brands. February 12. www.beveragedigest.com/editorial/980212.html, accessed January 28, 2003.

———. 1997. 1996 Top-10 U.S. CDS Numbers: Coca-Cola Co. Up Sharply. Colas Sluggish. February 7. www.beverage-digest.com/editorial/970207.html, accessed July 11, 2002.

Beverage Industry. 1998. Truck Graphics Help Level Playing Field. 89 (10): 68–70.

———. 1996. 1940s: Industry in Transition. 87 (6): 16–17.

Beverage Industry/Annual Manual. 1990/91.

Beverage World. 2001. When Competing Gets Doubly Tough. 120 (1701) April 15: 26.

Bloom, Paul N., Gregory T. Gundlach, and Joseph P. Cannon. 2000. Slotting Allowances and Fees: Schools of Thought and the Views of Practicing Managers. *Journal of Marketing,* 64 (2): 92–108.

Bodinet, Elizabeth. 2001. Personal interview, March 5, Milwaukee, WI.

Burdette, Dick. 2001. Bottles Keep 'Em Returning. *Lexington Herald-Leader.* April 4: B3.

Butler, Rachael. 2000. Always Coca-Cola. *Beverage World,* 199 (1688) March 15: 66–69.

Christensen, C. Roland. 1977. Note on the Soft Drink Industry in the United States. *Harvard Business School* (#377–213). HBS Case Services, Boston.

Chura, Hillary. 2001. Soft Drinks: Leading Brands Hold Own, but Flavored Drinks Gaining. *Advertising Age.* 72 (September 24): 8.

Davis, Michael. 1991. Double Swims for Far Shores, Plans Splash in U.S. Cola Race. *The Chattanooga Times.* November 28: C1.

DeSpain, Joseph. 2003. Telephone interview (January 14) and email correspondence.

————. 2001. Personal correspondence by email (March to August) and personal interview May 30, Greensburg, KY.

Dunagan, J. Conrad. 2001. Sort-Drink Industry. *The Handbook of Texas Online.* www.tsha.utexas.chu/handbook/online/articles/view/SS/disyk.htm, accessed July 19, 2002.

Federal Trade Commission. 2002. Commission Denial of Petitioners' Request Regarding Slotting Allowance Guidelines. www.ftc.gov/opa/2002/06/fyi0236.htm, accessed July 15, 2002.

————. 2001. Federal Trade Commission Workshop on Slotting Allowances and Other Marketing Practices in the Grocery Industry. A Report by the Federal Trade Commission Staff, February 15. www.FTC.gov/bc/slotting/index.htm, accessed June 20, 2002.

Govan, G. E. and J. W. Livingood. 1977. *The Chattanooga Country 1540–1976,* 3rd ed. Knoxville: University of Tennessee Press.

Gulley, Phillip. 2001. *Home Town Tales: Recollections of Peace, Love, and Joy.* San Francisco: Harper.

Hammond, Claude. 2001. Small and Sweet. *The Lane Report,* www.kybiz.com/lanereport/departments/entrepreneurs, accessed July 11, 2002.

Hays, Constance L. 2000. How Coke Pushed Rivals Off the Shelf: Texas Lawsuit Reveals Some Hardball Tactics, *The New York Times,* August 6, Section 3: 1, 11.

Heritage Report. 2002. The Story of Coca-Cola. www.heritage.coca-cola.com/heritage_index.html, Accessed July 16, 2002.

Irwin, Constance L. and Andrall E. Pearson. 1987a. Note on the U.S. Soft Drink in 1986. *Harvard Business School (#9–387107).* HBS Case Services, Boston).

————. 1987b. Coca-Cola Versus Pepsi-Cola (A). *Harvard Business School* (#9–387–108). HBS Case Services, Boston.

Kelley, Kristine Portno. 1994. Double Challenge. *Beverage Industry.* 85 (2): 26–29.

Kirby, John. 1992. Telephone interview, August 2. (Kirby was VP of Sales for the Double-Cola Co. at the time of the interview.)

Levin, Lawrence R. 1994. Antitrust: Competitors vs. Competition. *Beverage World,* 113 (1562): 128–130.

————. 1991. CMAs: Competitive Merchandising Agreements or Catastrophic Methods of Aggression? *Beverage World.* 110 (1505): 49–50.

Martin, W. 1989. Sun States Officials Believe Dreams Don't Have to Fizzle. *The Times* [Gainesville, GA], August 20: C5.

McGehee, Larry. 2000. Subconscious Allegiances. *What's New.* www.wofford.edu.southernseen/2000archieve/20000612.htm, accessed July 22, 2002.

McKay, Betsy and Luhnow, David. 2002. Mexico Finds Coke and Its Bottlers Guilty of Abusing Dominant Position in Market. *Wall Street Journal,* March 8: B3.

Mitchell, Cynthia 1994a. Coca-Cola Tells Stock Analysts Private Labels Not a Major Threat. *The Atlanta Journal-Constitution,* March 17: K3.

————. 1994b. Private Label Drink Makers " Parasites," Ivester Says. *The Atlanta Journal-Constitution,* October 26: G1.

Phillips, Kent 2000. Retailer Rebates; The Death of a Salesman? Or of an Industry? *Beverage World.* 119 (October): 162–163.

Prince, Greg. 2001. The Big Picture: America Makes Its Beverage Choices. *Beverage World,* 120 (1706): 12, 14.

————. 2000. Industry Considers its Private Parts. *Beverage World,* August 15, 199 (1693): 28.

Ricks, Thomas E. 1985. Guess Who's Losing the Great Cola War: Hint: It's Not Coke and It's Not Pepsi. *Wall Street Journal,* May 8, Eastern Edition: 1, 3.

Russo, Laurie. 1998. Redesign to Denim Makes Double Play, Double's Day. *Beverage World,* 117 (1669), Periscope Edition: 1, 4.

Schreiner, Bruce. 2001. Bottler Keeps Soda Tradition Alive: Double-Cola and Ski Maintain a Loyal Customer Base in Kentucky. *The Courier-Journal, Louisville, KY.* www.courier-journal . . . localnews/20001/04/12. accessed July 12, 2002.

Senate Committee on Small Business. 1999. Bond says "Slotting Fees" Threaten Small Manufacturers, Consumer Choice. www.senate.gov/~sbc/106press/spet1499.htm, accessed February 9, 2000.

Shanks, L. Edward. 1992. Telephone interview, July 23. (Shanks was President of the Double-Cola Co. at the time of the interview.)

Sooder, Karl 1992. Personal Interview. July 21, Chattanooga, TN. (Sooder was VP of Marketing for the Double-Cola Co. at the time of the interview.)

Stake, Robert E. 1994. Case Studies (Chapter 14). In *Handbook of Qualitative Research,* edited by Norman K. Denzin and Yvonna S. Lincoln (pp. 236–247). Thousand Oaks, CA: Sage Publications.

Steinriede, Kent. 1998. Fountain War Heats Up. *Beverage Industry.* 89 (10): 32–36.

Tannenbaum, Jeffery A. 2001. Beverage Marketers See Refreshing Distribution Possibilities—PepsiCo's Acquisition of South Beach Leaves Greater Room for Lesser-Known Brands. *Wall Street Journal* (May 29): B2.

Tom, Willard K. 1999. Slotting Allowances and the Antitrust Laws. Testimony of the Federal Trade Commission before the Committee on the Judiciary U.S. House of Representatives, Washington, DC. (October 20). www.ftc.gov/os/1999/9910/slotting991020.htm, accessed June 20, 2002.

Weir, Tom. 2001. More Pressure from the Feds? *Supermarket Business,* 56 (4): 23–25.

———. 1999. Senators vs. Slotting. *Supermarket Business,* 54 (10): 1, 14–16.

Wilson, J. 1980. Chattanooga's Story. *The Chattanooga News-Free Press,* September 7.

Wolburg, Joyce M. 1993. Double-Cola–The Story of the Underdog in an Oligopoly Market. In *Contemporary Marketing History: Proceedings of the Sixth Conference on Historical Research in Marketing and Marketing Thought,* edited by Jeffrey B. Schmidt, Stanley C. Hollander, Terence Nevett, and Jagdish N. Sheth (pp. 59–68). East Lansing, MI: Michigan State University.

www.coca-cola.com. Corporate website accessed July 18, 2002.

www.double-cola.com. Corporate website accessed July 17, 2002.

www.pepsico.com. Corporate website accessed July 18, 2002.

CHAPTER 13

ECONOMIC CENSORSHIP AND FREE SPEECH
The Circle of Communication Between Advertisers, Media, and Consumers

JEF I. RICHARDS AND JOHN H. MURPHY II

> Private economic censorship occurs when an advertiser formally or functionally dictates to the mass media what the public shall or shall not hear. (Collins 1992a)

Advertising and its practitioners are criticized for causing a multitude of society's ills. Critics suggest advertisements manipulate consumers, make them materialistic, and encourage them to abandon traditional values, along with a litany of other unattractive effects (Pollay 1986). Recently, the ad industry has been characterized as a serious threat to our "free press," using its financial leverage to dictate media content and censor the information received by the populace.

The purpose of this article is to assess the advertising industry's responsibility in "economic censorship" (EC). We will begin by reviewing the relationship between advertising and the media vehicles in which it appears.

USING MONEY TO CENSOR

Pressure from Advertisers

Advertising provides the primary source of revenue for most news and entertainment media in this country (Bagdikian 1992, p. 115). This is both the blessing and the bane of modern media management. Because it is advertising that pays the bills, managers of newspapers, magazines, television, and radio stations must keep their advertisers happy: a task not unlike feeding crocodiles. The inherent danger is that advertisers might use their economic influence to act as unofficial censors of "the press," thereby barring media from publishing or broadcasting certain material.

An illustration of this problem is found in an article by Wolf (1992), in which he describes a hypothetical fact situation:

> An explosion rocks a clinic that performs abortions. A reporter from the Los Angeles Times is sent to the scene, where pickets from both pro-choice and pro-life groups are present.

From *Journal of Current Issues and Research in Advertising,* vol. 18, no. 1 (Spring 1996). Copyright © 1996 by CtC Press. Reprinted with permission.

He interviews both sides, determined to come up with a story that is both objective and thought-provoking.

As the reporter is writing the article, the paper's publisher receives a call from not one, not two, but six of the paper's largest advertisers saying that they are pulling their advertising from tomorrow's edition if any story about the abortion clinic bombing, no matter how objective, appears. Their attitude is polite but firm—they do not wish to be associated with such an issue. (Wolf 1992)

The publisher has two options: (1) run the story and risk losing a large percent of the paper's revenue, or (2) accede to the advertisers' wishes and risk the possibility that many readers will never learn about this bombing.

While this particular situation is fictional, similar circumstances are relatively common. Wolf points out that when his television show, NBC's "Law and Order," ran an episode about the bombing of an abortion clinic, $500,000 worth of advertising was pulled from the show, and an episode about assisted suicide for AIDS victims resulted in an a $350,000 pullout (Wolf 1992). All three of the major television networks have experienced advertiser pull-outs of this sort. Exhibit 13.1 includes a few of the situations, publicly attributed to advertiser pull-outs, where networks incurred financial losses.

Exhibit 13.1
Examples of Economic Censorship—Television

- In 1973, CBS re-ran an episode of "Maude," in which the leading character obtained an abortion. No national sponsors purchased ad time, and approximately 39 CBS affiliates even refused to run the episode (Hoffman 1992).
- When "Jesus of Nazareth" was broadcast by NBC in 1977, General Motors withdrew its ads after fundamentalist religious groups—that had not even seen the program—protested. However, the program turned out to be a big hit (Rosenberg 1987).
- ABC claims its series "Soap," which ran from 1977 to 1981, lost $3 million per year as the result of advertisers refusing to sponsor it. "Soap" was subject to pickets, threatened boycotts, and a letter-writing campaign, mostly inspired by several religious organizations upset at early reports of sexual content in the series (Margulies 1985).
- McDonald's restaurant chain sent a memo to its franchise holders advising them to keep ad spots out of ABC's mini-series, "The Thorn Birds," in 1983. The series dealt with a Catholic priest involved in a love affair with a girl he had practically raised from childhood (Clark 1983).
- The ABC mini-series "Amerika," in 1987, depicted an America ruled by the Kremlin. It was subjected to heavy criticism by a variety of special-interest groups. Chrysler Corporation, while denying it was motivated by those criticisms, withdrew $5,000,000 worth of advertising from the show (Rosenberg 1987).

- In 1989, ABC's "Thirtysomething" lost over $1 million when an episode depicted two gay men in bed together, and lost another $500,000 when the gay couple appeared in a later episode (Weinstein 1990).
- ABC's "Geraldo" talk show, which frequently dealt with controversial issues, also met with advertising losses (Mahler 1990).
- Mennen Company withdrew advertising from ABC's "Heartbeat" medical drama because the show included a lesbian nurse (Blau 1989).
- IBM, Acura, Anheuser-Busch, Toyota, Sharp Electronics, and Spalding all decided to withdraw or reduce their advertising commitments to ABC and/or ESPN telecasts of the 1990 PGA Championship golf tournament when the founder of an Alabama country club announced that his club would not be pressured into admitting blacks (McManus 1990).
- A few years ago Domino's Pizza Inc. pulled advertising from NBC's "Saturday Night Live" because of its allegedly "offensive" skits (Blau 1989).
- More recently Mazda pulled its advertising from "Saturday Night Live" for ostensibly the same reasons (Du Brow 1991).
- Ralston Purina backed out of the same show because in one skit the word "penis" was mentioned several times (Carton 1989).
- A made-for-TV movie about a Chicago lawyer who dies of AIDS, "An Early Frost," cost NBC $600,000 worth of advertising revenue when it first ran in 1985, even though it garnered respectable ratings, and lost another $1 million when it was rerun about six months later (McDougal 1991b).
- NBC's "Quantum Leap," a show that has won many awards, also faced advertiser withdrawals amounting to $500,000 when an episode dealt with homosexuality in a military school (Rosenberg 1992).
- NBC incurred a similar loss when it aired an episode of "Lifestories" that discussed gay television reporter and his battle against AIDS (Weinstein 1990).
- NBC also lost advertisers when it ran a movie about the controversial "Roe v. Wade" Supreme Court decision on abortion (Rosenberg 1992).
- CBS, too, has lost advertisers as the result of "controversial" programming. For example, advertisers have pulled out of two of the network's most popular series: "Murphy Brown" and "Northern Exposure" (Du Brow 1991).
- An episode of "China Beach" that dealt with abortion also experienced advertiser pull-outs, and was not rerun (Carman 1990).
- Robert Iger, president of ABC Entertainment, claimed that research showed ABC lost $14 million in the 1989–90 season, $9 million of which was attributable to controversial programming. He claimed that ABC lost over $1 million in one movie about Rock Hudson that dealt with his homosexuality (Carman 1990).
- In 1994, "NYPD Blue" won more Emmy nominations than any series in history (Pergament 1994), won both People's Choice and Golden Globe awards, and consistently ranked in the "top 20" shows on television. But, because of controversy surrounding the show's occasional depictions of nude rear-ends and use of salty language, ABC was unable to attract major advertisers and consequently lost money on the show (Miller 1994).

Although the evidence is primarily anecdotal, it is conceivable that in some cases the losses result from poor management rather than advertiser withdrawals. However, the sheer number of losses and the circumstances surrounding each is strongly suggestive of EC.

That EC is behind these losses is particularly likely in light of modern media buying practices. It is well established that advertisers now systematically avoid shows that deal with certain "hot-button issues," such as abortion and homosexuality (Silverman 1991; Du Brow 1991). In fact, many major advertisers employ outside firms to pre-screen advance tapes of programs in which their commercials are scheduled to appear (Carter 1990; Wolf 1992). One screener explains, "Basically, we look for what we call the Big Six: sex, violence, profanity, drugs, alcohol and religion" (Carter 1990).

Some of those companies maintain "hit lists" of programs they advise clients to avoid. One screening firm, Telerep, reportedly had a 36-page hit list in 1990, that included some of the most popular shows on television (Mahler 1990). For example, one of the most popular syndicated shows in America, "A Current Affair," appeared on Telerep's list and was avoided by 94 potential sponsors (Mahler 1990). Today, advertisers have contract stipulations that allow them to back out of a media purchase if, after pre-screening a network show, they are uncomfortable with its content (Wolf 1992).

While the most publicized advertiser withdrawals revolve around programs with controversial subject matter, pull-outs are not limited to controversies. They commonly result from stories or television scripts that reflect poorly on the advertiser. For example, a "Saturday Night Live" script, co-written by Phil Hartman and guest host Tom Arnold, poked fun at Ford and General Motors (GM) executives. When a GM subsidiary reviewed the script and balked, references to Ford and GM were replaced with fictitious names (Piccoli 1992). Reflecting similar corporate concerns, one media buyer admitted, "We had a problem with an episode of 'Little House on the Prairie' because wild dogs were chasing a girl and we had a Puppy-Chow ad. We have to pull cat food commercials out of 'Alf' because Alf is constantly trying to eat the cat" (Kleinfield 1989).

Neither are advertiser pull-outs (or threats to pull-out) limited to television. Exhibit 13.2 provides a list of some known advertiser defections from newspapers and magazines.

Again, many of these offer only circumstantial evidence of EC, and some advertisers deny punative intent. However, some of these cases leave little room for doubt. For example, Procter & Gamble reportedly warned it would pull ads from any newspaper or magazine—as well as broadcast stations—to run stories that singled out its products in what it considered to be an unfair manner (Ramirez 1990). And when the Vice President of Advertising for Radio Shack became upset by a story that appeared in *InfoWorld,* he ordered his Media Department to cancel all contracts for ad placement in that magazine and 60 other publications owned by the same company. His letter of complaint, announcing that decision, was published in the magazine (Beckerman 1985).

There is little question that a great deal of pressure is being placed on media managers to modify (or eliminate) programming and editorial content that advertisers find objectionable. Whether media are obliging these requests is somewhat more difficult to determine, since they are unlikely to publicize such facts.

Media Acquiescence

Robert N. O'Neil, director of the Thomas Jefferson Center for the Protection of Free Expression, acknowledges, "There is increased evidence" that the media do censor news stories about advertisers (Riley 1992). Gloria Steinem states, "I don't think anyone questions whether or not advertisers influence the editorial content of most women's magazines. It's already taken for granted that they do" (Enrico 1990). And Richard Kipling, of the Los Angeles Times, admits:

> I get calls from reporters across the country who are fearful . . . about the increasing pressure to do stories pleasing to advertisers. They've questioned the journalistic value of these 'stories' and have been told simply to find a way to make the 'stories' work. They're panicked that their careers are in jeopardy, that they have only once choice—do the advertiser-friendly stories or join the burgeoning ranks of the journalistic unemployed. (Collins 1992b)

These allegations are supported by a recent survey of 147 daily newspapers that found more than 90% of editors have been pressured by advertisers and more than one-third of them claimed advertisers had succeeded in influencing news at their papers (Soley and Craig 1992). A recent study of almost 100 magazines, covering a span of 25 years, found that magazines relying heavily on cigarette advertising are far less likely than others to publish stories about the health hazards associated with smoking (Lipman 1992). And some of the examples in Exhibits 13.1 and 13.2 strongly suggest that media do, indeed, acquiesce to advertiser demands on occasion.

Advertising can, of course, be used as a vehicle for free speech. Businesses and citizens, alike, can use it to voice opinions and convey information that the editorial content of media omits, assuming these same media will publish the ad. In years past, such ads were called "advertorials" (Rotzoll, Haefner, and Sandage 1976, p. 134). But today the term "advertorials" represents yet another sign that advertiser influence is growing, because the word has taken on a new meaning: commercial advertisements that masquerade as editorial content (Fahri 1991). Media companies seem to have no objection to advertisers disguising promotional messages as "news." "Infomercials," "documercials," product placement in television shows, and commercial video news releases all represent instances where media allow advertisers to hide a marketing message in the clothing of non-advertising content (Collins and Skover 1993, p. 718).

It also has become commonplace to find special advertising sections of newspapers and magazines: automotive, real estate and travel sections of newspapers that run only "positive" stories about those products and services (Topping 1992). For example, the *advertising* department of the *Houston Chronicle* reportedly provides all the "news" for the following sections of the paper: home, townhouse, apartments, travel, technology, livestock, and swimming pools (Bagdikian 1992, p. 165).

This is not to suggest that all vehicles do advertisers' bidding. Indeed, when Macy's confronted *The New York Times* (see Exhibit 13.2), the *Times* refused to give-in (Dorfman 1989). NBC went forward with its made-for-TV movie, "Roe vs. Wade," in spite of anticipated advertiser pull-outs (Graham 1989). In fact, most of the television series episodes mentioned in Exhibit 13.1 were run, even though the networks incurred significant losses. Undoubtedly many, if not most, media vehicles resist all or most attempts by advertisers to dictate news and entertainment content.

To date, it appears that television networks and magazines are more prone to such EC than newspapers (Goerne 1992), and women's magazines are especially susceptible (Henry 1979). However, even where there are no tangible signs that media are giving-in, pressure from advertisers may be resulting in a less visible form of censorship: a chilling effect (Baker 1992; Baker 1994; Kurtz 1991). That is, reporters and producers may avoid stories critical of advertisers or about controversial topics—consciously or subconsciously—even where media owners and managers make no such demands on them. One producer remarked, "This kind of climate alters the way you think. You find yourself censoring yourself. You start to edit yourself around controversial areas you might want to be examining" (Silverman 1991).

Exhibit 13.2

Examples of Economic Censorship—Print Media

- A few years ago R.H. Macy & Co., one of *The New York Times*' three biggest advertisers, told the *Times* to remove a reporter from Macy's beat after the reporter published a book critical of the retailer (Dorfman 1989).
- The *Seattle Times* experienced a sharp reduction in advertising for Nordstrom stores after it published a series of articles about the retailer's labor problems (Zachary 1992).
- *Ms.* magazine closed its doors for failure to attract sufficient advertising. One reason: Advertisers were concerned about appearing in a magazine that took a strong stand on issues like abortion and sexual preference (Enrico 1990).
- After a bad review of "Patriot Games" appeared in *Daily Variety,* and a series of articles questioning exploitative marketing for "Juice" ran in the *Hollywood Reporter,* Paramount Pictures decided not to place its traditional congratulatory ads for "Patriot Games" in those publications (Welkos 1992).
- The *Arkansas Democrat* was chided for telling a columnist not to criticize advertisers. John Robert Star, managing editor of that paper, declared, "Our policy is no different from every other paper I know about: People hired as columnists by the paper don't trash advertisers" (Horovitz 1992).
- *Omni* magazine lost two of its top editors in 1990. They quit because the magazine's management acquiesced to the desires of an advertiser and ran an ad on the front cover of the publication (Donaton 1990).
- In 1993, Mercedes-Benz of North American warned 30 magazines not to print its ads in any issue containing an article that portrayed Germany or Mercedes-Benz in a negative light (Associated Press 1993).
- In the late 1980s, Reverend Donald Wildmon's American Family Association began a campaign against *Playboy* magazine—because of what Wildmon felt was obscene content—encouraging a boycott and letter-writing campaign targeted at the magazine's advertisers. Chrysler received hundreds of letters, and subsequently pulled its ads from *Playboy* (Farhi 1991).
- In the early 1980s, a major advertiser insisted that a press release concerning its financial problems be published exactly as written in the *Trenton Times.* A reporter who re-wrote the release was subsequently fired (Shaw 1987).
- Several years ago the *Atlanta Journal* published a story about Eastern Airline's baggage handling system at the Atlanta airport. The paper lost an estimated $100,000 in advertising by Eastern as a result (Shaw 1987).
- In the mid-1980s the *Wall Street Journal* ran a some stories about Mobil Oil Company and its executives. The company stopped advertising in the *Journal,* even though it had run $500,000 worth of ads in the paper the prior year (Shaw 1987).
- The *Umpqua Weekly Examiner,* in Oregon, was forced out of business after running a series of stories critical of the timber industry and others. The publisher blamed ad withdrawals, resulting from the efforts of Douglas Timber Operators urging advertisers to pull their ads dollars from the paper (Robertson 1993).

- WFLD-Channel 32 general manager Stacey Marks-Bronner was the subject of a critical article that appeared in the *Chicago Tribune* in 1994. The station pulled $42,000 worth of ads in protest (Feder 1994).
- In 1992, the Duluth, Minnesota, *News-Tribune* published a column that advised readers how to sell their home without using a real estate agent. As a result, the paper lost nearly half of its real estate agency advertising (Cox 1992).
- More than 40 automobile dealers cancelled their ads in the *San Jose Mercury News* when an article titled "A car buyer's guide to sanity" appeared in the paper. The dealers objected to the tone of the article, which they felt implied car sellers should be considered unethical adversaries in the negotiation process (Simon 1994).
- When the Hartford *Courant* newspaper ran an article that urged "buyer wariness" of car dealers, local dealers began an advertising boycott (Zachary 1992).
- When the Ogden, Utah, *Evening Standard* ran a full-page story that featured an auto dealer in another city, dealers in the Ogden area were outraged and withdrew their advertising (Stein 1992).
- In December 1985, the Federal Trade Commission charged 105 automobile dealerships, including some in the Detroit area, with antitrust violations. When the *Detroit Free Press* reported the story, several local dealerships cancelled their ads (*Washington Post 1986*).

Whether because of direct pressure from advertisers, or as a result of self-censorship by editors, reporters, and producers, clearly some editorial and entertainment content in today's media has been filtered or even biased. The ultimate consequence is that consumers of those media are receiving limited information.

The Danger

The impact of pocketbook censorship on the citizenry is no less pernicious than government censorship. As Baker recognized:

> Anything preventing the press from effectively providing information and commentary that the public would want or that an "independent" press would conclude the public needs, is a serious threat to sound social policy and a properly functioning democracy. (Baker 1992, p. 2153)

While the First Amendment holds no sway over non-governmental censorship, any practice restricting public viewing, listening, or reading options—regardless of who initiated that policy—directly conflicts with the fundamental democratic principle on which that Amendment is predicated: to encourage public debate and diversity of ideas. This is evident in judicial recognition of "a profound national commitment to the principle that debate on public issues should be uninhibited, robust and wide-open" (*New York Times v. Sullivan* 1964). Our democracy is predicated on the idea that objective "truth" can be found only through the exposition of an unhindered variety of subjective opinions (*United States v. Associated Press* 1943; Mill 1859).

This principle may be especially important where, as is frequently the case with EC, controversial matter is screened from public consideration. The Supreme Court has noted that "a function of free speech . . . is to invite dispute. It may indeed best serve its high purpose when it induces a condition of unrest, creates dissatisfaction with conditions as they are, or even stirs people to anger" (*Terminiello v. Chicago* 1949).

EC, therefore, is a serious threat to this cornerstone of our society, and should not be taken lightly. An obvious solution, of course, would be to prohibit such activity just as the First Amendment forbids government-instituted censorship. In fact, some commentators recently have suggested that regulatory response is needed, and that the primary target of those regulations should be advertisers (Collins 1992a; Baker 1992; Baker 1994). The remainder of this article will discuss the propriety of this approach.

REGULATING ECONOMIC CENSORSHIP

Placing the Blame

There is a tendency to blame much of this censorship on advertisers. A renowned observer of advertising, Sid Bernstein, once commented that there are people "who are absolutely certain that advertisers, individually and collectively, have a stranglehold on the neck of all advertising media, both print and broadcast" (Bernstein 1991). If advertisers are in control, clearly they are to blame for this EC.

Television producer Richard Kramer decried, "I'm really sickened by this and feel we're being censored by advertisers who are not equipped to make this judgment. At this point in history, it's up to organizations like ABC to show they will not be victims of advertisers' whims" (Rosenberg 1990). Radio Moscow commentator Vladimir Posner criticized American media for lack of diversity in its news broadcasts, concluding that the sponsors ultimately were responsible for this "political and social desert" (Colford 1990).

Law professor C. Edwin Baker also pins most of the blame on advertisers. He declares, "[P]rivate entities in general and advertisers in particular constitute the most consistent and the most pernicious 'censors' of media content" (Baker 1992). As a solution he recommends a special tax on advertising, designed to shift the power from advertisers to readers.

Communication professors Soley and Craig (1992) seem to agree that the ad industry is responsible. They note, "The assertion that advertisers attempt to influence what the public sees, hears, and reads in the mass media is perhaps the most damning of all criticisms of advertising, but this criticism isn't acknowledged in most advertising textbooks." They suggest this is an ethical issue that should be taught to advertising students.

Even reports that do not explicitly name the guilty tend to imply the ad industry is the root of the problem. One news story refers to "the taint of advertiser influence" (Topping 1992), one discusses TV network attempts to "withstand advertiser pressures" (Silverman 1991), and yet another talks about it being counterproductive for networks to "knuckle under to the pressure of sponsor defections" (Weinstein 1990). And one media ethics book refers to the "advertiser onslaught" facing the press (Day 1991, p. 184). The clear message is that advertisers are in control, and consequently bear the responsibility.

A recent report published by the Center for the Study of Commercialism (CSC) placed this blame more squarely on the shoulders of advertisers (Collins 1992a). That report stated:

> Who controls the press? The answer should be apparent—ultimately, those who control the purse. . . . In contemporary America, advertisers wield much of this monetary might, meaning that much press independence is potentially surrendered in their name. (p. 1)

It concluded that "[s]elf-censorship represents a victory of advertising influence over editorial integrity, of commercialism over content" (p. 31), and recommended several actions to rectify this problem, including laws aimed at (1) prohibiting advertisers from exerting influence, and (2) protecting journalists who blow the whistle on such influence. That report received considerable media attention (e.g., Goerne 1992; Horovitz 1992; Collins 1992b), leading to additional negative publicity for the advertising industry.

Most of these commentators, including the CSC report, acknowledge that advertising is not solely responsible. After all, advertisers would have no power if the media refused to cooperate. Yet the picture being painted is that economic realities are placing media at the mercy of advertisers, if they are to survive (e.g., Silverman 1991; Rosenberg 1990).

The model implied by this process is top-down and linear, from advertisers to consumers (see Exhibit 13.3). Under this model it is consumers who are the victims of advertiser force and media acquiescence. Advertisers are seen as imposing their collective will upon media, thereby infringing on the "freedom of the press," and limiting the free flow of information to consumers. This viewpoint, however, idealizes media as an altruistic endeavor to provide citizens with news, art, and entertainment, without respect to its free-market nature.

The relationship between these three parties is much more symbiotic than suggested in Exhibit 13.3. To the contrary, each party has the power (whether or not that power is exercised) to influence the other two, as illustrated by the "circle of communication" in Exhibit 13.4. Communication, in this model, encompasses all means of persuasion, by which the three parties influence the actions of the others. This includes, among others, the choice of editorial and entertainment matter in the media, the advertisements, the products sold by the advertisers, consumer complaints, and consumers' actions when buying or refusing to buy products.

The role that each of these parties plays in so-called "economic censorship" is discussed below. We will begin by considering the alleged victims of this censorship: consumers.

Vocal Consumers

It is indisputable that consumers often receive sterilized, biased, information from some media. But, in large part, this is a condition of their own making. Advertiser withdrawal from, or avoidance of, media virtually always results from feared consumer response to those media. And in many cases, consumers are actively petitioning advertisers to avoid certain media content.

Conservative consumer groups, collectively dubbed the "New Puritans," have bombarded advertisers with threats and complaints (Elliott 1992). "I call it advertising terrorism," says Jack Trout, of Trout & Ries. "A lot of folks have realized they can get their point of view across by jumping on the phones and threatening a boycott [of advertised products]" (Farhi 1989).

One conservative consumer group, Christian Leaders for Responsible Television [CLeaR-TV], was established by a Methodist minister named Donald Wildmon in 1986. Since then CLeaR-TV has spearheaded numerous boycotts—or threats of boycotts—against advertisers that sponsor television programs the organization identified as "un-Christian," sinful, or otherwise objectionable (Mahler 1990; Cox 1989). Wildmon says, for example, that he does not want to see homosexuality on television (Enrico 1990).

Another group, the National Coalition on Television Violence [NCTV], likewise has been involved in writing to advertisers about sponsorship of shows its members feel contain excessive violence, gratuitous sex, and Satanic overtones (Mahler 1990). Americans for Responsible Television (Silverman 1991) and Concerned Citizens for Quality Television (McDougal 1991a)

Figure 13.3 **Top-down Model of the Communication Process**

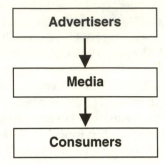

Figure 13.4 **Circle of Communication Model of Influences on Media Content**

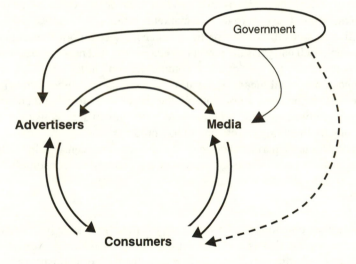

are yet two more such organizations. Each of these groups claims many victories in convincing advertisers to avoid buying time on certain shows (e.g., Fahey 1991, p. 657).

Conservative groups are not the only vocal consumers. There are, for instance, a variety of special interest groups that champion "politically correct" media content (Kurtz 1991). One example, the Nurses Association, successfully took on Chrysler and Sears for advertising on the show "Nightingales," because of its depiction of nurses as "boy-toys" (Clark 1989). Peter Tortorici, executive vice president of CBS Entertainment, admits that some things "All in the Family" used to do—especially the racist and sexist comments of its main character, Archie Bunker—might not get on the air today (Du Brow 1991).

In at least one instance an entire industry threatened an advertiser. Stroh Brewery withdrew sponsorship of an environmental program, *Ancient Forests: Rage Over Trees,* when the timber industry planned to boycott the company (Fahey 1991).

This proactive approach of consumers is not a new phenomenon, but has become more popular in recent years. In the distant past consumers relied heavily on government regulation to block "offensive" communication content, but a series of First Amendment cases have placed limits on government's ability to restrict material that offends some people (Schechter 1992). The result has been an increased popularity of advertiser boycotts. Reagan Administration deregulation of broadcast media may have been an additional catalyst for groups feeling they must rely on their own initiative rather than on government action (Hill and Beaver 1991).

Even where consumers are not *actively* trying to affect media content, they may well play a *passive* role. Advertisers, like politicians, want to alienate no one. Where they suspect consumers will be offended by media content, advertisers will avoid placing their ads in that context, even if no one threatens a boycott.

Consumers clearly do have a voice in EC, by expressing their desires to advertisers. They also have the power to actively voice those preferences directly to the media, but that approach is rare (Hill and Beaver 1991). They tend to declare their opinions to media passively, through rating points. If they dislike a program or a vehicle, they simply choose a different one.

The reason why consumers reserve active protests for advertisers rather than media is subject to speculation. It has been suggested this is because advertisers hold the purse strings (Collins 1992a), but this ignores the fact that an effective boycott of the medium or program would reduce ratings and therefore make the medium less attractive to advertisers. Consequently, the same effect could be realized by communicating directly with media rather than advertisers.

A more logical explanation is that boycotters are not trying to change the media *they* use, but rather to restrict what *other people* see and hear in the media (Fahey 1991, p. 654). After all, if boycotters are bothered by the content of media they use, they have the option of simply changing media. But if those protesters are not regular viewers of a particular program, their refusal to watch that program will have no measurable effect on program ratings. In this case, they have no leverage with which to control media content. Boycotting the advertisers, on the other hand, permits them leverage over such content.

Of course, these vocal consumers do not represent all consumers. So one might argue that the silent majority has no voice in this circle of communication, and that it is these silent consumers who are victimized by EC. In reality, if they were to take a more active role and collectively demand that media address controversial issues, both advertisers and media would readily comply. Alternatively, if these "victims" are sufficiently upset about the lack of information caused by EC, they can send a message to advertisers and media by giving preference to those media that accept no advertising. If they neither protest nor switch to alternative media, we can assume that most consumers are willing to accept the limitations of their current media.

Contrary to representations of advertiser-as-dictator, consumers command significant power in this process. Indeed, much of the recent EC is a direct result of consumers exercising that power. But it would be unfair to place the full blame for EC on consumers, because media also hold a share of power.

Free-Market Media

Collins (1992a; 1992b) and Baker (1992; 1994) claim that, as a result of advertiser pressure, the press is no longer "free." But the press *is* free. It is free to sell to advertisers, or solely to consumers. If a medium wishes to avoid advertiser influence, it could avoid selling ad space and finance its efforts strictly through consumer subscriptions. A "free press" refers to the rights of the press, not the rights of the audience. These commentators seem to confuse the right of the press to publish what it wants with the right of consumers to get untarnished information. To think these two rights coterminous is to romanticize media. What most media want to publish is whatever will make the most money.

Media companies are businesses. Most contemporary media have chosen to finance their businesses by selling ad space or time. And that space or time is worthless without readers, listeners, or viewers, which means these businesses serve two groups of customers: advertisers and consumers. While individual vehicles have complete freedom to print or broadcast whatever they desire, and to refuse the requests of advertisers and consumers, the principles of business require that they serve the wants and needs of those customers. This may not be what many envision as the ideal "free press," but it is good business.

In their efforts to remain fiscally strong, media sometimes find it advantageous to avoid certain content. But advertisers' demands are not their only concern. At times media alter content for the benefit of their other customers, the readers or viewers. In fact, even advertisers—who pay the bills—sometimes find their interests subjugated to those of the readers and viewers, when media choose to censor *ad* content. Quintessence, for example, recently ran afoul of NBC and CBS with an ad for its Jovan fragrance. The ad was a spoof of network censors, and the networks saw little humor in it (Hume 1992). Such content could reflect poorly on viewers' attitudes toward the networks.

Benetton Services, which has built a reputation for controversial advertising, recently had similar problems with *The New Yorker.* A Benetton ad scheduled to run in an issue of the magazine depicted an albino Zulu woman among a large group of other Zulu women. The albino woman looks embarrassed, and the others seem to be shunning her. Tina Brown, editor of *The New Yorker,* rejected the ad for the issue in which it was to appear; an issue containing an article about Malcolm X. She explained, "This ad is seeming to address the same issue, but obviously in a very punchy, advertising way. We wanted to make sure we didn't seem to be mixing advertising and editorial" (Elliott 1992). Again, it was readers rather than the advertiser that Tina Brown felt compelled to keep happy.

In 1991, Fox became the first and only network to accept condom advertising. In spite of national concerns about AIDS, other social diseases, and teenage pregnancy, the three established networks held fast to a universal policy against accepting these ads. The reason, of course, was a fear that the public would be offended and, hence, stop watching that network (Kitman 1991).

Another, particularly notable, instance of advertising being censored was the recent flurry of debate over whether or not college newspapers should publish advertisements by Bradley R. Smith (Bishop 1991). What makes this case especially important is that the ads in question were not "commercial" in nature, but rather were paid "editorial" or "opinion" ads. In late 1991 and early 1992 two full-page ads were sent by Smith to college newspapers around the country, in an attempt to publish them. The first ad was entitled, "The Holocaust Controversy: The Case For Open Debate," and the second was labelled, "Falsus in Uno, Falsus in Omnibus . . . The "Human Soap" Holocaust Myth." Both ads argued that popular historical accounts of Jews being executed en masse during World War II are exaggerated. On virtually all college campuses where the ads were considered, heated disputes resulted. In the end, several campus accepted the ad and several rejected it (Oshinskky and Curtis 1991; Warlick 1992; UPI 1992; Brooks 1992).

The debate at the University of Texas was particularly heated. Following a series of decisions that went back and forth, regarding whether to run the ads, students and faculty associated with the newspaper were called names, received death threats, and warned of potential lawsuits. Clearly, many readers did not want the ad published. Leaders of the campus Student Association even threatened to withhold the newspaper's funding if it should run the ad (Brooks 1992).

Further evidence that media business decisions adversely affect advertising—rather than just news and entertainment—content is the existence of advertising acceptability departments at many newspapers, magazines, and broadcast companies. Though some of these acceptability standards reflect legal concerns, many are designed to avoid offending readers or viewers.

Like consumers, the press clearly shares the power in this triad. That power is used to determine how best to serve all its customers, which sometimes requires limiting content desired by either consumers *or* advertisers. It has been suggested that advertisers have disproportionate power in this relationship, but the fact that ad content is also subject to EC seems to disconfirm that hypothesis. To substantiate this disproportionate power, critics point to such things as the special ad sections (e.g., real estate) that are commonplace in newspapers and magazines. But these special sections are not the result of advertiser demands; media offer them to create new opportunities for ad sales.

These are all reasonable (if not sound) business decisions, and media companies are businesses. Since advertisers are also subject to the rules of the marketplace, their decisions are very much like those of the press.

Advertisers

Baker (1992; 1994) argues there is an imbalance of power. He contends, "Of course, the medium's attempt to obtain advertising revenue leads it to tilt media content toward what advertisers, not readers or viewers, want" (Baker 1992, p. 2180). However, these two wants are not mutually exclusive. A medium is only beneficial to advertisers if consumers use it, and consumers will not use a medium if they are unhappy with its content. Consequently, a smart advertiser will never make demands of a medium that will reduce audience satisfaction.

Quite the contrary, advertisers seek to attract the largest possible numbers of consumers. In addition, they want those consumers to like their brands. A Coca-Cola spokesperson explains, "We are in the business to make friends" (Hill and Beaver 1991). Consequently, it is not surprising that advertisers tend to avoid content that might cause some consumers to either change vehicles or develop negative attitudes toward the sponsor. Betsy Frank, of the Saatchi & Saatchi advertising agency, explains:

> When we use TV, we're not using it to support First Amendment rights or artistic freedoms, we're using it because it's a good business decision for our client, and nobody wants the result of a business decision to be loss of customers rather than gains. (Silverman 1991)

If placing their ad in a vehicle will cause them to lose money, it makes no sense for them to buy that particular ad space. Consumers are not forced to buy products they do not want, and neither should advertisers be coerced to buy undesired ad space. But that is precisely what would happen if, as Collins (1992a; 1992b) suggests, advertisers were prohibited from engaging in pull-outs or expressing their likes/dislikes to publishers and producers.

Media purchases frequently are made before content is known, based on expected ratings. When the content is known, the advertiser may anticipate a loss of value and decide to pull out. This is no different than consumers agreeing to buy an automobile on the basis of an inspection, then when they go to pick it up they discover the engine has been removed. Advertisers should have the same right to back out of a deal that individual consumers enjoy.

Normally, there are literally thousands of media buys that can fulfill their needs, so if one vehicle becomes unattractive it is both easy and sensible to switch to another (Baker 1992, p. 2161). Because advertisers seldom sponsor an entire television show the way they did 40 years ago, but simply purchase time, they have no commitment to the shows (or magazines, etc.) in which they place their ads (Hill and Beaver 1991).

There are two types of content that may reduce the value of a vehicle: (1) material that is offensive to viewers and therefore indirectly reflects on the sponsors, and (2) stories that directly, negatively, reflect on the company or product. In both cases the obvious fear is bad publicity, which can quickly damage a product's reputation (Schechter 1992). Since advertising is an investment in a positive reputation, the potential costs outweigh the minimal benefits offered by any specific vehicle.

And consumer boycotts have made advertisers feel that consumers will desert them if they support certain content. John McNulty, General Motors' vice president of public relations, claims that even a single offended viewer may represent a loss of car sales for years to come (Mahler 1990). In 1989 a lone housewife, by writing letters to sponsors, convinced several advertisers to pull out of the Fox network's "Married . . . With Children." She complained the show was replete with "soft-core pornography" (Stein 1989; Clark 1990). It appears advertisers fear that if one viewer is sufficiently upset to write, there probably are many more who were equally angry but did not act on those feelings.

This places advertisers in a precarious position, since attack can come from groups of consumers with conflicting agendas. For instance, it is not inconceivable for a television show to be boycotted by the gay community for negatively portraying homosexuals, and by conservative forces for any positive aspects of that portrayal (Fahey 1991, p. 678). Advertisers are in jeopardy no matter how homosexuals are depicted. They seem to be in a "no win" situation.

For many advertisers the benefits offered by a particular vehicle are few. They see the vehicle as simply an audience, and rarely is that audience unique. However, the potential costs, whether real or imagined, are great. Under those circumstances, it is easy to understand why advertisers might readily engage in EC. When consumers refuse to buy an advertiser's product it is called an economic *boycott,* but when advertisers refuse to buy a media vehicle's product it is deemed economic *censorship.*

Like the press, advertisers have the freedom to ignore the other two parties, but that would not be a good business decision. Advertisers are merely trying to operate at a profit. But, as compared to consumers, neither advertisers nor press are completely free to engage in unrestricted expression, because both are subject to some governmental intervention.

Government Restrictions on Advertisers and Media

All participants in this society—individuals and businesses, alike—are subject to some limitations on their expressive freedom. For example, "obscene" programming can be prohibited even if consumers, advertisers, and media want it broadcast *(Miller v. California* 1973). But businesses are generally subject to regulations not imposed on individuals, and those restrictions can make their ability to communicate less "free" than individuals.

Advertisers communicate with consumers through their advertising, sales promotions, sales force, packaging, product instructions, and even the product itself. Yet all of these are subject to varying degrees of government control. Unlike the expression of the consumers, who are free to write what they desire in letters of complaint and to engage in boycotts, "commercial speech" by advertisers receives limited protection under the First Amendment (*Central Hudson Gas v. Public Service Commission of New York* 1980). Indeed, advertisers' marketing communications are scrutinized, and frequently regulated, by the Federal Trade Commission, the Food and Drug Administration, the Securities Exchange Commission, and others. In addition, in response to the threat of regulation, many of those communications are reviewed and altered by the advertiser's legal counsel.

The advertised product, too, is subject to some limits imposed by government. State and federal authorities dictate safety and environmental standards for products and their manufacture. Toys must be safe for children to put in their mouths and must not be flammable, wireless transmitters must be licensed for a given radio frequency, insecticides must not poison their users, bedding materials must meet several composition standards, etc. Thus, the ability of advertisers to communicate through the medium of their products is severely constrained by government.

Media are somewhat less encumbered by regulation, because their product is communication and their speech generally is not considered "commercial speech." Quite the contrary, information flowing from the media typically is considered to fall squarely under the protection of the "press" clause of the First Amendment (e.g., *Miami Herald Publishing v. Tornillo* 1974). However, broadcast media are subject to several restrictions, under the auspices of the Federal Communications Commission. For example, bearing directly on the "controversial issues" involved in EC, "indecent" language that is not "obscene" is nonetheless subject to limitation by that agency (*F.C.C. v. Pacifica Foundation* 1978). And even print media are restrainted in ways individuals are not, including regulation of the ink and paper on which they print, the employees they hire, and distribution through the mails.

Although within the circle of communication each of the three parties is free to express themselves, in their own best interests, that freedom is neither absolute nor equal. Consumers are subject to far fewer limitations than either media or advertisers. Indeed, among these parties, the most consistently and heavily regulated are the advertisers.

CONCLUSIONS

That EC occurs is beyond dispute. The question is where to lay the blame. Advertisers are popular targets of social critics, so it should come as no surprise that advertisers are charged with responsibility for EC. In fact, two of the most vocal commentators who blame advertisers for EC also have criticized the ad industry for other societal ills. Collins (1992a) is a co-founder of the CSC, an advocacy group that explicitly "exposes and opposes commercialism" (Ibid.), and has charged advertising with subjugating rational consumer decision making to the service of selling (Collins and Skover 1993). Baker (1994) elsewhere has argued that the profit motive behind advertising makes it unworthy of First Amendment protection (Baker 1976).

If one starts from the premise that the chain-of-events leading to EC begins with advertisers, the conclusion that advertisers bear primary responsibility is a *fait accompli.* But it is equally arguable that this process starts with consumers or with media. As with any circle, the process of EC has no definite beginning or end; it is a continuing and complex dynamic among all the participants. Consequently, they all bear some blame for EC.

But is EC really a cause for *serious* concern? Today consumers have a wide choice of media vehicles, and the number is expanding at a breathtaking rate. Since not all advertisers and media vehicles engage in EC, and probably none of them use it frequently, it is doubtful that great collective harm results from this process. Especially in light of new electronic data communication technologies, it is hard to imagine that a newspaper or broadcast station decision to avoid a topic will severely handicap an audience member's ability to obtain that information.

Finally, EC should never become too pervasive. When currently passive consumers become sufficiently unhappy about EC and more actively exercise their rights (e.g., change vehicles or boycott advertisers), media bias should be diminished. In short, the dangers of EC seem somewhat overstated.

BIBLIOGRAPHY

Associated Press (1993), "Mercedes magazine request raises censorship questions," *Austin American-Statesman,* (September 17), E3.
Bagdikian, Ben H. (1992), *The Media Monopoly* (4th Ed.), Boston: Beacon Press.

Baker, C. Edwin (1976), "Commercial Speech: A Problem in the Theory of Freedom," *Iowa Law Review*, 62, 1–56.
———— (1994), *Advertising and a Democratic Press*, Princeton, NJ: Princeton University Press.
———— (1992), "Advertising and a Democratic Press," *University of Pennsylvania Law Review*, 140, 2097–2243.
Beckerman, David M. (1985), "Tandy Pulls Its Ads," *InfoWorld*, (August 5), 6.
Bernstein, Sid (1991), "Who's afraid of advertisers?" *Advertising Age*, (March 11), 17.
Bishop, Katherine (1991), "Ads on Holocaust 'I Ioax' Inspire Campus Debates," *The New York Times*, (December 23), A12.
Blau, Eleanor (1989), "Domino's Pizza Cancels Ads on 'Saturday Night,'" *New York Times*, (April 11), Y45.
Brooks, A. Phillips (1992), "Free speech, responsible journalism at odds in bitter Holocaust ad debate," *Austin American-Statesman*, (May 10), B1.
Carman, John (1990), "Topics That Cost ABC Big Bucks," *The San Francisco Chronicle*, (July 25), E1.
Carter, Bill (1990), "Screeners Help Advertisers Avoid Prime-Time Trouble," *The New York Times*, (January 29), D1.
Carton, Barbara (1989), "Lashing back at TV sleaze; Outraged viewers gird to boycott advertisers," *The Boston Globe*, (April 23), A1.
Central Hudson Gas v. Public Service Commission of New York, 447 U.S. 557 (1980).
Clark, Kenneth R. (1989), "Will boycott fever affect television's disposition for fall?" *Chicago Tribune*, (May 4), Tempo section, 1.
———— (1990), "Housewife/lobbyist eyes TV 'raunch hour,'" *Chicago Tribune*, (August 2), Tempo section, 1.
———— (1983), "Church, advertisers criticize 'The Thorn Birds,'" United Press International, (March 23), wire story.
Colford, Steven W. (1990), "A Soviet view of U.S. advertising," *Advertising Age*, (May 7), 62.
Collins, Ronald K.L. (1992a), *Dictating Content: How Advertising Pressure Can Corrupt a Free Press*, Washington, D.C.: The Center for the Study of Commercialism.
———— (1992b), "Press Freedom vs. Advertising Pressure," *The Seattle Times*, (April 4), A19.
———— and David M. Skover (1993), "Commerce & Communication," *Texas Law Review*, 71, 697–746.
Cox, James (1992), "'Herald' controversy flares, Cuban exile leaders doubt bomb threats," *USA Today*, (February 5), 2B.
———— (1989), "Rev. Donald Wildmon; Mississippi minister takes on TV networks," *USA Today*, (July 17), 6B.
Danzig, Fred (1990), "This wall must stay; Editors shouldn't be censors of ads," *Advertising Age*, (January 8), 22.
Day, Louis A. (1991), *Ethics in Media Communications: Cases and Controversies*, Belmont, CA: Wadsworth, Inc.
Donaton, Scott (1990), "Two editors quit over 'Omni' ad flap," *Advertising Age*, (October 22), 54.
Dorfman, Dan (1989), "Macy's ad clout fails to sway 'N.Y. Times,'" *USA Today*, (February 13), 2B.
Du Brow, Rick (1991), "When Does TV Cross the Line?; Censorship vs. Good Taste—The debate continues as the networks get pressed tighter in the Iron Triangle of viewers, advertisers and the folks who create those prime-time shows," *Los Angeles Times*, (November 3), 7.
Elliott, Stuart (1992), "Group Seeks to Curb Advertisers' Power," *The New York Times*, (March 13), D6.
Enrico, Dottie (1990), "Ms., Minus Ads, Makes Debut Today," *Newsday*, (July 30), 2.
Fahey, Patrick M. (1991), "Advocacy Group Boycotting of Network Television Advertisers and Its Effects on Programming Content," *University of Pennsylvania Law Review*, 140, 647–709.
Farhi, Paul (1991), "Chrysler to Halt Ads in Playboy: Auto Firm Acts After Getting Complaints," *Washington Post*, (February 22), C1.
———— (1989), "Pan Am Grounds an Ad after Listener Complaint," *The Washington Post*, (April 14), F1.
F.C.C. v. Pacifica Foundation, 438 U.S. 726 (1978).
Feder, Robert (1994), "Channel 32 Pulls Newspaper's Ads," *Chicago Sun-Times*, (August 29), 31.
Goerne, Carrie (1992), "Study blasts advertisers, fearful media for suppressing news," *Marketing News*, (April 27), 8.
Graham, Judith (1989), "NBC's 'Roe' may turn off advertisers," *Advertising Age*, (May 1), 1.
Henry, Nancy (1979), "Women's Mags: The Chic Sell," in *The Commercial Connection: Advertising & the American Mass Media*, John W. Wright, ed., New York: Dell Publishing Company, 251–255.

Hill, Ronald Paul and Andrea L. Beaver (1991), "Advocacy Groups and Television Advertisers," *Journal of Advertising,* 20(1), 18–27.

Hoffman, Jan (1992), "TV Shouts 'Baby' (and Barely Whispers 'Abortion')," *The New York Times,* (May 31), Sect. 2, 1.

Horovitz, Bruce (1992), "Advertisers Influence Media More, Report says," *Los Angeles Times,* (March 12), D2.

Hume, Scott (1992), "What is censored? Quintessence won't change Jovan ad," *Advertising Age,* (February 17), 58.

Kitman, Marvin (1991), "Advertising as a Fact of Life," *Newsday,* (November 21), 81.

Kleinfield, N.R. (1989), "Television That Makes Advertisers Dive for Cover," *The New York Times,* (March 6), D8.

Kurtz, Howard (1991), "Our Politically Correct Press; More and More Stories Seem Too Touchy For Journalists," *The Washington Post,* (January 20), B1.

Lipman, Joanne (1992), "Media Content Is Linked to Cigarette Ads," *The Wall Street Journal,* (January 30), B5.

Mahler, Richard (1990), "The New Power of TV Advertisers; The increasing clout of sponsors has been seen more and more this season as 'objectionable' shows make some hit lists," *Los Angeles Times,* (May 6), 4.

Margulies, Lee (1985), "'Hail to the Chief' Goes to a Quiet Death on ABC," *Los Angeles Times,* (May 21), Part 6, 1.

McDougal, Dennis (1991a), "Hitting TV With the Off Switch," *Los Angeles Times,* (October 28), F1.

——— (1991b), "AIDS and airwaves: It's still a hard sell," *The Toronto Star,* (November 19), D4.

McManus, John (1990), "Furor over PGA cite sinks golf sponsors," *Advertising Age,* (July 30), 2.

Miami Herald Publishing v. Tornillo, 418 U.S. 241 (1974).

Mill, John Stuart (1859), *On Liberty,* Baltimore, MD: Penguin, (reprint 1974).

Miller, Cyndee (1994), "Advertisers in middle of the battle over 'Blue': 'Quality TV' counterattacks 'American Family,'" *Marketing News,* 28(10), 1.

Miller v. California, 413 U.S. 15 (1973).

New York Times v. Sullivan, 376 U.S. 254 (1964).

Oshinsky, David M. and Michael Curtis (1991), "The truth appears to be, with regard to the alleged extermination of the European Jews, that there was no order, no plan, no budget, no weapon . . .—From advertisements in college newspapers," *The New York Times,* (December 11), A27.

Pergament, Alan (1994), "'NYPD Blue's' 26 Nominations Leave Others Green with Envy," *The Buffalo News,* (July 22), Lifestyles Section, 10.

Piccoli, Sean (1992), "Taming the TV Watch Dog; Once-mighty censors give in to nervous admen, competition," *The Washington Times,* (May 3), D1.

Pollay, Richard W. (1986), "The Distorted Mirror: Reflections on the Unintended Consequences of Advertising," *Journal of Marketing,* 50 (April), 18–36.

Ramirez, Anthony (1990), "Procter & Gamble Pulls Some TV Ads Over Slur to Coffee," *The New York Times,* (May 12), 1.

Riley, Karen (1992), "Media back down from advertisers, critics say," *The Washington Times,* (March 12), C1.

Robertson, Lance (1993), "Timber group ruined paper, publisher says," *Eugene Register-Guard,* (March 18), Business.

Rosenberg, Howard (1992), "NBC Takes Hit Over Gay Issue on 'Leap' Show," *Los Angeles Times,* (January 17), F1.

——— (1990), "ABC Pulls Plug on a Rerun of 'Thirtysomething,'" *Los Angeles Times,* (July 19), F1.

——— (1987), "Howard Rosenberg: The 'Amerika' Controversy: Let America Decide," *Los Angeles Times,* (January 30), Part 6, 1.

Rotzoll, Kim B., James E. Haefner, and Charles H. Sandage (1976), *Advertising in Contemporary Society: Perspectives Toward Understanding,* Columbus, OH: Grid, Inc.

Shaw, David (1987), "Credibility vs. Sensitivity: High, Thick Wall Divides Editors and Advertisers," *Los Angeles Times,* (February 16), 1.

Silverman, Jeff (1991), "TV's Creators Face a New Caution," *The New York Times,* (December 8), Sect. 2, 1.

Simon, Mark (1994), "Mercury News Ad Dispute Cooling Off: Advertisers return while reporters stew," *San Francisco Chronicle,* (July 15), B1.

Soley, Lawrence C. and Robert L. Craig (1992), "Advertising Pressure on Newspapers: A Survey," *Journal of Advertising,* 21 (December), 1.

Stein, M.L. (1992), "Dinner ends boycott: Auto dealers pull ads from Utah daily; publisher buys them dinner, they come back," *Editor & Publisher Magazine,* (October 10), 38.

Stein, Sharman (1989), "And Now, a Few More Words to the Sponsors," *Newsday,* (March 6), 2.

Terminiello v. Chicago, 337 U.S. 1 (1949).

Topping, Seymour (1992), "Another wall crumbles; Editors tear 'taint of advertiser influence,'" *Advertising Age,* (May 11), 32.

United States v. Associated Press, 52 F.Supp. 362 (S.D.N.Y. 1943).

UPI (1992), "Ohio State refuses controverial ad," United Press International, (January 23), wire story.

Valentine v. Chrestensen, 316 U.S. 52 (1942).

Virginia State Board of Pharmacy v. Virginia Citizens Consumer Council, 425 U.S. 748 (1976).

Warlick, Debra (1992), "ETC," *The Atlanta Journal and Constitution* (February 29), E6.

Washington Post (1986), "Detroit Car Dealers Pull Ads in Protest," (May 28), G1.

Weinstein, Steve (1990), "When Gay Means Loss of Revenue, *Los Angeles Times,* (December 22), F1.

Welkos, Robert W. (1992), "Paramount Pulls Ads in Dispute with Trade Papers," *Los Angeles Times,* (June 10), F2.

Wolf, Dick (1992), "Hot Topics Get Chilly Ad Reception," *Los Angeles Times,* (September 1). F1.

Zachary, G. Pascal (1992), "Many Journalists See a Growing Reluctance To Criticize Advertisers," *The Wall Street Journal,* (February 6), A1.

CHAPTER 14

READERS' PERSPECTIVES ON ADVERTISING'S INFLUENCE IN WOMEN'S MAGAZINES
Thoughts on Two Practices

J. ERIC HALEY AND ANNE CUNNINGHAM

This study explores how consumers react to advertisers' attempts to influence editorial content of media. Two practices are explored: complementary editorial (magazines giving editorial mentions to advertisers' products or services) and attempts at content censorship. Specifically, the study looks at how adult female readers of women's magazines make sense of the 2 aforementioned practices. Findings indicate that women believe editorial mentions of advertisers' products and services can be useful. Based on what the women in this study stated, attempts by advertisers to prevent media content from being published has greater potential to damage the credibility of both the advertiser and the magazine. Participants drew a basic distinction between the practices of complementary editorial and advertiser influence to prevent content: Editorial provides information, but advertiser influence to prevent content denies information.

In the United States, the media need money to operate, and advertisers have the money. Advertisers need the media, as well, as vehicles through which to deliver messages to marketers' intended audiences. Although this relationship is mutually beneficial, it is not without conflicts, which may arise when advertisers attempt to gain the upper hand by influencing media content.

Advertisers influence content when they encourage the removal of "controversial" material or refuse to buy spots in shows they feel are too controversial. This practice was exemplified by Chrysler's advertising agency when it demanded magazines alert the Chrysler Corporation in advance of any and all editorial content that may be considered provocative or offensive (Knecht, 1997, A1).

Another way advertisers influence content is by requesting that specific material be included in media content, to showcase the marketers' product. Examples of this practice are product placements and editorial mentions of the product within editorial content.

It has been suggested that attempts at editorial influence may be more common and successful in tougher economic times (Lasek & Martin, 1990). That is, magazines may be more willing to entertain advertiser requests when advertising dollars are falling.

This study explores how consumers react to advertisers' attempts to influence editorial content

From *Mass Communication and Society,* vol. 6, no. 2 (May 2003). Copyright © 2003 by the Mass Communication and Society Division of the Association for Education in Journalism and Mass Communication (AEJMC). Reprinted with permission.

of media. Two practices are explored: complementary editorial (magazines giving editorial mentions to advertisers' products or services) and attempts at content censorship. Specifically, the study looks at how adult female readers of women's magazines understand and react to the two aforementioned practices.

LITERATURE

This study is part of a body of literature dealing with the advertising-editorial relationship. This literature has covered issues such as product placements in movies and television (e.g., Ferraro and Avery, 2000; DeLorme & Reid, 1999), the marketing/advertising paradigm's influence on the production of news and its subsequent impact on society (e.g., McManus, 1994), the relationship between the advertising and editorial departments of U.S. media and policy formulation regarding advertising practices that impact editorial credibility (e.g., Cameron & Haley, 1992), and general pressures felt from advertisers by the editorial staffs of U.S. media (Bagdikian, 1992; Hays & Reisner, 1990; Howland, 1989; Soley & Craig, 1992). Some researchers have even debated the First Amendment implications of advertiser control over editorial content (Lau, 2000; Parkinson, 2001).

In both the academic literature and trade press, women's and trade magazines have the reputation of catering to their advertisers' demands (Cunningham & Haley, 2000; Howland, 1989; Hoyt, 1990; Lasek & Martin, 1990; Orenstein, 1990; Potenzano, 1990; Steinem, 1990; Waldman, 1991). For example, no study has attempted to document the frequency of advertiser attempts at censorship, but Cunningham and Haley (2000) revealed that editors of Ms. magazine felt such practices as requesting complementary editorial and advertiser attempts at censorship were not uncommon.

Among editorial staffs, one underlying assumption is that media will lose credibility with readers/viewers if advertisers have influence over media content (Cameron & Haley, 1992; Cunningham & Haley, 2000). However, this contention has not been explored among readers/consumers. What is missing from the academic literature regarding the advertising—editorial relationship is the consumer's voice. With the exception of DeLorme and Reid (1999), whose study found that viewers at times enjoyed product placements in movies, studies thus far have focused on the attitudes and opinions of media and advertising professionals. Because credibility is ascribed by readers/consumers, it is necessary to talk with them specifically, to see how they understand and react to advertising practices that influence the content of media that readers use. This study seeks to fill the gap in the literature by studying how adult female readers of women's magazines understand and react to two advertising practices that influence the editorial content of women's magazines: complementary editorial and advertiser censorship.

PARADIGM AND METHOD

Seeking understanding is a research goal of phenomenological paradigms. The particular paradigm driving this study is that of constructivism (Guba, 1990), which is defined by a relativist ontology and subjectivist epistemology. Ontologically, constructivism holds that realities are multiple, socially constructed, and bound by time and context. Realities do not exist within objects, but rather in human interpretations of objects. Epistemologically, all knowledge is assumed to be a co-creation of researcher and participant. This paradigm holds that people are active creators of realities. Thus, the ultimate goal of a constructivist investigation is to uncover the various realities of a phenomenon, by focusing on the various meanings people ascribe to it. As such, what is essential is that the chosen research methodology allow individual constructions of reality and individual meanings to be revealed.

The long interview was the data collection method chosen for this study. The long interview gives researchers a way to see the logical scaffolding with which people construct their understanding of a phenomenon (McCracken, 1988). Because the research question asked how women understand and react to advertising practices, the long interview allows researchers the flexibility to explore the rationale behind the thoughts and feelings of study participants. Individual interviews were chosen, instead of the more time-efficient focus groups, because magazine consumption is an individual rather than a group activity.

For this study, adult women who read at least one female-targeted magazine were defined as the population of study. Rather than enumerating how prevalently particular beliefs are held, the goal of this study was to uncover the variety and structure of the realities female readers ascribe to the advertising practices of interest, as they relate to magazines they read.

Information saturation, or redundancy, is the appropriate criterion for determining how many interviews is enough to fulfill the research goal of a qualitative investigation (Taylor, 1994). Information redundancy refers to the point in a study when the variety of constructions of a phenomenon are repeated, despite attempts to modify recruitment of participants to find new realities. Information redundancy may be reached quickly, if the population of interest is relatively homogeneous. Here, homogeneity is defined in relation to worldview, rather than demographically. For example, McCracken (1988) has suggested that, in homogeneous populations, as few as eight interviews may be enough to ensure redundancy. If the population is more diverse in mindset, then a higher number of interviews should be expected.

Given the goal of covering the logical scaffolding, or structure of beliefs, it was important to employ a flexible, semistructured interview as part of the study's emergent design. The semistructured interview allowed interviewers to introduce discussion topics, but gave them the flexibility to move with the participants' responses, probing when appropriate, and allowing participants to define topics for discussion, as well (McCracken, 1988). To ensure trustworthiness of the study, interviews were tape-recorded and transcribed word-for-word.

Data were analyzed using analytic induction and comparative analysis, to look for recurring themes (Huberman & Miles, 1994; Strauss & Corbin, 1990). Analytic induction and comparative analysis involve reading the data line-by-line for themes and categories, developing a working schema from examination of initial cases, then modifying and refining the schema, based on subsequent cases. Negative instances that do not fit the initial constructs are sought, to expand, adapt, or restrict the original construction. Emphasis is on category construction, rather than enumeration. The findings presented are supported by exemplary quotations from participants, which summarize the particular theme of discussion. Using participants' words to support the analysis is an additional means of ensuring the trustworthiness of the study.

FINDINGS

The findings reported in this study are based on interviews with 47 adult women between the ages of 18 and 59 years. Although the majority of the women live in the southeastern United States, the geographic span of interviewees reaches as far as the northeastern United States and Europe. Despite the wide age and geographic ranges, information redundancy became apparent within very few interviews. When redundancy was noticed, the researchers recruited women of ages and backgrounds different than those already recruited. However, the common culture among all the women was reading women's magazines, which probably explains the redundancy across the diverse geographic locations and ages of participants in this study.

Understandings of Complementary Editorial

The women in this study were generally accepting of complementary editorial. However, this acceptance was not without limits.

It's just business. "I can understand why an advertiser would want it," responded one woman, when asked what she thought of advertisers getting editorial mentions in magazines in which they advertise. She continued, "They [advertisers] pay a lot of money, I would think, so of course they would like to have as much exposure as possible in the magazine." This captures a prominent theme among the female magazine readers; that is, they felt that magazines offering editorial mentions to advertisers was just part of doing business. "The magazines need the advertisers and the advertisers need the magazines, so I guess I can understand why both sides would benefit," commented another.

It's more information. Beyond understanding the business reasons for complementary editorial, the participants were asked if and how the practice affected them and their evaluation of the magazines they read. On the whole, women were receptive to complementary editorial because it provided information. One participant expressed the general consensus as follows: "I read the magazines like Cosmo for tips, anyway. It's just more information. I know I have to be the ultimate judge, no matter who is recommending something."

Another supported the idea that complementary editorial provides more information, giving credit to the judgment of magazine editors:

> My favorite magazines are my favorite magazines because I like what's in them. The people who put those magazines together know what their readers like. They know they have to have readers to stay in business, so they are not going to put things in there that we don't like. So, I guess I trust them to put in information that's useful, whether or not it's due to a business deal or just a writer's opinion.

The topic matters, though. Some women were accepting of the complementary editorial practice, regardless of topic or publication. However, there was a strong theme within most of the interviews that the topic and the type of publication do matter when evaluating whether complementary editorial is an acceptable practice. The following quotations from two different women summarize well the participants' views:

> Most women's magazines just aren't all that serious to begin with, so it really doesn't matter. But Time or a financial magazine, now that could be different. The material is just more important, or I mean, potentially more important, I guess. A mutual fund buy is more important than buying lipstick—although, with the price of some lipsticks, you sort of wonder (laugh).
>
> It's not only the audiences they [different magazines] seek, but also how they feel about their reputations. In Cosmo, I would expect it, but if I saw it in National Geographic, I would write a letter to the editor.
>
> For serious information, you want to think the recommendation is unbiased, or at least as unbiased as possible. It's different if you know an advertiser indirectly paid for the recommendation.
>
> You still have to be the judge, no matter who tells you something, but it would help you make that decision or judgment if you knew who the things were coming from.
>
> If it were prescription drugs or something, that would be a little different than a pack of

bubblegum. I'd think less of a prescription drug, because that has more of an effect on a person than a pack of bubblegum.

I would think less of my magazine. Very few women in the study said that knowing a magazine engaged in complementary editorial would change their opinions of the magazine. However, some did. The following quotations illustrate their rationales:

I think I'd think a little less of the magazine if I knew. I guess it doesn't really hurt anything, but I'd sort of feel like I'd been cheated or misled.

You see things in the magazines all the time that say "advertisement" or "special advertising section." That's ok. You know who it's from, and the information can be pretty interesting, you know, or useful. I think a lot of women read magazines like Glamour and even Better Homes and Gardens for the ads, anyway. I know I like the ads just as much as the articles. I get useful stuff from both. I guess I'd wish the magazine would not do it [complementary editorial], when they could just put it in one of those special advertising sections and be more honest about it.

I might think less, but I wouldn't drop my subscription. Even those women who said they would think less of their favorite publication, in light of the complementary editorial practice, said that knowing a magazine gave complementary editorial to advertisers would not make them drop their subscriptions to their favorite magazines. The participants explained:

Generally, I don't take the magazine[s] too seriously, anyway.

I just enjoy them.

Yeah, I guess I would think a little less of the editors, and maybe even the advertisers, for asking for it or accepting it, but if it's a magazine I'm already subscribing to, I obviously subscribe to it because I like it. So I guess I'd still subscribe.

I'd drop the magazine if the content was consistently offensive to me, but I don't think much of anything that would be in, what did you call it, complementary mentions, would really be offensive.

Advertisers Use of Influence to Prevent Content

These women were generally accepting of complementary editorial, but the issue of advertisers attempting to prevent certain content from being printed in magazines caused mixed and often strongly stated feelings. As with complementary editorial, some women viewed advertisers wanting to prevent certain types of content as "just business." One representative participant said, "I can see why an advertiser wouldn't want the magazine to offend anybody or say something bad about their product." However, very few women in the study were as accepting of advertisers trying to prevent content as they were of complementary editorial.

I can think for myself. Women who expressed the strongest negative feelings toward advertisers' attempts to prevent content were uncomfortable with the idea of media censorship. The following quotations summarize the ideas discussed:

It's the advertiser's job to tell me about the things they have for sale. It's not their job to decide what gets printed in a magazine. That's what the writers get paid to do. It seems to me the writers would know more what their readers want to read about than the advertisers do.

I don't think it's right for rich businesses to prevent me from getting information. Let me decide if the information is offensive or bad. I can think for myself. It's just another example of how much power we've let big business have in this country. It's way out of control.

If I see something I don't like in a magazine or on TV or something, I turn it off or I watch it anyway and gripe about it. It's sort of fun to have something to gripe about every once in a while. You know, if I don't see things that I don't like, how do I know how I really feel? Anyway, I sure don't think to call up the advertiser and blame them because Cosmo writes an article that is insulting to women. You know, if I'm reading Cosmo or watching a show like South Park—you know the sort of gross-out animated thing on cable—I probably like it and am not offended by it to start with, or I wouldn't be watching it.

I think it's really unfair for an advertiser to threaten to pull their ads if they don't like something that is going to be published.

A tough issue. Women who expressed mixed feelings about advertisers attempting to prevent media content were torn between having distaste for censorship and believing that a company has the right to express a view. The follow quotations illustrate these conflicting feelings:

That's a hard one. I don't like anybody telling me what I can or can't read. I get so mad at these other parents who want to keep books out of the school library, instead of teaching their kids how to decide for themselves what's good and bad. But I can understand an advertiser not wanting to have to align themselves with an idea presented in a show or a magazine that they really don't believe in. Boy, that's hard.

I guess, if you're buying ads, you have the right to say you won't advertise if there is stuff in the magazine you don't like. But that's sort of the same thing as censorship. If the magazine needs your ads to pay the bills, I guess you have the upper hand. I guess I understand it, but I don't like it.

Every once in a while, my preacher tells us to write letters to advertisers or not buy things from advertisers who buy ads in shows that are harmful. I've never really felt comfortable with that. I know that we should be vocal in making sure our views are heard, and I don't like a lot of what I see on TV. Since advertisers pay for the shows, I know that letting our feelings be known to them can be effective for us. But I just don't like the idea of having somebody else be in control of what I see or hear. I guess there is always somebody else in control of that, but I don't know. I've never actually done it, just because I'm not comfortable with it. I think I'd rather see something bad, and have the chance to explain why I think it's bad to my kids, than to not ever expose them to things. Christians have to live in the world, so it pays to not be naïve.

Both magazines and advertisers have something to lose. "You know, this whole thing is just bad for both sides. I think both magazines and advertisers have something to lose here." The preceding comment summarizes the ill effects consumers' knowledge of advertiser-induced censorship of media content could have on both advertisers and magazines. Although a few women said the practice would not adversely affect their views of either the advertiser or the magazine, the majority of the participants felt differently. They tended to feel both advertisers and editors are in the wrong:

I would be disappointed in my magazines if I knew they caved in. Yeah, I'd probably stop reading them. But if everybody caves in, I don't know what would be left to read.

> I think I'd be more angry with the advertiser than the magazine.
>
> The magazine sort of has a gun to its head, and the advertiser is the one holding it, you know. So I just don't think a company should try to keep me from seeing information. It's like they are telling me I'm too stupid to make up my own mind, or maybe that's what they are afraid of, that I can make up my own mind. Either way, I have a gun, too. I don't have to buy their products. Advertisers shouldn't threaten people, and magazines should not change editorial content for fear of losing advertisers.

Readers can see fault on both sides of the advertiser-editor relationship, but the women in this study seemed to feel that the magazines ultimately shoulder the responsibility for advertiser influence on magazine content:

> I would definitely blame the editor, because, in the end, it's the editor's responsibility how the magazine is presented to the consumer. And I think the advertiser is going to want anything they can get. They're going to push the limits as far as they can to get their products out on the market in the eye of the public. So I think it's the editor's responsibility to be sure they practice ethically. . . . When I look at the magazine, I don't think, "Oh, this advertiser snuck in here." It's the editor's responsibility, so I look badly on the magazine, not the advertiser.
>
> [Advertisers] can express concern, but if you [editors] allow advertisers to do that, then you set a precedent, and every time there is something they don't like, whether it is a valid reason or not, they have control over your publication. Ultimately, the consumer gets hurt, because he or she is not getting the news that they need or desire. People are trusting [editors] to give more accurate information, and they are not expecting them to be filtered.
>
> Like I said, it is [the magazines'] responsibility to let readers know what is going [on] in the world. If they upset their advertisers, then they should get new ones. If they lose their readers, that would be more detrimental to the magazine. It's like a kid asking their parents for candy. It's the parents' fault if they give it to them and their teeth rot and fall out, you know? . . . I think that's a child's way of just testing their parents, testing their authority to see how far they can go. . . . And I think it might be the same way for advertisers.

Credibility has already been lost. Findings indicate that women already question the credibility of women's publications and tend to take what they read in these magazines "with a grain of salt." For this reason, they are neither shocked nor overly worried about advertisers limiting content, as the following quotations illustrate:

> Especially magazines like the kind I read, like People and stuff, you can take what you read and cut it in half. And then maybe you believe half of what you read. I guess, you know, I really don't take everything to heart. So it wouldn't really affect me. I know this is a very biased view, but, in women's magazines, I just don't give them as much credit as Time and Newsweek, because I feel these last two have more information. It doesn't surprise me that it happens in Cosmo.
>
> Nothing is fair. [Advertisers] can threaten to do that [pull ads], but I think, if the magazine is worth its salt, they will do what they want to do. But they won't kowtow to advertisers. . . . Trashy magazines get trashy advertisers.

If only I knew. . . . Although women feel confident that they can identify complementary editorial when they see it, they admit there is no way to know when a magazine is withholding content.

As the following quotations illustrate, they would think less of those publications that withhold content to please advertisers. However, without any way of knowing if they do, women are going to keep on reading:

> The sad part of this is that you will never know just how much influence the advertisers have had over what we don't see. Unless it's reported in the news media or something, we'll just never know, so maybe it's pointless to get upset about it. Still, I think both, no, we all have something to lose with this. What I mean by that is people would be angry with magazines and advertisers if they knew—I know I would be. So I think people would not think highly of magazines and advertisers, so they lose. Everybody else loses, because we don't get to see potentially important information that we just might need sometime.

> I guess it would be interesting to know just how much we don't see because of advertisers. I guess you can never really know that. But if it's a lot, then I'd definitely think less of the magazines I read.

> I think that, if a magazine pulled a story . . . that would withhold information from the people. Not that I would know, but I would think less of a magazine, if I did.

> I would rather read a magazine that would let the readers be the voice of the magazine, and, realistically, that probably doesn't happen now. I can't say that I would not read this magazine, because, if I'm still reading it, I must not notice that this is going on.

DISCUSSION AND FUTURE DIRECTIONS

Theoretical Implications

One of the major contributions of qualitative investigation, in general, is its ability to provide insights that allow theoretical development to be grounded in the experience of a phenomenon's participants (Strauss & Corbin, 1990). This study provides a foundation for the development of a theoretical model explaining audience evaluations of the advertiser-editorial relationship. In so doing, this study provides an important addition to the existing literature that addresses advertisers,' magazine editors,' and journalists' perspectives.

Based on the findings of this study, information flow appears to be a central concern for magazine readers. Looking across the two practices of interest in this study, reader acceptance of advertiser influence on magazine content is mediated by whether the influence provides or denies information. Based on the findings, women seem more tolerant of complementary editorial (an activity that they see as adding information) than they are of advertiser attempts at media censorship (activities they see as denying information). Based on the importance of this differentiation to the women in this study, future research should include the dimension of information supplying versus information denying, in further study of media audience acceptance of advertiser influence over media content. The line between providing and denying information seems to define one boundary of acceptance or rejection by readers.

Acceptance of a practice that provides information, for example, complementary editorial, is not automatic. Specifically, the women in this study illustrate a latitude of acceptance of the practice of complementary editorial. Acceptance of the practice seems to be mediated by issue saliency. The findings show that complementary editorial about issues individuals perceive as more important (e.g., parenting, finance, news, etc.) is less likely to be accepted than complementary editorial about issues individuals perceive as less important (e.g., fashion, hobbies, etc.). The women in this study similarly differentiated among magazines by perceived importance of the topics in the magazines. Time was seen as a more important publication than Cosmo; thus, participants often cited complementary editorial in Time to be less tolerable than in Cosmo. In fact, many of the women were accepting of complementary fashion editorial, because they considered the advertising to be as informational as the articles.

Because this study suggests differential evaluations of complementary editorial, based on publication and story content, future research could test the effects of media type and story content on reader/viewer evaluations of the practice. Previous research indicates that audiences tend to find television less credible than the Internet, and the Internet less credible than newspapers (Kiousis, 2001). Our study suggests that women tend to find fault with the practice of complementary editorial, based mostly on the credibility they otherwise ascribe to the publications. It would therefore be interesting to examine the relationship between perceived media credibility and audience valuation of complementary editorial practices. Similarly, our findings suggest that women approach some magazines with very little expectation of finding news content and therefore are not bothered by advertiser influence. It may be useful to examine in greater detail how the audience's use of a media vehicle relates to the valuation of complementary content.

Another area for future theoretical exploration is the role of individual differences. There was strong consensus among women regarding the themes presented in the Findings section of this study, but individual differences can be seen in the ways study participants rationalized their evaluations of the two practices. It would be interesting to look more closely at those psychological and personality factors that might predict readers' reactions to practices like complementary editorial and attempted advertiser censorship of media content. Why are some women upset when others are not? Why can some simply dismiss the practices as "business," while others feel cheated by both the magazines and the advertisers? The words of the women in this study suggest at least three areas for the future study of the role of individual differences.

For example, women who were not particularly upset about complementary editorial offered their ability to discern what is and is not complementary editorial as one reason for their ambivalence. The participants were more upset over advertiser-imposed censorship of media content because they felt there was really no way of knowing what did not make it into print in their favorite magazines as a result of advertising influence. From this, it could be postulated that perceived ability to discern the practice (media savvy) may impact evaluation of the practice.

A second area of possible influence of individual differences may be perceived ability to effect change in the practice. This was apparent within the discussions of advertiser-imposed censorship of media content. The few women in our study who claimed not to be upset about advertiser-imposed censorship cited their inability to impact the situation, as a reason for not being upset. These women said things such as "It's just business" and "That's just the way it is." Women who were more upset about the practice suggested that they had a voice and the power to influence practices through their buying. Still, they were frustrated at the likelihood they would never know the extent of the practice of advertiser-imposed censorship.

A third area of individual differences suggested by the present study is in the faith readers placed in the magazine editor. Several women who said they did not worry about abuses of complementary editorial and advertiser-imposed censorship placed great faith in magazine editors' ability to guard against such practices.

Managerial and Social Implications

Based on the findings of this investigation, advertisers and women's fashion and lifestyle magazines can be confident that engaging in complementary editorial will not significantly erode the credibility of advertisers or the magazine. In fact, some women in this study suggested that editorial mentions of advertisers' products and services can be useful. Although some wished that the information could be set aside in special advertising sections, no one said that she would drop a current subscription for a magazine she already liked, if she learned the magazine engaged in complementary editorial. Earlier findings suggest that female magazine readers like advertising, at least in part, because it adds an appealing visual element to the publication (Cunningham & Haley, 2000). This study further suggests that women often go to women's magazines for product/fashion information. Whether that information is packaged as advertising or editorial does not seem to matter.

The implications beyond women's lifestyle and fashion magazines are less clear. A strong theme in the interviews with female readers is that certain types of information are more important than others. Women cited financial, news, parenting, and health magazines as types of publications in which they would not want to find complementary editorial, because these publications cover topics of more significant impact in their own and others' lives than most of the material covered in lifestyle magazines. However, our study further suggests that women are not very concerned with this practice, in large part because they believe they are able to identify complementary editorial when they see it.

Based on what the women in this study stated, attempts by advertisers to prevent media content has greater potential to damage the credibility of both the advertiser and the magazine. The basic difference uncovered by this study is women's perception that complementary editorial provides information, but advertiser influence to prevent certain content denies information. Researchers warn that such practice can jeopardize overall public confidence in the media (Cameron & Haley, 1992; Hays & Reisner, 1990; Hoyt, 1990). This study indicates that this has already happened with women's lifestyle and fashion magazines, that is, women already see these magazines as less credible than news and other types of magazines. Nevertheless, they continue to read them.

The research in the area of advertising's editorial impact generally expresses the fear that a stifled media will lead to an uninformed and stagnant society (Bagdikian, 1992; Hays & Reisner, 1990; Howland, 1989; Soley & Craig, 1992). The women in this study expressed similar concerns, although not as strongly as one often hears in academic circles. The participants in this study seem to be less concerned, for a few reasons: (a) They recognized the business incentive for both advertisers and media, and (b) they viewed themselves as savvy media consumers who knew which publications they could trust and which were purely for entertainment. However, as the earlier quotations illustrate, readers admitted that they have little way of knowing when such censorship occurs.

These women also showed a strong understanding of the relationship between a magazine's ability to attract an audience and ad sales. As one woman, who was quoted earlier, said:

> Like I said, it is [the magazines'] responsibility to let readers know what is going [on] in the world. If they upset their advertisers, then they should get new ones. If they lose their readers, that would be more detrimental to the magazine.

The participants in this study offer what may be good advice to advertisers: Trust editors both to know their audiences and to provide the appropriate content for them. In fact, the women in this study tended to place ultimate blame on the editors for abuses of advertiser influence in magazines.

As long as advertisers provide the economic basis for media, the relationship between advertisers and editors will be potentially difficult to manage. Although seemingly at odds in many cases, both parties have a common vested interest. That is, each depends on the magazine readers for survival. Much of the research concerning the advertising-editorial relationship has not included the voice of the one group that is most important to each party—the readers. Perhaps this study, and the suggested additional studies, can bring the important voice of the readers to the table, to inform the dialog about the increasingly difficult advertiser-editorial relationship in the U.S. media.

REFERENCES

Bagdikian, B. H. (1992). *The media monopoly* (4th ed.). Boston: Beacon Press.

Cameron, G. T., & Haley, J. E. (1992). Feature advertising: Policies and attitudes in print media. *Journal of Advertising*, 21(3), 47–56.

Cunningham, A., & Haley, J. E. (2000). A look inside the world of advertising-free publishing: A case study of Ms. magazine. *Journal of Current Issues and Research in Advertising* 22(2), 17–30.

DeLorme, D. E., & Reid, L. N. (1999). Moviegoers' experiences and interpretations of brands in films revisited. *Journal of Advertising*, 28(2), 71–95.

Ferraro, R., & Avery, R. J. (2000). Brand appearances on prime-time television. *Journal of Current Issues and Research in Advertising*, 22(2), 1–16.

Guba, E. G. (1990). The alternative paradigm dialog. In E. G. Guba (Ed.), *The paradigm dialog* (pp. 17–27). Newbury Park: Sage.

Hays, R. G., & Reisner, A. E. (1990). Feeling the heat from advertisers: Farm magazine writers and ethical pressures. *Journalism Quarterly*, 67(4), 936–942.

Howland, J. (1989, December). Ad vs. edit: The pressure mounts. *Folio*, 92–100.

Hoyt, M. (1990, March/April). When the walls come tumbling down. *Columbia Journalism Review*, 28 (6), 35–41.

Huberman, A. M., & Miles, M. B. (1994). Data management and analysis methods. In N. K. Denzin & Y. S. Lincoln (Eds.), *Handbook of Qualitative Research* (pp. 428–444). Thousand Oaks, CA: Sage.

Kiousis, S. (2001). Public trust or mistrust? Perceptions of media credibility in the information age. *Mass Communication and Society*, 4(4), 381.

Knecht, G. B. (1997, April 30). Magazine advertisers demand prior notice of "offensive" articles. *The Wall Street Journal*, pp. A1, A6.

Lasek, A., & Martin, K. (1990, October 29). New ad-editorial bridge goes up: As ad pages slide down publishers grow cozier. *Advertising Age*, 61(45), 28–29.

Lau, A. K. (2000). Advertiser control over editorial content: An emerging first amendment issue. *Southwestern Mass Communication Journal*, 15(2), 13–23.

McCracken, G. (1988). *The long interview*. Thousand Oaks, CA: Sage.

McManus, J. H. (1994). *Market-driven journalism: Let the citizen beware?* Thousand Oaks, CA: Sage.

Orenstein, P. (1990, November/December). Ms. fights for its life: the last-gasp strategy is to return to its roots. But are they still there? *Mother Jones*, 15(7), 32–36, 81–83, 91.

Parkinson, M. (2001). Advertiser attempts to control editorial content: A constitutionally protected right. *Southwestern Mass Communication Journal*, 17(1), 1–8.

Potenzano, J. (1990, June). Magazines: The added value of added-value. *Marketing and Media Decisions*, 25(6), 58–59.

Soley, L. C., & Craig, R. L. (1992). Advertising pressures on newspapers: A survey. *Journal of Advertising*, 21(4), 1–10.

Steinem, G. (1990, July/August). Sex, lies & advertising. *Ms.*, 1(1), 19–28.

Strauss, A., & Corbin, J. (1990). *Basic qualitative research: Grounded theory procedures and techniques*. Thousand Oaks, CA: Sage.

Taylor, R. E. (1994). Qualitative research. In M. W. Singletary (Ed.), *Mass Communication Research* (pp. 265–279). White Plains, NY: Longman.

Waldman, S. (1991, May 20). Consumer news blues; are advertisers stifling local TV reporting? *Newsweek*, 117(20), 48.

CHAPTER 15

SEX, LIES, & ADVERTISING

GLORIA STEINEM

About three years ago, as *glasnost* was beginning and *Ms.* seemed to be ending, I was invited to a press lunch for a Soviet official. He entertained us with anecdotes about new problems of democracy in his country. Local Communist leaders were being criticized in their media for the first time, he explained, and they were angry.

"So I'll have to ask my American friends," he finished pointedly, "how more *subtly* to control the press." In the silence that followed, I said, "Advertising."

The reporters laughed, but later, one of them took me aside: How *dare* I suggest that freedom of the press was limited? How dare I imply that his newsweekly could be influenced by ads?

I explained that I was thinking of advertising's media-wide influence on most of what we read. Even newsmagazines use "soft" cover stories to sell ads, confuse readers with "advertorials," and occasionally self-censor on subjects known to be a problem with big advertisers.

But, I also explained, I was thinking especially of women's magazines. There, it isn't just a little content that's devoted to attracting ads, it's almost all of it. That's why advertisers—not readers—have always been the problem for *Ms.* As the only women's magazine that didn't supply what the ad world euphemistically describes as "supportive editorial atmosphere" or "complementary copy" (for instance, articles that praise food/fashion/beauty subjects to "support" and "complement" food/fashion/beauty ads), *Ms.* could never attract enough advertising to break even.

"Oh, *women's* magazines," the journalist said with contempt. "Everybody knows they're catalogs—but who cares? They have nothing to do with journalism."

I can't tell you how many times I've had this argument in 25 years of working for many kinds of publications. Except as moneymaking machines—"cash cows" as they are so elegantly called in the trade—women's magazines are rarely taken seriously. Though changes being made by women have been called more far-reaching than the industrial revolution—and though many editors try hard to reflect some of them in the few pages left to them after all the ad-related subjects have been covered—the magazines serving the female half of this country are still far below the journalistic and ethical standards of news and general interest publications. Most depressing of all, this doesn't even rate an exposé.

If *Time* and *Newsweek* had to lavish praise on cars in general and credit General Motors in particular to get GM ads, there would be a scandal—maybe a criminal investigation. When women's magazines from *Seventeen* to *Lear's* praise beauty products in general and credit Revlon in particular to get ads, it's just business as usual.

I.

When *Ms.* began, we didn't consider *not* taking ads. The most important reason was keeping the price of a feminist magazine low enough for most women to afford. But the second and almost equal reason was providing a forum where women and advertisers could talk to each other and improve advertising itself. After all, it was (and still is) as potent a source of information in this country as news or TV and movie dramas.

We decided to proceed in two stages. First, we would convince makers of "people products" used by both men and women but advertised mostly to men—cars, credit cards, insurance, sound equipment, financial services, and the like—that their ads should be placed in a women's magazine. Since they were accustomed to the division between editorial and advertising in news and general interest magazines, this would allow our editorial content to be free and diverse. Second, we would add the best ads for whatever traditional "women's products" (clothes, shampoo, fragrance, food, and so on) that surveys showed *Ms.* readers used. But we would ask them to come in *without* the usual quid pro quo of "complementary copy."

We knew the second step might be harder. Food advertisers have always demanded that women's magazines publish recipes and articles on entertaining (preferably ones that name their products) in return for their ads; clothing advertisers expect to be surrounded by fashion spreads (especially ones that credit their designers); and shampoo, fragrance, and beauty products in general usually insist on positive editorial coverage of beauty subjects, plus photo credits besides. That's why women's magazines look the way they do. But if we could break this link between ads and editorial content, then we wanted good ads for "women's products," too.

By playing their part in this unprecedented mix of *all* the things our readers need and use, advertisers also would be rewarded: ads for products like cars and mutual funds would find a new growth market; the best ads for women's products would no longer be lost in oceans of ads for the same category; and both would have access to a laboratory of smart and caring readers whose response would help create effective ads for other media as well.

I thought then that our main problem would be the imagery in ads themselves. Carmakers were still draping blondes in evening gowns over the hoods like ornaments. Authority figures were almost always male, even in ads for products that only women used. Sadistic, he-man campaigns even won industry praise. (For instance, *Advertising Age* had hailed the infamous Silva Thin cigarette theme, "How to Get a Woman's Attention: Ignore Her," as "brilliant.") Even in medical journals, tranquilizer ads showed depressed housewives standing beside piles of dirty dishes and promised to get them back to work.

Obviously, *Ms.* would have to avoid such ads and seek out the best ones—but this didn't seem impossible. *The New Yorker* had been selecting ads for aesthetic reasons for years, a practice that only seemed to make advertisers more eager to be in its pages. *Ebony* and *Essence* were asking for ads with positive black images, and though their struggle was hard, they weren't being called unreasonable.

Clearly, what *Ms.* needed was a very special publisher and ad sales staff. I could think of only one woman with experience on the business side of magazines—Patricia Carbine, who recently had become a vice president of *McCall's* as well as its editor in chief—and the reason I knew her name was a good omen. She had been managing editor at *Look* (really *the* editor, but its owner refused to put a female name at the top of his masthead) when I was writing a column there. After I did an early interview with Cesar Chavez, then just emerging as a leader of migrant labor, and the publisher turned it down because he was worried about ads from Sunkist, Pat was the one who intervened. As I learned later, she had told the publisher she would resign if the interview wasn't published. Mainly because *Look* couldn't afford to lose Pat, it *was* published (and the ads from Sunkist never arrived).

Though I barely knew this woman, she had done two things I always remembered: put her job on the line in a way that editors often talk about but rarely do, and been so loyal to her colleagues that she never told me or anyone outside *Look* that she had done so.

Fortunately, Pat did agree to leave *McCall's* and take a huge cut in salary to become publisher of *Ms.* She became responsible for training and inspiring generations of young women who joined the *Ms.* ad sales force, many of whom went on to become "firsts" at the top of publishing. When *Ms.* first started, however, there were so few women with experience selling space that Pat and I made the rounds of ad agencies ourselves. Later, the fact that *Ms.* was asking companies to do business in a different way meant our saleswomen had to make many times the usual number of calls—first to convince agencies and then client companies besides—and to present endless amounts of research. I was often asked to do a final ad presentation, or see some higher decision-maker, or speak to women employees so executives could see the interest of women they worked with. That's why I spent more time persuading advertisers than editing or writing for *Ms.* and why I ended up with an unsentimental education in the seamy underside of publishing that few writers see (and even fewer magazines can publish).

Let me take you with us through some experiences, just as they happened:

• Cheered on by early support from Volkswagen and one or two other car companies, we scrape together time and money to put on a major reception in Detroit. We know U.S. carmakers firmly believe that women choose the upholstery, not the car, but we are armed with statistics and reader mail to prove the contrary: a car is an important purchase for women, one that symbolizes mobility and freedom.

But almost nobody comes. We are left with many pounds of shrimp on the table, and quite a lot of egg on our face. We blame ourselves for not guessing that there would be a baseball pennant play-off on the same day, but executives go out of their way to explain they wouldn't have come anyway. Thus begins ten years of knocking on hostile doors, presenting endless documentation, and hiring a full-time saleswoman in Detroit; all necessary before Ms. gets any real results.

This long saga has a semi happy ending: foreign and, later, domestic carmakers eventually provided Ms. with enough advertising to make cars one of our top sources of ad revenue. Slowly, Detroit began to take the women's market seriously enough to put car ads in other women's magazines, too, thus freeing a few pages from the hothouse of fashion-beauty-food ads.

But long after figures showed a third, even a half, of many car models being bought by women, U.S. makers continued to be uncomfortable addressing women. Unlike foreign carmakers, Detroit never quite learned the secret of creating intelligent ads that exclude no one, and then placing them in women's magazines to overcome past exclusion. (*Ms.* readers were so grateful for a routine Honda ad featuring rack and pinion steering, for instance, that they sent fan mail.) Even now, Detroit continues to ask, "Should we make special ads for women?" Perhaps that's why some foreign cars still have a disproportionate share of the U.S. women's market.

• In the *Ms.* Gazette, we do a brief report on a congressional hearing into chemicals used in hair dyes that are absorbed through the skin and may be carcinogenic. Newspapers report this too, but Clairol, a Bristol-Myers subsidiary that makes dozens of products—a few of which have just begun to advertise in *Ms.*—is outraged. Not at newspapers or newsmagazines, just at us. It's bad enough that *Ms.* is the only women's magazine refusing to provide the usual "complementary" articles and beauty photos, but to criticize one of their categories—*that* is going too far.

We offer to publish a letter from Clairol telling its side of the story. In an excess of solicitousness, we even put this letter in the Gazette, not in Letters to the Editors where it belongs. Nonetheless—and in spite of surveys that show *Ms.* readers are active women who use more of almost everything Clairol makes than do the readers of any other women's magazine—*Ms.* gets almost none of these ads for the rest of its natural life.

Meanwhile, Clairol changes its hair coloring formula, apparently in response to the hearings we reported.

• Our saleswomen set out early to attract ads for consumer electronics: sound equipment, calculators, computers, VCRs, and the like. We know that our readers are determined to be included in the technological revolution. We know from reader surveys that *Ms.* readers are buying this stuff in numbers as high as those of magazines like *Playboy;* or "men 18 to 34," the prime targets of the consumer electronics industry. Moreover, unlike traditional women's products that our readers buy but don't need to read articles about, these are subjects they want covered in our pages. There actually *is* a supportive editorial atmosphere.

"But women don't understand technology," say executives at the end of ad presentations. "Maybe not," we respond, "but neither do men—and we all buy it."

"If women *do* buy it," say the decision-makers, "they're asking their husbands and boyfriends what to buy first." We produce letters from *Ms.* readers saying how turned off they are when salesmen say things like "Let me know when your husband can come in."

After several years of this, we get a few ads for compact sound systems. Some of them come from JVC, whose vice president, Harry Elias, is trying to convince his Japanese bosses that there is something called a women's market. At his invitation, I find myself speaking at huge trade shows in Chicago and Las Vegas, trying to persuade JVC dealers that showrooms don't have to be locker rooms where women are made to feel unwelcome. But as it turns out, the shows themselves are part of the problem. In Las Vegas, the only women around the technology displays are seminude models serving champagne. In Chicago, the big attraction is Marilyn Chambers, who followed Linda Lovelace of *Deep Throat* fame as Chuck Traynor's captive and/or employee. VCRs are being demonstrated with her porn videos.

In the end, we get ads for a car stereo now and then, but no VCRs; some IBM personal computers, but no Apple or Japanese ones. We notice that office magazines like *Working Woman* and *Savvy* don't benefit as much as they should from office equipment ads either. In the electronics world, women and technology seem mutually exclusive. It remains a decade behind even Detroit.

• Because we get letters from little girls who love toy trains, and who ask our help in changing ads and box-top photos that feature little boys only, we try to get toy-train ads from Lionel. It turns out that Lionel executives *have* been concerned about little girls. They made a pink train, and were surprised when it didn't sell.

Lionel bows to consumer pressure with a photograph of a boy *and* a girl—but only on some of their boxes. They fear that, if trains are associated with girls, they will be devalued in the minds of boys. Needless to say, *Ms.* gets no train ads, and little girls remain a mostly unexplored market. By 1986, Lionel is put up for sale.

But for different reasons, we haven't had much luck with other kinds of toys either. In spite of many articles on child-rearing; an annual listing of nonsexist, multi-racial toys by Letty Cottin Pogrebin; Stories for Free Children, a regular feature also edited by Letty; and other prizewinning features for or about children, we get virtually no toy ads. Generations of *Ms.* saleswomen explain to toy manufacturers that a larger proportion of *Ms.* readers have preschool children than do the readers of other women's magazines, but this industry can't believe feminists have or care about children.

• When *Ms.* begins, the staff decides not to accept ads for feminine hygiene sprays or cigarettes: they are damaging and carry no appropriate health warnings. Though we don't think we should tell our readers what to do, we do think we should provide facts so they can decide for themselves. Since the antismoking lobby has been pressing for health warnings on cigarette ads, we decide to take them only as they comply.

Philip Morris is among the first to do so. One of its brands, Virginia Slims, is also sponsoring women's tennis and the first national polls of women's opinions. On the other hand, the Virginia Slims theme, "You've come a long way, baby," has more than a "baby" problem. It makes smoking a symbol of progress for women.

We explain to Philip Morris that this slogan won't do well in our pages, but they are convinced its success with some women means it will work with *all* women. Finally, we agree to publish an ad for a Virginia Slims calendar as a test. The letters from readers are critical—and smart. For instance: Would you show a black man picking cotton, the same man in a Cardin suit, and symbolize the antislavery and civil rights movements by smoking? Of course not. But instead of honoring the test results, the Philip Morris people seem angry to be proven wrong. They take away ads for *all* their many brands.

This costs *Ms.* about $250,000 the first year. After five years, we can no longer keep track. Occasionally, a new set of executives listens to *Ms.* saleswomen, but because we won't take Virginia Slims, not one Philip Morris product returns to our pages for the next 16 years.

Gradually, we also realize our naiveté in thinking we *could* decide against taking cigarette ads. They became a disproportionate support of magazines the moment they were banned on television, and few magazines could compete and survive without them; certainly not *Ms.*, which lacks so many other categories. By the time statistics in the 1980s showed that women's rate of lung cancer was approaching men's, the necessity of taking cigarette ads has become a kind of prison.

• General Mills, Pillsbury, Carnation, DelMonte, Dole, Kraft, Stouffer, Hormel, Nabisco: you name the food giant, we try it. But no matter how desirable the *Ms.* readership, our lack of recipes is lethal.

We explain to them that placing food ads *only* next to recipes associates food with work. For many women, it is a negative that works *against* the ads. Why not place food ads in diverse media without recipes (thus reaching more men, who are now a third of the shoppers in supermarkets anyway), and leave the recipes to specialty magazines like *Gourmet* (a third of whose readers are also men)?

These arguments elicit interest, but except for an occasional ad for a convenience food, instant coffee, diet drinks, yogurt, or such extras as avocados and almonds, this mainstay of the publishing industry stays closed to us. Period.

• Traditionally, wines and liquors didn't advertise to women: men were thought to make the brand decisions, even if women did the buying. But after endless presentations, we begin to make a dent in this category. Thanks to the unconventional Michel Roux of Carillon Importers (distributors of Grand Marnier, Absolut Vodka, and others), who assumes that food and drink have no gender, some ads are leaving their men's club.

Beermakers are still selling masculinity. It takes *Ms.* fully eight years to get its first beer ad (Michelob). In general, however, liquor ads are less stereotyped in their imagery—and far less controlling of the editorial content around them—than are women's products. But given the underrepresentation of other categories, these very facts tend to create a disproportionate number of alcohol ads in the pages of *Ms.* This in turn dismays readers worried about women and alcoholism.

• We hear in 1980 that women in the Soviet Union have been producing feminist *samizdat* (underground, self-published books) and circulating them throughout the country. As punishment, four of the leaders have been exiled. Though we are operating on our usual shoestring, we solicit individual contributions to send Robin Morgan to interview these women in Vienna.

The result is an exclusive cover story that includes the first news of a populist peace movement against the Afghanistan occupation, a prediction of *glasnost* to come, and a grass-roots, intimate view of Soviet women's lives. From the popular press to women's studies courses, the response is great. The story wins a Front Page award.

Nonetheless, this journalistic coup undoes years of efforts to get an ad schedule from Revlon. Why? Because the Soviet women on our cover *are not wearing makeup.*

• Four years of research and presentations go into convincing airlines that women now make travel choices and business trips. United, the first airline to advertise in *Ms.*, is so impressed with the response from our readers that one of its executives appears in a film for our ad presentations. As usual, good ads get great results.

But we have problems unrelated to such results. For instance: because American Airlines flight attendants include among their labor demands the stipulation that they could choose to have their last names preceded by "Ms." on their name tags—in a long-delayed revolt against the standard, "I am your pilot, Captain Rothgart, and this is your flight attendant, Cindy Sue"—American officials seem to hold the magazine responsible. We get no ads.

There is still a different problem at Eastern. A vice president cancels subscriptions for thousands of copies on Eastern flights. Why? Because he is offended by ads for lesbian poetry journals in the *Ms.* Classified. A "family airline," as he explains to me coldly on the phone, has to "draw the line somewhere."

It's obvious that *Ms.* can't exclude lesbians and serve women. We've been trying to make that point ever since our first issue included an article by and about lesbians, and both Suzanne Levine, our managing editor, and I were lectured by such heavy hitters as Ed Kosner, then editor of *Newsweek* (and now of *New York Magazine*), who insisted that *Ms.* should "position" itself *against* lesbians. But our advertisers have paid to reach a guaranteed number of readers, and soliciting new subscriptions to compensate for Eastern would cost $150,000, plus rebating money in the meantime.

Like almost everything ad-related, this presents an elaborate organizing problem. After days of searching for sympathetic members of the Eastern board, Frank Thomas, president of the Ford Foundation, kindly offers to call Roswell Gilpatrick, a director of Eastern. I talk with Mr. Gilpatrick, who calls Frank Borman, then the president of Eastern. Frank Borman calls me to say that his airline is not in the business of censoring magazines: *Ms.* will be returned to Eastern flights.

• Women's access to insurance and credit is vital, but with the exception of Equitable and a few other ad pioneers, such financial services address men. For almost a decade after the Equal Credit Opportunity Act passes in 1974, we try to convince American Express that women are a growth market—but nothing works.

Finally, a former professor of Russian named Jerry Welsh becomes head of marketing. He assumes that women should be cardholders, and persuades his colleagues to feature women in a campaign. Thanks to this 1980s series, the growth rate for female cardholders surpasses that for men.

For this article, I asked Jerry Welsh if he would explain why American Express waited so long. "Sure," he said, "they were afraid of having a 'pink' card."

• Women of color read *Ms.* in disproportionate numbers. This is a source of pride to *Ms.* staffers, who are also more racially representative than the editors of other women's magazines. But this reality is obscured by ads filled with enough white women to make a reader snowblind.

Pat Carbine remembers mostly "astonishment" when she requested African American, Hispanic, Asian, and other diverse images. Marcia Ann Gillespie, a *Ms.* editor who was previously the editor in chief of *Essence,* witnesses ad bias a second time: having tried for *Essence* to get white advertisers to use black images (Revlon did so eventually, but L'Oréal, Lauder, Chanel, and other companies never did), she sees similar problems getting integrated ads for an integrated magazine. Indeed, the ad world often creates black and Hispanic ads only for black and Hispanic media. In an exact parallel of the fear that marketing a product to women will endanger its appeal to men, the response is usually, "But your [white] readers won't identify."

In fact, those we are able to get—for instance, a Max Factor ad made for *Essence* that Linda Wachner gives us after she becomes president—are praised by white readers, too. But there are pathetically few such images.

• By the end of 1986, production and mailing costs have risen astronomically, ad income is flat, and competition for ads is stiffer than ever. The 60/40 preponderance of edit over ads that we promised to readers becomes 50/50; children's stories, most poetry, and some fiction are casualties of less space; in order to get variety into limited pages, the length (and sometimes the depth) of articles suffers; and, though we do refuse most of the ads that would look like a parody in our pages, we get so worn down that some slip through. (See this issue's No Comment.) Still, readers perform miracles. Though we haven't been able to afford a subscription mailing in two years, they maintain our guaranteed circulation of 450,000.

Nonetheless, media reports on *Ms.* often insist that our unprofitability must be due to reader disinterest. The myth that advertisers simply follow readers is very strong. Not one reporter notes that other comparable magazines our size (say, *Vanity Fair* or *The Atlantic*) have been losing more money in one year than *Ms.* has lost in 16 years. No matter how much never-to-be-recovered cash is poured into starting a magazine or keeping one going, appearances seem to be all that matter. (Which is why we haven't been able to explain our fragile state in public. Nothing causes ad-flight like the smell of nonsuccess.)

My healthy response is anger. My not-so-healthy response is constant worry. Also an obsession with finding one more rescue. There is hardly a night when I don't wake up with sweaty palms and pounding heart, scared that we won't be able to pay the printer or the post office; scared most of all that closing our doors will hurt the women's movement.

Out of chutzpah and desperation, I arrange a lunch with Leonard Lauder, president of Estée Lauder. With the exception of Clinique (the brainchild of Carol Phillips), none of Lauder's hundreds of products has been advertised in *Ms.* A year's schedule of ads for just three or four of them could save us. Indeed, as the scion of a family-owned company whose ad practices are followed by the beauty industry, he is one of the few men who could liberate many pages in all women's magazines just by changing his mind about "complementary copy."

Over a lunch that costs more than we can pay for some articles, I explain the need for his leadership. I also lay out the record of *Ms.:* more literary and journalistic prizes won, more new issues introduced into the mainstream, new writers discovered, and impact on society than any other magazine; more articles that became books, stories that became movies, ideas that became television series, and newly advertised products that became profitable; and, most important for him, a place for his ads to reach women who aren't reachable through any other women's magazine. Indeed, if there is one constant characteristic of the ever-changing *Ms.* readership, it is their impact as leaders. Whether it's waiting until later to have first babies, or pioneering PABA as sun protection in cosmetics, *whatever* they are doing today, a third to a half of American women will be doing three to five years from now. It's never failed.

But, he says, *Ms.* readers are not *our* women. They're not interested in things like fragrance and blush-on. If they were, *Ms.* would write articles about them.

On the contrary, I explain, surveys show they are more likely to buy such things than the readers of, say, *Cosmopolitan* or *Vogue*. They're good customers because they're out in the world enough to need several sets of everything: home, work, purse, travel, gym, and so on. They just don't need to read articles about these things. Would he ask a men's magazine to publish monthly columns on how to shave before he advertised Aramis products (his line for men)?

He concedes that beauty features are often concocted more for advertisers than readers. But *Ms.* isn't appropriate for his ads anyway, he explains. Why? Because Estée Lauder is selling "a kept-woman mentality."

I can't quite believe this. Sixty percent of the users of his products are salaried, and generally resemble *Ms.* readers. Besides, his company has the appeal of having been started by a creative and hardworking woman, his mother, Estée Lauder.

That doesn't matter, he says. He knows his customers, and they would *like* to be kept women. That's why he will never advertise in *Ms.*

In November 1987, by vote of the Ms. Foundation for Education and Communication (*Ms.*'s owner and publisher, the media subsidiary of the Ms. Foundation for Women), *Ms.* was sold to a company whose officers. Australian feminists Sandra Yates and Anne Summers, raised the investment money in their country that *Ms.* couldn't find in its own. They also started *Sassy* for teenage women.

In their two-year tenure, circulation was raised to 550,000 by investment in circulation mailings, and, to the dismay of some readers, editorial features on clothes and new products made a more traditional bid for ads. Nonetheless, ad pages fell below previous levels. In addition, *Sassy,* whose fresh voice and sexual frankness were an unprecedented success with young readers, was targeted by two mothers from Indiana who began, as one of them put it, "calling every Christian organization I could think of." In response to this controversy, several crucial advertisers pulled out.

Such links between ads and editorial content was a problem in Australia, too, but to a lesser degree. "Our readers pay two times more for their magazines," Anne explained, "so advertisers have less power to threaten a magazine's viability."

"I was shocked," said Sandra Yates with characteristic directness. "In Australia, we think you have freedom of the press—but you don't."

Since Anne and Sandra had not met their budget's projections for ad revenue, their investors forced a sale. In October 1989, *Ms.* and *Sassy* were bought by Dale Lang, owner of *Working Mother, Working Woman,* and one of the few independent publishing companies left among the conglomerates. In response to a request from the original *Ms.* staff—as well as to reader letters urging that *Ms.* continue, plus his own belief that *Ms.* would benefit his other magazines by blazing a trail—he agreed to try the ad-free, reader-supported *Ms.* you hold now and to give us complete editorial control.

II.

Do you think, as I once did, that advertisers make decisions based on solid research? Well, think again. "Broadly speaking," says Joseph Smith of Oxtoby-Smith, Inc., a consumer research firm, "there is no persuasive evidence that the editorial context of an ad matters."

Advertisers who demand such "complementary copy," even in the absence of respectable studies, clearly are operating under a double standard. The same food companies place ads in *People* with no recipes. Cosmetics companies support *The New Yorker* with no regular beauty columns. So where does this habit of controlling the content of women's magazines come from?

Tradition. Ever since *Ladies Magazine* debuted in Boston in 1828, editorial copy directed to women has been informed by something other than its readers' wishes. There were no ads then, but in an age when married women were legal minors with no right to their own money, there was another revenue source to be kept in mind: husbands. "Husbands may rest assured," wrote editor Sarah Josepha Hale, "that nothing found in these pages shall cause her [his wife] to be less assiduous in preparing for his reception or encourage her to 'usurp station' or encroach upon prerogatives of men."

Hale went on to become the editor of *Godey's Lady's Book,* a magazine featuring "fashion plates": engravings of dresses for readers to take to their seamstresses or copy themselves. Hale added "how to" articles, which set the tone for women's service magazines for years to come: how to write politely, avoid sunburn, and—in no fewer than 1,200 words—how to maintain a goose quill pen. She advocated education for women but avoided controversy. Just as most women's magazines now avoid politics, poll their readers on issues like abortion but rarely take a stand, and praise socially approved lifestyles, Hale saw to it that *Godey's* avoided the hot topics of its day: slavery, abolition, and women's suffrage.

What definitively turned women's magazines into catalogs, however, were two events: Ellen Butterick's invention of the clothing pattern in 1863 and the mass manufacture of patent medicines containing everything from colored water to cocaine. For the first time, readers could purchase what magazines encouraged them to want. As such magazines became more profitable, they also began to attract men as editors. (Most women's magazines continued to have men as top editors until the feminist 1970s.) Edward Bok, who became editor of *The Ladies' Home Journal* in 1889, discovered the power of advertisers when he rejected ads for patent medicines and found that other advertisers canceled in retribution. In the early 20th century, *Good Housekeeping* started its Institute to "test and approve" products. Its Seal of Approval became the grandfather of current "value added" programs that offer advertisers such bonuses as product sampling and department store promotions.

By the time suffragists finally won the vote in 1920, women's magazines had become too entrenched as catalogs to help women learn how to use it. The main function was to create a desire for products, teach how to use products, and make products a crucial part of gaining social approval, pleasing a husband, and performing as a homemaker. Some unrelated articles and short stories were included to persuade women to pay for these catalogs. But articles were neither consumerist nor rebellious. Even fiction was usually subject to formula: if a woman had any sexual life outside marriage, she was supposed to come to a bad end.

In 1965, Helen Gurley Brown began to change part of that formula by bringing "the sexual revolution" to women's magazines—but in an ad-oriented way. Attracting multiple men required even more consumerism, as the Cosmo Girl made clear, than finding one husband.

In response to the workplace revolution of the 1970s, traditional women's magazines—that is, "trade books" for women working at home—were joined by *Savvy, Working Woman,* and other trade books for women working in offices. But by keeping the fashion/beauty/entertaining articles necessary to get traditional ads and then adding career articles besides, they inadvertently produced the antifeminist stereotype of Super Woman. The male-imitative, dress-for-success woman carrying a briefcase became the media image of a woman worker, even though a blue-collar woman's salary was often higher than her glorified secretarial sister's, and though women at a real briefcase level are statistically rare. Needless to say, these dress-for-success women were also thin, white, and beautiful.

In recent years, advertisers' control over the editorial content of women's magazines has become so institutionalized that it is written into "insertion orders" or dictated to ad salespeople as official policy. The following are recent typical orders to women's magazines:

- Dow's Cleaning Products stipulates that ads for its Vivid and Spray 'n Wash products should be adjacent to "children or fashion editorial"; ads for Bathroom Cleaner should be next to "home furnishing/family" features; and so on for other brands. "If a magazine fails for 1/2 the brands or more," the Dow order warns, "it will be omitted from further consideration."
- Bristol-Myers, the parent of Clairol, Windex, Drano, Bufferin, and much more, stipulates that ads be placed next to "a full page of compatible editorial."
- S.C. Johnson & Son, makers of Johnson Wax, lawn and laundry products, insect sprays, hair sprays, and so on, orders that its ads *should not be opposite extremely controversial features or material antithetical to the nature/copy of the advertised product."* (Italics theirs.)
- Maidenform, manufacturer of bras and other apparel, leaves a blank for the particular product and states: "The creative concept of the _____ campaign, and the very nature of the product itself appeal to the positive emotions of the reader/consumer. Therefore, it is imperative that all editorial adjacencies reflect that same positive tone. The editorial must not be negative in content or lend itself contrary to the _____ product imagery/message (e.g. *editorial relating to illness, disillusionment, large size fashion, etc.*)." (Italics mine.)

The De Beers diamond company, a big seller of engagement rings, prohibits magazines from placing its ads with "adjacencies to hard news or anti/love-romance themed editorial."

Procter & Gamble, one of this country's most powerful and diversified advertisers, stands out in the memory of Anne Summers and Sandra Yates (no mean feat in this context): its products were not to be placed in *any* issue that included *any* material on gun control, abortion, the occult, cults, or the disparagement of religion. Caution was also demanded in any issue covering sex or drugs, even for educational purposes.

Those are the most obvious chains around women's magazines. There are also rules so clear they needn't be written down: for instance, an overall "look" compatible with beauty and fashion ads. Even "real" nonmodel women photographed for a woman's magazine are usually made up, dressed in credited clothes, and retouched out of all reality. When editors do include articles on less-than-cheerful subjects (for instance, domestic violence), they tend to keep them short and unillustrated. The point is to be "upbeat." Just as women in the street are asked, "Why don't you smile, honey?" women's magazines acquire an institutional smile.

Within the text itself, praise for advertisers' products has become so ritualized that fields like "beauty writing" have been invented. One of its frequent practitioners explained seriously that "It's a difficult art. How many new adjectives can you find? How much greater can you make a lipstick sound? The FDA restricts what companies can say on labels, but we create illusion. And ad agencies are on the phone all the time pushing you to get their product in. A lot of them keep the business based on how many editorial clippings they produce every month. The worst are products," like Lauder's as the writer confirmed, "with their own name involved. It's all ego."

Often, editorial becomes one giant ad. Last November, for instance, *Lear's* featured an elegant woman executive on the cover. On the contents page, we learned she was wearing Guerlain makeup and Samsara, a new fragrance by Guerlain. Inside were full-page ads for Samsara and Guerlain antiwrinkle cream. In the cover profile, we learned that this executive was responsible for launching Samsara and is Guerlain's director of public relations. When the *Columbia Journalism Review* did one of the few articles to include women's magazines in coverage of the influence of ads, editor Frances Lear was quoted as defending her magazine because "this kind of thing is done all the time."

Often, advertisers also plunge odd-shaped ads into the text, no matter what the cost to the readers. At *Woman's Day,* a magazine originally founded by a supermarket chain, editor in chief Ellen Levine said, "The day the copy had to rag around a chicken leg was not a happy one."

Advertisers are also adamant about where in a magazine their ads appear. When Revlon was not placed as the first beauty ad in one Hearst magazine, for instance, Revlon pulled its ads from *all* Hearst magazines. Ruth Whitney, editor in chief of *Glamour,* attributes some of these demands to "ad agencies wanting to prove to a client that they've squeezed the last drop of blood out of a magazine." She also is, she says, "sick and tired of hearing that women's magazines are controlled by cigarette ads." Relatively speaking, she's right. To be as censoring as are many advertisers for women's products, tobacco companies would have to demand articles in praise of smoking and expect glamorous photos of beautiful women smoking their brands.

I don't mean to imply that the editors I quote here share my objections to ads: most assume that women's magazines have to be the way they are. But it's also true that only former editors can be completely honest. "Most of the pressure came in the form of direct product mentions," explains Sey Chassler, who was editor in chief of *Redbook* from the sixties to the eighties. "We got threats from the big guys, the Revlons, blackmail threats. They wouldn't run ads unless we credited them.

"But it's not fair to single out the beauty advertisers because these pressures came from everybody. Advertisers want to know two things: What are you going to charge me? What *else* are you going to do for me? It's a holdup. For instance, management felt that fiction took up too much space. They couldn't put any advertising in that. For the last ten years, the number of fiction entries into the National Magazine Awards has declined.

"And pressures are getting worse. More magazines are more bottom-line oriented because they have been taken over by companies with no interest in publishing.

"I also think advertisers do this to women's magazines especially," he concluded, "because of the general disrespect they have for women."

Even media experts who don't give a damn about women's magazines are alarmed by the spread of this ad-edit linkage. In a climate *The Wall Street Journal* describes as an unacknowledged Depression for media, women's products are increasingly able to take their low standards wherever they go. For instance: newsweeklies publish uncritical stories on fashion and fitness. *The New York Times Magazine* recently ran an article on "firming creams," complete with mentions of advertisers. *Vanity Fair* published a profile of one major advertiser, Ralph Lauren, illustrated by the same photographer who does his ads, and turned the lifestyle of another, Calvin Klein, into a cover story. Even the outrageous *Spy* has toned down since it began to go after fashion ads.

And just to make us really worry, films and books, the last media that go directly to the public without having to attract ads first, are in danger, too. Producers are beginning to depend on payments for displaying products in movies, and books are now being commissioned by companies like Federal Express.

But the truth is that women's products—like women's magazines—have never been the subjects of much serious reporting anyway. News and general interest publications, including the "style" or "living" sections of newspapers, write about food and clothing as cooking and fashion, and almost never evaluate such products by brand name. Though chemical additives, pesticides, and animal fats are major health risks in the United States, and clothes, shoddy or not, absorb more consumer dollars than cars, this lack of information is serious. So is ignoring the contents of beauty products that are absorbed into our bodies through our skins, and that have profit margins so big they would make a loan shark blush.

III.

What could women's magazines be like if they were as free as books? as realistic as newspapers? as creative as films? as diverse as women's lives? We don't know.

But we'll only find out if we take women's magazines seriously. If readers were to act in a concerted way to change traditional practices of *all* women's magazines and the marketing of *all* women's products, we could do it. After all, they are operating on our consumer dollars; money that we now control. You and I could:

- write to editors and publishers (with copies to advertisers) that we're willing to pay *more* for magazines with editorial independence, but will *not* continue to pay for those that are just editorial extensions of ads;
- write to advertisers (with copies to editors and publishers) that we want fiction, political reporting, consumer reporting—whatever is, or is not, supported by their ads;
- put as much energy into breaking advertising's control over content as into changing the images in ads, or protesting ads for harmful products like cigarettes;
- support only those women's magazines and products that take *us* seriously as readers and consumers.

Those of us in the magazine world can also use the carrot-and-stick technique. For instance: pointing out that, if magazines were a regulated medium like television, the demands of advertisers would be against FCC rules. Payola and extortion could be punished. As it is, there are probably illegalities. A magazine's postal rates are determined by the ratio of ad to edit pages, and the former costs more than the latter. So much for the stick.

The carrot means appealing to enlightened self-interest. For instance: there are many studies showing that the greatest factor in determining an ad's effectiveness is the credibility of its surroundings. The "higher the rating of editorial believability," concluded a 1987 survey by the *Journal of Advertising Research,* "the higher the rating of the advertising." Thus, an impenetrable wall between edit and ads would also be in the best interest of advertisers.

Unfortunately, few agencies or clients hear such arguments. Editors often maintain the false purity of refusing to talk to them at all. Instead, they see ad salespeople who know little about editorial, are trained in business as usual, and are usually paid by commission. Editors might also band together to take on controversy. That happened once when all the major women's magazines did articles in the same month on the Equal Rights Amendment. It could happen again.

It's almost three years away from life between the grindstones of advertising pressures and readers' needs. I'm just beginning to realize how edges got smoothed down—in spite of all our resistance.

I remember feeling put upon when I changed "Porsche" to "car" in a piece about Nazi imagery in German pornography by Andrea Dworkin—feeling sure Andrea would understand that Volkswagen, the distributor of Porsche and one of our few supportive advertisers, asked only to be far away from Nazi subjects. It's taken me all this time to realize that Andrea was the one with a right to feel put upon.

Even as I write this, I get a call from a writer for *Elle,* who is doing a whole article on where women part their hair. Why, she wants to know, do I part mine in the middle?

It's all so familiar. A writer trying to make something of a nothing assignment; an editor laboring to think of new ways to attract ads; readers assuming that other women must want this ridiculous stuff; more women suffering for lack of information, insight, creativity, and laughter that could be on these same pages.

I ask you: Can't we do better than this?

PART 3

ADVERTISING RIGHTS
AND RESPONSIBILITIES

Protecting Consumers in a Consumer Culture
and a Global Economy

Central to Part 3 is the regulation of advertising in a consumer culture where the interests of free speech must constantly be weighed against the information needs of individuals and society. Several unique issues are raised under the competing interests of the public's right to know and the public's right to be protected from potentially harmful information. Nowhere is this conundrum better illustrated than in the debates surrounding first amendment rights as they apply to children.

Also at issue are the different values inherent in advertising self-regulation versus regulation by state, national, and international bodies. The practical and philosophical need for both forms of regulation (industry regulation of itself and governmental controls) are, in turn, addressed given the ideological base established earlier in this book. Implicit and explicit in Part 3 are the ethical issues inherent in the regulation of advertising and the protection of consumers.

The first two articles approach regulation in the broadest of terms. Hoefges provides a comprehensive review of Supreme Court decisions in cases involving advertising and the First Amendment. Preston looks at the problem of antifactual content (known as "puffery") in advertising and the resulting consequences for consumers.

The next article in Part 3 concentrates on industry self-regulation. General opportunities for protection of consumers through advertising industry self-regulation are addressed in Edelstein's article, which explains the strengths and weakness of the U.S. advertising self-regulation process.

Protection of vulnerable audiences then becomes the focus of Part 3. The first article addresses children while the subsequent article looks at inner-city minorities. French versus American efforts to protect children through advertising self-regulation are compared by Taylor and Cunningham; implicit in this article is the effect culture has on how advertising professionals perceive the potentially vulnerable nature of children. Part 3 concludes with Brenkert's chronicle of the ethical and moral issues involved in the marketing of PowerMaster (a high-alcohol content beverage) to inner-city minorities. At issue is the advertiser's moral and ethical responsibility to an audience that is heavily targeted with messages promoting dangerous and/or addictive products. One of the issues raised is whether advertisers are merely implementing textbook marketing strategies directed at consenting adults; or, whether advertisers are exploiting the environmental, economical, and psychological conditions influencing a particular audience.

CHAPTER 16

PROTECTING TOBACCO ADVERTISING UNDER THE COMMERCIAL SPEECH DOCTRINE
The Constitutional Impact of *Lorillard Tobacco Co.*

MICHAEL HOEFGES

Since 1980, the Supreme Court of the United States has utilized a unique and complex test of intermediate constitutional scrutiny when commercial speech regulations are challenged on First Amendment grounds. Established in 1980 in *Central Hudson Gas & Electric Corp. v. Public Service Commission*[1] this test—known as the *Central Hudson* analysis—has been applied by the Court with varying degrees of rigor, as noted by several legal commentators.[2] For instance, writing recently in the *UCLA Law Review,* one commentator called the Court's commercial speech doctrine a "notoriously unstable and contentious domain of American jurisprudence," stating that "[n]o other realm of First Amendment law has proved as divisive."[3]

Over the last two decades, the level of First Amendment protection for advertising has plummeted to nearly non-existent[4] and, more recently, has risen to its highest level, rendering it difficult for the government to constitutionally regulate truthful and non-deceptive advertising.[5] Arguably, the Court's recent commercial speech decisions have nearly eliminated the gap between commercial speech and fully protected non-commercial speech under the hierarchy of expression established by the Court.[6]

In recent cases, the Supreme Court employed an increasingly rigorous version of the *Central Hudson* analysis to strike down federal restrictions on beer label content,[7] state restrictions on retail price liquor advertising,[8] and federal restrictions on broadcast advertising for casino gambling.[9] As commentators have pointed out, these cases involved so-called "vice" advertising for products and activities that are legal for adults but carry harmful secondary effects for society, including minors.[10] The Court's approach in these cases departed significantly from its approach in earlier vice advertising cases in which the Court had rejected constitutional challenges to gambling advertising laws.[11]

In *Lorillard Tobacco Co. v. Reilly,*[12] decided in 2001, the Court addressed for the first time the constitutionality of state restrictions on retail tobacco advertising. The *Lorillard Tobacco* Court utilized a combination of federal pre-emption principles and the *Central Hudson* analysis to strike down state regulations that served to ban most outdoor and point-of-sale tobacco advertising. The justices split on several of the key rulings in the case, and Justice Sandra Day O'Connor, who wrote the majority opinion, was quoted stating that readers would need a "roadmap" to follow their votes.[13] However, she assured onlookers that there was a majority of the Court for each part of the decision.[14]

The *Lorillard Tobacco* opinion is significant on a number of points to the development of the commercial speech doctrine and to efforts by the government to regulate harmful product advertising. The case has legal and historical significance as the first in which the Supreme Court decided the constitutionality of an advertising restriction aimed at protecting children, and the first in which the Court directly decided the constitutionality of government attempts to restrict tobacco advertising. From a broader constitutional perspective, the case is important as reaffirmation of the *Central Hudson* analysis as constitutional doctrine despite concerns about its continued validity among members of the current Court. From a legislative perspective, the case is also significant for stringently interpreting the federal pre-emption provisions of the Federal Cigarette Labeling and Advertising Act (FCLAA)[15] in a manner that severely limits the legal capacity of states to regulate cigarette advertising absent further revision to the FCLAA by Congress.

This article first explores the commercial speech doctrine with emphasis on recent Supreme Court decisions leading to *Lorillard Tobacco*. Next, it sets out the national regulatory framework for tobacco advertising, which provides relevant context for the subsequent discussion and analysis of the *Lorillard Tobacco* case. The article then analyzes the Court's *Lorillard Tobacco* opinion and traces its progeny in lower federal and state court cases. Finally, the article provides analysis of the impact *of Lorillard Tobacco* on the commercial speech doctrine and seeks to derive the parameters of constitutionally permissible government regulation of protected commercial speech.

THE COMMERCIAL SPEECH DOCTRINE AND
CENTRAL HUDSON ANALYSIS

In the early 1970s, the Supreme Court had not fully assimilated advertising into the First Amendment as a form of constitutionally-protected speech.[16] In 1976, the Court decided *Virginia State Board of Pharmacy v. Virginia Citizens Consumer Council, Inc.,*[17] and shifted its position. In *Virginia State Board,* the Court ruled for the first time that pure commercial speech—meaning expression that does no more than "propose a commercial transaction"—is protected by the First Amendment, albeit not as fully as non-commercial political and social speech.[18] The *Virginia State Board* Court grounded its rationale on the informational value of advertising to consumers and found this to be a significant First Amendment interest. For instance, the Court stated: "Advertising, however tasteless and excessive it sometimes may seem, nonetheless is the dissemination of information as to who is producing and selling what product and for what reason."[19]

In *Virginia State Board,* the Court struck down a Virginia regulation that banned state-licensed pharmacists from advertising prescription drug prices to consumers. For the first time, the Court held specifically that the First Amendment protects not only a commercial speaker's right to speak but also the public's right to receive commercial information. Writing for the Court, Justice Harry A. Blackmun stated:

> So long as we preserve a predominantly free enterprise economy, the allocation of our resources in large measure will be made through numerous private economic decisions. It is a matter of public interest that those decisions, in the aggregate, be intelligent and well informed. To this end, the free flow of commercial information is indispensable.[20]

The Court was far more generous in its constitutional treatment of pure commercial speech in *Virginia State Board* than in prior decisions, yet still did not extend full First Amendment protection to commercial speech. As Justice Blackmun pointed out, the *Virginia State Board* opinion still allowed government to regulate commercial speech more extensively than non-commercial political and social speech.[21] In addition, the Court specifically refused First Amendment protection for false or deceptive commercial speech or commercial speech proposing an illegal transaction, and thus segregated protected and unprotected commercial speech based on these criteria.[22] After *Virginia State Board,* the government remained largely unrestricted to regulate unprotected commercial speech.[23] Still, the *Virginia State Board* decision remains significant for extending First Amendment protection to pure commercial speech that proposes a legal transaction and is truthful and non-deceptive.[24]

Establishment of the *Central Hudson* Analysis

The *Virginia State Board* Court did not specifically address the constitutional parameters of permissible government regulation on protected commercial speech. However, the Court faced that issue in *Central Hudson* in striking down a New York state regulation that prohibited public utility companies from using promotional advertising that encouraged energy consumption.[25] In doing so, Justice Lewis F. Powell, Jr., writing for the Court, set out a four-factor analysis to test the constitutionality of government restrictions on commercial speech:

> [First], we must determine whether the expression is protected by the First Amendment. For commercial speech to come within that provision, it at least must concern a lawful activity and not be misleading. [Second], we ask whether the asserted governmental interest is substantial. If both inquiries yield positive answers, we must [third] determine whether the regulation directly advances the governmental interest asserted, and [fourth] whether it is not more extensive than is necessary to serve that interest.[26]

Applying this four-step analysis to the regulation at issue, the Court concluded that the power company's advertising was protected commercial speech and thus applied the final three factors.[27] Under the second factor, the Court concluded that New York had demonstrated sufficiently "clear and substantial" regulatory interests in promoting energy conservation and fair and efficient utility rates.[28]

Applying the third factor, the Court found that the state's ban directly advanced the goal of energy conservation.[29] Based on the assumption that promotional utility advertising would stimulate consumer demand, the Court concluded that banning advertising would have the opposite effect.[30] Justice Blackmun—who had written the majority opinion in *Virginia State Board*—disagreed with the majority that an advertising ban was a constitutional means for the state to promote energy conservation.[31] He noted that the majority had not cited any empirical evidence in concluding that advertising bans effectively curb consumer demand and consumption.[32] Ultimately, the majority found the ban was not narrowly tailored under the fourth prong because New York had not proven that "less speech restrictive" means were unavailable or ineffective.[33] So, the evidentiary issue under the direct advancement factor was not dispositive.

The *Central Hudson* opinion is significant for establishing the four-factor analysis. The opinion is also remarkable because the Court clearly recognized the strong public policy interest in protecting free flowing commercial information, extending that rationale from its *Virginia State Board* opinion.[34] On this point, Justice Powell wrote:

> The First Amendment . . . protects commercial speech from unwarranted governmental regulation. Commercial expression not only serves the economic interest of the speaker, but

also assists consumers and furthers the societal interest in the fullest possible dissemination of information. . . . [W]e have rejected the 'highly paternalistic' view that government has complete power to suppress or regulate commercial speech.[35]

Three justices disagreed with the majority approach in *Central Hudson*. In a concurring opinion joined by Justice William J. Brennan, Jr., Justice Blackmun wrote that non-misleading advertising should receive full First Amendment protection—similar to non-commercial political and social speech—when the regulatory motive is to keep people ignorant on consumer protectionism grounds.[36] "No differences between commercial speech and other protected speech justify suppression of commercial speech in order to influence public conduct through manipulation of the availability of information," he wrote.[37] On the other end of the spectrum, Justice William H. Rehnquist dissented, concluding that the majority approach would "unduly impair" the ability of government to enact economic regulations.[38] However, despite these opposing concerns, the four-factor analysis was adopted by the Supreme Court as the appropriate form of intermediate constitutional scrutiny for government regulations of commercial speech and has been utilized by the Court ever since.[39]

Typically, once the Court has determined that a regulation restricts protected commercial speech under the first *Central Hudson* factor, it has been fairly liberal in finding that an asserted government interest is sufficiently "clear and substantial" under the second factor. Leading up to the *Lorillard Tobacco* decision, the Court had accepted asserted interests in promoting traffic safety and city aesthetics in zoning cases,[40] protecting family privacy regarding birth control in a contraception direct-mail advertising case,[41] protecting the public "health, safety, and welfare" in gambling and alcohol advertising and labeling cases,[42] protecting the gambling policies of individual states in gambling advertising cases[43] and preventing fraud and protecting individual privacy in lawyer and accountant solicitation cases.[44] Indeed, to date the Court has only found two asserted regulatory interests insufficient under the second *Central Hudson* factor: shielding recipients from mail they might find "offensive"[45] and preserving general "state authority" over alcohol sales and marketing.[46]

Instead, most of the Court's commercial speech decisions applying the *Central Hudson* test have turned on application of the third and fourth factors. As previously indicated, these require the government to demonstrate that the challenged regulation "directly advances" the regulatory interest, and that the government has selected a regulatory means that is "not more extensive than necessary" to achieve its goals. Leading up to the *Lorillard Tobacco* opinion, these requirements proved problematic in application as evidenced by inconsistency in Supreme Court opinions.

Third *Central Hudson* Factor: The "Direct-advancement" Requirement

The *Central Hudson* Court held that the third factor focuses on the "relationship" between the asserted government interest and the challenged advertising regulation.[47] In *Edenfield v. Fane,*[48] decided in 1993, the Court seemed to tighten the requirements of the third factor and then apply even more stringent versions in *Rubin v. Coors Brewing Co.*[49] in 1995, *44 Liquormart, Inc. v. Rhode Island*[50] in 1996 and *Greater New Orleans Broadcasting Association v. United States*[51] in 1999 However, in 1995, in *Florida Bar v. Went For It, Inc.,*[52] the Court applied a looser version that seemed to veer from the mandate in *Edenfield*. The Court split dramatically on the application of the third factor in *Went For It* and would do so again in the *Lorillard Tobacco* opinion.

In *Edenfield,* the Supreme Court struck down a Florida regulation that prohibited in-person solicitations by state-licensed certified public accountants.[53] In an opinion written by Justice Anthony M.

Kennedy, the Court held that the Florida ban was unconstitutional under the third *Central Hudson* factor because there was no evidence in the record that the regulation advanced the state's interest in preventing fraud and overreaching by CPAs.[54] Justice Kennedy wrote that the third factor—which he called the "penultimate prong of the *Central Hudson* test"—required the government to demonstrate that its regulation advanced the asserted regulatory interest in a "direct and material way."[55] He explained: "This burden is not satisfied by mere speculation or conjecture; rather, a governmental body seeking to sustain a restriction on commercial speech must demonstrate that the harms are real and that its restrictions will in fact alleviate them to a material degree."[56]

In *Coors Brewing,* the Court unanimously struck down a federal law that prohibited alcohol content percentage information in beer labeling.[57] The government argued that the ban was needed to keep beer manufacturers from marketing products on the basis of alcohol strength, which the government asserted would lead to increased consumption of high-alcohol beer and harmful secondary effects such as increased rates of alcoholism.[58] Although the Court ruled that the government had a sufficiently substantial interest in curbing problems related to excessive alcohol consumption, the Court concluded that the regulation did not directly advance the asserted interest under the third *Central Hudson* factor. First, the Court found that the ban was part of an irrational regulatory scheme that forbade alcohol content information in beer labeling but allowed and mandated it for wine and liquor labeling and advertising.[59] Second, the Court found no evidence in the record proving or even suggesting that lifting the ban would lead to strength war marketing.[60] Thus, the Court concluded that the government had not satisfied its burden of proving "direct advancement" under *Central Hudson.*[61]

In *44 Liquormart,* the Court struck down a Rhode Island law that had for years banned retail price advertising for liquor.[62] The state claimed that the ban helped promote temperance, arguing that liquor price advertising would lead to price competition among retailers, lower liquor prices, and, ultimately, increased alcohol consumption.[63] In the principal opinion, written by Justice John Paul Stevens, the Court accepted Rhode Island's regulatory interest of encouraging temperance as sufficiently substantial, but found the state had failed to present any evidence of the ban's effectiveness in curbing overall liquor consumption.[64] Indeed, Justice Stevens pointed out, the evidence in the record actually suggested otherwise.[65]

In *Greater New Orleans Broadcasting,* the Court struck down part of a federal regulation that banned broadcast advertising for casino gambling.[66] In doing so, the Court held that the ban was unconstitutional as applied to broadcast licensees in states that had legalized gambling even though the government had a sufficiently substantial regulatory interest in reducing excessive gambling and associated social harms.[67]

Ultimately, the Court held that the broadcast advertising ban failed the third *Central Hudson* factor because it was too "pierced with exemptions and inconsistencies" to directly advance the government's regulatory goal.[68] Writing for the Court, Justice Stevens pointed out that the ban did not apply to casinos operated by Native Americans or non-profit organizations, or to state-run lotteries. In addition, Justice Stevens wrote, the government had not provided clear evidence of a causal connection between broadcast advertising and the harmful effects of gambling.[69] However, Justice Stevens said it was unnecessary to determine whether the lack of evidence was fatal to the government's case under the third factor because the regulatory scheme was too irrational to be otherwise salvaged.[70]

The Court dealt for the first time with the sufficiency of an evidentiary record under the third *Central Hudson* factor in *Went For It.*[71] In that case, the Court, by a 5–4 vote, upheld a Florida state restriction on targeted, direct-mail solicitations by lawyers to accident victims within thirty days of their accidents.[72] Florida argued that the thirty-day ban served to protect the privacy of accident victims and reputations of lawyers,[73] which the Court found to be sufficiently substantial regulatory interests under the second *Central Hudson* factor.[74]

Under the third *Central Hudson* factor, the *Went For It* Court accepted Florida's summaries of empirical and qualitative studies of lawyer advertising as sufficient evidence of direct advancement.[75] For example, in one survey summarized by Florida, more than half of the adult respondents reportedly agreed that contacting accident victims is a privacy invasion.[76] In another summarized survey, approximately 25% of responding accident victims reportedly agreed the solicitations they received were an invasion of their privacy and lowered their opinions of lawyers and the judicial system.[77]

Writing for the 5–4 majority, Justice O'Connor concluded that Florida's summaries were sufficient to prove direct advancement and that the Court did not need to review the actual studies.[78] She found it persuasive that Florida's key study was commissioned by a nationally known consulting firm and pointed out that in prior speech restriction cases, the Court had allowed the parties to refer to studies without proving their methodological soundness.[79] In speech cases, she wrote, empirical data did not need to be presented with a "surfeit of background information" to be given weight.[80] In a sharp dissent, Justice Kennedy chastised the majority for not demanding better proof from Florida before upholding the thirty-day solicitation ban, concluding that the Court had no way of verifying such things as sample size, statistical universe or survey methodology of the studies upon which Florida had relied.[81]

After the *Greater New Orleans Broadcasting* decision, it seemed clear that the Court would not tolerate legislative irrationality under the third *Central Hudson* factor and would strike down regulations of protected commercial speech on that ground. Otherwise, the Court seemed to be demanding evidence that a regulation of protected commercial speech was efficacious in meeting the asserted regulatory goal. Even so, as the *Went For It* case suggests, the Court remained deeply divided on the quantity and quality of the evidence needed to meet the burden of proving direct advancement. This issue is important. In the *Lorillard Tobacco* case, the Court would again split on the issue of the sufficiency of evidence needed to establish "direct advancement" under the *Central Hudson* analysis like it had in *Went For It,* with both opinions written by Justice O'Connor.

Fourth *Central Hudson* Factor: The "Narrowly-tailored" Requirement

The fourth step in the *Central Hudson* analysis examines whether a regulation of commercial speech is "more extensive than . . . necessary" to achieve the asserted regulatory interest.[82] As Justice Powell wrote for the Court in *Central Hudson,* the "regulatory technique may extend only as far as the interest it serves."[83] In addition, he concluded that complete bans on commercial speech are highly suspect under the First Amendment and need to be reviewed with "special care" when the government tries to impact consumer behavior by suppressing information.[84] In 1993, the *Edenfield* Court echoed this point, concluding that "prophylactic" bans on protected commercial speech violate First Amendment policy aimed at facilitating broad public access to "complete and accurate commercial information."[85]

In *Central Hudson,* the Court did not decide the level of rigor with which the fourth factor should be applied. In 1989, in *Board of Trustees v. Fox,* the Court held that narrow tailoring under the fourth factor does not mean that the government must employ the least speech restrictive regulatory means available.[86] For the Court, Justice Scalia pointed out that *Central Hudson* requires only a reasonable, and not a perfect, fit between the asserted regulatory goals and the legislation.[87] "Within those bounds," he wrote, "we leave it to governmental decisionmakers to judge what manner of regulation may be best employed."[88]

Arguably, the *Fox* Court weakened the fourth *Central Hudson* factor, as commentators have pointed out.[89] The Court could have required that government utilize the least speech-restrictive regulatory means but clearly rejected that more stringent approach. In more recent commercial speech cases, however, the Court has significantly tightened the fourth factor. In those cases, the Court has required the government to demonstrate that a regulation of protected commercial speech was necessary because direct regulation of conduct itself was either unavailable or would be ineffective. As pointed out by Justice Clarence Thomas in his concurrence in *44 Liquormart*, this rendered it more difficult—if not highly unlikely—for government to demonstrate narrow tailoring under the fourth factor.[90]

For instance, in *Coors Brewing,* the Court concluded that the federal ban on alcohol content percentages in beer labeling was not narrowly tailored because the government had more direct means to curb "strength war" marketing than restricting speech.[91] The Court suggested that the government could impose direct limits on beer alcohol content.[92] Similarly, in *44 Liquormart,* a plurality of the Court held that the state ban on retail liquor price advertising was not sufficiently narrow because Rhode Island had more direct means available to curb liquor consumption than banning advertising.[93] In the principal opinion in *44 Liquormart,* Justice Stevens concluded that it is "perfectly obvious" that Rhode Island could have enacted minimum price levels or imposed taxes on liquor sales to keep prices artificially high.[94] Likewise, the *Greater New Orleans Broadcasting* Court concluded that the ban on broadcast casino gambling advertising was too broad because government could directly regulate casinos with betting limits, for instance, to potentially curb the problems associated with excessive gambling.[95]

After the *Coors Brewing, 44 Liquormart* and *Greater New Orleans Broadcasting* decisions, it was clear that the government had to prove narrow tailoring by demonstrating that less speech-restrictive means would not effectively meet legislative goals. As Justice Thomas wrote in his concurrence in *44 Liquormart:* "[I]t would seem that directly banning a product (or rationing it, taxing it, controlling its price, or otherwise restricting its sale in specific ways) would virtually always be at least as effective in discouraging consumption as merely restricting advertising . . . and thus all restrictions [aimed at dampening demand by legal users] would fail the fourth [factor]."[96] But, as with the third factor, it was not entirely clear what level of evidence would suffice for the government to prove narrow tailoring. These issues would surface again in the *Lorillard Tobacco* case that was on the horizon.

"Vice" Advertising Under the First Amendment

Another important issue leading up to the *Lorillard Tobacco* opinion was whether the government had added constitutional leeway to regulate harmful product advertising. In a 1986 case dealing with casino gambling advertising[97] and a 1993 case dealing with state lottery advertising,[98] the Supreme Court strongly suggested that the government's power to ban so-called vice products or activities included the lesser power to ban advertising about these products or activities. However, the Court largely abandoned that approach in *Coors Brewing* in 1995,[99] *44 Liquormart* in 1996[100] and *Greater New Orleans Broadcasting* in 1999.[101]

In *Posadas de Puerto Rico Associates v. Tourism Co. of Puerto Rico,* decided in 1986, the Court upheld Puerto Rico's ban on casino gambling advertising targeted to the local Puerto Rican population.[102] Puerto Rico argued that the ban served to protect the population from the social ills of compulsive gambling, which the Court accepted as a sufficiently substantial regulatory interest.[103] In an opinion by Justice Rehnquist, the Court assumed without evidence that the ban would directly advance Puerto Rico's asserted regulatory goal of reducing social harms related to compulsive gambling.[104] In *United States v. Edge Broadcasting Co.,* decided in 1993, the Court upheld a federal broadcast ban on state lottery advertising carried by broadcast licensees located in non-lottery states and, in doing so, relied heavily on its *Posadas* rationale.[105]

In both *Posadas* and *Edge Broadcasting,* the principal opinions suggested that because gambling was not a constitutionally-protected right and could be banned by government as a "vice" activity, advertising regulations should be viewed with greater deference to legislative goals than for other "non-vice" activities or products. For instance, in *Posadas,* Justice Rehnquist wrote for the Court: "It would be a strange constitutional doctrine indeed which would concede to the legislature the authority to totally ban a product or activity, but deny . . . authority to forbid the stimulation or demand for the product or activity through advertising."[106] This clearly echoed his dissent in *Central Hudson,* in which he suggested that the Court should have given greater constitutional deference to New York in regulating advertising by public utilities.[107] In *Posadas,* the Court split 5–4, and the dissenters were sharply critical of the majority's approach. For instance, Justice Stevens concluded that the advertising ban was blatantly discriminatory and flatly unconstitutional.[108] Likewise, in his dissent in *Edge Broadcasting,* Justice Stevens called the federal broadcast ban "extremely paternalistic" and "patently unconstitutional."[109]

Retreating from *Posadas* and, arguably, *Edge Broadcasting,* the *Coors Brewing* Court rejected the idea that the *Central Hudson* analysis is more lenient for government regulation of vice product advertising.[110] Likewise, in *44 Liquormart,* a majority of the Court clearly rejected the so-called "greater-includes-the-lesser" rationale that had been utilized in *Posadas,* with Justice Stevens concluding for the Court that legislatures should not have the "broad discretion to suppress truthful, nonmisleading information for paternalistic purposes that the *Posadas* majority was willing to tolerate."[111] In a concurring opinion joined by Justices Rehnquist, David H. Souter and Stephen Breyer, Justice O'Connor agreed with Justice Stevens that the deferential approach of the *Posadas* Court was invalid.[112] Continuing that trend, the *Greater New Orleans Broadcasting* Court confirmed its rejection of the *Posadas* rationale. Writing for the majority in that case in 1999, Justice Stevens echoed his position from *44 Liquormart* and concluded that the "power to prohibit or to regulate particular *conduct* does not necessarily include the power to prohibit or regulate speech about that conduct."[113]

In *Posadas* and *Edge Broadcasting,* the Court arguably utilized its most deferential versions of the *Central Hudson* analysis to date. Indeed, one commentator called the *Posadas* decision the "quintessential example of *Central Hudson* gone awry."[114] Other commentators concluded that after *Greater New Orleans Broadcasting,* the vice distinction retained little if any First Amendment significance in the context of lawful adult purchases and consumption.[115] However, the Court still had not addressed the evidentiary issue in the context of tobacco advertising restrictions, nor had the Court utilized the *Central Hudson* analysis in a case involving regulations aimed at shielding children from harmful product advertising or preventing unlawful activities like tobacco product purchases and usage by minors. Thus, the question remained how the Court would utilize the *Central Hudson* analysis in such a case—if at all.

TOBACCO ADVERTISING: NATIONAL REGULATORY FRAMEWORK

Tobacco advertising has been one of the most controversial public issues of recent years. Recent data indicate that tobacco manufacturers have continued to promote their products heavily. For instance, according to the most recent Federal Trade Commission figures, cigarette manufacturers spent $9.57 billion in the United States in 2000 on advertising and promotion, which was an increase of 16.2% increase over 1999 expenditures and a 139% increase over those in 1990.[116]

Until deciding the *Lorillard Tobacco* case, the Supreme Court had not ruled directly on the constitutionality of government curbs on tobacco advertising. In striking down state tobacco advertising restrictions in that case, the Court relied in part on the presence of a national regulatory framework, including federal laws requiring health warnings for tobacco product advertising and labeling and banning tobacco advertising from electronic media regulated by the Federal Communications Commission.[117]

Federally-Mandated Warnings in Tobacco Labeling and Advertising

The Federal Cigarette Labeling and Advertising Act (FCLAA)[118] requires that cigarettes sold or distributed in the United States include health warnings on packaging[119] and in print advertising.[120] Generally, Congress intended for these warnings to inform the public about "any adverse health effects" of smoking cigarettes.[121] Under the FCLAA, cigarette manufacturers and importers must adhere to a compliance plan approved by the Federal Trade Commission.[122]

Under the FCLAA, warnings in cigarette packaging and advertising must be conspicuous, as defined by the act[123] and described more fully in official FTC compliance guidelines.[124] In addition, cigarette manufacturers and importers must use ali of the required warnings on a rotating basis,[125] also more fully detailed in the official compliance guidelines.[126] The 1986 Comprehensive Smokeless Tobacco Health Education Act (Smokeless Tobacco Act),[127] includes similar package and advertising labeling requirements for smokeless tobacco products,[128] except that outdoor advertising for smokeless tobacco products is exempt from the warning requirements.[129]

The FCLAA also contains federal pre-emption provisions that prohibit states from enacting warning requirements for packaging[130] or "advertising or promotion" of cigarette products covered by the FCLAA.[131] As a matter of public policy, Congress intended for these pre-emption provisions to protect "commerce and the national economy" from being "impeded by diverse, nonuniform, and confusing cigarette labeling and advertising regulations."[132] Similarly, the Smokeless Tobacco Act pre-empts states from enacting their own package or labeling requirements for smokeless tobacco except in outdoor advertising.[133]

Tobacco Advertising Ban in Federally-Regulated Electronic Media

The FCLAA also bans advertising for cigarettes and little cigars on electronic media licensed and regulated by the FCC,[134] and the Smokeless Tobacco Act includes a similar ban for smokeless tobacco products.[135] To date, there is no legislation that places the Internet under the broad regulatory jurisdiction of the FCC, and the Supreme Court has strongly suggested that the Internet cannot be constitutionally regulated in the same manner as broadcast and other FCC-licensed electronic media.[136]

In 1971, a federal appeals court rejected a First Amendment challenge to the original cigarette advertising ban for regulated electronic media.[137] In 1972, the Supreme Court affirmed the lower federal court ruling without issuing an opinion and, thus, allowed the broadcast ban to stand.[138] This occurred some four years before the Court decided *Virginia Board* in 1976 and assimilated advertising into the First Amendment, and some eight years before the Court created the *Central Hudson* analysis in 1980. How the Supreme Court might decide the constitutional fate of the tobacco advertising ban on regulated electronic media is an issue that merits additional legal and policy research. One commentator recently concluded that the ban probably is unconstitutional under the *Central Hudson* analysis, but suggested that courts would be reluctant to overturn such a well-established regulation.[139]

FDA Regulations (1996) and Master Settlement Agreement (1998)

In 1996, the Food and Drug Administration issued regulations that would have substantially limited the sale, distribution and advertising of tobacco products in the United States (Final Rule).[140] Ultimately, the Supreme Court held that the FDA did not have the legal authority to regulate tobacco,[141] and the regulations in the Final Rule never went into effect. However, in a 1998 agreement with forty-six states, the nation's largest tobacco companies agreed to adhere to a set of sales, distribution and advertising restrictions similar to many of the regulations in the Final Rule.[142]

In enacting the Final Rule in 1996, the FDA concluded that advertising regulations were necessary to curb the appeal of cigarettes and smokeless tobacco products to minors and to curb demand and illegal underage consumption of tobacco products.[143] For instance, regulations proposed in the Final Rule would have limited tobacco advertising in print media to black text on a white background[144] with an exception for tobacco advertising in an "adult publication," defined as a publication whose underage readership (readers younger than 18 years old) is less than 15% of the publication's total readership and does not otherwise exceed two million underage readers.[145] In addition, the regulations would have banned outdoor advertising for cigarette and smokeless tobacco within 1,000 feet of schools and public playgrounds, and limited all other such advertising to black text on a white background.[146] Other regulations in the Final Rule would have limited cigarette and smokeless tobacco advertising in retail establishments (point-of-sale advertising) to black text on a white background except when located in "adult establishments" that ban minors, and the ads are placed so as to be not visible from outside the establishment.[147]

In supporting documentation, the FDA concluded that its tobacco advertising restrictions would pass muster under the *Central Hudson* analysis.[148] Specifically, under the third *Central Hudson* factor, the FDA asserted that it had collected enough evidence to establish that the advertising regulations would directly and materially advance its goal of reducing underage tobacco use.[149] In particular, the FDA concluded that its review of relevant social science research allowed the conclusion that "expert opinion, surveys and studies provide sufficient support for the inference that advertising does play a material role in children's tobacco use."[150] In addition, the FDA concluded that the proposed advertising regulations were sufficiently narrow under the fourth *Central Hudson* factor, claiming that the regulations still allowed tobacco manufacturers and retailers to communicate with adult purchasers while curbing advertising likely to be viewed by minors.[151]

The FDA admitted in the record that it could cite no single study that established a direct causal connection between advertising and the decision by minors to begin using tobacco. However, based on documentation the FDA reviewed, it concluded that advertising was instrumental in leading minors to use tobacco products.[152] For instance, the FDA concluded that "young people are aware of, respond favorably to, and are influenced by cigarette advertising,"[153] relying heavily on a social psychological theory suggesting that children can be particularly susceptible to "peripheral" cues in advertising such as colorful graphics and imagery.[154] The FDA's supporting documentation is indeed remarkable for its extensive review of the social science literature on advertising and tobacco usage. This is important because the Supreme Court ultimately relied on the FDA record when considering whether there is a sufficient connection between advertising and underage tobacco use under the third *Central Hudson* factor in *Lorillard Tobacco*.[155]

The FDA regulations were challenged, and the Supreme Court ultimately struck down the entire regulatory scheme in *Food and Drug Administration v. Brown & Williamson Tobacco Corp.*[156] There, the Court held that the FDA did not have authority from Congress to regulate tobacco products under the Food, Drug and Cosmetic Act.[157] In deciding the case, the Court found it unnecessary to reach First Amendment claims that the FDA regulations were unconstitutional. Following the decision in *Brown & Williamson,* the FDA withdrew all of its proposed tobacco regulations adopted in the Final Rule.[158] In addition, after the *Brown & Williamson* decision was handed down, three bills were introduced and remain pending in Congress to amend the Food, Drug and Cosmetic Act and give the FDA legislative authority to regulate tobacco products.[159]

In 1998, while the federal court challenge to the Final Rule was pending, forty-six states entered into a settlement agreement (Master Settlement Agreement) with the largest U.S. tobacco companies.[160] To settle claims by the states seeking various costs connected with the treatment of smoking-related illnesses, the tobacco manufacturers agreed to pay more than $200 billion and adhere to marketing and advertising restrictions similar to those contained in the invalidated the FDA regulations. For instance, the Master Settlement Agreement restricts tobacco brand name sponsorships for such events as concerts and athletic contests[161] and seeks to eliminate most outdoor and transit tobacco advertising.[162] The agreement has exceptions, however, such as provisions that allow outdoor tobacco advertising when it is located on the property of retail establishments that sell tobacco products.[163]

Although the Supreme Court avoided the First Amendment issues in *Brown & Williamson,* it took the opportunity to address some of them when it decided *Lorillard Tobacco* in 2001. In that case, the Supreme Court addressed the constitutionality of state tobacco advertising restrictions patterned in part after the failed FDA regulations. The Court utilized the *Central Hudson* analysis for the first time in a tobacco advertising case and, also for the first time, dealt with a regulatory scheme in which advertising for adults was being restricted on grounds of protecting minors from a harmful product.

LORILLARD TOBACCO CO. V. REILLY

In *Lorillard Tobacco,*[164] the Supreme Court struck down state regulations limiting outdoor and retail point-of-sale tobacco advertising. The regulations prohibited as an "unfair act or practice" any "outdoor advertising" for cigarettes, smokeless tobacco and cigars located within a 1,000-foot radius of a school or playground.[165] "Outdoor advertising" included in-stadium and in-store signs visible from outside these facilities. The regulations also required point-of-sale advertising to be placed five-feet or higher in retail operations that allowed children and were covered by the 1,000-foot rule.[166] These regulations acted to close loopholes in the Master Settlement Agreement that allowed outdoor and point-of-sale tobacco advertising on the property of tobacco retailers.[167]

A coalition of tobacco manufacturers and retailers that included the top four U.S. cigarette manufacturers—Philip Morris Cos., Inc.; R.J. Reynolds Tobacco Holdings, Inc.; Brown & Williamson Tobacco Co.; and Lorillard Tobacco Co.—challenged the advertising regulations in federal district court, arguing that the FCLAA's pre-emption provisions prevented the state from regulating cigarette advertising and, in any event, that all of the advertising regulations were unconstitutional under the First Amendment. In two separate opinions, the federal district court rejected the pre-emption argument,[168] and most of the First Amendment claims, finding only the five-foot height rule unconstitutional under the *Central Hudson* analysis.[169]

On appeal, the United States Court of Appeals for the First Circuit affirmed on the pre-emption issue.[170] The appeals court concluded that the cigarette advertising restrictions governed only the "location" of advertising—similar to a zoning regulation—and did not interfere with the labeling and advertising scheme set up by Congress in the FCLAA.[171] In addition, the appeals court upheld all the tobacco regulations, including the five-foot height rule, under the *Central Hudson* analysis.[172] The tobacco companies appealed to the Supreme Court, which reversed in an opinion written by Justice O'Connor. The opinion was viewed as having significant implications for the government's ability to regulate tobacco advertising and signage outside the terms and provisions of the 1998 Master Settlement Agreement.[173]

Pre-Emption Issue

The Court ruled 5–4 that the FCLAA pre-empted Massachusetts from regulating outdoor and retail point-of-sale cigarette advertising.[174] Writing for the Court, Justice O'Connor concluded that Congress had exclusive legislative control over cigarette advertising under the FCLAA, and Massachusetts had unlawfully targeted cigarette advertising in its regulations. She was careful to explain that the pre-emption ruling in the case was narrow and would not prevent states from enacting general billboard zoning regulations or laws that prohibited conduct such as underage possession of cigarettes or unlawful sales of cigarettes to minors.[175]

On the other hand, Justice Stevens wrote for the dissenters that it was not clear that Congress intended to keep the states from regulating the locations of tobacco billboards. Instead, he wrote, Massachusetts and other states should have been allowed to utilize zoning ordinances to protect children from cigarette advertising.[176] However, Justice Stevens only mustered three additional votes on this point—Justices Ruth Bader Ginsburg, Breyer and Souter—which was insufficient to create a majority on that part of the decision.

Application of the *Central Hudson* Analysis

The Court did not reach the First Amendment claim as applied to the cigarette advertising restrictions because the pre-emption ruling made it unnecessary. However, the pre-emption ruling did not apply to the restrictions on cigar and smokeless tobacco advertising because Congress had not enacted pre-emption provisions as to those products.[177] Thus, it was necessary for the Court to reach the constitutional issues on cigar and smokeless advertising.

The tobacco companies urged the Court to abandon the *Central Hudson* analysis in favor of strict constitutional scrutiny, which would have required that the regulations serve a compelling government interest and employ the least speech-restrictive means.[178] The Court refused.[179] Writing for the majority, Justice O'Connor concluded that the *Central Hudson* analysis was adequate to decide the First Amendment issues in the case without the need to abandon such a well-established constitutional test.[180] With some reservation, the Court thus reaffirmed the distinct constitutional treatment of commercial speech under the First Amendment and upheld the *Central Hudson* analysis as the appropriate constitutional test for advertising regulations.[181]

Not surprisingly, the Court found no issues under the first two *Central Hudson* factors. For purposes of summary judgment, Massachusetts had conceded that the regulations banned protected commercial speech under the first factor, and the tobacco companies had conceded that the state had a sufficiently substantial regulatory interest in reducing tobacco use by minors under the second factor.[182] As with most of the Court's commercial speech decisions, the *Lorillard Tobacco* opinion turned on the application of the critical third and fourth factors to the 1,000-foot rule for outdoor advertising and the five-foot height restrictions for retail point-of-sale advertising for smokeless tobacco and cigars.

Application of the Third *Central Hudson* Factor: Direct Advancement

Under the third *Central Hudson* factor, Justice O'Connor reiterated from *Greater New Orleans Broadcasting* that Massachusetts had to demonstrate that its regulations advanced the asserted regulatory interest.[183] She also pointed out that the Court's prior decision in *Edenfield* required the state to come forward with more than "mere speculation or conjecture" and to "'demonstrate that the harms it recites are real and that its restrictions will in fact alleviate them to a material degree.'"[184] The tobacco companies argued that Massachusetts had not met its burden of proof because it failed to prove a causal link between advertising and underage use of smokeless tobacco and cigars or that minors were even using these products to a significant degree.[185]

The Court held 5–4 that the state had met its burden under the third factor as to the 1,000-foot rule for outdoor advertising.[186] Writing for the Court, Justice O'Connor concluded that Massachusetts had cited a sufficient number of studies that established a seeming relationship between advertising and underage tobacco use including those reviewed in the extensive record developed by the FDA in its failed attempt to regulate tobacco advertising in 1996.[187] Justice O'Connor also noted that in previous cases, the Court had presumed without the necessity of evidence that advertising stimulates consumer demand and that "suppressed advertising" accomplishes the contrary.[188] Based on this, the majority was satisfied that the state had sufficiently established "direct advancement" under the third *Central Hudson* factor in the case. As Justice O'Connor summarized: "[W]e disagree with [the tobacco parties] that there is *no* evidence that preventing targeted campaigns and limiting youth exposure to advertising will decrease underage use of smokeless tobacco and cigars."[189]

On the other hand, the *Lorillard Tobacco* Court ruled 6–3 that the five-foot height rule for point-of-sale smokeless tobacco and cigar advertising failed the third *Central Hudson* requirement. Justice O'Connor concluded that the five-foot height rule was obviously ineffective because many children are taller than five feet and those who are not, certainly can look up.[190] Justice O'Connor pointed out that *Edenfield* required more than "ineffective or remote support for the government's purpose" and that *Greater New Orleans Broadcasting* required more than just a mere chance that a regulation would be effective.[191] She concluded that the height restrictions failed to pass muster under these standards and did not directly advance the state's asserted interest in curbing underage use of cigars and smokeless tobacco.

Application of Fourth *Central Hudson* Factor: Narrow Tailoring

Turning to the fourth *Central Hudson* factor, the *Lorillard Tobacco* Court held that the outdoor and point-of-sale regulations were too broad to survive constitutional scrutiny.[192] Writing for the Court, Justice O'Connor pointed out that Massachusetts had not considered the effective impact of the 1,000-foot rule in metropolitan areas like Boston, where high concentrations of schools and playgrounds would effectively ban tobacco billboards. She also said the regulations were too broad because they banned tobacco billboards of all sizes and types and did not target high visibility billboards or those with youth-oriented appeals.[193]

She wrote that Massachusetts could not broadly suppress speech directed to adults in order to protect children.[194] On this point, she relied on *Reno v. American Civil Liberties Union,* a 1997 decision in which the Court struck down federal restrictions on non-obscene sexual material on the Internet despite a strong government interest in preventing access by minors.[195] The *Reno* Court had concluded that non-obscene sexual material was protected speech that adults had a First Amendment right to access on the Internet.[196] Similarly, in *Lorillard Tobacco,* Justice O'Connor concluded that tobacco manufacturers and retailers had a First Amendment right to communicate with adults about their products, and that adults had a First Amendment right to receive these communications. She also wrote that the Massachusetts regulations would unfairly quash the only means that some retailers—like small, independent store-owners—had to communicate with passing customers.[197] The FDA had rejected similar concerns raised by comments submitted when the agency was considering final passage of the Final Rule in 1996.[198] At that time, the FDA took the position that clamping the tobacco advertising of some retailers was a necessary and constitutional cost of protecting minors from exposure to any tobacco advertising within those designated zones.[199] However, the *Lorillard Tobacco* opinion suggests that the Court would not agree with the FDA on this point.

Four justices—Breyer, Ginsburg, Souter and Stevens—concluded that the majority ruling on the fourth factor in *Lorillard Tobacco* was premature, arguing that more evidence and data were needed.[200] Justice Stevens expressed concern that there was no evidence of the regulations' impact including the numbers or percentages of billboards banned in various areas of the state, qualitative descriptions of areas in which billboards were banned, and descriptions of actual advertising alternatives for tobacco manufacturers and retailers.[201] He concluded that the Court should have remanded the case for further evidentiary development, but still expressed his concern that the outdoor restrictions would harm the ability of tobacco manufacturers to communicate lawfully with adult customers.[202] Thus, it seems clear that the Court continues to wrestle with the level of evidentiary sufficiency required under the *Central Hudson* analysis.

Justice Thomas and the Rejection of the *Central Hudson* Analysis

Justice Thomas concurred with the judgment in *Lorillard Tobacco*. In doing so, however, he strongly opposed the Court's continued use of the *Central Hudson* test for regulations aimed at restricting protected commercial speech in order to suppress information and manipulate consumer choices. Indeed, he concluded that the Court should have scrapped the *Central Hudson* analysis in favor of strict constitutional scrutiny under the circumstances of the case.[203]

Generally, Justice Thomas agreed with the Court that the cigarette advertising restrictions were pre-empted by the FCLAA and that the other regulations failed intermediate scrutiny under the *Central Hudson* analysis.[204] However, he wrote that the Court should have applied strict constitutional scrutiny to the advertising regulations.[205] He cited two principal reasons for his position.

First, he argued that it was illogical to treat commercial speech differently from non-commercial speech under the First Amendment. In fact, he expressly doubted whether such a distinction is ever logical or pragmatic.[206] Secondly, he concluded that the Massachusetts regulations were a form of content-based discrimination against non-misleading tobacco advertising. On this point, he wrote: "I continue to believe that when the government seeks to restrict truthful speech in order to suppress the ideas it conveys, strict scrutiny is appropriate whether or not the speech in question may be characterized as 'commercial.' "[207] He argued that the government could only constitutionally regulate advertising to prevent "commercial harms" such as consumer-related risks associated with deceptive or misleading advertising.[208]

Justice Thomas applied strict scrutiny and concluded, first, that the state had a sufficiently compelling interest in reducing underage use of tobacco.[209] However, he questioned whether the regulations possibly could be an effective means of advancing that interest.[210] Regardless, he wrote, the regulations were far too broad and, thus, unconstitutional for that reason alone.[211] He wrote that the state should have tried more direct means of curbing underage tobacco use like better enforcement of laws against selling tobacco to minors and enactment of laws against underage possession and use of tobacco products.[212]

Justice Thomas suggested that Massachusetts was improperly seeking a vice exception to the First Amendment that would more liberally allow states to regulate advertising for legal but potentially harmful products such as tobacco and alcohol.[213] However, he concluded that such an exception did not exist in the Court's commercial speech jurisprudence and could not be used as a means of salvaging otherwise unconstitutional restrictions on protected advertising.[214] In addition, he pointed out that government policies to ban advertising to protect children's health, if allowed, could just as logically be applied to lawful products like high-calorie and high-fat foods and alcoholic beverages.[215]

Of those justices who wrote opinions in *Lorillard Tobacco,* Justice Thomas wrote most strongly about the important historical role of the First Amendment as the protector of objectionable and even harmful expression. And, in a particularly remarkable passage, he applied that notion to tobacco advertising. He wrote:

> No legislature has ever sought to restrict speech about an activity it regarded as harmless and inoffensive. Calls for limits on expression always are made when the specter of some threatened harm is looming. The identity of the harm may vary. People will be inspired by totalitarian dogmas and subvert the Republic. They will be inflamed by racial demagoguery and embrace hatred and bigotry. Or they will be enticed by cigarette advertisements and choose to smoke, risking disease. It is therefore no answer for the State to say that the makers of cigarettes are doing harm: perhaps they are. But in that respect they are no different from the purveyors of other harmful products, or the advocates of harmful ideas. When the State seeks to silence them, they are all entitled to the protection of the First Amendment.[216]

Although this was the strongest statement to date on his commercial speech position, Justice Thomas had taken similar positions in previous cases.[217] For instance, in his concurring opinion in *44 Liquormart,* he asserted that it is *"per se* illegitimate" for government to manipulate lawful consumer choices by suppressing protected commercial speech.[218] He made similar statements in a concurring opinion in *Greater New Orleans Broadcasting,* taking the position in that case that the Court should have applied strict constitutional scrutiny to federal restrictions on casino gambling advertising.[219] While Justice Thomas seems to be the lone justice at this time calling explicitly for the abandonment of the *Central Hudson* analysis, Justices Blackmun, joined by Justice Brennan, made a similar argument in his concurring opinion in the *Central Hudson* opinion itself.[220]

Impact of *Lorillard Tobacco* in the Lower Courts

Not long after the Supreme Court handed down its decision in *Lorillard Tobacco,* lower courts began to apply its principles in constitutional challenges to various outdoor advertising restrictions. So far, the critical factor in the decisions has been whether the challenged regulations target specific content, like tobacco or alcohol advertising, or could be considered content-neutral zoning ordinances. Courts have typically upheld general zoning regulations but struck down specific regulations of alcohol or tobacco advertising on either federal pre-emption or First Amendment grounds, much like the majority approach in *Lorillard Tobacco.*

In two cases, a federal appeals court and a district court upheld general outdoor advertising ordinances in court challenges filed on First Amendment grounds. In *Long Island Board of Realtors, Inc. v. Village of Massapequa Park,* decided in 2002, the Second Circuit Court of Appeals upheld a town ordinance that prohibited almost all commercial signage on residential properties.[221] Similarly, in *Infinity Outdoor, Inc. v. City of New York,* decided in 2001, a New York federal district court upheld a city ordinance that prohibited all off-site commercial billboards within 200 feet of all highways and parks.[222] In both cases, the courts acknowledged the *Lorillard Tobacco* decision and found that the ordinances in question directly advanced sufficiently substantial interests in traffic safety or aesthetics in a reasonable manner without unconstitutionally targeting specific commercial content.[223]

Within a month of *Lorillard Tobacco,* the Tenth Circuit Court of Appeals decided *Utah Licensed Beverage Association v. Leavitt,*[224] and struck down state regulations that banned most liquor advertising in Utah.[225] Under the first *Central Hudson* factor, the court concluded that the regulations banned truthful, non-misleading commercial speech and had to be tested under the three remaining factors.[226] Under the second factor, the court found that the state had a sufficiently substantial regulatory interest in reducing social ills related to alcohol use like drunk driving and underage alcohol consumption.[227]

But the Tenth Circuit ruled that Utah's regulations were irrational and thus unconstitutional under the third *Central Hudson* factor because they banned advertising for one form of alcoholic beverages (liquor) and not others (beer and wine). The court relied on *Lorillard Tobacco, Greater New Orleans Broadcasting* and *44 Liquormart* in finding that Utah had not carefully weighed the impact of a near-total ban on speech and had not demonstrated that "nonspeech regulations" would be ineffective in meeting the state's goals.[228]

Similarly, in *Jones v. Vilsack,* also decided in 2001, the Eighth Circuit Court of Appeals relied on *Lorillard Tobacco* to invalidate key provisions of the Iowa Tobacco Use Prevention and Control Act (Control Act) under the preemption provisions of the FCLAA.[229] The Control Act prohibited retailers and wholesalers from giving away tobacco products and providing any "free articles, products, commodities, gifts, or concessions" in connection with any tobacco purchases.[230] The appeals court held that the FCLAA prevented states from regulating cigarette advertising or promotion, and the Control Act sought to regulate activities within the plain meaning of the term "promotion" in the FCLAA.[231] The court relied on *Lorillard Tobacco,* noting that in that case, the Court required that the terms "advertising or promotion" in the FCLAA must be given their "plain and ordinary" meanings.[232] Because the pre-emption ruling only applied to cigarette advertising, the appeals court sent the case back to the trial court to determine if the regulations violate the First Amendment as to other tobacco products.[233]

In *Eller Media Company v. City of Cleveland,* an Ohio federal district court struck down a city ordinance that prohibited outdoor alcohol advertising in Cleveland.[234] The ordinance criminalized alcoholic beverage advertising in "publicly visible locations" except for signage in industrial areas, temporary signage and billboards only visible from certain interstates.[235] The court concluded that the ordinance would effectively ban most outdoor alcohol advertising in the city's densely populated areas.[236]

Applying the *Central Hudson* analysis, the *Eller Media* court found that the ordinance banned protected commercial speech under the first factor and the city had a sufficiently substantial regulatory interest in curbing illegal underage drinking under the second factor.[237] Thus, as in *Lorillard Tobacco,* the *Eller Media* decision turned on application of the third and fourth *Central Hudson* factors.[238]

Under the third factor, the court used Justice O'Connor's liberal approach from *Lorillard Tobacco* and concluded that Cleveland had cited enough studies to find a sufficient connection between advertising and underage alcohol consumption for purposes of the *Central Hudson* analysis.[239] However, under the fourth factor, the court found the ordinance overly broad because it operated geographically as an effective ban much like the Massachusetts regulations struck down in *Lorillard Tobacco.*[240] In addition, the court found the ordinance overly broad because it banned all alcohol advertising and not just advertising most likely to be particularly appealing to children.[241] Echoing the *Lorillard Tobacco* majority, the *Eller Media* court held that Cleveland had unconstitutionally infringed upon the right of manufacturers and retailers to advertise lawful alcoholic products to adults and the right of adults to receive these communications.[242]

In yet another case, the *Lorillard Tobacco* decision prompted Chicago to voluntarily repeal a local ordinance that generally prohibited outdoor advertising for alcoholic beverages and cigarettes.[243] The Federation of Advertising Industry Representatives (FAIR), an advertising industry trade organization, had challenged the ordinance on First Amendment grounds. A federal trial judge had ruled in 1998 that the provisions as applied to cigarette advertising were pre-empted by the FCLAA and invalidated the entire ordinance on that ground alone.[244] The Seventh Circuit Court of Appeals reversed the federal district court on the pre-emption issue,[245] and the Supreme Court refused to review the decision.[246] After the Supreme Court handed down its decision in *Lorillard Tobacco,* Chicago dropped the matter without receiving a ruling from the federal trial court on the pre-emption or constitutional issues raised by FAIR.

ANALYSIS AND DISCUSSION

As indicated, the *Lorillard Tobacco* decision had a fairly immediate impact in the lower courts and prompted responses from federal legislators seeking to grant the FDA regulatory authority over tobacco. The case is also significant from a constitutional perspective because it marks the first time the Supreme Court applied the *Central Hudson* test in a tobacco advertising case. In addition, the decision effectively places tobacco advertising on the same constitutional level as advertising for other lawful goods and services under the First Amendment and creates a strong likelihood that laws restricting the flow of protected commercial speech in order to manipulate consumer behavior are likely to be struck down as unconstitutional despite a compelling regulatory interest such as protecting the health of minors. More importantly, the *Lorillard Tobacco* decision has added insights to the Court's handling of advertising regulations under the critical third and fourth *Central Hudson* factors, the regulation of harmful product advertising and the continued validity of the *Central Hudson* analysis itself.

Third *Central Hudson* Factor

Under the third *Central Hudson* factor, which requires the government to demonstrate that its regulation directly advances a substantial regulatory goal in a direct and material way, it is increasingly clear that the government needs to submit a sufficient evidentiary record in support of its case. The Supreme Court considered the extent of the evidentiary record under this factor in *Coors Brewing, 44 Liquormart* and *Greater New Orleans Broadcasting,* and did so again in *Lorillard Tobacco.* The Court abandoned in those cases the more deferential approach taken in *Posadas* and *Edge Broadcasting,* in which the Court had accepted the government's claims of direct advancement with little or no evidence. Even so, the Court's approach in all of these cases is mitigated by the rather loose evidentiary standard it has taken when determining the sufficiency of government evidence supporting claims of direct advancement under the third factor.

As indicated, the *Lorillard Tobacco* Court narrowly adopted Justice O'Connor's approach from *Went For It* when considering the evidentiary record. In other words, the Court seems willing to accept government summaries of empirical studies and anecdotal evidence as proof of direct advancement without the need to establish methodological soundness as the dissenters in those cases would have demanded. Such an approach arguably weakens the third *Central Hudson* factor by easing the government's burden of proof under the third *Central Hudson* factor.[247] As a result, the amount and sufficiency of evidence of direct advancement remains somewhat unclear and arguably subject to the discretion and whims of courts reviewing commercial speech cases.[248]

However, it seems equally clear that the Court will not tolerate "irrational" regulatory schemes under the third *Central Hudson* factor. The Court struck down irrational regulatory schemes in both *Coors Brewing* and *Greater New Orleans Broadcasting*. In addition, the Court in *Lorillard Tobacco* concluded that the Massachusetts height restrictions also were irrational and thus fatally flawed on that point alone. Arguably, when restricting protected commercial speech, legislatures must not only craft a sufficient legislative record but also must ensure that regulations are not undermined or controverted by other regulatory provisions. In other words, the Court seems unwilling to liberally defer to legislative judgment when protected commercial speech is at issue.

Fourth *Central Hudson* Factor

When considering the fourth *Central Hudson* factor, the *Lorillard Tobacco* Court focused primarily on the broad sweep of the Massachusetts regulations and treated them as an effective ban on all outdoor tobacco advertising in the state's major metropolitan areas. Clearly the Court seems unwilling to tolerate such broad suppression of protected commercial speech when narrower, more precise regulations have not been considered. But it remains to be seen how the Court might handle more exacting regulations under the fourth *Central Hudson* factor.

In the majority opinion, Justice O'Connor suggested that regulations more specifically aimed at restricting youth-oriented tobacco appeals in highly-visible outdoor advertising might be sufficiently narrow under the fourth *Central Hudson* factor.[249] Justice Thomas made a similar point in the majority opinion in *Coors Brewing* in 1995. He suggested that a regulation prohibiting specific advertising appeals based on high alcohol content might be a sufficiently narrow alternative under the fourth factor to banning all alcohol percentage information on beer labels.[250] Thus, the issue of how the Court will deal with narrower, more specific advertising regulations than those considered in cases like *Coors Brewing* and *Lorillard Tobacco* remains uncertain.

Also under the fourth factor, the *Lorillard Tobacco* Court continued its trend of requiring the government to seek out more direct means of accomplishing regulatory goals than restricting protected commercial speech. In other words, a regulation of protected commercial speech is unlikely to be considered narrowly tailored if there are direct regulatory means available that government has not tried or has tried and found ineffective. As indicated previously, this was the approach of the Court in striking down the regulations at issue in *Coors Brewing*,[251] *44 Liquormart*[252] and *Greater New Orleans Broadcasting*.[253] The Court took a similar approach in 2002 in its most recent commercial speech case, *Thompson v. Western States Medical Center*.[254] In that case, the Court struck down a federal ban on direct-to-consumer advertising by pharmacies, pharmacists and physicians for legal compounded prescription drugs.[255] The Court concluded that the government could more directly regulate the manufacture and sale of compounded prescription drugs and better alleviate regulatory concerns about the sale of compounded prescription drugs for purposes not approved by the FDA.[256]

It also is important to note that the *Lorillard Tobacco* Court was divided on the sufficiency of the evidence needed to decide whether the Massachusetts regulations were narrowly tailored under that factor. Justices Breyer, Ginsburg, Souter and Stevens concluded that more substantial evidence of the impact of the regulations was needed before deciding that issue.[257] Thus, the current Court remains divided over the sufficiency of evidence needed to decide both direct advancement under the third factor and narrow tailoring under the fourth factor. Unless the Supreme Court abandons the *Central Hudson* analysis, these evidentiary issues are likely to resurface as litigants in commercial speech cases develop more sophisticated evidentiary records in support of their claims under both the third and fourth factors.

Continued Rejection of the "Vice" Advertising Exception

The *Lorillard Tobacco* opinion is also significant for again clearly rejecting the "greater-includes-the-lesser" rationale from the *Posadas* and *Edge Broadcasting* cases. Without question, the power of the government to ban a vice product or activity is not alone sufficient to justify otherwise unconstitutional regulations of advertising. As commentators have pointed out, in *Coors Brewing, 44 Liquormart* and *Greater New Orleans Broadcasting,* the Court seemed to have virtually eliminated the "vice" category from its commercial speech jurisprudence to the extent that it ever was firmly implanted.[258] Still, after *Greater New Orleans Broadcasting,* there was some question about whether the Court would take a different approach with tobacco advertising because of the substantial health risks associated with underage tobacco use. However, the *Lorillard Tobacco* Court made it clear that even a compelling interest in protecting children's health would not allow government to overly burden the flow of lawful communication to adults about tobacco products. The current Court seems willing to apply the *Central Hudson* analysis—when applicable—with equal rigor to all advertising for lawful products, including so-called "vice" products and activities like alcohol, gambling and, now, tobacco.

For instance, commentators in the *Journal of the American Medical Association* recently concluded the following about the impact of the *Lorillard Tobacco* decision: "[T]he Supreme Court, in effect, has left public health authorities with little room to craft tobacco advertising restrictions that are both demonstrably effective and likely to be deemed constitutionally acceptable by the current Supreme Court."[259] These commentators proposed a three-pronged regulatory scheme consisting of a federal tax on tobacco advertising and promotion,[260] public health warnings in print advertisements equal in size to half of the advertising space,[261] and required graphic depictions of the results of smoking damage on cigarette packages like those required in Canada.[262] One can surmise that regulatory proposals that seek other methods than banning protected commercial speech are precisely the results the Supreme Court intended through its recent line of commercial speech decisions.

The result of a constitutional challenge to such proposed regulations remains uncertain and worthy of further exploration should such proposals be strongly considered by lawmakers. In addition, as indicated, proposed federal legislation would provide Congressional authority to the FDA to regulate tobacco.[263] Provisions in this proposed legislation also seek to remove the federal pre-emption provisions of the FCLAA and enact the FDA's 1996 tobacco advertising and promotion regulations as federal law.[264] Thus, evidence clearly indicates that federal lawmakers have not abandoned their efforts to curb tobacco advertising on a national scale. Should this proposed legislation be signed into law, constitutional challenges in court would be certain to follow. Thus, a fresh look at the FDA's 1996 Final Rule through the lens of the Supreme Court's current commercial speech doctrine seems worthy of additional research and analysis.

Continued Validity of the *Central Hudson* Analysis

Finally, it is important to note that the current Court remains ambiguous about the *Central Hudson* analysis in situations where the government enacts regulations restricting protected commercial speech in order to manipulate lawful consumer choices by suppressing the flow of commercial information in the marketplace. As previously indicated, in *Lorillard Tobacco,* Justice O'Connor expressed her ambivalence over the continued validity of the *Central Hudson* analysis under these circumstances, as did Justice Stevens in his concurrence. Justice Thomas continues to be the lone justice who clearly favors abandoning the *Central Hudson* analysis in favor of strict scrutiny, the position he took in *44 Liquormart, Greater New Orleans Broadcasting* and *Lorillard Tobacco.* Regardless of whether the Court abandons the *Central Hudson* analysis, its recent trend of strengthened constitutional protection for truthful, non-misleading advertising about lawful products and services seems unlikely to be interrupted.

CONCLUSION

The Supreme Court remains divided on how to apply the *Central Hudson* analysis in commercial speech cases, especially when it comes to the sufficiency of evidence needed to establish "direct advancement" under the third factor and "narrow tailoring" under the fourth factor. Despite this, however, the *Lorillard Tobacco* Court clearly continued a trend of providing strong First Amendment protection for non-misleading advertising including tobacco advertising. In addition, the Court made it clear that the First Amendment will not allow the government to substantially disrupt the flow of lawful commercial information to adult consumers even when a compelling regulatory goal of protecting children from the harms of tobacco usage exists. The pragmatic effect for advertisers and marketers is that government has little constitutional leeway to broadly restrict non-misleading commercial communication about lawful products and services.[265] In short, the Court continues to suggest that legislators look seriously and carefully at more direct, narrow and efficacious means of solving serious social and political problems like underage use of tobacco products than banning protected commercial speech.

NOTES

1. 447 U.S. 557 (1980).

2. *See, e.g.,* Karl A. Boedecker, Fred W. Morgan & Linda Berns Wright, *The Evolution of First Amendment Protection for Commercial Speech,* 59 J. MARKETING 38 (1995); Michael Hoefges & Milagros Rivera-Sanchez, *"Vice" Advertising Under the Supreme Court's Commercial Speech Doctrine: The Shifting Central Hudson Analysis,* 22 HASTINGS COMM. & ENT. L. J. 350 (2000); Arlen W. Langvardt, *The Incremental Strengthening of First Amendment Protection for Commercial Speech: Lessons From Greater New Orleans Broadcasting,* 37 AM. BUS. L. J. 587 (2000); Robert Post, *The Constitutional Status of Commercial Speech,* 48 UCLA L. REV. 1 (2000); Jef I. Richards, *Is 44 Liquormart a Turning Point?,* 16 J. PUB. POL'Y & MARKETING 156 (1997); and Daniel E. Troy, *Advertising Not "Low Value" Speech,* 16 YALE J. REG. 85 (1999).

3. Post, *supra* note 2, at 2.

4. *See generally* United States v. Edge Broad. Co., 509 U.S. 418 (1993); Posadas de Puerto Rico Assocs. v. Tourism Co. of Puerto Rico, 478 U.S. 328 (1986).

5. *See generally* Thompson v. W. States Med. Ctr., 535 U.S. 357 (2002); Lorillard Tobacco Co. v. Reilly, 533 U.S. 525 (2001); Greater New Orleans Broad. Ass'n v. United States, 527 U.S. 173 (1999); 44 Liquormart, Inc. v. Rhode Island, 517 U.S. 484 (1996); Rubin v. Coors Brewing Co., 514 U.S. 476 (1995).

6. *See, e.g.,* Langvardt, *supra* note 2, at 650.

7. Rubin v. Coors Brewing Co., 514 U.S. 476 (1995).

8. 44 Liquormart, Inc. v. Rhode Island, 517 U.S. 484 (1996).

9. Greater New Orleans Broad. Ass'n v. United States, 527 U.S. 173 (1999).

10. *See generally* Hoefges & Rivera-Sanchez, *supra* note 2 (concluding that the Supreme Court has virtually eliminated the constitutional distinction between truthful non-misleading advertising for legal "vice" products and services like alcoholic beverages and gambling that are legal for adults, and advertising for other lawful products and services).

11. *See* United States v. Edge Broad. Co., 509 U.S. 418 (1993) (upholding federal broadcast ban on state lottery advertising by broadcast licensees located in non-lottery states); Posadas de Puerto Rico Assocs. v.

Tourism Co. of Puerto Rico, 478 U.S. 328 (1986) (upholding Puerto Rico's ban on casino gambling advertising targeted to the local Puerto Rican population).

12. 533 U.S. 525 (2001). One media account described the opinion as "mix-and-match." Mary Leonard, *Limits on Tobacco Ads Lifted,*" BOSTON GLOBE, June 29, 2001, at A1, *available at* 2001 WL 3940373. Another called it "tangled." Tony Mauro, *Mix-and-Match Majority Finds Tobacco-Ad Rules Too Restrictive,* FREEDOMFORUM.ORG, June 21, 2001, *at* http://www.freedomforum.org/templates/ document. asp?documentID=14292.

13. Mauro, *supra* note 12.

14. *Id.*

15. 15 U.S.C. §§ 1333, *et seq.* (2002).

16. *See* Pittsburgh Press Co. v. Pittsburgh Comm'n on Human Relations, 413 U.S. 376 (1973); Breard v. City of Alexandria, 341 U.S. 622 (1951); Valentine v. Chrestensen, 316 U.S. 52 (1942).

17. 425 U.S. 748 (1976).

18. *Id.* at 762 (quoting *Pittsburgh Press Co.,* 413 U.S. at 385).

19. *Id.* at 765.

20. *Id.*

21. *Id.* at 770–73. For instance, in a footnote Justice Blackmun wrote, "Even if the differences [between commercial and non-commercial speech] do not justify the conclusion that commercial speech is valueless, and thus subject to complete suppression by [government], they nonetheless suggest that a different degree of protection is necessary to insure that the flow of truthful and legitimate commercial information is unimpaired." *Id.* at 771 n.24.

22. *Id.* at 771. Justice Blackmun pointed out in *Virginia State Board* that even commercial speech that "is not provably false, or even wholly false, but only deceptive or misleading" would fall outside the ambit of First Amendment protection for commercial speech and be subject to government regulation. He wrote: "We foresee no obstacle to a State's dealing effectively with this problem." *Id.*

23. *See id.* Justice Blackmun wrote, "The First Amendment, as we construe it today does not prohibit the State from insuring that the stream of commercial information flow cleanly as well as freely." *Id.* at 771–72.

24. Justice Blackmun pointed out that even commercial advertising could have important content of interest to the general public. *Id.* at 764–65. For instance, he noted, in a prior case, the Court had struck down a state ban that prohibited a referral service in Virginia—where abortions were illegal at the time—from publicizing legal abortion services in New York. *Id.* at 764 (citing Bigelow v. Virginia, 421 U.S. 809 (1975)). However, Justice Blackmun carefully pointed out that, the *Virginia State Board* Court was not holding that it was not necessary for advertising to carry such important public information to merit First Amendment protection. *Id.* at 764–65. For instance, he went on, it would not be necessary for prescription drug price advertising to include discussion about the "store-to-store disparities in drug prices" to be protected. *Id.*

25. 447 U.S. 557, 560–61 (1980).

26. *Id.* at 566.

27. *Id.* The Court noted that New York was not claiming that the "expression at issue is inaccurate or relates to unlawful activity." *Id.* at 566.

28. *Id.* 568–69. In addition, near the end of the opinion, the majority stated, "We accept without reservation the argument that conservation, as well as the development of alternative energy sources, is an imperative national goal." *Id.* at 571.

29. *Id.* at 569–70.

30. *Id.* Justice Powell wrote: "There is an immediate connection between advertising and demand for electricity. Central Hudson would not contest the advertising ban unless it believed that promotion would increase its sales." *Id.* at 569. On this point, Justice Blackmun—who had written the majority opinion in *Virginia State Board*—disagreed with the *Central Hudson* majority that a ban on protected commercial speech was a permissible way for the state to advance its goal of promoting energy conservation. *Id.* at 573–74 (Blackmun, J., concurring in the judgment). He concluded that the First Amendment would not tolerate regulations that sought to manipulate consumer demand for lawful products and services by suppressing information. *Id.* at 574–75 (Blackmun, J., concurring in the judgment).

31. *See id.* at 573 (Blackmunn, J., concurring in the judgment). Justice Blackmun concluded that the *Central Hudson* test was not appropriate "when a State seeks to suppress information about a product in order to manipulate a private economic decision that the State cannot or has not regulated or outlawed directly." *Id.* (Blackmun, J., concurring in the judgment).

32. *Id.* (Blackmun, J., concurring in the judgment).

33. *Id.* at 571.

34. *Id.* at 561–62.

35. *Id.* (internal citation to *Virginia St. Bd. of Pharmacy v. Va. Citizens Council, Inc.,* 425 U.S. 748, 761–62 (1976) omitted).

36. *Id.* at 578 (Blackmun, J., concurring in the judgment).

37. *Id.* (Blackmun, J., concurring in the judgment). Justice Stevens, also joined by Justice Brennan, took the position that government should not be permitted to regulate truthful, non-misleading advertising simply because it fears that the public will find the message persuasive. *Id.* at 581 (Stevens, J., concurring).

38. *Id.* at 584–85 (Rehnquist, J., dissenting).

39. It should be noted that the Court has not always applied the *Central Hudson* analysis in cases in which commercial speech is involved. For instance, in *Glickman v. Wileman Bros. & Elliott, Inc.,* the Supreme Court upheld a federal marketing order that required California growers of certain tree fruit to contribute to a fund that was in part used to subsidize generic advertising for California tree fruit. 521 U.S. 457, 463, 466–67 (1997). The majority concluded that the marketing order did not raise a significant First Amendment issue because it was part of a larger regulatory scheme that furthered the collective economic interests of tree fruit growers. *Id.* at 469–70, 475. Thus, the majority concluded that constitutional scrutiny—even the less stringent *Central Hudson* test—was inappropriate. *Id.* at 474–75. Writing for the majority, Justice Stevens concluded that generic advertising was not likely to create a "crisis of conscience" for tree fruit producers who objected to their payments being used to subsidize the advertising. *Id.* at 472.

Subsequently, in *United States v. United Foods, Inc.,* the Court struck down on First Amendment grounds a provision in the federal Mushroom Promotion, Research and Consumer Information Act that assessed fresh mushroom handlers with a fee that was used to subsidize government-funded generic advertising promoting mushroom sales. 533 U.S. 405, 408–409 (2001). Writing for the Court, Justice Anthony Kennedy character-ized the assessment as a form of compelled speech because it was used to sponsor government expression with a certain viewpoint and applied the more stringent strict scrutiny instead of the less rigorous *Central Hudson* analysis. *Id.* at 410–11. The majority concluded that the mushroom assessment in *United Foods* was different than the tree fruit assessment in *Wileman Bros.* Justice Kennedy pointed out that the tree fruit assessment was part of larger regulatory scheme aimed at fostering a cooperative market for tree fruit while the mushroom assessment was not. *Id.* at 415. In a dissenting opinion, Justice Stephen Breyer concluded that the assessment was a form of economic regulation that did not interfere with the speech rights of mushroom handlers sufficiently enough to raise First Amendment concerns. *Id.* at 425–26 (Breyer, J., dissenting) (joined by Justice Ginsburg on this point). Even so, he concluded, the regulations passed constitutional muster under the *Central Hudson* analysis. *Id.* at 429 (Breyer, J., dissenting) (joined by Justices Ginsburg and O'Connor on this point). One federal district court recently followed the majority approach in *United Foods* in a case dealing with subsidies for generic beef advertising. *See Livestock Marketing Ass'n v. United States Dept. of Agriculture,* 207 F.Supp.2d 992 (D. S.D. 2002).

40. *See* City of Cincinnati v. Discovery Network, Inc., 507 U.S. 410 (1993); Metromedia, Inc. v. City of San Diego, 453 U.S. 490 (1981).

41. *See* Bolger v. Youngs Drug Products Corp., 463 U.S. 60 (1983).

42. *See* Greater New Orleans Broad. Ass'n v. United States, 527 U.S. 173 (1999); 44 Liquormart, Inc. v. Rhode Island, 517 U.S. 484 (1996); Rubin v. Coors Brewing Co., 514 U.S. 476 (1995); Posadas de Puerto Rico Assocs. v. Tourism Co. of Puerto Rico, 478 U.S. 328 (1986).

43. *See* Greater New Orleans Broad. Ass'n v. United States, 527 U.S. 173 (1999); United States v. Edge Broad. Co., 509 U.S. 418 (1993).

44. *See* Florida Bar v. Went For It, Inc., 515 U.S. 618 (1995); Edenfield v. Fane, 507 U.S. 761 (1993).

45. *See* Bolger v. Youngs Drug Prods. Corp., 463 U.S. 60, 72 (1983).

46. *See* Rubin v. Coors Brewing Co., 514 U.S. 476, 486 (1995).

47. Central Hudson Gas & Elec. Corp. v. Public Serv. Comm'n, 447 U.S. 557, 570 (1980).

48. 507 U.S. 761 (1993).

49. 514 U.S. 476 (1995).

50. 517 U.S. 484 (1996).

51. 527 U.S. 173 (1999).

52. 515 U.S. 618 (1995).

53. 507 U.S. at 763.

54. *Id.* at 770–71.

55. *Id.*

56. *Id.* at 771.

57. 514 U.S. 476, 478, 491 (1995).

58. *Id.* at 487–88.

59. *Id.* at 488–89. The Court described the regulatory scheme as "unique and puzzling" and concluded that the government's asserted regulatory interest in furtherance of the beer labeling ban was undermined by labeling and advertising requirements for wine and liquor. *Id.* at 489.

60. *Id.* at 489–90. The Court concluded that the "Government did not offer any convincing evidence that the labeling ban has inhibited strength wars." *Id.* at 490.

61. *Id.*

62. 517 U.S. 484, 489–90 (1996).

63. *Id.* at 504–05.

64. *Id.* at 505–06, 508.

65. *Id.* at 506 (citing the district court opinion in *44 Liquortmart, Inc. v. Racine,* 829 F. Supp. 543, 549 (D. R.I. 1993)). Justice Stevens concluded that evidence in the record suggested that excessive drinkers and alcoholics were not likely to be deterred by higher prices. *Id.*

66. 527 U.S. 173, 176, 195–96 (1999).

67. *Id.* at 176, 185, 195–96.

68. *Id.* at 190.

69. *Id.* at 188–89

70. *Id.* at 190.

71. 515 U.S. 618 (1995).

72. *Id.* at 621–22, 635.

73. *Id.* at 624–25.

74. *Id.* at 625.

75. *Id.* 625–29. The Florida Bar submitted a 106-page summary of a two-year study of advertising that contained both summaries of empirical research in the form of polls and anecdotal accounts of lawyer solicitations of accident victims. For descriptions of the studies recounted in the summary submitted by Florida, see generally, *id.*

76. *Id.* at 627.

77. *Id.*

78. *Id.* at 628.

79. *Id.* at 628–29 (citing Renton v. Playtime Theatres, Inc., 475 U.S. 41, 50–51 (1986); Barnes v. Glen Theatre, Inc., 501 U.S. 560, 584–85 (Souter, J., concurring in the judgment); Burson v. Freeman, 504 U.S. 191, 211 (1992)).

80. *Id.*

81. *Id.* at 640–41 (Kennedy, J., dissenting) (joined by Justices Stevens, Souter and Ginsburg) (calling Florida's summary a "selective synopsis of unvalidated studies"). *See also* John Phillips, *Six Years After Florida Bar v. Went For It, Inc., The Continual Erosion of First Amendment Rights,* 14 GEO. J. LEGAL ETH-ICS 197, 197 (2000) (stating that the principle study relied upon by Florida was a "rather questionable and extremely narrow survey").

82. 447 U.S. 557, 566 (1980).

83. *Id.* at 565.

84. *Id.* at 566 n.9.

85. 507 U.S. 761, 765–66 (1993) (citations omitted).

86. 492 U.S. 469, 477–78, 480 (1989).

87. *Id.* at 480.

88. *Id.*

89. *See, e.g.,* Langvardt, *supra* note 2, at 610

90. 517 U.S. 484, 524–25 (1996) (Thomas, J., concurring). On this point, Justice Thomas wrote: "The opinions [in *44 Liquormart*] would appear to commit the courts to striking down restrictions on speech whenever a direct regulation (i.e., a regulation involving no restriction on speech regarding a lawful activity at all) would be an equally effective method of dampening demand by legal users." *Id.* at 524.

91. Rubin v. Coors Brewing Co., 514 U.S. 476, 490–91 (1995).

92. *Id.*

93. 517 U.S. at 507–508.

94. *Id.* at 507.

95. 527 U.S. 173, 192–93 (1999).

96. 517 U.S. at 524–25 (Thomas, J., concurring).

97. Posadas de Puerto Rico Assocs. v. Tourism Co. Puerto Rico, 478 U.S. 328 (1986).

98. United States v. Edge Broad. Co., 509 U.S. 418 (1993).

99. 514 U.S. 476 (1995).

100. 517 U.S. 484 (1996).

101. 527 U.S. 173 (1999).

102. 478 U.S. 328, 331, 346 (1986)

103. *Id.* at 341.

104. *Id.* at 341–42. On this point, Justice Rehnquist wrote:

> The Puerto Rico Legislature obviously believed, when it enacted the advertising restrictions at issue here, that advertising of casino gambling aimed at the residents of Puerto Rico would serve to increase the demand for the product advertised. We think the legislature's belief is a reasonable one and the fact that appellant has chosen to litigate this case all the way to this Court indicates that appellant shares the legislature's view.

Id.

105. 509 U.S. 418, 426, 428, 432–35 (1993).

106. 478 U.S. at 346.

107. 447 U.S. at 603–04 (Rehnquist, J., dissenting).

108. 478 U.S. at 359 (Stevens, J., dissenting).

109. 509 U.S. at 437, 439 (Stevens, J., dissenting).

110. 514 U.S. 476, 482 n.2 (1995) (stating that "[n]either *Edge Broadcasting* nor *Posadas* compels us to craft an exception to the *Central Hudson* standard [for vice product advertising]").

111. 517 U.S. 484, 510 (1996) (joined by Justices Kennedy, Thomas and Ginsburg). Justice Stevens, wrote further:

> Moreover, the scope of any "vice" exception to the protection afforded by the First Amendment would be difficult, if not impossible, to define. Almost any product that poses some threat to public health or public morals might reasonably be characterized by a state legislature as relating to "vice activity." Such characterization, however, is anomalous when applied to products such as alcoholic beverages, lottery tickets, or playing cards, that may be lawfully purchased on the open market. The recognition of such an exception would also have the unfortunate consequence of either allowing state legislatures to justify censorship by the simple expedient of placing the "vice" label on selected lawful activities, or requiring the federal courts to establish a federal common law of vice. For these reasons, a "vice" label that is unaccompanied by a corresponding prohibition against the commercial behavior at issue fails to provide a principled justification for the regulation of commercial speech about that activity.

Id. at 514.

112. *Id.* 531–32 (O'Connor, J., concurring).

113. 527 U.S. 173, 193 (1996) (emphasis added).

114. Troy, *supra* note 2, at 132.

115. *See generally* Hoefges and Rivera-Sanchez, *supra* note 2.

116. FED. TRADE COMM'N, CIGARETTE REF. FOR 2000 1, Table 2A, Table 2B (2002), *available at* http://www.ftc.gov/os/2002cigrpt.pdf. The Federal Trade Commission has reported these data to Congress annually since 1967. *Id.* According to the data reported by the FTC, the cigarette industry spent more than $700 million on newspaper, magazine, outdoor, transit, point-of-sale and Internet advertising. *Id.* Table 2B. The rest of the expenditures were devoted promotional allowances, sampling distribution, specialty item distribution, public entertainment, direct mail and coupons, among other types of promotional activities. *Id.*

Although advertising and promotional expenditures have increased every year since 1963, total U.S. cigarette sales in dollars have not. According to data reported by the FTC, cigarette sales in the United States totaled $413.5 billion, which represented a 0.5% increase over 1999 sales ($411.3 billion) but a 21% decrease when compared to 1990 sales ($523.7 billion). *Id.* at Table 1. Since 1963, the first year for which the FTC reported data, 2000 marked the second lowest total of U.S. cigarette sales ahead of 1999. *Id.*

117. *See generally* Lorillard Tobacco Co. v. Reilly, 533 U.S. 525, 540–51 (2001).

118. 15 U.S.C. §§ 1333, *et seq.* (2002).

119. *Id.* at § 1333(a)(1). The current set of required packaging warnings are as follows: "SURGEON

GENERAL'S WARNING: Smoking Causes Lung Cancer, Heart Disease, Emphysema, And May Complicate Pregnancy;" "SURGEON GENERAL'S WARNING: Quitting Smoking Now Greatly Reduces Serious Risks to Your Health;" "SURGEON GENERAL'S WARNING: Smoking By Pregnant Women May Result in Fetal Injury, Premature Birth, And Low Birth Weight;" and "SURGEON GENERAL'S WARNING: Cigarette Smoke Contains Carbon Monoxide." *Id.*

120. *Id.* at § 1333(a)(2), (3). The FCLAA distinguishes between printed advertisements in magazines and newspapers and those on outdoor billboards. *See id.* at § 1333(a)(2), (3). The current set of required warnings for print advertisements (non-billboard) are the same as those required for package labels. *See supra* note 119. The required set of cigarette warnings for outdoor billboard advertising are as follows: "SURGEON GENERAL'S WARNING: Smoking Causes Lung Cancer, Heart Disease, And Emphysema;" "SURGEON GENERAL'S WARNING: Quitting Smoking Now Greatly Reduces Serious Health Risks;" "SURGEON GENERAL'S WARNING: Pregnant Women Who Smoke Risk Fetal Injury and Premature Birth;" and "SUR-GEON GENERAL'S WARNING: Cigarette Smoke Contains Carbon Monoxide." *Id.* at § 1333(a)(3).

121. *Id.* at § 1331(1).

122. *Id.* at § 1333(c).

123. *Id.* at § 1333(b).

124. *See generally* Fed. Trade Comm'n, Div. of Adver Practices, "Memorandum to Potential Cigarette Manufacturers or Importers," Oct. 1, 2002, *available at* http://www. ftc. gov/ bcp/policystmt/cigarette-memo.htm.

125. 15 U.S.C. § 1333(c) (2002).

126. *See generally* Fed. Trade Comm'n, *supra* note 124.

127. 70 U.S.C. § 4401, *et seq.* (2002).

128. *Id.* at § 4402. Smokeless tobacco packaging and advertising must include one of the following warnings: "WARNING: THIS PRODUCT MAY CAUSE MOUTH CANCER;" "WARNING: THIS PRODUCT MAY CAUSE GUM DISEASE AND TOOTH LOSS;" "WARNING: THIS PRODUCT IS NOT A SAFE ALTER-NATIVE TO CIGARETTES." *Id.* at § 4402(a)(1). The warnings must be "conspicuous and prominent" as further defined by guidelines that the Federal Trade Commission promulgates. *Id.* at § 4402(b). Smokeless tobacco manufacturers, packagers and importers must use the warnings on a rotating basis according to a compliance plan that they must submit to the FTC for approval. *Id.* at § 4402(c), (d).

129. *Id.* at § 4402(a)(2).

130. 15 U.S.C. § 1334(a).

131. *Id.* at § 1334(b).

132. *Id.* at § 1331(2).

133. 70 U.S.C. § 4406 (2002). It should be noted that smokeless tobacco manufacturers do not utilize outdoor advertising as extensively as other forms of advertising and promotion. According to the most recently available figures from Congress, the five major smokeless tobacco manufacturers spent a total of $170.2 million on advertising and promotion in 1999 but only $7,258 on outdoor advertising that year. *See* FEDERAL TRADE COMM'N, REF. TO CONGRESS FOR THE YEARS 1998–1999 PURSUANT TO THE COMPREHENSIVE SMOKELESS TOBACCO HEALTH EDUCATION ACT OF 1986 (2001), *available at* http://www.ftc.gov/reports/tobacco/smoke-less98_99.htm. According to the FTC, smokeless tobacco advertisers spent $30,756,608 (or 18% of the total of all advertising and promotion dollars) on promotions, $26,092,942 (15.3%) on point-of-sale advertising, $24,221,899 (14.2%) on coupons, $22,136,453 (13%) on public entertainment and $18,436,630 (10.8%) on magazine advertising. *Id.* at Table 2E. These categories accounted for the top five smokeless tobacco advertising and promotional expenditure categories in 1999. *Id.*

134. 15 U.S.C. § 1335 (2002).

135. 70 U.S.C. § 4402 (2002).

136. *See generally* Reno v. American Civil Liberties Union, 521 U.S. 844 (1997).

137. Capitol Broad. Co. v. Mitchell, 333 F. Supp. 582, 585–86 (D.C. Cir. 1971), *aff'd without opinion sub nom.* Capitol Broad. v. Kleindienst, 405 U.S. 1000 (1972). The ban was challenged by a coalition of broadcasters.

138. Capitol Broad. Co. v. Kliendienst, 405 U.S. 1000 (1972).

139. Martin H. Redish, *Tobacco Advertising and the First Amendment,* 81 IOWA L. REV. 589, 632–34 (1996). Professor Redish stated that the electronic media bans on tobacco advertising were "subject to serious constitutional question" and likely would not survive scrutiny under "modern doctrinal standards of commercial speech protection." *Id.* at 633–34. However, he concluded that because the bans are so well-established, the courts would not be likely to overturn them on constitutional grounds. *Id.*

140. *Regulations Restricting the Sale and Distribution of Cigarettes and Smokeless Tobacco to Protect Children and Adolescents,* Final Rule, 61 Fed. Reg. 44,396 (Aug. 28, 1996) (hereinafter "Final Rule").

141. Food and Drug Administration v. Williamson Tobacco Corp., 529 U.S. 120, 126, 161 (2000).

142. *See generally* Master Settlement Agreement (Nov. 23, 1988), *available at* http://www.naag.org/upload/1040655230_lstmsa.pdf.

143. *See generally* Final Rule, 61 Fed. Reg. 44,396, 44, 465–69 (Aug. 28, 1996). In the introduction to the advertising section of the Final Rule, the FDA wrote: "The purpose of the advertising regulations is to decrease young people's use of tobacco products by ensuring that the restrictions on access are not undermined by the product appeal that advertising for these products creates for young people." *Id.* at 44,465 (citing Central Hudson Gas & Elec. Corp. v. Public Serv. Comm'n of New York, 447 U.S. 557, 569 (1980)).

144. 21 C.F.R. § 897.32(a) (1996) (revoked 2000). *See generally* Final Rule, 61 Fed. Reg. at 44,508–14 § VI.E.4 (Aug. 28, 1996).

145. 21 C.F.R. § 897.32(a)(2), (a)(2)(i)–(ii) (1996) (revoked 2000). *See generally* Final Rule, 61 Fed. Reg. at 44,514–19 § VI.E.5 (Aug. 28, 1996).

146. 21 C.F.R. § 897.30(b) (1996) (revoked 2000). *See generally* Final Rule, 61 Fed. Reg. 44,396, 44,502–08 § VI.E.3 (Aug. 28, 1996).

147. 21 C.F.R. § 897.16(c) (1996) (revoked 2000); § 897.32(a)(1) (revoked 2000). *See generally* Final Rule, 61 Fed. Reg. at 44,508–14 § VI.E.4 (Aug. 28, 1996).

148. Final Rule, 61 Fed. Reg. at 44,471–513 (Aug. 28, 1996). The FDA claimed that it had a sufficiently substantial regulatory interest in curbing use of cigarettes and smokeless tobacco products by minors to protect their health under the second *Central Hudson* factor. *See generally id.* at 44,472–74. In addition, the FDA claimed that its proposed regulations of cigarette and smokeless tobacco advertising and marketing directly advanced this regulatory interest and were narrowly tailored under the fourth *Central Hudson* factor. *See generally id.* at 44–474096, 44,496–500.

149. *Id.* at 44,474–96.

150. *Id.* at 44,474–96 § VI.D. As to the proposed advertising restrictions, the FDA concluded in a subsequent section that the "evidence amassed during this investigation and provided by comments [to the proposed Final Rule] provides ample support for its requirement that all forms of advertising that children see and are exposed to can have an effect upon their attitudes about tobacco use." *Id.* at 44,513.

151. *Id.* at 44,472 (asserting that the restrictions would "have virtually no effect on the core informational function of commercial speech" and were "designed . . . to ensure that adults can continue to be informed by the information in tobacco advertising while restricting the noninformative aspects of advertising that appeal to [minors]"), 44,496–500 § VI.E.2.

152. *Id.* at 44,466.

153. *Id.* at 44,475–76. The FDA cited the following studies in support of this conclusion: S. Chapman & B. Fitzgerald, *Brand Preference and Advertising Recall in Adolescent Smokers: Some Implications for Health Promotion,* 72 AM. J. PUB. HEALTH 491 (1982); P. P. Aitken & D. R. Eadie, *Reinforcing Effects of Cigarette Advertising on Under-Age Smoking,* 85 BRIT. J. ADDICTION 399 (1990); A. O. Goldstein et al., *Relationship Between High School Student Smoking and Recognition of Cigarette Advertisements,* 110 J. PEDIATRICS 488 (1987); G. L. Botvin et al., *Smoking Behavior of Adolescents Exposed to Cigarette Advertising,* 108 PUB. HEALTH REP. 217 (1993); M. Klitzner et al., *Cigarette Advertising and Adolescent Experimentation With Smoking,* 86 BRIT. J. ADDICTION 287 (1991); P. P. Aitken et al., *Predisposing Effects of Cigarette Advertising on Children's Intentions to Smoke When Older,* 86 BRIT. J. ADDICTION 383 (1991); D. L. O'Connell et al., *Cigarette Smoking and Drug Use in Schoolchildren: II. Factors Associated With Smoking,* 10 INT'L J. EPIDE-MIOLOGY 223 (1981); H. M. Alexander et al., *Cigarette Smoking and Drug Use in Schoolchildren: IV. Factors Associated With Changes in Smoking Behaviour,* 12 INT'L J. EPIDEMIOLOGY 59 (1983). *Id.* at 44,476 n.99.

The FDA relied on studies to conclude that advertising contributes to children's overestimation of smoking prevalence in society. *Id.* 44,476 n.102 (citing L. Chassin et al., *Predicting the Onset of Cigarette Smoking in Adolescents: A Longitudinal Study,* 14 J. APPLIED SOC. PSYCHOL. 224 (1984); L. M. Collins et al., *Psychosocial Predictors of Young Adolescent Cigarette Smoking: A Sixteen-Month, Three-Wave Longitudinal Study,* 17 J. APPLIED SOC. PSYCHOL. 554 (1987); S. Sussman et al., *Adolescent Nonsmokers, Triers, and Regular Smokers' Estimates of Cigarette Smoking Prevalence: When do Overestimations Occur and by Whom?,* 18 J. APPLIED SOC. PSYCHOL. 537 (1988); S. J. Sherman et al., *The False Consensus Effect in Estimates of Smoking Prevalence: Underlying Mechanisms,* 9 PERSONALITY AND SOC. PSYCHOL. BULL. 197 (1983); G. J. Botvin et al., *Smoking Behavior of Adolescents Exposed to Cigarette Advertising,* 108 PUB. HEALTH REP. 217 (1993)).

In addition, the FDA reviewed studies indicating that certain advertising campaigns are well-recalled by children. *Id.* at 44,476 n.103 (citing J. P. Pierce et al., *Does Tobacco Advertising Target Young People to Start Smoking?*, 266 J. AM. MED. ASS'N 3154 (1991); P. M. Fischer et al., *Brand Logo Recognition by Children Aged 3 to 6 Years: Mickey Mouse and Old Joe Camel*, 266 J. AM. MED. ASS'N 3145 (1991); G. B. Hastings et al., *Cigarette Advertising and Children's Smoking: Why Reg Was Withdrawn*, 309 BRIT. MED. J. 933 (1994); J. P. Pierce et al., *Smoking Initiation by Adolescent Girls, 1944 Through 1988: An Association With Targeted Advertising*, 271 J. AM. MED. ASS'N 608 (1991). The FDA also concluded that studies indicated that the "Joe Camel" campaign was particularly well-known by subject children. *Id.* at 44,476 n.104 (citing P. M. Fischer et al., *Brand Logo Recognition by Children Aged 3 to 6 Years: Mickey Mouse and Old Joe the Camel*, 266 J. AM. MED. ASS'N 3145 (1991); J. P. Pierce et al., *Does Tobacco Advertising Target Young People to Start Smoking?* 226 J. AM. MED. ASS'N 3154 (1991)).

154. *Id.* at 44,468 (citing R. E. PETTY & J. T. CACIOPPO, COMMUNICATION AND PERSUASION: CENTRAL AND PERIPHERAL ROUTES TO ATTITUDE CHANGE (1986)). The FDA cited the Elaboration Likelihood Model, which is based on a social psychological theory that suggests that people process information more or less thoroughly and deeply depending on various factors including cognitive development. Under this model, the FDA explained, persuasion can be accomplished through the "peripheral" or the "central" route:

> The *central route* refers to the process by which a person reads the messages or information contained in the advertisement and thinks carefully about it and is influenced by the strength of its arguments. *The peripheral route is a process in which individuals, particularly young people, are more likely to pay attention and be persuaded by peripheral cues such as attractive models, color and scenery, which are unrelated to the primary parts of the message.* Therefore, a young person, or anyone who is unmotivated or unable to carefully consider the arguments in a message, is likely to be persuaded via the peripheral route.

Id. (emphasis added).

155. *See generally* Lorillard Tobacco Co. v. Reilly, 533 U.S. 525, 556–61 (2001).

156. 529 U.S. 120 (2000).

157. *Id.* at 131–32 (rejecting the FDA's assertion that it had regulatory jurisdiction over nicotine as a "drug" and tobacco products as "drug delivery devices").

158. Regulations Restricting the Sale and Distribution of Cigarettes and Smokeless Tobacco to Protect Children and Adolescents; Revocation, 65 Fed. Reg. 17,135 (2000) (Food and Drug Administration, HHS), *available at* http://www.fda.gov/OHRMS_DOCKETS/98fr/033100c.txt.

159. Youth Smoking Prevention and Public Health Protection Act, S. 2626, 107th Congress (2002), *available at* http://thomas.loc.gov/cgi-bin/bdquery/z?d107:s.02626: (introduced by Sen. Edward Kennedy (D-MA) on June 14, 2002, and referred that date to the Senate Committee on Health, Education, Labor and Pensions, where it remains pending); National Cancer Act of 2002, S. 1976, 107th Congress (2002), *available at* http://thomas.loc.gov/cgi-bin/bdquery/z?d107:s.01976: (introduced by Sen. Dianne Feinstein (D-CA) on Feb. 28, 2002, and referred that date to the Senate Committee on Health, Education, Labor and Pensions, where it remains pending); FDA Tobacco Authority Amendments Act, H.R. 1097, 107th Congress (2001), *available at* http://thomas.loc.gov/cgi-bin/bdquery/z?d107:h.r.01097: (introduced by Rep. Greg Ganske (R-IA) on March 20, 2001, and referred on April 2, 2001, to the House Subcommittee on Health, where it remains pending).

160. Master Settlement Agreement, *supra* note 142. In addition, four other states—Florida, Minnesota, Texas and Mississippi—entered into similar separate settlement agreements with tobacco manufacturers. *See* National Association of Attorneys General, *NAAG Projects: Tobacco, at* http://naag.org/issues/issue-tobacco. php (last visited Jan. 20, 2003). For a discussion of the constitutionality of holding non-signing tobacco manufacturers to the terms and provisions of the Master Settlement Agreement, *see generally* Lori Ann Lukas, Note, *The Tobacco Industry and the First Amendment: An Analysis of the 1998 Master Settlement Agreement*, 14 J.L. & HEALTH 297 (1999/2000).

161. Master Agreement, *supra* note 142, at 14–20 pt. III (c).

162. *Id.* at 17 pt. III (d). The MSA defines "outdoor advertising" as including billboards and signs and placards in arenas, stadiums, shopping malls and video game arcades unless located in an "adult-only" location where those under the legal age are prohibited. *Id.* at 7–8 pt. II (ii). It should be noted that the MSA excludes outdoor advertising that is less than fourteen square feet, located on a tobacco manufacturing facility, or located on the property of retail establishments that sell tobacco products. *Id.*

163. *See id.* at 8 pt. II (ii).

164. 533 U.S. 525 (2001).

165. MASS. REGS. CODE tit. 940, §§ 21.04, 21.06 (2000).

166. *Id.*

167. *See supra* notes 162 and 163 and accompanying text. Massachusetts was one of the signatory states to the Master Settlement Agreement.

168. Lorillard Tobacco Co. v. Reilly, 76 F. Supp. 2d 124 (D. Mass. 1999) (Lorillard I), *aff'd in part and rev'd in part sub nom.* Consolidated Cigar Corp. v. Reilly, 218 F.3d 30 (1st Cir. 2000), *aff'd in part and rev'd in part,* 533 U.S. 525 (2001).

169. Lorillard Tobacco Co. v. Reilly, 84 F. Supp. 2d 180 (D. Mass. 2000) (Lorillard II), *aff'd in part and rev'd in part sub nom.* Consolidated Cigar Corp. v. Reilly, 218 F.3d 30 (1st Cir. 2000), *aff'd in part and rev'd in part* Lorillard Tobacco Co. v. Reilly, 533 U.S. 525 (2001).

170. Consolidated Cigar Corp. v. Reilly, 218 F.3d 30 (1st Cir. 2000), *aff'd in part and rev'd in part sub nom.* Lorillard Tobacco Co. v. Reilly, 533 U.S. 525 (2001).

171. *Id.* at 41.

172. *Id.* at 53.

173. *See* Steve Jarvis, *Big Tobacco's Marketing Practices Challenged by States,* MARKETING NEWS, May 21, 2001, at 11.

174. *Lorillard Tobacco Co.,* 533 U.S. at 551 (Chief Justice Rehnquist and Justices Scalia, Kennedy and Thomas joined Justice O'Connor in the holding on the pre-emption issue).

175. *Id.* at 551–52.

176. *Id.* at 597–98 (Stevens, J., concurring in part, concurring in the judgment, and dissenting in part) (joined in this part by Justices Ginsburg, Breyer and Souter).

177. *Id.* at 553.

178. *Id.* at 554.

179. *Id.* at 554–55.

180. *Id.* (joined by Chief Justice Rehnquist and Justices Kennedy, Scalia, Souter and Thomas on this point). In a concurring opinion, Justice Kennedy, joined by Justice Scalia, expressed concern that the *Central Hudson* test failed to adequately protect truthful, non-misleading commercial speech. *Id.* at 571–72 (Kennedy, J., concurring in part and concurring in the judgment). However, he agreed with Justice O'Connor that it was not necessary to the disposition of the case to consider abandoning the test in favor another constitutional standard. *Id.*

181. *Id.*

182. *Id.* at 555.

183. *Id.* (citing Greater New Orleans Broad. Ass'n v. United States, 527 U.S. 173, 188 (1999) (quoting Edenfield v. Fane, 507 U.S. 761, 770–71 (1993)).

184. *Id.*

185. *Id.* at 556–57.

186. *Id.* at 557–561.

187. *Id.* Justice O'Connor stated that the FDA had "considered several studies of tobacco advertising and trends in the use of various tobacco products" and had "made specific findings with respect to smokeless tobacco." *Id.* at 558–59.

188. *Id.* at 557.

189. *Id.* at 561 (emphasis added). In a concurring opinion joined by Justice Scalia, Justice Kennedy concluded that the majority's ruling under the third *Central Hudson* factor was unnecessary and therefore gratuitous. *Id.* at 571–72 (Kennedy, J., concurring in part and concurring in the judgment). He concluded that because the regulations were clearly unconstitutional under the fourth *Central Hudson* factor alone, application of the third factor was not needed. *Id.*

190. *Id.* at 566.

191. *Id.* at 556.

192. *Id.* at 561 (Justice O'Connor was joined on this point by Chief Justice Rehnquist and Justices Scalia, Kennedy and Thomas).

193. *Id.* at 563.

194. *Id.* at 564.

195. *Id.* (relying on Reno v. Am. Civil Liberties Union, 521 U.S. 844, 875 (1997)).

196. *See Reno,* 521 U.S. at 849.

197. Lorillard Tobacco Co. v. Reilly, 533 U.S. 525, 565 (2001).

198. Final Rule, 61 Fed. Reg. 44,396, 44,506 (Aug. 28, 1996).

199. *Id.* (noting that small retailers would be unable to communicate to passing adults that tobacco products were sold inside but stating that the ban was "necessary to keep outdoor advertising away from areas where children are likely to congregate daily").

200. *Lorillard Tobacco Co.,* 533 U.S. at 601–03 (Stevens, J., concurring in part, concurring in the judgment in part, and dissenting in part), 590 (Souter, J., concurring in part and dissenting in part). Justice Stevens was joined by Justices Ginsburg and Breyer.

201. *Id.* at 601–02 (Stevens, J., concurring in part, concurring in the judgment in part, and dissenting in part).

202. *Id.* at 601 (Stevens, J., concurring in part, concurring in the judgment in part, and dissenting in part).

203. *Id.* at 572 (Thomas, J., concurring in part and concurring in the judgment). Justices Kennedy and Scalia expressed concern that the *Central Hudson* test provided too little protection for protected commercial speech but agreed with Justice O'Connor that it was not necessary to adopt a new constitutional standard in the case. *See supra* note 180.

204. *Id.* at 572 (Stevens, J., concurring in part, concurring in the judgment in part, and dissenting in part).

205. *Id.* (Thomas, J., concurring in part and concurring in the judgment).

206. *Id.* at 575 (Thomas, J., concurring in part and concurring in the judgment).

207. *Id.* at 573 (Thomas, J., concurring in part and concurring in the judgment).

208. *Id.* at 576–77 (Thomas, J., concurring in part and concurring in the judgment).

209. *Id.* (Thomas, J., concurring in part and concurring in the judgment).

210. *Id.* at 582–83 (Thomas, J., concurring in part and concurring in the judgment).

211. *Id.* at 584–85 (Thomas, J., concurring in part and concurring in the judgment).

212. *Id.* (Thomas, J., concurring in part and concurring in the judgment).

213. *See id.* at 589–90 (Thomas, J., concurring in part and concurring in the judgment).

214. *Id.* (Thomas, J., concurring in part and concurring in the judgment).

215. *Id.* at 590 (Thomas, J., concurring in part and concurring in the judgment) (suggesting that "no principle of law or logic . . . would preclude the imposition of restrictions on fast food and alcohol advertising similar to those [the State of Massachusetts] seeks to impose on tobacco advertising").

216. *Id.* (Thomas, J., concurring in part and concurring in the judgment).

217. For discussion of Justice Thomas' positions in commercial speech decisions, *see generally* Hoefges and Rivera-Sanchez, *supra* note 2 at 363–85; David L. Hudson, Essay, *Justice Clarence Thomas: The Emergence of a Commercial-Speech Protector,* 35 CREIGHTON L. REV. 485 (2002) (including discussion of Justice Thomas' position in *Lorillard Tobacco*).

218. 44 Liquormart, Inc. v. Rhode Island, 517 U.S. 484, 518 (Thomas, J., concurring in part and concurring in the judgment). This position was described by one commentator as the most "radical" taken by any of the justices on the Supreme Court regarding the commercial speech doctrine. Kathleen M. Sullivan, *Cheap Spirits, Cigarettes, and Free Speech: The Implications of 44 Liquormart,* 1996 SUP. CT. REV. 123, 141–42 (1996).

219. Greater New Orleans Broad. Ass'n v. United States, 527 U.S. 173, 197 (1999) (Thomas, J., concurring in the judgment). Justice Thomas citied to his concurring opinion in *44 Liquormart. Id.* (citing 44 Liquormart, Inc. v. Rhode Island, 517 U.S. 484, 518 (1996)).

220. Central Hudson Gas & Elec. Corp. v. Public Serv. Comm'n, 447 U.S. 557, 573 (1980) (Blackmun, J., concurring in the judgment) (stating that the *Central Hudson* test is not appropriate when the government "seeks to suppress information about a product in order to manipulate a private economic decision that [the government] cannot or has not regulated or outlawed directly"). Likewise, at least one commentator has suggested that the *Central Hudson* analysis fails to provide adequate constitutional protection for commercial speech against legislation seeking to influence lawful consumer decisions in the marketplace against "subjective evaluations of individual administrators, legislators, and judges." Troy, *supra* note 2, at 142.

221. 277 F.3d 622, 624–25 (2d Cir. 2002).

222. 165 F. Supp. 2d 403, 408–11, 422 (E.D. N.Y. 2001).

223. *See Long Island Bd. of Realtors,* 277 F.2d at 626; *Infinity Outdoor, Inc.,* 165 F. Supp. 2d at 414–15. *Cf.* Horizon Outdoor, LLC v. City of Industry, California, 228 F. Supp. 2d 1113 (C.D. Cal. 2002) (temporarily enjoining enforcement of city ordinance that required permission of certain city or state officials before erecting outdoor signs or advertising).

224. 256 F.3d 1061 (8th Cir. 2001).

225. *Id.* at 1076–77. The regulations in question prohibited with limited exceptions "advertising or use of any means or media to induce persons to buy liquor." *Id.* at 1068 (quoting UTAH CODE ANN. § 32A-12–401(6) (2000)).

226. *Id.* at 1069.

227. *Id.* at 1069–70.

228. *Id.* at 1075.

229. 272 F.3d 1030, 1032 (8th Cir. 2001).

230. *Id.* at 1032 (quoting IOWA CODE § 142A.6(6) (2000)).

231. *Id.* at 1037.

232. *Id.* at 1035.

233. *Id.* at 1039.

234. 161 F. Supp. 2d 796, 808, 799, 811–12 (N.D. Ohio 2001). The court found that the city ordinance was preempted by an Ohio state law that provided that only the state government can regulate alcohol advertising in Ohio. *Id.* at 802–02, 808. However, the court found the ordinance unconstitutional under the First Amendment utilizing the *Central Hudson* analysis. *Id.* at 808–12.

235. *Id.* at 798–99.

236. *Id.* at 812.

237. *Id.* at 808–10.

238. *Id.* at 810–12.

239. *Id.* at 811.

240. *Id* at 811–12.

241. *Id.*

242. *Id.*

243. *See* Fed. of Adver. Indus. Representatives, Inc. v. City of Chicago, 2002 WL 398531 (N.D. Ill. 2002) (No. 97 C 7619) (published order in the case denying the challengers' motion for attorneys' fees after Chicago repealed the ordinance in question and rendered the First Amendment challenge moot). The ordinance in question banned alcohol and cigarette advertisements in a "publicly visible location" although the ordinance provided exceptions for alcohol and cigarette advertising near designated retail establishments, on city transit vehicles, on property owned by the state sports facility authority, on property adjacent to interstate highways, in certain industrial zones, and at Comiskey Park, Soldier Field, the United Center and Wrigley Field. Fed'n of Adver. Indus. Representatives, Inc. v. City of Chicago, 189 F.3d 633, 634 n.1 (7th Cir. 1999) (setting out the text of CHICAGO MUNICIPAL CODE, tit. 17, § 5.17).

244. Fed'n of Adver. Indus. Representatives, Inc. v. City of Chicago, 12 F. Supp. 2d 844, 852, 853 (N.D. Ill. 1998), *aff'd in part, rev'd in part,* 189 F.3d 633 (7th Cir. 1999) (also finding that the alcohol advertising provisions were not severable from the cigarette advertising provisions of the ordinance).

245. *Fed'n of Adver. Indus. Representatives,* 189 F.3d at 640. The Seventh Circuit also reversed the federal district court on the severability issue. *Id.*

246. Fed. of Adver. Indus. Representatives, Inc. v. City of Chicago, 529 U.S. 1066 (2000).

247. This point may be tempered somewhat because of the posture in which the case arrived at the Court. The *Lorillard Tobacco* case was decided by the Court on appeal from summary judgment, which required the Court to view the evidence most favorably to the non-moving party—the state. Justice O'Connor pointed this out in the majority opinion when she concluded that the state's regulatory scheme seemed to be based on more than "mere speculation and conjecture." Lorillard Tobacco Co. v. Reilly, 533 U.S. 525, 561 (2001).

248. In the only commercial speech case decided by the Supreme Court to date after *Lorillard Tobacco,* the Court avoided the evidentiary issue under the third *Central Hudson* factor. In that case, the Court struck down a federal ban on direct-to-consumer advertising by pharmacists for compounded prescription drugs. *See* Thompson v. W. States Med. Ctr., 535 U.S. 357, 122 S.Ct. 1497, 1500 (2002). Compounding is the lawful practice by a doctor or pharmacist that "combines, mixes, or alters ingredients to create a medication tailored to the needs of an individual patient" such as removing a particular ingredient to which a specific patient might have an allergy. *Id.* The regulations in question were added by Congress in 1997 to the Federal Food, Drug and Cosmetic Act and specifically stated that pharmacies, licensed pharmacists and licensed physicians could not lawfully "advertise or promote the compounding of any particular drug, class of drug, or type of drug" but could "advertise or promote the compounding service." *Id.* at 1502 (citing the Food and Drug Modernization Act of 1997, tit. 21 U.S.C. at § 353a(c)). In an opinion by Justice O'Connor, the *Western States* Court ruled that the federal ban was not sufficiently narrow under the fourth *Central Hudson* factor and unconstitutional on that ground alone. *Id.* at 1506. The Court thus found it unnecessary to make a conclusive

ruling on the issue of whether the government had established that the advertising ban for compounded drugs directly advanced the governmental interest in preventing the development of a mass demand for compounded prescription drugs that had not been specifically approved by the FDA. *Id.* at 1506.

In two cases involving the constitutionality of government regulations that require producers of agricultural products to subsidize generic advertising for those products, the Supreme Court issued rulings that avoided application of First Amendment commercial speech principles including the *Central Hudson* analysis. See *supra* note 39.

249. *See Thompson,* 122 S.Ct. at 2426.

250. *See* Rubin v. Coors Brewing Co., 514 U.S. 476, 490–91 (1995).

251. *See supra* note 110 and accompanying text.

252. *See supra* notes 111 and 112, and accompanying text.

253. *See supra* note 113 and accompanying text.

254. 535 U.S. 357, 122 S.Ct. 1497 (2002).

255. 12 S.Ct. at 1500.

256. *Id.* at 1507.

257. *See supra* notes 200–201 and accompanying text.

258. *See* Hoefges & Rivera-Sanchez, *supra* note 2.

259. Ronald Bayer et al., *Tobacco Advertising in the United States: A Proposal for a Constitutionally Acceptable Form of Regulation,* 287 J. AM. MED. ASSOC. 2990, 2994 (2002).

260. *Id.* at 2994. The authors noted that the neither the Supreme Court nor any lower courts had decided the constitutionality of a "content-based tax on commercial speech." *Id.*

261. *Id.* at 2994–95. The authors took that position that such requirements would require an amendment to the Federal Cigarette Labeling and Advertising Act and would constitute a form of "social marketing-informed messages designed to neutralize the seductive impact of the advertisements themselves." *Id.* at 2995.

262. *Id.* at 2995. The authors proposed "that one full side of each cigarette package be devoted to a graphic depiction of the dangers of smoking." *Id.* The authors noted that this and their other proposed regulations "were designed to combat bad speech with more speech" but would "evoke the full resistance of the tobacco industry and its allies in the Congress." *Id.* They noted that the Canadian regulations that required graphic visual warnings on cigarettes have been challenged in the Canadian courts by the tobacco industry. *Id.*

263. *See supra* note 159.

264. *See id.*

265. *See* Troy, *supra* note 2, at 142.

CHAPTER 17

A PROBLEM IGNORED
Dilution and Negation of Consumer Information by Antifactual Content

IVAN L. PRESTON

This first of two articles argues that a type of message content used frequently in advertising and other promotional communication has been ignored in research and public policy on consumer information. It is called *antifactual content* because, rather than being informative, i.e., a true fact claim, about the product or service, it is either noninformative, providing no fact at all about the item, or misinformative, providing a false fact about it. Consideration of such claims should be incorporated into analysis of consumer information.

Antifactual claims are those that in explicit form are not factual about the item. Claims may be made both explicitly and impliedly, with "explicit" content being what is literally stated, such as the words of this sentence as they appear on this page. "Implied" refers to what consumers see the message to be saying and to mean, which thus are the words of the sentence as they appear in the consumer's perception.

While the implied content may include the explicit, what is most significant for analysis is that it also may exclude or distort some or all of the explicit content and may include additional content that can be far afield from what was explicitly stated. In the old cliché of Freudian psychology, I say "Hello" to you and my intended implication is merely that I am engaging in common courtesy, but you may hear me saying "I like you" or "I don't like you."

In consumer information a claim that is explicitly factual may imply additional fact claims. In some instances the implied fact may be false even though the explicit fact is true. In a recent deceptive advertising case, the true explicit claim was that Doan's had a special ingredient for back pain that other pain relievers did not. The implied claim found false was that Doan's was thereby more effective for back pain than the others (Novartis 1999).

More pertinent here is that a claim that is *not* explicitly factual about the advertised item, an antifactual claim, may also be less than truthful about the item. The first of three such types this article identifies is explicitly opinion, which means the explicit wording, as in "Our bread is the best you can buy," states a subjective evaluation rather than objective fact. The second type is a claim, often called a joke or spoof claim, that consumers may be thought to take as obviously false in explicit form. The third type is a claim explicitly about the consumer rather than the advertised

From *The Journal of Consumer Affairs,* vol. 36, no. 2 (Winter 2002). Copyright © 2002 by The American Council on Consumer Interests. Reprinted with permission.

item, for example the famous "You deserve a break today." All of these claims may imply facts about the item that may be false, making them misinformative, or, if they imply no fact at all, noninformative. In either of the latter two cases, which I argue here occur often, the claims are antifactual, meaning they may detract from information rather than add to it.

Despite such possibilities, what I believe to be the most prominent lines of research and government policymaking on consumer information interpret such information as coming almost entirely from explicitly factual claims about the item. The antifactual claims and their potential impacts are scarcely mentioned in research on advertising information, or in regulatory policies that try to improve quantity and quality of information for consumers. Such omission leads researchers to conclude that ads are higher in information, and leads regulators to conclude that they are lower in deceptiveness, than is thought here to be accurate.

This article proposes that there is no justification for that traditional handling. Rather, failure to acknowledge all content pertinent to consumer information is detrimental to the acquisition of knowledge about it, to policy efforts to improve it, to advertisers' credibility as suppliers of it, and especially to consumers' opportunities to obtain and use information in their buying and consumption activities. Assessments of amount and quality of an ad's information will be more correct and useful when they include the effects of all claims. The value of claims would then be seen to involve not merely positive assessments of information value, but also neutral and negative ones, which surely exist.

The article's focus is theoretical and hypothetical, and as such is more a matter of suggesting questions than of answering them conclusively. The intent is to provoke inquiries that this author, now retired, will not be pursuing. Much of the analysis relied on is already published, and because it thus may be discussed here in lesser detail, readers may need to consult the cited sources for further background. Although the communication content examined here is mass media advertising, the topic has implications for all consumer information, for example content such as labels and even salespeople's claims made orally. This article's criterion for usefulness to consumers is strictly informativeness, stemming from factualness. Advertising claims may be entertaining, inspiring, motivating, and other things that are useful to sellers and often also to consumers, but they are simply not part of the topic here.

ANTIFACTUAL CONTENT IN ADVERTISING

This analysis identifies antifactual content as what I originally discussed as puffery, the marketplace term for claims explicitly of opinion rather than fact about the advertised item (Preston 1994, 1996, 1997). More recently I have added two additional types (Preston 1998). One is the obviously false claim, presumably readily seen as such by consumers by being tongue-in-cheek or otherwise humorous, or by being physically impossible. The other is the lifestyle claim, which is about the consumer to whom the advertised item is targeted rather than about the item. While more is said below on these claims, readers may want to consult Preston (1998) for additional detail.

I call these three types "loophole claims" to indicate that the law excuses advertisers from prosecution of them even when they are false, including when consciously and intentionally so (1998). Regulators, principally the Federal Trade Commission, examine only explicit form and so excuse these claims as nondeceptive because explicitly they state either no facts or else only obviously false facts about the advertised item. In the 1998 article I say that such position is wrong and creates a loophole enabling deceptiveness to go undetected because the law does not seek to determine what these claims imply. I argue that the claims may imply facts about the advertised item that may be false.

The Potential for Loophole Claims to Imply Facts

I argue not that loophole claims always imply facts, but that puffery often does and that obviously false and lifestyle claims sometimes do. For puffery, the suggested factual and often false implication that consumers could draw is that the advertiser knows of underlying facts that serve as a basis for these claims, such as that Goodyear makes the best tires. A typology of puffery claims suggests that they come in six categories from strongest to weakest: "best," "best possible," "better," "specially good," "good," and "subjective qualities," from strongest to weakest (Preston 1998). "Strongest" means having the greatest tendency to imply facts, "weakest" means having the least. An example of the weakest category would be that BMW is "the ultimate driving machine."

For obvious falsity, the suggestion is that consumers sometimes may not see the falsity as obvious and so possibly take the claim seriously, as either explicitly or impliedly true. An example is an IBM commercial run before Christmas in 1999 and 2000 showing parents on Christmas Eve assembling a bicycle. Their youngster, sneaking out of bed and peering over a railing, hears her father say he can't find the instructions. She rushes to her room, finds the instructions on her computer, prints them, floats the sheet over the railing, hears her father say, "Oh, here they are," and returns to bed. The possibility that the instructions could be found so quickly, or even found at all, seems very remote and essentially false. The advertiser, if investigated, might well defend the claim as obviously false, yet there is reason to think many consumers might take it at face value and be fooled. Many U.S. households are not yet on the web and so would not have the background to recognize the depicted product benefit as unlikely to exist.

The third type is lifestyle claims, which I earlier called "social and psychological" claims (Preston 1996, and in original ed., 1975). These claims might imply factual and sometimes false claims by tying the advertised item to the consumer's personal characteristics. An article described how Michael Saylor of MicroStrategy wanted to create a device that, if your house was on fire, "would page you . . . and automatically phone the fire department." Noting that people might or might not be consciously fearful of events such as a fire while away from home, Saylor said, "Even if you're not afraid of these things, the beauty is, with proper marketing, we can make you afraid" (MacFarquhar 2000). Yet while Saylor essentially admits that he would be willing to imply falsely that such need exists objectively for consumers, the company would be able to defend the reference to anxiety about security as saying nothing that consumers would take to be about the product.

My argument for implied meanings is based on advertiser as well as consumer behavior (Preston 1998). The loophole claims offer sellers free rein to create factual implications so as to favorably affect consumers' purchasing decisions. The result is two alternatives rather than only one in cases where factually true claims will not suffice to distinguish a brand. Rather than being factually false about the item, i.e., misinformative, thus vulnerable to prosecution for deceptiveness, advertisers may choose instead to be noninformative, neither true nor false, which regulators do not prosecute.

The argument is also based on other evidence too extensive to be repeated here; see Preston (1998). In particular, there is consumer research, principally on puffery, showing that consumers see facts implied. There are also various aspects of reasoning which argue why consumers can see loophole claims as impliedly factual, including that ad claims should be interpreted as involving mass rather than individual opinion. That suggests that consumers may see the claims to imply beliefs held by the public generally rather than merely by individual consumers personally, which can make the claims more persuasive. More recently than the 1998 article, Kelly, Slater and Karan (2000) provided empirical evidence that factual meanings are implied by lifestyle ads.

Potential Noninformativeness of Loophole Claims

The focus of this article is not only on whether the loophole claims are deceptive. Although I argue that they may imply facts and be deceptive, misinformative, when those facts are false, I disavow that examining consumer perceptions would find that result in all cases (Preston 1998). However, I have not previously stressed that when the loophole claims, which by definition are not factual explicitly, imply nothing to consumers, they are thus factually meaningless, noninformative, about the advertised item.

The significance of being noninformative is that the analysis of loophole claims does not end with deciding whether they are deceptive. If the latter were so, then the claims would be considered damaging to consumer information if deceptive, but simply not damaging if not deceptive. This article proposes a different view, however, because when the loophole claims are not deceptive it is because they are factually meaningless and thus noninformative.

Later sections describe how the loopholes are defended exactly as that by those who wish to interpret them as not deceptive. But to be noninformative is not at all benign to consumer information, but rather another way of being damaging to it. The loophole claims are either misinformative or noninformative, and either way these antifactual claims are contrary to being informative. Switching from being deceptive to being noninformative just raises the claims' information quality from being seriously negative to the higher level of being merely worthless.

Frequent Occurrence of Loophole Claims

The issues in this article are enhanced in significance because so many loophole claims exist. I have done a modest content analysis of prime-time television ads for national brands to count the incidence of loophole claims in relation to fact claims. Ads were selected from May 11–17, 2000, one hour each day, two from each of ABC, CBS, and NBC, one from Fox, two from each of the 8–9 and 10–11 p.m. hours, and three from the 9–10 hour (EDT). Coded were the numbers and percentages of ads having at least one of any of Resnik and Stern's (1977) fourteen types of information claims (price, performance, nutrition, safety, etc.), one loophole claim of any type, and/or one of each individual loophole type.

I also examined ads for national brands on the 1999 and 2000 Super Bowls. They are nontypical, of course, but in a potentially interesting way, with business lore saying the purpose is to show advertisers' best work to their largest audiences. With the two Super Bowls combined, the results were:

	May 2000	Super Bowls
Total Ads	175	107
Any Claim	175 (100%)	107 (100%)
Any Information Claim	138 (79%)	61 (57%)
Any Loophole Claim	149 (85%)	101 (94%)
Puffery	117 (67%)	65 (61%)
Obvious Falsity	30 (17%)	33 (31%)
Lifestyle	65 (37%)	46 (43%)

Because the coding was done by myself alone, and without other formal controls, it is offered as suggesting no more than that the loophole claims are plentiful. Probably their substantial incidence is already taken for granted by readers, and can be checked by anyone informally by casually examining consumer advertising. In the process I also noted frequent elements that seemed best described as explicit nonclaim content. Although not factual, they are not noninformative claims because, unlike the information and loophole claims discussed, they state no explicit claim at all. Many are attention-getting devices, such as attractive people, scenery, graphic designs, etc. Because such content might also relate to assessments of information, proposals for handling it are discussed in a second article to appear in the Summer 2003 issue of this journal.

Despite the apparent high incidence of loophole claims, major research and public policy activities, as shown in the next two sections, fail to incorporate such claims into their considerations of consumer information. A later section elaborates on reasons for including them. Proposals for incorporating the claims in research, policy, and marketplace activity are discussed in the second article.

AN AREA OF INFORMATION RESEARCH NOT RECOGNIZING LOOPHOLE CLAIMS AS PERTINENT INFORMATION

Fifty-nine items of research were summarized in meta-analyses by Abernethy and Franke (1996, 1998). All identified and quantified the information content of advertising by the definitions of Resnik and Stern (1977), in which only fourteen types of explicit fact claims are called information. Such work constitutes a major portion of research on the incidence of information in advertising, and it received enhanced attention when the meta-analyses earned awards for best article of the year in both journals where they were published.

Yet such research examines only some ad content. A key discrepancy, in this author's view, is that the research does not recognize the relevance to information of the loophole claims or of the implications of any claims: "The approach is explicitly a measure of objective information *content* and not the consumer's subjective experience with the ad" (Abernethy and Franke 1996). In personal communication, Abernethy (2000) confirmed that while each Resnik and Stern fact statement counted as one item of information, no other content did so. He said puffs not only were not facts but were not even considered claims in such content analyses.

While the studies clearly note such restraints, I suggest in contrast that the Resnik and Stern claims, or indeed all explicit fact claims, do not incorporate all content that may affect consumers' perceptions of quantity and quality of information. Studies of information that do not consider implied claims and loophole claims are simply incomplete.

AN AREA OF PUBLIC POLICY ON INFORMATION NOT RECOGNIZING LOOPHOLE CLAIMS AS PERTINENT TO INFORMATION

Pertinent Federal Trade Commission (FTC) cases do not count information claims but decide whether claims legally are deceptive (FTC 1984a). The emphasis here, however, is on the similar factual findings on which both groups base their decisions. The Commission, just as the information researchers, says loophole claims are not fact claims (thus, in effect, not information), and so excused from deceptiveness prosecutions:

> The term "puffing" refers generally to an expression of opinion not made as a representation of fact (FTC 1984a).

> [T]here is a category of advertising themes, in the nature of puffing or other hyperbole, which do not amount to the type of affirmative product claims for which either the Commission or the consumer would expect documentation (FTC 1984a).

The Commission generally will not pursue cases involving obviously exaggerated or puffing representations, i.e., those that the ordinary consumers do not take seriously (FTC 1984a).

FTC does not pursue subjective claims or puffery—claims like "this is the best hairspray in the world" (Starek 1996).

Although silent on the topic, the Commission appears to apply the above comments to all three types of loophole claims, in effect calling them all puffery. This is the first of several conclusions I will draw on matters about which the FTC has nothing on the written record. I cannot give citations to steps for which there is no printed source, but I will state what I have seen and my reasoning for my conclusions. I use as a basis my personal experience in working fulltime at the Commission as a marketing consultant in 1979, and in ensuing years contacting its people and studying its cases and other published materials.

Treating the three types of loopholes similarly is logical in the sense of showing how they share the trait of not being explicitly factual about the advertised item. I have cited that similarity myself in suggesting that more than opinion could be included in a conception of puffery wider than the strictly legal (Preston 1996). At present, however, I want to emphasize the legal sense by noting that the loophole claims differ in their explicit content. They are either (1) opinion (puffery), (2) obviously false about the item, or (3) about consumers rather than the item (lifestyle).

With only the first explicitly being opinion, the others technically are not traditional puffery. The Deception Statement (FTC 1984a) does not comment on obvious falsity and lifestyle claims, but their characteristics suggest the Commission regards all three as not factual and so not information about the advertised item, and not taken seriously by consumers regarding the item.

Unlike the information researchers, the Commission recognizes claims as consumers perceive them, identifying not only explicit but also implied fact claims, the latter often from survey evidence of what claims consumers take from the ads (FTC 1984a, Owen and Plyler 1991, Preston 1987, Yao and Vecchi 1992). The strong tendency to make such findings is illustrated in cases such as Novartis (1999), Kraft (1991), and Stouffer (1994). However, the agency, again without comment, appears to limit its recognition of implications to those taken from explicit fact claims (Preston 1989, 1998), apparently by assuming that the loophole claims can imply nothing factual about the advertised item, and so are informative about it neither explicitly nor impliedly. More details about such policy, and reasons for it, are provided in the next subsection.

While deceptiveness for the FTC is mainly a matter of finding claims to be likely to mislead a reasonable consumer, it must also find them material, which means "likely to affect a consumer's choice of or conduct regarding a product" (FTC 1984a). Without comment, the Commission appears to assume that the loopholes, not explicitly being factual about the item, imply nothing about it and are not material. The same applies to the agency's substantiation rule, by which it finds claims likely to mislead not only for falsity but for having no reasonable basis (FTC 1984b). Claims not factual need no substantiation.

FTC's Different Treatment of Loophole Claims

The different treatment, in this article's view, creates a major problem for distinctions between deceptive and nondeceptive claims. The FTC often explores what explicit fact claims may imply by using evidence apart from the ad, i.e., "extrinsic evidence," often consumer surveys (Thompson Medical 1984). But it typically uses no such direct evidence when it decides what the loopholes mean to consumers. Rather, it appears inexplicably to assume that statements not explicitly factual about the item cannot be impliedly factual about it either. While silent on the matter, it appears to decide by virtually automatic assumption, usually at an early investigation stage where it examines only the claims themselves ("intrinsic evidence") (Thompson Medical 1984). It sees that certain claims, such as "Advil works better," explicitly have the semantic form of opinion or evaluation rather than of objective fact. From that it defines them as puffery, and from that says they are ones that "ordinary consumers do not take seriously" or for which "the consumer would not expect documentation" (FTC 1984a). It thus finds the loophole claims nondeceptive only by defining them as such, not by knowing, declining even to try to consider that they may be deceptive. That is why they are "loopholes."

A recent unofficial comment said: "The FTC's Peeler [C. Lee Peeler, head of Advertising Practices] calls puffery 'a claim that doesn't mean anything to consumers, and therefore is not actionable'" (Savan 2000). While that invites the belief that the FTC first determines factually how consumers respond, finds those claims that mean nothing to consumers, and defines them as puffery, the agency actually finds the opposite. It finds not that consumers reject a claim so it must be puffery, but rather that it's puffery so consumers must reject it. In my own experience working fulltime on the FTC staff, as a member of the "monitoring" committee that examined current claims in search of candidates for investigation, I saw exactly that happen. It is remindful of Justice Potter Stewart's famous means of identifying "hard-core pornography": "I know it when I see it . . ." (Jacobellis v. Ohio 1964).

Typically the Commission doesn't know at all. Its sheer definitional method works only at the explicit level, where we can use semantic form to decide, for example, that "Water is made of hydrogen and oxygen" is explicitly factual, while "Advil works better" is not. But when we want to define claims as those to which consumers respond in a certain way, and we do not observe consumer response, we can make no decision on such response and therefore do no defining. What would work would be to (1) define puffs as opinion or evaluative claims that may or may not taken as factual and/or imply facts, and then (2) observe consumer response to an opinion or value claim to see what factual content consumers see, if any, and whether such facts are true or false.

These remarks are not significantly qualified by the fact that the FTC *has* made rulings on loophole claims in two types of situations. First, it has done so when advertisers assert the puffery defense, which forces the Commission to respond, typically by ruling that the claim is not puffery, again typically by assumption rather than evidence. There are a number of such cases (Preston 1989), but, for the vast number of loophole claims, the agency has made no such ruling.

Second, the FTC has occasionally brought up puffery when advertisers use both a puff and a false fact claim, prompting the agency to prohibit both because the factual falsity has infected the puff (see cases identified in Preston 1998). The Commission also has sought to prohibit lifestyle claims twice, but not since the 1970s, and both times only in conjunction with false fact claims. It succeeded in one case, though only by consent rather than litigation, and failed in the other (Preston 1996, pp. 155–56).

In such ways, the FTC and regulators enforcing other laws (e.g., the Lanham Act in Pizza Hut v. Papa John's 2000) have prohibited claims defended as puffery for not being puffery at all or else not puffery as it customarily occurs, meaning unaccompanied by facts. Such prohibitions, however, have involved no more than a miniscule proportion of those claims that may by semantic form be defined as loophole claims. Nor are they pertinent to what regulators do when they decide a claim *is* typical puffery, which is to excuse it along with the other loophole claims as factually meaningless, deciding by assumption rather than actual observation.

Result of the Differing Treatments: The Split View

The FTC's treatment of loophole claims has a distinctly different impact on amount and quality of information available to consumers than does its treatment of explicitly factual claims. The Commission highlighted its efforts with the latter at least as early as 1979 in its briefing book, *Consumer Information Remedies,* which indicated a dedication to maximize the Commission's efforts to get consumers a good "quality, quantity, and variety of marketplace information" (FTC 1979, p. 2). The Commission felt it could counter actions by market participants that block or slow the information stream: "Information remedies have the direct benefit of improving the free flow of truthful commercial information. This result allows consumers to improve the quality of marketplace decisions . . ." (p. 14). "Consumer information is an issue which has been a central focus of Commission concern from the beginning," the introduction said, discussing many past efforts and proposals for further improvement.

How the FTC has since addressed those concerns is evidenced by far too many cases and publications to cite here; however, an excellent way to identify them is to examine the subject indexes of the *Journal of Public Policy and Marketing,* in which items about efforts to increase information include 32 under "nutritional information," 18 under "health and warning labels," 23 under "warnings," 27 under "information disclosures," and 11 under "affirmative disclosures," across 20 volumes for 1982–2001. The Director of the FTC's Bureau of Consumer Protection, Joan Z. Bernstein, noting issues on which the Commission needs research, identified the first as "Disclosures, disclosures and more disclosures" (1996). A search for "disclosures" at the FTC web site, <www.ftc.gov>, on March 13, 2001, identified 2921 documents.

However, despite such favorable attitudes and efforts to increase consumer information, the treatment of loophole claims suggests the FTC simultaneously is encouraging advertisers to use content that negates those goals. The Deception Statement's descriptions of the loophole claims (FTC 1984a) indicate that it considers them to be factually meaningless and thus noninformative and nontruthful—not false, but not truthful either, since they are taken to mean nothing factual. For the Commission to say also that it will "not pursue cases involving [such] representations" (FTC 1984a) means that it affirmatively encourages advertisers to run significant amounts of such noninformation at the same time it is otherwise making efforts to increase information.

Such activity reveals a split rather than consistent view toward different types of content. With factual content the FTC considers consumers' information needs, obtains direct evidence of consumer perception, and creates remedies. Yet for the loophole claims it forgoes direct evidence of consumers' perceptions and thus ignores information effects. This combination of events makes it difficult to interpret FTC statements such as the recent one of Ms. Bernstein that "Consumers should be able to rely on advertising for solid information when they're making purchasing decisions. If they can't trust the claims in the ads, they're in a tough spot. . . ." (FTC 2000). While on the one hand the Commission clearly promotes consumer trust, on the other it promotes distrust.

This split view was called to the commissioners' attention as long ago as publication of its staff's briefing book (FTC 1979):

> Traces of the caveat emptor doctrine remain in FTC law [and] may have contributed to the apparent tendency of advertising to emphasize subjective appeals at the expense of objective data (p. 146).

> It could be said that FTC insistence on strict factual accuracy in advertising has created an incentive for advertisers to use "nonfacts" to sell goods and services (p. 155).

[A]d substantiation enforcement in practice has focused on factual claims [and this] may have contributed to the skewing of advertising content toward ephemeral and nonsubstantiable subjective claims (p. 170).

[T]he risk of an FTC order or a prolonged court battle can be viewed as a "cost" placed on purely factual advertising. . . . [T]he economically rational seller would naturally prefer ads which were both effective sales vehicles and free from the risk of litigation. Ironically, then, the drive for consumer protection through the regulation of false advertising claims may have accelerated the shift away from objective data in advertising . . . (p. 156).

When a seller expresses an opinion on value . . . there may be an implied factual claim. It could be assumed by a reasonable buyer . . . that the seller based his opinion of value on specific offers by others to buy the product, on a consensus of expert opinion, or on the going market price. If the seller knows that the implied factual basis . . . contradicts his proferred opinion, then there is a conscious intent to deceive . . . and not simply an exaggerated opinion (p. 148).

Recent empirical evidence has shown . . . that puffery does have a potential for deception (p. 149).

Nonetheless, the FTC retains the split view, on the one hand encouraging factual and informative claims by recognizing effects but on the other hand encouraging nonfactual noninformative ones by ignoring effects. This article's position, in contrast, is that all claims should be incorporated when considering consumers' perceptions and use of information.

A ROLE FOR EXPLICITLY NONFACTUAL CLAIMS IN CONSIDERATIONS OF CONSUMER PERCEPTIONS OF INFORMATION

Discussion thus far has shown how antifactual loophole claims go unrecognized as being or pertaining to consumer information by researchers and regulators who play key roles in our knowledge of an area very central to consumer welfare. The topic of this section is how much the omission matters. Can acknowledging these claims result in better information about information, improving how we understand it, regulate it, and supply it, so as to produce increased consumer satisfaction?

Surely the answer is that with respect to consumer information the loophole claims are not nothing, they are something. Accordingly, they should be counted as claims that are antifactual, i.e., they may dilute or negate information, in contrast to the Resnik and Stern (1977) and other explicit fact claims. Only by considering all claims can there be accurate assessments of the usefulness of advertising's information, letting us understand that perceived quantity and quality may be affected by advertising content in neutral and negative as well as positive ways.

Possible Impacts of Loophole Claims on Consumers' Perceptions

Consider two ads, one with one true fact and no other claims, the other with the same true fact and five loophole claims. By judgment of the information researchers and regulators, the two ads do not differ in information content, because for each the fact claim is evaluated positively as one piece of information, and no other differences pertinent to information are recognized. Such conclusion would be inappropriate, however, if consumers perceived information value in the loophole claims, and if they considered that value in conjunction or combination with the value of the fact claim. The resulting perception might be positive, negative, or neutral.

The loopholes could have a positive impact if consumers see them as informative, negative if seen as misinformative, and neutral if seen as noninformative. My own analysis to date has focused mainly on how they may be misinformative (Preston 1998 and previous work). I emphasized their potential to be deceptive, by being factually meaningful via implied facts that could be false. I did not emphasize the other possibilities.

Might the loophole claims be informative, which could occur if they imply true facts? That seems doubtful, on the grounds that advertisers having true supporting facts are likely to state them explicitly in conjunction with, or instead of, their loophole claims. Thus the occurrence of the loopholes in the way they typically occur, which means unaccompanied by supporting facts, suggests that no such supporting facts exist. The possibility, then, of being informative by implying true facts, while not ruled out, should not be accorded high probability.

In contrast, there is much support for arguing that the loopholes may be informationally neutral. The position discussed above of the information researchers and regulators is that consumers interpret such claims as factually meaningless, noninformative, which implies neutrality. Advertisers also support that conclusion by frequently using the loopholes, hence acting in a way which is incompatible with a sense of legal vulnerability, and also by the defense their national organizations mounted against proposed changes to the Uniform Commercial Code that threaten puffery (Preston 1998). Those concerted actions suggest that industry leaders clearly want to maintain their traditional privilege of using loophole claims without fear of prosecution, a hope that can be based only on the continuing legal conclusion that the claims have no perceived factual meaning. The advertisers' concern for such outcome is consistent with their need to differentiate their brands, which often cannot be accomplished with true facts because so many truths are equally available to competitors.

Another support group for concluding that loophole claims are perceived as meaningless, and thus as informationally neutral, consists of economists who contend that people are essentially rational and skeptical (Calfee 1997, Calfee and Ringold 1994, Ford, Smith and Swasy 1990, Smith, Ford and Swasy 1990). By such thinking, consumers are unlikely to accept unsupported or otherwise inaccurate implications, e.g., "Several of the findings of this study suggest that consumers are not misled by implied health claims" (Mitra et al. 1999; see also Ford et al. 1996).

In total that is a large array of believers that the loophole claims are taken as meaningless. However, those parties also appear to assume that the claims therefore are simply irrelevant to considerations of information, i.e., not claims at all (Abernethy 2000). That, however, is not what "neutral" and "noninformative" necessarily mean. In keeping with the idea proposed above that the loophole claims are something, not nothing, the suggestion here is that consumers' perceptions of claims as "neutral" may well include their seeing the claims as relevant to information. And further, they may see the claims, by the *failure* to contribute to information, as tending to *dilute* or *negate* the information consumers see an ad to convey.

Compare again the ad with one fact claim to the ad with one fact and five loophole claims. Could not consumers see the first ad to be entirely factual while seeing the second to be only weakly so? Could they even see the second ad as predominantly noninformative and thus neutral in its contribution to information, or even essentially as negative in the sense of failing to take the opportunity to be useful?

Those are questions for research to be discussed further in proposals made in the second article. The current article continues with examination of possible other types of impacts of loophole claims.

Consumer Perceptions of Information Sources

Consumers' perceptions of information based on loophole claims might also affect evaluations of information sources. The economics of information literature observes that consumers' skepticism, deriving from assumed rational behavior, protects them (Calfee 1997, Calfee and Ringold 1994, Ford, Smith and Swasy 1990, Smith, Ford and Swasy 1990). However, while information "involves messages that reduce uncertainty" (Abernethy and Franke 1996), would not skepticism increase uncertainty? Consumers could come thereby to see an advertiser as a poor information source, including to the extent of utter rejection, often within a context of scarcity of such sources. After similar occurrences with multiple advertisers, consumers might direct the same attitude toward advertising in general. As a result, they might perceive a more limited opportunity to obtain information.

Such effects could override the positive aspects of rejecting claims, and might even supersede them to produce an overall negative informational impact of the ad, or all advertising, even all marketing. That could make the results of consumer skepticism essentially negative rather than positive, a possibility that seems little emphasized in discussions of skepticism.

Evidence of skepticism comes from many surveys (Calfee and Ringold 1994). Of them the FTC's Lee Peeler recently said, in the context of the Commission's dismissal of puffery's impact, "Most of the polls I've seen have found that consumers have a very healthy level of skepticism about ad claims" (Savan 2000). The surveys, however, typically probe advertising in general rather than specific claims (Calfee and Ringold 1994), and thus do not refute the chance that skepticism could be much less for the latter.

The most recent Gallup poll (Gallup 2001) rated "the honesty and ethical standards of people in [various] fields—very high, high, average, low or very low." Results were based on combined percentages for "very high" and "high" for 1993 through 2001. Twenty-five professions were evaluated through 1998, while for 1999 through 2001, 45, 32, and 23 professions, respectively, were covered. In the past three years "advertising practitioners" have been consistently next-to-last, ahead only of "car salesmen." In previous years they were in the same or about the same position; changes in number of professions made no difference. The other fields included "nurses," "clergy," "judges," "school teachers," "labor union leaders," "real estate agents," and "auto mechanics."

While the relationship of the loopholes to low scores on "honesty and ethical standards" is not established, arguably cause and effect may exist. Deceptive claims might also be causes, but regulators' prosecution of the latter leaves fewer of them, and for shorter times. Also, consumers might be more likely to recognize that a loophole claim isn't explicitly factual about the advertised item, which could be a major reason to reject reliance on it, while being less likely to recognize an explicit fact claim as false. Factual falsity often can be detected only with the help of additional information beyond the ad, additional information that consumers often don't have.

The ideal result of consumer skepticism should be to damage only those ads using deceptive or meaningless claims, allowing the cream of factually trustworthy ads to rise to the top. That could favorably affect the marketplace, supporting the suggestion that skepticism makes regulation less necessary or unnecessary (Calfee 1997). The Gallup data, however, suggest consumers may take their skepticism even farther, potentially producing additional effects hurtful to marketplace transactions.

Potential Impact on Freedom of Commercial Speech

A separate effect consumer rejection can have on information stems from potential impact on the Supreme Court's currently favorable position on freedom of commercial speech. While the

Court's basis for expanding freedom is the public's interest in the speech's information value, the perception of such value could lessen drastically if the Court ever considers the quantity and quality of the loophole claims. While the requirement for avoiding deceptiveness is only that claims not be factually false, the requirement for deserving Constitutional protection is that they be informationally useful. Claims avoiding factual falsity only by meaninglessness might thus have an unfavorable impact on freedom of speech as well as on consumer behavior. Much more can be said on this topic; for citations see Preston (1998).

Combining the Effects of Noninformativeness and Misinformativeness

No loophole claim can be both noninformative (factually meaningless) and misinformative (deceptive) for the same person at the same moment, but the theoretical view here predicts significant occurrence of both effects across all consumers. Analyses therefore should assume that they can occur simultaneously.

If, to speculate, there are about as many fact claims as loopholes, but most fact claims are not deceptive, then advertising probably has more meaninglessness than deceptiveness. Deceptiveness, however, is potentially more harmful to consumer welfare by being misinformative rather than noninformative. Skepticism is said to counteract deceptiveness, but, along with possibly being less so for particular claims than for ads in general, it may also be less for fact than for loophole claims.

If deceptiveness is harder to recognize than meaninglessness, it will be less of a trigger toward being skeptical and therefore toward protecting consumers. Thus while it may occur less frequently than meaninglessness, it may be more likely to be damaging when it does occur. Also, it may contribute additional strength to the effects discussed above of prompting consumers to discount the credibility of ads, advertising, and marketing.

A Broader Social View of Information Impacts

With the effects of both meaninglessness and deceptiveness in mind, the hypothesized view of the loopholes' effects can be expanded beyond marketplace decisions, into a broader impact on society. A way to do that involves a parallel to developments in the New York Police Department. In 1994, after Rudolph Giuliani became mayor, the NYPD shifted to "intensive quality-of-life enforcement":

> [I]nstead of merely reacting to individual crimes as they occur [it] established proactive strategies for confronting the problems of [various crimes] [and] responded to problems like public drinking, boom-box cars, street prostitution, street-level drug dealing, and the notorious "squeegee pests." Two years later, neighborhoods feel safer, as . . . New Yorkers are feeling less fear rather than more in the city's public spaces (Andrews 1996).

> The NYPD's stunning success [is] based on the "broken window" theory [which] holds that disorder is a contagion: If a broken window remains unrepaired, soon there will be many broken windows [and eventually] a menacing sense of anarchy, driving law-abiding citizens indoors and ceding the streets to predators (Will 1999).

Thus even minor forms of unruly or lawless activity can lead to public perception that lawlessness is acceptable, which can lead in turn to more serious matters such as robbery and assault. But removing those sights of undesirable behavior can give a perception of lawfulness that helps prevent the unwanted acceleration. While there is no rigorous proof that such results were caused by the NYPD's actions, the relationship is widely publicized (Will 1999) and suggests an analogy.

Without implying that marketplace activities are as bad as street crimes, the analogy is based on unruly actors in the streets being encouraged by success to expand into more heinous crimes. Similarly, marketplace actors can be encouraged, by the right to create the mild unruliness of running noninformative loophole claims, to expand into the more serious matter of running misinformative deceptive fact claims. Further, just as control of the lower-level offenses in the streets can lead to a reduction of higher-level offenses, so can control of the loophole claims lead to dissuading advertisers from accelerating their activities in the direction of harder-core deceptiveness.

Because there has been no Guiliani-like control of the loophole claims, there is no reason to expect that advertisers always take pains to use them only in nondeceptive ways. No actual knowledge is implied here that any specific advertiser in any specific instance has consciously lied when using loophole claims, which, after all, is a state of mind rarely observed. What can be said, however, is that for regulators to decline to investigate the loopholes is to invite advertisers to use them in any way they choose. Those uses certainly can include fraudulent falsity, i.e., conscious lying (Preston 1998), and we should reasonably expect that what is possible will sometimes happen. All it takes is to call one's brand superior while knowingly having a factual basis for believing otherwise. The points discussed here support a speculation that such steps are being taken every day.

Further, the immunity the law grants to the loophole claims gives advertisers a cover to assert that they cannot be lying. The possibility is illustrated in a comment about President Clinton's impeachment: "It is the . . . irony of his career that Clinton is now in a position of having to defend himself against the charge that he is a liar by arguing that he is only a bullshit artist" (Menand 1998). The myriad of cases involving puffery (Preston 1989, Richards 1990) shows that advertisers defend themselves in the same way. They are, in fact, even luckier because they enjoy the protection of the law's assertion that the lower level of lying represented by the loopholes is no level of lying at all.

SUMMARY

In summary, this theoretical examination suggests much can be learned should researchers and policymakers consider information as consumers do. The preceding section has discussed potential effects on consumer information from perceiving claims as informative, misinformative, or noninformative. While consumers will often see information in a positive sense, they can also see dilution or negation of it. The latter can indicate levels of consumer information far lower than is assumed by other sources, along with lowered credibility for advertisers and advertising, and perhaps also a lowered opinion by the Supreme Court of advertising's value as commercial speech.

The second of these two articles, appearing in the Summer 2003 issue of this journal, offers proposals for incorporating antifactual content into studies and decisions about consumer information by researchers, public policymakers, advertisers, and consumers.

REFERENCES

Abernethy, Avery M. 2000. Personal communication. April 15.

Abernethy. Avery M. and George R. Franke. 1998. FTC Regulatory Activity and the Information Content of Advertising. *Journal of Public Policy and Marketing*, 17(Fall):239–256.

———. 1996. The Information Content of Advertising: A Meta-Analysis. *Journal of Advertising,* 25(Summer):1–17.

Andrews, William. 1996. The New NYPD. Online at <www.ci.nyc.ny.us/html/nypd/html/3100/newnypd.html>.

Bernstein. Joan Z. 1996. Federal Trade Commission Solicits Consumer Research. *Advances in Consumer Research.* Edited by Kim P. Corfman and John G. Lynch. Jr., 23:313–15.

Calfee, John E. 1997. *Fear of Persuasion: A New Perspective on Advertising and Regulation.* Washington, DC: AEI Press of American Enterprise Institute.

Calfee, John E. and Debra Jones Ringold. 1994. The 70% Majority: Enduring Consumer Beliefs About Advertising. *Journal of Public Policy and Marketing,* 13(Fall):228–38.

Federal Trade Commission (FTC). 2000. *FTC Charges Marketer of Dietary Supplement with Making Unsubstantiated ADHD Treatment Claims.* Press release, Aug. 16. online at <www.ftc.gov/opa/2000/08/natorganics.htm>.

———. 1984a. Policy Statement on Deception, *FTC Decisions.* 103:174–184 (originally letter from FTC to Cong. John D. Dingell, Oct. 14, 1983).

———. 1984b. Policy Statement Regarding Advertising Substantiation. *FTC Decisions,* 104:839–842.

———. 1979. *Consumer Information Remedies.* 23 authors drawn from staff and consultants of Bureau of Consumer Protection.

Ford, Gary T., Darlene B. Smith, and John L. Swasy. 1990. Consumer Skepticism of Advertising Claims: Testing Hypotheses from Economics of Information. *Journal of Consumer Research,* 16(March):433–41.

Ford, Gary T., Manoj Hastak, Anusree Mitra, and Debra Jones Ringold. 1996. Can Consumers Interpret Nutrition Information in the Presence of a Health Claim? A Laboratory Investigation. *Journal of Public Policy and Marketing,* 15(1):16–27.

Gallup Organization. 2001. *Honesty/Ethics in Professions.* Online at <www.gallup.com/poll/topics/hnsty_ethcs.asp>.

Jacobellis v. Ohio. 1964. *U.S. Reports,* 378:184, 197 (Stewart, J., concurring).

Kelly, Kathleen J., Michael D. Slater, and David Karan. 2000. The Effects of Tombostone Advertisements on Adolescents' Attitudes Toward Ad, Brand and Product Category: Evidence for a "Lifestyle" Ad Influence on Attitude about Cigarettes and Beer. Paper at Public Policy and Marketing Conference, Washington DC.

Kraft Foods. 1991. *FTC Decisions,* 114:40–55, aff'd. 970 F.2d 311 (7th Cir. 1992).

MacFarquhar, Larissa. 2000. Caesar.com. *New Yorker,* 76(Apr. 3):34–40.

Mitra, Anu, Manoj Hastak, Gary T. Ford, and Debra Jones Ringold. 1999. Can the Educationally Disadvantaged Interpret the FDA-Mandated Nutrition Facts Panel in the Presence of an Implied Health Claim? *Journal of Public Policy and Marketing,* 18(1):106–117.

Owen, Debra K. and Joyce E. Plyler. 1991. The Role of Empirical Evidence in the Federal Regulation of Advertising. *Journal of Public Policy and Marketing,* 10(Spring):1–14.

Novartis. 1999. FTC Docket No. 9279. Online at <www.ftc.gov/os/1999/9905/novartisopin.pdf> (to be published in *FTC Decisions*).

Peeler. C. Lee. 1997. Telephone communication. January 24.

Pizza Hut v. Papa John's. 2000. Civil Action No. 3:98cv 1902-AH, U.S. District Ct. for the Northern District of Texas. Jan. 3. Online at <lexis-nexis@prod.lexis-nexis.com>.

Preston, Ivan L. 1998. Puffery and Other "Loophole" Claims: How the Law's "Don't Ask, Don't Tell" Policy Condones Fraudulent Falsity in Advertising. *Journal of Law and Commerce,* 18(Fall):49–114.

———. 1997. Regulatory Positions Toward Advertising Puffery of the Uniform Commercial Code and the Federal Trade Commission. *Journal of Public Policy and Marketing,* 16(Fall):336–44.

———. 1996. *The Great American Blow-Up: Puffery in Advertising and Selling.* Madison, WI: University of Wisconsin Press, revised ed. (original ed., 1975).

————. 1994. *The Tangled Web They Weave.* Madison, WI: University of Wisconsin Press.

————. 1989. The Federal Trade Commission's Identification of Implications as Constituting Deceptive Advertising. *University of Cincinnati Law Review,* 57(4):1243–1310.

————. 1987. Extrinsic Evidence in Federal Trade Commission Deceptiveness Cases. *Columbia Business Law Review.* 1987 (3):633–94.

Resnik, Alan and Bruce L. Stern. 1977. An Analysis of Information Content in Television Advertising. *Journal of Marketing*, 41(Jan.):50–53.

Savan, Leslie. 2000. Truth in Advertising? *Brill's Content,* 3(March):62–63, 114.

Smith, Darlene B., Gary T. Ford, and John L. Swasy. 1990. The Economics of Information: Research Issues. *Marketing and Advertising Regulation.* Edited by Patrick E. Murphy and William L. Wilkie, 300–12.

Starek, Roscoe B. 1996. Myths and Half-Truths About Deceptive Advertising. Unpublished speech to Nat'l Infomercial Mktg. Assn., Oct 15. Online at <www.ftc.gov/speeches/starek/nima96d4.htm>.

Stouffer Foods. 1994. *F.T.C.Decisions,* 118:746–810.

Thomspon Medical. 1984. *F.T.C. Decisions.* 104:648–844.

Yao, Dennis A. and Christa Van Anh Vecchi. 1992. Information and Decisionmaking at the Federal Trade Commission. *Journal of Public Policy and Marketing,* 11(Fall):1–11.

CHAPTER 18

SELF-REGULATION OF ADVERTISING
An Alternative to Litigation and Government Action

JEFFREY S. EDELSTEIN

I. OVERVIEW

The advertising industry in the United States has established an extensive system of self-regulation. The primary purposes of self-regulation are to ensure that (1) advertising is truthful, accurate, and not misleading or deceptive, (2) all claims are adequately substantiated, and (3) there is compliance with federal, state, and local laws and regulations.

The major components of advertising industry self-regulation are: the National Advertising Division of the Council of Better Business Bureaus, Inc., its appellate body, the National Advertising Review Board, and its children's division, the Children's Advertising Review Unit; the national television networks; and trade associations in many industries. Advertising is also regulated by some magazines and newspapers, some station and cable television groups, and local Better Business Bureaus. There are also controls by advertisers and advertising agencies.

The advertising industry engages in self-regulation for a number of reasons. Advertisers and advertising agencies have long recognized that truthful advertising promotes consumer confidence in advertising claims, benefiting all advertisers. Truthful advertising also promotes fair competition between advertisers, provides useful information to consumers enabling them to make rational choices among competing products, and spurs product innovation and improvement.

On the other hand, false advertising erodes consumer trust in advertising, reducing the effectiveness of advertising in general. False or deceptive advertising can subject the advertiser and advertising agency to intervention by the Federal Trade Commission ("FTC"), the Food and Drug Administration ("FDA"), and other federal, state, and local governmental agencies, as well as private lawsuits by competitors and consumers. The media can also be liable for false advertising, although liability is rarely found. The television networks have a statutory obligation, as licensees of their owned and operated stations with the Federal Communications Commission ("FCC"), to prevent their facilities from being used for the dissemination of false or misleading advertising.[1]

Self-regulation reduces the time and expense of governmental regulation of advertising and private lawsuits. In addition, self-regulation helps maintain high standards of truth and accuracy in advertising. When advertising is reviewed prior to dissemination to ensure that it is truthful and that all claims are adequately substantiated, such as by the television networks, legal viola-

---

From *IDEA—The Journal of Law and Technology*, vol. 43, no. 3 (2003). Copyright © 2003 by the Franklin Pierce Law Center. Reprinted with permission.

tions can be prevented before they occur. The FTC has expressed its support for self-regulation for many years.[2]

II. AUTHORITY FOR SELF-REGULATION

A. First Amendment

As a general rule, the broadcast and print media have a First Amendment right to determine what advertising they will disseminate. In *Columbia Broad. Sys., Inc. v. Democratic Natl. Comm.*,[3] the United States Supreme Court ruled that the television networks had broad discretion to accept or reject advertising. The Supreme Court recognized the editorial discretion of a publisher to decide what to print in *Miami Herald Publg. Co. v. Tornillo,*[4] upholding the publisher's right to refuse to run editorial replies by political candidates whose records had been criticized by the newspaper. The editorial discretion of publishers has been applied to commercial advertising.[5]

The media is not permitted to reject advertising if the rejection results in unlawful discrimination,[6] violates a statute, such as the Sherman Act,[7] or constitutes unreasonable editorial discretion.[8]

B. Media Liability for False Advertising

The media's obligation to review advertising submitted for broadcast or publication is underscored by the legal rule that a medium is subject to liability if it knowingly or recklessly publishes false advertising.[9] The general rule is:

> [I]f a newspaper publishes false and misleading advertisements maliciously or with the intention to harm another or so recklessly and without regard to its consequences that a reasonably prudent person would anticipate the damage, that newspaper should be held accountable for its conduct in the same manner as is any other person who commits such a tortious act.[10]

The courts have refused to impose liability upon the media for failing to conduct investigations of the truth or falsity of advertisements, since this would place an onus upon them.[11] In addition, many state statutes exempt the media from liability for false advertising in the absence of knowledge or recklessness.[12]

As a result of these general principles, there have been few false advertising lawsuits against the media, and fewer still have been successful. The media have, however, occasionally been held liable for false advertising. In one case, a publisher of a magazine was held potentially liable for carrying an advertisement that it knew or had reason to know was deceptive, according to the court.[13] In another case, a magazine publisher was held liable in a false advertising suit brought by the New York Attorney General for damages, restitution, civil penalties, and an injunction.[14] Another magazine publisher was held liable for an advertisement that on its face would alert a reasonably prudent publisher to a clearly identifiable unreasonable risk of harm to the public posed by the advertisement.[15]

III. HISTORY OF SELF-REGULATION

Newspapers and magazines began to review advertisements which were submitted to them for publication around 1900, in response to complaints from muckrakers about phony advertisements, particularly for patented medicines. Probably the first self-regulation advertising code was the "Curtis Advertising Code," which was printed in 1910 by the publisher Cyrus H.K. Curtis. Its purpose was "to protect both our advertisers and our readers from all copy that is fraudulent or deceptive."[16]

In 1911, George P. Rowell, founder of Printer's Ink Magazine, published a model statute entitled "The Printer's Ink Statute." The statute made it a criminal misdemeanor to advertise a representation that was untrue, deceptive, or misleading.[17] Approximately thirty-seven states passed some version of it.[18] The statute was ineffective because of lax law enforcement and because it applied only to definitive misrepresentations of fact.[19] Another important development was the issuance, in 1914, of the "Standards of Newspaper Practice" by the newspaper division of the Associated Advertising Clubs of the World.[20] Since then, newspaper and magazine publishers have exercised some review over advertisements placed with them, with varying degrees of scrutiny.

In 1952, the National Association of Broadcasters ("NAB"), a trade association consisting of the three major television networks, the radio networks, and most commercial broadcasters, adopted the Television Code. This code established rules regulating the content of both television advertising and programming. The NAB had also established a Radio Code for the same purpose. The Codes were enforced by the Television and Radio Code purpose. The Codes were enforced by the Television and Radio Code Authorities, respectively, which had great influence over the content of advertising on television and radio. Over a thirty-year period they issued many rules, guides, and interpretations regarding the acceptability of advertising for the NAB members.

In an antitrust action brought against the NAB by the Justice Department, the Multiple Product Announcement Rule of the NAB Code was held to be a *per se* violation of the Sherman Act in 1982. The decision enjoined further enforcement of the Rule, which had prohibited advertisers from promoting more than one product in a 30-second commercial.[21] While an appeal was pending, the NAB's Executive Committee decided to suspend enforcement of the entire NAB Code. The Television and Radio Codes, as well as the Code Authorities, were terminated.

Shortly after they began operating in the early 1950s, the ABC, CBS, and NBC television networks established broadcast standards and practices departments to review commercials submitted for broadcast. While the NAB Code Authorities were in operation, the networks used the Code and its interpretations in their review of proposed advertising. After the termination of the NAB Code, each of these television networks issued its own set of advertising standards and guidelines. They were modeled after the Code, but contained many differences from the Code and from each other. Since the issuance of these guidelines, each of the networks has issued revisions periodically.[22] In addition, the Fox Broadcasting Company issued its guidelines for the first time in 2001.[23]

IV. NATIONAL ADVERTISING DIVISION AND NATIONAL ADVERTISING REVIEW BOARD

The National Advertising Division ("NAD") and the National Advertising Review Board ("NARB") were created in 1971 to serve as a self-regulatory mechanism for the advertising industry. The NAD and the NARB were established by four major associations: the Council of Better Business Bureaus, the American Association of Advertising Agencies, the American Advertising Federation, and the Association of National Advertisers. The Children's Advertising Review Unit ("CARU") was created in 1974 as a division of NAD. The NAD/CARU/NARB mechanism has gained widespread acceptance in the advertising industry. This voluntary self-regulatory process has handled over 4000 cases.[24]

NAD investigates complaints about the truth and accuracy of national advertising. As stated in the NAD/NARB/CARU Procedures, NAD is "responsible for receiving or initiating, evaluating, investigating, analyzing . . . and holding negotiations with an advertiser, and resolving complaints or questions from any source involving the truth or accuracy of national advertising."[25]

A. NAD Jurisdiction

NAD has jurisdiction over national advertising, whether it is addressed to consumers, professionals, or business entities.[26] "National advertising" is defined as:

> [A]ny paid commercial message, in any medium (including labeling), if it has the purpose of inducing a sale or other commercial transaction or persuading the audience of the value or usefulness of a company, product or service; if it is disseminated nationally or to a substantial portion of the United States, or is test market advertising prepared for national campaigns; and if the content is controlled by the advertiser.[27]

NAD will not accept a complaint about advertising if, in its judgment, the advertising is:

> [N]ot national in character; the subject of pending litigation or an order by a court; the subject of a federal government agency consent decree or order; permanently withdrawn from use prior to the date of the complaint and NAD/CARU receives the advertiser's assurance, in writing, that the representation(s) at issue will not be used by the advertiser in any future advertising for the product or service; of such technical character that NAD/CARU could not conduct a meaningful analysis of the issues; without sufficient merit to warrant the expenditure of NAD/CARU's resources; . . . regarding specific language in an advertisement, or on product packaging or labels, when that language is mandated or expressly approved by federal law or regulation; political and issue advertising; and raising questions of taste and morality (unless raising questions under *CARU's Self-Regulatory Guidelines for Children's Advertising*).[28]

Even if NAD/CARU has jurisdiction over the advertising which has been challenged, it reserves the right to refuse to handle a case if the challenger publicizes the fact that specific advertising has been referred to NAD/CARU.[29] The purpose of this provision is to maintain a professional atmosphere in which NAD/CARU "can affect a timely and lasting resolution to a case in the spirit of furthering voluntary self-regulation of advertising and the voluntary cooperation of the parties involved."[30] In addition, if the advertising is false, deceptive, or misleading, and the advertiser will not participate in the self-regulatory process, NAD/CARU will prepare a review of the facts with relevant exhibits and, after consultation with the NARB Chairman, will forward them to the appropriate federal or state law enforcement agency.[31]

B. NAD Procedures

A complaint regarding national advertising may be submitted by any person or legal entity, including NAD/CARU itself.[32] The complaint should be as detailed as possible, describing the nature of the alleged misrepresentations and providing complete data supporting the challenge.[33] NAD/CARU will not consider any data submitted by a complainant which the complainant will not make available to the advertiser, and any materials submitted by a complainant on condition that they are not shown to the advertiser will promptly be returned. Studies, tests, polls, and other forms of research must be sufficiently complete to permit expert evaluation.[34]

A complainant may, with the consent of the advertiser, request that NAD/CARU conduct expedited review of the challenged advertising.[35] The complainant may make this request in the original challenge letter, which, if the request is made, may not exceed four double-spaced pages.[36] NAD/CARU determines, based on the complexity of the challenge, whether or not to grant expedited review. If NAD/CARU decides to grant the complainant's request, the complainant automatically waives its right to submit a reply to the advertiser's response. If expedited proceedings are initiated, NAD must issue a summary decision within 15 business days after the record is closed. The record is considered closed as of the date the advertiser submits its response or the date by which the parties submit any additional information requested by NAD. If NAD recommends that the challenged advertising be modified or discontinued, the advertiser may request a full review and a detailed decision. If the advertiser makes this request, it is required to discontinue the challenged advertising until NAD issues the final decision. If the parties agree to expedited proceedings, the parties will not have a right to appeal NAD's decision unless the advertiser requests a full review and a full decision is issued.[37]

If NAD/CARU determines to open an investigation of the advertising, it will promptly forward the complaint to the advertiser for its response.[38] In all cases, NAD/CARU will advise the advertiser of the identity of the complainant.[39] Prior to the transfer of data to the advertiser (or from the advertiser to the complainant), NAD/CARU will obtain assurances that the recipients agree that the materials are provided exclusively for the purpose of furthering NAD/CARU's inquiry, circulation will be restricted to persons directly involved, and all copies must be returned if requested on the completion of the inquiry.[40]

The advertiser must submit "a written response that provides substantiation for any advertising claims or representations challenged" within 15 business days after it receives the complaint.[41] The response, in its transmittal letter, should also deal with any issues raised by the challenger or by NAD/CARU. The advertiser may submit data to NAD/CARU with the request that the data not be made available to the complainant. The advertiser must clearly identify which materials are confidential, redact any confidential portions from one copy of the materials, state the basis of its request for confidentiality, and affirm that the information for which confidentiality is claimed is not publicly available. In addition, the advertiser seeking to protect confidential materials should provide a comprehensive summary of such materials and the principal arguments submitted by the advertiser in its rebuttal of the challenge.[42]

If the advertiser submits a substantial written response, NAD/CARU will promptly forward it to the complainant, except for any material designated as confidential, and the complainant may submit a reply within ten business days.[43] If the complainant wishes to expedite the proceedings, it has the option to waive its right to submit a reply by notifying NAD/CARU in writing. NAD will then proceed to formulate a decision upon the expiration of the complainant's reply deadline.[44] If the complainant submits a reply, NAD/CARU will promptly forward it to the advertiser, which is entitled to submit a response within ten business days.[45] If NAD/CARU requests further information, the advertiser or complainant has six business days to respond, and NAD/CARU will forward the additional response to the other party, which has six business days to respond.[46] Unless NAD/CARU requests further information, NAD will not accept any additional submissions as part of the case record, and it will return any such submissions to the sender.[47]

At its discretion, NAD/CARU may participate in a meeting (either in person or via teleconference) in addition to accepting written responses.[48] "In the event that NAD/CARU participates in a meeting in which only one party participates, NAD/CARU shall notify the other party that a teleconference or meeting has been scheduled to take place and after the meeting shall summarize the substance of the information exchanged for the other party."[49]

Within 15 business days of its receipt of the last document authorized by the NAD/NARB/CARU Procedures, NAD/CARU must formulate its decision on the truth and accuracy of the claims at issue or consistency with CARU's *Self-Regulatory Guidelines for Children's Advertising.*[50] During this period, NAD/CARU must prepare the "final case decision," send a copy to the advertiser, and invite the advertiser to add an Advertiser's Statement within five business days of receiving the decision.[51] If NAD/CARU decides that any of the advertising claims at issue are not substantiated, the Advertiser's Statement must state whether the advertiser agrees to modify or discontinue the advertising or chooses to appeal to the NARB. NAD/CARU must then immediately provide the parties with the final case decision and make copies available to the public.[52]

NAD/CARU's decisions are announced in press releases and are published in monthly reports entitled the NAD Case Reports. They are published under the headings Advertising Substantiated, Advertising Referred to NARB, Advertising Modified or Discontinued, Administrative Closing, Advertising Referred to Government Agency, No Substantiation Received, or Compliance.[53] The NAD/CARU Case Reports identify the advertiser, the product, the advertising agency, the advertising claims at issue, NAD/CARU's decision, and the rationale for the decision. NAD/CARU publishes an NAD Case Report for all investigations that are opened; none are settled privately.[54]

Extensions of time in NAD/CARU proceedings are permitted with the consent of NAD/CARU and the other party. If an advertiser fails to file a substantial written response within 15 business days, NAD/CARU issues a press release noting the advertiser's failure to substantively respond.[55] If the advertiser does not substantively respond within an additional 15 business days, NAD/CARU may refer the file to the appropriate government agency, issue a press release, and report the referral in the next monthly Case Reports.[56] NAD/CARU has made referrals to the FTC, which are discussed in Section IV(E). If the complainant fails to file a reply within ten business days, or an advertiser fails to file a response to that reply within ten business days, the untimely document will not be considered by NAD/CARU, or by any NARB panel.[57]

NAD identified the following categories of recurring issues in its 2002 cases: comparative performance claims; consumer surveys; defamatory/false claims; disclosure; efficacy claims; establishment claims; exclusivity claims; express claims; health and safety claims; implied claims/ consumer perception; ingredient content/nutrition claims; labeling/product packaging claims; online advertising; parity claims; performance claims; pricing/discounts/sales claims; product demonstration/testing; product description; puffery; superiority claims; taste/sensory claims; and testimonials.[58]

C. NARB Procedures

When an advertiser does not agree to comply with NAD/CARU's decision, the advertiser is entitled to appeal to the NARB. In those cases, NAD publishes the referral among cases closed in the current period, specifying the issues to be decided by the NARB panel. The advertiser is entitled to add an Advertiser's Statement.[59]

Unlike an advertiser, a complainant does not have an automatic right to NARB review of an NAD decision. A complainant may request review by the NARB by filing a letter with the NARB Chairman explaining its reasons within ten business days of publication of the final case decision.[60] A copy of this letter is sent to the advertiser and to the NAD/CARU, each of which has ten business days to respond.[61] The letters are reviewed by the NARB Chairman, who has ten business days to determine if there is "no substantial likelihood that a panel would reach a decision different from NAD/CARU's decision," in which case the request for NARB review is denied, or proceed to appoint a review panel.[62] The NARB Chairman reserves the right to extend these time intervals for good cause.[63]

Upon receipt of an appeal by an advertiser or upon granting an appeal by the complainant, the NARB Chairman appoints a panel of five qualified members, designating one to serve as panel chairman.[64] Each panel consists of one public member, one advertising agency member, and three advertiser members. Alternates may be used where required. NARB members are not qualified if their employer is involved with a product or service which directly competes with a product or service sold by the advertiser, or if for any reason arising out of past or present employment or affiliation they cannot reach a completely unbiased decision.[65] The advertiser and complainant each have the right to object for cause to the inclusion of individual panel members. Such objections are decided by the NARB Chairman.[66]

If the advertiser appeals to the NARB, or if the NARB Chairman grants a complainant's request for NARB review, NAD/CARU forwards the case record to the NARB within five business days.[67] The NARB then mails the case record to the parties, with the exception of confidential portions, which are not sent to the complainant unless the advertiser consents.[68] The party appealing must submit a letter explaining its position to the NARB Chairman within ten business days.[69] A copy of the letter is sent to the other parties, each of which has ten business days to submit a response. No other submissions may be made.[70]

The panel is directed by the NAD/NARB/CARU Procedures to "proceed with informality and speed."[71] Within ten business days after receiving copies of the appeal, the panel members fix the time schedule and procedures for the appeal, and give all parties ten days notice of the meeting at which the matter is to be presented to the panel.[72] The case record in NAD/NARB proceedings is considered closed upon publication of NAD/CARU's final case decision.[73] "No factual evidence, arguments or issues will be considered within the case record if they are introduced after that date."[74]

The decision of an NARB panel is based upon the case record before it, the submissions to it by the parties, and any summaries of the facts and arguments presented to the panel during its meeting with the parties.[75] At the hearing, a party may present representatives to summarize facts and arguments that were presented to the NAD, and the panel members may question these persons. "The panel will consider no facts or arguments if they are outside the facts presented to, or inconsistent with the arguments made before, NAD/CARU."[76] The complainant is excluded from the meeting during the time when any confidential substantiation submitted by the advertiser is being discussed by the panel with NAD/CARU and the advertiser.[77] If any newly discovered evidence that is germane to the issues to be decided by the panel becomes available, the panel may remand the case back to NAD/CARU for its further consideration and decision.[78]

When the NARB panel has reached a decision, it notifies the NARB Chairman of its decision and the rationale behind it in writing, and "shall endeavor to do so within 15 business days" of the NARB hearing.[79] The NARB Chairman transmits the written decision to NAD/CARU and then to the advertiser, which has five business days to respond indicating its acceptance, rejection, or any comments it wishes to make on the decision.[80] The NARB Chairman then notifies the other parties of the decision, and makes the decision public. The Chairman will issue a Notice of Intent to the advertiser that the record of the case will be referred to the appropriate government agency if a panel has determined that an advertisement is unsubstantiated or is untruthful or inaccurate, and the advertiser fails to indicate that the advertisement will be withdrawn or modified in accordance with the panel's findings within a time period appropriate to the circumstances of the case.[81] If the advertiser fails to respond or does not agree to comply with the panel's decision within ten business days of the issuance of the Notice of Intent, the Chairman will so inform the appropriate government agency, offer the complete NARB file to the agency upon request, and publicly release his letter.[82]

When a case has been concluded with the publication of an NAD/CARU decision, or when a panel has turned over a decision to the NARB Chairman, the case will be closed and, "absent extraordinary circumstances, no further materially similar complaints on the claim(s) in question shall be accepted by NAD/CARU or NARB."[83]

D. CARU Procedures

The Children's Advertising Review Unit ("CARU"), a division of the NAD, is responsible for monitoring and reviewing national advertising directed to children under 12 for consistency with CARU's Self-Regulatory Guidelines for Children's Advertising.[84] CARU publishes in the monthly NAD Case Reports a summary of its actions, other than formal cases, during the preceding month. These reports include summaries of informal inquiries, summaries of proposed advertising submitted to it for pre-screening, and commentaries, consisting of news or policy that CARU believes is appropriate to disseminate to its readership.[85] Formal cases are also published in the NAD Case Reports.

CARU first published its Self-Regulatory Guidelines for Children's Advertising in 1972. Since then, they have been revised a number of times, most recently in December of 2001. The guidelines cover such subjects as: sales pressure, comparative advertising, required disclosures and disclaimers, endorsements, sweepstakes and premium offers, host-selling, and product safety. Guidelines covering the use of telemarketing and pay-per-call 900/976 telephone number marketing directed to children were adopted by CARU in 1989 and were incorporated in the guidelines in 1991. In 1996, CARU added Guidelines for Interactive Electronic Media. In 1999, CARU adopted guidelines for data collection and privacy on the Internet. In January 2001, CARU's Guidelines became the first Safe-Harbor program approved by the FTC under the Children's Online Privacy Protection Act of 1998 ("COPPA"). An advertiser who complies with the Guidelines is deemed to be in compliance with COPPA and, provided the advertiser continues to comply with the Safe-Harbor program requirements, is likely protected against FTC enforcement action.[86]

CARU follows the same procedures for formal cases as the NAD and also has a provision for expedited procedures. If the advertiser responds within five business days to a letter of inquiry from CARU and the advertising is substantiated, or if the advertising is modified to comply with CARU's guidelines within an additional five business days, no formal case will be opened, and the results will be published in the CARU Activity Report.[87]

Most CARU investigations are informal inquiries. However, about one-third are published in the NAD Case Reports. Currently, the vast majority of investigations involve web sites.[88]

E. Compliance With NAD and NARB Decisions

There has been a high degree of compliance with NAD (including CARU) and NARB decisions. Advertisers, advertising agencies, and courts have recognized the expertise and importance of the NAD/NARB/CARU mechanism as the self-regulatory body of the advertising industry. In 1985, one court stated:

> The value of this [procedure] lies largely in the particular experience and skill of the NAD as a resolver of disputes. In the [then] fourteen years since its formation, the NAD has

developed its own process of reviewing complaints of deceptiveness, coupling relative informality and confidentiality with safeguards to ensure procedural fairness. . . . As the NAD puts it: "Speed, informality and modest cost are three chief benefits of [this] self-regulatory system." . . . To these advantages . . . is added the unique ability of the NAD to decide what is fair in advertising. A judge might make this inquiry, but ultimately it would have to defer to the very expertise that NAD offers without resort to the courts.[89]

That same court also stated: "Voluntary compliance with NAD's decisions has been universal. Reportedly no advertiser who has participated in the complete process of an NAD investigation and NARB appeal has declined to abide by the decision."[90] That is no longer the case. NAD usually refers several cases per year to the FTC, whose former Chairman has stated that it takes such referrals "seriously."[91]

Despite an occasional exception there is still a high level of compliance with NAD, CARU, and NARB decisions, given the number of cases handled. As of March 2003, NAD, CARU, and NARB together had resolved over 4000 cases.[92] Of these, less than 5% have been referred to government agencies. Most recently, in 2002, NAD referred six cases to the FTC and other government agencies.[93] Altogether, of the 412 cases decided in the last four years, twenty-one (five in 1999, two in 2000, eight in 2001, and six in 2002) were referred to a government agency for action.[94] Since NARB's formation in 1971, the NARB had adjudicated 114 cases, and only a few advertisers have refused to abide by NARB's decision.[95]

In 1994, the United States Department of Transportation encouraged the airline industry to cooperate with NAD in settling disputes about advertising claims.[96]

F. Effect of NAD Decisions on Litigation

A decision of the NAD is not legally binding upon the participants and it is not binding upon a court of law, even when a court reviews the exact same issues. However, a decision of NAD can play an influential role with the federal courts. There have been a number of cases in which NAD decisions were cited by federal courts, although none have cited an NAD decision as grounds for the ultimate holding. Nevertheless, one court noted the benefits of alternative resolution methods such as NAD and required a party to comply with an agreement with a competitor to obtain a "non-binding advisory opinion in a dispute over the proprietary of advertising claims."[97]

In another case, a court dismissed a false advertising claim under § 43(a) of the Lanham Act,[98] noting that NAD, as well as the television networks, had rejected the challenge and that the self-regulatory process should be encouraged.[99]

NAD's high stature with the federal judiciary was recognized when a federal district court in New Jersey confirmed a settlement agreement under which the parties consented to referral of their case to NAD.[100] While it is too early to tell whether such referrals will become commonplace, it seems likely that the courts will continue to recognize the expertise of NAD in advertising cases.

G. Code of Advertising

The Council of Better Business Bureaus has issued a Code of Advertising, consisting of basic advertising standards for the guidance of advertisers, advertising agencies, and the advertising media. The Code covers the following topics: comparative price, value, and savings claims; "free" claims; "cents-off" sales; trade-in allowances; credit; extra charges; bait advertising and selling; warranties and guarantees; layouts and illustrations; asterisks; abbreviations; use or condition disclosures; superiority claims-comparatives-disparagement; superlative claims-puffery; testimonials and endorsements; rebates; company name or trade style; contests and games of chance, claimed results; and unassembled merchandise.[101] The Council also publishes a publication entitled *Do's and Don'ts in Advertising,* a comprehensive loose-leaf volume covering many advertising topics, which is updated periodically.

V. TELEVISION NETWORKS

A. Commercial Clearance

The four major television networks require advertisers to submit storyboards or scripts of their proposed commercials for review prior to production, along with substantiation for all claims.[102] These materials are reviewed by each network's broadcast standards department[103] for compliance with the network's advertising guidelines and policies as well as applicable laws and regulations. Each department has editors assigned to different product categories, who make the initial decisions. Appeals from the editors' decisions can be made to the department's vice president. Following review, the network may approve or reject the commercial, request revisions or request further substantiation. Final approval of a commercial is contingent upon review of the finished commercial.[104]

The networks will not permit a commercial to air unless it has been approved by its broadcast standards department. Therefore, no commercial scheduled for broadcast on a network should be produced unless prior approval has been obtained for the storyboard or script. Otherwise, a finished commercial may have to be modified or may not be allowed to run at all, resulting in substantial costs which could have been avoided.

The four major networks require adequate substantiation for all claims made in proposed commercials.[105] The networks' guidelines cover acceptable and unacceptable subject matter, disclosure requirements for certain types of advertising, and special standards that apply to different product categories. All four networks permit comparative advertising as long as the claims are truthful and adequately substantiated.[106] The networks do not permit false disparagement or "ash-canning," *i.e.,* falsely claiming that a competitive product has little or no value.[107] The networks' guidelines are particularly detailed in some areas, such as children's advertising, personal products, and medical products. Advertising for certain product categories and certain types of advertising are prohibited by the networks' guidelines, such as advertising for distilled spirits and firearms, advocacy advertising involving controversial issues, and subliminal advertising.[108]

Each of the four networks makes independent decisions on proposed commercials submitted to them. It is not uncommon for a commercial to be accepted by only one or two networks. Different versions sometimes appear on the four networks, with different copy, disclaimers, or visuals. Although this can be frustrating to advertisers and advertising agencies, and can impose additional expenses, it is necessary for the networks to make independent decisions for antitrust reasons.

The advertising standards, guidelines, and policies of the networks are followed locally by the stations that are owned and operated by the networks. Network affiliates also tend to follow them, but not consistently because they are permitted to make their own decisions.

B. Network Challenge Procedures

The four major networks permit companies to challenge advertising by their competitors.[109] Any commercial aired on the networks can be challenged. The challenges are handled by each network's broadcast standards department at ABC, CBS and NBC, and by the legal department at Fox.

The networks require that a challenge be made in writing in a form that permits it, along with any supporting data, to be transmitted to the challenged advertiser for a response.[110] If the challenger considers any challenge material to be confidential, the challenger can make a specific designation of that material; the networks will honor the request that such material not be transmitted if the material is non-public and proprietary.

Upon receipt, all challenges are reviewed by each network's broadcast standards department. If, in the department's opinion, the challenge appears to have merit (*i.e.*, on its face the challenge has substance), it will be sent to the challenged advertiser for a response. A challenge will be dismissed outright if it is considered without merit or non-substantive, or if it involves advertising that has completed its schedule and is not scheduled to air again. If the challenge is made to advertising which has not yet been approved by the network, the substantive matters raised will generally be considered during the clearance process.

When a challenge is transmitted to the advertiser, the networks usually request a response within 14 days, although a different deadline may be established if the circumstances warrant.[111] The networks will speed up the process if a matter is urgent or relatively simple, and will grant reasonable requests for extensions of time for good cause.[112]

Each of the networks will maintain the confidentiality of the substantiation originally submitted by the challenged advertiser to support the claims made in the advertising.[113] Advertisers, though, are encouraged by the networks to submit a response, with supporting data, in a form that can be transmitted to the challenger.

The networks will generally permit a challenged commercial to continue to run until a response is received and the challenge is fully resolved. However, in extraordinary circumstances, approval may be withdrawn or airing may be suspended immediately after receipt of a challenge. Some commercials are accepted "subject to challenge"; this indicates borderline approval, and may result in either withdrawal of approval upon receipt of a responsible complaint or a short deadline for response to a challenge. If approval is withdrawn or suspended, the advertiser may still proceed with the challenge and try to persuade the network to change its mind and reinstate the advertising.

When the advertiser's response is received, the networks will review it and will transmit it to the challenger for rebuttal if this appears to be useful in resolving the challenge (*e.g.* if more information is needed, new arguments have been made, or new issues have been raised).[114] The networks apply the same criteria in deciding whether to transmit the challenger's rebuttal to the advertiser. Each side generally is given an opportunity to respond to and rebut the other side.

A meeting with network personnel to discuss the challenge may be requested by the advertiser, the challenger or the network. These meetings are always *ex parte;* the network meets with the advertiser or challenger alone, without the other side present.[115] The networks may seek to encourage the parties to obtain a resolution from an acceptable third party if they feel that they do not have the expertise necessary to make a judgment.

At the end of the process, the networks' broadcast standards departments make independent decisions to resolve challenges. Since they act independently, each may reach a different judgment on the same challenge. They will permit a challenged commercial to continue to run unless: (1) it is voluntarily withdrawn by the challenged advertiser; (2) the challenged advertiser refuses to cooperate with the challenge procedures; or (3) a determination is made against the challenged advertiser by the network, by a third party to whom the matter has been referred, or by a government agency or an appropriate court, with finality.[116] A brief letter setting forth the decision is sent to each side. Where changes are requested in the challenged advertising, network practice is to advise the challenger of that fact without detailing the requested changes. The advertiser is given a reasonable period of time to effectuate the requested changes.

C. Effect of Network Decisions on Litigation

In some cases, the courts have looked to the challenge process of the television networks as a source of guidance on the issue of false or deceptive advertising. In *McNeilab, Inc. v. Am. Home Products Corp.*,[117] the court noted that a party's knowledge of the deceptive nature of its advertising could be shown by the fact that a network had objected to the commercial.[118] There, the advertiser submitted the commercial to ABC's Broadcast Standards and Practices Department, which found a claim to be "highly misleading."[119] The court stated that this objection gave the defendant "reason to be aware of the 'highly questionable' nature of its approach to advertising [its product]."[120] The court criticized the defendant because it "did not take steps to ensure that its advertising would not confuse consumers."[121]

Several other cases have noted the network clearance process but did not discuss the effect, if any, the process had on their decisions.[122] On the other hand, one court dismissed a false advertising action under § 43(a) of the Lanham Act, noting that ABC, CBS, and NBC had each rejected challenges to the advertising and that the NAD had found it to be adequately substantiated.[123] The court ruled that the alleged false advertising was not actionable under the Lanham Act; however, the decision was reversed on appeal on the basis that § 43(a) encompasses a competitor's misrepresentations of the quality of its product.[124]

VI. PROS AND CONS OF DIFFERENT TYPES OF CHALLENGES

Allegedly false or deceptive advertising can be challenged with NAD or with the networks; challenges can be made with individual stations or station groups which have aired a commercial; a complaint can be filed with the FTC; and a lawsuit can be filed against false comparative advertising under § 43(a) of the Lanham Act or under state laws. These actions can be taken separately or in any combination. The following are the pros and cons of these options.

Network challenges are usually resolved more quickly than the other types of complaints. They tend to be less expensive, and are resolved by professionals who are highly experienced in the advertising field, particularly with network advertising standards and guidelines. NAD challenges are similarly resolved by professionals who are highly experienced in the advertising field. NAD had been criticized in the past regarding the time it took to resolve some challenges,[125] but its decision-making time has been shortened by the changes in the NAD rules which became effective on April 1, 1990, setting strict time limits on each stage of NAD challenges. Under the current rules,[126] provided both the parties and NAD abide by the timing guidelines, NAD cases are generally decided within 60 days. However, NAD does not have the authority to remove advertising from dissemination, whereas the networks can withdraw a commercial from the air.

Section 43(a) of the Lanham Act[127] provides a cause of action to a competitor for false advertising. A Lanham Act suit can produce the fastest result if a federal district court (or a court of appeals on appeal) is willing to grant a temporary restraining order or a preliminary injunction. An additional advantage is that a plaintiff can obtain the defendant's relevant documents and depose witnesses during discovery, whereas the complainant in an NAD or network challenge has no subpoena power. Moreover, a successful plaintiff can receive damages, including treble damages, attorneys fees, and court costs in appropriate cases. However, there are drawbacks to a private civil suit. There are difficult elements of proof. If a temporary restraining order or a preliminary injunction is not obtained, discovery is likely to be lengthy, time consuming, and expensive. The discovery process may give each party access to the other party's marketing information and other sensitive data. Employees may be requested to give depositions, which can be disruptive to a company's business. Outside experts may be required to make analyses of evidence and give testimony.

Judges are not as familiar with advertising as NAD or network broadcast standards personnel, since they do not deal with it on a day-to-day basis. They will not apply their own "expertise" to identify implied claims that are alleged to be false; they generally must rely upon consumer perception surveys.

Network challenges can be based upon alleged violations of network policies, such as taste standards, as well as allegations of falsity or deceptiveness. NAD will only consider complaints involving the truth and accuracy of advertising. The courts in Lanham Act cases will only consider whether the advertising makes misrepresentations in violation of the law. In addition, Lanham Act suits must contain a number of allegations necessary to state a claim upon which relief can be granted, such as that the plaintiff has been or is likely to be injured as a result of the defendant's false advertising. The plaintiff has the burden of proving that the advertising is false or misleading.

The networks will only handle challenges of commercials broadcast by them; they will not consider advertising in other media, even if it is part of the same campaign. NAD will handle challenges of advertising in all media, including broadcast, print, and Internet advertising, as well as labeling, as long as the advertising meets its criteria for national advertising. The courts in Lanham Act cases and the FTC have jurisdiction over all advertising in interstate commerce.

Section 5 of the Federal Trade Commission Act[128] prohibits "unfair or deceptive acts or practices in or affecting commerce." Section 5 encompasses false advertising. In addition, § 12 of the FTC Act[129] gives the FTC authority over false advertising of foods, drugs, devices, services, and cosmetics. The FTC will only consider alleged violations of the FTC Act. It has limited resources, and will only pursue a small percentage of the complaints it receives. In addition, the FTC has a policy of not involving itself in private disputes between competitors; instead, it takes law enforcement action only when it has reason to believe that the public interest warrants it.

If a network challenge is upheld, the network advertising will be withdrawn from broadcast on the entire network, including all owned and operated and affiliated stations. The affiliated stations, as well as independent stations, are free however, to run locally placed commercials, even if those commercials have been successfully challenged on a network. Challenges with individual stations can be filed. While usually expeditious, they only affect the broadcast schedule of those stations.

Filing a challenge with NAD and the networks has its limitations. Neither NAD nor the networks have subpoena power or other discovery procedures; they must rely on the information voluntarily submitted by the parties. This information, of course, may not tell the whole story. The judicial rules of evidence and due process do not apply. Except for NARB hearings, there is no hearing at which both sides appear together and present arguments. Sanctions are limited. No monetary damages are permitted. The networks' ultimate sanction is to refuse to carry the challenged advertising, and NAD's and the NARB's ultimate sanction is to refer the matter to the appropriate government agency. The networks may reach different results from each other and from NAD on the same matter.

Successfully challenging a network commercial is generally no easy matter. If the commercial has aired, the network has already cleared it; the challenger is asking the network to revoke clearance, based on the network's own standards. The network is being asked, in essence, to change its mind. In addition, since the networks are in competition for a share of total advertising dollars, they have an institutional interest in favor of accepting advertising and keeping it on the air, rather than rejecting it or taking it off the air.

The networks have as broad discretion in ruling upon challenges as they do in reviewing proposed commercials. They reserve the right to accept or reject at any time advertising for any product or service broadcast over their facilities.

An NAD or network challenge should present arguments and facts as strongly as possible. It should be as well written, organized, and supported as a brief. It need not be lengthy, but it should be complete. If comparative product testing has been conducted to disprove a claim in a commercial, the protocol and results should be submitted. Particular network standards or guidelines, NAD precedents, or governmental laws or regulations which are alleged to be violated, should be specified. Both the challenger and the advertiser should permit as much information as feasible to be transmitted to the opposing side. The process gets bogged down when the parties do not allow material to be passed on, since then NAD or the networks do not have the benefit of informed adversarial comment. Finally, it is prudent to retain competent counsel to prosecute or defend a challenge.

VII. TRADE ASSOCIATION REGULATION OF ADVERTISING

Many industries have established advertising codes for their members through their industry or trade associations. These codes generally contain moral or ethical proscriptions instead of legal restrictions.

For example, the Consumer Healthcare Products Association ("CHPA"), a trade association which represents U.S. manufacturers and distributors of nonprescription, over-the-counter drugs and dietary supplements, has a Code of Advertising Practices for Nonprescription Medicines.

The Preamble to the CHPA Code states that:

> [A]dvertising should truthfully reflect the goals of self-medication and the safety and efficacy of nonprescription medicines. Untruthful or misleading claims or comparisons, which are inconsistent with the role of self-medication or with the safety and effectiveness of nonpre-scription medicines, are to be avoided. They do not serve the interests of consumers and cast doubt on both the appropriateness of self-medication and the industry's willingness to live up to its public trust.[130]

The Code requires compliance with FDA and FTC labeling and advertising requirements, and contains many other requirements and prohibitions. The CHPA reviews complaints regarding alleged violations, and takes appropriate action to resolve them.

Other prominent industry codes are the "Code of Good Practice" of the Distilled Spirits Council of the United States, Inc.[131] and the Direct Marketing Association Guidelines for Ethical Business Practice.[132] These codes generally are effective self-regulatory mechanisms. Voluntary compliance by members of each trade association tends to be high due to the force placed upon the codes by the industry's imprimatur.

VIII. OTHER ADVERTISING INDUSTRY SELF-REGULATION

A. Better Business Bureaus and Local Advertising Review Boards

The Council of Better Business Bureaus consists of local Better Business Bureaus throughout the United States. The local BBB's receive and attempt to resolve consumer complaints against local advertisers and businesses.[133] They keep records of the number and status of these complaints, and provide this information to consumers upon request.[134] They generally do not make public comments or judgments about the business practices involved.[135] Most lawsuits brought against local BBB's for defamation have failed.[136]

The first BBB's began operating in 1912. There were originally "Vigilance Committees" of Advertising Clubs, established to correct abuses in advertising. Over the years they broadened their function to monitor other marketplace activities and business performance. Today, there are 145 BBB's in the United States, with more than 24 million consumer and business contacts each year.[137]

The Council of Better Business Bureaus has encouraged the establishment of local advertising review boards ("LARB's") to investigate the truth and accuracy of local advertising. The Council has drafted guidelines for the establishment of such boards, and is active in trying to induce its members to form them.[138] As with lawsuits against local BBB's, lawsuits seeking to suppress actions by LARB's have been unsuccessful.[139]

B. Advertising Regulation by Other Media

Although most media entities do not review advertising and enforce advertising standards and guidelines as rigorously as the four major television networks, some media entities do review substantiation for claims made in advertising submitted to them, and review challenges to advertising. Among these media entities are some station and cable television groups, individual stations, and a few publications such as *Good Housekeeping* and *The New York Times*. In fact, *Good Housekeeping* not only reviews proposed advertising and claim support, but also conducts testing of products at the *Good Housekeeping Institute*.

C. Controls by Advertisers and Advertising Agencies

Many advertisers and advertising agencies engage in self-regulation by having their proposed advertising reviewed by in-house or outside counsel prior to dissemination. Advertising is reviewed for truth, accuracy, substantiation for claims, and compliance with legal requirements. Since both the advertiser and its advertising agency can be liable for false or deceptive advertising, this legal review is extremely important in helping to prevent costly and time-consuming legal problems. Advertising agencies are frequently named as respondents along with advertisers in proceedings instituted by the FTC, and are occasionally named as respondents in false advertising suits brought by competitors of their clients.

A study conducted by the Association of National Advertisers found that reviews of proposed advertising claims by many national advertisers take place both before submission to the advertising agency and after the proposed advertising comes back from the agency.[140] Many national advertisers police their advertising for compliance with legal requirements and with the advertising guidelines of their industry or trade associations, as well as any applicable guidelines of the media to which the advertising will be submitted.

Many advertising agencies typically submit prospective advertising to counsel for the same purposes as it is submitted to counsel for advertisers. Agencies look to their clients for proper substantiation of claims. Contracts with clients customarily indemnify agencies for any losses or expenses incurred due to lack of adequate substantiation of claims. However, such indemnities do not protect agencies from being named as co-respondents in governmental actions instituted by the FTC or other agencies, such as state attorneys general.

IX. CONCLUSION

The system of self-regulation established by the advertising industry in the United States is extensive and effective. Its effectiveness is due to the following factors: (1) it is well known, understood, and accepted by all major advertisers and advertising agencies; (2) it is strongly supported by the primary federal regulator of advertising, the FTC; (3) there is a long history of advertising industry self-regulation; (4) the system operates at many levels, from local to national; (5) the system is generally faster and less expensive than litigation and governmental regulation; and (6) there are legal sanctions for failure to abide by the decisions of NAD, CARU, and the NARB.

In a speech to the advertising industry, FTC Commissioner Sheila T. Anthony stated:

> I want to echo [former] Chairman Pitofsky's past comments that the BBB's National Advertising Division has really set the model for independent, objective, public and enforceable self regulation. . . .
>
> Because of your past efforts, there is a real acceptance within the Commission of the effectiveness of self-regulation as an alternative to government action. Our attitude is that, in many instances, self-regulatory initiatives can address consumer concerns in a more flexible manner and in a much shorter period of time than government regulation.[141]

Despite the success of the advertising industry's self-regulation system, there is room for improvement. Commissioner Anthony pointed to three areas where more and better self-regulation is needed: (1) dietary supplement advertising, in which "many advertisers . . . use exaggerated and unsubstantiated claims"; (2) "media screening for deceptive advertising, [which] has long been an important goal of the advertising industry's self-regulatory program," (but the FTC "is concerned that too many deceptive ads are slipping through)"; and (3) Internet privacy, where the FTC has "actively encouraged effective self-regulation."[142] Based on an extensive survey of commercial web sites which found that few children's sites were disclosing their information practices or providing for parental consent, as required by the CARU Guidelines discussed above, the FTC reported the results of its survey to Congress in June 1998, and recommended that Congress enact legislation to protect children's privacy online.[143] On October 21, 1998, Congress enacted COPPA,[144] which provides for uniform national regulation of the collection, use, and disclosure of individually identifiable information obtained online from children under the age 13. The FTC's final rules implementing COPPA became effective on April 21, 2000.[145]

Nonetheless, the system of self-regulation established by the advertising industry in the United States has served as an effective alternative to litigation and government action, and provides a useful model for other industries and other countries.

NOTES

1. The FCC's basic policy regarding broadcaster responsibility for what is broadcast was set forth in its 1960 policy statement:

> Broadcasting licensees must assume responsibility for all material which is broadcast through their facilities. This includes all programs and advertising material which they present to the public. With respect to advertising material, the licensee has the additional responsibility to take all reasonable measures to eliminate any false, misleading, or deceptive matter. . . . This duty is personal to the licensee and may not be delegated.

Report and Statement of Policy, 44 FCC 2303 (1960).

The FCC referenced this basic responsibility in 1986, when it deregulated its specific policies that previously regulated broadcasters' practices regarding false and misleading advertising, stating: "Broadcast licensees . . . continue to be responsible for all material broadcast through their facilities, including advertising, but the method of compliance now will be left to the discretion of licensees." *In the Matter of Elimination of Unnecessary Broad. Regulation,* 57 Rad. Reg. 2d (P & F) 1, 40–41 n. 26 (F.C.C 1985), *aff'd, sub nom., Telecomm. Research and Action Ctr. v. FCC,* 800 F.2d 1181 (D.C. Cir. 1986).

2. In 1964, the FTC stated: "[I]f the Commission could persuade business to do its own housecleaning, the public interest would be served just as well, faster, and at a fraction of the cost." 1964 FTC Ann. Rep. at 1. In 1994, the Associate Director of the FTC's Division of Advertising Practices declared: "The Commission appreciates the important support the advertising industry's self-regulation system gives to our own regulatory and enforcement efforts to help ensure that consumers receive truthful and substantiated claims on advertising." C. Lee Peeler, Remarks, *Remarks Before the National Advertising Review Board* (N.Y.C., Dec. 7, 1994), in *Advertising Topics, Council of Better Business Bureaus, Inc.*, Supp. 541, at 1. In 1998, Robert Pitofsky, the former Chairman of the FTC, said: "We have recognized for over a generation that self-regulation can serve as an important complement to our consumer protection enforcement efforts. . . . On several occasions, I have described the advertising industry's self-regulatory program as an effective model." Robert Pitofsky, Remarks, *Self-Regulation and Antitrust*, (Washington, D.C., Feb. 18, 1998), available at, Federal Trade Commission, *FTC News Releases, Publications & Speeches, Speeches* <www.ftc.gov/opa/1998/9802/selfreg.htm> (accessed March 28, 2003).

In 2001, Timothy J. Muris, the current Chairman of the FTC, said:

> [W]hen faced with an increasingly active FTC and a concerned public the advertising industry responded by creating the National Advertising Review Board, or NARB, in 1971. One of the first principles the NARB announced was that advertisers must possess reasonable substantiation for their objective claims. The NARB today remains a model of self-regulation, a vital supplement to government law enforcement efforts, and one of the many accomplishments for which Bob Pitofsky can genuinely be proud.

Timothy J. Muris, Remarks, *Robert Pitofsky: Public Servant and Scholar* (Washington, D.C., June 12, 2001), available at, Federal Trade Commission, *FTC News Releases, Publication & Speeches, Speeches* <www.ftc.gov/speeches/muris/muris010612.htm> (accessed April 15, 2003).

3. *Columbia Broad. Sys., Inc.*, 412 U.S. 94 (1973). The case concerned the policy of the major television networks (ABC, CBS, and NBC) to refuse to sell editorial advertising time to individuals or groups wishing to speak out on controversial issues of public importance. *Id.* at 98. The Court ruled in favor of the networks, holding that there is no "private right of access" to the broadcast media. *Id.* at 129. The opinion's language affirming the broad discretion given to broadcast licensees to meet their "public trustee" obligations applies to commercial as well as editorial advertising.

Likewise, in *Rokus v. Am. Broad. Co.*, 616 F. Supp. 110 (S.D.N.Y. 1984), a federal district court upheld ABC's refusal to broadcast a commercial for "editorial reasons" despite the advertiser's willingness to delete the portions of the commercial which had been questioned by the network. *Id.* at 113–14.

4. 418 U.S. 241, 258 (1974).

5. *See e.g. Chi. Jt. Bd., Amalgamated Clothing Workers of Am. v. Chi. Tribune Co.*, 435 F.2d 470, 478 (7th Cir. 1970), *cert. denied*, 402 U.S. 973 (1971) (upholding newspaper's refusal to print union advertisement stating opposition to the sale of foreign-made clothing); *Person v. New York Post Corp.*, 427 F. Supp 1297 (E.D.N.Y. 1977), *aff'd without opinion*, 573 F.2d 1294, 1309 (7th Cir. 1977) (upholding newspaper's refusal to print attorney's advertisement selling shares in a lawsuit).

6. *Pitt. Press Co. v. Pitt. Commn. of Human Rel.*, 413 U.S. 376, 391 (1973).

7. *Lorian J. Co. v. U.S.*, 342 U.S. 143, 155–56 (1951); *Home Placement Serv. v. Providence J. Co.*, 682 F.2d 274, 281 (1st Cir. 1982), *cert. denied*, 460 U.S. 1028 (1983).

8. *Penthouse Intl., Ltd. v. Koch*, 599 F. Supp 1338, 1351 (S.D.N.Y. 1984) (refusal by New York City Transit Authority to accept advertisement for New York City subway system showing scantily clad caricature of presidential candidate Walter Mondale on basis that advertisement was "offensive to good taste" held to be unconstitutional because standard was "too vague and subjective to meaningfully circumscribe the discretion of subway officials.")

9. *Goldstein v. Garlick*, 318 N.Y.S.2d 370, 374 (Sup. Ct. 1971); *Suarez v. Underwood*, 426 N.Y.S.2d 208, 210 (Sup. Ct. 1980), *aff'd*, 449 N.Y.S.2d 438 (2d Dept. 1981).

10. *Goldstein*, 318 N.Y.S.2d at 375.

11. *Id.* at 375–76 ("Such a rule would make a newspaper an arbiter of the conflicting claims of competing advertisers and would impose an intolerable burden upon newspapers and would, in the end, have a chilling effect upon them since they would have to refuse many items submitted because of the possibility that publication would lead to liability."). *See also Yuhas v. Mudge*, 322 A.2d 824, 825 (N.J. Super. App. Div. 1974) (holding that magazine publisher was not liable for injuries sustained from fireworks purchased by defendants through paid advertisements in magazine. The court concluded that the publisher did not guarantee, warrant or endorse the product, even though the magazine was allegedly a pseudoscientific publication which had acquired a sense of authority in the public mind).

12. The media exemption for liability for deceptive advertising applies in the following states only to media with no knowledge of the deceptiveness of the advertisement and no financial stake in the profits from the sale of the advertised product: Alaska, Alaska Stat. § 42–110c (2001); Connecticut, Conn. Gen. Stat. § 42-110c (2001); District of Columbia, D.C. Code Ann. § 28–3903 (2002); Georgia, Ga. Code Ann. § 10–1-421 (2002); Louisiana, La. R.S. 51:1406 (2003); Michigan, Mich. Comp. Laws § 445.358 (2002); Minnesota, Minn. Stat. Ann. § 325E.42 (West 2002); Mississippi, Miss. Code Ann. § 75–24–7 (2002); Montana, Mont. Code Ann. § 30–14–105 (2002); South Carolina, S.C. Code Ann. § 39–5-40 (2002); Texas, Tex. Bus. & Com. Code Ann. § 17.49 (2002); and West Virginia, W. Va. Code § 46A-6–105 (2003).

Most of the remaining state statutes grant media an even broader exemption by requiring only a lack of knowledge of the deceptive nature of the advertising: Alabama, Ala. Code § 13A-9–44 (2002); Arizona, Ariz. Rev. Stat. Ann. § 44–1523 (West 2002); California, Cal. Civ. Code § 1755 (West 2003); Colorado, Colo. Rev. Stat. § 6–1-106 (2002); Delaware, Del. Code Ann. tit. 6, § 2513 (2002); Florida, Fla. Stat. § 817.43 (2002); Hawaii, Haw. Rev. Stat. § 481A-5 (2002); Idaho, Idaho Code § 48–605 (2002); Illinois, 815 III. Comp. Stat. § 505/10b (2002).; Iowa, Iowa Code. § 714.16 (2002); Kansas, Kan. Stat. Ann. § 21–4403 (2001); Kentucky, Ky. Rev. Stat. Ann. § 367.180 (2002); Maine, 17 Me. Rev. Stat. Ann. § 901 (2001); Maryland, Md. Comm. Law Code Ann. § 11–702 (2002); Massachusetts, Mass. Gen. Laws ch. 266, § 91 (2002); Missouri, Mo. Rev. Stat.§ 407.020 (2002); Nebraska, Neb. Rev. Stat. § 87–304 (2002); Nevada, Nev. Rev. Stat. Ann § 207.172 (LEXIS L. Publg. 2002); New Hampshire, N.H. Rev. Stat. Ann. § 358-A:3 (2002); New Jersey, N.J. Stat. Ann. § 56:8–2 (2002); New York, N.Y. Gen. Bus. Law § 349 (Consol. 2002); North Carolina, N.C. Gen. Stat. § 75–1.1 (2002); North Dakota, N.D. Cent. Code § 51–12–09 (2002); Ohio, Ohio. Rev. Code Ann. § 1345. 12 (Anderson 2002); Oklahoma, Okla. Stat. tit. 15, § 754 (2003); Oregon, Or. Rev. Stat. Ann. § 646.612 (2001); Pennsylvania, Pa. Stat. Ann. tit. 73, § 201–3 (West 2002); Rhode Island, R.I. Gen. Laws § 11–18–11 (2002); South Dakota, S.D. Codified Laws § 22–41–12 (2002); Tennessee, Tenn. Code Ann. § 47–18–111 (2002); Utah, Utah Code Ann. § 13–11a-5 (2003); Vermont, Vt. Stat. Ann. tit. 9, § 2452 (2002); Virginia, Va. Code Ann. § 59.1–199 (2002); Washington, Wash. Rev. Code Ann. § 9.04.010 (West 2002); Wisconsin, Wis. Stat. § 100.18 (2002); and Wyoming, Wyo. Stat. Ann. § 40–12–110 (2002). In New Mexico, N.M. Stat. Ann. § 57–15–10 (2002), the statute on its face unconditionally exempts the media from liability for false advertising.

The only state that does not exempt media is Indiana. Ind. Code § 24–5-0.5–3 (2002).

13. *Thomas v. Times Mirror Mag., Inc.*, 159 Cal. Rptr. 711 (1979), *hr'g denied and ordered not to be officially published* (Dec. 20, 1979). The publisher of *Popular Science Magazine* was held liable for publishing a classified advertisement for the personal services of an engineer who held himself out as a "licensed professional patent engineer," when the publisher had received letters from readers pointing out that he had been disbarred from practice before the Patent Office a number of years earlier, and a magazine article had been published regarding his disbarment. With respect to the liability of the media company, the court stated:

> We are aware that by virtue of [California] Business and Professions Code section 17502, the statutory proscription of false and misleading advertising at issue does not apply to the publisher of a magazine who "publishes an advertisement in goo[d] faith, without knowledge of its false, deceptive, or misleading character." In view of the just recounted proof regarding Popular Science's possible knowledge of the false, deceptive and misleading character of the patent services advertising of Spector that it was carrying, we hold that triable issues of fact did exist regarding the good faith of Popular Science in publishing this advertising and the knowledge that Popular Science may have possessed of its false, deceptive and misleading character.

Id. at 715–16.

14. *State of New York v. Ginzburg,* 428 N.Y.S.2d 132, 136 (Sup. Ct. 1980) (repetition of false advertising that constituted persistent fraud actionable as fraudulent enterprise).

15. *Braun v. Soldier of Fortune Mag., Inc.*, 968 F.2d 1110 (11th Cir. 1992), *cert. denied,* 506 U.S. 1071 (1993). The magazine had run a personal service advertisement stating: "GUN FOR HIRE: 37 year old professional mercenary desires jobs. Vietnam Veteran. Discrete [sic] and very private. Body guard, courier, and other special skills. All jobs considered." *Id.* at 1112. The magazine was held liable in a wrongful death action brought by the sons of a murder victim who was killed by an assassin hired by their father's business partner through the advertisement. *Id.* at 1122.

16. George Eric Rosden & Peter Eric Rosden, *The Law of Advertising* vol. 4, § 40.02, 40–4 (Matthew Bender 2002).

17. *Id.*

18. *Id.*

19. *Id.*

20. *Id.*

21. *U.S. v. Natl. Assn. of Broadcasters,* 536 F. Supp. 149, 170 (D.D.C. 1982). The court found that this provision forced advertisers to buy more broadcast time than they might have desired and that it artificially increased the demand for broadcast time, thereby increasing its price and the revenue of broadcasters.

22. American Broadcasting Company Television Network Advertising Standards and Guidelines (July 2002 ed.) [hereinafter *ABC Guidelines*]; CBS Broadcasting, Inc., Television Network Advertising Guidelines (Oct. 1990 ed.) [hereinafter *CBS Guidelines*]; National Broadcasting Company Broadcast Standards for Television (May 1993 ed.) [hereinafter *NBC Guidelines*]. The ABC Guidelines are available online by sending an e-mail request to <ABC.BSP.2002.Advertising.Guidelines@abc.com> with "new info" in the subject line.

23. *Fox Broadcasting Company Advertising Guidelines* (Oct. 2001) [hereinafter *Fox Guidelines*]. In addition, Fox issued separate Guidelines for Advertising to Young Children in July of 1998. The *Fox Guidelines* were revised in March 2003.

24. *See* CBBB-NAD Case Reports Online, available at <www.cbbb.org/join/nadonline.asp> (accessed March 20, 2003).

25. National Advertising Division/National Advertising Review Board/Children's Advertising Review Unit Procedures § 2.1(A) (May 1, 2002) [hereinafter *NAD/NARB/CARU Procedures*].

26. *Id.* at § 2.2(A).

27. *Id.* at § 1.1(A).

28. *Id.* at § 2.2(B)(i)(vi).

29. *Id.* at § 2.2(B)(vii).

30. *Id.*

31. NAD/NARB/CARU Procedures at § 2.1 (E).

32. *Id.* at § 2.2(A). In 2002, NAD decided 100 cases: 18 resulted from NAD monitoring, 81 from competitor challenges, 6 from local Better Business Bureau challenges, and 5 from consumer challenges. In 2001, NAD decided 117 cases: 18 resulted from NAD monitoring, 77 from competitor challenges, 6 from local Better Business Bureau challenges, and 16 from consumer challenges. In 2000, NAD decided 98 cases: 7 resulted from NAD monitoring, 75 from competitor challenges, 4 from local Better Business Bureau challenges, and 12 from consumer challenges. In 1999, NAD decided 97 cases: 5 resulted from NAD monitoring, 88 from competitor challenges, 1 from local Better Business Bureau challenges, and 3 from consumer challenges. *National Advertising Division Case Reports,* (Jan. 2003, Jan. 2002, Jan. 2001, and Jan. 2000) [hereinafter *NAD Case Reports*].

Recently, NAD imposed a filing fee to help defray some of the costs associated with the review process. Accordingly, the complaint must be accompanied by a check, payable to the Council of Better Business Bureaus, Inc., in the amount of $1,500, if the complainant is a member of the Council, or $2,500, if the complainant is not a member. The President of the National Advertising Review Council has the discretion to waive the fee for anyone who can demonstrate economic hardship. NAD/NARB/CARU Procedures at 2.2(A)(i).

33. *Id.* at § 2.4(C).

34. *Id.*

35. *Id.* at § 2.1.

36. *Id.*

37. *Id.* at § 2.11.

38. NAD/NARB/CARU Procedures at § 2.2(B)(v).

39. *Id.* at § 2.2(D)

40. *Id.* at § 2.4(E).

41. *Id.* at § 2.5.

42. *Id.* at §§ 2.4(D), 2.5.

43. *Id.* at § 2.6(A).

44. NAD/NARB/CARU Procedures at § 2.6(B).

45. *Id.* at § 2.7.

46. *Id.* at § 2.8(A).

47. *Id.*

48. *Id.* at § 2.8(B).

49. *Id.*

50. NAD/NARB/CARU Procedures at § 2.9(A).

51. *Id.*

52. *Id.* at § 2.9. "Whether an advertiser intends to comply or appeal, an advertiser may include in this statement an explanation of why it disagrees with NAD/CARU. However, this is not the venue to reargue the merits of the case, bring in new facts, or restate or summarize NAD/CARU's conclusions. NAD/CARU reserves the right, upon consultation with the advertiser, to edit for length or inappropriate material." *Id.* at § 2.9(B).

53. *Id.* at § 2.9(D).

54. NAD Case Reports are available online on a subscription basis at <www.nadreview.org>.

55. NAD/NARB/CARU Procedures at § 2.10(A).

56. *Id.* at § 2.10(B).

57. *Id.* at § 2.10(C).

58. NAD Case Reports (Jan. 2003).

59. NAD/NARB/CARU Procedures at § 3.1(A).

60. *Id.* at § 3.1(B).

61. *Id.*

62. *Id.*

63. *Id.*

64. *Id.* at § 3.2.

65. NAD/NARB/CARU Procedures at § 3.3.

66. *Id.*

67. *Id.* at § 3.1(C).

68. *Id.*

69. *Id.*

70. *Id.*

71. NAD/NARB/CARU Procedures at § 3.5(B).

72. *Id.* at §§ 3.5(A), (B).

73. *Id.* at § 3.5(C).

74. *Id.*

75. *Id.* at § 3.5(D).

76. *Id.*

77. NAD/NARB/CARU Procedures at § 3.5(D).

78. *Id.*

79. *Id.* at § 3.6.

80. *Id.*

81. *Id.*

82. *Id.*

83. NAD/NARB/CARU Procedures at § 3.7.

84. *Id.* at § 2.1(B).

85. *Id.* at § 2.1(C)(i)-(iii).

86. The Children's Advertising Review Unit Self-Regulatory Guidelines for Children's Advertising <www. caru.org> (last updated Dec. 2001).

87. NAD/NARB/CARU Procedures at § 2.12.

88. In 2001, CARU initiated 89 informal inquiries and commenced 43 formal cases. Of the 43 formal cases, 38 advertisers agreed to either modify or discontinue the activity in question and three cases were referred to the government. By and large, CARU focused on web sites targeted to children under 13 or web sites whose operators had a reasonable expectation that children under 13 accessed the site. Of the 43 formal cases, 39 focused on web sites: five involved food/beverage; 12 involved entertainment (*i.e.,* editorials or movies, celebrities, etc.); five involved general interest web sites (*i.e.,*www.yahoo.com); eight involved consumer products (*i.e.,* make-up) two involved sports (*i.e.,* www.sportsline.com); and six involved music/musicians (*i.e.,* www.lilromeo.com). Many of the web sites contained a non-compliant privacy policy, ineffective age screening. no tracking mechanisms to deter age falsification, and non-compliant parental consent forms. Of the four non-web site cases, one involved packaging (product presentation and claims) and the other three involved television commercials (product presentation and claims). NAD Case Reports (Jan.–Dec. 2001).

89. *AMF Inc. v. Brunswick Corp.,* 621 F. Supp. 456, 462 (E.D.N.Y. 1985).

90. *Id.* at 458.

91. Pitofsky, *supra* n. 2. "When an advertiser refuses to abide by an NAD decision, this matter is often referred to the Commission. We take referrals seriously but engage in our own investigation and review of

the issues under Section 5 of the FTC Act." *Id.* For example, in May 1991, NAD referred a complaint against Nutro Products regarding the advertising of Nutro Max dog foods to the FTC after the advertiser failed to respond adequately to a complaint which Alpo Pet Foods, Inc. had submitted to NAD. Alpo had challenged superiority, exclusivity, and health claims. According to NAD, Nutro's only response to NAD's request for substantiation consisted of the statement, "The Alpo complaint is without merit and should not be considered by you as a valid complaint." *See Nutro Products, Inc./Nutro Max Dog Foods,* NAD Case Reports, March 1991 (#2857). Shortly after NAD referred the matter to the FTC, the FTC initiated an investigation. Nutro received and complied with a request for information from the FTC. The fact that the FTC began its investigation shortly after receiving the NAD referral indicates that the prospect of an NAD/CARU/NARB referral of a complaint against a recalcitrant advertiser to the FTC is not an idle threat.

92. In 1999, NAD made decisions in 97 cases. The advertising was found to be substantiated in 8 cases (8%); NAD recommended that the advertising be modified or discontinued in 56 cases (58%); 22 cases (23%) were administratively closed, 6 cases (6%) were compliance proceedings; and 5 cases (5%) were referred to a government agency. In 2000, NAD disposed of 98 cases. The advertising was found to be substantiated in 11 cases (11%); NAD recommended that it be modified or discontinued in 57 cases (58%); 2 cases (2%) were referred to a government agency; 21 cases (21%) were administratively closed; and 7 cases (7%) were compliance proceedings. In 2001, NAD made 117 decisions. The advertising was found to be substantiated in 17 cases (15%); NAD recommended that the advertising be modified or discontinued in71 cases (61%); 13 cases (11%) were administratively closed; 8 cases (7%) were compliance proceedings; and 8 cases (7%) were referred to a government agency. In 2002, NAD made 100 decisions. The advertising was found to be substantiated in 5 cases (5%); NAD recommended that the advertising be modified or discontinued in 59 cases (59%); 18 cases (18%); were administratively closed; 12 cases (12%) were compliance proceedings; and 6 cases (6%) were referred to a government agency. NAD Case Reports (Jan. 2000, Jan. 2001, Jan. 2002, and Jan. 2003).

93. NAD Case Reports (Jan. 2003).

94. NAD Case Reports (Jan. 2000, Jan. 2001, Jan. 2002, and Jan. 2003).

95. In December 1993, it was reported that for the first time in its 22-year history, the NARB had referred a case to the FTC because the advertiser had refused to withdraw a commercial. *See* Steven W. Colford, *Paper Tiger Litmus Test: FTC Gets Eggland's, its First NARB Case,* Advertising Age 2, 2 (Dec. 20, 1993). At issue was a television commercial that claimed clinical tests prove that eating a dozen of Eggland's Best eggs per week as part of a low-fact diet will not increase serum cholesterol. The NARB agreed with NAD that the commercial suggested a favorable comparison of Eggland's Best to other eggs, when the clinical study offered as support did not make any comparison between different brands of eggs. The NARB panel recommended the commercial be discontinued, but the advertiser refused. In 1994, the FTC gave final approval to a consent order against Eggland's Best, Inc., settling charges that its advertising and promotional materials deceptively represented that Eggland's eggs will not increase consumers' serum cholesterol, and that they are superior to regular eggs in that respect. *Eggland's Best, Inc.,* FTC Docket No. C-3520 (August 24, 1994). In 1996, the Department of Justice and the FTC obtained a stipulated permanent injunction and a $100,000 civil penalty against Eggland's Best for violation of the consent order. *United States v. Eggland's Best, Inc.,* No. 96 CV-1983 (E.D.Pa. Mar. 12, 1996).

Most recently, NAD referred a case involving Joint-Ritis Arthritis Pain Reliever to the FTC after the advertiser failed to comply with NAD's decision recommending that the advertiser modify its packaging and advertisements to avoid conveying an inaccurate message that the ingredients glucosamine and chondroitin provide a pain relief benefit and discontinue the use of consumer endorsements claiming extraordinary or permanent relief of moderate or severe arthritis pain. NAD's decision was upheld by NARB. *See* National Advertising Division, *NAD NEWS, NAD Refers Advertising Claims by NLII to the FTC,* (July 8, 2002) <www.nadreview.org> (accessed April 18, 2003).

96. *NAD Gets Boost From Gov't in Airline Case,* Advertising Age 16, 16 (Mar. 14, 1994). Continental Airlines had refused to participate in an NAD investigation resulting from a challenge by Virgin Airlines on the grounds that such disputes should be handled solely by the federal government. NAD referred the dispute to the Transportation Department, which wrote a letter to Continental stating: "Our resources are limited. The public would be better served if complaints against air carriers could be resolved informally and without involvement of federal enforcement personnel. Therefore, we again urge Continental to cooperate with NAD . . . in the event of any future controversies like this one." *Id.*

97. *AMF,* 621 F. Supp. at 462. AMF sought to compel Brunswick to comply with the agreement. These two manufacturers of electronic and automatic machinery for bowling centers had entered into a settlement

agreement in earlier litigation which provided that future disputes involving an advertised claim of "data-based comparative superiority" of any bowling product would be submitted to NAD to determine if there was adequate support for the claim. The court held that the agreement to submit the controversy to NAD was enforceable under the Federal Arbitration Act.

98. Codified as amended at 15 U.S.C. § 1125(a) (2000).

99. *Coca-Cola Co. v. Procter & Gamble Co.*, 642 F. Supp. 936, 939 (S.D. Ohio 1986), *rev'd on jurisdictional grounds*, 822 F.2d 28 (6th Cir. 1987). In this dispute between two competitors over advertising for orange juice, the court cited the fact that all three networks and NAD had reviewed the commercial and found it not to be misleading as partial justification for the court's refusal to expand its jurisdiction over an advertising dispute where no likelihood of consumer confusion was alleged.

See also Am. Home Prods. Corp. v. Johnson & Johnson, 436 F. Supp. 785, 789 (S.D.N.Y. 1977), *aff'd,* 577 F.2d 160, 163 (2d Cir. 1978), where the court noted the fact that NAD had previously rendered a decision. The court observed that the competitor's challenge to advertising with the networks and NAD had led it to file for injunctive relief.

But see Abbott Laboratories v. Gerber Prods. Co., 979 F.Supp. 569 (W.D. Mich. 1997), where the court observed: "This Court notes that these NAD decisions were analyzed on a case-by-case basis, looking at the specific advertisement, product, and tests conducted. These decisions do not contain hard and fast rules regarding choice of test participants in taste tests." *Id.* at 575

100. *Campbell Soup Co. v. ConAgra, Inc.,* Civ. No. 91–4100 (D.N.J. 1991). The district court retained jurisdiction to enforce the settlement agreement.

101. Council of Better Business Bureaus, Inc., Code of Advertising (2003).

102. ABC Guidelines at 2; CBS Guidelines at 2; NBC Guidelines at 1; Fox Guidelines at 1.

103. These departments are named Broadcast Standards and Practices at ABC and Fox Advertising Standards at NBC, and Program Practices at CBS.

104. ABC Guidelines at 2; CBS Guidelines at 2; NBC Guidelines at 1; Fox Guidelines at 1.

105. The ABC Guidelines state: "All advertising claims must be substantiated with scientific, valid, and reliable research. Substantiation may include such research methods as laboratory testing, clinical studies, market research, surveys, and field tests." ABC Guidelines at 20. The CBS Guidelines provide: "A reasonable basis must be established for all claims prior to broadcast. Adequate documentation must also be provided for all demonstrations, testimonials and endorsements in advance of broadcast." CBS Guidelines at 3. The NBC Guidelines require that "substantiation for all material claims" must be submitted in order for a commercial to be approved. NBC Guidelines at 1. The Fox Guidelines provide that the network will review "advertising for truth, taste, and legal requirements" and that "[a]11 claims made in comparative advertising must be documented to the satisfaction of [Fox]." Fox Guidelines at 1, 4.

106. The ABC Guidelines deal with the proper identification of competitors, permissible comparative claims, price comparisons, and the substantiation required. ABC Guidelines at 27–29. The ABC Guidelines state: "Truthful and fair comparative advertising can provide consumers with useful information and aid them in making a rational choice between competitive products or services." *Id.* at 27. The CBS Guidelines provide: "There is no restriction on commercials which draw meaningful comparisons, however strong, with specific competing products or services as long as these comparisons are fair and are based on true and adequately substantiated information." CBS Guidelines at 20. The NBC Guidelines state: NBC will accept comparative advertising which identifies, directly or by implication, a competing product or service. As with all other advertising, each substantive claim, direct or implied, must be substantiated. NBC Guidelines at 3. According to the Fox Guidelines, "Comparative advertising may not distort or exaggerate differences between competitive products or services or otherwise create a false, deceptive or misleading impression. False or services or otherwise create a false, deceptive or misleading impression. False or misleading disparagement of competitive products or services is not acceptable." Fox Guidelines, at 4.

107. *See e.g.* ABC Guidelines at 27.

108. *Id.* at 5, 43, 34, 96; CBS Guidelines at 8, 6; NBC Guidelines at 17, 7, 16; Fox Guidelines at 3, 19, 7.

109. ABC Guidelines at 10–11; NBC Guidelines at 4–6; CBS Guidelines at 21. Fox also permits challenges, but does not have written procedures.

110. ABC Guidelines at 10; NBC Guidelines at 5; CBS Guidelines at 21, 22.

111. ABC Guidelines at 10. The CBS Guidelines state: "Upon consent by the challenger, the challenge materials will be sent to the challengee with a request for a response—usually within 10 business days." CBS Guidelines at 22.

112. ABC Guidelines at 10; CBC Guidelines at 22.

113. ABC Guidelines at 10; NBC Guidelines at 5. CBS also keeps substantiation originally submitted with the advertising confidential.

114. The CBS Guidelines state: "Upon request by a challenger or where determined that a fair and thorough resolution of the challenge warrants it, CBS will forward the response to the challenger for rebuttal." CBS Guidelines at 22.

115. "In order to resolve the issues raised by a challenge, it may be necessary to require the challenger and/or the advertiser to respond in person to the arguments and data presented." ABC Guidelines at 11.

116. *Id.;* NBC Guidelines at 5. The CBS Guidelines state: "During the challenge process, the challenged advertising will generally remain approved for broadcast. If the challenge is upheld, the advertising will usually remain approved for broadcast for a grace period of ten business days from the date of the resolution letter." CBS Guidelines at 22.

117. 501 F. Supp. 517 (S.D.N.Y. 1980).

118. *Id.* at 531.

119. *Id.*

120. *Id.*

121. *Id.*

122. *See e.g. LensCrafters, Inc. v. Vision World, Inc.,* 943 F. Supp. 1481, 1501 (D. Minn, 1996) (advertiser granted summary judgment on its claim that its lenses could stand up to steel wool; court noted that the commercial satisfied the major networks' substantiation guidelines); *Borden, Inc. v. Kraft, Inc.,* 224 U.S.P.Q. 811, 814 (N.D. Ill. 1984) (a commercial challenged in a § 43(a) false advertising lawsuit had been cleared by all three networks; the commercial was not enjoined); *Vidal Sassoon, Inc. v. Bristol-Myers Co.,* 661 F.2d 272, 276 n.6 (2d Cir. 1981) (during the clearance process, ABC had objected to a proposed commercial as potentially deceptive but had cleared it subject to challenge; the commercial was enjoined by the court in a § 43(a) Lanham Act false advertising action); *Am. Home Products Corp. v. Johnson & Johnson,* 436 F. Supp. 785, 789, 803 (S.D.N.Y. 1977) (the court enjoined a commercial that had been accepted by the networks).

123. *Coca-Cola Co. v. Procter & Gamble Co.,* 642 F. Supp. 936, 939 (S.D. Ohio 1980), *rev'd on other grounds,* 822 F.2d 28 (6th Cir. 1987). See also *Huhtamaki Foodservice, Inc. v. Georgia-Pacific Corp.,* CV-02-N-1485-S (N.D. Ala. 2002) (denying plaintiff's request for a preliminary injunction under § 43(a) of the Lanham Act and noting that the major networks approved the commercial).

124. *See Coca-Cola Co. v. Procter & Gamble,* 822 F.2d 28, 31 (6th Cir. 1987).

125. *See* S.W. Colford, *Speed Up the NAD, Industry Unit Told,* Advertising Age 3 (May 1, 1989).

126. *See* NAD/NARB/CARU Procedures.

127. Codified as amended at 15 U.S.C. § 1125(a).

128. 15 U.S.C. § 45.

129. *Id.* § 52.

130. The full text of the CHPA Code is available online at <www.chpainfo.org/aboutchpa/Voluntary_Codes. asp> (accessed March 2, 2003).

131. *See* <http://www.discus.org/industry/code/code.htm> (accessed March 20, 2003).

132. *See* <http://www.the-dma.org/guidelines/ethicalguidelines.shtml> (accessed March 20, 2003).

133. *See* Rosden & Rosden, *supra* n. 16, at § 42.01.

134. *Id.*

135. *Id.*

136. *See e.g. Sunshine Sportswear & Electronics, Inc. v. WSOC Television, Inc.,* 738 F. Supp. 1499, 1509 (D.S.C. 1989) (libel action against the BBB of Southern Piedmont dismissed because plaintiff was a limited public figure and did not establish actual malice); *Audition Div., Ltd. v. Better Bus. Bureau of Metro. Chi., Inc.,* 458 N.E.2d 115, 118–19 (Ill. App. Ct. 1983) (BBB reports not libelous per se when capable of innocent interpretation); *N. Energy Products v. Better Bus. Bureau of Minn., Inc.,* 7 B.R. 473 (Bankr. D. Minn. 1980) (BBB report that plaintiff filed Chapter 11 proceedings was truthful and therefore did not constitute libel or slander; complaint dismissed); *Econ. Carpet Mfrs. & Distributors v. Better Bus. Bureau of Baton Rouge Area, Inc.,* 361 So. 2d 234 (La. Ct. App. 1978), *cert. denied,* 440 U.S. 915 (1979) ($1 million judgment against local BBB reversed on appeal since BBB bulletin contained opinion rather than defamatory false statements of fact).

137. *See* <www.bbb.org/bnd/bbbsystem.asp> (accessed on March 2, 2003).

138. *See* Rosden & Rosden, *supra* n. 16, at § 42.04.

139. *See e.g. Ve-Ri-Tas, Inc. v. Advert. Rev. Council & Metro. Denver, Inc.,* 411 F. Supp. 1012, 1016, 1018

(D. Colo. 1976) (weight reduction clinic sought injunction and damages against local advertising review board which had released statement saying clinic's advertising was misleading and unethical; trial court dismissed all claims and denied relief), *aff'd*, 567 F.2d 963 (10th Cir. 1977), *cert. denied*, 436 U.S. 906 (1978).

140. *See* Rosden & Rosden, *supra* n. 16, at § 41.01.

141. Sheila T. Anthony, *The Federal Trade Commission's Advertising Program: A Big Stick, a Keen Eye, and Some Help from Our Friends* (address at a meeting of the American Advertising Federation) (March 25, 1999) (available on the FTC Web site at www.ftc.gov/speeches).

142. *Id.*

143. Federal Trade Commission, *Privacy Online: A Report to Congress* 17 (June 1998).

144. *See* 15 U.S.C. §§ 6501 *et seq.*

145. *See* 16 C.F.R. pt. 312 (available on the FTC Web site at <www.ftc.gov> (accessed April 13, 2003)).

CHAPTER 19

PROTECTING THE CHILDREN
A Comparative Analysis of French and American Advertising Self-Regulation

RONALD E. TAYLOR AND ANNE CUNNINGHAM

INTRODUCTION

A French automobile tire manufacturer runs an advertising campaign in the United States that features infants and toddlers floating about on the tires in rainy and snowy conditions. An adult voice-over appeals to viewers' fears about safety for their children while traveling in hazardous conditions. Ironically, this commercial could not air in the manufacturer's own country because it features children in advertising for a product that they themselves would not buy, and it depicts children outside the surroundings of their everyday lives.

That children in their role as consumers deserve special protection from overzealous and sometimes manipulative advertisers generally goes unquestioned today in the United States and in many Western European countries. However, the notion that it may be exploitative to use children as spokespersons or as images in commercials for products not directly related to them is more a European idea than an American one.

PURPOSE

The International Advertising Association has spent several decades trying to foster a greater understanding of the national differences in advertising self-regulation in order to promote the "internationalization of advertising regulation" (Stridsberg, 1974, p. 38). Numerous surveys have been conducted by or in conjunction with the IAA comparing guidelines. Finally, some 23 years after the IAA's initial report suggested that further research was needed to examine substantive issues such as advertising to children such a study has been undertaken.

The purpose of this paper is to analyze and compare advertising self-regulations regarding children in the United States and in France. France was selected as the country for comparison because it has one of the most developed system of advertising self-regulation in Western Europe (Baudot, 1989, p. 13). Furthermore, France is a leader in the European Advertising Standards Alliance, and its regulations are often used as a model by other European countries. By mak-

Originally presented at the National Conference of the Association for Education in Journalism and Mass Communication: Advertising, July 30–August 2, 1997, Chicago, Illinois.

ing the comparison, the authors hope to re-open the discussion about regulations protecting children and bring to the forefront some potential areas of protection that have been ignored in the United States.

DATA

Data for this paper come from (1) examination of the National Advertising Division's (NAD) Children Advertising Review Unit (CARU) advertising guidelines and all cases involving children reported by CARU in 1994 and 1995, (2) examination (and translation) of all mentions of children in the French *Bureau de Vérification de la Publicité's Le Recueil des Recommandations* and all cases involving children reported in 1994 and 1995 in the *BVP Echo,* the newsletter of the BVP.

PROTECTING CHILDREN IN THE UNITED STATES

The belief that children deserve special protection from advertisers is fairly new in the United States. The earliest media codes in the United States saw a need to protect children from certain types of programming, but advertising directed to children drew no special attention. For example, The Radio Code, established in 1937, noted that programming should contribute to the healthy development of personality and character, that depiction of conflict and material reflective of sexual considerations should be handled with sensitivity, and that programming should convey a reasonable range of the realities that exist in the world to help children make the transition to adulthood.

The one mention regarding children and promotion cautioned that "programming should avoid appeals urging children to purchase the product specifically for the purpose of keeping the program on the air or which, for any reasons, encourage children to enter inappropriate places" (Radio Code, 1937). Direct appeals to children to buy products, to encourage children to ask their parents to buy the product for them, or phrases such as "mother will be glad to have you fix . . . all you want" (Radio transcript, 1940) were not considered problematic.

After 1950, American society's perception of children changed so that they came to be seen as distinct individuals with rights, opinions, and the power to purchase. Seeing this change as a golden opportunity, advertisers began to target children more heavily as a market (Alexander, 1994). With this increase in advertising directed toward children came an increase in public policy concerns about the effects such practices might have. In his book, *A Bibliography of Research and Writings on Marketing and Advertising to Children* (1991), McNeal writes, "Prior to 1960, there was hardly anything written on the subject of children's consumer behavior. Throughout the 1960s, interest in the topic of children as a market continued at a low level." With the exception of a slight drop-off in the early 1980s, children and advertising have become an increasingly popular topic for scholars and laypeople alike.

Most of the research has focused on children as recipients of advertising messages rather than as participants. One notable exception is the handful of studies that have looked at gender stereotypes of children in toy advertising (Ungar, 1982; O'Kelly, 1974). Not surprisingly, such studies generally have found that advertising reinforces society's traditional sex-role stereotypes.

Recognizing that children deserve protection beyond that afforded to adults was firmly established in the United States by 1974 when the National Advertising Division of the Council of Better Business Bureaus (CBBB) formed the Children's Advertising Review Unit (CARU) to "promote truthful, accurate advertising to children which is sensitive to the special nature of its audience" (CBBB, 1993, Section 2.801). In its *Do's and Don'ts in Advertising* the CBBB explains that "children are not simply little adults. Because their view and understanding of the world is different from that of adults, and their experience in the marketplace is limited, important considerations must be taken into account when communicating advertising messages to children" (CBBB, 1993, Section 2.801).

CARU regulates advertising directed toward children in three basic ways: providing guidelines, offering advice to those who seek it, and monitoring media and investigating complaints. CARU informs advertisers of questionable practices by publishing and updating its *Self-Regulatory Guidelines for Children's Advertising.* In addition to the guidelines, CARU reports all case decisions monthly in the *NAD Case Reports,* which includes the *CARU Activity Report* summarizing inquiries, prescreening submissions, and commentaries.

CARU's Academic Advisory panel, made up of academics distinguished in the fields of child development, nutrition, and children and the media, offers general guidance to advertisers and advertising agencies regarding issues concerning children's advertising. Furthermore, CARU will prescreen storyboards or videotapes of proposed advertising to see that it meets the CARU guidelines. Still, CARU does not prescreen all advertising and, therefore, must rely on networks to do so or wait until after an advertisement has aired or been published to determine if it is questionable.

CARU enforces its guidelines primarily through its own systematic monitoring of cable and broadcast television, radio, children's magazines, and comic books. Other advertisers and the concerned public can also bring complaints to CARU for review. When advertising is found to be questionable, the advertiser is notified and given five days to substantiate its claims or ten days to modify the advertising before a formal case is opened. An advertiser who disagrees with CARU's decision can appeal to the National Advertising Review Board (NARB), a peer-review panel composed of members affiliated either with advertisers, agencies, or the public. Finally, if a case is deemed to violate the law or if the advertiser fails to respond to CARU's decision, the case may be turned over to the appropriate government agency.

PROTECTING CHILDREN IN FRANCE

At what age does a child become an adult? In the United States, CARU regulations apply to children ages 12 and under. The International Chamber of Commerce, however, in its advertising code defines a child, or minor, as one under the age of 14. Most European countries have used this definition in their codes. In some areas of product regulation such as with tobacco and alcohol, a child is often defined as one under age 18. France uses the ICC Code definition of 14 or under.

French advertising self-regulation dates to 1902 with the creation of *la Corporation des techniciens de la publicité* and to 1905 with the creation of the parallel *la Chambre syndicale de la publicité.* These two organizations merged in 1934 to create the *Fédération française de la publicité.* In 1935 French advertisers formed the BVP, an organization created to "purify" advertising practice. The association's original name was *Office de Contrôle des Annonces* and it cited three objectives: (1) assuring the sincerity of advertising, (2) informing print media about misleading advertisements (*les annonces trompeuses*) that had appeared in print, and (3) rendering advice on the morality and legality of advertising projects submitted to it (Greffe and Greffe, 1995).

In 1953 it changed its name to *le Bureau de Vérification de la Publicité* and its charter to include "leading in the interest of public respect actions in favor of advertising that was fair, truthful, and beneficial (*loyale, véridique et saine*).

Table 19.1

Comparison of CARU and BVP Procedures

Activity	CARU	BVP
Issues guidelines	Yes	Yes
Offers legal advice	No	Yes
Monitors advertising	Yes	Yes
Will review advertising before production	Yes	Yes
Approves advertising before airing on television	No	Yes
Receives and investigates consumers' and competitors' complaints	Yes	Yes
If unsuccessful in negotiations with advertiser, refers case to government body	Yes	Yes
Publicizes decisions	Yes	Yes, but often without advertiser's name. Considers brand mention as publicity for advertiser.
Specific regulations for children	Yes	Yes

Today BVP membership is made up advertisers, advertising agencies, media, and related organizations. It regulates advertising in five ways: (1) issuing guidelines (much like the Better Business Bureau's *Do's and Don'ts in Advertising*), which are based on interpretations of French law or industry codes (*déontologie*), (2) offering legal advice when requested by advertisers and agencies, (3) monitoring claims in newspapers, radio, movie theatre, and poster advertising (much like the monitoring function of the Federal Trade Commission and the NARB), (4) reviewing all television commercials before they are aired (much like the network television clearance process in the United States), and (5) receiving and investigating consumers' and competitors' complaints about specific advertising. The CARU and the BVP operate in very similar fashion. There are, however, three notable differences. First, the BVP is empowered to enforce various industry codes, which CARU is not. For example, BVP enforces the French Automobile Advertising Code that prohibits emphasizing vehicular speed in a commercial. Second, the BVP serves, at the government's request, as the official clearance agency for all television advertising; and third, BVP offers legal advice to its members. Table 19.1 summarizes the similarities in the operating procedures of CARU and BVP.

The French government did not allow brand advertising on television until 1968. For that reason, French regulations providing special protection for children from advertising came much later than in the United States. The first French regulations dealing specifically with children, *L'article 6 du décret du 26 janvier 1987,* prohibited children and adolescents from being spokespersons for products or services in advertising and forbade their being principal actors in commercials unless there was a direct relationship between them and the advertised product. In addition, the 1987 law forbade advertising generally from exploiting the inexperience or credulity of children and adolescents. The BVP immediately included the provisions of the law in its *Recommandations*. In 1989, the BVP added recommendations prohibiting direct appeals to children to buy the product (although it later explained that appeals to children are acceptable when the product, such as a toy, is within the child's field of knowledge), appeals to children to persuade their parents or friends to buy a product, or appeals that undermine the trust relationship between children and their parents, their teachers, or other persons. Despite its later development, French law and self-regulation are more protective of children than is the case in the United States.

REGULATED AREAS

Table 19.2 summarizes the areas where both countries have regulations in place and areas unique to each country. Self-regulations in both countries generally prohibit misleading descriptions and representations about what is offered and how a product performs. Both, for example, insist that the actual size of the product be indicated, that items to be purchased separately must be indicated as such, that the need for batteries be stated, that any product assembly be noted, that appropriate age groups be shown using the product, and that the product and what is being advertised not be misrepresented in any way.

In addition, both countries prohibit suggestions that owning the advertised product will make the child superior in any way, advertising that would challenge parents' authority or judgment, or messages that encourage children to ask their parents to buy the product for them. For example, a 1994 CARU decision against Kenner Products' Nerf weapon series cited the company for promoting anti-social behavior and encouraging the notion that possession of a toy leads to superiority. A commercial aired during children's programming featured a "spokes kid" saying "Face it! You're at one end of Nerf or the other" as a group of other children begin firing on a child who is without a Nerf weapon. This unarmed child runs away as the others continue playing among themselves. The commercial ends with the group of kids staring into a garbage can, presumably at the unarmed child, as the spokes kid says, "Don't ya get it? It's Nerf or Nothin!" (NAD Case Reports, 1994, pp. 23–24).

CARU ruled that this commercial violated its guidelines against implying superiority of a child with the toy over one without and against misleading children as to the benefits of possessing the toy. As the case report explained, "In the commercial the clear message is that if you don't have a Nerf weapon you will be excluded rather than accepted . . . In fact, in this commercial, the import of the "Nerf or Nothin!" tag line seems to have evolved from meaning if you don't have Nerf you *have* nothing, to meaning if you don't have Nerf you *are* nothing" (NAD Case Reports, 1994, p. 24). Because the advertising flight had ended by the time CARU's decision was made, Kenner Products was not forced to take action. However, CARU stressed that subsequent advertising should be modified to avoid the promotion of anti-social behavior among children.

Both countries require that children not be shown engaging in unsafe practices and activities or that children be shown in dangerous situations. The French *Code de la Route* (highway safety law), for example, requires that motorcyclist wear safety helmets; similarly, any depictions of motorcyclists in French advertising must show them wearing helmets. Likewise, children under the age of 10 must use specified security systems inside automobiles, and when shown in advertising, the security systems must be in use. The BVP sought and accomplished a change in a print ad that showed a young child strapped into a child's safety seat but only a seat belt was used. The French regulations require that shoulder harnesses be used, and the advertiser re-shot the photograph to comply with the regulation (*Protegeons les enfants de la pub!* 1996).

Regulations unique to France. French regulation prohibits showing a child of less than age 3 consuming the advertised product. The reasoning is that such depictions may give the impression that the advertised product provides the nutritional elements and nourishment that children under this age need.

Children in commercials are not permitted to say the brand name of the product, and it is suggested that children not appear in clothing that has the initials or colors of the advertised product. However, adolescents older than age 16 and who would be perceived as such may appear as principal actors in commercials and may make recommendations in the commercial.

Television commercials may not encourage children to call toll numbers but may include a

Table 19.2

Common and Unique Areas of Regulation

Areas Common to France and the U.S.	Areas Unique to France	Areas Unique to United States
Advertising to children MUST: • Clearly indicate actual product size. • Clearly indicate the knowledge/maturity level that is appropriate for product use. • Identify items that are to be purchased separately. • Note if batteries are included. • State that assembly is required. • Demonstrate proper, safe use of the product. **Advertising to children MUST NOT:** • Misrepresent the size, speed, or durability of the product. • Imply that children possessing the advertised product are, in any way, superior. • Challenge parents' authority or judgment. • Not encourage children to pressure parents.	• Advertising for pornographic films cannot appear in theatres or media where children are likely to see the advertisement. • Advertising for any product that encourages purchasing through the mail or on credit or any advertising that features a toll call to get information. • Children may not appear in alcoholic beverage advertising. • Children may not say the brand name of the product. • Children may not appear as principal actor in a commercial for which they have no direct knowledge or use of the product. • Children under age 3 may not be shown eating the advertised product. • Telephone sales calls may not be directed to children.	• The use of program tie-ins or program characters in advertising during the character's show is prohibited. • The use of fantasy must not exploit the imaginations of children. • Advertising for medicines and vitamins should not be directed toward children. • Advertising of food must promote healthful eating habits. • The use of premiums, kids' clubs, sweepstakes and teleprograms is limited. • Advertising should avoid excessive violence. • Advertising should avoid representations of "bad manners" and promote positive social behavior.

toll-free number (*numero verte*). Alcoholic-beverage advertising, which is banned from television, may not appear in publications specifically aimed at children, and ads may not show children consuming alcohol or invite consumption of the product.

Regulations unique to the United States. Because advertising in the United States is aired throughout the programming, as opposed to French advertising which occurs in blocks between programs, American regulations prohibit the use of program characters in a commercial within their own program. Title characters cannot be used in ads within their own print publication. These regulations are meant to protect children who have difficulty distinguishing programming from advertising. Similarly, children are thought to have greater difficulty distinguishing reality from the imaginary. Therefore, advertisers are cautioned to use fantasy carefully, avoiding unrealistic expectations of product performance.

Products considered inappropriate for children such as medications and vitamins should not be advertised to children. When directing food advertising to children, advertisers must avoid promoting poor eating habits. Products must be shown within the framework of a balanced diet. Advertisements must not suggest that one food can supply all the necessary nutrients of a well-balanced meal and must not suggest over-consumption of the product.

American advertising self-regulations allow the use of premiums, sweepstakes, and other promotions when targeting children but offer some guidelines. Premium offers must be secondary to the product message and conditions for receiving the premium must be clearly stated in terms a child can understand. Kid's clubs are to be distinguished from simple premium offers by the fact that membership is interactive, continuous, and exclusive. Sweepstakes must clearly state, in terms understandable to a child, the chances of winning and offer prizes appropriate to children.

Teleprograms directed to children are allowed but are required to: emphasize that parents must okay any telephone calls; state that children will hear a message about the Easter Bunny, rock star, etc. rather than actually speak to the character; consist of self-contained story lines without cliff hangers or references to other products or teleprograms.

SUMMARY

As advertisers in the latter half of this century began to identify children as potential markets, governments and self-regulatory bodies in the United States and France began to implement policies to protect children from excessive manipulation by advertisers. The thrust of the American regulation came about in the early 1970s and the thrust of the French regulation occurred in the late 1980s.

Today both American and French self-regulatory bodies have in place a number of policies designed to protect children as consumers. The two countries are concerned about how products are described and shown in advertising. But unlike American policy, French self-regulations have extended to areas of children's appearance in commercials. While the United States bans the use of children in commercials for medical products intended for adults, France prohibits using children as principal actors in advertising for any product for which there is not a direct relationship between the product and the everyday life of the child. Thus, while the United States protects children as consumers, France protects children not only as consumers but also as actors in commercials.

CONCLUSION: DO AMERICAN CHILDREN
DESERVE GREATER PROTECTION?

Controversy ensued when Calvin Klein launched his summer 1995 campaign for CK jeans featuring teens in poses many found suggestive of child pornography. But because American self-regulations fail to address age-inappropriate uses of children and completely ignore adolescents, there was no basis for censuring Klein's advertising. Compare this to the European treatment of Klein's 1994 Obsession for Men campaign featuring waif-like Kate Moss lying naked on a sofa. Calling the advertising inappropriate and irresponsible, the British Advertising Standards Authority demanded that the ad be pulled, not because the 20 year-old model was naked but because she resembled a child. The ASA's decision was later adopted by the BVP.

As this example and the review of French self-regulation pertaining to children demonstrates, Europeans tend to afford greater protection to their young from commercial exploitation than Americans do. We can learn from France's example and should consider areas for improvement in the existing system. It is not enough to concern ourselves with marketing to children, we must also avoid exploiting children in order to sell products. Too often the fragile bond between child and parent is preyed upon in order to sell everything from life insurance to tires. Such emotional manipulation is impossible in France where children cannot be featured in advertising for products not directly related to children.

French self-regulation has the additional advantage of requiring that all television advertising, including that directed toward children, be prescreened. CARU, on the other hand, relies on the networks, which have a financial stake in approving advertising, to prescreen children's advertising. Commercials placed on cable channels are likely to avoid screening altogether. As seen in the example of Kenner Products' Nerf weapons series, by the time CARU discovered the problematic commercial and decided that the it violated children's advertising guidelines the campaign had run its course. Greater cooperation is needed between the media and CARU if guidelines are to be enforced. If it is unrealistic to expect networks to refuse profitable advertising even if it violates guidelines, then perhaps the responsibility should be turned over to CARU.

By restricting how children appear and what use is made of them in commercials, the U.S. advertising industry could help to improve its own image at home. Children would no longer be used to hawk everything from dishwashers in network spots to "My daddy's used car lot" in local television spots. No longer would tots belt out over the airwaves "My bologna has a first name. . . ." and the industry might get closer to something stated long ago by CARU: Children are not simply little adults.

REFERENCES

Alexander, Victoria D. (1994), "The Images of Children in Magazine Advertisements from 1905 to 1990," *Communication* Research, 21 (6), 742–765.

Baudot, Barbara (1989), *International Advertising Handbook,* Lexington, Mass.: Lexington Books.

Bureau de vérification de la publicité (1992), *BVP Recommandations.*

Council of Better Business Bureaus, Inc. (1993), *Do's and Don'ts in Advertising,* October/November, Section 2.

Greffe, Pierre and Francois Greffe (1995) *La Publicite & La Loi,* Paris: Litec.

McNeal, James U. (1991), *A Bibliography of Research and Writings on Marketing and Advertising to Children,* New York: Lexington Books.

NAD Case Reports (1994), "Kenner Products," April, 23–24.

O'Kelley, Charlotte G. (1974). "Sexism in Children's Television," *Journalism Quarterly* 51:722–724.

Protegeons les enfants de la pub! BVP Echos, No. 148/Mars/Avril (1966, np).

Radio transcript (1940) for "Orphan Annie Shake-Up Mug." Transcribed from Radio Reruns, "50 Radio Commercials," Minneapolis, n.d.

The complete transcript reads:

What's happening to you these days? Having lots of fun? Believe me, I know some folks that are into some fun–those early bird friends of Annie who've already sent for their new 1940 model Orphan Annie Shake-Up Mugs. You know all of Annie's friends who drink sweet chocolate-flavored Ovaltine can get these swell new shake-up mugs free, and, boy, are they beauties! Wait til you see 'em! They're made of genuine vitaware in brand new colors, a beautiful deep green and a bright flashing scarlet and every mug has a big colored picture of Orphan Annie and her dog, Sandy, right on the front. Now don't forget, this shaker-upper is a two-in-one gift. When you put the top on, it makes a keen shaker for mixing your ice cold chocolate-flavored Ovaltine shake-up. And then when you take the bright red top off, presto, the shaker turns into a swell big drinking mug. Holding a creamy bubbly shake-up all ready for you to drink. Man alive, what fun you'll have with that new shaker-upper. Playing a shake-up game with your friends and having shake-up parties–making a picnic out of every meal this summer. Think of having a delicious ice cold shake-up drink anytime you want it made with fresh cold milk and sweet chocolate flavored Ovaltine. Mmmm, what a treat on a warm summer day! And, of course, *mother will be glad to have you fix all the shake-ups you want* because she knows how much extra pep and energy food there is in every single Ovaltine shake-up. Loads of extra vitamins, minerals and other things every body needs to be healthy and husky the way we all want to be. So here's the thing, Annie wants all her friends to have one of these swell new 1940 model shake-up mugs. And you want to get one, I know, especially when Annie has fixed it so that fellows and girls who drink Ovaltine can get one absolutely free even though our regular price is 50 cents. So listen closely, here's what to do. Simply sit down after tonight's adventure and print your name and address plainly on a piece of paper, send it in along with the thin metal foil seal from under the lid of a can of sweet chocolate-flavored Ovaltine. Mail it to Orphan Annie, Chicago, Ill. and she'll send you your new 1940 model shake-up mug absolutely free. Now don't put it off, will ya. Ask mother to get you a can of sweet chocolate-flavored Ovaltine right now and send in that seal for your free shake-up mug tonight. Mail it to Orphan Annie, Chicago, Ill. I'm sorry but she can offer this wonderful shake-up mug only to you and your friends in the United States. But if you do live in the United States, send in tonight.

Stridsberg, Albert B. (1974), *Effective Advertising Self-Regulation,* New York: International Advertising Association, 38.

Ungar, Sheldon B. (1982), "The Sex-Typing of Adult and Child Behavior in Toy Sales," *Sex Roles 8:251–160.*

CHAPTER 20

MARKETING TO INNER-CITY BLACKS
PowerMaster and Moral Responsibility

GEORGE G. BRENKERT

I. INTRODUCTION

The nature and extent of marketers' moral obligations is a matter of considerable debate. This is particularly the case when those who are targeted by marketers live in disadvantaged circumstances and suffer various problems disproportionately with other members of the same society. An interesting opportunity to explore this difficult area of marketing ethics is presented by Heileman Brewing Company's failed effort to market PowerMaster, a malt liquor, to inner-city blacks. The story of PowerMaster is relatively simple and short. Its ethical dimensions are much more complicated.[1]

In the following, I wish to consider the moral aspects of this case within the context of a market society such as the U.S. which permits the forms of advertising it presently does.[2] To do so, I first briefly evaluate three kinds of objections made to the marketing of PowerMaster. I contend that none of these objections taken by itself clearly justifies the criticism leveled at Heileman. Heileman might reasonably claim that it was fulfilling its economic, social, and moral responsibilities in the same manner as were other brewers and marketers.

Accordingly, I argue that only if we look to the collective effects of all marketers of malt liquor to the inner-city can we identify morally defensible grounds for the complaints against marketing campaigns such as that of PowerMaster. The upshot of this argument is that marketers must recognize not only their individual moral responsibilities to those they target, but also a collective responsibility of all marketers for those market segments they jointly target. It is on this basis that Heileman's marketing of PowerMaster may be faulted. This result is noteworthy in that it introduces a new kind of moral consideration which has rarely been considered in discussions of corporate moral responsibilities.

II. HEILEMAN AND POWERMASTER

G. Heileman Brewing Co. is a Wisconsin brewer which produces a number of beers and malt liquors, including Colt Dry, Colt 45, and Mickey's. In the early 1990s, competition amongst such brewers was increasingly intense. In January 1991, Heileman was facing such economic diffi-

---

From *Business Ethics Quarterly,* vol. 8, no. 1 (January 1998): 1–18. Copyright © 1998 by Society for Business Ethics. Reprinted with permission.

culties that it filed for protection from creditors under Chapter 11 of the U.S. Bankruptcy Code (Horovitz, 1991, D1). To improve its financial situation, Heileman sought to market, beginning in June 1991, a new malt liquor called "PowerMaster." At that time there was considerable growth in the "up-strength malt liquor category." In fact, "this higher-alcohol segment of the business [had] been growing at an explosive 25% to 30% a year" (Freedman, 1991a: B1). To attempt to capitalize on this market segment, Heileman produced PowerMaster, a malt liquor that contained 5.9% alcohol, 31% more alcohol than Heileman's top-selling Colt 45 (4.5% alcohol). Reportedly, when introduced, only one other malt liquor (St. Ides) offered such a powerful malt as PowerMaster (Freedman, 1991a: B1).

Further, since malt liquor had become "the drink of choice among many in the inner-city," Heileman focused a significant amount of its marketing efforts on inner-city blacks.[3] Heileman's ad campaign played to this group with posters and billboards using black male models. Advertisements assured consumers that PowerMaster was "Bold Not Harsh." Hugh Nelson, Heileman's marketing director, was reported to have claimed that "the company's research . . . shows that consumers will opt for PowerMaster not on basis of its alcohol content but because of its flavor. The higher alcohol content gives PowerMaster a 'bold not nasty' taste . . ." (Freedman, 1991a: B4).

In response, a wide variety of individuals and groups protested against Heileman's actions. Critics claimed that both advertisements and the name "PowerMaster" suggested the alcoholic strength of the drink and the "buzz" that those who consumed it could get. Surgeon General Antonia Novello criticized the PowerMaster marketing scheme as "insensitive" (Milloy, 1991: B3). Reports in *The Wall Street Journal* spoke of community activists and alcohol critics branding Heileman's marketing campaign as "socially irresponsible" (Freedman, 1991b: B1). "Twenty-one consumer and health groups, including the Center for Science in the Public Interest, also publicly called for Heileman to halt the marketing of PowerMaster and for BATF to limit the alcohol content of malt liquor" (Colford and Teinowitz, 1991: 29). A reporter for the *L.A. Times* wrote that "at issue is growing resentment by blacks and other minorities who feel that they are being unfairly targeted—if not exploited—by marketers of beer, liquor and tobacco products" (Horovitz, 1991: D6). Another reporter for the same paper claimed that "[a]nti-alcohol activists contend that alcoholic beverage manufacturers are taking advantage of minority groups and exacerbating inner-city problems by targeting them with high-powered blends" (Lacey, 1992: A32). And Reverend Calvin Butts of the Abyssinian Baptist Church in New York's Harlem said that "this [Heileman] is obviously a company that has no sense of moral or social responsibility" (Freedman, 1991a: B1).

Though the Bureau of Alcohol, Tobacco, and Firearms (BATF) initially approved the use of "PowerMaster" as the name for the new malt liquor, in light of the above protests it "reacted by enforcing a beer law that prohibits labels 'considered to be statements of alcoholic content'" (Milloy, 1991: B3). It insisted that the word "Power" be removed from the "PowerMaster" name (Freedman, 1991b: B1). As a consequence of the actions of the BATF and the preceding complaints, Heileman decided not to market PowerMaster.

III. THE OBJECTIONS

The PowerMaster marketing campaign evoked three distinct kinds of moral objections:[4]

First, because its advertisements drew upon images and themes related to power and boldness, they were criticized as promoting satisfactions only artificially and distortedly associated with the real needs of those targeted. As such, the PowerMaster marketing campaign was charged with fostering a form of moral illusion.[5]

Second, Heileman was said to lack concern for the harm likely to be caused by its product.

Blacks suffer disproportionately from cirrhosis of the liver and other liver diseases brought on by alcohol. In addition, alcohol-related social problems such as violence and crime are also prominent in the inner-city. Accordingly, Heileman was attacked for its lack of moral sensitivity.

Third, Heileman was accused of taking unfair advantage of those in the inner-city whom they had targeted. Inner-city blacks were said to be especially vulnerable, due to their life circumstances, to advertisements and promotions formulated in terms of power, self-assertion, and sexual success. Hence, to target them in the manner they did with a product such as PowerMaster was a form of exploitation. In short, questions of justice were raised.

It is important not only for corporations such as Heileman but also for others concerned with such marketing practices to determine whether these objections show that the PowerMaster marketing program was morally unjustified. The economic losses in failed marketing efforts such as PowerMaster are considerable. In addition, if the above objections are justified, the moral losses are also significant.

The first objection maintained that by emphasizing power Heileman was, in effect, offering a cruel substitute for a real lack in the lives of inner-city blacks. PowerMaster's slogan, "Bold Not Harsh," was said to project an image of potency. "The brewers' shrewd marketing," one critic maintained, "has turned malt liquor into an element of machismo" (Lacey, 1992: A1). George Hacker, Director of the National Coalition to Prevent Impaired Driving, commented that "the real irony of marketing PowerMaster to inner-city blacks is that this population is among the most lacking in power in this society" (Freedman, 1991a, B1).

This kind of criticism has been made against many forms of advertising. The linking of one's product with power, fame, and success not to mention sex is nothing new in advertising.[6] Most all those targeted by marketers lack (or at least want) those goods or values associated with the products being promoted. Further, other malt liquor marketing campaigns had referred to power. For example, another malt liquor, Olde English "800," claimed that "It's the Power." The Schlitz Red Bull was associated with the phrase "The Real Power" (Colford and Tenowitz, 1991:1). Nevertheless, they were not singled out for attack or boycott as PowerMaster was.

Accordingly, however objectionable it may be for marketers to link a product with something which its potential customers (significantly) lack and which the product can only symbolically or indirectly satisfy, this feature of the PowerMaster marketing campaign does not uniquely explain or justify the complaints that were raised against the marketing of PowerMaster. In short, this objection appears far too general in scope to justify the particular attention given PowerMaster. Heileman could not have reasonably concluded, on its basis, that it was being particularly morally irresponsible. It was simply doing what others had done and for which they had not been boycotted or against which such an outcry had not been raised. It is difficult to see how Heileman could have concluded that it was preparing a marketing program that would generate the social and moral protest it did, simply from an examination of its own plan or the similar individual marketing programs of other brewers.

The second objection was that the marketers of PowerMaster showed an especial lack of sensitivity in that a malt liquor with the potency of PowerMaster would likely cause additional harm to inner-city blacks. According to various reports, "alcoholism and other alcohol-related diseases extract a disproportionate toll on blacks. A 1978 study by the National Institute on Alcohol Abuse and Alcoholism found that black men between the ages of 25 and 44 are 10 times more likely than the general population to have cirrhosis of the liver" (N.Y. Times, 1991). Fortune reported that "The Department of Health and Human Services last spring released figures showing a decline in life expectancy for blacks for the fourth straight year—down to 69.2 years, vs. 75.6 years for whites. Although much of the drop is attributable to homicide and AIDS, blacks also suffer higher instances of . . . alcohol-related illnesses than whites" (*Fortune,* 1991: 100). Further, due to the combined use of alcohol and cigarettes, blacks suffer cancer of the esophagus at a disproportional rate than the rest of the population.[7] Similarly, assuming that black women would drink PowerMaster, it is relevant that the impact of alcohol use in the inner-city is also manifested in an increased infant mortality rate and by new born children with fetal alcohol syndrome (*The Workbook,* 1991:18). Finally, a malt liquor with a high percentage of alcohol was expected to have additional harmful effects on the levels of social ills, such as violence, crime, and spousal abuse. As such, PowerMaster would be further destructive of the social fabric of the inner-city.[8]

Under these circumstances, the second objection maintained, anyone who marketed a product which would further increase these harms was being morally obtuse to the problems inner-city blacks suffer. Accordingly, Heileman's PowerMaster marketing campaign was an instance of such moral insensitivity.

Nevertheless, this objection does not seem clearly applicable when pointed simply at Power-Master. Surely inner-city blacks are adults and should be allowed, as such, to make their own choices, even if those choices harm themselves, so long as they are not deceived or coerced when making those choices and they do not harm others. Since neither deception nor coercion were involved in PowerMaster's marketing campaign, it is an unacceptable form of moral paternalism to deny them what they might otherwise wish to choose.

Further, those who raised the above complaints were not those who would have drunk Pow-erMaster, but leaders of various associations both within and outside the inner-city concerned with alcohol abuse and consumption.[9] This was not a consumer-led protest. Reports of the outcry over PowerMaster contain no objections from those whom Heileman had targeted. No evidence was presented that these individuals would have found PowerMaster unsatisfactory. Argument is needed, for example, that these individuals had (or should have had) overriding interests in healthy livers. Obviously there are many people (black as well as white) who claim that their interests are better fulfilled by drinking rather than abstinence.

Finally, argument is also needed to show that this increase in alcoholic content would have any significant effects on the targeted group. It might be that any noteworthy effects would be limited because the increased alcoholic content would prove undesirable to those targeted since they would become intoxicated too quickly. "Overly rapid intoxication undercuts sales volume and annoys consumers," *The Wall Street Journal* reported (Freedman, 1991a: B1). Supposedly this consequence led one malt brewer to lower the alcoholic content of its product (Freedman, 1991a: B1). Furthermore, malt liquor is hardly the strongest alcohol which blacks (or others) drink. Reportedly, "blacks buy more than half the cognac sold in the United States" (*The Workbook,* 1991:18). Cheap forms of wine and hard liquor are readily available. Thus, it is far from obvious what significant effects PowerMaster alone would have in the inner-city.

One possible response to the preceding replies brings us to the third objection. This response is that, though inner-city blacks might not be deceived or coerced into drinking PowerMaster, they were particularly vulnerable to the marketing campaign which Heileman proposed. Because of this, Heileman's marketing campaign (wittingly or unwittingly) would take unfair advantage of inner-city blacks.

Little, if any attempt, has been made to defend or to explore this charge. I suggest that there are at least three ways in which inner-city blacks—or anyone else, for that matter—might be said to be specially vulnerable.

A person would be cognitively vulnerable if he or she lacked certain levels of ability to cognitively process information or to be aware that certain information was being withheld or manipulated in deceptive ways. Thus, if people were not able to process information about the effects of malt liquor on themselves or on their society in ways in which others could, they would be cognitively vulnerable.

A person would be motivationally vulnerable if he or she could not resist ordinary temptations and/or enticements due to his or her own individual characteristics. Thus, if people were unable, as normal individuals are, to resist various advertisements and marketing ploys, they would be motivationally vulnerable.

And people would be socially vulnerable when their social situation renders them significantly less able than others to resist various enticements. For example, due to the poverty within which they live, they might have developed various needs or attitudes which rendered them less able to resist various marketing programs.

Nevertheless, none of these forms of vulnerability was explored or defended as the basis of the unfair advantage which the PowerMaster marketers were said to seek.[10] And indeed it is difficult to see what account could be given which would explain how the use of the name "PowerMaster," and billboards with a black model, a bottle of PowerMaster, and the slogan "Bold Not Harsh" would be enough to subvert the decision making or motivational capacities of inner-city blacks. To the extent that they are adults and not under the care or protection of other individuals or agencies due to the state of their cognitive or motivational abilities, there is a prima facie case that they are not so vulnerable. Accordingly, the vulnerability objection raises the legitimate concern that some form of unjustified moral paternalism lurks behind it.

In short, if we consider simply the individual marketing program of PowerMaster, it is difficult to see that the three preceding objections justified the outcry against Heileman. Heileman was seeking to satisfy its customers. As noted above, none of the reported complaints came from them. Heileman was also seeking to enhance its own bottom line. But in doing so it was not engaged in fraud, deception, or coercion. The marketing of PowerMaster was not like other morally objectionable individual marketing programs which have used factually deceptive advertisements (e.g., some past shaving commercials), taken advantage of the target group's special vulnerabilities (e.g., certain television advertisements to children who are cognitively vulnerable), or led to unusual harm for the group targeted (e.g., Nestlé's infant formula promotions to Third World mothers). Black inner-city residents are not obviously cognitively vulnerable and are not, in the use of malt liquor, uniformly faced with a single significant problem such as Third World Mothers are (viz., the care of their infants). As such, it is mistaken to think that PowerMaster's marketing campaign was morally offensive or objectionable in ways in which other such campaigns have been. From this perspective, then, it appears that Heileman could be said to be fulfilling its individual corporate responsibilities.

IV. ASSOCIATED GROUPS AND COLLECTIVE RESPONSIBILITY

So long as we remain simply at the level of the individual marketing campaign of PowerMaster, it is doubtful that we can grasp the basis upon which the complaints against PowerMaster might be justified. To do so, we must look to the social level and the collection of marketing programs of which PowerMaster was simply one part. By pushing on the bounds within which other marketers had remained,[11] PowerMaster was merely the spark which ignited a great deal of resentment which stemmed more generally from the group of malt liquor marketers coming into the inner-city from outside, aggressively marketing products which disproportionately harmed those in the inner-city (both those who consume the product and others), and creating marketing campaigns that took advantage of their vulnerabilities.[12]

As such, this case might better be understood as one involving the collective responsibility of the group of marketers who target inner-city blacks rather than simply the individual responsibility of this or that marketer. By "collective responsibility" I refer to the responsibility which attaches to a group (or collective), rather than to the individual members of the group, even though it is only through the joint action (or inaction) of group members that a particular collective action or consequence results. The objections of the critics could then more plausibly be recast in the form that the *collection* of the marketers' campaigns was consuming or wasting public health or welfare understood in a twofold sense: first, as the lack of illness, violence, and crime, and, second, as the presence of a sense of individual self that is based on the genuine gratification of real needs. When the individual marketers of a group (e.g., of brewers) engage in their own individual marketing campaigns they may not necessarily cause significant harms—or if they do create harm, the customers may have willingly accepted certain levels of individual risk of harm. However, their efforts may collectively result in significant harms not consciously assumed by anyone.

Similarly, though the individual marketing efforts may not be significant enough to expose the vulnerabilities of individuals composing their market segment, their marketing efforts may collectively create a climate within which the vulnerabilities of those targeted may play a role in the collective effect of those marketing campaigns. Thus, it is not the presence of this or that billboard from PowerMaster which may be objectionable so much as the large total number of billboards in the inner-city which advertise alcohol and to which PowerMaster contributed. For example, it has been reported that "in Baltimore, 76 percent of the billboards located in low-income neighborhoods advertise alcohol and cigarettes; in middle and upper-income neighborhoods it is 20 percent" (*The Workbook,* 1991: 18). This "saturation advertising" may have an effect different from the effect of any single advertisement. Similarly, it is not PowerMaster's presence on the market as such, which raises moral questions. Rather, it is that alcohol marketers particularly target a group which not only buys " . . . more than half the cognac sold in the United States and . . . consume[s] more than one-third of all malt liquor . . ." (*The Workbook,* 1991: 18), but also disproportionately suffers health problems associated with alcohol. The connection between the amount of alcohol consumed and the alcohol related health problems is hardly coincidental. Further, if the level of alcohol consumption is significantly related to conditions of poverty and racism, and the consequent vulnerabilities people living in these conditions may suffer, then targeting such individuals may also be an instance of attempting to take unfair advantage of them.[13]

Now to make this case, it must be allowed that individual persons are not the only ones capable of being responsible for the effects of their actions. A variety of arguments have been given, for example, that corporations can be morally responsible for their actions. These arguments need not be recited here since even if they were successful, as I think some of them are, the marketers who target inner-city blacks do not themselves constitute a corporation. Hence, a different kind of argument is needed.

Can there be subjects of responsibility other than individuals and corporations? Virginia Held has argued that under certain conditions random collections of individuals can be held morally responsible. She has argued that when it would be obvious to the reasonable person what a random collection of individuals ought to do and when the expected outcome of such an action is clearly favorable, then that random collection can be held morally responsible (Held, 1970: 476).

However, again the marketers of malt liquor to inner city blacks do not seem to fit this argument since they are not simply a random collection of individuals. According to Held, a random collection of individuals " . . . is a set of persons distinguishable by some characteristics from the set of all persons, but lacking a decision method for taking action that is distinguishable from such decisions methods, if there are any, as are possessed by all persons" (Held, 1970: 471). The examples she gives, "passengers on a train" and "pedestrians on a sidewalk," fit this definition but are also compatible with a stronger definition of a group of individuals than the one she offers. For example, her definition would include collections of individuals with no temporal, spatial, or teleological connection. Clearly marketers of malt liquor to inner-city blacks constitute a group or collection of individuals in a stronger sense than Held's random collection of individuals.

Consequently, I shall speak of a group such as the marketers who target inner-city blacks as an associated group. Such groups are not corporations. Nor are they simply random collections of individuals (in Held's sense). They are groups in a weaker sense than corporations, but a stronger sense than a random collections of individuals. I shall argue that such groups may also be the subject of moral responsibility. This view is based upon the following characteristics of such groups.

First, an associated group is constituted by agents, whether they be corporate or personal, who share certain characteristics related to a common set of activities in which they engage. Thus, the marketers who target inner-city blacks share the characteristic that they (and no one else) target this particular market segment with malt liquor. They engage in competition with each other to sell their malt liquor according to the rules of the (relatively) free market. Though they themselves do not occupy some single spatial location, the focus of their activities, the ends they seek, and their temporal relatedness (i.e., marketing to the inner-city in the same time period) are clearly sufficient to constitute them as a group.

Second, though such associated groups do not have a formal decision-making structure which unites them, Stanley Bates has reminded us that "there are other group decision methods, [that] . . . are not formal . . ." (Bates, 1971: 345).[14] For example, the brewers presently at issue might engage in various forms of implicit bargaining. These informal and implicit group decision methods may involve unstructured discussions of topics of mutual interest, individual group member monitoring of the expectations and intuitions of other group members, and recognition of mutual understandings that may serve to coordinate the expectations of group members (cf. Schelling, 1963). Further, brewers in the United States have created The Beer Institute, which is their Washington-based trade group, one of whose main purposes is to protect "the market environment allowing for brewers to sell beer profitably, free from what the group views as unfair burdens imposed by government bodies."[15] The Beer Institute provides its members with a forum within which they may meet annually, engage in workshops, discuss issues of mutual concern, agree on which issues will be lobbied before Congress on their behalf, and may voluntarily adopt an advertising code to guide their activities.[16] Such informal decision-making methods amongst these brewers and suppliers are means whereby group decisions can be made.

Third, members of associated groups can be said to have other morally relevant characteristics which foster a group "solidarity" and thereby also unify them as a group capable of moral responsibility (cf. Feinberg, 1974: 234). These characteristics take three different forms. (a) Members of the group share a community of interests. For example, they all wish to sell their products to inner-city blacks.[17] They all seek to operate with minimal restrictions from the government on their marketing activities within the inner-city. They all are attempting to develop popular malt liquors. They all strive to keep the costs of their operations as low as possible. (b) Further, they are joined by bonds of sentiment linked with their valuing of independent action and successfully selling their products. Though they may try to out-compete each other, they may also respect their competitors when they perform well in the marketplace. (c) Finally, they can be said to share a common lot in that actions by one brewer that bring public condemnation upon that brewer may also extend public attention and condemnation to the other brewers as well—as happened in the PowerMaster case. Similarly, regulations imposed on one typically also affect the others. Thus, heavy regulation tends to reduce all their profits, whereas light regulation tends to have the opposite effect.

The unity or solidarity constituted by the preceding characteristics among the various marketers would be openly manifested, for example, if the government were to try to deny them all access to the inner-city market segment. In such a circumstance, they would openly resist, take the government to court, and protest with united voice against the injustice done to them, both individually and as a group. In this sense, there is (at the least) a latent sense of solidarity among such marketers (cf. May, 1987: 37). When they act, then each acts in solidarity with the others and each does those things which accord with the kinds of actions fellow group members are inclined to take. All this may occur without the need for votes being taken or explicit directions given among the various brewers (cf. May, 1987: 40).

Fourth, associated groups like inner-city marketers can investigate the harms or benefits that their products and marketing programs jointly do to those who are targeted. They can also study the overall effects of their own individual efforts. They could do so both as individual businesses and as a group. In the latter case, The Beer Institute might undertake such studies. Similarly, these marketers might jointly commission some other organization to study these effects. In short, they are capable both as individual businesses and as a group, of receiving notice as to the effects of their individual and collective actions. In short, communication amongst the group members is possible.

Finally, associated groups can modify their activities. They are not simply inevitably or necessarily trapped into acting certain ways. For example, the inner-city malt liquor marketers might voluntarily reduce the number of billboards they use within the inner-city. They might not advertise in certain settings or in certain forms of media. They might not use certain appeals, e.g., touting the high alcoholic content of their products. As such, they could take actions to prevent the harms or injustices of which they are accused. At present brewers subscribe to an advertising code of ethics which The Beer Institute makes available and has recently updated. The Beer Institute might even lobby the government on behalf of this group for certain limitations on marketing programs so as to eliminate moral objections raised against such marketing programs.

The preceding indicates that this group can act: it has set up The Beer Institute; it may react with unanimity against new regulations; it may defend the actions of its members; it may investigate the effects its group members have on those market segments which they have targeted. It does not act as a group in marketing particular malt liquors. The law prevents such collective actions. However, marketing malt liquor to particular groups is an action which this group may approve or disapprove.[18] The group lobbies Congress on behalf of its members' interests. The group has organized itself such that through development and support of The Beer Institute its interests are protected. There is no reason, then, that such a group may not also be morally responsible for the overall consequences of its members' marketing.

Does the preceding argument suggest that the group of marketers would run afoul of concerns about restraint of trade? The above argument need not imply that inner-city marketers are always a group capable of moral action and responsibility—only that under certain circumstances it could be. Hence, the above argument does not suggest that this group constitutes anything like a cartel. In addition, the above argument does not suggest that marketers agree on pricing formulas, on reserving certain distributional areas for this or that marketer, or similar actions which would constitute classic forms of restraint of trade. Further, the preceding argument leaves open what mechanisms might be legally used whereby these moral responsibilities are discharged. It might be that individual marketers voluntarily agree to such actions as they presently do with their advertising code. On the other hand, they might collectively appeal to the government to approve certain general conditions such that the playing field within which they compete would be altered to alleviate moral objections to their marketing campaigns, but would remain relatively level in comparison with their situations prior to the imposition of such conditions.

If the preceding is correct, then given the assumption that basic items of public welfare (e.g., health, safety, decision-making abilities, etc.) ought not to be harmed, two important conclusions follow regarding the marketing of malt liquor to inner-city blacks.

First, malt liquor marketers have a collective responsibility to monitor the effects of their activities and to ensure that they jointly do not unnecessarily cause harm to those they target or trade on their vulnerabilities. Assuming that malt liquor does harm inner-city blacks and that the marketing programs through which malt liquor is sold to this market segment play some significant causal role in creating this harm, then they have an obligation to alter their marketing to inner-city blacks in such a way that the vulnerabilities of inner-city blacks are not exploited and that unnecessary harm does not come to them.

Second, where the collective consequences of individual marketing efforts create the harms claimed for alcohol among inner-city blacks, and marketers as a group do not discharge the preceding collective responsibility, then there is a need for some agency outside those individual marketers to oversee or regulate their actions. Obviously, one form this may take is that of an industry or professional oversight committee; another form might be that of government intervention.

Two objections might be noted. It might be objected that the preceding line of argument faces the difficulty of determining the extent of harm which each marketer of malt liquor causes to the market segment targeted. Since this will be hard to determine, marketers of malt liquor may seek to escape the responsibility attributed to them. This difficulty, however, is no different in kind from other instances in which the actions of individual persons or businesses jointly produce a common problem. If the heavy trucks of several businesses regularly ply the city's streets contributing to the creation of potholes and broken asphalt, it will be difficult to determine the causal responsibility of each business. In all such instances there are difficult empirical and conceptual issues involved in establishing that harm has occurred, the levels at which it has occurred and the attendant moral responsibility. However, this is not to deny that such determinations can be made. I assume that similar determinations can be made in the present case.

Further, though it may be difficult to determine the harm which the marketing of a particular product may cause, it is less difficult—though by no means unproblematic—to determine the harm caused by the collection of marketing programs aimed at a particular market segment. Thus, though particular marketers may seek to escape individual responsibility for their actions, it will be much harder for them to escape their collective responsibilities. Still, we may anticipate that, in some cases, the results will be that an individual marketer has met his or her individual *and* collective responsibilities.

It might also be objected that this group cannot be responsible since it lacks control of its members. However, various forms of moral control are available to this group. They may try to persuade each other to change their course of action. And indeed, this occurred in the Power-Master case: "Patrick Stokes, president of Anheuser-Busch Cos.' Anheuser-Busch Inc. unit and chairman of The Beer Institute, asked . . . Heileman's president, to reconsider the strategy for PowerMaster, which 'appears to be intentionally marketed to emphasize high alcohol content'" (Freedman, 1991b: B1). They might seek to expel a member from The Beer Institute and the benefits which such membership carries.[19] Conceivably, they could turn to the public media to expose unethical practices on the part of that member. They might even, as with other groups within a nation state, seek outside help from the government. More positively, they could praise and hold up as models of marketing responsibility the marketing programs of certain group members. Thus, this group can be said to be able to exercise moral influence and control over its members which is not dissimilar to that which is exercised by other similar groups and more generally within society as a whole.

V. COLLECTIVE RESPONSIBILITY AND SHARED RESPONSIBILITY

The nature of the collective responsibility discussed in the preceding section deserves further elaboration. Why, for example, should we not consider the responsibility attributed above to all marketers who target inner-city blacks as a form of shared (rather than collective) responsibility? By shared responsibility I understand that the responsibility for a certain event (or series of events) is shared or divided among a number of agents (personal or corporate). Shared or divided responsibility does not require that we are able to identify any group which could be said to be itself responsible for that (or those) event(s). As such, under shared responsibility each of those identified is, at least partially, responsible for the event(s). Shared responsibility, then, is a distributional concept. Each agent involved is assumed to have played some causal role in the occurrence of the event(s) in question. This does not mean that each agent had to have done exactly what the others did. One person might have knowingly and secretly loaded a truck with toxic chemicals, another might have driven the truck to an unauthorized and dangerous dump site, and a third pulled the lever to dump the chemicals. Each one did something different, yet they all played contributory causal roles in the immoral (and illegal) dumping of toxic chemicals. They share responsibility for this event and their responsibility exhausts the responsibility which may be attributed under these circumstances. Such shared responsibility differs from individual responsibility in that when a number of moral agents participate together in the production of some event (or series of events) it may not be possible to determine what the contribution of each agent was and hence to establish the nature or extent of their individual responsibility (cf. May, 1992: 39). Thus, if several corporations each make one of their marketing experts available to solve a problem confronting a regional council on tourism, it may not be possible to determine the exact contribution of each expert or each corporation to the resolution of this problem. Still, to the extent that each corporation (and each marketing expert) contributed and was a necessary part of the solution, they all share responsibility for the solution.[20]

With collective responsibility, on the other hand, we must be able to identify some collective or group which itself has responsibility for the event (or series of events). Collective responsibility may or may not be distributional. Thus, some members of a group might be individually responsible as well as collectively responsible for what happens. In other instances, they may not be individually responsible, but only the group of which they are members be collectively responsible. For example, the members of some group might agree, by a divided vote, to undertake some project. Later, those who voted for the project may have died or left the group, while the negative voters (and others who have replaced the former members) remain. Still, that group remains responsible for (the completion of) the project, even though its individual members do not themselves have individual responsibilities for that project.[21]

Now with regard to the group of marketers who target inner-city blacks, we have seen that we can refer to this as a group, which, though it does not have a formal decision-making structure, may still act. Its members have common interests; they communicate with each other regarding those interests; they share a solidarity which unites them in approving various things their fellow members do and defending those members when criticized. Further, within this group we may distinguish four situations concerning the marketing program of individual brewers: (1) It itself harms inner-city blacks; (2) It contributes to the harm of inner-city blacks; (3) It is indeterminate in its harm, or contributory harm, to inner-city blacks; and (4) It does not itself harm, or contribute to the harm of, inner-city blacks. In the first case, the marketer is individually responsible for such harm as is caused. In the second case, the marketer has a shared responsibility with other marketers of this group. However, in the last two cases, though we may not speak of the individual or shared responsibility of the marketer, we may still speak of the collective responsibility of the group of marketers of which the last two are a part. We may also bring those in the first two cases under the same collective responsibility. The reason (in each of these cases) is that the group or collective of which they are members—whether they are individually responsible, share responsibility, or are responsible in neither of these cases—can collectively act, and could reduce such harms or evils by taking a stance against marketing practices which produce or foster them. For example, if Heileman dramatically revised its marketing campaign to inner-city blacks, but Pabst and Anheuser-Busch did not, then there might be little change in the results for inner-city blacks. Hence, it is only if the members of this group act in concert, as a group, that the objections raised against the marketing of malt liquors such as PowerMaster be responded to. This collective responsibility of the group of marketers will mean that individual marketers incur other individual responsibilities to act in certain ways as members of that group, e.g., to bring the harm created to the attention of other group members, to work within the group to develop ways to reduce or eliminate marketing practices which foster such harm, and to act in concert with other group members to reduce harm to targeted groups. Accordingly, it seems reasonable to attribute a collective responsibility to the group of these marketers, and not simply a shared responsibility.

It is also correct to say that the moral responsibility of the group of inner-city marketers does not replace or negate the individual responsibility of the members of this group. Still, the collective responsibility of this group does not simply reduce to the individual responsibility of its members in that, as argued above, an individual member of this group might fulfill his/her individual moral responsibilities and still the group not fulfill its collective responsibilities. Accordingly, marketers of alcohol to inner-city blacks may have individual, shared and collective responsibilities to which they must attend.

VI. IMPLICATIONS AND CONCLUSION

The implications of this social approach to the PowerMaster case are significant.

First, marketers cannot simply look at their own individual marketing campaigns to judge their moral level. Instead, they must also look at their campaign within the context of all the marketing campaigns which target the market segment at which they are aiming. This accords with Garrett Hardin's suggestion that "the morality of an act is a function of the state of the system at the time it is performed" (Hardin, 1968: 1245; emphasis omitted). It is possible that marketers could fulfill their individual responsibilities but not their collective responsibilities.

Second, when the products targeted at particular market segments cause consumers to suffer disproportionately in comparison with other comparable market segments, marketers must determine the role which their products and marketing programs play in this situation. If they play a contributory role, they should (both individually and as a group) consider measures to reduce the harm produced. One means of doing this is to voluntarily restrict or modify their appeals to that market segment. In the present case, industry organizations such as The Beer Institute might play a leading role in identifying problems and recommending countermeasures. Otherwise when harm occurs disproportionately to a market segment, or members of that segment are especially vulnerable, outside oversight and regulation may be appropriate.

Third, marketers have a joint or collective responsibility to the entire market segment they target, not simply for the effects of their own products and marketing campaigns, but more generally for the effects of the combined marketing which is being done to that segment. The protests against PowerMaster are best understood against the background of this collective responsibility.

Thus, when we think of responsibility in the market we must look beyond simply the responsibility of individual agents (be they personal or corporate). We must look to the responsibility of groups of persons as well as groups of corporations. Such responsibility is not personal or individual, but collective. Examination of the case of PowerMaster helps us to see this.

Accordingly, the preceding analysis helps to explain both why PowerMaster was attacked as it was and also why it seemed simply to be doing what other marketers had previously done. Further, it helps us to understand the circumstances under which the above objections against marketing malt liquor to inner-city blacks might be justified. However, much more analysis of this form of collective harm and the vulnerability which is said to characterize inner-city blacks needs to be undertaken.

Finally, it should be emphasized that this paper advocates recognition of a new subject of moral responsibility in the market. Heretofore, moral responsibility has been attributed to individuals and corporations. Random collections of individuals have little applicability in business ethics. However the concept of associated groups and their collective responsibility has not been previously explored. It adds a new dimension to talk about responsibility within current discussions in business ethics.[22]

NOTES

1. Though the case of PowerMaster is admittedly several years old, its importance for this paper lies in gaining a better understanding of the moral responsibilities of marketers, rather than in the case itself.

2. As such, I do not attempt to raise far broader moral questions concerning the moral legitimacy of advertising itself. Instead, I wish to examine the marketing of PowerMaster as much as possible within the current, albeit vague, moral limits of advertising.

3. Lacey, 1992: 1. Lacey also noted that "Blacks, who make up 12% of the U.S. population, represent 10% of beer drinkers but 28% of malt liquor consumers, according to a study by Shanken Communications Inc. of New York City" (ibid.). It should be noted that Heileman was only one of a number of malt liquor manufacturers who directed marketing campaigns at this market segment.

4. This paper does not consider this legal aspect of the case. However, critics said that the reference to power in "PowerMaster" referred to the alcoholic strength of the drink. Such references were prohibited by a law passed in 1935. It was on this basis that BATF required that Heileman drop the word "power" from the name "PowerMaster."

5. The phrase "moral illusion" is not intended to suggest that those targeted by PowerMaster would have affirmed, had they been asked, that they gained the power they lacked by purchasing this malt liquor. On the other hand, critics did contend that an illegitimate form of value displacement or substitution was encouraged by advertisements such as those of PowerMaster.

6. It might be noted that the name "Powermaster" has been used for other products. Kleer-Flo uses it for water-based cleaning stations and Runnerless Molding Technology uses it for a filtering system designed to reroute electrical and nonelectrical disturbances. Needless to say, neither of these companies has been the object of protests against the use of the name "Powermaster."

7. The Reverend Jesse W. Brown claims that "African-Americans are twice as likely to die from cirrhosis of the liver than whites, and the rate of cancer of the esophagus is ten times higher for African-American males than for white males" (Brown, 1992: 17). These figures differ from others reported in this paper. I can only assume that they are due to differing "populations" being surveyed and different times during which the surveys were conducted.

8. An additional aspect of the objections against PowerMaster which only came out indirectly was the implication that the firms doing the marketing were based outside the inner-cities and were (presumably) predominately white. Thus, the impression given was that of outside whites marketing a product which might further harm poor blacks within the inner-city.

9. "'This is an activist reaction' to the product, said Heileman President Thomas Rattigan. 'I'm not sure anyone has a feel of the public reaction'" (Teinowitz and Colford, 1991, p. 35).

10. Among the questions we need to ask are: Is everyone in the inner-city vulnerable? Are they all vulnerable in the same way(s)? Are those who drink malt liquor specially vulnerable in a way relevant for the present case? Is their vulnerability the only relevant one for this case?

11. It did this by placing the word "power" within its name and not simply the various advertisements for its product. It also pushed the bounds by raising the alcohol content to the highest (or one of the highest) level(s) of malt liquors.

12. Suppose that malt liquors had harmed inner-city blacks *proportionately*—their rates of cirrhosis of the liver and other diseases were at the same levels of other people in society, whether whites, Hispanics, or Asians and whether upper class, middle class, or lower class. The upshot would be that one part of the present complex web of criticisms would have to be modified. It might still be, however, that the level of harm was unacceptably high in comparison with those who did not drink.

This modification, however, would not, in itself, affect the other two criticisms having to do with the artificial gratifications being offered by the advertisements and with the vulnerability of those targeted. In the end, it appears, the vulnerability criticism is the criticism basic to this dispute.

13. Stanley I. Benn also distinguishes between the effects of individual advertisements and "the cumulative influence of an environment filled with a variety of advertisements all with the same underlying message . . ." Stanley I. Benn, "Freedom and Persuasion," *The Australasian Journal of Philosophy*, vol. 45 (1967), p. 274. Benn maintains that the former might be resistible, whereas the latter might not be.

14. Bates refers to the work of Thomas Schelling, *The Strategy of Conflict* (New York: Oxford University Press, 1963), in making this point.

15. "The Beer Institute," *Encyclopedia of Associations*, Carolyn A. Fischer and Carol A. Schwartz (eds.), vol. 1 (New York: Gale Research Inc., 1995), p. 27.

16. In 1995, The Beer Institute claimed to have 280 members (*ibid.*).

17. I leave vague here any more specific statement of this common interest: e.g., to make more profit, to fulfill the needs of their customers, to enlarge their market share, etc. etc. On the importance of a common interest or outlook to define a(n) (unorganized) group see May, 1987: 33.

18. When PowerMaster was under attack, the President of The Beer Institute defended Heileman's marketing of PowerMaster: "The strange inference drawn from these charges is that this product is somehow being marketed unfairly. That's not true. Everyone sells his product to the people who prefer them . . . People can make up their own minds about what product they prefer" (Farhi, 1991: A4).

19. In fact, this has never happened. One reason is that The Beer Institute might be sued by the expelled member for attempting to restrain trade.

20. The example is inspired by Michael J. Zimmerman, "Sharing Responsibility," *American Philosophical Quarterly*, vol. 22, no. 2 (April 1985).

21. This example is influenced by one from Joel Feinberg, "Collective Responsibility," in *Doing & Deserving* (Princeton: Princeton University Press, 1974), p. 249.

22. I am indebted to the following individuals for their helpful comments: James Bennett, Kathy Bohstedt, John Hardwig, John McCall, Betsy Postow, Leonard J. Weber, Andy Wicks, and an anonymous reviewer for *Business Ethics Quarterly*. Barry Danilowitz helped in the identification and collection of relevant materials concerning the PowerMaster case.

BIBLIOGRAPHY

Bates, Stanley (1971), "The Responsibility of 'Random Collections,'" *Ethics,* 81, 343–349.

Benn, Stanley I. (1967), "Freedom and Persuasion," *The Australasian Journal of Philosophy,* 45, 259–275.

Brown, Jesse W. (1992), "Marketing Exploitation," *Business and Society Review,* Issue 83 (Fall), p. 17.

Colford, Steven W. and Teinowitz, Ira (1991), "Malt liquor 'power' failure," *Advertising Age,* July 1, pp. 1, 29.

Farhi, Paul (1991), "Surgeon General Hits New Malt Liquor's Name, Ads," *Washington Post,* June 26, pp. A1, A4.

Feinberg, Joel (1974), "Collective Responsibility," in *Doing & Deserving* Princeton: Princeton University Press, pp. 222–251.

Fortune (1991), "Selling Sin to Blacks," October 21, p. 100.

Freedman, Alix (1991a), "Potent, New Heileman Malt Is Brewing Fierce Industry and Social Criticism," *Wall Street Journal,* June 17, pp. B1, B4.

———. (1991b), "Heileman, Under Pressure, Scuttles PowerMaster Malt," *Wall Street Journal,* July 5, pp. B1, B3.

Hardin, Garrett (1968), "The Tragedy of the Commons," *Science,* 162, 1243–1248.

Held, Virginia (1970), "Can a Random Collection of Individuals Be Morally Responsible?," *The Journal of Philosophy,* 67, 471–481.

Horovitz, Bruce (1991), "Brewer Faces Boycott Over Marketing of Potent Malt Liquor," *L.A. Times,* June 25, pp. D1, D6.

Lacey, Marc (1992), "Marketing of Malt Liquor Fuels Debate," *L.A. Times,* December 15, pp. A32, A34.

May, Larry (1987), *The Morality of Groups* Notre Dame: University of Notre Dame Press.

May, Larry (1992), *Sharing Responsibility* Chicago: The University of Chicago Press.

Milloy, Courland (1991), "Race, Beer Don't Mix," *The Washington Post,* July 9, p. B3.

New York Times, The (1991), "The Threat of Power Master," July 1, p. A12.

Schelling, Thomas (1963), *The Strategy of Conflict* New York: Oxford University Press.

Teinowitz, Ira and Colford, Steven W. (1991), "Targeting Woes in PowerMaster Wake," *Advertising Age,* July 8, 1991, p. 35.

"The Beer Institute," *Encyclopedia of Associations* (1995), Carolyn A. Fischer and Carol A Schwartz (eds.), vol. 1 New York: Gale Research Inc.

Workbook, The (1991), "Marketing Booze to Blacks," Spring, 16, 18–19.

Zimmerman, Michael J. (1985), "Sharing Responsibility," *American Philosophical Quarterly,* 22, 115–122.

PART 4

ADVERTISING AUDIENCES

The Consumers in a Consumer Culture
and the Ethics of Cultural Materialism

Part 4 extends the questions raised in Part 3 about the protection and rights of advertisers and consumers by pursuing the discussion of ethical and moral issues often raised regarding the role of advertising in consumer culture. Beginning with the classic and very broad debate between Pollay and Holbrook, Part 4 then elaborates on some of the enduring cultural and ideological controversies in advertising. Pollay organizes the many ways advertising has been criticized: morally, economically, and socially. Holbrook's response, on the other hand, is more typical of the way advertisers respond to economic and social criticisms.

Some advertising elicits criticism based on the product it is promoting. This is the case with alcoholic beverage advertising, one of those products often considered a "vice product." Wolburg, Hovland, and Hopson explore strategies used to promote beer in television commercials, then suggest ways to help those who suffer from alcohol addiction deal with beer advertising.

Articles are presented about gender and racial stereotypes, issues that were initially introduced in Part 2. These articles focus on how advertising communicates ideologies about gender and race that support consumer culture, perhaps at the expense of alternative gender and race ideologies. Jones, Stanaland, and Gelb deal with stereotypes of males, while Kates and Shaw-Garlock offer insight into the portrayals of women.

Part 4 concludes with a look at cross-cultural issues within and beyond U.S. borders. Taylor and Stern explore the stereotypic portrayals of the so-called model majority, Asian Americans in American television.

The collection of readings concludes with a very broad subset of articles that run the gamut of controversies involving racial and gender stereotypes, addictive products, and concludes with cross-cultural issues on domestic and international levels. Implicit in these studies are broad questions of ethics on issues of free speech, consumer rights and responsibilities, and international consumer culture.

CHAPTER 21

THE DISTORTED MIRROR
Reflections on the Unintended Consequences of Advertising

RICHARD W. POLLAY

> It is worth recognizing that the advertising man in some respects is as much a
> brain alterer as is the brain surgeon, but his tools and instruments are different.
> *Advertising Age (1957).*

While the metaphor of brain surgery may be hyperbole, the inflated rhetoric so characteristic of advertising, it still contains an element of truth. Advertising is without doubt a formative influence within our culture, even though we do not yet know its exact effects. Given its pervasive and persuasive character, it is hard to argue otherwise. The proliferation and the intrusion of various media into the everyday lives of the citizenry make advertising environmental in nature, persistently encountered, and involuntarily experienced by the entire population. It surrounds us no matter where we turn, intruding into our communication media, our streets, and our very homes. It is designed to attract attention, to be readily intelligible, to change attitudes, and to command our behavior. Clearly not every advertisement accomplishes all of these aims, but just as clearly, much of it must—otherwise, advertisers are financially extravagant fools.

The applied behavioral technologies for consumer behavior and advertising research, like most technologies today, have grown increasingly sophisticated and elaborate. This gives at least the major advertiser a large arsenal of information and the technique with which to fine-tune a message, aided by an army of experienced professionals running market research surveys, focus groups, copy testing procedures, recall and awareness tests, and test markets. As Marshall McLuhan (1951, p. v) once commented: "Ours is the first age in which many thousands of the best trained minds have made it a full-time business to get inside the collective public mind . . . to get inside in order to manipulate, exploit, and control." Even if individual efforts often fail, the indirect effects of the overall system deserve careful consideration.

This consideration is all too rarely given to advertising by those most sophisticated in their knowledge of the processes of advertising strategy formation and advertisement creation. These scholars and practitioners, including those of us trained in the more general fields of consumer behavior and marketing, are by tradition focused on the study of advertising's practical consequence, sales promotion: everything that stimulates the purchase act or the intermediary steps toward that objective. Knowledge of the unintended social consequences of advertising, the social by-products of the exhortations to "buy products," is less helpful in professional school teaching or consulting. It is also potentially far more challenging. Advertising's unintended consequences are seen by many as a pollution of our psychological and social ecology, which raises more alarm and tempts a defensive reaction from those of us whose expertise and sense of personal worth is drawn from our knowledge of, and at least implicit assistance in, the processes of persuasion. Thus, the concerns of nonbusiness academics and the general public are too often dismissed with a wave of the ideological wand. Commonly we appeal to some alternative value, as in the claim that unregulated advertising is a freedom of speech or essential to the efficient functioning of the economy, hardly perceiving that this is distractive argumentation.

Not all scholars assume that mass advertising of the character and scale we now experience is either inevitable or benign. Indeed, those from a wide range of disciplines have given the matter thought, including a surprising number of individuals whose fame and influence extend beyond their academic boundaries. This article reviews this scholarly thought. A priori such a review has the potential for setting a research agenda, for suggesting public policy, and for revising our ideas about the interplay between advertising and the social system in which it operates. This revised perspective may in turn lead to an increased sense of moral duty or social responsibility for individuals and organizations, professional and academic.

WHO ARE THESE PEOPLE?

This survey of the literature encompasses all North American authors known to have written on the cultural character of advertising. While this study excludes the European Marxist tradition, the research process is otherwise a survey rather than a sampling, with no authors knowingly excluded. Those whose writings have been reviewed represent academic fields with diverse theoretical and methodological perspectives. While few of these authors have in-depth knowledge of advertising or marketing, they are far from ignorant observers. Generally, they are scholars of stature and include many who have already influenced our culture's intellectual history far more than anyone in the professional disciplines. Although the ideas reported here are echoed in multiple sources, the passages selected are primarily from those writers who are more famous, articulate, and influential.

A particularly strong example is historian Daniel Boorstin. His prolific and often profound output has propelled him from a distinguished chaired professorship at the University of Chicago, to serving as Librarian of Congress. Author of the trilogy, *The Americans* (1973), he has won the Bancroft prize and the Pulitzer Prize and, at last count, has garnered 18 honorary degrees. Some, like John Kenneth Galbraith, Margaret Mead, and Marshall McLuhan, have been honored with public attention and have had broad influence, while the fame and following of others, like Erich Fromm, George Katona, Clyde Kluckhohn, or Henry Steele Commager, lie mainly in their own and closely allied fields.

This review includes (1) psychologists who view advertising as a source of learning or conditioning, with cognitive and affective results, (2) sociologists who emphasize the role modeling aspects of advertising and its impact on social behaviors, (3) anthropologists who see advertising in terms of rituals and symbols—incantations to give meaning to material objects and artifacts, (4) educators who question the influence of advertising on child development, and (5) communications specialists who view ads as propaganda and question their role within and influence upon mass media. Also represented is the work of linguists, semanticists, philosophers, theologians, political scientists, economists, and, perhaps the most integrative of the social scientists, historians. Information regarding the areas and distinctions of some of those surveyed appears in Figure 21.1, while the names and work of others appear only in the references and consulted sources listings.

Most of the criticism of advertising comes from those who focus on advertising's social role, whereas most of its defense comes from those who emphasize its economic functions. Still, not all economists are sanguine about advertising, nor are all other social scientists alarmed. This disparity of perspectives prevents an effective exchange of ideas, as the two sides (if there are but two sides) talk past one another, raising wholly different issues and reaching judgments on wholly different criteria. It will be of no surprise, then, that raising serious questions about advertising's social role is an inherently critical process. To ponder what advertising as an institution is doing to us as individuals or as a community; to wonder if it aids or impedes rational thought; to ask how it redirects our aspirations, or channels and prompts our emotions; to assess how it may alter our values and morality; to question any of these things is to cast doubt on the social value of advertising. Thus, we should fully expect this inquiry to illuminate those ways in which advertising might be a less than ideal cultural influence. What may be shocking, however, is the veritable absence of perceived positive influence.

WHAT ARE THEY SAYING ABOUT ADVERTISING?

It is difficult to summarize the overall critique of advertising's social role without occasionally simplifying the arguments of the original authors. Further, while this summary requires a broad examination of proposed consequences, it should be clear that every author would not fully subscribe to each effect. Also, the relative importance of some issues may have changed. These caveats notwithstanding, the current nonbusiness scholarly views about advertising's role in society are synthesized in Figure 21.2. It need not be repeated here, beyond a summary provided by UNESCO:

> Regarded as a form of communication, it (advertising) has been criticized for playing on emotions, simplifying real human situations into stereotypes, exploiting anxieties, and employing techniques of intensive persuasion that amount to manipulation. Many social critics have stated that advertising is essentially concerned with exalting the materialistic virtues of consumption by exploiting achievement drives and emulative anxieties, employing tactics of hidden manipulation, playing on emotions, maximizing appeal and minimizing information, trivializing, eliminating objective considerations, contriving illogical situations, and generally reducing men, women, and children to the role of irrational consumer. Criticism expressed in such a way may be overstated but it cannot be entirely brushed aside (MacBride 1980, p. 154).

These allegations are not very different in character from the listing of unintended consequences of advertising in a major review of advertising's effects on children (National Science Foundation 1978, pp. 145–146). This report listed, among others, the "possible outcomes" of encouragement of unsafe behavior, confused assessment of products, encouragement of inappropriate standards for choice, promotion of parent-child conflict, modeling of hazardous behavior (especially malnutrition and drug abuse), and reinforcement of sex role stereotypes, cynicism, and selfishness. The only positive effect suggested was the development of consumer skills, but this tautologically presumes the desirability of socializing citizens as consumers.

The review of the evidence and arguments submitted to the FTC (Howard and Hulbert 1973) say very little in response to these charges. Despite the volume of submissions reviewed, some 105 pages of annotated bibliography, the report looked only at influences directly related to buying behavior. Submissions pertaining to broader social effects were systematically excluded, even

Figure 21.1

Select Biographical Highlights

Name	Field	Distinctions*
Barnouw, Erik	Communications History	Professional advertising experience
		Editor, Columbia University Press
		Chief, Broadcasting Division, Library of Congress
		George Polk Award; Frank Luther Mott Award; Bancroft Prize in American History
Bell, Daniel	Sociology	Professor, Harvard University
		Editor, *The Public Interest, Daedalus*
		Fellow, Center for Advanced Studies in Behavioral Sciences
		Honorary degrees
Berman, Ronald	Humanities	Chair, National Endowment for the Humanities
		Chair, Federal Council on Arts and Humanities
		Gold Medal (Phi Beta Kappa)
Boorstin, Daniel	American History	Distinguished Professor of American History, University of Chicago
		Librarian of Congress
		Chair of American History, Sorbonne
		Presidential Task Force of Arts and Humanities
		Pulitzer Prize; Dexter Prize; Bancroft Prize; Frances Parkman Prize
		Honorary degrees (18)
Commager, Henry Steele	American History	Bullitt Professor, University of Washington
		Gold Medal, American Academy of Arts and Letters
		Herbert B. Adams Prize (AHA)
		Honorary degrees (45)
Galbraith, John Kenneth	Economics	Paul M. Warburg Professor, Harvard University
		Fellow, Social Science Research Council
		Fellow, Academy of Arts and Sciences
		President, American Economic Association
		Ambassador to India
Hayakawa, S.I.	Semantics	President, San Francisco State College
		U.S. Senator
		Honorary degrees (4)
Heilbroner, Robert	Economics	Norman Thomas Professor, New School for Social Research
Horney, Karen	Psychoanalysis	Dean, American Institute for Psychoanalysis

Name	Field	Distinctions*
Krutch, Joseph Wood	Literature	National Book Award
		Editor, *The Nation*
		Founder, The Literary Guild of America
		Honorary degrees (4)
Lasch, Christopher	History	Watson Professor, University of Rochester
MacBride, Sean	Law, Politics	Chair, UNESCO, Communications Problems
		Nobel Peace Prize
		Lenin Peace Prize
		American Medal of Justice
McLuhan, Marshall	Literature	Albert Schweitzer Professor of Humanities, Fordham University
		Chairman, Ford Foundation, Culture and Communications
		Governor General Award (Canada)
		Honorary degrees (9)
Mead, Margaret	Anthropology	Curator Emeritus, American Museum of Natural History
		Numerous awards and prizes
		Honorary degrees (12)
Potter, David	History	Coe Professor of American History, Stanford University
		President, American Historical Association
		President, Organization of American Historians
		Pulizer Prize
Silber, John Robert	Philosophy	Wilbur Lucas Cross Medal, Yale University
		Executive Board, National Humanities Institute
		President, Boston University

*As of 1984. All have terminal academic degrees, and those still active continue to accumulate distinctions.
Sources: *American Men and Women of Science; Social and Behavioral Sciences; Contemporary Authors; Directory of American Scholars; International Who's Who; National Cyclopedia of American Biography; Who's Who in America.*

though these effects were held to be "of obvious importance." The criterion of importance, however, gave way to the criteria of manageability and measurability, a reflection of the prevailing scientific bias. But clearly it is not acceptable for our entire discipline to avoid addressing questions merely because certain constructs are difficult to measure. Many of the most important aspects of life elude simple measurement. Indeed, measurability may be highly correlated with triviality.

Discussion of the broader social impact of advertising certainly continues with some vigor in allied disciplines. In order to flesh out the arguments outlined in Figure 21.2 and to more faithfully capture the tone of the original works, excerpts will be extensively used. The positions advocated by those cited do not necessarily represent the opinion of the author, other academics, or the marketing profession generally. It is, however, the prevailing opinion in wider circles having no vested interest in advertising.

Figure 21.2

Reflections on "The Distorted Mirror"

		Representative Authors*
I. Because Advertising Works:	**It Is a Process of:**	
A. To persuade and introduce	A. Change for cognitions, attitudes, behaviors, and values	
B. Within a cultural context	B. Selective reinforcement of those styles, roles, and values	
	—readily commercialized	
	—easily linked to products	
	—dramatically visualized	
	—reliably responded to	

II. Because Advertising Is Characteristically:	**Its Presumed Unintended Effects Are:**	
A. Pervasive and persuasive	A.1 Profound	A.1 Bell
—in proliferated media	—social, political, cultural	Berman
—penetrating everyday life	—moral and spiritual	Potter
—relentless over time	—not just personal, practical	Toronto School of Theology
—professionally executed	A.2 Environmental	
	—hard to detect and measure	A.2 Barnouw
	—impossible to avoid	Kuhns
	—affecting all (despite myth of personal immunity)	McLuhan
	A.3 Intrusive and dominating	
	—setting agenda and goals	A.3 Commager
	—specifying alternatives	Hayakawa
	—specifying criteria for choice	McLuhan
	—prompting passivity, "copy-shock"	Schiller
	B. Materialistic	
B. Promoting of goods (objects)	—belief that consumption is the route to happiness, meaning, and the solution to most personal problems	B. Fromm
	—reification; displacement of feeling from people to objects	Galbraith
	—displacing spiritual development with secular hedonism	Krutch
	—distorted political priorities; private goods vs. public goods; gross economic goals vs. justice, peace, etc.	Leiss
	—ecological wastefulness and damage	Skolimowski
C. Advocative	C.1 Cynical	
C.1 —incomplete information, half truths, or careful deceptions	—distrust of authority	C.1 Heilbroner
	—anomie; disbelief of received cultural wisdom and norms	Henry
		Skornia

C.2 —insistent, exhortative, emphatic

C.2 Irrational
—hypnoid, neurotic compulsiveness to consume
—indulgence vs. deferral of gratification
—shortsighted here and now attitudes, with reduced perceived responsibility for consequences

C.2 Fromm
McLuhan
Schiller
Skolimowski

D. Appealing to the individual

D. Greedy and selfish
—loss of community ethic, cooperation, charity, and compassion

D. Berman
Lasch
Toronto School of Theology

E. Easily understandable, using:
E.1 modal characterizations

E.1 Reinforcing social stereotypes
—dehumanizing interpersonal relations
—encouraging simplistic social analyses
—aggravating sexism, racism, ageism, etc.

E.1 Commager
Fromm
Mannes

E.2 strong symbols, poetry

E.2 Trivializing of language
—debasing currency of community and communion
—degrading spiritual symbols, e.g., secularizing of Christmas
—thinning of experience

E.2 Boorstin
Hayakawa
Heilbroner
Nouwen

F. Idealizing "the good life"

F. Perpetually dissatisfying
—economic treadmill, rat race
—loss of self-esteem, self-respect
—inadequacy, marginality, powerlessness
—frustration, displacement, and criminality

F. Horney
Lasch
Mead
Myers

III. And When Advertising Employs Appeals to:

It also promotes:

A. Mass markets

A. Conformity

A. Baran and Sweezy
McLuhan

B. Status

B. Social competitiveness, envy, false pride

B. Barnouw
Krutch

C. Fears

C. Anxieties, insecurities

C. Larsch
Mannes

D. Newness

D. Disrespect for experience, tradition, and history

D. Leiss
Real

E. Youth

E. Reduced family authority, disrespect for age

E. Fisher
Mannes

F. Sexuality

F. Sexual preoccupations and dissatisfaction, pornography

F. Kuhns
Slater

*This classification is suggestive only of those apparently influential and ignores many others. Most authors offer comprehensive commentary beyond indicated themes. While this identifies starting points, serious scholars should read broadly.

The Subtleties of Seduction

Advertising is seen as having profound consequences, despite the fact that its intent is clearly the pedestrian one of affecting sales, and despite the fact that many of the forms of advertising are transparent in intent to even quite unsophisticated subjects. The intent of advertising, especially in the aggregate, is to preoccupy society with material concerns, seeing commercially available goods or services as the path to happiness and the solution to virtually all problems and needs. In so doing, advertising makes consumption a top-of-mind behavior. This state of mind seems natural or rational because this persuasion also provides a world view with a value scheme that rationalizes such behavior and presents itself as commonplace. Commercial persuasion appears to program not only our shopping and product use behavior but also the larger domain of our social roles, language, goals, values, and the sources of meaning in our culture.

The potential for advertising to penetrate our consciousness and channel our very modes of thinking is seen as highly likely, if not for individual ads, then at least for advertising in the aggregate. Several reasons are offered to explain advertising's effect: It is (1) pervasive, appearing in many modes and media; (2) repetitive, reinforcing the same or similar ideas relentlessly; (3) professionally developed, with all of the attendant research sophistications to improve the probabilities of attention, comprehension, retention, and/or behavioral impact; and (4) delivered to an audience that is increasingly detached from traditional sources of cultural influence like families, churches, or schools.

It is further argued that the more profound impacts of an intensely commercialized culture may be readily underestimated because, viewing the culture from within, we cannot see the forest for the trees. As McLuhan and Fiore (1967) noted, "Environments are invisible. Their ground rules, pervasive structure, and overall patterns elude easy perception." In addition, we like to think of ourselves as personally immune to advertising's inducements. This is clearly a delusion for some or perhaps many or even most of the public. This myth of personal immunity gets generalized into an attitude that advertising is of little import to anyone, a view that seems roughly consistent with the obvious banalities of some advertising. Advertising operates successfully despite the cynics, virtually all of whom feel sufficiently sophisticated so as to be immune.

> The creators of advertising can claim that no one takes it all very seriously; it is all more or less in fun. The viewer can adopt a similar attitude. The viewer's self-respect requires a rejection of most commercials on the conscious level, along with some ridicule. Beneath the ridicule the commercial does its work (Barnouw 1978, p. 83).

The myth of immunity from persuasion may do more to protect self-respect than accurately comprehend the subtleties and implications of influence.

> Advertising begins to play a more subtle role in changing habits than merely stimulating wants. . . . Though at first the changes were primarily in manners, dress, taste, and food habits, sooner or later they began to affect more basic patterns: the structure of authority in the family, the role of children and young adults as independent consumers in the society, the pattern of morals, and the different meanings of achievement in the society (Bell 1976, p. 69).

This cultural role of advertising may have profound, pervasive dimensions, and while this might be overestimated, it is more commonly underestimated. As Galbraith (1967) noted, it is hard for solemn social scientists to take seriously anything so patently self-serving as commercials. But as

Daniel Boorstin notes, the attitude of critical but callous disregard by some scholars limits their perception of the often very fundamental impact of advertising in providing us with the concepts and criteria with which we view our experience.

> Our frenetic earnestness to attack advertising, our fear of advertising, and our inability to fit advertising into old-time familiar cubbyholes of our experience—all these prevent us from seeing its all-encompassing significance as a touchstone of our changing concept of knowledge and of reality (Boorstin 1962, p. 211).

> Advertising utilizes both modes effectively—the informational and the mythic—as a socializing agent structuring assumptions, feelings, attitudes, and beliefs in the internal consciousness of contemporary individuals. . . . As a system, advertising cumulatively conveys an integrated value structure determining individual and group living (Real 1977, p. 29).

It is ironic that it is advertising's very omnipresence that contributes to its being taken for granted. Like all environments, its impact may be profound—certainly beyond the obvious.

> To think that the effects of advertising, such a potent environment in any industrialized country, could be limited to economics, is as absurd as assuming that the effects of a hot climate upon a culture could be limited to tropical diseases (Kuhns 1970).

Giving symbolic significance to prosaic products is what anthropologists describe as the magic of ritual. In this sense, ads are rituals, incantations to make inert objects meaningful, to convert products into "goods" and, occasionally, to convert the needs into "taboos," elevating their social significance.

> We see advertising actually creating and naming taboos. The most famous, B.O. and Halitosis, are archaeological specimens from an age which we might fix as either Late Iron Tonic or Early Soap. . . . Bad breath and body odor have always existed, of course, but as individual matters. To transfer them from personal idiosyncrasies into tribal taboos is a magicianly trick indeed (Gossage 1967, p. 366).

> It is clear that we have a cultural pattern in which the objects are not enough but must be validated, if only in fantasy, by association with social and personal meanings which in a different cultural pattern might be more directly available. The short description of the pattern we have is magic: a highly organized and professional system of magical inducements and satisfactions, functionally very similar to magical systems in simpler societies, but rather strangely coexistent with a highly developed scientific technology (Williams 1960, p. 27).

Advertising has influence in part because it normally addresses many of life's common issues, while other institutions seem to fade in relevance.

> The institutions of family, religion, and education have grown noticeably weaker over each of the past three generations. The world itself seems to have grown more complex. In the absence of traditional authority, advertising has become a kind of social guide. It depicts us in all the myriad situations possible to a life of free choice. It provides ideas about style, morality, behavior (Berman 1981, p. 13).

> It reiterates the essential problems of life—good and evil, life and death, happiness and misery, etc.—and simultaneously solves them. To the constant anxieties of life, advertising gives a simple answer. In consuming certain products, one buys not only a "thing" but also an image, an image which invokes the belief and the hope of having the good rather than the bad, happiness rather than misery, success rather than failure, life rather than death. And the more anxious, confused, uncertain, and bewildered modern society gets, the stronger will be the role played by advertising (Leymore 1975, p. x).

Since its impact on culture may be penetrating, we need to question the selective influence pattern of ads.

> I don't think the advertisers have any real idea of their power not only to reflect but to mold society. . . . And if you reflect us incorrectly, as I believe you are doing, you are raising a generation of children with cockeyed values as to what men and women and life and family really are. You may be training them as consumers, but you are certainly not educating them as people (Mannes 1964, p. 32).

Consequences of Commercialism

Given the position that advertising, a propaganda for products, might have penetrating consequences, much of the discussion attempts to identify just what these consequences might be. Many authors, including the UNESCO Commission concerned with advertising's impact in the Third World, readily admit that some of these consequences are potentially beneficial, such as facilitating marketplace efficiencies and helping media to be autonomous from politics, even if not autonomous from commerce. But when considering the impact on the cultural character or the modal personality, it is less clear to most observers that the effects of a highly commercialized culture are beneficial. There is no reason to presume a virtuous cultural impact, critics argue, because the institutions of advertising are inherently amoral, serving their self-interests and with no ennobling social purpose. Just as it seems unwise to assume that advertising has no long-term effects whatsoever, the UNESCO report holds that it would be unwise to assume that such effects are wholly beneficial (MacBride 1980, p. 154).

> Advertising undoubtedly has positive features. It is used to promote desirable social aims, like savings and investment, family planning, purchases of fertilizer to improve agricultural output, etc. It provides the consumer with information about possible patterns of expenditure . . . and equips him to make choices; this could not be done, or would be done in a much more limited way, without advertising. Finally, since the advertising revenue of a newspaper or a broadcaster comes from multiple sources, it fosters economic health and independence, enabling the enterprise to defy pressure from any single economic interest or from political authorities (ibid., p. 110).

At the least, advertising is seen as inducing us to keep working in order to be able to keep spending, keeping us on a treadmill, chasing new and improved carrots with no less vigor, even though our basic needs may be well met. This impact was manifest in an unusual personal admission by a famous Yale psychologist (Dollard 1960, p. 307) that "advertising makes me miserable" by an intensified pursuit of goals that would not have been imagined save for advertising. Thus, advertising's most fundamental impact may be that it induces people to keep productive in order to keep consuming, to work in order to buy.

Advertising and its related arts thus help develop the kind of man the goals of the industrial system require—one that reliably spends his income and works reliably because he is always in need of more. . . . In the absence of the massive and artful persuasion that accompanies the management of demand, increasing abundance might well have reduced the interest of people in acquiring more goods. . . . Being not pressed by the need for these things, they would have spent less reliably of their income and worked less reliably to get more. The consequence—a lower and less reliable propensity to consume—would have been awkward for the industrial system (Galbraith 1967, p. 219).

This maintenance of our propensity to consume is accomplished, in part, by channeling our psychological needs and ambitions into consumption behaviors by romanticizing goods. But this romantic attitude toward objects is seen as having serious side effects for our personalities; a social effect of displacing affect from people to objects and an alienating effect where the self is perceived not as a child of God or as an element in community, but as an exchange commodity. Whatever advertising's economic contributions, these do not invalidate concern for its influence on our personalities and values.

For material things cannot in themselves achieve anything. They count only where there is a will to use them, and whether they count for weal or woe depends upon the way that they are used. What is, in the end, of decisive importance are the intangible factors that we call character: . . . the ideals that are held up to children and the pattern of conduct that is fixed for them, the moral standards that are accepted and the moral values that are cherished (Commager 1947, p. vii).

There is a reluctance to simply presume innocence or influence on our character. This is rooted in a view of advertising as inherently amoral, acting only for its own ends and without more ennobling goals. A late Stanford historian, highly influential in his discipline, expressed it as follows:

Though it wields an immense social influence, comparable to the influence of religion and learning, it has no social goals and no social responsibility for what it does with its influence, so long as it refrains from palpable violations of truth and decency. It is this lack of institutional responsibility, this lack of inherent social purpose to balance social power, which, I would argue, is a basic cause for concern about the role of advertising (Potter 1954, p. 177).

A simple materialistic orientation without compensating values is seen as problematic, for a romantic attitude toward goods comes at some cost. As most thoroughly discussed by Leiss (1976), the transfer of feeling toward goods and away from people, the reification of abstract meaning into objects, and the simultaneous objectification of personal relations, are manifestations of this materialism.

I should like to suggest that perhaps a transfer of attitudes through the change of the semantic environment has taken place. Previously, highly emotional expressions were applied to human beings. Nowadays, they are constantly and massively applied by the admen to objects. . . . It is quite natural that when we become more and more emotionally involved with objects, we tend to be less and less involved with people. . . . In love, in friendship, and in the multitude of other human relations, detachment, lack of interest, and coldness seem to prevail. Human beings are treated like objects (Skolimowski 1977, p. 97).

The objectification of self has been explicitly described in personality theory as a "marketing orientation," where a person is mannered for mercenary motivations and has a detached view of self as a commodity.

> In this orientation, man experiences himself as a thing to be employed successfully on the market. He does not experience himself as an active agent, as the bearer of human powers. He is alienated from these powers. His aim is to sell himself successfully on the market. . . . His body, his mind, and his soul are his capital, and his task in life is to invest it favorably, to make a profit of himself. Human qualities like friendliness, courtesy, kindness are transformed into commodities, into assets of the "personality package," conducive to a higher price on the personality market (Fromm 1955, pp. 140, 142).

Intrusion and Irrationality

Advertising is designed to be intrusive. Indeed, intrusiveness is one of the concepts currently in vogue in pre-testing the effectiveness of television commercials. This successful commanding of attention makes the attempt to concentrate on the remaining content of media "like trying to do your algebra homework in Times Square on New Year's Eve" (Hayakawa 1964, p. 265). Such intrusion, first into our consciousness and then into our inner voices, distracts us from the serenity of solitude and thereby inhibits self-awareness. Preoccupied with commercial blandishments, what passes for common culture in our affluent society are sets of jingles, slogans, and selling phrases which are perhaps more uniformly known than any other creed, ideology, or set of myths.

The repetitive, fantastic, one-sided, and often exhortative rhetorical styles of advertising combine, it is felt, to blur the distinction between reality and fantasy, producing hypnoid states of uncritical consciousness wherein the subject is reduced to passivity and a relative sense of powerlessness. Being inundated with propaganda for products, only "an exceptional degree of awareness and an especial heroism of effort" can free the individual from becoming the "supine consumer of processed goods" (McLuhan 1951, p. 211). In this view, such autonomous awareness is unlikely, not only because of the monopolizing presence of commercial coercions but because their character is "anti-rational" or precipitates irrationalities. Thus, intellectual submission seems almost inescapable, given the omnipresence of advertising and the success with which its ideas, phrases, and melodies are implanted in our minds.

> And so we are denied chances to discover the value of silence and nothingness, an environment conducive to contemplation. Advertising has taken quiet away from us, has made the choice impossible. Our minds become jammed with bits and pieces of jingles, buzz words, products, ad images, brand names, and slogans so there is no room for meditation and little room for self-confrontation (Schrank 1977, p. 90).

The one-sided rhetorical styles of advertising seem to inhibit rationality and common sense, as does the repetitive nature of claims and encouragements.

> The nature of any communication in which the actual information conveyed is less significant than the manner of its presentation is, to say the least, illogical. The illogical man is what advertising is after. This is why advertising is so anti-rational; this is why it aims at uprooting not only the rationality of man but his common sense (Skolimowski 1977, p. 95).

We have become so groggy, so passive, so helpless amidst the endless barrage of appeals that "we go about our business," as we say. But the business of the advertiser is to see that we go about our business with some magic spell or tune or slogan throbbing quietly in the background of our minds. . . . Today our whole society is reeling from copy-writer's shock as much as any soldier ever felt battle-shock (McLuhan 1953, p. 557).

A vast sector of modern advertising . . . does not appeal to reason but to emotion; like any other kind of hypnoid suggestion, it tries to impress its objects emotionally and then make them submit intellectually. This type of advertising impresses the customer by all sorts of means: by repetition, . . . by attracting the customer and at the same time weakening his critical abilities by the sex appeal of a pretty girl; . . . by terrorizing him with (a) threat; . . . or yet again by stimulating daydreams about a sudden change in one's whole course of life. All these methods are essentially irrational; they have nothing to do with the qualities of the merchandise, and they smother and kill the critical capacities of the customer like an opiate or outright hypnosis. They give him a certain satisfaction by their daydreaming qualities just as the movies do, but at the same time they increase his feeling of smallness and powerlessness (Fromm 1976, p. 110).

Mirroring and Modeling

Advertising models a pattern of behavior that is held out to be "the good life," with the props, of course, for sale, and this is shown to be the ideal for all to strive toward. Indeed, the lifestyles displayed are ideal from a consumption perspective, and they probably provide a fair portrayal of a materialist's hedonic conception of utopia or heaven. Such conceptions may be increasingly common and unquestioned. As Potter (1954) notes, the stimulation and rehearsal of materialistic drives and emulative anxieties inevitably involve processes of validation, sanctioning, and standardization of the drives as accepted criteria of social value.

But the behaviors displayed often appear less than ideal judged from other perspectives. To most observers, the image presented in the cultural mirror of advertising is not unambiguously worth imitating. Even if it were, imitation requires some effort, perhaps frustrating, and the prior acceptance of an unworthiness of one's own life experiences.

Strictly considered, however, modern advertising seeks to promote not so much self-indulgence as self-doubt. It seeks to create needs, not to fulfill them; to generate new anxieties instead of allaying old ones. By surrounding the consumer with images of the good life, . . . the propaganda of commodities simultaneously makes him acutely unhappy with his lot. By fostering grandiose aspirations, it also fosters self-denigration and self-contempt (Lasch 1978, p. 180).

It addresses itself to the spiritual desolation of modern life and proposes consumption as the cure. It not only promises to palliate all the old unhappiness to which flesh is heir; it creates or exacerbates new forms of unhappiness—personal insecurity, status anxiety, anxiety in parents. . . . Advertising institutionalizes envy and its attendant anxieties (ibid., p. 73).

Whether or not people are very successful in pursuing the ideals offered, they may more easily suffer self-denigration and doubt. By constantly showing us that the grass seems greener elsewhere, we're led to look askance at our immediate environment and experience. We may not be sure where the action is, but we suspect it's almost always somewhere else.

This fear that advertising instills a sense of inadequacy has been particularly expressed with respect to women's self-concepts.

> Advertisers in general bear a large part of the responsibility for the deep feelings of inadequacy that drive women to psychiatrists, pills, or the bottle. You keep telling us over and over that if we could use that or have this or look like that, we would be forever desirable, forever happy. So we spend our time worrying over the grey streak or the extra pound or the dry skin instead of our minds, our hearts, and our fellow men (Mannes 1964, p. 31).

Women are not the only segment that feels stress when confronted by advertising imagery. The elderly, like other minorities not glamorized in advertising, have self-concepts threatened by the gospel of advertising.

> The exploitation of age, fear, and social acceptance are so closely interwoven that it is difficult to separate them for the purposes of examination. But exploited they are, ruthlessly and continually wearing away at this image we have of ourselves. Our society's values are being corrupted by advertising's insistence on the equation: Youth equals popularity, popularity equals success, success equals happiness (Fisher 1968, p. 117).

We are all potential victims of the invidious comparisons of reality to the world seen in advertising. Once convinced that the grass is greener elsewhere, one's own life pales in comparison and seems a life half-lived.

> So people do worry, feel inferior, inadequate, guilty. They sense that they live without living, that life runs through their hands like sand (Fromm 1955, p. 166).

> Advertising, using "ideal types," can lead the receiver to be dissatisfied with the realities of his everyday world—his wife, his friends, his job, even his life itself. Fantasies are a loaded gun. They *may* sweeten life and advance culture; they *may* also destroy life in a reckless pursuit of impossible accomplishments (Toronto School of Theology 1972, p. 22).

Simplistic, symbolic stereotypes, chosen for their clarity and conciseness, serve as poor models and inhibit sympathetic understanding of individual differences. This position has been articulated in detail regarding the portrayal of women, but the problem is universal, as ads can reinforce stereotypes for not just the sexes, but also for races, ages, occupations, family relations, etc. To the extent that these images are disrespectful or unworthy of emulation, they are socially divisive.

> Advertisers should be made much more sensitive to the fall-out from their ads (using strong stereotypes). . . . Such advertising is disseminating offensive and deleterious images which cannot be laughed off as mere harmless buffoonery (ibid., p. 17).

Few would argue that advertising faithfully mirrors reality. What are the supposed consequences of confronting the imagery in the mirror of advertising? What strains are felt facing the distortions inherent in selective feedback? While some worry about mass persuasion creating conformity, more worry more about the nature of norms that we may be conforming to. One fear is that the advertising system will create the kind of consumer citizen it seems to assume or prefer.

> [These would be] insatiably desiring, infinitely plastic, totally passive, and always a little bit sleepy; unpredictably labile and disloyal (to products); basically wooly-minded (Henry 1963, p. 79).

> American society, as popular advertisements portrayed it, was a nightmare of fear and jealousy, gossip and slander, envy and ambition, greed and lust. . . . The typical American, as they pictured him, lived in a torment of anxiety and cupidity and regulated his conduct entirely by ulterior considerations. . . . To the advertisers nothing was sacred and nothing private; they levied impartially upon filial devotion, marriage, religion, health, and cleanliness. . . . Love, as they portrayed it, was purely competitive. . . . Friendship, too, was for sale . . . (Commager 1950, pp. 416–417).

Social Change and Social Problems

The education to abundance by advertising has already, it is claimed, induced cultural change.

> Commercials have worked—with success—toward revision of many traditional tenets of our society. As we have seen, reverence for nature has been replaced by a determination to process it. Thrift has been replaced by the duty to buy. The work ethic has been replaced by the consumption ethic. . . . Modesty has been exorcised with help from the sexual sell. Restraint of ego has lost standing (Barnouw 1978, p. 98).

Ironically, commercials often romanticize the life being lost, just as museums encapsulate ways of life no longer possible.

> This background texture is often composed of traditional images of well-being drawn from social situations which have largely disappeared from everyday life: a slower pace of life, quiet and serenity, open space, and closeness to the natural environment (images of rural life); contributing to the happiness of loved ones (images of family life); attainment of goals set in accordance with personal rather than institutional demands (images of success in noninstitutional settings); a sense of familiarity and security in purchasing goods (images of craft skills); a concern for quality and good judgment (images of discerning tastes) (Leiss 1976, p. 89).

In most western cultures, families are nearly sacred and seen as the basic social unit. Yet, family composition and character are changing for many social reasons. Nowhere may interpersonal relations be more affected by advertising than in the home, as the roles of both women and children as consumers get expanded and redefined.

> The advertising industry thus encourages the pseudo-emancipation of women, flattering them with its insinuating reminder, "You've come a long way, baby," and disguising the freedom to consume as genuine autonomy. Similarly it flatters and glorifies youth in the hope of elevating young people to the status of full-fledged consumers in their own right (Lasch 1978, p. 74).

> If advertising has invaded the judgment of children, it has also forced its way into the family, an insolent usurper of parental function, degrading parents to mere intermediaries between their children and the market. This indeed is a social revolution in our time! (Henry 1963, p. 76)

Relations with neighbors, the proverbial Joneses we strive to keep up with, are increasingly based on envy, emulation, and competition (Krutch 1959, p. 34). But social competition can turn asocial and precipitate violence and theft.

> Two processes could be involved in this type of response. First, the inaccessibility of the products being offered may create in some viewers feelings of frustration sufficient to make them engage in antisocial acts. Second, the arousal process associated with the ad itself may have behavioral consequences about which very little is known. Much advertising is designed to gain attention and build positive attitudes to brands essentially by a tension-arousal and tension-reduction process. . . . If, for a number of reasons, frustration is an outcome of such a process, it is possible . . . that aggressive acts of one kind or another may follow (Myers 1978, p. 176).

Other social problems that have been linked to advertising are those of ecology and pornography. Since there is rarely consumption without waste and unintended by-products, promotion of consumption also promotes pollution.

> The squandering of resources only begins the problem. The consumption hinge which television has done so much to push has been fouling air, water, roads, streets, fields, and forests—a trend we failed or declined to recognize until almost irreversible. It has given us garbage statistics as staggering as our consumption statistics, and closely related to them (Barnouw 1978, p. 156).

Advertising, for almost as long as it has existed, has used some sort of sexual sell, sometimes promising seductive capacities, sometimes more simply attracting our attention with sexual stimuli, even if irrelevant to the product or the selling point. This provocation, while less graphic than more extreme pornography, is far more public in exposure. The difficulty seems to be that these sexual stimuli are frequent, very hard to avoid, and employed for a broad range of products. This makes them inevitably offensive to some and potentially jading. To all, advertising is more of a tease than a whore, for sexual stimulation is moderated and channeled. As Slater (1970) discusses, a modest arousal commands our attention and can be harnessed for instrumental purposes, while too strong an arousal might not. For at least some of the public, however, sexual ads represent a challenge to standards of decency and are in a real sense pornographic. Not everyone enjoys confronting near nudes on their streets' billboards or seeing things that flaunt conventional propriety on their living room TV. Certainly conventions of intimacy are frequently violated. Barnouw (1978, p. 98) notes as an example that we now see women caressing their bodies in showers with a frequency and reverence of attention that makes "self-love a consecrated ritual." This would have been unheard of only a few years ago. So too with the TV selling of women's sanitary products. Standards of public decency have changed much in the twentieth century, and advertising has been one of the elements contributing to changed norms.

It is also argued that our capacities for political responsiveness to social problems like these may be reduced by virtue of living in a commercial culture, as consumers grow indifferent to either communications generally or the plight of others in their communities.

Exhortations to buy assail everyone from every possible direction. Subways, highways, the airwaves, the mail, and the sky itself (skywriting) are vehicles for advertising's unrelenting offensives. The total indifference with which advertising treats any political or social event, insisting on intruding no matter what else is being presented, reduces all social phenomena to bizarre and meaningless happenings. . . . The result is individual passivity, a state of inertia that precludes action (Schiller 1973, p. 25).

Encouraged in our inclination to self-centeredness, our personal political priorities seem to reflect private economic goals with diminished counterbalancing social consciences. Our collective political priorities shift to economic goals more exclusively, despite our lip service that doing so is simplistic. We tolerate higher and higher levels of unemployment and welfare needs as long as sales and profits are maintained by aggregate consumer demand. We maximize GNP, with little concern for economic justice.

Every feature and facet of every product having been studied for selling points, these are then described with talent, gravity, and an aspect of profound concern as the source of health, happiness, social achievement, or improved community standing. Even minor qualities of unimportant commodities are enlarged upon with solemnity which would not be unbecoming in an announcement of the combined return of Christ and all the apostles. . . . The consequence is that while goods become ever more abundant, they do not seem to be any less important. On the contrary, it requires an act of will to imagine that anything else is so important. Morally, we agree that the supply of goods is not a measure of human achievement; in fact, we take for granted that it will be so regarded (Galbraith 1967, p. 219).

Of course, if propaganda for products is a concern to the cultures within which it has gradually evolved, it is even more threatening as a cultural intervention in economically less developed societies.

Advertising is seen by many as a threat to the cultural identity and self-realization of many developing countries: it brings to many people alien ethical values; it may deviate consumer demands in developing countries to areas which can inhibit development priorities; it affects and can often deform ways of life and lifestyles (MacBride 1980, p. 111).

Credibility, Cynicism, and Community

Language is of vital cultural significance. The ability to trust in the validity of what is comprehended verbally is a cornerstone of one's mode of acting in the world—the ability to accumulate knowledge, build community, and establish a relationship with God. These are possible only with faith in words. Words can be poetry for everyone; the richness of language can, with inspiration, express our passions, politics, praise, and prayers.

Our language is potentially affected by advertising in two ways. Advertising provides us with vocabulary: a set of words and the concepts they express with which we structure our perceptions and judgments, defining in large measure how "reality" is conceived. All language does this. What advertising does is give some words and concepts greater emphasis. But it also affects the credibility of language, and so simultaneously cheapens its own currency.

Poetic language is used so constantly and relentlessly for the purposes of salesmanship that it has become almost impossible to say anything with enthusiasm or joy or conviction without running into the danger of sounding as if you were selling something.

To repeat, advertising is a symbol-manipulating occupation. The symbols of fashion and elegance are used to glamorize clothing and cosmetics. The symbols of youthful gaiety sell soft drinks and candy bars. The symbols of adventure and sportsmanship are used to promote cigarettes and liquor. . . . Advertising is a tremendous creator and devourer of symbols. Even the symbols of patriotism are used for the purposes of salesmanship. . . . Not even the symbols of religion are off limits—Christmas and Easter are so strenuously exploited commercially that they almost lose their religious significance (Hayakawa 1964, pp. 268–269).

Now we pay intellectual talent a high price to amplify ambiguities, distort thought, and bury reality. All languages are deductive systems with a vast truth-telling potential imbedded in vocabulary, syntax, and morphology, yet no language is so perfect that men may not use it for the opposite purpose. One of the discoveries of the twentieth century is the enormous variety of ways of compelling language to lie (Henry 1963, p. 91).

Because virtually all citizens seem to recognize this tendency of ad language to distort, advertising seems to turn us into a community of cynics, and we doubt advertisers, the media, and authority in all its forms. Thus, we may also distrust other received wisdoms from political authorities, community elders, religious leaders, and teachers of all kinds. As Heilbroner (1976, p. 113) wondered: "How strong, deep, or sustaining can be the values generated by a civilization that generates a ceaseless flow of half-truths and careful deceptions?"

In fact, perhaps one of the most powerful effects of television has been to teach a national tolerance of falsehood, exaggeration, and distortion. Parents who ask their children to tell the truth must explain that of course a certain cereal will not transform them into great athletes, as the highly paid announcer says, nor will the drug mentioned really cure hemorroids, or cancer, or arthritis. The announcer is really lying. . . . Somehow the parent must explain that truth is to be expected of the child individually, but that a huge industry can be based on falsity, exaggeration, and distortion (Skornia 1965, p. 158).

Riesman, Glazier, and Denny (1950, p. 294) once asked: "Isn't it possible that advertising as a whole is a fantastic fraud, presenting an image of America taken seriously by no one?" It may be possible, despite industry attempts to attain credibility, but even frauds have serious consequences. The consequence of extreme cynicism, the rejection or doubt of all offered values, is the norm-lessness known as anomie. This faithless position trusts no one and no word. Without a reliance on words and a faith in truth, we lack the mortar for social cohesion. Without trustworthy communication, there is no communion, no community, only an aggregation of increasingly isolated individuals, alone in the mass.

There was a time not too long ago without radios and televisions, . . . signs, bumper stickers, and the everpresent announcements indicating price increases or special sales. There was a time without the advertisements which now cover whole cities with words. . . . The result is that the main function of the word, communication, is no longer realized. The word no longer communicates, no longer fosters communion, no longer creates community, and therefore no longer gives life. The word no longer offers trustworthy ground on which people can meet each other and build society (Nouwen 1980, p. 22).

Ironically, the anomic isolation of the individual creates some needs that well-advertised goods might meet. Identification with society, or at least the appropriation of lifestyle roles therein, is easily affected. It requires only the wit to buy recognized brands with symbolic value. Today, such brands, badges providing identity, are proudly displayed on shoes and shirts, on pants and hats—from tip to toe, from fronts to backs.

> To use a brand of car, drink, smoke, or food that is nationally advertised gives a man the feeling that he belongs to something bigger than himself. He is part of a process or a culture that contains and nourishes him. And the irrational basis of the appeals made to him by the ads reinforces his sense of mystic communion (McLuhan 1953, p. 555).

Rites, Religion, and Morality

The criticism of advertising on moral grounds, seeing it often as a social force opposed to the values of religion, is not new. Indeed, such observations were probably more frequent and came from more varied sources at the turn of the century. The emergence of the more secular, urban, and mediated society stood in some contrast to the preceding gilded age. Here, for example, is the thought on vulgar advertising by a copywriter/poet writing in a magazine of the old style, a literary journal for the "gentle reader."

> On the moral side, it is thoroughly false and harmful. It breeds vulgarity, hypnotizes the imagination and the will, fosters covetousness, envy, hatred, and underhand competition (Logan 1907, p. 333).

Spiritually based observations are probably less frequent in today's more secular society, but commentary is still very evident in major places, as witness those below by presidents of colleges, major theologians, schools of theology, etc. Their concerns have intensified because of two features of advertising in the postwar era. Seeing advertising promoting not only goods but a whole life-style and accompanying rationalizing attitudes, they see it as moral (or immoral) instruction that contains injunctions about how life should be led. Because they also witness this instruction being aimed and delivered to children, primarily through television, they see this secular conditioning as directly competitive with the instruction and ideals of religious teachings. Hence, they see the prideful self-interest of the commercial creed as impeding spiritual development. Faith in litanies such as, "Me, I'm the one. I deserve a break today! I'll go for the gusto, and taste the good life," is hardly conducive to reverence, humility, or grace.

It shouldn't surprise us that the temptations to which the flesh is heir are seen as problematic. Nor then should we be surprised when the persistent, emphatic presentation of these temptations is seen as seductive to the soul, the promising of immediate pleasures in lieu of the rewards of a spiritual life, which seem more remote, even if potentially far richer and enduring. "Love things above all else, learn to want more and more, waste rather than conserve, spend what you do not have" is a repugnant injunction, but, as Krutch (1959, p. 37) notes, it is repugnant in part because we realize just how vulnerable we are to responding to it.

We are called in this way at an early age. Our commercial education begins early with jingles, slogans, and catch phrases, the total commercial catechism, so that children learn the "rite words in rote order."

The slogans, catchwords, values, mottoes, and other lessons tattooed on young minds even before young people learn to read are not educational but commercial. They displace, contradict, and cancel, in many cases, in advance, those lessons and values which education seeks and will seek at public expense to teach and inculcate (Skornia 1965, p. 158).

Advertising commonly employs direct exhortations, literally a series of commandments, a secular litany that Barzun (1946, p. 53) identified as the "revealed religion of the twentieth century."

(This is) usurpation of moral instruction by cynical television advertisers. . . . Schlitz, a firm with license to brew but none to preach, intones, "You only go around once in life; therefore, get all the gusto you can!" These are not statements about beer, but a theological claim and moral injunction (Silber 1982, p. 203).

Much of modern advertising offers a display of lifestyle attitudes as its focal point, so this is one of several possible examples of such exhortation toward unconflicted self-indulgence. Of course, the temptations are rarely presented in a way that would make their moral character too obvious.

Lust, sloth, greed and pride. . . . In the advertising community these words are frowned upon. They have a bad connotation, so they must be changed. Lust becomes the desire to be sexually attractive. Certainly no one can complain if a woman desires to be sexually attractive; it is her birthright. Sloth becomes the desire for leisure—for rest and recreation—and certainly all of us are entitled to that. Greed becomes the desire to enjoy the good things of this world. Why were they put here if not for us to enjoy? Pride, of course, becomes the desire for social status (Mayer 1961, p. 128).

The common use of these four of the seven deadly sins makes the effective morality of materialism, the gospel of goods, suspect in the eyes of those faithful to almost any spiritual creed. The Christian perspective on materialism has its roots in Biblical warnings about the spiritual bankruptcy of self-indulgence, and the socially corruptive consequences of its practice.

Self-indulgence is the opposite of the Spirit. . . . When self-indulgence is at work, the results are obvious; fornication, gross indecency, and sexual irresponsibility; idolatry and sorcery; feuds and wrangling, jealousy, bad temper, and quarrels; disagreements, factions, envy; drunkenness, orgies, and similar things. . . . What the Spirit brings is very different: love, joy, peace, patience, kindness, goodness, trustfulness, gentleness, and self-control . . . if he sows in the field of self-indulgence, he will get a harvest of corruption (Gal. 5:17–23; 6:8).

Advertising also seems subversive of morality when judged from the perspective of a secular liberal humanism.

If I were asked to name the deadliest subversive force within capitalism, the single greatest source of its waning morality—I would without hesitation name advertising. How else should one identify a force that debases language, drains thought, and undoes dignity? (Heilbroner 1981, p. 40)

WHAT RESEARCH IS IN ORDER?

It is not clear now how to separate cause and effect when discussing the relation between advertising and social character. Historians recognize the complexities of our evolution as a society and point out that our culture had materialistic leanings long before the emergence of modern advertising. As modern advertising emerged around the turn of the century, many other aspects of society were also in flux—most notably urbanization, industrial expansion, geographic and status mobility, splintering of the extended family, increases in literacy and education, etc. See Boorstin (1973) for a particularly broad perspective, or any of several excellent treatments more focused on advertising by Fox (1984), Pope (1983), Potter (1954), or Schudson (1984).

None of the critics cited would argue that advertising alone is responsible for the conditions discussed, corrupting an otherwise innocent and perfect culture and precipitating a condition previously nonexistent. Even the neo-Marxist historian of advertising (Ewen 1976), in an otherwise flawed work, recognized this. Whatever their focus or theoretical bent, even the most critical historians would allow that there were many preconditions to the emergence of advertising and that advertising has evolved coincident with other social changes which make it impossible to determine causality unambiguously. Advertising is also clearly not alone in its attempts to influence our thinking and behavior.

Recognition of this historical complexity does not invalidate our concern about advertising's continuing cultural role. While we may not be able to untangle the historical fabric to trace the threads of influence, we can still question the extent to which today's advertising perpetuates and/or exacerbates the alleged effects. More rooted in the present, such research is less likely to dwell on recriminations and remorse and is more readily directed toward proactive policy.

The Need for Research

> If one can justifiably say that advertising has joined the charmed circle of institutions which fix the values and standards of society, . . . then it becomes necessary to consider with special care the extent and nature of its influence—how far it extends and in what way it makes itself felt (Potter 1954, p. 177).

> There is a real need for an independent, comprehensive, and systematic comparative enquiry into advertising in all its many aspects. Such an enquiry, which is long overdue, should ascertain both the direct and indirect, the intended and the unintended effects, and should provide the base for decisions that are found to be required and any new policies that may result from them (MacBride 1980, p. 155).

It is clearly appropriate for us to take these assertions about advertising's unintended consequences seriously. Despite the relative lack of data based research to date, despite the occasional naiveté of some authors with respect to the processes of strategy formation and advertising execution, and despite the challenge this indictment represents to our own vested interests and ideologies, the charges are much too serious to dismiss cavalierly. The convergence of thought among intellectual leaders of so many diverse disciplines demands our attention and research as allied academics.

These ideas also deserve consideration because of their sobering and substantial nature. Taken as a whole, they constitute a major indictment of advertising. It should be acknowledged, however, that while this indictment is the result of the reflective ruminations of senior, highly respected scholars, the conclusions are typically arrived at deductively. While their insights are sometimes self-evident and their rhetoric is often very persuasive, few of the alleged effects are directly observed, nor is the causal role of advertising certain. Thus, the ideas constitute the conventional wisdom of nonbusiness academics and are better thought of as hypotheses than conclusions.

Potential Research Approaches

It is all too easy to let suspicions or defensiveness preclude more definitive research on these hypotheses. Doing nothing, however, accepts ideology in lieu of academic inquiry and information. Polemic stands on all sides of this issue are potentially tempered by research findings, which should illuminate our understanding of both the institution of advertising and the character of its target, the consumer. But how many of the consequences are readily researched, especially with traditional consumer research methodologies? The traditional research methods of consumer behavior are drawn from psychology, and, to a far lesser degree, from other social science disciplines. Viewed from the perspective of psychology, the research agenda suggested by the views reported involves study of both the stimulus materials and the responses, i.e., the ads and the behaviors to which they might be causally linked.

Content analysis of systematically drawn samples of ads can provide insight into the nature of the stimuli. Such a sample could be measured for its value content (Pollay 1983), and these results correlated with the findings of Rokeach (1973) or others to test the idea that advertising replicates the value hierarchy of the population. Data on cultural change might be examined for movement toward reinforced values. Content analysis can also identify the relative frequencies of tactics in order to establish some measure of the relative import of the various concerns listed in Figure 21.2 and to establish subsequent research priorities (Pollay 1985). Behaviors most commonly role modeled and encouraged can also be identified and their frequencies observed. While this, of course, is not equivalent to researching behaviors that might actually result from the exhortations of advertising, it would nonetheless identify the patterning of behaviors attempted. Systematically selected advertising copy is excellent grist for the historian's mill, and there is no reason why it would not also prove valuable for contemporary studies by marketing scholars.

Traditional experiments can more directly test the questions of effects produced by examining the extent to which various types of advertising stimuli produce various kinds of responses. For example, we could verify the supposed tendencies of status appeals, fear appeals, or sexual sells to produce envy and social competitiveness, anxieties and insecurities, and sexual preoccupations and dissatisfactions, respectively. There is no shortage of measures for dependent variables, and treatments and experimental designs should be quite straightforward. Our experimental paradigms, however, look to short-term impacts of specific stimuli rather than the longer-term results of repeated treatments. Thus, while internal validity can be highly controlled, some issue of external validity will remain.

Experimental paradigms can also be used to examine the extent to which ads work to set agendas, chanelling behavior by specifying the "evoked set" of alternatives and providing the criteria employed to choose from that evoked set. Nutritionists, for example, worry that our response to thirst is increasingly imagery of packaged goods and that, as a consequence, the "market share" for water is declining. (One once suggested to me in jest that maybe we needed to package water and brand it in order to compete with drinks of sugar, alcohol, or caffeine, ironically presaging the bottled water successes of recent years.) Protocol measures, unaided recall, or other free response methods are probably the best tools for validating the general issues of agenda setting, but forced choice techniques could identify the perceived relative importance of criteria after exposure.

At first glance it might seem that survey methods and other cross-sectional descriptive data about the population, such as that used in segmentation studies, might be helpful. Unfortunately, while these might prove descriptive of the current status of the American character and, hence, be valuable as a base line for future measures of change, this sort of data is of limited value in addressing the issues of causality and social change. It often lacks historical reference points and contains weak evidence, if any, regarding attribution for any phenomena noticed. Even direct questions which ask individuals the "why" questions are likely to fall far short of the mark, for individuals are probably unable to specify the reasons for cultural evolution of attitudes, norms of behavior, or relative values. We know full well how much difficulty respondents have reconstructing the determinants of even an isolated major consumer purchase of recent occurrence.

Even more unfortunately, it would seem that our research paradigms are at quite a loss in dealing with fundamental questions in the macromarket's evolution, only partially due to the hypotheses and their specification. Most of the variables in question are potentially measurable with existing or creative metric tools which social science has recently produced in such abundance. A less tractable problem is our inability to effectively research environmental issues from within the environment. No major longitudinal experiments are possible, as all individuals are already very heavily "treated." The few "unexposed" individuals are those with major differences on a wide variety of other significant dimensions—like those in total institutions, remote geographic locations, foreign cultures, primitive economies, or in some combination of these conditions. Hence, natural or quasi experiments aren't possible, as significant variation in advertising exposure isn't likely without naturally occurring covariation in other major variables, and it would seem quite difficult to sort the covariance in order to isolate relative determination.

But the shortcomings of our traditional techniques only suggest again that we need to broaden our concept of consumer behavior. Perhaps we should be drawing on a far broader base of research tools, employing techniques of historians, sociologists, anthropologists, or psycholinguists, and encouraging our students in these directions. It might also mean abandoning the academic concept of the consumer as a complex information processor, however dignified and morally reassuring that image. Instead of our current focus on short-term responses of individual consumers to specific configurations of stimuli, we need methods which deal with the long-term effects of aggregated stimuli. We need to supplement our focus on microphenomena with macro concerns, and our methods must expand accordingly.

Values and Research Objectivity

A common defense of advertising against criticisms of its cultural role is that it must, of necessity, be in harmony with its culture; messages must employ symbols and cultural values that are readily understood and accepted by the intended audience. In this view, advertising is seen as a mirror that only reflects and exposes existing cultural values and behaviors. It is argued from this perspective that to find fault with advertising is simply to display a cultural alienation. But this argument typically ignores several key points: (1) any culture is a mosaic of multiple values, (2) a culture is characterized in substantial measure by the relative importance of these values, and (3) not all cultural values are employed and echoed in advertising.

Not all values are equally suited for use in commercials. Some are more plausibly linked to the products in current production, some are more dramatically visualized, and some are more reliably responded to by the consuming public. Thus, in the aggregate, some of our cultural values are reinforced far more frequently than others. Hence, while it may be true that advertising reflects cultural values, it does so on a very selective basis, echoing and reinforcing certain attitudes, behaviors, and values far more frequently than others. Thus, it becomes a serious research question, which values are subjected to this selective reinforcement and which suffer from neglect, however benign?

The possible distortion of the relative importance of various values may have far-reaching consequences. Most serious social decisions involve conflict between competing value premises, and it is the relative importance of the competing values that tips the balance and precipitates wholly different patterns of behavior and paths of history. Political processes, for example, are typically the weighing of the relative importance of a series of values, each one of which in isolation would be endorsed by virtually all citizens. But it is the balancing of these valued considerations (like democracy, prosperity, the sanctity of family life, religious freedom, civil rights, national security, etc.) that leads to critical decisions and separates the various political parties and policies. The same can be said for individuals and their balancing of values when confronted with nontrivial decisions and moral quandaries. Thus, identifying the value profile of advertising seems a research priority and is allowed by recent methodological developments (Pollay 1983, 1984).

Many contentions about advertising's impact and the defensive responses to them are inherently ideological in nature (Greyser 1972). Authors note critically those ways in which they feel advertising leads to deviations from their concept of an improved or ideal society, and this unavoidably involves value judgments. But having said as much, it is not adequate, as so often seems to be implied, therefore to disregard the allegations and to accept the conservative tautology that "what is, is good." While it may be difficult to conduct a value-free inquiry into the effects of advertising, in large measure because advertising is itself so value laden, such an inquiry should be attempted. When that inquiry reaches its limits of providing information and insight, its data and conclusions must then form the basis of a better informed judgment. In the end, however, both research and moral judgment seem necessary. The issues are too important to tolerate uninformed or amoral attitudes.

Greed, lust, sloth, and pride were identified earlier as common ad themes. One might also consider the extent to which advertising encourages envy and gluttony. If anger were added to this list, we would have what are popularly known as the seven deadly sins. We could do far worse in our research agenda, as in our moral reflections, than to consider the extent to which advertising fosters these, or, in balance, encourages the seven cardinal virtues of wisdom, justice, temperance, courage, faith, hope, and love. This criterion set at least transcends personal value preferences of different researchers.

A Last Call to Research

The need for this research, even at the risk of embarrassing discoveries, has been recognized by famous professionals, including a copywriter chief executive and an advertising researcher who is a frequent industry spokesman.

> Criticism is much more welcome, because much more helpful, than praise. Criticism stimulates the nerve ends; praise merely lards with cholesterol the mental arteries. . . . In my opinion, we in advertising should be more concerned with those in our profession, or outside it, who lack the interest to criticize, who lack the urge to improve (Weir 1963, pp. 179–180).

> We should be enlisting the support of cultural critics and historians, as well as psychiatrists, to study the influence of advertising on the fantasy life of the public, on its conscious

aspirations and unconscious motives. We should be probing the symbolism evoked by the models and scenes depicted in advertising to see what impact they have had on the national character (Bogart 1969, p. 10).

Despite calls for this sort of research from professionals and despite nearly four decades of prodding from parallel social science paradigms, to date our discipline has produced shamefully little in response. Perhaps this reflects the immaturity of marketing and consumer behavior as autonomous academic disciplines. We have been quite preoccupied with either professional practicalities and/or mimicking the established sciences, afraid, it would seem, of alienating either constituency. Yet, this inhibition often precipitates the most pedestrian and pedantic of research, ignoring questions meaningful to the larger communities of scholars and citizens. Hopefully, as we mature into a more truly scholarly tradition, our scope and courage will enlarge.

This is entirely possible for individuals as their careers mature and as their concerns and perspective also mature. As the methodologies of the discipline evolve, it also becomes more feasible to undertake research with the promise of its being satisfying. The meaningfulness of the questions increases the satisfactions to the researcher, and improved methods make the research product more satisfying to others. While research on these topics is hardly simple, it is potentially significant.

Critical inquiry does not require researchers to believe that advertising will be absolved of all charges as much as it requires having faith that the institutions of advertising have some potential for self-correction and a capacity for moral action in the light of new knowledge. Let us hope that marketing and advertising scholars have this faith and carry out the needed research. Let us also hope that such faith is well-founded.

Failure to initiate this research would suggest that academics are servants to marketing practice rather than scholars of it. Intellectual detachment suggests that we should study the consumer in the marketing environment as the biologist studies the fish. As suggested by Tucker (1974), all too often our perspective has been exclusively that of the fisherman.

REFERENCES

Advertising Age (1957), "Editorial," 28 (February 11), 12.

Barnouw, Erik (1978), *The Sponsor: Notes on a Modern Potentate,* New York: Oxford University Press.

Barzun, Jacques (1946), "Myths for Materialists," *Chimera,* 4 (No. 3), 52–62.

Bell, Daniel (1976), *The Cultural Contradictions of Capitalism,* New York: Basic Books.

Berman, Ronald (1981), *Advertising and Social Change,* Beverly Hills, CA: Sage.

Bogart, Leo (1969), "Where Does Advertising Research Go from Here?" *Journal of Advertising Research,* 9 (No. 1), 3–12.

Boorstin, Daniel J. (1962), *The Image,* New York: Atheneum.

———— (1973), *The Americans: The Democratic Experience*, New York: Random House.

Commager, Henry Steele (1947), *America in Perspective,* New York: Random House.

———— (1950), *The American Mind,* New Haven, CT: Yale University Press.

Dollard, John (1960), "Fear of Advertising," in *The Role of Advertising,* C. H. Sandage and V. Fryburger, eds., Homewood, IL: Irwin, 307–317.

Ewen, Stuart (1976), *Captains of Consciousness: Advertising and the Social Roots of the Consumer Culture*, New York: McGraw-Hill.

Fisher, John (1968), *The Plot to Make You Buy,* New York: McGraw-Hill.

Fox, Stephen (1984), *The Mirror Makers: A History of Twentieth Century American Advertising*, New York: Morrow.

Fromm, Erich (1955), *The Sane Society,* New York: Holt.

———— (1976), *To Have or To Be?* New York: Harper.

Galbraith, John Kenneth (1967), *The New Industrial State,* Boston: Houghton Mifflin.

Gossage, Howard Luck (1967), "The Gilded Bough: Magic and Advertising," in *The Human Dialogue:*

Perspectives on Communication, Floyd W. Matson and Ashley Montagu, eds., New York: Free Press, 363–370.

Greyser, Stephen A. (1972), "Advertising: Attacks and Counters," *Harvard Business Review,* 50 (March–April), 22–28ff.

Hayakawa, S. I. (1964), *Language in Thought and Action,* New York: Harcourt.

Heilbroner, Robert L. (1976), *Business Civilization in Decline.* New York: Norton.

——— (1981), "Demand for the Supply Side," *New York Review of Books,* 38 (June 11), 37–41.

Henry, Jules (1963), *Culture against Man,* New York: Random House.

Howard, John A. and James Hulbert (1973), *Advertising and the Public Interest: A Staff Report to the Federal Trade Commission,* Chicago: Crain.

Jerusalem Bible, New Testament (1966), Garden City, NY: Doubleday.

Krutch, Joseph Wood (1959), *Human Nature and the Human Condition,* New York: Random House.

Kuhns, William (1970), *Waysteps to Eden: Ads and Commercials,* New York: Herder and Herder.

Lasch, Cristopher (1978), *The Culture of Narcissism: American Life in an Age of Diminishing Expectations,* New York: Norton.

Leiss, William (1976), *The Limits of Satisfaction,* Toronto: University of Toronto Press.

Leymore, Varda Langholz (1975), *Hidden Myth: Structure and Symbolism in Advertising,* New York: Basic Books.

Logan, John Danier (1907), "Social Evolution and Advertising," *Canadian Magazine,* 28 (No. 4), 330–334.

MacBride, Sean (1980), *Many Voices, One World: Communication and Society, Today and Tomorrow,* New York: Unipub (UNESCO).

McLuhan, Marshall (1951), *The Mechanical Bride,* Boston: Beacon.

——— (1953), "The Age of Advertising," *Commonweal,* 58 (September), 555–557.

——— and Quentin Fiore (1967), *The Medium Is the Message: An Inventory of Effects,* New York: Random House.

Mannes, Marya (1964), *But Will It Sell?* New York: Lippincott.

Mayer, Martin (1961), "The American Myth and the Myths of Advertising," in *The Promise of Advertising,* C. H. Sandage, ed., Homewood, IL: Irwin, 125–133.

Myers, John G. (1978), "Advertising and Socialization," in *Research in Marketing,* Vol. 1, J. Sheth, ed., Greenwich, CT: JAI Press, 169–199.

National Science Foundation (1978), *Research on the Effects of Television Advertising on Children: A Review of the Literature and Recommendations for Future Research,* Washington, DC: NSF.

Nouwen, Henri (1980), "Silence, the Portable Cell," *Sojourners,* 9 (July), 22ff.

Pollay, Richard W. (1983), "Measuring the Cultural Values Manifest in Advertising," in *Current Issues and Research in Advertising,* James H. Leigh and Claude R. Martin, Jr., eds., Ann Arbor: University of Mich., Graduate School of Business, 71–92.

——— (1984), "The Identification and Distribution of Values Manifest in Print Advertising, 1900–1980," in *Personal Values and Consumer Behavior,* A. G. Woodside and R. Pitts, eds., Lexington, MA: Lexington Books, 111–135.

——— (1985), "The Subsiding Sizzle: A Descriptive History of Print Advertising, 1900–1980," *Journal of Marketing,* 49 (Summer), 24–37.

Pope, Daniel (1983), *The Making of Modern Advertising,* New York: Basic Books.

Potter, David M. (1954), *People of Plenty,* Chicago: University of Chicago Press.

Real, Michael R. (1977), *Mass-Mediated Culture,* Englewood Cliffs, NJ: Prentice-Hall.

Riesman, David, Nathan Glazier, and Rauel Denny (1950), *The Lonely Crowd,* New Haven, CT: Yale University Press.

Rokeach, Milton (1973), *The Nature of Human Values,* New York: Free Press.

Schiller, Herbert I. (1973), *The Mind Managers,* Boston: Beacon.

Schrank, Jeffrey (1977), *Snap, Crackle, and Popular Taste: The Illusion of Free Choice in America,* New York: Delacorte.

Schudson, Michael (1984), *Advertising, The Uneasy Persuasion: Its Dubious Impact on American Society,* New York: Basic Books.

Silber, John R. (1982), *Democracy: Its Counterfeits and Promises.* Quoted in Lewis Kornfeld, *To Catch a Mouse, Make a Noise Like a Cheese,* Englewood Cliffs, NJ: Prentice-Hall.

Skolimowski, Henryk (1977), "The Semantic Environment in the Age of Advertising," in *The New Languages:*

A Rhetorical Approach to the Mass Media and Popular Culture, Thomas H. Ohlbren and L. M. Berk, eds., Englewood Cliffs, NJ: Prentice-Hall, 91–101.

Skornia, Harry J. (1965), *Television and Society,* New York: McGraw-Hill.

Slater, Philip E. (1970), *The Pursuit of Loneliness: American Culture at the Breaking Point*, Boston: Beacon.

Toronto School of Theology (1972), *Truth in Advertising: A Symposium,* New York: Harper.

Tucker, W. T. (1974), "Future Directions in Marketing Theory," *Journal of Marketing,* 38 (April), 30–35.

Weir, Walter (1963), *Truth in Advertising and Other Heresies,* New York: McGraw-Hill.

Williams, Raymond (1960), "The Magic System," *New Left Review,* 4 (July–August), 27–32.

CONSULTED SOURCES

Arendt, Hannah (1959), *The Human Condition,* Garden City, NY: Doubleday.

Baran, Paul A. and Paul M. Sweezy (1964), "Theses on Advertising," *Science and Society,* 28, 20–30.

Bell, Daniel (1960), "The Impact of Advertising," in *The Role of Advertising,* C. H. Sandage and V. Fryburger, eds., Homewood, IL: Irwin, 280–285.

Bernbach, William (1980), "A Creative Credo for the Advertising Business," *Advertising Age,* 51 (April 30), 206ff.

Boorstin, Daniel J. (1974a), "The Thinner Things of Life," in *Advertising's Role in Society,* John S. Wright and John E. Mertes, eds., New York: West, 111–116.

———— (1974b), "Advertising and American Civilization," in *Advertising and Society,* Yale Brozen, ed., New York: New York University Press. 11–23.

Boulding, Kenneth (1956), *The Image,* Ann Arbor: University of Michigan Press.

Buzzi, Giancarlo (1968), *Advertising: Its Cultural and Political Effects,* Minneapolis: University of Minnesota Press.

Coleman, James (1982), *The Asymmetrical Society,* Syracuse: Syracuse University Press.

Doob, Leonard W. (1948), *Public Opinion and Propaganda,* New York: Holt.

Douglas, Mary and Baron Isherwood (1979), *The World of Goods,* New York: Basic Books.

Dyer, Gillian (1982), Advertising as Communication; Advertising and the Social Roots of the Consumer Culture, London: Methuen.

Fox, Richard W. and T.J. Jackson Lears, eds. (1983), *The Culture of Consumption: Critical Essays in American History*, 1880–1980, New York: Pantheon.

Fritsch, Albert J. (1974), *The Contrasumers,* New York: Praeger.

Galbraith, John Kenneth (1958), *The Affluent Society,* Boston: Houghton Mifflin.

Glick, Ira O. and Sidney J. Levy (1962), "The Love and Fear of Commercials," in *Living with Television,* Chicago: Aldine, 204–228.

Griff, Mason (1969), "Advertising: The Central Institution of Mass Society," *Diogenes,* 68 (Winter), 120–137.

Hanan, Mark (1960), *The Pacifiers: The Six Symbols We Live By,* Boston: Little, Brown.

Heilbroner, Robert L. (1977), *The Economic Transformation of America,* New York: Harcourt.

Horney, Karen (1937), *The Neurotic Personality of Our Time,* New York: Norton.

Jarrell, Randall (1961), "A Sad Heart at the Supermarket," in *Culture for the Millions,* Norman Jacobs, ed., Boston: Beacon, 97–110.

Jellinek, J. Stephan (1977), *The Inner Editor: The Offense and Defense of Communication*, New York: Stein and Day.

Johnson, Harry G. (1968), "The Consumer and Madison Avenue," in *Social Issues in Marketing,* Lee E. Preston, ed., Glenview, IL: Scott, Foresman, 253–259.

Jones, Mary G. (1970), "The Cultural and Social Impact of Advertising on American Society," *Osgoode Hall Law Journal,* 8 (No. 1) 65–89.

Katona, George (1964), *The Mass Consumption Society,* New York: McGraw-Hill.

———— (1974), "Artificially Created Wants," in *Advertising's Role in Society,* John S. Wright and John E. Mertes, eds., New York: West, 126–132.

————, Bernhard Strumpel, and Ernest Zahn (1971), *Aspirations and Affluence: Comparative Studies in the United States and Western Europe*, New York: McGraw-Hill.

Kavanagh, John Francis (1981), *Following Christ in a Consumer Society: The Spirituality of Cultural Resistance*, Maryknoll, NY: Orbis.

Kaysen, Carl (1967), "The Business Corporation as a Creator of Values," in *Human Values and Economic Policy,* Sidney Hook, ed., New York: New York University Press.

Kluckhohn, Clyde (1949), *Mirror for Man,* New York: McGraw-Hill.

Levitt, Theodore (1960), "Are Advertising and Marketing Corrupting Society? It's Not Your Worry," in *The Role of Advertising,* C. H. Sandage and V. Fryburger, eds., Homewood. IL: Irwin, 442–450.

—— (1970), "The Morality (?) of Advertising," *Harvard Business Review,* 48 (July–August), 84–92.

Linden, Eugene (1979), *Affluence and Discontent: The Anatomy of Consumer Societies,* New York: Viking.

Mander, Jerry (1978), *Four Arguments for the Elimination of Television,* New York: Morrow.

McLuhan, Marshall (1947), "American Advertising," *Horizon,* No. 93–94 (October), 132–141.

—— (1966), *Understanding Media: The Extensions of Man,* New York: New American.

Mead, Margaret (1960), "The Worm of Self-Consciousness in American Culture," in *The Role of Advertising,* C. H. Sandage and V. Fryburger, eds., Homewood, IL: Irwin, 286–293.

Patai, Raphael (1972), *Myth and Modern Man,* Englewood Cliffs, NJ: Prentice-Hall.

Payne, Richard J. and Robert Heyer (1969), *Discovery in Advertising,* New York: Paulist Press.

Pease, Otis (1958), *The Responsibilities of American Advertising: Private Control and Public Influence,* 1920–1940, New Haven, CT: Yale University Press.

Pollay, Richard W. (1984), "Twentieth Century Magazine Advertising: Determinants of Informativeness," *Written Communication,* 1 (No. 1), 56–77.

Price, Jonathan (1978), *The Best Thing on TV: Commercials,* New York: Penguin.

Rosten, Leo (1961), "The Intellectual and the Mass Media," in *Culture for the Millions,* Norman Jacobs, ed., Boston: Beacon, 71–84.

Royal Commission on Consumer Problems (1974), "Social Effects of Advertising," in *Advertising's Role in Society,* John S. Wright and John E. Mertes, eds., New York: West, 117–120.

Schramm, Wilbur (1960), "The Effects of Mass Communications," in *The Role of Advertising,* C. H. Sandage and V. Fryburger, eds., Homewood, IL: Irwin, 204–221.

Schwartz, Anthony (1973), *The Responsive Chord,* Garden City, NY: Anchor Press/Doubleday.

Seldin, Joseph J. (1965), *The Golden Fleece: Advertising in American Life,* New York: Marzani and Munsell.

Shils, Edward (1961), "Mass Society and Its Culture," in *Culture for the Millions,* Norman Jacobs, ed., Boston: Beacon, 1–27.

Warne, Colston E. (1962), "Advertising—A Critic's View," *Journal of Marketing,* 26 (October), 10–14.

White, Irving S. (1960), "The Functions of Advertising in Our Culture," in *The Role of Advertising,* C.H. Sandage and V. Fryburger, eds., Homewood, IL: Irwin, 195–203.

Whitehead, Frank (1964), "Advertising," in *Discrimination and Popular Culture,* Denys Thompson, ed., Baltimore: Penguin, 23–49.

Whorf, Benjamin Lee (1956), *Language, Thought, and Reality,* New York: Wiley.

Williams, Raymond (1974), *Television: Technology and Cultural Form,* Fontana, Great Britain: Collins.

Winich, Charles (1971), "Sex and Advertising," *Sexual Behavior,* 1 (April), 36ff.

CHAPTER 22

MIRROR, MIRROR, ON THE WALL, WHAT'S UNFAIR IN THE REFLECTIONS ON ADVERTISING?

MORRIS B. HOLBROOK

[RESPONSE TO RICHARD W. POLLAY, "THE DISTORTED MIRROR"]

In his recent "reflections" on the role of advertising in American society, Pollay (1986) summarizes some attacks on the unintended consequences of television or radio commercials, print ads, and other forms of promotional messages. In general, Pollay assembles quotations from humanists and social scientists who see advertising as a socially destructive force and whose collective ideas constitute what Pollay regards as "a major indictment of advertising" (p. 31).*

In many ways, Pollay's essay provides a unique and valuable contribution to the marketing literature. It describes the charges against advertising with admirable breadth and clarity. It documents the case against ads and commercials with citations that reveal an impressive command of the relevant literature. Surely this essay deserves wide circulation and careful scrutiny by marketing scholars. One might argue, however, that by virtue of its persuasive force it may seriously mislead many readers who may respond sympathetically to the rhetorical power of the charges against advertising without adequately examining the logic of the arguments underlying the attacks.

The Conventional Wisdom or Prevailing Opinion (CWOPO)

Rather than revealing his own views, Pollay portrays what he calls the "conventional wisdom" or "prevailing opinion." The following discussion addresses that conventional wisdom or prevailing opinion—hereafter referred to by the acronym "CWOPO"—as Pollay describes it.

Mirror, Mirror

Mirror imagery is a common literary device. Classical and neoclassical critics, for example, believed that written communications should hold a mirror up to nature—that is, they should accurately reflect or represent the world around them (Abrams 1953). As Pollay himself acknowledges, many

---

From *Journal of Marketing,* vol. 51 (July 1987). Copyright © 1987 by the American Marketing Association. Reprinted with permission.

* Page references are to Pollay's original article.

Figure 22.1   **A Reconstruction of CWOPO's Implicit Arguments**

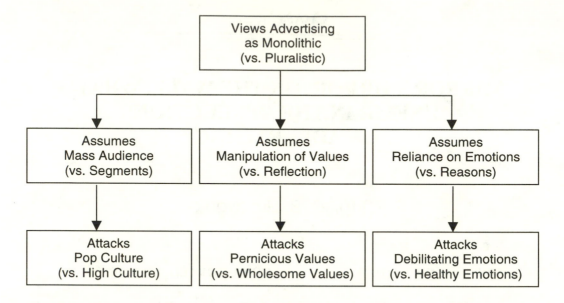

people feel that advertising can, does, and in fact must perform that function in modern free societies and that, indeed, it would fail if it did not accurately reflect prevailing cultural values and norms. As suggested by Pollay's title, however, CWOPO argues that advertising trivializes reality, distorts societal values, engenders dangerous or debilitating emotions, and thereby produces unintended consequences that are due cause for alarm. To someone who sees advertising as a mirror, it is as though CWOPO dislikes the reflections found there and now might want to smash that mirror.

Weak Logical Threads

Unfortunately, the logic by which CWOPO arrives at such a conclusion seems rather obscure and lends itself better to enumeration than to coherent argumentation. For example, in the list provided by Pollay's Figure 21.2, CWOPO's arguments appear to lack the kind of structure that might convey a logical progression from premises or assumptions to deductions or inferences to conclusions or implications. If we search through Pollay's discussion to find the slender logical threads that underlie CWOPO's attack on advertising, we might discover that they fail to support its heavy weight. Let us therefore attempt to reconstruct the underlying logic of CWOPO's argument so that we can examine whether it commands our acquiescence.

THE STRANDS IN CWOPO'S LOGICAL THREAD

An attempt to reconstruct CWOPO's argument by finding the logical thread implicit in Pollay's discussion is shown in Figure 22.1. From the top, CWOPO appears to adopt a tacit view of advertising as a *monolithic institution* that somehow (whether intentionally or unintentionally) acts in concert to pursue certain shared ends via a set of common means. Thus, Pollay speaks repeatedly of "advertising as an institution" (p. 19), "advertising in the aggregate" (p. 21), "the indirect effects of the overall system" (p. 18), and "advertising's social and cultural consequences"

(p. 18) to suggest that, collectively, "advertising is without doubt a formative influence within our culture" (p. 18). Hence, in spite of occasional hedges about the unintended nature of its consequences, CWOPO implicitly espouses a view of advertising as a monolithic institution exerting global effects. For example, in his highly sophisticated and generally well-balanced account of the CWOPO perspective, Schudson (1984, p. 5) comments:

> My subject is not advertisements but advertising: advertising as an institution that plays a role in the marketing of consumer goods, advertising as an industry that manufactures the cultural products called advertisements and commercials, and advertising as an omnipresent system of symbols, a pervasive and bald propaganda for consumer culture.

This description enables Schudson to discuss "advertising's . . . general role in shaping consciousness and providing a framework for thought and feeling" (p. 43), to view advertising as "a general cultural encouragement toward materialism" (p. 130), and to conclude sweepingly that "advertising is capitalism's way of saying 'I love you' to itself'" (p. 232).

Figure 22.1 further indicates three inferences that stem from this view of advertising as a monolith. First, on the left, CWOPO's conception of advertising as somehow collective, univocal, and global in its impact coheres with the assumption of a *mass audience* characterized by innumerable homogeneous receivers of its promotional message (see Pollay's Figure 21.2, III, A). Pollay's focus on this mass audience enables him to register CWOPO's apparent contempt for *pop culture* (p. 26).

> What passes for common culture in our affluent society are sets of jingles, slogans, and selling phrases which are perhaps more uniformly known than any other creed, ideology, or set of myths.

> Sociologists such as Gans (1974) have coped painfully with the conflict between their perception as intellectuals that pop culture is inherently inferior to high culture and their desire as social scientists to avoid imposing their own elite value judgments on their subject matter. However, Pollay avoids this kind of sociological angst by simply revealing CWOPO's disdain for the common characteristics of pop culture that show up in advertising. For example, CWOPO attacks the propensities of advertising toward repetition and stereotyping.

> The repetitive, fantastic, one-sided, and often exhortative rhetorical styles of advertising (p. 26);

> Simplistic, symbolic stereotypes, chosen for their clarity and conciseness, . . . stereotypes for not just the sexes, but also for races, ages, occupations, family relations, etc. (p. 27).

In the center of Figure 22.1, CWOPO's monolithic view of advertising also enables it to assume that this institution works toward the *manipulation of social values* in a direction favorable to its own selfish business interests. In other words, CWOPO assumes that advertising operates less like a mirror that reflects prevailing societal norms and more like a mold that shapes those values toward its own ulterior ends. Pollay does acknowledge that this molding process may work by means of selective reinforcement rather than direct inculcation, but the overall effect remains roughly the same—a distortion of the prevailing value hierarchy.

. . . in the aggregate, some of our cultural values are reinforced far more frequently than others. Hence, . . . advertising reflects cultural values . . . on a very selective basis, echoing and reinforcing certain . . . values far more frequently than others. . . . The possible distortion of the relative importance of various values may have far-reaching consequences (p. 33).

Pollay enumerates several *pernicious values* that CWOPO finds reinforced by advertising. They include conspicuous consumption, envy, emulation, self-centeredness, unconflicted self-indulgence, vulgarity, covetousness, hatred, underhand competition, and especially pollution and pornography (p. 28). Perhaps most saliently, materialism occupies a position high on CWOPO's list of offensive values encouraged by advertising.

Thus advertising's most fundamental impact may be that it induces people to keep productive in order to keep consuming, to work in order to buy . . . the transfer of feeling toward goods and away from people, the reification of abstract meaning into objects, and the simultaneous objectification of personal relations, are manifestations of this materialism (p. 25).

Ultimately, Pollay draws upon the *Holy Bible* to bring the force of religious rectitude down on the values espoused by advertising.

Greed, lust, sloth, and pride were identified earlier as common ad themes. One might also consider the extent to which advertising encourages envy and gluttony. If anger were added to this list, we would have what are popularly known as the seven deadly sins (p. 33).

On the right side of Figure 22.1, CWOPO's contention that advertising works collectively toward the molding or shaping of values supports the complementary assumption that it *relies heavily on its emotional impact*. Thus, Pollay concentrates primarily on people's emotional reactions to advertising rather than on their potential use of advertising information as a guide to reasoned action. Here, he represents the claim that "the one-sided rhetorical styles of advertising seem to inhibit rationality" (p. 26) by citing such sources as Fromm (1976), who contended, "A vast sector of modern advertising . . . does not appeal to reason but to emotion" (p. 110). In describing the nature of this emotional impact, Pollay focuses on such *debilitating emotions* as terror, self-doubt, anxiety, unhappiness, self-contempt, spiritual desolation, envy, inadequacy, fear, guilt, inferiority, dissatisfaction, sexual frustration, and cynicism. In sum, CWOPO dwells on a long list of negative emotions and blames advertising for their deleterious effects.

THIN STRANDS, WEAK THREAD

CWOPO's indictment of advertising follows only the weakest thread of logic, which tends to break from the burden Pollay places upon it. Overall, when closely examined, the arguments mustered by Pollay on behalf of CWOPO cannot support the heavy weight of CWOPO's charges against advertising. Let us return to Figure 22.1 and reconsider each claim in turn.

Monolithic Versus Pluralistic Advertising

CWOPO's tacit but often emergent assumption that advertising acts like a monolithic institution holds implicitly that advertising works as a collective, univocal, and global force in which media, ad agencies, and marketing strategists somehow manage (whether intentionally or unintentionally) to create television commercials, print ads, and other promotional communications that join in concert to foster certain common ends and objectives. Yet most of the institutions involved in advertising appear on closer examination to be bastions of pluralism, characterized by in-fighting, checks and balances, and various other contrapuntal tendencies. In particular, one notes the unwritten laws that guide the behavior of most ad agencies and marketing departments (e.g., see Ries and Trout 1981): (1) be different, (2) seek a unique niche, (3) avoid head-to-head competition, and (4) protect proprietary secrets. In this climate of jealous competitive secrecy and internecine business strategizing, one sees little of advertising as a monolithic institution in which everybody preaches the party line in perfectly synchronized unison or harmony. Rather, one sees advertisers —that is, media, agencies, and their organizational clients—as a vast particularistic assortment of atomistic elements, each engaged in a sort of communicational random walk that contributes to the informational chaos of the overall cluttered spectacle. A communication system based on self-interest rather than central planning could not be otherwise.

Admittedly, advocates of CWOPO might find this emphasis on pluralism somewhat naïve. For example, Schudson (1984) speaks of "the seductiveness of pluralism" and argues that, "advertising may influence cultural life in the large even when it is not doing much to sell goods piece by piece" (p. 10). Elsewhere, however, Schudson himself adopts a more pluralistic view (p. 65).

> Advertising practice employs a vast array of notions of the consumer and ideas of human nature in an utterly ad hoc and opportunistic way. Whatever frightful characteristics one may attribute to the American advertising industry, consistency is not one of them.

This recognition underscores the fact that we need some specific link—something more than a sociological wave of the hand—to forge a connection between the highly atomistic practices of the advertising profession and their assumed effects as a monolithic force. Schudson attempts to provide such a linkage via an intriguing but perhaps overdrawn account of advertising as a form of "capitalist realism" in which "the parallels are strong between what socialist realism is designed to do and what advertising in capitalist society intends to do" (p. 215).

Unfortunately, Pollay's account of CWOPO proposes no such connecting link, however tenuous. Rather, in Pollay's treatment, CWOPO seems simply to assume the monolithic impact of advertising as an article of faith. This assumption will strike many people as unacceptable. If advertisers did somehow magically act in concert to exalt the worst aspects of pop culture, encourage pernicious values, and engender debilitating emotions, we would echo Johnny Carson by asking incredulously, "How dey do dat?" At best, this issue warrants serious discussion —something that seems to be missing in Pollay's representation of CWOPO. At worst, but perhaps most plausibly, this question strikes a blow at the very foundations on which the rest of CWOPO so shakily depends.

Mass Audience Versus Segments

One reason we need not worry excessively about the dangers of a monolithic advertising institution is the general repudiation of mass marketing in favor of some form of market segmentation. Marketing wisdom recognizes the fallacies of assuming the existence of a mass market of homogeneous customers, all of whom will respond favorably to some offering or marketing mix. Rather, a fundamental marketing principle holds that customers differ and stresses the importance of catering to their differing needs and wants by the design of different offerings to appeal to different market segments via different promotional communication strategies in different media. In short, everywhere, the emphasis is on differences. Conversely, everywhere, marketing practitioners and scholars regard the assumption of a homogeneous mass market or mass audience as a fallacy.

Pop Culture Versus High Culture

We cannot safely conclude that advertising appeals only to the lowest common denominator of pop culture by dealing excessively in social stereotypes. Departures from stereotypes abound in advertising of all kinds—the tough-minded little old lady who asks "Where's the beef ?," the crusty baseball manager who befriends the rookie umpire, the football coach who fears airplanes and good cameras, and the husband who prepares an elaborate gourmet meal for his wife only to be told that he has "ring around the collar." Such examples suggest that advertising does not necessarily involve stereotyping.

Nevertheless, some studies have supported the charge that television in general and advertising in particular do tend, on balance, to present a stereotypical view of the world. For example, prime-time television shows underrepresent blue collar and service workers (Gerbner and Signorielli 1982) and overrepresent millionaires (Stein 1982). Meanwhile, advertising undoubtedly emphasizes elegant homes, beautiful people, and shiny cars (Millum 1975) while neglecting death, suffering, and hardship (McCracken and Pollay 1981). However, proportional representation seems a rather unfair criterion of veridicality. Any artist must select some subject matter to hold up as an object for the audience's attention or admiration. The valid criterion is whether this material is handled truthfully, and that question cannot be decided by means of simple counting rules.

Notice that the treatment of advertising copywriters as artists implies that—partly by virtue of aiming at narrow market segments—some advertising escapes the pop-culture level of entertainment to approach the high-culture status of Art. This judgment is reinforced by the recent decision of New York's Cooper-Hewitt Museum to present an exhibition of television commercials and print ads entitled "Advertising America." Even some advocates of CWOPO agree that advertising can be artistic.

> . . . advertising is . . . clearly *art*. . . . The difference between fashion photography and photography as art is subtle, if it exists at all, and certainly the techniques and innovations in fashion photography influence photography as fine art as often as the other way around. In recent years, television commercial techniques have influenced film and commercial directors have become makers of feature films (Schudson 1984, p. 222).

Thus, one would be hard-pressed to find better dramaturgical examples of minimalist expressionism than, say, the famous Mean Joe Green commercial ("Have a Coke and a smile"), the celebrated familial telephone ads ("He called just to say, 'I love you, Mom' "), or the brilliantly compressed love story that appears in one 30-second spot for Dodge ("Do you like trucks?"). These little video episodes might be regarded as minor but nonetheless genuine artistic masterpieces—comparable to full-length PBS productions in much the same way that the novels of Jane Austen compare with those of Charles Dickens or the Bach fugues compare with Bruckner's late symphonies. They are beautifully crafted little miniatures whose jewel-like production values radiantly outshine many longer, more sprawling attempts at grandeur. Critics of art and literature have accepted the possibility of finding the artistically sublime in the small fragments prized by Longinus, the brief "touchstones" regarded by Matthew Arnold as exemplars of high seriousness, or what Abrams (1953) calls "the short and incandescent passage as the manifestation of poetry at its highest" (p. 134). Similarly, many viewers will sense a clear artistic integrity in the complex contrapuntal qualities of the Sears commercial with the little girl, her new bicycle, and an operatic chorus intoning, "There's more for your life at Sears." In short, one finds little reason to denounce advertising as a merely entertaining specimen of popular culture fallen from the graces of High Art. Rather, as should not be surprising in light of the tremendous creative talent and energy that go into them, some advertising masterpieces endure—for example, the Ajax, Texaco, Vitalis, and M&M commercials from the 1950s.

Manipulation Versus Reflection of Values

Other researchers have considered whether advertising does or should try to manipulate values (like a mold) or should only reflect values that already exist (like a mirror). For example, Boyd, Ray, and Strong (1972) have outlined contrasting strategic postures in this respect. Simplifying somewhat, we can condense their argument into the context of a simple multiattribute joint space model and can focus on advertising intended to increase selective (rather than primary) demand for some brand of a mature (as opposed to a new) product category—in other words, the most typical type of advertising. Within this framework, advertising copy might attempt to improve the position of a brand by (1) altering the dimensions of the market space (to make some new attribute more salient in the buyer's set of choice criteria), (2) changing beliefs (to move the perceived position of this or a competitor's brand closer to or farther away from some segment's ideal point), or (3) manipulating values (to shift the locations of the ideal points themselves). For example, a Buick ad might attempt to (1) convince people to consider safety in choosing a car (on which, perhaps, Buick excels), (2) demonstrate that a Buick gets better gas mileage than a Toyota (presumably a desirable feature for at least some segment(s) of the market), or (3) persuade customers that conspicuous consumption is desirable and therefore that low fuel economy should be preferred (thereby shifting their ideal points on the gas-mileage dimension to favor big cars). Only the third strategy clearly involves the manipulation of values in that it causes people to redefine their conception of what is desirable. By contrast, the second strategy alters just perceptions while leaving values intact, and the first strategy changes only the relative salience of values in a particular context by making some choice criterion more (or less) salient for a given product category. Notice that this shift in salience or relative importance differs markedly from any sort of manipulative distortion of values—first because it leaves the value intact while only shifting its priority, second because it applies to just one product category, and third because an ad for some other brand or product may work in exactly the opposite direction by arguing for a diametrically opposed increase or decrease in the salience of that very same value.

Traditional thinking and slender empirical evidence suggest that (1) early in the product life cycle when evaluative criteria are in flux, changing the relative salience of product attributes may contribute to successful persuasion but that (2) late in the cycle when the dimensions of the market space have crystalized, working on perceptions proves more effective than trying to shift the importance or to manipulate the content of values (Holbrook and Howard 1977). Thus, because most products are in the mature stages of their life cycles, augmenting or repositioning people's beliefs usually appears more fruitful than trying to alter their choice criteria or attempting to move their ideal points—precisely because those choice criteria and ideal points are anchored in value systems that are themselves the products of extensive long-time socialization or acculturation. For example, Aaker and Myers (1975, p. 548) conclude:

> . . . advertising does not have the power to dominate other forces (i.e., family, church, literature, etc.) that contribute to the values of society. . . . the values of society have evolved

over centuries and have been influenced by philosophers, poets, statesmen, and others. It is unrealistic to expect advertising to have a dominant impact on them.

In short, no matter how hard a company or advertising agency tried to alter the salience or content of people's values, it would *not* convince them that friendliness and cuisine are more important than routes and scheduling in choosing an airline or that they should prefer dangerous and fuel-wasting rather than safe and economical automobiles. For this reason, most advertising appears to mirror or reflect rather than to mold or shape the values of its target audience. Thus, many scholars (including Pollay himself at times) have regarded the content analysis of advertising as a useful index of social norms (Pollay 1985). Here, however, we might question CWOPO's assessment of the values that tend to dominate advertising messages.

Pernicious Versus Wholesome Values

For Pollay's version of CWOPO's conventional wisdom, reading print ads or watching TV commercials is the moral equivalent of sticking one's head in a toilet. According to this view, advertising espouses greed, lust, sloth, pride, and a few other deadly sins. Ads praise conspicuous consumption, wasteful pollution, and pornographic display. Promotional communications threaten religion and morality by replacing spiritual reverence with a kind of materialistic anti-Christ.

Thus conceived, advertising becomes the target of those critics who would blame it for what they see as an increase in modern American materialism. However, we might pause to ask whether we really are growing increasingly materialistic. For example, using content analysis of American novels as his criterion, Friedman (1985) demonstrated an increase (since World War II) in commercialism (the use of brand names) but *not* in materialism (the mention of product categories). Moreover, informal observation suggests that, like some Americans, citizens of Communist countries can show nearly obsessive levels of preoccupation with material goods. Russians will stand in line for hours, risk imprisonment by dealing on the black market, or harass tourists to distraction to obtain a new pair of shoes, a jazz record, or a buttondown shirt. Further, ethnographic evidence suggests that primal societies may equal or even surpass more civilized cultures in their tendency to use luxury goods as weapons of social exclusion. For example, Douglas (1979) reports that the Yurok—a small tribe of fishers and hunters studied by Kroeber in the 1920s—were concerned with personal property "above all else" and had a culture "as commercial in outlook as any modern industrial society today" (p. 132). Finally, it appears that, even without the benefit of advertising, primates can be almost as materialistic as humans. Chimpanzees in the wild will neglect their offspring in order to sit for three or more hours at a time using a blade of grass to fish for termites (Goodall 1971, p. 162).

Aside from these moot questions of materialism, the crux of CWOPO's charge against pernicious values is the aforementioned view of advertising as little more than a vulgar encouragement of sin and degradation. However, with the possible exceptions of the old National Airlines, Calvin Klein, and Harvey's Bristol Cream commercials (two of which aroused storms of protest precisely because they *were* inconsistent with widely shared values), one is hard-pressed to think of advertising that supports Pollay's presentation of CWOPO's rather prissy perceptions. In sharp contrast to CWOPO's claims, most ads seem to reflect fairly wholesome values such as sociability (AT&T's "reach out and touch someone"), affection (Kodak's "decorate your home with love"), generosity (Hallmark's "you care enough to send the very best"), health (the dairy industry's "you never outgrow your need for milk"), patriotism (Chevy's "see the USA in your Chevrolet"), ecumenism (Coke's "I'd like to teach the world to sing in perfect harmony"), personal enrichment (the Army's "be all that you can be"), security (State Farm's "like a good neighbor, State Farm is there"), or temperance (LA Beer's "the secret to carryin' on is not gettin' carried away").

Subjectively, it appears that such examples of wholesome (God, mother, and country) values found in advertising could be multiplied almost without limit whereas the noxious or deleterious counterexamples are relatively few and far between. One must concede that, as suggested by Pollay (1986, p. 31), such an issue lends itself to investigation by means of systematic content analysis (Kassarjian 1977; Pollay 1983). Surely, however, such a content analysis should be conducted with detachment from the viewpoints advocated by CWOPO.

The dangers inherent in using content analysis to test CWOPO's hypotheses seem to surface in an otherwise imaginative and valuable study by Belk and Pollay (1985). These authors examine American magazine advertising from 1900 to 1980 and conclude (p. 895):

> Appeals to luxury and pleasure have increased in frequency while the use of practical and functional appeals has decreased. Themes involving having or terminal materialism have also lately increased at the expense of doing or instrumental materialism. On the basis of these findings, it appears that ads . . . increasingly employed pleasure, luxury, and terminal materialism to sell their products and services.

Clearly, if valid, this conclusion supports CWOPO. However, one can accept this view of the results only at the expense of making three rather precarious assumptions: (1) that "luxury/pleasure" appeals (p. 893) involve such characteristics as taste in food (something that could be regarded as a rather practical or functional aspect of eating), (2) that we can safely "ignore . . . the 1960s" (p. 894) during which themes of terminal materialism were actually fewer than in 1915 (perhaps as a reflection of the hippy ethos described by Belk 1986), and (3) that the fairly minor increase in terminal materialism matters more than the fact that themes of doing greatly outnumbered themes of having (p. 895) *during the entire period* (so that *never* did the most objectionable form of materialism predominate). The difficulty in justifying these three assumptions hints at the problems that might arise in looking at the world through CWOPO-colored glasses.

Reliance on Emotions Versus Reasons

Increased attention recently has focused on the fact that much advertising works by means of emotional appeals (Holbrook and O'Shaughnessy 1984). In essence, this type of strategy draws on classical conditioning by assuming that the frequent pairing of a brand name with an experienced emotion eventually will result in the tendency of one to evoke the other and will thereby predispose the consumer toward buying certain brands (e.g., Gorn 1982; Shimp 1981). However, Holbrook and O'Shaughnessy (1984) found many researchers and practitioners subscribe to a contingency model in which emotional appeals work best for some situations, products, or people, whereas rational appeals work best for others (Berger 1981; Vaughn 1980). For example, under conditions of high involvement, one might assume the careful processing of message arguments to form beliefs as the basis for reasoned action (Petty, Cacioppo, and Schumann 1983; Ray and Batra 1983; Shimp 1981). Under such circumstances, one returns to the familiar models of rational behavior employing means in the service of ends (Ajzen and Fishbein 1980).

These findings suggest that much advertising does attempt to supply reasons as the basis for action (O'Shaughnessy 1987). Most advertising that seeks to attain a differential advantage works in such a manner. Reeves' (1961) classic discussion of the unique selling proposition or USP contains numerous examples: Listerine's "stops halitosis," Lucky Strike's "Lucky Strike means fine tobacco," Colgate's "cleans your breath while it cleans your teeth," and Wonder Bread's "helps build strong bodies 12 ways." More recent examples are "Dodge trucks are ram tough," "at Ford, quality is Job 1," "the Citi never sleeps," and "nobody compares with Atari."

Interestingly, Pollay (1985, p. 33) himself found a long-term tendency toward a shift from more emotional to more rational print advertising in the period from 1900 to 1980.

> A postwar pattern, identified here as the "subsiding sizzle," begins in the 1950s with a growth rather than decline of the number of ads whose rhetorical style is that of logos, straight and sober textual styles. . . . Thus, in the postwar era, print ads are less likely to portray human users and use situations, less likely to push benefits of consumption, and less likely to use emotive rhetorical styles.

Though one suspects that in the 1980s the role of emotion in advertising has once again increased in importance (Holbrook and O'Shaughnessy 1984), especially in television commercials, one also notes that much advertising continues to contain highly rational content aimed at providing reasons for brand selection.

Debilitating Versus Healthy Emotions

Even if we momentarily ignore the fact that not all advertising relies on emotional appeals, we still find cause for concern in Pollay's discussion of CWOPO's attack on advertising-related emotions as primarily debilitating. According to CWOPO's view of the world, advertising fills its victims with fear, self-doubt, guilt, envy, sexual lust, cynicism, dissatisfaction, and other negative emotions. Overall, however, this seems a rather unbalanced, one-sided perspective from which to interpret most print ads and television commercials.

For example, a recent study of emotional responses to television commercials (Holbrook and Westwood 1987) does show that some ads prompt sadness and fear (e.g., Bayer, Poligrip, Prudential) or anger and disgust (Calvin Klein, Chanel #5, Crazy Eddie). However, other commercials elicit feelings of anticipation (British Air, U.S. Army), acceptance (Atari, G.E.), and joyfulness (Coke, Dr. Pepper, Kellogg's, Budweiser). Other studies could be cited to support the same conclusion (Holbrook and Batra 1987). It therefore seems somewhat churlish to single-mindedly attack the negative aspects of emotional advertising without giving balanced attention to the capacity of ads for evoking happiness ("It's the Pepsi generation"), gratification ("You deserve a break today"), pride ("Raise your hand if you're sure"), love ("He called just to say, 'I love you, Mom' "), appreciation ("Gee, thanks, Mean Joe"), and any number of other healthy positive emotions. Ask yourself which would leave you feeling more cheerful, watching two hours of randomly selected television commercials or viewing 10 minutes of the evening news.

THE MIRROR CRACKED

In conclusion, the thin strands of CWOPO's implicit arguments for the conventional wisdom or prevailing opinion form a weak logical thread that snaps in several places from the burden of trying to tie together its multifarious attacks on advertising. CWOPO claims that advertising acts to oversimplify reality, distort social values, and evoke unhealthy emotions. One might reply that these assertions tend to smash or at least to crack the mirror that advertising holds up to social mores, norms, and values by multiplying accusations that are misleading or even unfair. The important question, then, is not what distorts whom but who distorts what. CWOPO's attacks on advertising are unnecessarily destructive.

Late in his essay, Pollay does suggest that many of the issues he raises warrant empirical exploration. While applauding the spirit of this concession to scientific investigation, one wonders whether many of the questions Pollay addresses are really susceptible to empirical inquiry by currently available methods. For example, it is difficult to imagine works with such titles as "Using LISREL to Demonstrate the Pernicious Effects of Advertising," "A Multivariate Analysis of the Process by Which TV Commercials Corrupt American Society," or "Maximum Likelihood Estimates of the Tendency for Print Ads to Encourage the Seven Deadly Sins in Late 19th Century New England." Pollay, too, seems to recognize that conventional methods may not be well suited to the problems he cares about. Thus, he arrives via a somewhat circuitous route at a conclusion with which many will wholeheartedly concur (p. 32).

> But the shortcomings of our traditional techniques only suggest again that we need to broaden our concept of consumer behavior. . . . It might also mean abandoning our academic concept of the consumer as a complex information processor, however dignified and morally reassuring that image. . . . We need to supplement our focus on microphenomena with macro concerns, and our methods must expand accordingly.

This conclusion places Pollay on the same wavelength as much recent work in consumer research that has attempted to break away from the old excessively rational model of buyer behavior (Hirschman and Holbrook 1982; Holbrook and Hirschman 1982). Thus, whatever their contrasting ideological origins, disparate paths may lead toward similar conclusions about the nature of the needed research on the role of advertising in society.

REFERENCES

Aaker, David A. and John G. Myers (1975), *Advertising Management*. Englewood Cliffs, NJ: Prentice-Hall, Inc.

Abrams, M. H. (1953), *The Mirror and the Lamp*. New York: Oxford University Press.

Ajzen, Icek and Martin Fishbein (1980), *Understanding Attitudes and Predicting Social Behavior*. Englewood Cliffs, NJ: Prentice-Hall, Inc.

Belk, Russell W. (1986), "Yuppies as Arbiters of the Emerging Consumption Style," in *Advances in Consumer Research*, Vol. 13, Richard J. Lutz, ed. Provo, UT: Association for Consumer Research, 514–19.

—— and Richard W. Pollay (1985), "Images of Ourselves: The Good Life in Twentieth Century Advertising," *Journal of Consumer Research*, 11 (March), 887–97.

Berger, D. (1981), "A Retrospective: FCB Recall Study," *Advertising Age* (October 26), S36–S37.

Boyd, Harper W., Jr., Michael L. Ray, and Edward C. Strong (1972), "An Attitudinal Framework for Advertising Strategy," *Journal of Marketing*, 36 (April), 27–33.

Douglas, Mary with Baron Isherwood (1979), *The World of Goods*. New York: W. W. Norton & Company.

Friedman, Monroe (1985), "The Changing Language of a Consumer Society: Brand Name Usage in Popular American Novels in the Postwar Era," *Journal of Consumer Research*, 11 (March), 927–38.

Fromm, Erich (1976), *To Have or To Be?* New York: Harper & Row Publishers, Inc.

Gans, Herbert J. (1974), *Popular Culture and High Culture*. New York: Basic Books, Inc.

Gerbner, George and Nancy Signorielli (1982), "The World According to Television," *American Demographics*, 4 (October), 14–17.

Goodall, Jane (1971), *In the Shadow of Man*. Boston: Houghton-Mifflin Company.

Gorn, Gerald J. (1982), "The Effects of Music in Advertising on Choice Behavior: A Classical Conditioning Approach," *Journal of Marketing*, 46 (1), 94–101.

Hirschman, Elizabeth C. and Morris B. Holbrook (1982), "Hedonic Consumption: Emerging Concepts, Methods and Propositions," *Journal of Marketing*, 46 (Summer), 92–101.

Holbrook, Morris B. and Rajeev Batra (1987), "Toward a Standardized Emotional Profile (SEP) Useful in Measuring Responses to the Nonverbal Components of Advertising," in *Nonverbal Communication in Advertising*, David W. Stewart and Sid Hecker, eds. Lexington, MA: D. C. Heath & Company.

———— and Elizabeth C. Hirschman (1982), "The Experiential Aspects of Consumption: Consumer Fantasies, Feelings, and Fun," *Journal of Consumer Research*, 9 (September), 132–40.

———— and John A. Howard (1977), "Frequently Purchased Nondurable Goods and Services," in *Selected Aspects of Consumer Behavior: A Summary from the Perspective of Different Disciplines*, Robert Ferber, ed. Washington, DC: National Science Foundation.

———— and John O'Shaughnessy (1984), "The Role of Emotion in Advertising," *Psychology & Marketing*, 1 (Summer), 45–64.

———— and Richard A. Westwood (1987), "The Role of Emotion in Advertising Revisited: Testing a Typology of Emotional Responses," in *Advertising and Consumer Psychology*, Pat Cafferata and Alice M. Tybout, eds. Lexington, MA: D. C. Heath & Company.

Kassarjian, Harold H. (1977), "Content Analysis in Consumer Research," *Journal of Consumer Research*, 3 (June), 8–18.

McCracken, Grant W. and Richard W. Pollay (1981), "Anthropological Analyses of Advertising," Working Paper #815, Faculty of Commerce and Business Administration, University of British Columbia.

Millum, Trevor (1975), *Images of Women*. Totowa, NJ: Bowman and Littlefield.

O'Shaughnessy, John (1987), *Why People Buy*. New York: Oxford University Press.

Petty, R. E., J. T. Cacioppo, and D. Schumann (1983), "Central and Peripheral Routes to Advertising Effectiveness: The Moderating Role of Involvement," *Journal of Consumer Research*, 10 (September), 135–46.

Pollay, Richard W. (1983), "Measuring the Cultural Values Manifest in Advertising," in *Current Issues and Research in Advertising 1983*, James H. Leigh and Claude R. Martin, Jr., eds. Ann Arbor: Division of Research, Graduate School of Business Administration, University of Michigan, 71–92.

———— (1985), "The Subsiding Sizzle: A Descriptive History of Print Advertising, 1900–1980," *Journal of Marketing*, 49 (Summer), 24–37.

———— (1986), "The Distorted Mirror: Reflections on the Unintended Consequences of Advertising," *Journal of Marketing*, 50 (April), 18–36.

Ray, Michael L. and Rajeev Batra (1983), "Emotion and Persuasion in Advertising: What We Do and Don't Know About Affect," in *Advances in Consumer Research*, Vol. 10, Richard P. Bagozzi and Alice M. Tybout, eds. Ann Arbor, MI: Association for Consumer Research.

Reeves, Rosser (1961), *Reality in Advertising*. New York: Alfred A. Knopf, Inc.

Ries, Al and Jack Trout (1981), *Positioning: The Battle for Your Mind*. New York: Warner Books.

Schudson, Michael (1984), *Advertising, the Uneasy Persuasion: Its Dubious Impact on American Society*. New York: Basic Books, Inc.

Shimp, Terrence A. (1981), "Attitude Toward the Ad as a Mediator of Consumer Brand Choice," *Journal of Advertising*, 10 (2), 9–15.

Stein, Benjamin (1982), "On T.V. These Days, the Really Rich Are Really In," *Wall Street Journal* (September 3), 17.

Vaughn, R. (1980), "How Advertising Works: A Planning Model," *Journal of Advertising Research*, 20 (5), 27–33.

CHAPTER 23

COGNITIVE RESTRUCTURING AS A RELAPSE PREVENTION STRATEGY
Teaching Alcoholics to Talk Back to Beer Ads

JOYCE M. WOLBURG, ROXANNE HOVLAND,
AND RONALD E. HOPSON

INTRODUCTION

While some disagreement exists about specific approaches to treatment of alcoholism, most experts agree that an essential stage of the recovery process is "maintenance," which begins the moment after the initiation of abstinence or control (Marlatt, 1985). From that point on, the alcoholic will be faced with a plethora of temptations, stressors, and the pull of powerful habitual behavior. Marlatt identifies a number of stressors, such as emotional states, social pressures, and temptations in the form of external stimuli, which include ads for alcoholic beverages.

Relapse Prevention

Despite the plethora of views regarding the etiology of alcohol addiction, the focus upon prevention, remediation, and maintenance of sobriety has gained in importance. A number of different approaches to maintenance are used including relapse prevention. Examples include coping with frustration and anger, drink-refusal training in social pressure situations, and learning how to cope with urges and cravings (Marlatt, 1985).

Marlatt and Gordon (1980) categorize relapse situations as intrapersonal-environmental determinants, such as coping with negative emotional states, enhancing positive emotional states, and giving in to temptations and urges; and interpersonal determinants, such as coping with interpersonal conflict, and responding to direct or indirect social pressure. "Substance cues" that can encourage one to give in to temptations and urges include ads for alcohol in addition to "passing by a liquor store" or "unexpectedly finding a bottle of one's favorite booze." While this determinant was not the most frequently rated high risk category, Marlatt and Gordon noted that it was identified in at least 11% of cases.

A variety of skill training methods are used to prepare alcoholics for dealing with high risk situations; however, Cooney et al. (1983) recommend combining cue exposure with cognitive restructuring methods to correct false beliefs. For example, many alcoholics falsely assume that all cravings and urges are manifestations of physical withdrawal symptoms that cannot be controlled. Therapists can counter such cognitive beliefs with the information that most urges are triggered by external factors. The alcoholic can then reframe the craving as a desire to cope with stress rather than a biological urge. A few of the many cognitive distortions that alcoholics are prone to experience are: (1) overgeneralizing, e.g., "if it's true in one case, it applies to any case . . . ," (2). excessive responsibility, e.g., "I am responsible for all bad things, failure, and so on," (3) catastrophizing, e.g., "always think of the worst. It's most likely to happen to you," and (4) dichotomous thinking, e.g., "everything is either one extreme or another" (Beck, Rush, Shaw, & Emery, 1979, p. 261).

Marlatt sums up the individual's dilemma in society as follows:

> . . . people are constantly bombarded with stimuli and cues arising from the observation of other people's behavior, from advertising and the media, from associations and memories of past behaviors, all of which form a strident chorus of voices urging the individual to "DRINK ME!" . . . How can we assist the client to cope with all of these tempting lures? Although it is tempting to follow the lead of Odysseus, who had the ears of his rowers plugged with wax to block out the Sirens' song of temptation, this solution hardly seems practical in contemporary society. Instead, a balanced presentation of cognitive and behavioral coping strategies may be the best weapon against temptation. (1985, p. 243)

We suggest that of all stimuli, alcohol advertising may play a key role as a "tempting lure" and that efforts at inoculating persons against the effects of alcohol advertising may be usefully informed by greater understanding of the psychological dynamics which may underlie the addictive experience.

Hopson's Study

Hopson's (1993; Hopson & Beaird-Spiller, 1995) understanding of the experience of addiction from the point of view of the addicted person offers a point of departure for developing strategies to assist the addicted person in dealing with alcohol advertising. His findings indicate that the addictive experience is characterized by four problematic modes: (1) intense feelings for which language is inadequate; (2) a disruption in the experience of time; (3) alienation from oneself and others; and (4) lack of sense of agency, self-efficacy, or capacity for self regulation. These four modes of experience serve as a foundation for the present study and are described below.

1. *Intense Feelings*. The life-world of the alcohol addicted person is set within intense feelings which form the context within which the person lives. The world is ordered by feelings, and actions are organized around an attempt to manage them. The feelings are often, though not always, negative, and are experienced as potentially overwhelming and always intense.
2. *Disruption in the Experience of Time*. Within the context of these wordless, intense, affective experiences, the sense of temporal flow is disrupted. The usual sense of temporality and flux is interrupted, and time moves exceedingly slowly or ceases to move at all.
3. *Alienation from Oneself and Others*. The third area of difficulty is that of intra/interpersonal relationships. The world of the addicted person is a world of disconnection from oneself and others and a sense of alienation.

4. *Lack of Sense of Agency, Self-Efficacy, and Capacity for Self Regulation.* The final area of difficulty relates to efficacy. The failure of words or time to adequately represent, symbolize, and modulate affective states appear to be related to a relative lack of sense of agency, self-efficacy, and capacity for self-regulation (Khan, 1983).

Hopson concludes that the addictive phenomenon is rooted in problematic modes of experience in these domains. As such, the addiction is an ineffective solution to the persistent experiential anomalies of the addicted person. We suggest that it is useful to consider alcohol advertising with attention to these modes of experience. If alcohol ads contain elements that are associated with these vulnerabilities, coping strategies ads should be advanced.

METHODOLOGY

The Interpretive Approach

A qualitative study was designed to investigate the relationship of the content of beer ads to the experience of addiction as suggested by Hopson. Document analysis was chosen in order to allow researchers to conduct an in-depth examination of the content of ads (Denzin, 1978; Taylor, 1994). Though a more subjective method than traditional content analysis, document analysis allows the coding categories to emerge from the data. Thus, instead of applying pre-existing categories used in previous research (none existed for the four experiential modes) or creating them prior to examining the data, the method allows the researcher to create categories while examining the data (Altheide, 1996). Tentative categories were tested and refined until final categories fit the data without being either too inclusive or too restrictive.

Because the three researchers brought different interests and expertise to the study including legal and social issues in advertising, existential-phenomenological psychology and clinical psychology, and advertising as a form of cultural communication, the researchers worked as a team in viewing and coding a sample of commercials. Known as "investigator triangulation" (Denzin, 1978, p. 245), the team approach in qualitative research benefits from expanding the interpretive base of the research by revealing elements of the phenomenon that are not necessarily seen by just one researcher. The researchers worked until reaching a consensus on all issues; thus, no unresolved differences occurred.

Since no previous research had examined how the four experiential modes might be depicted in ads, the researchers examined sources of creative strategy in ad development to generate initial ideas concerning the relationship of Hopson's categories. Advertising strategies have been classified as either transformational or informational, with the former based on emotion and the latter based on logic (Lasky, Day, & Crask, 1989). A standard list of advertising appeals includes a number of emotions such as excitement, fear, love, and pleasure, which are commonly used in ads as part of the creative strategy (Moriarty, 1991). These emotional appeals suggest that addicted persons may be especially vulnerable to beer ads due to the difficulty with affect management which characterizes the addictive phenomena (mode #1).

An advertising study that identified five ways in which time is depicted in ads (Wolburg & Taylor, 1998) suggested a possible relationship between presentation strategies in beer commercials and problems with the experience of time as exemplified in mode #2. According to the study, time was expressed as: (1) a commodity that can be saved or spent; (2) an orientation to past, present, and future; (3) something that "marks" events including birthdays and anniversaries; (4) a way of noting pace through editing; and (5) a way of privileging passage (new is superior to old). These provided a basis for examining time messages in the beer and car product ads.

The advertising appeals also included the need for affiliation or belonging, which seems to resonate with mode #3—alienation from oneself and others. Finally, appeals to challenge, achievement, and accomplishment resonate with mode #4—the lack of sense of agency or self-efficacy. These sources generated initial ideas prior to viewing the ads, and during the process of viewing the ads themselves the researchers continued to refine the list of elements that pertain to each mode.

Obtaining the Sample

The sample was drawn from weekend television sports programming including professional football games, basketball games, and car racing on cable and broadcast channels over a four month period. Sports programming was chosen due to the large volume of beer advertising and for its appeal to men, who represent about 60% of beer consumers and are the primary target market (Simmons Market Research Bureau, 1996). Figures also support the choice of television as a medium, since 83% of beer ads are placed on TV (Leading National Advertisers, 1996). Fifty unduplicated beer ads and 50 unduplicated ads for automotive products and services (motor oil, batteries, fuel additives, etc.) were compiled, which required the taping of 41 hours of programming. The auto products and services ads were selected as a control product, since they are advertised to the same demographic group at the same frequency. After compiling the tapes, the ads were transcribed.

Although auto products and services are quite dissimilar to beer as a product category, products more similar to beer, such as soft drinks, are targeted to different demographic groups, e.g., both males and females including teens. Since no ideal comparison product exists, the use of a comparison product was included primarily for illustrative purposes.

The Research Questions

The study posed four research questions, each of which directed a stage of the analytical process. The four questions are presented together, and the stages are presented afterward.

RQ1: Does beer advertising contain any elements that directly relate to Hopson's four problematic modes of experience for people recovering from alcohol addiction?

RQ2: If so, when beer advertising depicts various situations and experiences, what key elements in the ads relate to these problematic modes?

RQ3: How does beer advertising differ from the advertising for other products in its use of the elements associated with the problematic modes?

RQ4: Can insight into beer advertising be applied to relapse prevention treatment for alcoholics? If so, how?

The Research Process

Stage 1. RQ1 asks if beer advertising contains elements related to the four modes. A preliminary viewing of the sample provided overwhelming support that beer ads do depict situations and experiences that can directly appeal to people who have difficulties with: (1) intense feelings; (2) disruption in the experience of time; (3) alienation from oneself and others; and (4) lack of agency, self-efficacy, or self-regulation.

The relationship between the ads and the modes of experience is complex. The ads make very few rational, testable statements of any kind—certainly no ads claim that consumption will help one overcome problematic modes, for problems are never acknowledged. However, by consistently showing beer as a product for popular fun-seekers who spend their time enjoying life, expressing emotions, celebrating occasions, and performing at high levels of skill, the ads focus upon the very qualities and experiences most elusive to those addicted to alcohol. The ads contain both verbal and visual elements that can make promises through imagery and encourage the belief that people who drink experience none of these problems. These initial findings directed the next stage.

Stage 2. RQ2 asked what specific elements relate to the modes. A more thorough viewing of the ads was required to address this question, and a coding sheet was created to capture the variety of advertising elements related to these modes (coding sheet is available upon request). Rather than presenting the coding sheet as a finite or exhaustive list of elements related to the problematic modes, it is offered as a list of the elements most apparent to the researchers.

Given that people with alcohol addiction experience intense feelings for which language is inadequate, both verbal and visual expressions of emotion were noted using Moriarty's (1991) list of appeals. In addition, actions that take the place of verbal communication were also abundant in the commercials exemplifying "act, don't think" behavior. Since alcohol addiction involves disturbance of the experience of the movement of time, the study tracked all verbal and visual references to time, including use of time for celebrations, prominent use of fast or slow paced music, and idealization of past, present, or future. Given the feelings of alienation, the study also noted all interaction, particularly the nature of the relationship (friendship, romance, etc.). Finally, in relation to a sense of lack of agency and self-efficacy, the study coded the overcoming of physical laws, including violation of rules of temporal and physical contiguity, e.g., instantaneous changes in location and state after opening the product, defiance of gravity, use of anthropomorphism, "scoring" in sports or in sex, and use of special effects.

Each ad for both product categories was viewed using the coding sheet in order to gain a count of how frequently each element occurred and to gain insight into their use. Examples of the elements are provided in the Findings section.

Stage 3. RQ3 asked how beer advertising differs from the advertising of other products. To address this question, differences in usage and frequency of the elements were noted and compared. Although the interpretation of qualitative research primarily relies on insight, the collection of numerical data allowed for Chi-Square analysis as well. In cases where cell values were less than ten, Yates' correction was applied.

Stage 4. RQ4 asked how insight into beer ads could benefit recovering alcoholics. To address this, the psychological literature on treatment and relapse prevention was examined to understand the role of advertising as a stressor. Coping strategies were evaluated.

FINDINGS

The following provides a description and analysis of how the elements were used in the ads. Results of the Chi-Square analysis are also included.

Intensity of Feelings

A number of elements in the ads addressed emotion, and the beer commercials outnumbered the car category commercials in both verbal and non-verbal expressions of emotion. Chi-Square analysis showed that the combined use of verbal and non-verbal emotion was significantly greater for beer ads (Table 23.1), as was the use of emotion in advertising appeals (Table 23.2). Emotional appeals as a whole and specific emotions of love (romance) and pleasure (humor) were also significantly greater for beer ads. However, the number does not do justice to the intensity of emotion. The following Bud Light ad expresses that emotional intensity using an editing style of quick cuts with various beach, boat, and pool scenes and a large cast of fun-loving sunbathers on a hot day.

Table 23.1

Frequency of Appeals

Appeals	Clarification of Some Appeals	Incidence in Beer Ads	Incidence Car Ads	Chi-Square
Aesthetics***	Appreciation of the beautiful	22 (44%)	0 (0%)	25.6
Affiliation**	Belonging to a group	16 (32%)	2 (4%)	11.4
Appetite**	Hunger, taste, cravings	7 (14%)	0 (0%)	5.52
Aspiration**	Achievement, accomplishment	14 (28%)	2 (4%)	9.00
Avoidance		1 (2%)	5 (10%)	2.83
Cleanliness		0 (0%)	3 (6%)	3.09
Convenience	Saving time and effort	0 (0%)	5 (10%)	3.36
Economy***	Saving money	0 (0%)	18 (36%)	19.5
Efficiency***		2 (4%)	32 (64%)	37.4
Egoism	Recognition, prestige	24 (48%)	23 (46%)	0.04
Total Emotions**		47 (94%)	36 (72%)	8.57
Excitement		10 (20%)	5 (10%)	1.96
Fear	Danger, embarrassment	0 (0%)	4 (8%)	2.34
Family	Love, protection	0 (0%)	4 (8%)	2.34
Love***	Affection, romance	12 (24%)	0 (0%)	13.6
Nostalgia		2 (4%)	0 (0%)	2.04
Pleasure*	Humor, happiness, laughter	23 (46%)	11 (22%)	6.41
Pride		9 (18%)	12 (24%)	0.54
Identification	Respect, hero worship	29 (58%)	21 (42%)	2.56
Mental stimulation	Curiosity, challenge	3 (6%)	0 (0%)	3.09
Responsibility		2 (4%)	4 (8%)	0.70
Safety/Security***		1 (2%)	16 (32%)	13.8
Sensory pleasure***	Touch, taste, sound, sight	28 (56%)	0 (0%)	38.8
Sex***		22 (44%)	1 (2%)	20.2
Thriftiness		0 (0%)	9 (18%)	9.89

*$p = <.05$; **$p = <.01$; ***$p = <.001$ for Chi-Square analysis with Yates' Correction for small cells.

ELEMENTS IN ADS BY PRODUCT CATEGORIES

Elements in Ads	Incidence in Beer Ads	Incidence in Car Part Ads	Chi-Square
Elements Associated with Relationships Continued			
Physical Contact	15 (30%)	8 (16%)	2.76
Identification Disclosed	4 (8%)	12 (24%)	3.64
Recognizable, Familiar Music	7 (14%)	2 (4%)	3.05
Elements Associated with Efficacy			
Total Limit Violations***	36 (72%)	9 (18%)	27.3
Anthropomorphism	7 (14%)	1 (2%)	3.39
Defiance of Gravity	5 (10%)	1 (2%)	2.83
Defiance of Nature***	24 (48%)	3 (6%)	20.2
Other special effects	12 (24%)	4 (8%)	3.64
Scoring***	30 (60%)	6 (12%)	22.9
Product as reward***	14 (28%)	0 (0%)	14.0
Product Empowers	9 (18%)	5 (10%)	1.32
Objectifying other people*	6 (12%)	0 (0%)	4.43
Others shown for validation*	6 (12%)	0 (0%)	4.43

*$p = <.05$; **$p = <.01$; ***$p = <.001$ for Chi-Square analysis with Yates' Correction for small cells.

Table 23.2

Elements in Ads by Product Category

Elements in Ads	Incidence in Beer Ads	Incidence in Car Part Ads	Chi-Square
Elements Associated with Intense Emotion			
Verbal Expression of Emotion	15 (30%)	8 (16%)	2.76
Nonverbal Expression of Emotion	23 (46%)	16 (32%)	2.05
Total Verbal & Non.Expression**	38 (76%)	24 (48%)	8.31
Emphasis on "act don't think"***	18 (36%)	2 (4%)	14.0
Elements Associated with Time			
Verbal References	16 (32%)	17 (34%)	0.04
Visual References	14 (28%)	7 (14%)	2.95
Celebrations*	14 (28%)	2 (4%)	6.49
Special Editing**	15 (30%)	4 (8%)	9.00
Compressed or non-real time*	40 (80%)	31 (62%)	3.93
Prominent use of music for pace**	27 (54%)	13 (26%)	8.16
Idealization of past, future, present	5 (10%)	0 (0%)	3.36
Time as a limited commodity***	0 (0%)	15 (30%)	15.3
Time passage, longevity	2 (4%)	5 (10%)	1.38
Elements Associated with Relationships			
No beings depicted	4 (8%)	9 (18%)	2.21
Single being depicted*	4 (8%)	14 (28%)	5.48
Non-human interaction	3 (6%)	1 (2%)	1.04
Total Human interaction**	39 (78%)	25 (50%)	8.50
Family members	0 (0%)	3 (6%)	3.09
Friends*	24 (48%)	3 (6%)	20.2
Acquaintances	6 (12%)	6 (12%)	0
Strangers	8 (16%)	6 (12%)	0.33
Co-workers, team members	1 (2%)	7 (14%)	3.39
Romantic Interest present***	22 (44%)	1 (2%)	13.8
Predator/Victim	4 (8%)	0 (0%)	2.34

Man:	Live from the beach, it's Bud Light!!!
Woman:	Where the weather's always hot and the Bud Light's cold!
Man:	Bud Light for all my friends!
Woman:	What if we get stranded???
Man:	Ha . . . (He implies that being stranded would be an opportunity to "score.")
Woman:	It's perfect on a cold winter day—like today! (In reality, it's hot).
Man:	Unbelievable! The official beer of winter. Sure beats rush hour. Bud Light!!!

The quick editing style, special effects, enthusiasm in their voices, and pulsating background music all gave the dizzying impression of emotion in the midst of intense activity.

Fast action for its own sake was even more prominent in a series of Coors Light ads that depicted swimming, rollerblading, and volleyball in one spot and skiing, ice skating, and hang gliding in another, all fused with dancing scenes and images of the Coors can breaking through a mountain of snow. The words "keep on movin' " were repeated while a voiceover sang:

And the Silver Bullet has the taste to keep it movin.' Coors Light. Naturally brewed for a taste that goes down easy. Coors Light. Keep on movin.'

The words "keep on movin" kept the pace rapid and depicted an action-packed life that left little time to reflect. The words contrast markedly with one alcoholic's description of wearing lead boots that make you feel "you can't move your feet" (Hopson, 1993).

The "act, don't think" theme occurred only in beer ads. While car product ads also used emotions, the nature of the emotions differed. For example, some car product ads played off the fear of injury to a family member by using the wrong brand. This use of occasional negative emotions for the car product category contrasted with the beer commercials' consistently positive tone. As a result, consumers know that there are risks in purchasing car products and services, such as the dissatisfaction that comes from buying a product that doesn't live up to expectations. Consumers may even overestimate the risk of physical injury from using a product of lower quality, e.g., having an accident for lack of Michelin tires. Ironically, the statistics leave no doubt that alcohol is a risky product, but the lack of negative emotions in beer ads effectively conceals any evidence of risk.

Time

A number of elements are associated with the passage of time, most of which were used significantly more often in beer ads including references to celebrations and prominent use of music for pace (Tables 23.1 and 23.2). Beer ads were also more likely to use special editing devices that either compressed time or presented the sequence of events as a montage of images rather than in "real" time. The use of time as a limited commodity was used significantly fewer times in beer ads than for car products commercials, which relied heavily on claims such as "while supplies last," "lifetime guarantee or your money back," and "quickest service around." These messages focus on "clock time," while one could say beer ads suspend clock time.

Miller beer has incorporated time in a long-standing campaign of ads using "Miller Time." One ad in the sample opened with the words to the song, "Time is on my side," while the visuals showed men quitting work at the auto shop and going to a bar to drink beer.

Song:	*Time is on my side. Yes it is. Time is on my side. Yes it is.*
VO:	*The time is 5:01. The beer is Miller High Life. And the reason is clear. When the time is your own, it must be Miller Time.*
Song:	*Time, time, time . . .*
VO:	*Miller Time. Miller Beer.*

Not only is the association with time meaningful, but the use of lyrics conveying that time is "on my side" encourages thinking that drinking Miller makes time "my friend" instead of the adversary that Hopson's participants described.

Michelob has also used a long-standing time-oriented campaign using the slogan, "Some days are better than others." In an ad that commemorated PGA golfers, a number of spectacularly executed golf shots were shown including one in which the ball bounced off the water and landed in the hole.

VO:	*Did you ever have one of those days that starts off with a bang?*
	When things take a turn for the best?
	When you practically walk on water?
VO:	*Michelob salutes the PGA golfers and golfers everywhere, and those special moments that make some days better than others.*

The ad sends two messages: first, by associating Michelob with success the ad encourages viewers to believe that "if I drink Michelob, things will take a turn for the best. Maybe I, too, can practically walk on water." Second, by "saluting . . . special moments that make some days better than others," the ad goes beyond the context of golf and encourages the belief that "Michelob can turn the ordinary moments of my life into special moments that make the days better." This could be a compelling message for the person who feels that time is never-ending.

Pace featured prominently in the ads through slow, sexy music; fast, rhythmic music; editing devices that changed the feel of the passage of time; and use of special content in visuals. For example, the Busch "be a mountain man" ads used music with a prominent beat, quick editing, and visuals that rushed the viewer to the mountains. The heavy reliance on pace and images of movement for Busch beer and the previously described Coors ads convey the notion that beer offers an escape from feeling "stuck" in time.

Hopson's participant who described feeling "trapped" implies a spatial component in addition to a temporal one. The mountain man ads not only transported people through time but literally to another *place*. The place metaphor was also vivid in Miller Genuine Draft's use of the line, "The world is a very cool place; get out of the old and into the cold," and in the Busch ads that worship the cowboy and idealize the land:

> There's no place on earth that I'd rather be, out in the open where it's all plain to see. The land is pure, unchained and free, and there's no place that I'd rather be. Come on, come on, head for the mountains of Busch Beer. Head for the mountains, it's cold and it's smooth, it's waiting for you. Come on, head for the mountains of Busch Beer.

Interpersonal Alienation

Since the participants in Hopson's study spoke of extreme loneliness and isolation from others, both sets of ads were examined for appeals to affiliation and the nature of interpersonal relationships. Overall, beer ads were significantly stronger in the appeal to affiliation, the portrayal of interaction, which was most commonly between friends, and sexual or romantic interest. Absence of any people or the use of a single spokesperson occurred significantly more often in car category ads, and when interaction occurred it was more often between co-workers or with customers (Tables 23.1 and 23.2).

Celebrity spokespersons rarely appeared in beer ads, probably a result of a regulation that only allows retired sports celebrities to appear while current sports figures cannot. Since these restrictions do not apply to car part and service commercials, more celebrities appeared. As a result, car category ads encouraged viewers to identify psychologically with an individual, e.g., Richard Petty or Mario Andretti, while the beer ads encouraged viewers to identify with a character type, e.g., "the mountain man" or "the modern day hero."

The vast majority of beer commercials presented the drinker in social settings. In contrast with the feelings of alienation experienced by people addicted to alcohol, many beer ads used casts in social settings where belonging was easy and befriending strangers was natural. Even when non-humans were shown, they were socializing (the Budweiser frogs, the Molson bears, people on billboards who came to life . . .).

Many beer ads emphasized friendship, and a Molson ad featured two anthropomorphized bears conversing as buddies in a humorous play on words.

> Bear 1:   Hey, whatcha doin' down there?
> Bear 2:   Trying to cool off.
> Bear 1:   Yeah, the heat's unbearable.
> Bear 2:   I was gonna hit the beach but it's a zoo on weekends.
> Bear 1:   Yeah, parking can get really hairy.
> Bear 2:   You know, I could go for a nice cold beer.
> Bear 1:   Hey, how'd you like to wrap your paws around a nice cold Molson?
> Bear 2:   Molson? Hey. Now you're talking.
> VO: Molson-of Canada. Because good friends deserve a great beer.
> Bear 1:   Whatcha wanna do tomorrow?
> Bear 2:   Hey, it's the weekend. Let's go scare some tourists.

While this exchange included bears, a Heineken ad with two men had the same degree of humor and male bonding.

Several ads used strong sexual innuendo, such as a Miller Genuine Draft ad played to the tune of "The Good, The Bad, and The Ugly." The ad featured a sweaty, sexy woman in a hot apartment who called a repairman to fix her air conditioner. She opened the door to a stranger wearing cowboy boots, who unplugged the AC and opened a bottle of MGD. Instantly the room became filled with snow and strong sexual undercurrents. The real repairman drove up, saw the snow coming from the apartment, and examined the bottle cap with an amused but knowing expression. Viewers heard the familiar words:

> . . . for those who've discovered its smooth draft taste, the world is a very cool place. So get out of the old and into the cold.

The ad is one of a series, all of which center on strong sexual attraction between a man and woman who are strangers, while a second male bystander, who is older, less attractive, not drinking, and presumably not "cool," watches with an expression of envy and surprise. In each ad, beer and sex are associated only with the attractive young man and woman, not the "outsider."

Other ads had a large cast of characters, such as the Bud Light series of beach party ads and the Busch mountain man ads. Each type of relationship depicted in the ad, whether it involved strong male bonding, intense male/female sexual attraction, or casual party scene encounters, showed an ease and naturalness as though beer was the essential element that brought people together. This could be a powerful association for those who experience extreme loneliness and feelings of isolation.

Agency and Self-Efficacy

The commercials were examined for evidence of efficacy through activities involving such things as skill, power, and accomplishments. Appeals to aspiration (accomplishment) and evidence of self-efficacy were significantly more frequent in the beer commercials, especially through "scoring" in sports and in sex (Tables 23.1 and 23.2). People in the beer ads operated at a high level of skill when athletic ability was required and easily succeeded in attracting members of the opposite sex.

In fact, people in beer ads had superhuman abilities, particularly through the use of "limit violations"—the stretching of reality beyond its limits. Examples included people in billboards who came to life and people who performed daredevil acts of skill that defied gravity. This took place in a world where beer cans forged through mountains, snowstorms came out of beer bottles, frogs and bears talked, monsters walked through cities while women watched in amusement, and buildings became bottle openers. Many beer ads combined the use of limit violations with a positioning of the product that either empowered or rewarded the user.

An example is a series of commercials that implied that Miller beer can do anything including resolving disagreements over which TV programs to watch. When one ad depicted a group of men arguing over whether to watch a cooking show or a wrestling match, the cook suddenly became part of the match and defeated the wrestler. A different ad in the series combined golf and football into a single sport. Both closed with the line, "Can your beer do this?"

Similarly, a series of Busch ads challenged viewers by asking if they have what it takes. The answer is "yes" for those who drink Busch. Each ad showed a young man picking up two kinds of Busch beer while young, attractive, admiring women were on hand.

> *Have you got what it takes to be a mountain man? All it really takes are the two cool beers of the mountain man. Smooth Busch Beer and easy drinking Busch Light. So, be a mountain man. All you gotta do is head for the mountains.*

An unspoken implication is that the Busch-drinking mountain man has "what it takes" to sexually satisfy the many women he attracts.

Foster's beer used a series of humorous ads that contained subtle limit violations. These ads identified objects in a very exaggerated way, either through understatement or overstatement. For example, one showed a shark and redefined it as a "guppy." Other ads redefined a sprig of parsley as "salad" and a crocodile's mouth as a "can opener." The next image in all ads showed a can of Foster's, which was defined as beer. When the same redefining process is used for beer, the ad encourages viewers to use their imagination to exaggerate the meaning of beer and redefine it in a new way.

The frogs who croak the Budweiser name and the talking Molson bears also lend their own brand of anthropomorphic humor to the limit violations. The use of humor in these ads makes them seem quite innocuous, but the unreality associated with the product remains.

Limit violations were significantly less frequent in car parts commercials. One featured an interview at a BP station with a man and a series of cars that "talk" about how clean their fuel injectors feel. Another showed a bottle of 4×4 Quaker State Oil breaking out of a box and turning into a 4×4 vehicle. While the ad recommends the "intelligent oil for hard working engines," the vehicle climbs over the merchandise in an auto parts store, hauls items, and breaks through ice.

Efficacy was observed to be a recurring theme in both beer and car products ads; however, in beer commercials the efficacy almost always enhanced the user, and limit violations were achieved as a result of using the product. The efficacy involved in the car product commercials predominantly referred to the product's efficacy in fulfilling its intended purpose. In other words, the car product empowered the car, not the driver. In a few instances the car product empowered the user by making him/her more competitive, but the product claims and imagery were within realistic limits, unlike the magical world of beer imagery.

SUMMARY AND CONCLUSIONS

Applications for the Treatment of Alcoholism

Given that advertising messages can act as stimuli for relapse and are targeted to heavy drinkers, some of whom are unavoidably alcoholics, inoculating the recovering alcoholic to beer commercials could become a significant part of the recovery process, particularly for those in the early stages. More research is needed to further explore the role of advertising during recovery; however, we offer the following preliminary suggestions as relapse prevention strategies. First, experts can make alcoholics aware of the four problematic experiential modes as reported by Hopson. Second, they can help alcoholics realize that beer ads contain images associated with these modes. And third, experts can help alcoholics develop coping strategies for responding to advertising messages.

Some coping strategies previously reported by alcoholics are avoiding the ads when possible; and reinterpreting advertising messages (Treise, Taylor, & Wells, 1994). To avoid ads or encounter fewer ads is impractical for some, and one can argue that trying to avoid advertising messages may result in empowering the ads; however, we offer some techniques for those who can benefit by this strategy. In order to avoid beer ads, it is necessary to know where they are found. According to 1996 figures from Leading National Advertisers and Simmons Market Research Bureau, the majority of beer ads are placed on television, primarily in sports programming; however, some also appear in late night talk shows and in programs on national cable networks that target men. While this study examined beer advertising, we mention in passing the media that carry ads for other forms of alcohol. Distilled spirits ads are primarily found in magazines and on billboards, while wine advertising appears in newspapers and in national broadcast spot ads on radio and on cable TV channels.

Other avoidance strategies that are admittedly inconvenient for long-term implementation but possibly worth the effort during high risk times include: taping a television program and zapping through commercials at the time of viewing; having a friend or family member cut ads out of magazines; or driving a different route to avoid a particularly appealing billboard.

Reinterpreting the message is an example of cognitive restructuring (Marlatt, 1985) and is a more realistic relapse prevention strategy for most alcoholics than avoidance. One approach is to counter the positive image portrayed in the ads with the negative but more realistic aspects of drinking. Treise, Taylor, and Wells (1994, p. 126) quoted one participant who reinterpreted the message by reminding himself that "beer commercials don't show . . . the ambulance . . . the families that are broken, or the pain . . . when you would do anything for a drink." Teaching alcoholics to restructure their beliefs could be done in a variety of ways; however, the results of this study suggest that a primary strategy should be to teach alcoholics to restructure advertising messages related to themes of time, self-efficacy, alienation from others, and emotion.

For example, an ad that addresses efficacy can be restructured in the following way. When beer ads equate drinking with feeling sexy, successful, or powerful, the alcoholic can "talk back to the ad" with examples of feeling powerless from his or her own experiences. An alcoholic might say, "Sure, the guy in the ad has women hanging onto him, and he's thinking how cool he is and that he's going to score. But how many women will want him if he spills his drink on her, gets sick and throws up on her, or gets arrested for drunk driving?"

Treatment personnel can encourage the addicted person to query the commercial for a reality check by asking, "Is that realistic, can that happen?" This may serve to make the exaggerations and limit violations more apparent to the viewer. Also this serves a psychological function of teaching self talk strategies, which may generalize to other situations in which the addicted person is inclined to experience emotions in an exaggerated form.

Beer ads typically show people interacting in a group, but the reality for many is drinking alone. Ads that tap into the alienation mode could be restructured using the same technique. The alcoholic could say, "Everyone in the ad has so many friends—no one is alone. But when I drink, there's no one. I'm all alone." Or, as the case may be, the alcoholic may not literally be alone but may feel alone. In that case the talking back dialogue may be, "When I drink, there's no one. I feel all alone, even though there are people all around." It may be useful to assist the addicted person in knowing that there is often a discrepancy between how things appear in the ad and what one experiences internally. The ads do not show the internal state.

Negative emotions are part of most alcoholics' experience; yet, ads are upbeat and humorous. The use of humor is deceptive in that it not only generates a false perception of reality but disarms viewers from taking ads seriously, since humorous ads *seem* harmless. Alcoholics who learn to talk back can break the illusion and turn humorous ads "inside out." By giving drinkers the tools to talk back to ads and counter the perception with the reality, alcoholics take power over the ads and gain a real sense of efficacy, not the false sense portrayed in ads.

It is often said colloquially of alcoholics that they have a problem with "people pleasing." This suggests that they may have difficulties challenging the dictates and preferences of others even when they may not agree with them. Ironically, as addicted persons are able to challenge the experience presented in the ads, they may be able to generalize this practice to relationships in their lives.

Another cognitive restructuring approach that may remove much of the appeal from an advertising message is to enlighten alcoholics to basic advertising strategy so they can "oppositionally decode" the ad (Steiner, 1991). Most people react negatively if they feel manipulated by advertisers (Bond & Kirshenbaum, 1998), and alcoholics may become resentful upon learning that advertisers target heavy users of alcohol through their demographic and psychographic characteristics. For example, upon viewing an appealing ad that associates drinking with good times, alcoholics could remind themselves that the ad is simply a sales pitch that an advertising agency created by knowing the right psychological buttons to push. Any technique that challenges the illusion in the ad may be helpful.

These techniques could either be taught individually or as a group exercise using role playing. The effectiveness of the various strategies will probably vary in effectiveness with different individuals, but we pose these preliminary suggestions and call for additional research.

Implications

With $800 million at stake in mass media advertising (Leading National Advertisers, 1996), many would claim that there is nothing inherently unethical or illegal about the tactics used by beer advertisers. Supporters might argue that beer advertisers are merely employing tactics available to all advertisers. Unfortunately, while beer advertising is aimed at a general audience, it reaches especially vulnerable audiences—those who are in the throes of alcohol addiction, heavy drinkers who have the potential to become alcoholics, and those in recovery programs who are actively committed to overcoming alcohol addiction. The traditional marketing notion of maximizing advertising efficiency by targeting those who are likely to consume relatively more of the product has unique implications when the product is addictive, and when the heaviest users include alcoholics.

Beer advertisers often defend their position by arguing that restrictions go against the utilitarian notion of the greatest good for the greatest number by putting the needs of a small group above those of the majority who otherwise have a right to see these ads. Since there is no indication that alcohol advertising will undergo any further restriction at this time, alcoholics will continue to have to deal with the presence of mass media messages that heavily target them and tap into their vulnerabilities. Recovering alcoholics may not be able to avoid advertising; however, they may reduce their risk of relapse by learning coping strategies such as cognitive restructuring.

This research constitutes a step toward understanding the unique interaction between advertising messages and the experience mode of the alcohol addicted consumer. Given the importance to individuals and society, it is essential to investigate the power of advertising for this group.

REFERENCES

Altheide, D.L. (1996). *Qualitative media analysis*. Thousand Oaks, CA: Sage.

Beck, A.T., Rush, A.J., Shaw, B.F., & Emery, G. (1979). *Cognitive therapy of depression*. New York: Guilford.

Bond, J., & R. Kirshenbaum, R. (1998). *Under the radar*. New York: John Wiley & Sons, Inc.

Cooney, N.L, Baker, L., & Pomerleau, O.F. (1983). Cue exposure for relapse prevention in alcohol treatment. In R.J. McMahon & K.D. Craig (Eds.), *Advances in clinical behavior therapy*. New York: Brunner/Mazel.

Denzin, N.K. (1978). *The research act: A theoretical introduction to sociological methods*. Englewood Cliffs, NJ: Prentice Hall.

Hopson, R.E. (1993). A thematic analysis of the addictive experience: Implications for psychotherapy. *Psychotherapy*, 30 (Fall), 481–494.

Hopson, R.E. & Beaird-Spiller, B. (1995). Why AA works: A psychological analysis of the addictive experience and the efficacy of alcoholics anonymous. *Alcoholism Treatment Quarterly*, 12 (3), 95 1–17.

Khan, M. (1983). *Hidden selves*. New York: International Universities Press.

Laskey, H.A., Day, E., & Crask, M. (1989). Typology of main message strategies for television commercials. *Journal of Advertising*, 18 (1), 36–41.

Leading National Advertisers/Ad Dollar Summary, Multi-Media Service (1996). New York: *Competitive Media Reporting and Magazine Publishers of America, Inc.*

Marlatt, G.A. (1985). Relapse prevention: Theoretical rationale and overview of the model. In G.A. Marlatt & J.R. Gordon (Eds.),, *Relapse prevention: Maintenance strategies in the treatment of addictive behaviors* (pp. 3–70). New York: Guilford.

Marlatt, G.A., & Gordon, J.R. (1980). Determinants of relapse: Implications for the maintenance of behavior change. In P.O. Davidson (Ed.), *Behavioral medicine: Changing health lifestyles*. New York: Brunner/Mazel, 1980.

Moriarty, S. E. (1991). *Creative advertising: Theory and practice*. Englewood Cliffs, NJ: Prentice Hall.

Simmons Market Research Bureau (1996). Vol P-14.

Steiner, L. (1991). Oppositional decoding as an act of resistance. In R.K. Avery & D. Eason (Eds.), *Critical perspectives on media and society* (pp. 329–345). New York: The Guilford Press.

Taylor, R.E. (1994). Qualitative research. In M.W. Singletary (Ed.), *Mass communication research* (pp. 265–279). New York: Longman.

Treise, D., Taylor, R.E., & Wells, L.G. (1994). How recovering alcoholics interpret alcoholic-beverage advertising. *Health Marketing Quarterly*, 12 (2), 125–139.

Wolburg, J.M. & Taylor, R.E. (1998). Celebrate the moments of your life: An investigation of time as a cultural value in American television advertising. In J.B. Ford & E.D. Honeycutt, Jr. (Eds.), *Developments in marketing science*, Vol XXI (pp. 363–367). Norfolk, VA: Academy of Marketing Science.

CHAPTER 24

BEEFCAKE AND CHEESECAKE
Insights for Advertisers

MARILYN Y. JONES, ANDREA J. S. STANALAND, AND BETSY D. GELB

Sex appeals in advertising now include eye-catching male models (Kuriansky 1995; Miller 1993) as well as cheesecake—sexy female models. Over the last 25 years, researchers investigating the effectiveness of sexy ads, most often cheesecake ads viewed by men, have reported mixed findings, in general concluding that such ads attract attention but do not improve either recall of or attitude toward the brand. The emergence of beefcake ads, ones with sexy male models, prompts the question of whether responses parallel those to cheesecake ads. Further, recent literature on differences between the sexes in responses to the same stimuli suggests that men and women may respond differently to any ad that makes a gender perspective salient.

Our study proceeded from two premises. The first was that we need to know more about responses to cheesecake ads. Both men and women may have evolved in their views of what is appropriate since previous research was conducted; therefore, previous findings may no longer apply. The second premise was that we need to know more about beefcake ads, as no model of advertising effects predicts whether or under what circumstances men's and women's responses to beefcake ads parallel those to cheesecake ads.

We therefore studied how both male and female viewers of an ad respond to advertising that is more versus less suggestive in its illustrations. We expected differences related to (1) the sex of the model and (2) whether the model is provocatively dressed. We expected those variables, interacting with sex of viewer, to affect attitudes toward the ad and the advertised brand, and also memorability of the ad and the brand.

The pattern of relationships expected was based on four overlapping streams of research. The first important stream consists of studies of sexy models in advertising. The second pertains to the interpretation of, and reaction to, the pictorial components of an ad. The third stream is represented by the deconstruction literature, and has been applied to understanding how consumers read ads (Scott 1994a, b; Stern 1993). That perspective, which sees individual reaction to a communication as dependent on situation and context, has contributed to the position that communication is inherently gendered; that is, it contains cues that readers recognize as representing statements about gender (Stern 1993). The fourth research stream pertains to the general formulations of advertising response. Of specific interest was the dual mediation hypothesis (MacKenzie, Lutz, and Belch 1986) that reaction to an advertised brand is influenced by cognitive processing of

From *Journal of Advertising*, vol. 27, no. 2 (Summer 1998). Copyright © 1998 by the American Academy of Advertising. Reprinted with permission from M.E. Sharpe, Inc.

advertised messages and the attitudes that such processing may in turn influence, but also that reaction is influenced directly by emotional response to the advertising.

PREVIOUS RESEARCH

Sexy Models in Advertising

The history of research in the field of sexy advertising is summarized in Table 24.1. That history has followed advertising practice. Beginning more than 50 years ago, an advertiser might occasionally or routinely place a scantily clad female model in an ad offering a utilitarian product to men, assuming that attention to the ad would thereby increase. Once researchers began testing the efficacy of including such a model as an attention-getter, they simply followed advertising practice: they conducted their research using a sexy female model and an audience of men. They measured the effects on not only attention, but also other variables, such as brand name and copy point recall.

As sophistication increased, researchers added women to their pool of respondents and included measures of attitude toward the ad, realizing that for women the attitudes could well be negative (Morrison and Sherman 1972; Baker and Churchill 1977; Chestnut, LaChance, and Lubitz 1977; Peterson and Kerin 1977). Then psychological researchers prompted further complexity by showing the interrelationships of attitudes and cognitive variables. At roughly the same time, other researchers perceived that men as well as women might respond negatively to sexual images unrelated to the advertised product. More complex relationships were tested. As the next step, research with male models as well as female models appeared, with male and female respondents, primarily focusing on attitudes and finding differences depending on sex of respondent.

Our study adds to the stream of literature by measuring responses to beefcake and cheesecake ads by both men and women, and examining both attitudes and cognitive (memorability) variables. We measured attitude toward the ad and brand, as well as recall and recognition of brand, illustration, and copy. From the work of gender theorists such as Stern (1993), we expected to find differences between men's and women's responses to the same stimuli.

We proceeded from the idea that sexiness of a model pictured in an ad is linked to measures of responses to the ad and the brand, and that the relationships are moderated by the match between the sex of the viewer and the sex of the model. Measures of attitude response to advertising have demonstrated the utility of the dual-mediation hypothesis (MacKenzie, Lutz, and Belch 1986), which posits the following three sets of links: cognitions about the ad influence attitudes toward it and attitudes toward the brand; attitude toward the ad affects the cognitions people generate about the brand and also the attitude toward the brand; and brand cognitions influence attitude toward the brand. Other responses to advertising include memory measures, with memory depending on the amount of attention and thought given to an ad.

In general, the research summarized in Table 24.1 supports the idea that sex of model and sex of viewer interact to influence response to advertising. However, the studies are not altogether consistent in their findings. One possible explanation is that sexiness has been operationalized in three major ways: physical attractiveness, nudity, and rated sexiness/suggestiveness. Hence, research results that appear to conflict may actually reflect responses to significantly different stimuli.

As the table shows, some studies have found that it is not the degree of sexiness (whether that be nudity or rated suggestiveness) but the presence or absence of a model that produces negative effects on recall and recognition (Alexander and Judd 1978; Judd and Alexander 1983). However, that conclusion is called into question by O'Connor et al. (1986), who found that brand recall did not diminish with the presence or absence of a model. Recall does appear to decline as an ad contains more nudity, but sexiness operationalized in a broader sense than nudity may or may not reduce recall.

Increasing nudity and/or sexiness historically has been found to influence attitude toward the ad. The most striking differences are between men and women, with female respondents reacting more negatively than men to sexiness. However, these results are based largely on studies employing only female models.

Visual Images in Advertising

A separate but related set of studies has considered the effects of visual images. Mitchell (1986) and Mitchell and Olson (1981) show evidence that the meanings derived from the pictures included with ads have a direct effect on attitude toward the ad and an indirect effect on attitude toward the brand. According to Mitchell (1986), the meanings conveyed by a picture in an ad may be affect laden and may influence attitude toward the ad and, by extension, alter the direct link between attitude toward the ad and attitude toward the brand as well as the brand cognitions that contribute to attitude toward the brand. Scott (1994a, b) notes that pictorial stimuli communicate meaning that they do not explicitly "show," as consumers interpret visual content through a dynamic system of symbols. One possibility, then, is that any ad with a model prominently illustrated is making a gender-salient statement based simply on the sex of the model. Another possibility is that in the case of sexy ads, an advertiser is perceived as communicating a wish to associate a brand with a sexy man or a sexy woman.

Understandably, differences in responses have been found between men and women. When Mick and Politi (1989) asked student subjects to relate their thoughts and feelings about a suggestive ad with a dominant visual content, the subjects reported a great variety of interpretations. Gender differences in interpretation were found and could be traced back to differences in sensitivity to symbolic meanings within the pictures. In contrast, Elliott et al. (1995) expected to find such differences but did not. They noted that many sexual images are ambiguous, giving rise to interpretations that vary between sexes, although their study results did not support their expectations of interpretive differences. Plausibly, then, if interpretations yield beliefs that influence memory of the ad and attitudes toward it, those variables will be influenced by the sex of the respondent interacting with the degree of sexiness in the ad and the gender of the model.

Sex of the Model and Deconstruction Literature

As Table 24.1 shows, gender differences within the audience for advertising have frequently been associated with differences in response. Few studies, however, have examined differences generated by varying the sex of the model in the stimulus ads, because few have explicitly examined beefcake advertising.

Among researchers who have used sexy male models are Simpson, Horton, and Brown (1996), who found an opposite-sex effect: female viewers liked beefcake better than male viewers did. Their study involved neither a comparison with cheesecake nor extensive measurement of cognitive variables, and our research was intended to fill those gaps.

Some earlier studies (Belch et al. 1981; Sciglimpaglia, Belch, and Cain 1978) had used nude male models and nude female models and found that respondents reacted more negatively to models of their own sex than to those of the opposite sex. However, later studies using models that were attractive but not sexy produced different results. Patzer (1983) tested for differences

Table 24.1

Previous Research on Sex Appeals in Advertising

Authors	Stimuli	Dependent Measures	Subjects	Results
Alexander and Judd (1978)	Five levels of nude female model	Brand name recall	181 male students	Brand recall higher for nonsexual scene than for nude female model
Baker and Churchill (1977)	Two levels of attractiveness, male or female model	Affective, cognitive, and conative components of attitude toward the ad	96 students	Higher affect for ads with opposite sex and/or attractive models
Belch et al. (1981)	Three levels of nudity; male, female, and couples; 3 levels of suggestiveness	Electrodermal response (GSR); measures of interest, appeal, offensiveness	30 students	Strong physiological response to nudity and suggestiveness; opposite sex was appealing; same sex nude was offensive
Bello, Pitts, and Etzel (1983)	Controversial sexy content vs. non-offensive content; TV programs coupled with TV commercials	Purchase intention, affect toward the brand, interest in program	217 student subjects	Controversy is more interesting; higher affect toward advertised product paired with noncontroversial program
Caballero and Solomon (1984)	Varied gender of model and attractiveness of model on point-of-purchase displays for beer and facial tissue	Purchase or non-purchase by customers who were exposed to the display	6492 shoppers were exposed to beer display, 6535 to facial tissue display	In general, point-of-purchase displays with a human model outperformed displays without; male models produced more beer sales among both male and female subjects than a female model or no model; the low attractiveness condition produced more sales of tissue than high attractiveness
Caballero, Lumpkin, and Madden (1989)	Three levels of spokesperson attractiveness, male or female spokesperson	Purchase intention	256 adult grocery shoppers	Subjects showed greater intention to purchase from spokesperson of same sex

Source	Stimulus	Measures	Sample	Findings
Chestnut, LaChance, and Lubitz (1977)	Print ads with decorative female vs. no model	Recognition for ad or recognition for brand name	100 subjects	Presence of decorative model enhances memory for model-related information
Judd and Alexander (1983)	Subjects chose from pairs of ads depicting either a pasture, clothed couple, nude breasts, or full nude female model	Affect toward each ad, preference between two ads, recall of products and brand names	96 students	Recall highest for pasture, lowest for nude female; female subjects showed more negative affect toward nudity than male students
LaTour (1990); LaTour, Pitts, and Snook-Luther (1990)	Perfume ads with three levels of nudity: seminude female model, nude female model, or fully clothed couple	Arousal, impressions of the ad	202 students	Men are energized by female nudity whereas women are made tense and fatigued; men had positive feelings associated with nudity but women had negative feelings
Morrison and Sherman (1972)	Cluster analysis performed on subjects who rated 100 advertisements	Subjects judged all 10 ads on degree of nudity, realism, romantic content, sexual overtones, and sexual arousal	100 men, 100 women	Suggestiveness of copy detected by women more than men; nudity not a major characteristic on which men discriminate between ads; women who rated the ads high in nudity also reported being sexually aroused by the ads
O'Conner et al. (1986)	Subjects viewed four ads: low sexuality-appropriate, low sexuality-inappropriate, high sexuality-appropriate, high sexuality-inappropriate	Unaided recall; attitude toward the ad	105 student subjects	Brand recall did not diminish with the presence of a model; brand recall highest for sexually inappropriate ads; product recall highest for sexually appropriate ads
Patzer (1979)	Sexy vs. nonsexy female communicators (determined by nudity) in advertisements for body soap	Three attitudinal components: cognitive, affective, and conative; perceived communicator credibility, intelligence, trustworthiness, expertise; perceived expensiveness of product, recall of copy	60 student subjects	Behavior of men positively influenced by sexiness of female communicator but behavior of women negatively influenced; for male subjects, source credibility higher for the sexy than for the nonsexy communicator; in general, for male subjects effects were consistently favorable to the sexy female communicator

Authors	Stimuli	Dependent Measures	Subjects	Results
Peterson and Kerin (1977)	Ads for body oil or ratchet set depicting "demure," "seductive," or nude female models (determined by level of nudity)	Perceptions of advertisement (appealing/unappealing), the product (high quality/low quality) and company (reputable/not reputable)	224 adult subjects	Across products and respondents, the ad containing a nude model was perceived as the least appealing, and the product and company were perceived as lowest quality and least reputable; men perceived the seductive model/body oil advertisement to be most appealing, whereas women evaluated the nude model/ratchet set as least appealing
Reid and Soley (1983)	Panel selected ads containing female model, male model, couple, or no model; all models determined to be "decorative" (one whose primary activity is to adorn the product as a sexual or attractive stimulus)	Starch readership scores of the magazines from which the ads were taken (*Time*, *Newsweek*, and *Sports Illustrated*)		Attention-getting value of an ad for male readers decreased as the model type moved from a female model portrayed alone, to a couple, to a male model portrayed alone; presence of decorative female model did *not* affect male readership of ad copy
Richmond and Hartman (1982)	50 adults classified ads, resulting in four dimensions: functional, fantasy, symbolism, and inappropriate (entire ad judged, not just model); ads targeted males or females	Aided recall: association of headline, copy, or illustration with brand or company name; classification of ads into dimensions	398 adult subjects	Ads deemed inappropriate (such as a suggestive ad for the Rice Council) elicited lowest recall of all ads viewed
Sciglimpaglia, Belch, and Cain (1978)	Ads depicting male *or* female models *or* couples nude, partially clothed, or fully clothed (couples were deemed to represent suggestiveness)	Subjects rated ads in terms of good taste, appealing, interesting, or offensive; attitudes toward sex, role portrayals in advertising, and personal role orientation	142 student subjects	Evaluation of sexual content became less positive as nudity increased; "suggestive" ads (depicting couples) judged to be in poor taste and were also offensive to women; men evaluated male nudity poorly whereas women evaluated male nudity positively and vice versa for female nudity

Study	Ads	Measures	Sample	Results
Severn, Belch, and Belch (1990)	Ads for shoes depicting couples with combinations of high/low sex and high/low information in copy	Brand name and product category recall (dummy ads were included in the experiment); thought listings; copy-point recall; attitudes toward brand and ad; purchase intentions	180 student subjects	Ability to recall brand name appeared to be more a function of information level than sexual explicitness; copy recall higher in no-sex than in explicit-sex conditions; more product-related thoughts generated in no-sex than in explicit conditions; more ad execution-related thoughts for explicit than for no-sex conditions
Simpson, Horton, and Brown (1996)	Ads for body oil or a ratchet set depicting product with no model, clothed male model, male model without a shirt, nude male model	Mood (pleasure and arousal), attitude toward advertiser, attitude toward ad, attitude toward brand, and purchase intention	341 student subjects	Women reacted most favorably to the suggestive ad on A_{ad}, mood, and $A_{advertiser}$; men responded most favorably to the fully clothed male model and least favorably to the male nude model on mood; in general there was an opposite sex effect: women responded more favorably than men to ads containing male models; nude and suggestive ads were viewed more favorably for body oil ads than for wrench set ads
Steadman (1969)	Subjects viewed ads with either no model (house, car, etc.) or a female model at varying stages of undress; subjects had 24 hours to view ads	Brand name recall, rankings of ads by suggestiveness, brand name recall seven days later; attitudes toward use of sexy illustrations in ads	60 male students	Greater recall for nonsexual ads than for sexual ads after seven days (no difference for immediate recall); subjects with attitudes favorable to the use of sexy illustrations in ads showed higher recall of brand names accompanying sexual illustrations
Weller, Roberts, and Neuhaus (1979)	Ads for four brands, each with three levels of "erotic content" (determined by researchers)	Recall of brand name 24 hours after viewing ads	30 adult subjects	Advertisements with low erotic content yielded the highest frequency of correct recalls and ads with high erotic content yielded the lowest (with medium erotic content between those values)
Wise, King, and Merenski (1974)	Respondents were asked their level of agreement with the statement, "Advertisers make too much use of sex appeals in their advertisements."	Likert scale of agreement with statement, demographics	621 student subjects and 589 parents	Parents showed significantly higher agreement than did students; female respondents showed significantly higher agreement than did male respondents.

between male and female viewers in liking for an ad with attractive (but not "sexy") models of each sex and found no difference by sex of viewer. Likewise, Caballero, Lumpkin, and Madden (1989) and Caballero and Solomon (1984) did not find an effect on purchase response for the viewer's sex in the presence of an attractive, but not sexy, model. The apparent lack of an opposite-sex effect for model attractiveness without sexiness suggests that the sexiness of the model may drive the effect.

More positive affective responses toward models of the opposite sex were found in studies by Belch et al. (1981), Sciglimpaglia, Belch, and Cain (1978), and Baker and Churchill (1977), particularly for a nude male model or a nude female model. Most prior work on gender differences supports an opposite-sex effect: sexy ads showing the opposite sex are viewed more favorably than are ads depicting a model of the viewer's own sex.

A broader conclusion, however, is that sexy ads evoke gender differences in measures of advertising effectiveness whether a study examines ads with same-sex illustrations, opposite-sex illustrations, or both. Explanations have alluded to a possible role of social and cultural factors in those differences. Scott (1994a, b) and Stern (1993) make the case for gender-specific interpretations of sexy advertising, and Thompson and Hirschman (1995) note that widespread social constructions might give rise to the meanings people bring to sexy, and other gendered, stimuli. Stern and Holbrook (1994) explain that gender must be considered when attempting to understand a consumer's "meaning-making process," as gender will interact with cultural context to influence consumer responses to communication.

Elliott et al. (1995), using discourse analysis, analyzed the conversations of separate male and female focus groups about four sexy ads. Four male and four female focus groups were conducted, each moderated by someone of the same sex as its participants. The researchers concluded that both male and female participants responded positively to equality in sexual images or to perceived artistic sexuality, and responded negatively to sex-role stereotyping and the objectification of women. Interestingly, they found little comment on the objectification of men for the one ad that contained a sexy male image rather than a female image. One could hypothesize that male reactions to beefcake parallel female reactions to cheesecake. However, we might not expect that to be true in view of the political loading imposed on sexy ads with female models. Elliott and his coworkers observed that the focus group reactions appeared to take social and political themes into account. The same political/social themes were voiced by both male and female participants, and not generalized to the ads containing male models by either gender. Hence, though there seem to be gender-specific interpretations of advertising (cf. Scott 1994a, b) and cultural context seems to play a role (cf. Stern and Holbrook 1994), we cannot necessarily infer a parallel reaction effect.

Contemporary Models of Advertising Effectiveness

The literature also suggests the possibility that sexy ads are processed differently from ones with less distracting illustrations; that is, attention goes to the ad rather than the product. Differences in processing would explain findings such as those of Alexander and Judd (1978), whose male subjects had lower recall of brand names from ads showing a nude female model than from ads showing a landscape. Consistent with those results, other studies have found higher recall for (1) ads depicting a pasture versus a nude female model (Judd and Alexander 1983), (2) ads with lower erotic content than comparison ads (Weller, Roberts, and Neuhaus 1979), (3) ads deemed nonsexy as opposed to sexy ads (Severn, Belch, and Belch 1990), and (4) ads deemed nonsexual as opposed to sexual ads, though only male subjects were included in the study (Steadman 1969).

Only O'Conner et al. (1986) found lower recall for an ad with no model than for an ad judged to be high in sexuality. However, they did find higher recall for a low sexuality condition (an ad containing a nonsexy model) than for a high sexuality condition. The discrepancy between the findings of O'Conner et al. and those of prior studies may be due to lack of control of stimuli; O'Conner et al. used actual ads judged as to sexuality, with no attempt to obtain uniform content, layout, or detail of copy.

Only Judd and Alexander (1983) and O'Conner et al. (1986) designed their studies to examine the effect of interaction between sex of viewer and type of ad on memory; neither found such interaction. However, their operationalizations may have affected the results: Judd and Alexander looked at nudity without consideration of "sexiness," whereas O'Conner et al. did not use consistent stimuli. Also, none of the previously cited researchers used beefcake to prompt the cognitive responses of interest; reaction was to female models only.

By contrast, our expectation of memory differences is based on theory about how ads are processed. Possibly viewers can be attracted by an eye-catching model and therefore associate favorable affect with the brand, but at the same time be annoyed by a sexist portrayal and feel unfavorable affect toward the ad. Alternatively, viewers can be puzzled by apparent incongruity between a sexy model and the product he or she is illustrating, experiencing unfavorable affect that is then associated with the brand. The theory suggesting the possibility of such scenarios comes from MacKenzie, Lutz, and Belch (1986), who tested four models of ad processing that included various paths between cognitive and affective processing of the ad itself and the cognitive and affective reactions to the brand. They demonstrated that not only do brand cognitions lead to brand attitudes, as posited in the most common models of advertising response, but that affective reactions to an ad influence brand attitudes both directly and indirectly, in the latter case by changing cognitions about the brand.

That is the dual mediation hypothesis, and a meta-analysis (Brown and Stayman 1992) of the many studies that have examined the influence of attitude toward the ad on brand attitudes and cognitions found strong support for the paths hypothesized by the dual mediation model. The research is particularly pertinent because sexy advertising evokes feelings and thoughts about the ad itself that not only may reflect on attitudes toward the brand, but also may influence cognitive processing of it. Hence, men and women may differ in their response processes given a female or male model, provocatively clothed or not–the basic combinations tested in our study. Stern (1993) notes several information processing effects whereby gender may influence affective response to the ad, perceptions of an ad, and inference making. Meyers-Levy and Maheswaran (1991) bring additional complexity to the issue by suggesting that the different processing approaches employed by men and by women afford another explanation for the expectation of different affective outcomes.

There is a precedent for attempting to blend such post-modern viewpoints with a cognitive-based communications model. Sujan, Bettman, and Baumgartner (1993) studied interplay between emotion-evoking stimuli and consumer judgments of those stimuli. Their results suggest that advertising cues often evoke autobiographical information; the self-referencing is associated with an emotional loading, shifting thought away from the product information in the ad. Further, autobiographical associations may carry over into evaluative judgments, such as attitude toward the ad and even attitude toward the brand if a link is established between the brand and the personal memories evoked. Thus, gender differences might prompt different responses to sexy advertising, including processing differences, because only ads using models matching one's own gender prompt self-referencing (pointing to a potential same-sex effect when cognition is measured).

On the basis of the literature, we tested a familiar idea in a more comprehensive way than had been attempted previously. Using not only cheesecake but also beefcake, and using not only affective but also memory measures of advertising effectiveness, we tested the overall idea that men and women respond differently to advertising, with the sex of a model and degree of provocative dress of the model contributing to the differences.

We tested the following specific hypotheses.

H1: The sex of a subject and the type of ad interact to influence men's and women's affective responses to ads.
   a. Women have less favorable attitudes than men toward cheesecake ads and brands advertised in cheesecake ads.
   b. Men have less favorable attitudes than women toward beefcake ads and brands advertised in beefcake ads.
   c. Women have more favorable attitudes toward beefcake ads than toward cheesecake ads, but even more favorable attitudes toward ads with nonsexy male models.
   d. Men will have more favorable attitudes toward cheesecake ads than toward beefcake ads, but even more favorable attitudes toward ads with nonsexy female models.

H2: The sex of a subject and the type of ad interact to influence men's and women's memory of advertising content.
   a. Women have lower recall and recognition scores than men for cheesecake ads.
   b. Men have lower recall and recognition scores than women for beefcake ads.
   c. Women have higher recall and recognition scores for beefcake ads than for cheesecake ads, and higher recall and recognition scores for nonsexy ads with a male model than for beefcake.
   d. Men have higher recall and recognition scores for cheesecake ads than for beefcake ads, and higher recall and recognition scores for nonsexy ads with a female model than for cheesecake.

METHOD

Design and Stimuli

The hypotheses were tested in an experiment with five treatment levels, resulting in a five (type of ad) by two (gender of subject) between-subjects design. The dependent variables tested were recall and recognition of claims in the copy, of the illustration, and of the brand name, as well as attitude toward the ad and its elements (? = .89) and attitude toward the brand (? = .90).

The stimulus ads were created from two pretests. One pretest was used to find a gender-neutral product. Subjects rated 16 different products for their intrinsic masculinity and femininity and rated them for the sex of the usual buyer. Bicycles were selected from the test as being neither inherently feminine nor masculine and as being purchased by either male or female consumers.

In a separate pretest, student subjects rated 10 photos of male models and 10 photos of female models for sexiness of the model and attractiveness of the model. The photos used, selected from actual ads, included models wearing a variety of clothing (from conservative streetwear to swimwear) and in a variety of poses. For the sexy ad stimuli in the experiment, the male and female models (with comparable clothing and poses) considered attractive and having the highest sexiness ratings were used. For the nonsexy ad stimuli, male and female models with comparable clothing and poses rated attractive but nonsexy were selected. We were aware that bicycles seemed an

Figure 24.1 **Ad with Sexy Male Model**

FIT FOR THE LONG HAUL

Our flagship fitness/cross bike

Powerful Superglide gearset

Well-balanced frame for
superb comfort

Extra lightweight frame

CIGNAL®

Men's models

available in

Black or Bright Yellow.

Ladies' in White or Rose.

unlikely match for a provocatively clothed model as the advertising illustration, but reasoned that previous research and frequent advertising practice have juxtaposed sexy illustrations with products for which their applicability is at least questionable. Further, bicycles were equally incongruous with the dress of the attractive but not sexy models, providing a control for the possible effect of perceived incongruity in the illustration across ads.

The ads, designed specifically for our study, promoted a fitness/cross-training bicycle. Each contained four claims (our flagship bike, powerful gearset, comfortable frame, and lightweight frame) as well as the colors available, a headline, and the brand name. All ads were identical in terms of copy and layout, differing only in the picture included with the bicycle. One of five pictures was used: a provocatively dressed (sexy) male model, a sexy female model, a nonsexy male model, a nonsexy female model, and a landscape. As in prior studies (Steadman 1969; LaTour 1990; LaTour, Pitts, and Snook-Luther 1990), the landscape was included as a control. Figure 24.1 is the beefcake ad; Figure 24.2 shows the alternative illustrations (clockwise from the top left: a nonsexy female model, cheesecake, landscape, and nonsexy male model).

Figure 24.2   **Pictures Used in Other Ads**

Sample and Procedures

Approximately 300 undergraduate students at a major southwestern university were enlisted as subjects in exchange for extra credit toward their grade in a course. Students were chosen to be subjects because of both availability and the compatibility of their age group and lifestyle with the product category, bicycles.

The one ad given to each student was selected randomly: sexy male model, sexy female model, nonsexy male model, nonsexy female model, or landscape. The students were given 15 seconds to study the ad and then told to put it in a manila envelope. They next filled out a series of questionnaires in prescribed sequence, with several monitors in the room to ensure that no one referred to the ad or to any preceding form while filling out his or her answers.

The first section of the questionnaire measured attitudes by asking for degree of agreement or disagreement with statements about perceptions of the brand and ad. It was followed by a blank layout of the ad and a request that subjects write in information that they remembered about the ad, a demonstration of recall. They also were asked to write in the brand name and to describe in their own words the picture in the advertisement. A final section of the questionnaire tested for recognition of brand name and copy points with true/false questions that included accurate and fictional statements.

Scores for attitude toward the ad and the brand were calculated as the sum of responses to a set of five 7-point Likert scales measuring strength of agreement or disagreement with statements such as "I thought this was an interesting ad" (for attitude toward the ad) and "I think the advertised bicycle is high quality" (for attitude toward the brand). That approach to tapping attitudes (including terms such as "likable," "quality," "interesting," and "good") is consistent with previous ad research on brand and ad evaluations (Edell and Staelin 1983; Keller 1987). The adjectives selected were those used previously by Baker and Churchill (1977) and by Bello, Pitts, and Etzel (1983).

Recall scores for each respondent were calculated by first coding responses into 11 possible categories of ad content, such as "flagship fitness bike," and then calculating the average number of correct items mentioned per category. Recognition scores were the average number of correct responses to the eight true/false questions about ad claims, such as "the frame is a medium-weight frame."

Data were analyzed by ANOVA to determine the effect of the independent variables on attitude toward the ad and the brand (affective responses) and on recall and recognition (cognitive responses) at the omnibus level. Planned simple and complex contrasts then were tested to pinpoint differences between specific sets or pairs of ads or sets of respondents (male vs. female). Initially, MANOVA had seemed appropriate, but we were unable to meet the assumption of homogeneity of variance-covariance matrices required for that technique.

RESULTS

A manipulation check verified that the sexy ads were, in fact, perceived as sexy by subjects who saw them. Subjects who looked at an ad with a provocatively clothed model mentioned sexiness on their blank-page comments significantly more often than subjects who were shown a nonsexy ad ($p < .0001$). Figures 24.3 and 24.4 show the results in graphic form.

Results from ANOVA and a priori contrasts, reported in Tables 24.2, 24.3, and 24.4, show partial support for both hypotheses. However, in general, the data show fewer significant results for cognitive responses and more for affective responses.

Figure 24.3 **Results for Attitude Measures**

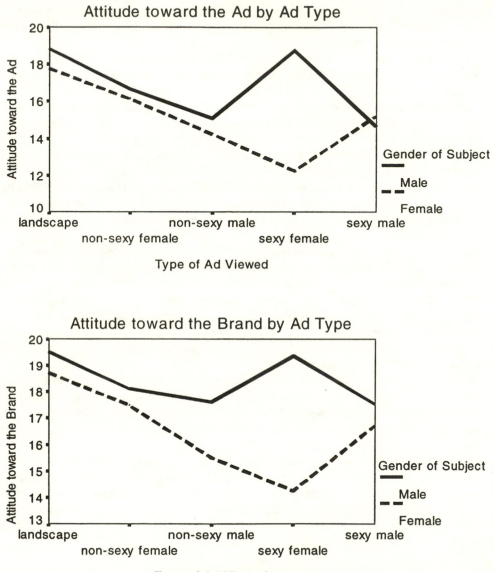

Figure 24.4 **Results for Cognitive Measures**

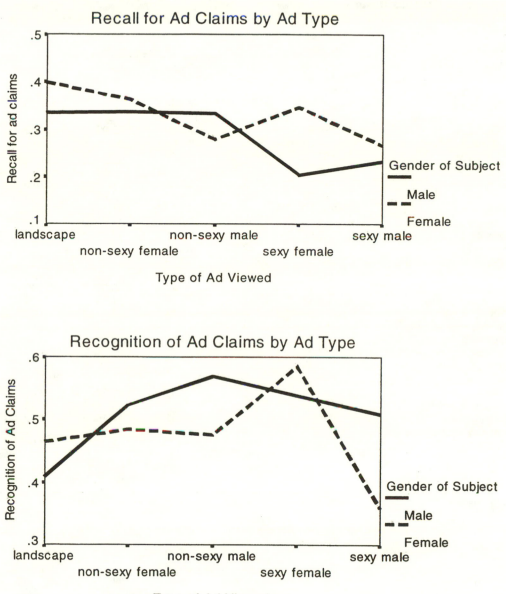

Table 24.2

Analysis of Variance Results

Source of variation	Sum of Squares	d.f.	Mean Square	F	Sig. of F
For A_{ad}					
Main effects	660.64	5	132.13	3.15	.009
Subject gender	202.04	1	202.04	4.82	.029
Type of ad	481.36	4	120.34	2.87	.023
Two-way interactions	454.08	4	113.52	2.71	.030
Explained	1125.83	9	125.09	2.99	.002
Residual	11729.29	280	41.89		
Total	12855.12	289	44.48		
For A_{brand}					
Main effects	464.29	5	92.86	2.73	.020
Subject gender	260.43	1	260.43	7.65	.006
Type of ad	232.66	4	58.17	1.71	.148
Two-way interactions	212.05	4	53.01	1.56	.186
Explained	685.47	9	76.16	2.24	.020
Residual	9599.52	282	34.04		
Total	10284.99	291	35.34		
For Recall					
Main effects	.70	5	.14	3.08	.010
Subject gender	.13	1	.13	2.88	.091
Type of ad	.55	4	.14	3.04	.018
Two-way interactions	.31	4	.08	1.70	.150
Explained	1.02	9	.11	2.49	.009
Residual	12.97	286	.05		
Total	13.98	295	.05		
For Recognition					
Main effects	.85	5	.17	3.87	.002
Subject gender	.10	1	.10	2.16	.142
Type of ad	.72	4	.18	4.10	.003
Two-way interactions	.46	4	.11	2.58	.038
Explained	1.33	9	.15	3.36	.001
Residual	12.60	286	.04		
Total	13.93	295	.05		

Table 24.3

A Priori Contrast Results for Women Versus Men

Measure		Mean Women	Men	Contrast Value	t Value	d.f.	Sig.
H1a	A_{ad} for cheesecake	12.25	18.75	6.50	3.70	58	.000
	A_{brand} for cheesecake	14.25	19.38	5.13	2.98	58	.004
H1b	A_{ad} for beefcake	15.20	14.64	−.55	−.32	57	.753
	A_{brand} for beefcake	16.71	17.54	.83	.50	57	.622
H2a	Recall for cheesecake	.35	.21	−.14	−3.02	58	.004*
	Recognition for cheesecake	.59	.54	−.05	−.96	58	.343
H2b	Recall for beefcake	.27	.23	−.03	−.58	57	.562
	Recognition for beefcake	.36	.51	.15	2.90	57	.005*

*Significance in direction opposite than hypothesized.

Table 24.4

A Priori Contrast Results for Four Types of Ads

Measure		Nonsexy male	Beef-cake	Cheese-cake	Nonsexy female	Contrast value	t Value	d.f.	Sig.
			Mean						
H1c	A_{ad} (women)	—	15.19	12.25	—	−2.94	−1.63	57	.108
	A_{brand} (women)	—	16.71	14.25	—	−2.46	−1.44	57	.157
	A_{ad} (women)	14.23	15.19	—	—	−.96	−.56	55	.575
	A_{brand} (women)	15.50	16.71	—	—	−1.21	−.81	55	.420
H1d	A_{ad} (men)	—	14.64	18.75	—	4.11	2.42	58	.019
	A_{brand} (men)	—	17.54	19.38	—	1.84	1.10	58	.275
	A_{ad} (men)	—	—	18.75	16.65	−2.10	−1.28	56	.205
	A_{brand} (men)	—	—	19.38	18.11	−1.26	−.76	57	.448
H2c	Recall (women)	—	.27	.35	—	.08	1.48	57	.144
	Recog (women)	—	.36	.59	—	.23	4.87	57	.000*
	Recall (women)	.28	.27	—	—	.01	.24	55	.811
	Recog (women)	.48	.36	—	—	.12	2.35	55	.022
H2d	Recall (men)	—	.23	.21	—	−.03	−.59	58	.560
	Recog (men)	—	.51	.54	—	.03	.57	58	.571
	Recall (men)	—	—	.21	.34	.13	2.60	57	.012
	Recog (men)	—	—	.54	.52	−.02	−.26	57	.795

Dash denotes means not included in the particular contrast tested.
*Significance in direction opposite than hypothesized.

Consistent with H1, we found women to have less favorable attitudes than men toward the cheesecake ad as well as the brand advertised in that ad. Also, male subjects had more favorable attitudes toward the cheesecake ad than to the beefcake ad. Those findings generally support the opposite-sex effect in the context of sexy stimuli. However, the differences seem to emerge primarily for the cheesecake ad. Male and female subjects showed no difference in their attitudes toward the beefcake ad or the brand advertised in it. Also, no difference appeared in the attitude scores of female subjects who saw a beefcake ad and those who saw an ad with a nonsexy male model.

Differences in attitude toward the ad and toward the brand between women who saw a beefcake ad and women who saw a cheesecake ad are not statistically significant but are in the hypothesized direction. Similarly, differences in attitude toward the brand between men who viewed a cheesecake ad and men who viewed a beefcake ad are not statistically significant but are in the expected direction.

H2 has only limited support. Women had higher recognition scores for the ad showing a nonsexy male model than for the beefcake ad; however, the contrast is not significant for the recall measure. Men had higher recall scores for the ad showing a nonsexy female model than for the cheesecake ad, but not higher recognition scores.

No other hypothesized memory differences were found. However, some findings opposite the ones expected can be seen in the tables. Women had *lower* recognition scores then men for the beefcake ad, and women viewing the cheesecake ad had *higher* recognition scores than women viewing the beefcake ad. Also, men had *lower* recall than women for the cheesecake ad.

CONCLUSIONS AND IMPLICATIONS

The chief limitations of our study—the classroom setting and university student subjects—may limit the findings to a young adult advertising audience. However, students' attitudes toward advertising have been found to be consistent with those of the general population (Barnes 1982; Zanot 1984), and students are deemed appropriate subjects for basic research on causal mechanisms (Kardes 1996). Also, a young adult audience may be a likely target for bicycle ads and beefcake or cheesecake ads. Nevertheless, given the limitations of the study, conclusions drawn from the results are only tentative.

Discussion of such conclusions begins with examination of the questions that prompted the study: Do previous findings about reactions to cheesecake ads still hold, for men and for women, given changes in the social climate? Do those findings apply symmetrically to beefcake? Are responses to an ad with a sexy model in its illustration influenced by the interaction of the sex of a model with the sex of the viewer? If attitude toward the ad is influenced by such interaction, are cognitive measures likewise influenced? We discuss each of those issues in turn.

The findings support the previously noted negative influence of cheesecake on women's attitudes toward the ad. However, men do not disparage beefcake. The results support the findings of Elliott et al. (1995) that a sexy male image evoked little comment. In our study, responses to beefcake differed from responses to an illustration of a fully clothed male model in only one hypothesized comparison. Scores on the recognition measure encompassing copy points, brand name, and illustration were higher for women who saw the clothed male model than for women who saw the beefcake ad.

The third issue guiding our study, the expectation that, for an ad with a provocatively clothed model, the sex of that model and the sex of the viewer would interact to influence attitudes and cognitive responses, is supported but not as expected. Women who saw a cheesecake ad recognized ad content more and viewed the brand significantly more negatively than those who saw other illustrations. Cheesecake boosted men's attitude toward the ad, as expected, but caused no discernable reduction in measures of memory of the ad. However, beefcake evoked significantly lower recognition of ad contents among women than did cheesecake or other illustrations. Hence, contrary to our expectation, we cannot conclude that same-sex sexy ads provoke indignation and therefore interfere with memory of the ad copy and brand name. For women, indignation about a cheesecake ad instead appears to help memorability, but indignation is unlikely to be the effect the advertiser intended.

The interaction does appear, but not as consistently as expected. Scores for men do not support the expectation that provocatively clothed models of one's own sex lead to disapproval that discourages cognitive processing. Possibly men simply are not interested in beefcake, and so processing is not influenced. The finding for women who viewed cheesecake was opposite the one hypothesized: cheesecake was more memorable than a nonsexy female model. Perhaps, disapproval of an illustration leads to a search in the ad copy for more to disapprove of.

In short, beefcake seems not to be as detrimental as cheesecake, but, with an audience in the age category that might be most attuned to a sexy stimulus, we found that ads with sexy models offered few of the effects an advertiser would seek. Of course, a bicycle is not a product with sex-laden associations, and Simpson, Horton, and Brown (1996) found differences between products in responses to the degree of male nudity in an ad. It is interesting to juxtapose our findings with those of Campbell (1995), who studied consumer inferences of "manipulative intent" in ads with attention-getting tactics and found that such intent was most often inferred when the tactic did not fit the product category.

Clearly, the nonsexy ads seemed to do the most good with the least harm. Affective responses to such ads did not parallel women's negative responses to cheesecake, and cognitive responses did not parallel women's low level of recognition for beefcake. We found no evidence that attitude toward the brand is helped by a sexy model of either sex with audience members of either sex.

Our study has several theoretical implications. The nonsymmetrical patterns of results suggest the presence of (1) other meanings that are being brought to bear on the pictorial stimuli and (2) gender-specific interpretations of the stimuli. If a sexy picture has just an opposite-sex effect, we should always find a difference by gender of viewer—we do not. If a sexy model is always more fun to look at, men should prefer the sexy female model to the nonsexy one (they do), and women should prefer the sexy male model to the nonsexy one (they do not). Men and women, as Mick and Politi (1989) show, may perceive rather different qualities in such portrayals and may relate to the portrayals with different underlying needs and life experiences. Similar notions apply to the memory data—men and women may have studied the ads differently. For example, over all of the ads, recognition is higher than recall, but there are cases where recognition is no higher for a specific ad (women viewing a beefcake ad). That finding suggests increased elaboration on a selected subset of the information such that all that was examined (the particular subset) can be recalled. What we do not know is the nature of the thought process and why that subset was the focus of the attention.

From the perspective of advertising research, the obvious lesson is to exercise considerable care in audience selection when testing ads that might be characterized as sexy. Apparently, for sexy men as well as sexy women in ads there are some significant differences in responses. We expected and found male versus female differences in both attitudinal responses and ability to remember advertising claims. Those differences may not be critical for products targeted to one gender or the other, but caution must be used in testing advertising for a product for which one gender constitutes product users or decision influencers, and therefore is selected as the audience for the advertising research, but the other gender often performs the actual purchase. With beer, for instance, brand preference among men is one goal, but women constitute the majority of supermarket beer purchasers (Dietrich 1992). If a male audience responds favorably to an ad test, a followup among women may be necessary.

The limitation of our study to visual print ads provides issues to be investigated in future research. How might sexy models influence attitudes and memory differently in television commercials? Would we find similar effects when measuring reactions to sexy voices in radio spots? How resilient are resulting brand attitudes over time, especially in light of a variety of subsequent messages? Such questions might guide further efforts in the evolving research on sex appeals in advertising.

REFERENCES

Alexander, M. Wayne and Ben Judd, Jr. (1978), "Do Nudes in Ads Enhance Brand Recall?" *Journal of Advertising Research,* 18 (1), 47–50.

Baker, Michael J. and Gilbert A. Churchill, Jr. (1977), "The Impact of Physically Attractive Models on Advertising Evaluations," *Journal of Marketing Research,* 14 (November), 538–555.

Barnes, M. (1982), "Public Attitudes to Advertising," *International Journal of Advertising,* 1 (April–June), 119–128.

Belch, Michael A., Barbro E. Holgerson, George E. Belch, and Jerry Koppman (1981), "Psychophysiological and Cognitive Responses to Sex in Advertising," *Advances in Consumer Research,* Vol. 9, Andrew A. Mitchell, ed., St. Louis: Association for Consumer Research, 424–427.

Bello, Daniel C., Robert E. Pitts, and Michael J. Etzel (1983), "The Communication Effects of Controversial Sexual Content in Television Programs and Commercials," *Journal of Advertising,* 12 (3), 32–42.

Brown, Steven P. and Douglas M. Stayman (1992), "Antecedents and Consequences of Attitude toward the Ad: A Meta-Analysis," *Journal of Consumer Research,* 19 (June), 34–51.

Caballero, Marjorie J., James R. Lumpkin, and Charles S. Madden (1989), "Using Physical Attractiveness as an Advertising Tool: An Empirical Test of the Attraction Phenomenon," *Journal of Advertising Research,* 29 (4), 16–22.

——— and Paul J. Solomon (1984), "Effects of Model Attractiveness on Sales Response," *Journal of Advertising,* 13 (1), 17–33.

Campbell, Margaret C. (1995), "When Attention-Getting Advertising Tactics Elicit Consumer Inferences of Manipulative Intent: The Importance of Balancing Benefits and Investments," *Journal of Consumer Psychology,* 4 (3), 225–254.

Chestnut, Robert W., Charles C. LaChance, and Amy Lubitz (1977), "The 'Decorative' Female Model: Sexual Stimuli and the Recognition of Advertisements," *Journal of Advertising,* 6 (4), 11–14.

Dietrich, Robert (1992), "Tracking the Invisible Men," *Progressive Grocer,* 71 (11), 69–82.

Edell, Julie A. and Richard Staelin (1983), "The Information Processing of Pictures in Print Advertisements," *Journal of Consumer Research,* 10 (June), 45–61.

Elliott, Richard, Abigail Jones, Andrew Benfield, and Matt Barlow (1995), "Overt Sexuality: A Discourse Analysis of Gender Responses," *Journal of Consumer Policy,* 18 (June), 187–217.

Judd, Ben B., Jr. and M. Wayne Alexander (1983), "On the Reduced Effectiveness of Some Sexually Suggestive Ads," *Journal of the Academy of Marketing Science,* 11 (2), 156–168.

Kardes, Frank R. (1996), "In Defense of Experimental Consumer Psychology," *Journal of Consumer Psychology,* 5 (3), 279–296.

Keller, Kevin Lane (1987), "Memory Factors in Advertising: The Effect of Advertising Retrieval Cues on Brand Evaluations," *Journal of Consumer Research,* 14 (3), 316–333.

Kuriansky, Judy (1995), "Sex Simmers, Still Sells," *Advertising Age,* 66 (special issue), 49.

LaTour, Michael S. (1990), "Female Nudity in Print Advertising: An Analysis of Gender Differences in Arousal and Ad Response," *Psychology & Marketing,* 7 (1), 65–81.

———, Robert E. Pitts, and David C. Snook-Luther (1990), "Female Nudity, Arousal, and Ad Response: An Experimental Investigation," *Journal of Advertising,* 19 (4), 51–62

MacKenzie, Scott B., Richard J. Lutz, and George E. Belch (1986), "The Role of Attitude Toward the Ad as a Mediator of Advertising Effectiveness: A Test of Competing Explanations," *Journal of Marketing Research,* 23 (May), 130–143.

Meyers-Levy, Joan and Durairaj Maheswaran (1991), "Exploring Differences in Males' and Females' Processing Strategies," *Journal of Consumer Research,* 18 (June), 63–70.

Mick, David Glen and Laura G. Politi (1989), "Consumers' Interpretations of Advertising Imagery: A Visit to the Hell of Connotation," in Elizabeth C. Hirschman, ed., *Interpretive Consumer Research,* Provo, UT: Association for Consumer Research, 85–96.

Miller, Cyndec (1993), "They're Macho, and They're Back," *Marketing News,* 27 (24), 1.

Mitchell, Andrew A. (1986), "The Effect of Verbal and Visual Components of Advertisements on Brand Attitudes and Attitude Toward the Advertisement," *Journal of Consumer Research,* 13 (June), 12–24.

——— and Jerry C. Olson (1981), "Are Product Attribute Beliefs the Only Mediator of Advertising Effects on Brand Attitude?" *Journal of Marketing Research,* 18 (August), 318–332.

Morrison, Bruce John and Richard C. Sherman (1972), "Who Responds to Sex in Advertising?" *Journal of Advertising Research,* 12 (2), 15–19.

O'Connor, P.J., Aylin Baher, Bosco Gong, and Elyse Kane (1986), "Recall Levels of Sexuality in Advertising," *American Marketing Association Educators' Proceedings,* Terence A. Shimp, Subhash Sharma, George John, John A. Quelch, John H. Lindgren, Jr., William Dillon, Meryl Paula Gardner, and Robert F. Dyer, eds., Chicago: American Marketing Association, 2–5.

Patzer, Gordon L. (1979), "A Comparison of Advertisement Effects: Sexy Female Communicator vs. Non-Sexy Female Communicator," *Advances in Consumer Research,* Vol. 7, Jerry C. Olson, ed., San Francisco: Association for Consumer Research, 359–364.

——— (1983), "Source Credibility as a Function of Communicator Physical Attractiveness," *Journal of Business Research,* 11 (2), 229–241.

Peterson, Robert A. and Roger A. Kerin (1977), "The Female Role in Advertisements: Some Experimental Evidence," *Journal of Marketing,* 41 (4), 59–63.

Reid, Leonard N. and Lawrence C. Soley (1983), "Decorative Models and the Readership of Magazine Ads," *Journal of Advertising Research,* 23 (2), 27–32.

Richmond, David and Timothy P. Hartman (1982), "Sex Appeal in Advertising," *Journal of Advertising Research,* 22 (5), 53–61.

Sciglimpaglia, Donald, Michael A. Belch, and Richard F. Cain (1978), "Demographic and Cognitive Factors Influencing Viewers' Evaluations of 'Sexy' Advertisements," *Advances in Consumer Research,* Vol. 6, William L. Wilkie, ed., Miami Beach: Association for Consumer Research, 62–65.

Scott, Linda M. (1994a), "Images in Advertising: The Need for a Theory of Visual Rhetoric," *Journal of Consumer Research,* 21 (September), 252–273.

―――― (1994b), "The Bridge from Text to Mind: Adapting Reader-Response Theory to Consumer Research," *Journal of Consumer Research,* 21 (December), 461–480.

Severn, Jessica, George E. Belch, and Michael A. Belch (1990), "The Effects of Sexual and Non-sexual Advertising Appeals and Information Level on Cognitive Processing and Communication Effectiveness," *Journal of Advertising,* 19 (1), 14–22.

Simpson, Penny M., Steve Horton, and Gene Brown (1996), "Male Nudity in Advertisements: A Modified Replication and Extension of Gender and Product Effects," *Journal of the Academy of Marketing Science,* 24 (3), 257–262.

Steadman, Major (1969), "How Sexy Illustrations Affect Brand Recall," *Journal of Advertising,* 9 (1), 15–19.

Stern, Barbara B. (1993), "Feminist Literary Criticism and the Deconstruction of Ads: A Postmodern View of Advertising and Consumer Responses," *Journal of Consumer Research,* 19 (March), 556–566.

―――― and Morris B. Holbrook (1994), "Gender and Genre in the Interpretation of Advertising Text," in *Gender Issues and Consumer Behavior,* Janeen Arnold Costa, ed., Thousand Oaks, CA: Sage Publications, 11–41.

Sujan, Mita, James R. Bettman, and Hans Baumgartner (1993), "Influencing Consumer Judgments Using Autobiographical Memories: A Self-Referencing Perspective," *Journal of Marketing Research,* 30 (November), 422–436.

Thompson, Craig J. and Elizabeth C. Hirschman (1995), "Understanding the Socialized Body: A Poststructuralist Analysis of Consumers" Self-Conceptions, Body Images, and Self-Care Practices,' *Journal of Consumer Research,* 22 (September), 139–153.

Weller, Ralph B., C. Richard Roberts, and Colin Neuhaus (1979), "A Longitudinal Study of the Effect of Erotic Content upon Advertising Brand Recall," *Current Issues and Research in Advertising,* James H. Leigh and Claude R. Martin, Jr., eds., Ann Arbor: The University of Michigan, 145–161.

Wise, Gordon L., Alan L. King, and J. Paul Merenski (1974), "Reactions to Sexy Ads Vary With Age," *Journal of Advertising Research, 14* (4), 11–16.

Zanot, E. J. (1984), "Public Attitudes Towards Advertising: The American Experience," *International Journal of Advertising, 3* (1), 3–15.

CHAPTER 25

THE EVER ENTANGLING WEB
A Study of Ideologies and Discourses in Advertising to Women

STEVEN M. KATES AND GLENDA SHAW-GARLOCK

> "When I use a word," Humpty Dumpty said, in a rather scornful tone, "it means just what I choose it to mean—neither more nor less."
>
> "The question is," said Alice, "whether you can make words mean so many different things."
>
> "The question is," said Humpty Dumpty, "which is to be master—that's all."
>
> (Lewis Carroll, *Through the Looking Glass*)

ADVERTISING AS REPRESENTATION

Representation involves the connection between things in the phenomenal world, concepts, and signs (Hall 1997). A magazine advertisement consisting of a two-dimensional image combined with text from which we can derive a particular meaning is the very essence of representation. Through culture, we learn that a photograph signifies something that exists in the real world, an abstract concept, or an imaginary thing. We can decode an ad by using cues found in representative systems of language such as physical gestures, clothing, set, lighting, tropes, and text. The meanings derived can be as simple as the identification of an object such as a toothbrush or chair or as abstract as the notion of the good life or love.

Ad interpretation is part of a larger system called "the circuit of culture" (Hall 1997). Indeed, to discuss representation requires that it be placed in the context of conventions and linguistic tropes that help us make sense of our social worlds (see Thompson and Haytko 1997). We represent something when we desire to share or express some idea, feeling, or concept that we carry in our heads. Loosely speaking, individuals are said to belong to the same culture, when they interpret the world in a broadly similar way and can express thoughts and feelings in such a way as to be understood. Culture also includes the organization and *regulation* of social practices, and it influences conduct by setting out the rules, norms, and conventions of social order (Foucault 1980).

From *Journal of Advertising,* vol. 28, no. 2 (Summer 1999). Copyright © 1999 by the American Academy of Advertising. Reprinted with permission from M.E. Sharpe, Inc.

Over time, ideological *codes* tend to fix and naturalize the relationships between conceptual maps and language systems and enable members of a culture to communicate effectively. The system of representation thus becomes a stable cultural convention that is taught and learned by members of a society. As a result, the preferred meaning (Hall 1980) of a cultural text such as an ad may "be this, but not the other."

We argue that despite recent important revisions to the traditional advertising communication model (Lasswell 1948; Stern 1994), it is still deficient, for it does not explicitly incorporate the critical dimensions of discourses and conventions that influence consumers' decoding processes (Stern 1994, p. 9). Examining the current model, we make two specific criticisms. First, the consumer is presumed to interpret the ad as text seemingly in the absence of representational codes and, conventions implying textual determinism. Second, the model does not incorporate the notion that texts invite *multiple* readings, and consumers are likely to forge their own negotiated meanings, albeit influenced by broad sociocultural viewpoints (see Byars 1991; Hirschman and Thompson 1997; Thompson 1996; Thompson and Haytko 1997). Overall, we explore the nature and importance of discourses in mediating ad interpretation; further, we propose revisions to the model, placing ad interpretation within broader social and historical contexts. Thus, we contend that cultural studies (Hall 1980, 1982; Turner 1996)—a diverse body of thought that has extensively addressed issues circumscribing ideology, discourse, representation, and interpretation—can make a contribution to our discipline.

As Humpty Dumpty's presumption suggests (see Hall 1997; Mick 1986), language is not a neutral medium (Stern 1996a). It may be described as social practice: "our private intended meanings, however personal to us, have to enter into the rules, codes and conventions of language to be shared and understood . . . neither things in themselves nor the individual users of language can fix meaning in language . . ." (Hall 1997, p. 25). We explicitly acknowledge the discursive aspects of ads as representation (Dreyfus and Rabinow 1982; Foucault 1970, 1980; Hall 1997) and draw upon British and American branches of cultural studies, which in turn have been influenced by poststructuralism (Foucault 1970, 1977, 1980; Hall 1997).

THE IMPORTANCE OF HISTORICAL AND IDEOLOGICAL CONTEXT: AN ILLUSTRATIVE DISCURSIVE ANALYSIS OF THE AD REPRESENTATIONS OF THE "LONE WOMAN"

An accepted criticism is that advertising is an important and pervasive cultural institution that represents women in a problematic and unacceptable way (Bordo 1993; Douglas 1994; Ferguson, Kreshel, and Tinkham 1990; Hirschman and Thompson 1997; Richins 1991; Stern 1993; Wolf 1991). Further, it is not particularly radical to argue that certain ads have co-opted feminist themes in order to market to women. For illustration, an ad for Evian portrays a woman *alone* in the frame, potentially suggesting themes of autonomy, arguably important to the feminist movement. The woman is not shown leaning on a man or surrounded by other women, depictions which might imply that she requires the company of others to legitimate her identity (see Stern 1993). The ad is good exemplar of many found in women's magazines such as *Vogue, Self, Elle,* and *Mademoiselle.*

What is the origin of the "lone woman" field of discourse? Traditionally, women have been positioned within discourse as relegated to the home (Ehrenreich and English 1979; Thompson 1996). Yet during the last few decades, feminist critique of the domestic role has entered mainstream social discourse. As women have crossed the boundary from the domestic sphere to the professional arena, expectations and representations of women have changed as well. Further, in some discourses, the stereotypic character traits attributed to women have shifted from weak and dependent to strong and autonomous. The market for women's magazines has fragmented accordingly, moving from the mass appeal of the older, more traditional magazines such as *Good Housekeeping* to the niched appeal of more recent entries such as *Cosmopolitan,* broadening the representations of women's pastimes (McCracken 1993). Ads now incorporate aspects of the broad sociocultural shifts in women's lives. The lone woman embodies, physically and figuratively, the cultural and historical shift from the home to the outside world. Perhaps she is the postmodern woman who constructs her identity "through eclectic borrowing of the fragments available in consumer culture. Women of this era are trained for growth and change; they are encouraged to develop wings, not roots" (Fournier 1998, p. 360).

The transformed social positioning(s) of women in North American society is perhaps the *most* important social development of this century. We argue that ad representations of the so-called "liberated" woman provide a rich discursive application and a springboard for a theoretical expansion of the advertising communication model. Further, we believe that our ad exemplar is constituted by discourses related to women in public life beyond the domestic sphere. But how is the transformed woman made intelligible by discourse? We draw perspective and substance from cultural studies (see Hall 1980, 1997) and feminist film criticism (see Byars 1991; Penley 1988; Pribram 1988) to develop a theoretical framework for interpreting the meanings of ads with the lone woman. Important previous research has addressed the same related set of topics; however, we offer a mode of interpreting advertising that explicitly incorporates the important issues: the problematic construction and positioning of the woman subject, the negotiation of meanings, the dialogic process of reading, and the problem of ideology.

METHOD

One objective of our study was to synthesize relevant research in the advertising and consumer literatures with work in cultural studies to build on the advertising communication model. Another was to identify women consumers' interpretive strategies, while demonstrating that the ad interpretations that emerge are informed discursively within a specific ideological context. We determined that qualitative data from an actual consumption context would best serve our purpose. We chose the consumption of women's special interest magazines, a frequent and everyday event in many women's lives (Ferguson, Kreshel, and Tinkham 1990; McCracken 1993; Wolf 1991). Another strong argument that reinforced our choice is that almost all such magazines carry numerous advertisements for a wide array of products targeted to female consumers. We followed McCracken's (1988) guidelines for long interviews, and therefore requested and received the co-operation of eight women who agreed to take part in tape-recorded interviews lasting one to two hours. The majority of the informants, virtual strangers to us, were former clients of a community agency that provides counseling and training courses for local businesses and entrepreneurs. Two informants were students at the local university. The ages of the women ranged from 20 to 33 years. Seven of the eight worked full-time outside the home. The eighth woman, Meena, worked part-time as a cosmetician and took university courses part time. Table 25.1 reports the women's names, ages, occupations, and some of their leisure interests.

For the interviews, the women brought some of their favorite magazines. We asked them to flip through the magazines as though they were reading them with a friend, which is not an uncommon event, as the majority of informants reported that they occasionally read magazines with friends. When they stopped at an ad that caught their attention, we asked them to talk about what they liked or disliked and what they thought and felt about the products and models featured.

Table 25.1

List of Informants

Name	Age	Occupation	Interests	Marital Status
Terry	26	Graphic Designer	Art, reading	Married
Polly	33	Dietician	Computers	Single
Denise	25	Clerk	Clothes, animals	Married
Jean	33	Public Relations	Skiing, gardening	Married, one son
Meena	20	Student/Cosmetician	Fashion, reading	Single
Lorna	30	Owns Fashion Agency	Sports, reading	Divorced, one daughter
Marilyn	28	Fundraising Consultant	Gardening, motorcycling	Single

Interviews were fluid, phenomenological, and rather unstructured, for informants set the agenda when inspired by the ads. Among the magazines read were *Cosmopolitan, Woman's Day, Us, Shape, Self, Elle,* and *Vogue.*

We took special care to let the data "speak" when identifying interpretive strategies and corresponding ad readings. First, we followed established protocols in protecting informants' privacy and identities, transcribing tapes, and asking broad questions about informants' lives to open the interviews. Our methodological approach was based on grounded theory (Geertz 1979; Lincoln and Guba 1985; Strauss and Corbin 1994), for our primary purpose was elaboration of theory through systematic analysis of empirical data (Glaser and Strauss 1967). Our approach was to relate the themes derived from the data to literature and a theoretical framework, an illuminating and useful approach that has been employed before (cf. Holt 1997; Thompson and Haytko 1997; Thompson and Hirschman 1995). We independently and jointly read through the data, seeking expressions of common thematic categories and important differences among informants, and subsequently employed interpretive tacking to understand informants' interpretive strategies (cf. Hirschman and Thompson 1997). This study was conducted in the spirit of both discovery and justification (Deshpande 1983). Whereas the etic, theoretical categories which compose the revised ad model do not flow directly from the data, we have taken care in our argument below to demonstrate that the data illustrates instantiated manifestations of broad cultural viewpoints, ideologies, or discourses (see Thompson, Pollio, and Locander 1994) and that there are linkages between the etic concepts of the model and the emic perspectives of the informants (cf. Thompson and Hirschman 1995).

THE UNSTABLE, "LEAKY" AND DYNAMIC TEXT: THEORIZING IDEOLOGICAL CONTEXT AND THE SIGNIFYING POTENTIAL OF ADVERTISEMENTS

Although many of us may disagree with Humpty Dumpty's philosophical assertion that meaning is necessarily the product of the historical subject's intention, he does provoke an important question: Why does an ad "mean this but not that?" In other words, how is it that certain interpretations of an ad garner more "cultural weight" (Turner 1996) than others? To gain insight to the question, we turn to the central contribution of cultural studies: its conceptualizations and applications of ideology. In terms of the revised ad communication model Figure 25.1, the constructs we explore below provide a mode of understanding the extratextual ideological context (Figure 25.2) in which ad interpretation takes place.

Figure 25.1 **Revised Advertising Communication Model**

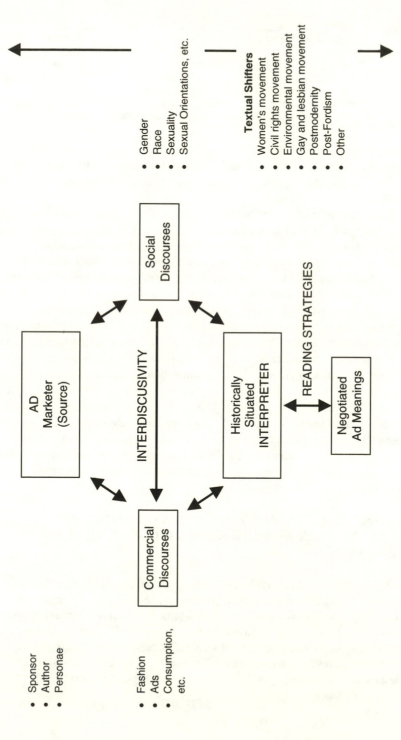

- Sponsor
- Author
- Personae

- Fashion
- Ads
- Consumption, etc.

- Gender
- Race
- Sexuality
- Sexual Orientations, etc.

Textual Shifters

- Women's movement
- Civil rights movement
- Environmental movement
- Gay and lesbian movement
- Postmodernity
- Post-Fordism
- Other

AD Marketer (Source)

Social Discourses

Commercial Discourses

Historically Situated INTERPRETER

Negotiated Ad Meanings

INTERDISCUSIVITY

READING STRATEGIES

Source: Adopted and synthesized from Stern (1994), Thompson and Haytko (1997), Hirschman and Thompson (1997), and Scott (1994a, b).

Figure 25.2   **Extratextual Ideological Context**

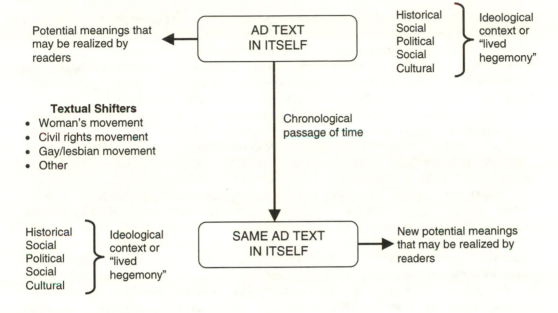

A Working Conceptualization of Ideology

Ideology is the central construct addressed by cultural studies (Turner 1996). Further, given recent work in advertising research and other disciplines which has productively and critically incorporated it (see Eagleton 1991; Hirschman 1993; Hirschman and Thompson 1997; Thompson and Haytko 1997; J. Thompson 1984; Warlaumont 1995), it appears to have considerable descriptive, analytical, and theoretical utility, despite challenge from postmodern perspectives (Dreyfus and Rabinow 1982; Foucault 1970, 1977, 1980; Hall 1986; Larrain 1994). We briefly summarize some of recent thought on ideology and justify just *how* ideological context is instrumental to the construction of ad meanings in a given historical moment.

Thompson (1984, p. 4) notes that ideology refers to the processes that legitimate the power of a dominant group or "the ways in which meaning (or signification) serves to sustain relations of domination." Eagleton (1991) argues that Thompson's definition is the one most widely accepted. A particular "worldview" is naturalized so that acceptable beliefs are rendered self-evident and act as impediments to knowledge, self-determination, or freedom (Hetrick and Lozada 1994). Further, dissenting beliefs are denigrated, obscured, and excluded from the realm of acceptable discourse (Eagleton 1991). The problem, as Eagleton points out, is that "not every body of belief which people term ideological is associated with a *dominant* political power" (p. 6; his emphasis). But Foucault's (1980) contribution is helpful in this regard, despite poststructuralist challenge of the concept itself (see Larrain 1994). Foucault noted that although power is dispersed throughout the social body, it is not necessarily dispersed *evenly*. Hence, we contend that multinational corporations with large advertising budgets that target female consumers *do* constitute a more powerful interest than that of one consumer. The implication is that although corporate advertising may significantly influence consumers' consciousness, it does not dominate it totally. Another implication is that there are several ideological positions from which an ad may be interpreted.

Ideologies and Ad Text

For textual analysis, one problem is that ideology may work through semiotic sleight of hand. Verbal and written propositions along with visual images may help to promote an ideological position if the former are familiar aspects of everyday experience. As Eagleton (1991) argues, an ideology that fails to do so would not last long. A successful ideological position embedded within advertisements must incorporate "true" propositions or images while simultaneously harboring the goal of selling a product. "Some at least of what we call ideological discourse is true at one level but not at another: true in its empirical content but deceptive in its force, or true in its surface meaning but false in its underlying assumptions" (Eagleton 1991, p. 16–17). On a deeper level, an ideology might be trying to persuade us to believe *in* something as opposed to simply believing something. In line with that notion, Althusser proposed that knowledge of one's social reality is produced through the effect of ideology (Althusser 1969, 1970; Williams 1977).

However, we argue that advertising researchers should be skeptical about such a modernist and conspiratorial view, for it is open to the criticisms of textual determinism and unproblematic authorial intention (see Barthes 1977). It is not appropriate to the complex and fragmented post-modern condition (Firat and Shultz 1997; Firat and Venkatesh 1995; Holt 1997). The ideological potential of advertisements may be largely an unconscious phenomenon in that images and text in ads are constructed in the *absence* of any intention to distort and oppress (Hall 1982) beyond the obvious goal of selling products (Scott 1994b). In other words, the advertising executives, brand managers, copywriters, and art directors who co-operatively produce a particular ad are not involved in a cloak and dagger conspiracy to oppress women. Rather, as historical subjects, they unconsciously and unwittingly "speak" dominant discourse(s) and adapt certain tacit, unquestioned ideological positions and conventions that render women intelligible. "Ideology is a function of the discourse and of the logic of social processes, *rather than an intention of the agent*" (Hall 1982, p. 88, italics added).

As a systemic phenomenon, ideological reproduction occurs at the level of the ad producer *and* the ad consumer. In the following passage, Denise's evaluation of female models in Calvin Klein ads provides an account of how the ad images in a women's magazine prompt the reinforcement of a common ideological position:

> The girls are so . . . natural . . . that Calvin Klein, natural kind of look and I'm about as un-natural as they come.[I: Talk about that.] Because I've always worn makeup all my life, I've always . . . this is the first time in my life I've not had nails (acrylic). I've always liked fake and bake tans—anything that I could do to change myself. Like if I could afford plastic surgery I would do it. [I: What would you have done?] I would have my breasts done . . . I would have liposuction . . . and would have abs put in . . . and I would have my ankles thinned. [I: Where does that need come from?] Because I've never felt beautiful . . . I don't feel like that. I don't feel that way about myself . . . and I'm very critical of myself and other people as well. And think that's just from being unhappy with myself. All my life I've felt that I have thick ankles. Always. I see pictures and I go "ewww!" I used to wear really high heels to make my legs look skinnier cause I used to hate that I had such big legs I guess. I always felt that I had big legs.

The passage reveals Denise's harsh, judgmental gaze (Foucault 1977; Thompson and Hirschman 1995), for she scrutinizes every facet of her appearance and finds herself lacking in comparison with a normative beauty ideal (cf. Richins 1991; Wolf 1991). She evaluates her appearance from a particular ideological position that goes virtually unproblematized. She is "speaking" within the confines of one dominant and entrenched gendered discourse about female bodies, that of the "natural look." In that context, "natural" assumes a particular connotation. It refers to her imperfect body in contrast to the "made up" one enabled by her use of cosmetics: "she [the model in an Ann Taylor design ad] is very natural looking to me. And that's not me at all. I'm made right up . . . I get up in the morning and I shower immediately, and I do my hair and my makeup . . . I'll do my makeup always always always. I never leave the house without makeup." Denise is made to feel lesser by her own mercilessly panoptic gaze.

Complex, stable, yet cultural conditions, and the variety of possible interpretive standpoints are conducive to key *performative contradictions*—"contradiction[s] between a meaning conveyed explicitly and a meaning conveyed by the act itself of conveying" (Turner 1983, p. 26) occur as the consumer interprets ads. The manner, executional elements, messages, or style of an ad may appear to be at odds with its preferred meaning(s), potentially alerting women to various other interpretations and inspiring the construction of negotiated readings of the ad (Hall 1980; Hirschman and Thompson 1997). In other words, a variety of interpretive positions and conflicting cultural meanings that may inform the everyday act of reading a woman's magazine (Rabine 1994; Thompson and Haytko 1997).

Diachronic Aspects of Ad Meanings: Textual Shifting

Discourse as a basis for speech and action implies that women have become intelligible in different ways at different historical junctures. Much mainstream discourse has been influenced by decades of feminist critique, political action, and women's presence in the workforce. Given that discourses transform, how is it that the ad text realizes a *particular* set of meanings? We acknowledge that ads invite many viable readings, but only some of them may be realized within a given historical, ideological context. Dyer (1982) rejects the notion of the "text in itself" and conceptualizes text and context as inseparable, broadening the text to include *extratextual* elements such as historical social discourses. The multitude of intertextual relations between various ads and discourses increases polysemic potential (Fiske 1987), allowing a great variety of meanings to be negotiated within actual contexts of use (see Holt 1997; Thompson and Haytko 1997). Figure 25.2 illustrates the effect of textual shifters on ad meanings.

Further, Bennett and Woollacott (1988) contend that the meaning potential of any text must be considered in relation to social conditions that frame its interpretation. Textual shifters are broad historical and sociocultural influences—such as the women's and civil rights movements in North America—that influence discourses and as thus, can foreground or background various aspects of the ad text (called "pieces of play"), helping it to realize some meanings while silencing others. Although it may have been acceptable fifty years ago to think of and speak about women exclusively in their domestic and childbearing roles, it is now deemed unacceptable to do so. The cultural position(s) of ads that represent women has been shifted to a radically changed ideological context. The shift constitutes more than just a change of context, for textual shifters, throughout the passage of time, alter the text itself (Bennett and Woolacott 1988; Turner 1996) in terms of its overall signifying potential. Therefore, we reject the formalist conceptualization of ad text that is implicitly grounded in the "container metaphor" (cf. Holt 1997) of meaning (i.e., meanings as immanent in ad text).

Synchronic Ad Meaning and Hegemonic Accommodation

As Byars (1991) convincingly argues, multiple ideological stances co-exist within the overall American ideology, for American society is quite complex. Therefore, Gramsci's (1971) work on hegemony—dominance attained by configurations of ideologies within the context of struggle and negotiation—is relevant here. Cultural leadership must be won and rewon continually, vying with various forms of cultural resistance by historical subjects and competing with other ideologies (Williams 1977). That contest has significant implications for the textual meanings in advertising. Stern (1989) provides a literary critique of a 1928 ad for Ivory Flakes detergent. The ad and Stern's argument strongly suggest that the ideological context of that era socially positioned female consumers as being preoccupied with "charming trifles," degrading the value of women's daily work within the home. Such an anachronistic advertising pitch would not work today, for it would be strikingly out of line with the relevant textual shifters. From our theoretical perspective, the fact that many advertisers use images of women living outside traditional gendered lines of shopping, childcare, housework, cooking, and caring-for-others roles may represent the genuine hegemonic accommodation of large corporations as they compete for cultural and commercial share of consciousness (cf. Hall 1982).

We cannot go back in time and gather data by showing 1990s ads to 1950s homemakers. However, Terry, who works as a graphic designer at a local newspaper, interprets an ad that strikes her as a "1950s Beaver Cleaver" sort of image and, somewhat paradoxically, inspires her intertextual allusion to the 1980s supermom/superwoman icon. Overall, the following passage affords an excellent example of the way texts shift in meaning over time as a result of the broad social shifts in women's experiences:

> This [ad for Lifetime network, "Television for Women," in *Cosmopolitan*, December 1997] is kind of a funny ad. It reads: "It's not easy to pull together the perfect holiday . . ." Well I guess some women think they have to do it all and that's kind of saying that if you watch this program you can [do it all]. Like in the olden days. What would that be . . . the 1950s? I think they are trying to say that women can do it all and if watch their show they'll show you how. How to be like a superwoman. [I: What do you think of the superwoman icon?] I think it's unrealistic and that it's hard on women. Because I think that you can either be domestic oriented or you can be more career oriented. Both of them are equal—but I don't think you can do both. Like I don't think I can do both. And I don't think that you should feel that you have to do both. Unless you have a partner that is doing both as well and then you can balance it out. I think one person doing it all is too overwhelming and unrealistic and not fair.

Terry refers to a recent ad in *Cosmopolitan* done in 1950s style with an impeccably dressed and coiffed mother (wearing pearl earrings, just like June Cleaver) who is serving a Thanksgiving dinner to her family. Dad is at the head of the perfect table, and the children are attractive in stereotypical "Beaver Cleaver family" style. In Terry's view, the ad execution provokes feelings of anxiety by eliciting an allusion to the 1980s supermom or superwoman icon. Given Terry's 1990s context of work commitments and home responsibilities, both June Cleaver and Superwoman are problematized as anachronistic and unrealistic. The ad may have made sense in the 1950s before feminism altered the gender[ed] landscape, and it may have fit the 1980s superwoman icon who tried to do it all, but its signifying possibilities are limited by more recent developments in gender expectations. Perhaps as a result of the women's movement's legacy, Terry expects women to have partners who share equitably in private household responsibilities. Hence, for Terry, the ad realizes negative meanings and is evaluated as incompatible with her own gender identity, for she does not identify with the image in the ad. Through a relevant textual shift and accompanying altered discourses, the ad assumes a different cultural position than it would have held in either the 1950s or in the 1980s. In a sense, the Lifetime ad is remarkably out of line with many advertisers' hegemonic accommodations of the recent past. Terry's interpretation is an example of how hegemonic process entails a struggle among a number of ideological positions within a historical juncture.

In sum, the realized meanings of ads depend on dynamic, *historically grounded* discourses. Further, hegemony is achieved through vying for a leading commercial interest. Dominant interests in society must be *genuinely* accommodative of opposing societal interests if they are to negotiate a position of leadership, producing the common sense view that social arrangements benefit the dominated (Gramsci 1971; Hall 1982; Turner 1996). For a lived hegemony (Williams 1977) to be relevant to advertising, the tacit cultural viewpoints that ads encompass must lend themselves to the easy development of situational, interpretive frameworks (Holt 1997) brought to bear within actual consumption contexts (such as examining an ad in one's favourite women's magazine). In the context of advertising to women *specifically,* meanings must resonate with market segments of women consumers and speak to their lived experience as women such as problematic relationships with food (Bordo 1993), one's body (Schouten 1991; Thompson and Hirschman 1995), or the "juggling" lifestyle (Thompson 1996). Finally, meanings and images must also appear familiar and friendly, drawn from a pool of other mass media vehicles such as television shows or films (Hirschman and Thompson 1997; Traube 1992).

A lived hegemony never remains static or in place. In our postmodern era, social conditions are complex, and so are the marketing environments of competing organizations and influential political lobbies. Countervailing and contradictory cultural perspectives (Thompson and Haytko 1997) are capable of inspiring clashing interpretive disjunctures. To make matters even more complicated, they are juxtaposed against individual differences and group interests based on gender, race, ethnicity, subculture, sexual orientations, lifestyles, taste, and so on (see Bourdieu 1984; Hebdige 1979; Holt 1997; Solomon 1996). Moreover, damning feminist critique of advertising has entered popular speech (Pollay 1986; Pollay and Mittal 1993). In sum, hegemonic process *negotiates* for leadership among diverse streams of thought. At any given time, however, certain potential ad meanings may achieve a higher degree of shared cultural weight and semiotic closure within contexts of use, interpretation, or conversation. Within that complexity, spaces are available for resistance and reading against the grain. As Holt (1997, p. 342) notes, "different social contexts and different historical periods produce specific sociocultural configurations of [social] categories. These classificatory regimes . . . structure cultural understandings . . ." Therefore, an ad's set of potential meanings changes because the world around it has changed. Here today, gone tomorrow.

We next flesh out the other components of our proposed ad communication model (Figure 25.1), which are drawn from previous research in advertising (Scott 1994a, b; Stern 1994; Thompson and Haytko 1997), cultural studies (Bennett and Woollacott 1988; Dyer 1982; Fiske 1987; Hall 1980, 1982; Turner 1996; Williams 1977), and our interview data.

COMMERCIAL AND SOCIAL DISCOURSES

"Discourses" are defined as sets of ideas that provide presuppositional understanding and "ways of speaking" about topics or subjects (Foucault 1977, 1978; Hall 1997; Holt 1997; Thompson and Haytko 1997). They are grounded in historical social practice, operate at the everyday level of lived experience, and are inextricably linked to relations of power (Foucault 1980; Hall 1997); Lorna's perspective of women's depictions in magazine ads illustrates the way that ad interpretions are constituted by social and commercial discourses.

I think this is one of the industries [modeling] where it's a role reversal where the male models don't make as much as the female models. That's kind of different. . . . They're a lot more conservative with men too—quite often. They don't often put them [men] in vulnerable situations and settings. I don't see too many. You know like what they put around them wouldn't make them weak or anything—it's always the strong attractive male. [I: And the women?] They're getting better . . . you can see these women are a little more no nonsense but having fun and "in charge" type attitudes no matter what the settings are—quite often. It's less and less the ones where you see the depressed, frail, fragile and totally helpless female—and I'm glad to see that. I don't like to see the totally helpless female. [I: Where has the totally helpless woman gone?] Probably women's attitudes of today. Because they are trying to become more independent. More chameleon type. . . . but more in charge in themselves and they want to be seen that way too or come across that way without being "butchy!" [I: What's butchy?] You know when the feminists say, "to be equal you had to be like a man" so you would dress, act and behave male almost. Which was kind of sad I think and I think you should be able to be a strong female and still be feminine. Women have evolved—you don't see them so much in the homemaker situation—not that there is anything wrong with that either, depending on what you choose—but it's not an expected or a given anymore. You see [women] in a whole variety of settings now, you see them in romantic settings, you see them in risqué settings, rebellious settings, and so on. . . . I like that variety. Not just the good housewife.

Although Lorna is speaking primarily about women's cultural positions, she also alludes to a more commercial discourse concerning the modeling industry, a phenomenon we identify as "interdiscursivity," a term describing how discourses intertwine in speech to inform the everyday act of reading women's magazines. Lorna's passage draws from a popular discourse of our time in describing the way women have become intelligible and distinct in contrast to men *and* "women of the past," the latter being a mythical, stereotypical construct—the unhappy, helpless homemaker. The Chameleon-like modern woman is versatile and competent in both domestic and professional spheres of life. Lorna also alludes to the construction of her own femininity by distancing herself from "butchy" types. (i.e. feminist, overly masculine, and possibly lesbian). The discourse about women is useful to Lorna because it helps her understand the differences between current and past generations of women. It also helps her construct her own gender identity, for it draws upon a discourse related to traditional and non-traditional conceptions of femininity (feminine and "butchy"). Although Lorna values various qualities associated with the women's movement ("controlled strength" and independence), she demonizes a construct she labels "butchy" feminism, a term also grounded in her understanding of the women's movement. The overall theoretical point is that understanding of ads emerges in relation to various discourses and is not textually determined as suggested by the current ad model.

Discourses about "What Advertising Is For"

One important category of commercial discourse relevant to the nature of advertising in women's magazines constitutes the character of acceptance versus skepticism toward ads (Scott 1994b) and the conditions of intelligibility (how advertising is regarded and understood) in general. Our informants made many comments about the nature of advertising such as "it's [an ad] extreme and sometimes trashy, like the stories in *Cosmo*" (Karen) or "it's light entertainment" (Jean). Other comments included "this [ad] doesn't do much for me. I can't relate to her at all. She's a waif" (Jean). Some informants noted that "things [ad depictions of women] are getting more fair."

These comments reflect intersecting types of discourses that influence the ways ads are to be understood. Ads in magazines may be appreciated for their color and physical beauty (a form of "entertainment"), or they may act as fashion arbiters or enablers, helping women to compose their images with fragments of consumer culture. They may be used as a means of reinforcing various aspects of self-concept, as a means of representing qualities one would like to cultivate, or even as a means of criticizing culturally entrenched beauty standards. Often, the women in our study referred to ads as "realistic and unrealistic," and that pattern of response requires some interpretation (cf. Schroeder and Borgerson 1998). Our informants' judgments suggest that consumers view pictures as true accounts (i.e., "objective reality") rather than as rhetoric (see Scott 1994a). That hegemonic aspect of ad representation does not go uncontested, however. For example, Jean reported that she feels very comfortable with her life and appearance, and asserted that "these ads are just a way of displaying clothes," implicitly acknowledging that ads, for her, are creative fictions. But overall, the magazine ads appear to play a key role in legitimating various authoritative beliefs about health and fitness, acceptable appearance criteria, and a mindset of comparison—all aspects of a traditional gendered discourse (see Bordo 1993; Thompson and Haytko 1997; Thompson and Hirschman 1995) that conflate appearance with self-worth and underlying personal character. To the extent that such implications go undetected and unchallenged, operations of disciplinary power are perpetuated (Foucault 1980).

Fashion Discourses

The "natural look" (Thompson and Haytko 1997) bears further comment as an important form of commercial fashion discourse. Most of our informants mentioned "natural" looks in the context of evaluating the ads in the magazines. When reading *Cosmopolitan,* Jean noted that "natural" refers to one particular reformulation of a beauty ideal: images that impress readers as real, authentic, warm, and healthy, and in contrast to "overly made up" gendered images that strike them as "plastic and phony" (Polly). "Natural" is a paradox because although it signifies freedom from fashion pressures, Terry and other informants note that achieving the seemingly effortless look demands and requires significant time investment and physical labour. "[Y]ou know 'cause [the ad is for] Noxzema and doesn't say anything, it doesn't tell you how to be. It just presents it [the product]." Yet, ironically, Noxzema is a required resource for the personal care rituals so characteristic of adherence to fashion norms! Terry's statement is an instance of disciplinary power's ideological capacity to "cover its tracks" (Foucault 1980), naturalizing certain fashion images over others and legitimating concrete self-care practices that are characteristic of disciplinary norms (cf. Thompson and Hirschman 1995).

Discourses and the Activities of Marketers

Discourses also influence the activities of marketers. Sales reports, marketing research surveys, letters of complaint or thanks, retailer reactions, conversations with channel intermediaries, boycotts, public outcries, and protests by interest groups are the various feedback mechanisms by which corporations learn about social change and which help shape their subsequent portrayals of women. The Calvin Klein ad campaign of 1995 provides an extreme example of that phenomenon (Goldman 1995). Klein had released a series of ads featuring ostensibly underage adolescents. Further, the skinny models were portrayed in a way that some critics labeled pedophilic. After public protests and threats of retailer withdrawal, the company cancelled the ads. The combined effect of current discourses about the acceptability of representations is instrumental in shaping how certain groups such as the young or women are depicted in future ads. Discourses do not simply funnel down, and they are not unilaterally imposed on consumers. Rather, discourses are grounded in social conditions and permeate the interactions among various stakeholder groups. Knowledge of discourses enables marketers to appropriate the meanings adhering to social movements and societal transformations, allowing for hegemonic accommodation (see Hall 1980, 1982; Thompson and Haytko 1997).

BRIDGING THE GAP FROM TEXT TO MIND: THE DISCURSIVE CONSTITUTION OF THE SOCIALLY, HISTORICALLY SITUATED INTERPRETING SUBJECT

The subject refers to a centred versus decentred understanding of self. *Subjectivism* finds its roots in the humanistic philosophical tradition that attributes a privileged and dominant status to the individual mind and thought: "*Cogito ergo sum.*" The subject in poststructuralist thought constitutes a reaction against humanist ideology that grants the preeminent status of "maker of meaning" to the individual (Hall 1997; Rice and Waugh 1996), a decidedly logocentric position (Derrida 1981). Foucault (1980) also theorized about the production of knowledges and the displaced subject in his discussion of discourse, and argued that discourse is the producer of knowledges (Foucault 1980). The relevant implication is that consumers become entangled within discourses when seeking to understand ads (see Foucault 1970, 1977, 1978, 1980; Hall 1997; see also Thompson and Hirschman 1995). Consequentially, some research in advertising is rather problematic. Note the following claim: "[r]eading as a consumer involves assembling textual cues, but also having the willingness to 'be' a particular fictive reader . . ." (Scott 1994b, p. 471). But willingness to "do" *what?* To "be" *what?* Discourse constitutes these important "whats." Although we acknowledge that consumers assume and reject multiple interpretive stances (Iser 1978; Scott 1994b, p. 473) during the interaction of text and reader, we conceptualize the reader of ads as someone who may "willingly" accept or reject the subject position created for him or her *and interprets the ad in relation to the associated social and commercial discourses* (Foucault 1970; Hall 1997; Thompson and Haytko 1997) or knowledge systems (Thompson and Hirschman 1995) in which s/he has been "entangled" (p. 145), such as normalized ideals of beauty (Bordo 1993), which provide bases of social comparison (Richins 1991; Wolf 1991).

Discourses render the woman subject understandable to self and others. They also inform consumers' various interpretive ad frameworks and self narratives which, in turn, highlight *some* experiences, meanings, and ad elements while backgrounding others (cf. Bennett and Woollacott 1988; Thompson 1997). The interpretive frameworks tend to be dynamic, for discourses and social conditions change, and they have relevance for the use of interpretive strategies and the construction of personalized ad meanings. Dialogically, negotiated ad meanings then facilitate the ongoing development of interpretive frameworks (Thompson 1997).

CONSUMER READING STRATEGIES AND NEGOTIATED AD MEANINGS

Although Hirschman and Thompson's (1997) empirically grounded reading strategies (inspiring/ aspiring, deconstructing/rejecting, and identifying/individualizing) are appropriate for understanding relationships between advertising and mass media, their categories are insufficient for describing *all* ad readings (cf. Brunsdon and Morley 1980; Hall 1980; Morley 1980, 1981), and subsequent research has established that a greater variety of reading strategies are employed. For example, some readings in media studies were not based on class as an organizing principle, and the dominant code was overlooked or ignored (Morley 1980, 1981). Further, ethnicity and gender emerged as important factors in text interpretation (see also Byars 1991). One cannot assume that all readers apply similar levels of sophistication, cultural knowledge, or symbolic capital when interpreting ads (Bourdieu 1984). Although consumers share similar cultural knowledge, they differ profoundly on the bases of race, ethnicity, gender, experience, and so on. Previous research (see Byars 1991; Thompson and Haytko 1997; Turner 1996) suggests that a reader may assume several ideological positions within the context of a lived hegemony. A consumer may use one of many reading strategies, as appropriate to the consumption context. Therefore, we reject the notion of preferred and oppositional readings in favor of a multitude of subtly negotiated ones.

Jean: An Idiographic Case Analysis

Jean, a married woman in her thirties, works full time as a public affairs officer in an insurance company, travels frequently for her job, has a three-year-old son, cycles, works out, gardens in summer, skis in winter, and takes a class at the local university. Her current position provides a maternity leave at work, and she is looking forward to "getting back" to part time work so she can spend more time with her son as "they [children] grow up like that and you could miss it." Her life is strikingly similar to those of the women described by Thompson (1996), for Jean "juggles" work, childcare, travel, exercise, household tasks, shopping, and rare personal time. Currently, she reads women's magazines while travelling, devoting an hour here and there to "flipping through" *Cosmopolitan, Chatelaine, Woman's Day,* and occasionally *Elle* and *Vogue*. She reports that price is an important factor, for her family is on a budget, and she and her husband spend a significant portion of the household income on daycare and other childcare expenses. Hence, she rarely reads the latter two magazines, for they are more expensive than the first three noted.

As our interview progressed, the second author understood that her general interpretive strategy is one which we call "aesthetic evaluation." She reads magazines to enjoy the artistry of advertisements, a pattern shared by other informants. Jean flips through until a particularly colorful and attractive ad "catches her eye" although some ads "do nothing for [her]." When a particularly colorful or "flashy" ad attracts her attention, she attempts to "relate" to the model, critiquing her hair, makeup, body type, and clothing, sometimes in light of previous knowledge of the model. If the model is older (a woman who appears to be in her late twenties or early thirties), wears more conservative clothing, and has subdued "natural" makeup and hairstyle, Jean feels she can easily relate to her and to the product. She then thinks about whether her family can afford the cosmetics or fashions depicted. Usually they cannot, and although Jean holds very positive evaluations of Lancome cosmetics, she asserts that they are too expensive for her and her family, but Estée Lauder, another favored brand, is much more affordable.

Although Jean claims that "light entertainment" is her primary goal in reading women's magazines and the ads, she employs several interpretive strategies. The screening strategy is her requirement that ads be colorful and eyecatching. Otherwise, she flips the page without a second look. Beyond that, she employs a strategy of relating to the model's style and the product's benefits to her own life themes and projects (Mick and Buhl 1992), reinforcing her self concept as a good (working) mother. Raising her son is her primary endeavour, and this concern influences Jean's strategies. Only sensible and affordable products are considered for her personal use. She evaluates ads for products suitable for a mother of a toddler. For example, she noted that an ad for Miller clothing in *Woman's Day* was for the "mom-ish kind of clothes," which are affordable, sensible, casual, and durable. Moreover, she carefully evaluates ads in *Woman's Day* which feature products for young children, such as one for Barney the Dinosaur movies which she has rented and might buy for her son. Secondarily, controlling her weight (she has been overweight before and does not like "feeling fat") and leading an active life are important life projects. Jean therefore attempts to identify with models only if they resemble a "type of look" that is older, casual, and "natural." Ads are immediately rejected as "unrealistic" or "silly" if the model looks "eight years old," "anorexic" or "like an airhead."

Throughout Jean's narrative, certain discursive currents can be identified. Foremost is a traditional, gendered discourse constituting the "good mother" illustrated by her efforts to find clothes suitable for "moms" and products for her toddler. Importantly, her commitment to motherhood and thriftiness affords her a critical position from which to critique ads. The tacit ideological position of working mother accords her licence to construct oppositional readings to certain ads: "When you have a family, it's not a priority to have [brand] names on [clothing]." Like many women, Jean feels caught between traditional notions of motherhood and domesticity and the more recent expanded formulations of women's gender roles (see Fournier 1998; Thompson 1996). In light of Jean's social and historical position as a working mother, certain meanings in the ad texts are accepted ("This is for mom-ish kind of clothes . . . practical and affordable. It's an awesome ad. I'm a mom, I relate to it because there's a kid in it. It's fun."), and others are rejected ("She [the model] looks eight years old. I don't relate to [the Jockey underwear ad] at all.") Overall, Jean constructs personalized ad meanings ("You can be attractive without being skinny and model gorgeous") which negotiate among culturally imposed beauty standards, feminist critique of those ideals, and conceptions of motherhood.

We next discuss other interpretive strategies gleaned from informants' interviews.

Godzilla versus Bambi?—NOT!: Knowledge versus Knowledge

Knowledge about fashion and beauty standards constructed from ads and articles is often countered, reinforced, or elaborated on by the knowledge developed in professional settings (cf. Bourdieu 1984; Holt 1998). Although consumers become entangled in knowledge systems as demonstrated by their reported beliefs, that condition is not without contradiction. Traditionally, women have been socialized into the domestic, consumer role (Stern 1989), but more recently, the traditional role has been supplemented by the newer professional one with corresponding changes in women's authoritative knowledges and interpretive frameworks.

Lorna, a co-owner of a modeling agency, evaluated a Pantene shampoo ad in *Mademoiselle* accordingly, drawing from her personal and professional experience:

> Nice hair but impossible. It's just too perfect. [I: This doesn't exist?] Oh I'm sure it does but it would cost a lot of expense and time . . . even though they're trying to say it's not. For someone like me who's tried a lot of different things and had a lot of disappointments based on that sort of thing . . . when I see things are too good to be true and almost guaranteed I am very skeptical—it's like, "I'll pass."

Generally, consumers gain personal experience with products that subsequently leads to a more critical disposition toward ads and their claims. However, Lorna's passage is a good example of the way one particular informant uses extensive work experience and insider knowledge to construct an oppositional interpretation. She does not reject the product, but she does reject the perceived simplicity of the rhetorical claim conveyed through vivid imagery.

Similarly, Terry works as a graphic designer in a newspaper, and is able to evaluate the technology that produces the so-called perfect images:

> I guess the only time it bothers me seeing models that I feel inadequate is like when it's for cellulite cream or something like and they're half naked and thinking "oh man . . . I think that's airbrushing but gee I wish my legs looked even close to that." [I: So you suspect they use airbrushing?] Yes. I know how the magazine industry works and I know what the computer technology is and stuff. [I: Can you show me an example?] You see her skin is flawless, right? [I: So knowing that then—does that alter the way you look at ads?] Slightly, but not as much as it should. I mean I know that, but I still think, "oh gee, you know." Its such an ideal, it doesn't really matter if she's real or not.

Terry's comments illustrate that professional knowledge, despite its authority, does not necessarily go unchallenged. Although she knows that ad images are manufactured and recognizes that the beauty standard is an unattainable ideal, Terry exhibits the qualities of "mythical thinking" (Barthes 1972; Thompson and Haytko 1997): "I know, but all the same . . ." On a conscious level, Terry gravitates toward the image but does not silence her critical voice. Underlying her passage is a tangled knot of popular discourses about fashion, beauty, and women's bodies, none of which can be completely discounted despite her years of professional career history. Mythical thinking represents an attempt to negotiate among countervailing cultural meanings to forge a personalized ad meaning. On the one hand, Terry has airbrushed photographs herself and understands the attempt to alter images and manipulate consumers' impressions. On the other hand, she aspires to emulate a fashion model in one respect. Although her own knowledge has gained legitimate currency, so has that of the fashion industry, as disseminated through the relevant gatekeepers: journalists, editors, and fashion icons. Therefore, personal and professional knowledges, combined with commercial discourses, inform negotiated personalized ad meanings. In the background is the relevant sociocultural influence—the transformed role of women—which places Terry in the public, professional sphere and affords her an ideological position from which to criticize and to invest confidence in her own evaluations.

Polly, a dietican, interpreting a "moustache" ad for skim milk, offers an instance of the way scientific knowledge of health practices is employed in an interpretation to counter an ad's possible preferred meaning:

> Stuff like this . . . what they are advertising kind of bores me. Because I have a nutrition background and, "yada, yada, yada . . ." They are talking about the word "fat" and they have such a negative connotation about fat and it's no good, and [reads ad]. [I: Is fat bad?] No, it has a place. But people don't believe that, they just say, and this ad is saying that it is no good. And it just chokes me, it's such a misconception even though fat has its place. Everything in moderation—and fat definitely in moderation. And you know without fat, we'd be dead. It's too extreme. People who don't have a nutrition background will go, "Oh my God! I'll never eat fat again." Especially young girls . . . I'm more worried about the younger generation. They might interpret that as, "I won't drink milk at all because it might have fat," if you read that the wrong way.

Polly interprets from a privileged position in relation to the ad sponsors and consumers who might believe the ad. Here, the body and self-care practices are sites of struggle and resistance among various health-related beliefs. Yet, Polly is still entangled in knowledge systems, and she speaks from a particular discursive position that esteems "balance and moderation," countering a more dominant popular discourse that she positions as more "extreme" and oppressive to women, particularly young ones. To be entangled in knowledge or discourse is not always a bad thing, for it helps consumers organize their social worlds, positions, and self-concepts. But Polly is not outside power relations, as her interpretation exemplifies the way power relations are knowledge productive (Foucault 1980). She rejects the extremity of eliminating fat, but is constrained by discourses that prescribe moderation for fitness.

COMPARISONS: CONSTRUCTING THE AVERAGE WOMAN

The natural look discussion was often related to a discourse concerning the "average woman" who, according to informants' reports, is not usually depicted in ads. Yet, in an exceptional instance, when evaluating an ad for Dove soap in *Cosmopolitan*, Polly remarks that she loves the ad and identifies with it, for it represents an "attainable and balanced" beauty:

> Yes, but when I say "average person," I don't mean not beautiful. I like that a lot. And I commend them for being . . . for going out there and doing the opposite of what one would expect for a commercial. It seems advertisers are going more and more that way. Hitting a clearer cross section of people in the world so that they can target people and have them relate to themselves and go, you know, that's kind of like me—that's more down to earth. That [the Dove ad] is more reality—realistic. "I can touch base with this [the Dove ad]," a person would say, [rather] than looking at something and going "this is so not me." And then they dream about it or whatever. This just touches home.

The average woman is a reformulation of the natural look; it does not undermine informants' self-esteem, and they can more easily identify with it. Moreover, Polly's aesthetic evaluations of the Dove model—a dignified, older looking African American woman—reflect concrete manifestations of damning feminist critique about the fashion industry's unattainable beauty ideals.

The average woman serves as an important touchstone for informants. Through comparison, she helps them to negotiate a key tension within postmodern consumer society: the requirement to conform and belong versus the one to be individual and special (cf. Thompson and Haytko 1997). The average woman provides an ego-defensive function, enabling informants to enjoy the ads in magazines as entertainment and as inspiration for their own fashion endeavours, relatively free from feelings of inadequacy. She helps informants distance themselves from images that threaten self-esteem or, conversely, helps them to aspire to images that enhance and reinforce key aspects of self-concept.

Polly's passage below illustrates the way that images can seem threatening to women consumers. However, rather than comparing herself with the image and feeling inferior, she employs a strategy of distancing herself from the image, using the construct of the average woman and denigrating the potential impact of the ad depiction. Thus, comparison processes are not straightforward (cf. Richins 1991; i.e., the actual woman comparing herself with the model). Rather, many informants compared the models with an abstract construction of an everyday woman and were able to preserve self-esteem while drawing on various *conflicting* discourses about what women should look like:

> It [depiction of women in ads] is changing . . . isn't there a magazine or something that's new . . . sure, I just heard about it. That's great . . . that will target normal people. Normal

meaning the average woman. I really think she's too skinny . . . but if you had asked me that question 10 years ago I would have said, "Yeah, she's [the woman depicted in the Revlon ad in *Allure* she's looking at] too skinny but gee wouldn't it be nice to look like that." [I: You don't think like that anymore?] No. Not like that. Because they are too skinny. I have an ideal about what I'd like to look like and this isn't it. [I: What's your ideal?] I went to the body building competition two weeks ago. I don't do body building, I don't believe in it . . . I don't believe in the steroids, it's against my professional ethics anyway. But the Ms. Fitness portion of it—with a focus on agility, flexibility, a bit of talent—that sort of thing. Its not like Ms. USA or anything. Those girls, they look beautiful! They are strong, they are worked out . . . their muscles are defined and they have wonderful symmetry and they are healthy . . . their bodies are the way they are and they just worked them out and eaten well and done a routine and they looked beautiful. That's where I want to be.

Mode Magazine targets women from sizes 4 to 24. The first issue featured eight cover models who were all size fourteens. Interestingly, *Mode* facilitates another comparison strategy: women may look at its large models and feel slim and superior by contrast, interpreting within the parameters of dominant gendered discourses. Thus, the average woman construct works flexibly in another way, for it allows consumers to position themselves as both similar to her and yet unique. Polly does so by aspiring to a "healthy, fit" ideal figure which contrasts with her perceptions of "skinny and unhealthy" fashion models and deviant "bodybuilders." Further, she positions herself a little farther from "the average woman" who is not as toned and "beautiful" as she hopes to be.

It is a comfort to our informants to "see" the average woman in depictions of fabulous super-models such as Cindy Crawford. Denise, who confessed that she does not have a positive body image, forges more positive self-related meanings from ads depicting famous models:

There's Cindy Crawford . . . there's a classic. She's a classic model. She's our age and isn't that scary. She's older than I normally would think for a model . . . and I think because blondes have been played up so much to be so glamorous and so beautiful and every blonde has a body and you just kinda go, "No they don't."

Sometimes, Denise reinforces positive aspects of self-concept by finding at least one quality (or flaw) of the average woman incorporated into idealized images and then shares in the glamour. She humanizes and subsequently individualizes her interpretations by talking about Crawford's "advanced age." Denise uses ads as meaning-full resources that, when conflated with average woman qualities, bring the supermodel to her level. Further, she uses the more humanized version of Crawford as a valued symbolic resource to counter another common manifestation of beauty discourses: the notion that blondes have more fun.

We propose that there is an intersection of conflicting discourses constructing the woman subject and underlying women's reading strategies. Certainly, some ideological positions contradict others (e.g., feminism's struggle for equality and traditional portrayals of women as subordinate), but the historical female subject is evolving too. Through practice, she acquires the know-how to negotiate the tensions of being a woman within patriarchal social relations. The multitude of tacit ideological positions underlying informants' interpretations reflect the contradictory historical juncture where contemporary women find themselves, in a complex ideology of consumption (Bocock 1993; Giddens 1991). Some ads do portray women in a manner interpreted as empowering, and they represent instances of hegemonic accommodation (Gramsci 1971; Hall 1982). Yet, sexist residual meanings are present too, undermining the ideal of gender equality. Such ads construct a woman subject who is not only more secure in her expanded societal roles, but also constrained within patriarchal institutions. Use of the product evokes perceptions of gender equality, perhaps perpetuating a cycle of felt tension (provoked by conflicting role expectations in social relations) and then temporary resolution of that tension. Reading strategies are the means by which discourses become interwoven in ad interpretations. When we juxtapose the counter-vailing interpretive positions of the natural look and of the average woman, we obtain insight to the intricate workings of hegemonic accommodation in the arena of competing ad meanings. In a paradoxical sense, naturalization and problematization of fashion ads exist side by side. The unquestioned acceptance of one fashion look (or practice) usually implies the challenge of another one that is seen as contrived—and vice versa.

DISCUSSION: DISCOURSE AND INTERPRETING ADVERTISING

We add to a stream of advertising research that explores the theoretical link between text and consumer (Scott 1994a, b; Stern 1989, 1993, 1994, 1996a) by incorporating a poststructuralist perspective on meaning construction through discursive appropriation (see Byars 1991; Foucault 1970, 1980; Hall 1997; Hirschman and Thompson 1997; Thompson and Haytko 1997; Thompson and Hirschman 1995), enhancing the ad communication model. The paradox of interpretation implies a socially and historically positioned subject-consumer who can construct webs of meaning of her own by shifting among different interpretive positions in the reading context and by understanding text and self in relation to various discourses. Consumers are the arbiters of meaning making, but simultaneously are subject to the limitations imposed by the (con)text and by relevant social and commercial discourses. We contend that the web metaphor suggests that people become immersed and entangled in webs of ideological meaning, implying the discursive constitution of the consumer subject (Thompson and Haytko 1997; Thompson and Hirschman 1995) and of negotiated ad meanings. Further, our revised framework is not inconsistent with de-constructive perspectives (see Stern 1996a, b): over time and space, sociocultural textual shifters alter ad meanings through mediating discourses. Thus, ad meaning is "slippery," dynamic, and constantly deferred, never achieving a timeless, transcendent status (Derrida 1982).

The revised ad model in Figure 25.1 constitutes a departure from conventional thought in that it is not an ad communication model; it is an ad *interpretation* model. We have attempted to problematize the interpreter/consumer and what s/he does with the text, enhancing the model with the critical element of discourse (cf. Stern 1994). Consumers do not "decode" ads with identifi-able and unproblematic conventions and in the determined ways that marketers "intend" or might desire. Rather, consumers *interpret* ads and negotiate personalized meanings, albeit constituted by discursive, cultural viewpoints. They accept, reject, subvert, alter, and ignore ads in a multitude of ways, but within the constraints of historical and ideological context.

The advertising academic discipline has undergone an important paradigmatic shift during the last decade or so. The idea that advertising may be conceptualized as literary text (Stern 1989, 1996a) or as visual rhetoric (Scott 1994a) is becoming increasingly accepted. Recent contributions indicate a shift from ad communication models to ad meaning models (see Mick and Buhl 1992; Scott 1994b). We urge researchers to broaden focus even further and incorporate our perspective, consolidating the new paradigm. For example, many best-selling advertising textbooks targeted to undergraduate commerce and MBA students incorporate a version of that model (such as Arens 1996; Batra, Myers, and Aaker 1996; Belch and Belch 1998; O'Guinn, Allen and Semenik 1998). In the future, our students will be better served by incorporation of the collective contribution onto which our revised model builds.

FUTURE RESEARCH

Advertising researchers have the opportunity to identify different kinds of nuanced interpretive strategies consumers use for different types of ads and ad contexts. We emphasize the chronological dimension of textual shifters and text-altering potentials, but future work may focus on changes in physical or cultural space and address a very important issue in international marketing. Employing our framework, we might ask: What meanings will an ad developed in Canada or the United States realize in Great Britain, Australia, or Israel? Further, given that postmodern North American society is fragmented into many ethnic groups, taste cultures, and subcultures (and other divisions), texts may be shifted by changing both temporal and cultural space.

REFERENCES

Althusser, Louis (1969), *For Marx,* London: Penguin Books.
——— (1970), "Ideology and Ideological State Apparatuses," in *Lenin and Philosophy and Other Essays,* trans. Ben Brewster, London: New Left Books.
Arens, Willam F. (1996), *Contemporary Advertising,* 6th ed., Toronto: Irwin.
Barthes, Roland (1972), *Mythologies,* trans. Annette Lavers, New York: Hill & Wang.
——— (1977), *Image-Music-Text,* Glasgow: Fontana.
Batra, Rajeev, John G. Myers, and David A. Aaker (1996), *Advertising Management,* 5th ed., Upper Saddle River, NJ: Prentice Hall.
Belch, George E. and Michael A. Belch (1998), *Advertising and Promotion,* 4th ed., New York: Irvin McGraw Hill.
Bennett, Tony and Janet Woollacott (1988), *Bond and Beyond: The Political Career of a Popular Hero,* London: Macmillan.
Bocock, Robert (1993), *Consumption,* London: Routledge.
Bordo, Susan (1993), *Unbearable Weight: Feminism, Western Culture, and the Body,* Berkeley: University of California Press.
Bourdieu, P. (1984), *Distinction: A Social Critique of the Judgment of Taste,* Cambridge, MA: Harvard University Press.
Brunsdon, Charlotte and David Morley (1980), *Everyday Television: "Nationwide,"* London: British Film Institution.
Byars, Jackie (1991), *All That Hollywood Allows: Re-Reading Gender in 1950's Melodrama,* Chapel Hill: University of North Carolina Press.
Derrida, Jacques (1981), *Positions,* Chicago: University of Chicago Press.
Deshpande, Rohit (1983), "Paradigms Lost: On Theory and Method in Research in Marketing," *Journal of Marketing,* 47 (Fall), 101–110.
Douglas, Susan (1994), *Where the Girls Are: Growing Up Female with the Mass Media,* New York: Times Books.
Dreyfus, Hubert L. and Paul Rabinow (1982), *Michel Foucault: Beyond Structuralism and Hermeneutics,* Chicago: University of Chicago Press.
Dyer, Richard (1982), *Stars,* London: BFI.
Eagleton, Terry (1991), *Ideology: An Introduction,* London: Verso.
Ehrenreich, Barbara and Deirdre English (1979), *For Her Own Good: 150 Years of the Experts' Advice to Women,* Garden City, NY: Anchor.
Ferguson, Jill Hicks, Peggy J. Kreshel, and Spencer F. Tinkham (1990), "In The Pages of Ms.: Sex Role Portrayals of Women in Advertising," *Journal of Advertising,* 19 (1), 40–51.
Firat, A. Fuat, and Alladi Venkatesh (1995), "Liberatory Postmodernism and the Reenchantment of Consumption," *Journal of Consumer Research,* 22 (3), 239–267.
——— and Clifford J. Shultz II (1997), "From Segmentation to Fragmentation: Markets and Marketing Strategy in the Postmodern Era," *European Journal of Marketing,* 31,(3/4), 183–207.
Fiske, John (1987), *Television Culture,* London: Methuen.
Foucault, Michel (1970), The Order of Things, London: Tavistock.
——— (1977), *Discipline and Punish,* London: Tavistock.

———— (1978), *The History of Sexuality, Part One,* Harmondsworth: Penguin.

———— (1980), *Power / Knowledge,* Brighton: Harvester.

Fournier, Susan (1998), Consumers and Their Brands: Developing Relationship Theory in Consumer Research," *Journal of Consumer Research,* 24 (March), 343–373.

Geertz, Clifford (1979), "From the Native's Point of View: On the Nature of Anthropological Understanding," in *Interpretive Social Science,* Paul Rabinow and William M. Sullivan, eds., Berkeley: University of California Press, 225–241.

Giddens, Anthony (1991), *Modernity and Self-Identity,* Stanford, CA: Stanford University Press.

Glaser, Barney G. and Anselm L. Strauss (1967), *The Discovery of Grounded Theory: Strategies for Qualitative Research,* New York: Aldine de Gruyter.

Goldman, Kevin (1995), "What Made Calvin Think Again," *Globe and Mail* (August 30), A13.

Gramsci, A. (1971), *Selections From the Prison Notebooks of Antonio Gramsci,* New York: International Publishers.

Hall, Stuart (1980), "Encoding and Decoding," in *Culture, Media, Language*, Stuart Hall et al., eds., London: Hutchinson.

———— (1982), "The Rediscovery of Ideology:" The Return of the 'Repressed' in Media Studies," in *Culture, Soceity and the Media,* Michael Gurevitch, Tony Bennett, James Curran and Janet Woollacott, eds., London: Methuen, 22–49.

———— (1986), "The Problem of Ideology: Marxism Without Guarantees," *Journal of Communication Enquiry,* 10, (2), 28–44.

———— (1997), "The Work of Representation," in *Representation: Cultural Representations and Signifying Practices,* Stuart Hall, ed., London: Sage.

Hebdige, Dick (1979), *Subculture: The Meaning of Style,* New York: Routledge.

Hetrick, William P. and Héctor Lozada (1994), "Construing the Critical Imagination: Comments and Necessary Diversions," *Journal of Consumer Research,* 21 (December), 548–558.

Hirschman, Elizabeth C. (1993), "Ideology in Consumer Research, 1980 and 1990: A Marxist and Feminist Critique," *Journal of Consumer Research,* 19 (4), 537–555.

———— and Craig J. Thompson (1997), "Why Media Matter: Toward a Richer Understanding of Consumers' Relationships with Advertising and Mass Media," *Journal of Advertising,* 26 (Spring), 43–60.

Holt, Douglas B. (1997), "Poststructuralist Lifestyle Analysis: Conceptualizing the Social Patterning of Consumption in Postmodernity," *Journal of Consumer Research,* 23 (March), 326–350.

———— (1998), "Does Cultural Capital Structure American Consumption?" *Journal of Consumer Research,* 25(June), 1–25.

Iser, Wolfgang (1978), *The Act of Reading,* Baltimore: Johns Hopkins University Press.

Larrain, Jorge (1994), "The Postmodern Critique of Ideology," *Sociological Review,* 42 (2), 289–314.

Lasswell, Harold D. (1948), "The Structure and Function of Communication in Society," in *The Process and Effects of Mass Communication,* Wilbur Schramm and Donald F. Roberts, eds., Urbana: University of Illinois Press, 84–99.

Lincoln, Yvonna S. and Egon G. Guba (1985), *Naturalistic Inquiry,* Beverly Hills, CA: Sage.

McCracken, Ellen (1993), *Decoding Women's Magazines: From Mademoiselle to Ms,* London: Macmillan.

McCracken, Grant (1986), "Culture and Consumption: A Theoretical Account of the Structure and Movement of the Cultural Meaning of Consumer Goods," *Journal of Consumer Research,* 13 (June), 71–84.

———— (1988), *The Long Interview,* Newbury Park: Sage.

Mick, David G. (1986), "Consumer Research and Semiotics: Exploring the Morphology of Signs, Symbols, and Significance," *Journal of Consumer Research,* 13 (June), 196–213.

———— and Claus Buhl (1992), "A Meaning-Based Model of Advertising Experiences," *Journal of Consumer Research,* 19 (December), 317–338.

Morley, David (1980), *The 'Nationwide' Audience,* London: British Film Institute.

———— (1981), "The "Nationwide Audience: A Critical Postscript," *Screen Education,* 39 (Summer), 3–14.

O'Guinn, Thomas C., Chris T. Allen and Richard J. Semenik (1998), *Advertising,* Cincinnati: Southwestern College Publishing.

Penley, Constance (1988), "Introduction—The Lady Doesn't Vanish: Feminism and Film Theory," *in Feminism and Film Theory,* Constance Penley, ed., New York: Routledge.

Pollay, Richard W. (1986), "The Distorted Mirror: Reflections on the Unintended Consequences of Advertising," *Journal of Marketing,* 50 (April), 18–36.

———— and Banwari Mittal (1993), "Here's the Beef: Factors, Determinants, and Segments in Consumer Criticism of Advertising," *Journal of Marketing,* 57 (July), 99–114.

Pribram, Deidre (1988), *Female Spectators: Looking at Film and Television,* New York: Verso.

Rabine, Leslie W. (1994), "A Woman's Two Bodies: Fashion Magazines, Consumerism, and Feminism," in *On Fashion,* Shari Benstock and Suzanne Feriss, eds., New Brunswick, NJ: Rutgers University Press.

Rice, Philip and Patricia Waugh (1996), *Modern Literary Theory,* 3rd ed., New York: Arnold.

Richins, Marsha (1991), "Social Comparison and the Idealized Images in Advertising," *Journal of Consumer Research,* 12 (December), 71–83.

Schouten, John. W. (1991), "Selves in Transition: Symbolic Consumption in Personal Rites of Passage and Identity Reconstruction," *Journal of Consumer Research,* 17 (March), 412–425.

Schroeder, Jonathan E. and Janet L. Borgerson (1998), "Marketing Images of Gender: A Visual Analysis," *Consumption, Markets and Culture,* forthcoming.

Scott, Linda M. (1994a), "Images in Advertising: The Need for a Theory of Visual Rhetoric," *Journal of Consumer Research,* 21 (September), 252–273.

———— (1994b), "The Bridge from Text to Mind: Adapting Reader-response Theory to Consumer Research, *Journal of Consumer Research,* 21 (December), 461–480.

Solomon, Michael R. (1996) *Consumer Behavior: Buying, Having, and Being,* Englewood Cliffs, NJ: Prentice Hall.

Stern, Barbara B. (1989), "Literary Criticism and Consumer Research: Overview and Illustrative Analysis," *Journal of Consumer Research,* 16 (December), 322–344.

———— (1993), "Feminist Literary Criticism and the Deconstruction of Ads: A Postmodern View of Advertising and Consumer Responses," *Journal of Consumer Research,* 19 (March), 556–566.

———— (1994), "A Revised Communication Model for Advertising: Multiple Dimensions of the Source, the Message, and the Recipient," *Journal of Advertising,* 23, (2), 5–15.

———— (1996a), "Textual Analysis in Advertising Research: Construction and Deconstruction of Meanings," *Journal of Advertising,* 25 (3), 61–73.

———— (1996b), "Deconstructive Strategy and Consumer Research: Concepts and Illustrative Exemplar," *Journal of Consumer Research,* 23 (September), 136–147.

Strauss, Anselm and Juliet Corbin (1994), "Grounded Theory Methodology," in *Handbook of Qualitative Research,* Norman K. Denzin and Yvonna S. Lincoln, eds., London: Sage, 273–285.

Thompson, Craig J. (1996), "Caring Consumers: Gendered Consumption Meanings and the Juggling Lifestyle," *Journal of Consumer Research,* 22 (March), 388–407.

———— (1997), "Interpreting Consumers: A Hermeneutical Framework for Deriving Marketing Insights from the Texts of Consumers' Consumption Stories," *Journal of Marketing Research,* 34 (November), 438–455.

———— and Diane L. Haytko (1997), "Speaking of Fashion: Consumers' Uses of Fashion Discourses and the Appropriation of Countervailing Cultural Meanings," *Journal of Consumer Research,* 23 (June), 15–42.

———— and Elizabeth C. Hirschman (1995), "Understanding the Socialized Body: A Poststructuralist Analysis of Consumers' Self-Conceptions, Body Images, and Self-Care Practices," *Journal of Consumer Research,* 22 (September), 139–153.

————, Howard R. Pollio, and William B. Locander (1994), "The Spoken and the Unspoken: A Hermeneutical Approach to Understanding the Cultural Viewpoints That Underlie Consumers' Expressed Meanings," *Journal of Consumer Research,* 21 (December), 432–452.

Thompson, John B. (1984), *Studies in the Theory of Ideology,* Cambridge: Polity Press.

Traube, Elizabeth G. (1992), *Dreaming Identities: Class, Gender, and Generation in 1980's Hollywood Movies,* Boulder:, CO: Westview Press.

Turner, Denys (1983), *Marxism and Christianity,* Oxford: Blackwell.

Turner, Graeme (1996), *British Cultural Studies: An Introduction,* 2nd ed., New York: Routledge.

Warlaumont, Hazel G. (1995), "Advertising Images: From Persuasion to Polysemy," *Journal of Current Issues and Research in Advertising,* 17 (Spring), 19–31.

Williams, Raymond (1977), *Marxism and Literature,* Oxford, UK: Oxford University Press.

Wolf, Naomi (1991), *The Beauty Myth,* New York: Anchor.

CHAPTER 26

ASIAN-AMERICANS
Television Advertising and the "Model Minority" Stereotype

CHARLES R. TAYLOR AND BARBARA B. STERN

[THE ASIAN-AMERICAN MARKET]

Asian-Americans are considered a "model minority" (Cohen 1992; Delener and Neelankavil 1990) whose premium demographic profile (Fisher 1994)—affluence, high education, and managerial/professional occupations—and rapid growth in number make them an attractive market. The market's size is impressive, for if Asians in the United States were viewed as a separate country, they would be among the larger members of the global family—eighty-fifth out of 220 nations (*Marketing Review* 1994, p. 8). Even as a minority, Asian-Americans represent the "fastest-growing and most affluent demographic segment" (Fisher 1994, S-2). Their rate of immigration outpaces that of any other group. It increased 108% from 1980 to 1990 and is projected to increase 64% from 1990 to 2000 (Fisher 1994), 11 times the rate of increase of the general U.S. population and twice that of the Hispanic population. The number of Asian-Americans in the U.S. population is predicted to jump from a current 9.4 million (3.6% of the total) to 16 million (6%) in 2010 and to 20 million (8%) in 2020 (Bureau of the Census 1996).

Rapid growth is accompanied by affluence. At present, although the Asian-American market is less than one third the size of the Hispanic-American market, the former has $125 billion in annual purchasing power, nearly two thirds of the latter's $200 billion. Further, Asian-Americans have a median household income of $44,460 a year, 19% more than the national average, which includes white as well as minority households. In 1990, 41% of Asian-American adults 25 years of age and older had at least a bachelor's degree in comparison with 22% for the rest of the population (Bureau of the Census 1996).

In addition, 53.3% of Asian-Americans occupy managerial or professional positions, a percentage higher than that of any other population group (Kern 1988). Further, 5.7% are entrepreneurs, more than double the percentage of any other minority group (Weisendanger 1993). Asian-Americans therefore form a segment "big enough to be meaningful to U.S. marketers" (*Marketing Review* 1994, p. 15) and "poised for growth" much as the Hispanic-American segment was 15 years ago (Fisher 1994, p. S-18).

The superlative demographic profile (Kern 1988) fuels the positive stereotyping of Asian-

---

Americans as intellectually gifted, mathematically skilled, technically competent, hard-working, serious, and well assimilated (Delener and Neelankavil 1990; Yim 1989). Delener and Neelankavil (1990) found that in general other Americans view Asian-Americans as hard-working and thrifty. Similarly, in a study comparing beliefs about Korean-Americans with beliefs about other Americans (Yim 1989), 99% of the respondents described Korean-Americans as intelligent, 98.6% described them as industrious, and 96.8% described them as self-disciplined in comparison with other Americans.

Paucity of Research: "If it ain't broke. . . ."

Ironically, the positive stereotyping of Asian-Americans may be one factor in the paucity of research on that minority—the portrayals do not appear problematic. Most prior research has addressed the consequences of negative stereotyping on the considerably larger African-American and Hispanic-American minorities (Bristor, Lee, and Hunt 1995; Taylor, Lee, and Stern 1995; Zinkhan, Qualls, and Biswas 1990), 30 million and 23.3 million, respectively.

The term "stereotype" is descriptive rather than derogatory—it may be positively or negatively valenced. "Stereotype" is defined as one group's generalized and widely accepted beliefs about the personal attributes of members of another group (Ashmore and Del Boca 1981; Dates and Barlow 1990), and its essence is the perception of group members as generic exemplar of a type rather than as individuals. The tendency to generalize is pervasive in advertising, for as Courtney and Whipple (1983, p. 205) point out, "advertising messages must employ stereotypes because stereotypes are a shorthand which helps to convey ideas and images quickly and clearly." We agree with their claim that despite the need for "an easily recognized stereotype," it is possible to create advertising that accepts the changes in society without apologizing for them, without explaining them away, without denigrating them, and without manipulating them" (p. 205). A compelling motivation for creating such advertising is that reliance on familiar stereotypes may have negative consequences unforeseen by the sponsors or creators of advertising. Hence, the following discussion is not intended to castigate advertising, but to heighten the industry's awareness of some problematic consequences of even positive stereotyping.

The few academic studies on advertising portrayals of Asian-Americans have found evidence of stereotyping in *print* media (magazines). One study was an experimental investigation of white consumers' attitudes toward Asian models (Cohen 1992) and two others were content analyses of the frequency and nature of Asian-American representation (Schmid and Bowen 1995; Taylor and Lee 1994). The latter two obtained different frequency counts (1.8% versus 4.0%), but similar findings about the presence and valence of stereotypes, with Asian-Americans depicted as technically competent, hard-working, self-disciplined, serious, and well-assimilated (Taylor and Lee 1994).

The evidence of stereotyping in print media suggests a need to extend content-analysis to *television* advertising (Pollay and Gallagher 1990), which affects and reflects public perceptions more profoundly than print does. Television has particular impact because the average American watches 30 hours of programming a week (*Statistical Abstract of the United States* 1994), with especially heavy viewing during prime time (8 to 11 p.m). In addition, viewing invokes the low-involvement processing mode that depresses cognitive responses and content screening (Krugman 1965). Passive viewing sustains uncritical acceptance of stereotypical portrayals such that advertising—albeit unintentionally—shapes the American public's view of minorities (Bristor, Lee, and Hunt 1995; Wilkes and Valencia 1989).

Insofar as television portrayals influence attitudes toward minorities, we must investigate the frequency and nature of Asian-American appearances in prime time advertising. We address those issues by framing research questions about representation, role prominence, and stereotypes and using content analysis to answer them. The most basic questions pertain to the frequency and role status of Asian-Americans in advertisements. They are followed by questions about social and contextual variables that reveal minority stereotypes in terms of the type of goods/services the models are shown using, the settings in which they appear, and the relationships in which they engage. We discuss each question to justify its value in eliciting information that will contribute to more informed understanding of advertising images of Asian-Americans.

RESEARCH QUESTIONS

Frequency of Representation

Q1:   Is the proportion of television commercials portraying Asian-American men and women higher or lower than the proportion of these groups in the U.S. population?

The purpose of the question is to discover the extent to which Asian-Americans are visible in advertisements. When a minority is not depicted, its capacity to assimilate with the host culture is diminished, for group members feel they are socially invisible. Minority consumers who fail to see anyone like themselves using products or services may conclude that society in general and marketers in particular barely register their existence.

The concept "frequency of representation" is evaluated by means of the proportionality criterion, which states that total minority representation should approximate the minority's proportion in the population (Faber, O'Guinn, and Meyer 1987). In our study of Asian-American portrayals, we disaggregated the data by sex because prior research has shown that representation of men and women is disproportionate (Courtney and Whipple 1983). We applied the proportionality criterion to Asian-American men and women separately in light of the following percentages of U.S. population: all Asian-Americans 3.58%, men 1.73%, and women 1.85%.

Our decision to disaggregate by sex was influenced by the pioneering study of gendered minority images in Bristor, Lee, and Hunt's (1995) work on African-Americans as was our decision to exclude age as a variable. Bristor et al. found that lack of representation in advertising (e.g., no scenes of African-American mothers playing with their children) is problematic, for absence reinforces commonly held stereotypes (e.g., broken African-American families). One of the more important commonalities across Asian cultures is adherence "to the Confucian core values of family . . . filial piety . . . and loyalty" (Cheng 1996, p. 12). Gender roles are highly traditional, and men and women typically occupy separate spheres (women in the home, men in the workplace). Despite cultural differences between minority groups, we anticipated underrepresentation of female Asian-Americans.

Regardless of the frequency of representation, Bristor, Lee, and Hunt (1995, p. 48) conclude that mere numbers do not eliminate "selective, partial, one-dimensional and distorted" stereotypes. Hence, it is necessary to move beyond the question of percentages to the meaning encoded in the portrayals.

Perceived Importance

Q2:   When male and female Asian-American models are present in a television commercial, do they appear most frequently in major roles, minor roles, or background roles?

The point of determining the types of roles in which male and female Asian models appear in is to obtain information about their perceived importance in society. Are they shown as full participants in the culture or as token representatives? A minority group consistently portrayed in background roles as opposed to major or minor ones is marginalized as peripheral. As Bristor, Lee, and Hunt (1995) point out, when minorities are not depicted as central ("tokenism"), the message is that the host culture considers them unimportant—on the fringes of social life, not at its center.

Media images of a minority in the background can retard the group's assimilation—the host culture's acceptance of the group as equal across all societal roles. Insofar as the viewing public tends to equate mass media images with reality (Gerbner et al. 1980), depictions of minorities as marginal reinforces their outsider status. That effect is especially damaging to the social fluidity of the nearly two-thirds of Asian-Americans in the U.S. who "want to assimilate as quickly and easily as possible" (Weisendanger 1993, p. 101).

Consistent portrayal of a group in background roles can work in tandem with stereotyping to slow a minority's acculturation (see Lee and Tse 1994), defined as "the general process of movement and adaptation to the consumer cultural environment in one country by persons from another country" (Penaloza 1994, p. 33). A minority group that is backgrounded and stereotyped may perceive the host culture as indifferent to its values (Faber, O'Guinn, and Meyer 1987).

Barriers to acculturation and assimilation are compounded by lack of first-hand familiarity. Cultivation theory (Gerbner et al. 1980) proposes that a host culture accepts distorted media portrayals (Signorielli and Morgan 1990) of a minority more readily when it has little contact with a group. The theory applies to Asian-Americans (Faber, O'Guinn, and Meyer 1987), who are isolated by geographic concentration. Three of every four live in just three states—California, New York, and Hawaii–and most are concentrated in six cities—Los Angeles, San Francisco, New York, Sacramento, Chicago, and Houston. Hence, Americans in many other parts of the country have little or no personal interaction with them and see only what the media depicts. The lack of direct contact increases the likelihood that the host culture will interpret the portrayals as accurate. As prior research suggests that Asian-Americans, like other minorities, occupy few important roles in advertisements, our next questions probe the kinds of roles they take.

Stereotyping Variables: Products, Places, Personal Relationships

Q3:   In association with what product categories are male and female Asian-American models commonly portrayed in television advertising?

Q4:   In what types of settings are male and female Asian-American models likely to be portrayed in television advertising?

Q5:   In what types of interpersonal relationships are male and female Asian-American models likely to be portrayed in television advertising?

The purpose of those questions is to elicit information about stereotypes in terms of the types of goods/services that Asian models are shown using, the settings in which they appear, and the relationships in which they engage. The constraints of positive stereotyping can be identified by investigating whether the minority is shown with full or limited access to products/services, settings, and relationships.

Product Category. Cohen (1992) hypothesized an association between Asian-American stereotypes and the product category being advertised. She proposed that white consumers' attitudes toward Asian versus white models would vary by product category, predicting that white consumers would respond more positively to Asian models in ads for technical products (stereo speakers) and more negatively or neutrally to Asian models in ads for nontechnical categories (food, men's suits). She confirmed those hypotheses in an experiment assessing the reaction of 208 subjects to advertising in which the race of the model was varied in advertisements for the same product.

Taylor and Lee (1994) built on Cohen's findings to determine whether magazine advertisements featured Asian models in some product categories more than others. Their study corroborated her results, for Asian models were found to be well-represented in technical product categories (automobiles, electronics, computers), but poorly represented in non-technical ones (food and beverages, clothing, health and beauty aids, toys and sporting goods, furniture, and retail outlets). We expected Asian-American representation to be similarly product-specific in television advertisements and thus limited to certain categories.

Settings and Relationships. Prior research has found that Asian models appear in business settings to the exclusion of others (home, social gatherings, restaurants). The "all work, no play" stereotype is reinforced by the absence of ads showing Asian-Americans engaged in leisure activities or having fun (Yim 1989). Taylor and Lee (1994) found that business settings were dominant in portrayals of Asian-Americans in magazine advertisements, with 60% of the Asian models featured at work. Settings correlate with relationships, for characters in business scenes are likely to be coworkers, whereas those elsewhere are likely to be family or friends.

Although the work ethic is valued positively in our society, the "workaholic" stereotype deindividuates all members of a group, those who conform as well as those who rebel. Expectancy theory (Jussim 1990) predicts that minorities are likely to behave in conformance to expectations established by stereotypes—a self-fulfilling prophecy. However, the stereotype of Asian-Americans as technologically gifted works against assimilation of nonconformists who do not fit into the high-achievement mold, such as artists (Lee 1996), skiers (Weisendanger 1993), or persons not interested in math or science. It also irritates many successful Asian-Americans who would prefer "to see themselves on screen as smart and successful at being Americans—and non-stereotypical" (*Marketing Review* 1994, p. 9). Thus, the positive stereotype offends both conformist and nonconformist Asian-Americans, for it ignores individual variability.

The potential for mass media stereotypes (see Courtney and Whipple 1983; Goffman 1979) to perpetuate prejudice and divisiveness must be considered in evaluating advertising portrayals of minority groups. According to social cognition theory, when individuals are perceived as generic, perceivers evaluate each person on the basis of a set of often incorrect beliefs about the entire group (see Folkes and Kiesler 1990). That is the source of "in-group bias"—the tendency to regard one's own group (the in-group) positively and to regard "other" groups (out-groups) negatively (Folkes and Kiesler 1990). Such bias sustains prejudice by fostering the evaluation of individuals on the basis of generic expectations ("all" x's are like that).

When the stereotyping is positive, it can lead to hostility on the part of other minorities and the majority culture. It can inhibit assimilation (Faber, O'Guinn, and Meyer 1987) by reinforcing the public perception of the minority as generic and unidimensional. For example, the stereotype of Asian-Americans as intellectually gifted (Cohen 1992; Delener and Neelankavil 1990) contributes to the perception that they are the educationally favored "in group" in a system that discriminates against Hispanics and African-Americans (Onishi 1996a,b).

METHOD

Sample

A content analysis of television advertisements from one full week of prime time programming (8 p.m. to 11 p.m.) on the four major television networks (ABC, CBS, Fox, NBC) was conducted. However, at the time of the recording, Fox offered only five nights of prime time network programming; hence, only five nights of programming from Fox were recorded. Our sample of network ads is consistent with the samples used in several previous studies, allowing for longitudinal comparisons (Stevenson and McIntyre 1995). Programming was taped off the air in the first week of June 1994, a time period with no major holidays and/or special events that could skew sample representativeness.

Only ads that included models were retained for analysis, and those not showing the model's face were excluded. The sample was edited to exclude local advertising and political advocacy messages. Following Wilkes and Valencia (1989) and Stevenson and McIntyre (1995), we retained duplicate ads in the sample to represent more accurately the number of Asian-Americans portrayed. Analyses showed no statistically significant differences in Asian-American representation between the duplicates and the rest of the sample.

Coding and Variables

Six undergraduate students who majored in marketing were recruited as coders, and they received course credit for their participation. Procedures recommended by Kolbe and Burnett (1991) to enhance reliability were used in the content analysis: giving the coders written rules and procedures, training the coders (over a 10-week period in one-hour sessions), using judges other than the researchers, and having judges code independently for reliability testing. Because of the large size of the sample, all six coders coded 225 ads (20% of the sample) to establish reliability. Coders were then placed into groups of two, so that each of the remaining 1088 ads in the sample would be recorded by two people. Reliability was also measured for each of the two-person groups.

Coders were given a codebook containing operational definitions of each variable. The items measured were the presence of Asian, African-American, Hispanic, and Caucasian models, the gender of the models, the perceived importance of models appearing in the ads, the setting of the ad, and the relationship among the characters. Coders were asked to classify the product category by using a list of 21 categories. They were allowed to pause and/or replay a commercial as many times as necessary to complete the task.

For the purpose of coding, Asian-Americans were defined as persons whose ancestry is rooted in any of the following Asian countries: Cambodia, China, Japan, Korea, Vietnam, Laos, Philippines, Taiwan, Thailand, Malaysia, and Hong Kong. The omission of other areas within the geographic boundaries of Asia was based on the idea that the U.S. public views immigrants from other countries as belonging to separate groups (e.g., Saudi Arabians are viewed as "Arabs"; Indians are viewed as a distinct group) rather than as Asian-Americans (Taylor and Lee 1994). The recording of African-American and Hispanic models as well as Caucasians was undertaken to afford comparisons.

For each group, coders were asked to use a scale ranging from "1" to "9 or more" to record the number of people portrayed in each ad. The scale was intended to prevent skewing of the data by a few outlier ads depicting crowd scenes (Wilkes and Valencia 1989). As in prior studies, coders were instructed to select the most prominent model and to record the role of that model in the ad for each minority group as "major," "minor," or "background" according to the operational definitions of those roles. Appendix 26.1 contains the coding scheme and operational definitions for settings and relationships, as well as the coding scheme for product categories.

FINDINGS

Reliability

To provide a rigorous test, we computed reliability estimates by using both Cohen's kappa and Perreault and Leigh's (1989) reliability index. As indicated by Hughes and Garrett (1990) and

Table 26.1

Breakdown of Sample by Program Type and Network

	# of Commercials	
	no.	%
Program Type		
Comedy series	407	31.0
Drama series	398	30.3
Newsmagazine	135	10.3
Reality programming	111	8.5
Movies	262	20.0
	1313	100.0
Network		
CBS	369	28.1
NBC	355	27.0
ABC	322	24.5
Fox	267	20.3
	1313	100.0

Franke (1992), the Cohen kappa measure has the advantages of taking the number of coding categories into account and correcting for chance agreement. It is therefore a more accurate quantitative measure of reliability than raw percentage agreement. The figures reported here represent average reliability across all three groups of coders. For all reported variables, the raw percentage agreement for each of the three coding groups is in excess of the .85 standard recommended by Kassarjian (1977). Reliability coefficients as measured by Cohen's kappa are .944 for presence of Asian models, .941 for presence of African-American models, .860 for presence of Hispanic models, .895 for product category, .765 for setting, and .901 for relationship of models.

Although most previous articles have reported either raw percentage agreement figures or Cohen's kappa (Franke 1992; Perreault and Leigh 1989), recent literature suggests that even Cohen's kappa has significant limitations (Rust and Cooil 1994). In particular, it has been criticized for being overly conservative (see Rust and Cooil 1994) and insensitive to qualitative factors associated with the coding process. Therefore, we also calculated reliability by using the Perreault and Leigh index. Estimates based on that index are .947 for presence of Asian models, .940 for presence of African-American models, .927 for presence of Hispanic models, .979 for product category, .840 for setting, and .935 for relationship of models. Rust and Cooil suggest that because the Perreault and Leigh index contains a qualitative component, it can be interpreted in a manner similar to Cronbach's alpha, which is widely employed in survey research.

General Sample Characteristics

Table 26.1 is a breakdown of the sample by program type and network. The sampling procedure provided a total of 1313 advertisements with human models. A variety of program types were represented, and CBS ran the most national commercials, followed by NBC, ABC, and Fox. The lower number of commercials from Fox is a consequence of programming schedule (Fox ran only five nights of programming at the time the sample was taken).

Table 26.2

Group Representation in Sample

	Asian-Americans		Hispanic-Americans		African-Americans		Caucasians	
	No.	%	No.	%	No.	%	No.	%
All Models* (male or female)	110	8.4	111	8.5	418	31.8	1283	97.7
Male Models*	79	6.0	80	6.1	314	23.9	1043	79.4
Female Models*	47	3.6	48	3.6	205	15.6	980	74.6

*Indicates a statistically significant difference in the relative frequency of group representation at $p < .001$ (n = 1313).

Question 1: Representation

Table 26.2 reports the representation of each minority group in comparison to its proportion of the population. A statistically significant difference was found in the relative frequency of minority group representation ($\chi^2 = 3084$; $p < .001$). Male and female Asian-Americans are represented in 8.4% of the advertisements (110 ads), which is more than double their proportion in the overall population (3.6%). Hence, representation exceeds the proportionality criterion. Additionally, representation is substantially higher in television commercials than in mainstream magazine advertising, which is 4% as reported by Taylor and Lee (1994) and 1.8% as reported by Schmid and Bowen (1995).

However, when the total is separated by sex, women are found to be less well represented than men. Female Asian models are present significantly less than male Asian models ($\chi^2 = 21.9$; $p < .01$). In raw numbers, only 47 advertisements, or 3.7% of the sample, include an Asian-American woman.

Question 2: Perceived Importance

Table 26.3 reports the relative frequency with which Asian-Americans, African-Americans, Hispanics, and Caucasians are portrayed in major, minor, or background roles. There is a significant difference in representation of the groups across perceived importance levels ($\chi^2 = 967$; $p < .001$). Notably, Caucasian models play a major role in 90.8% of the ads in which they appear, nearly twice the percentage found for Asian models (47.1%).

Asian models occupy major roles in almost half of the commercials in which they appear (52, or 47.2% of appearances), but when perceived importance is broken down by sex, a male-female disparity becomes evident. The number of Asian female models in major roles, just 16 (14.6% of appearances), is significantly lower than the number of Asian male models in major roles, 42 (38.2%). In comparison, Hispanic female models (the next lowest group) appear in major roles in 25 commercials (52.1% of ads in which a Hispanic woman is present).

A related finding is that Asian-Americans, especially women, tend to be minor or background figures more frequently than other minorities. Asian-American male and female models are shown in minor roles in 28 (25%) of the ads in which an Asian model appears and in background roles in 30 (27.4%) of those ads. The latter figure is substantially higher than that for African-Americans

Table 26.3

Perceived Importance of Models

	Asian-Americans		Hispanic-Americans		African-Americans		Caucasians	
	Number of Portrayals (% of Sample)	% of Group Portrayals	Number of Portrayals (% of Sample)	% of Group Portrayals	Number of Portrayals (% of Sample)	% of Group Portrayals	Number of Portrayals (% of Sample)	% of Group Portrayals
All Models*								
Major role	52 (4.0)	47.6	52 (4.0)	47.1	223 (16.9)	53.3	1165 (88.7)	90.8
Minor role	28 (2.1)	25.0	45 (3.4)	40.0	127 (9.7)	30.4	105 (8.0)	8.2
Background	30 (2.3)	27.4	14 (1.1)	12.9	68 (5.2)	16.3	14 (1.1)	1.1
		100.0		100.0		100.0		100.0
Male Models*								
Major role	42 (3.2)	53.1	33 (2.5)	41.3	156 (11.9)	49.8	936 (71.3)	89.7
Minor role	18 (1.4)	22.8	33 (2.5)	41.3	105 (8.0)	33.1	93 (7.9)	9.0
Background	30 (2.3)	24.1	14 (1.1)	17.5	53 (4.0)	17.0	14 (1.1)	1.3
		100.0		100.0		100.0		100.0
Female Models*								
Major role	16 (1.2)	34.0	25 (1.9)	52.1	119 (9.1)	58.1	880 (67.0)	89.8
Minor role	14 (1.1)	29.8	21 (1.6)	43.8	57 (4.3)	27.8	90 (6.9)	9.2
Background	17 (1.3)	36.2	2 (0.2)	4.2	29 (2.2)	14.1	10 (1.3)	1.0
		100.0		100.0		100.0		100.0

*Indicates a statistically significant difference in the distribution of racial groups across levels of perceived importance at $p < .001$

(16.3%) or Hispanic Americans (12.9%). The results are especially skewed for Asian women, who appear in background roles in 17 (36.2%) of the ads in which they appear, the highest proportion of any group. The higher incidence of backgrounding suggests that Asian models are more likely to be given token representation than other minority group models.

In summary, even though Asian-Americans are overrepresented in television advertising in terms of proportion of the population, they appear less frequently than whites in major roles and appear more frequently than other minorities in background roles. When gender is taken into account, Asian women are less well represented and perceived as less important than any other minority men or women; when they appear, they are most often in the background.

Question 3: Product Category

Table 26.4 provides data on the representation of male and female models in all groups by product category. The top eight categories are those with 60 or more ads, comprising 93.6% of the sample (1229). The category list (see Appendix) replicates the one used in a study of magazine advertisements (Taylor and Lee 1994), although some product categories found in magazine ads (Taylor and Lee 1994) are absent or nearly so in television commercials. In fact, several of the categories that are closely associated with Asian-American stereotypes appeared very infrequently in our sample of television commercials (office supplies 0, home computers, 1, electronics 8).

However, despite this difference, in television commercials as in magazine ads, Asian-American representation by product category is skewed toward products/services consistent with affluence and work orientation. It differs significantly from that of other groups in the sample (χ^2 = 48.8; p < .001), for Asian-Americans are more represented in ads for items associated with affluence and work life (banks, telecommunications, retail outlets) and less represented in ads for items associated with home or social life (apparel, food/beverages, and household supplies).

Further, when distribution by product category for Asian-Americans is broken down by sex (χ^2 = 75.6; p < .001), we see a statistically significant difference between Asian women and all other women. That is, Asian women's representation in product categories resembles that of Asian men, but differs from that of other women.

Question 4: Settings

Table 26.5 reports the distribution of settings by racial group. A statistically significant difference is present for both total racial group representation by setting (χ^2 = 122; p < .001) and the distributions for men (χ^2 = 127.5; p < .001) and women (χ^2 = 118.2; p < .001). Asian models appear in a variety of settings, and the differences in representation across settings are statistically significant (χ^2 = 26.9; p < .001). Notably, that difference does not appear to be due to a dramatic overrepresentation in business settings (see Table 26.5). Underrepresentation of Asian models in home settings is more noteworthy than overrepresentation in business situations. The least used setting for all Asian models is the home; only 17 ads, or 15.4% of the ads with Asian models have the home as a setting. When gender is taken into account, the finding is even more skewed toward severe underrepresentation of Asian female models. The raw number is striking: Asian female models appear in home settings in just four (.3%) of the 1313 ads in the overall sample. That finding, coupled with lack of representation in "homey" product categories such as food, drugstore items, and cleaning supplies, implies that Asian women are restricted to the workplace—an interesting reversal of the more usual depiction of woman's "place" as in the home.

Table 26.4

Minority Group Representation in Leading Product Categories

	N	Asian-Americans		Hispanic-Americans		African-Americans		Caucasians	
		No.	%	No.	%	No.	%	No.	%
All Models									
1. Food/beverage	334	20	6.0	24	7.1	97	29.0	330	98.1
2. OTC drugs	214	11	5.1	55	25.7	1	0.5	210	98.1
3. Cosmetics	185	19	10.2	29	15.7	7	3.8	182	98.3
4. Retailers	182	20	10.9	70	38.5	29	15.9	178	97.8
5. Automotive	106	5	4.7	55	51.9	13	12.3	98	92.4
6. Telecommunications	84	8	9.5	24	28.5	9	10.7	81	96.7
7. Household/lawn and garden supplies	64	5	7.8	15	23.4	2	3.1	62	96.9
8. Banking/finance	60	6	10.0	32	53.3	11	18.3	58	96.6
Male Models									
1. Food/beverage	334	15	4.5	82	24.6	14	4.2	283	84.7
2. OTC drugs	214	5	2.3	31	14.5	1	0.5	156	72.9
3. Cosmetics	185	13	7.0	15	8.10	3	1.6	114	61.7
4. Retailers	182	15	8.2	48	26.4	24	13.2	156	85.7
5. Automotive	106	3	2.8	49	46.2	11	10.4	94	88.7
6. Telecommunications	84	4	4.8	15	17.9	9	10.7	63	75.0
7. Household/lawn and garden supplies	64	4	6.2	8	12.5	1	1.6	44	68.8
8. Banking/finance	60	5	8.3	27	45.0	10	16.7	57	95.0
Female Models									
1. Food/beverage	334	4	1.1	38	11.4	14	4.2	255	76.3
2. OTC drugs	214	7	3.2	33	15.4	0	0.0	153	71.5
3. Cosmetics	185	6	3.2	22	11.9	4	2.2	153	82.7
4. Retailers	182	10	5.4	34	18.7	12	6.6	124	68.1
5. Automotive	106	2	1.8	19	17.9	3	2.8	75	70.8
6. Telecommunications	84	5	5.9	16	19.0	10	1.2	65	77.4
7. Household/lawn and garden supplies	64	1	1.5	7	10.9	2	3.1	48	75.0
8. Banking/finance	60	4	6.6	12	20.0	11	18.3	7	11.7

Question 5: Relationships

Table 26.5 provides data showing that the distribution of models of different racial groups across types of relationships is statistically significant for all models ($\chi^2 = 349.1$; $p < .001$), male models ($\chi^2 = 243.8$; $p < .001$), and female models ($\chi^2 = 99.6$; $p < .01$).

Not surprisingly, when a relationship is depicted between an Asian model and another model, it is most likely to be a business one. If we look only at ads in which a relationship is depicted (i.e., drop ads in the "impersonal" category), Asians appear as coworkers in the majority of the ads in which they appear. That is more often than any other minority group and more than twice as often as Caucasians. Here, the data are more skewed for Asian men, who appear as coworkers in 23 (58.9%) of the 40 cases in which a relationship is portrayed.

DISCUSSION

Our study shows that Asian-Americans are overrepresented in television ads according to the proportionality criterion, but the portrayals raise questions about stereotyping, tokenism, and gender asymmetry. Advertisers probably do not intend to produce any of those consequences, for on the surface the portrayals show the group exhibiting positive traits. Nevertheless, constant reiteration of positive images can have a negative impact on the self-perceptions of minority individuals, as well as on the attitudes of other cultural groups toward those individuals.

Stereotyping

Heightened sensitivity to possible unwanted effects of Asian-American portrayals would be beneficial to both the advertising industry and society as a whole. For advertisers, portrayal of Asians in product categories, settings, and relationships not associated with the "success image" has the potential to generate positive reactions among Asian-Americans and other social groups. Additionally, more common inclusion and more prominent portrayal of Asian models, particularly in ads in product categories for which they have not traditionally been included, have the potential to attract attention and break through clutter. Thus, advertisers may benefit by portraying Asian-Americans in nonstereotypical ways.

For society as a whole, nonstereotypical portrayals of Asian-Americans can help expose other groups to Asians in contexts in which they have not often been portrayed. Through exposure to portrayals that contradict the stereotype, members of society may be encouraged to question the stereotype and perhaps gain a better understanding of Asian-Americans.

An example of how nonstereotypical portrayals may help at a societal level involves the lack of portrayals of Asian-Americans in family and social situations. The collective absence of Asian models in such situations sends a message that is counter to American core beliefs. Ironically, the message is false and may contribute to the misunderstanding of Eastern cultures, in which family identity is a long-standing tradition. If advertisers begin depicting Asian models in family and social situations, however, viewers will be exposed to images that counter the "all work, no play" stereotype.

As reverence for the family is rarely depicted, creators of advertising may be missing an opportunity to build pan-Asian messages around that theme. Indeed, most marketers overlook the commonly held values of the Asian-American market, focusing instead on its diversity as a barrier to national advertising (Fisher 1994, p. S-2). To date, only banks and insurance companies have tapped into the family theme, probably because security and protection relate to attributes

Table 26.5

Settings and Relationships Depicted by Racal Groups

	Asian-Americans		Hispanic-Americans		African-Americans		Caucasians	
	No.	%	No.	%	No.	%	No.	%
Settings								
All Models*								
Business	24	21.9	26	23.4	124	29.7	258	20.1
Home	17	15.4	16	14.4	78	18.7	423	33.0
Outdoors	26	23.6	29	26.1	84	20.1	237	18.5
Social	26	23.6	22	19.9	67	16.0	160	12.5
Other	17	15.5	18	16.2	65	15.5	204	15.9
	110	100.0	111	100.0	418	100.0	1283	100.0
Male Models*								
Business	18	22.8	21	26.3	92	29.3	232	22.2
Home	13	16.5	10	12.5	54	17.2	306	29.3
Outdoors	14	17.7	21	26.3	67	21.3	201	19.3
Social	22	27.8	14	17.5	52	16.6	153	14.7
Other	12	15.2	14	17.5	50	16.0	151	14.5
	79	100.0	80	100.0	314	100.0	1043	100.0
Female Models*								
Business	11	23.4	6	12.5	62	30.2	200	20.4
Home	4	8.5	9	18.8	38	18.5	328	33.5
Outdoors	17	36.2	20	41.6	39	19.0	177	18.1
Social	9	19.1	8	16.7	33	16.1	131	13.4
Other	6	12.8	5	10.4	33	16.1	143	14.6
	47	100.0	48	100.0	205	100.0	980	100.0
Relationships								
All Models*								
Business	28	25.4	29	26.1	93	22.2	231	18.0
Family	4	3.6	1	0.9	33	7.9	300	23.4
Social	22	20.1	41	37.1	127	30.4	325	25.3
Impersonal	50	50.9	40	35.9	165	39.5	427	33.3
	110	100.0	111	100.0	418	100.0	1283	100.0
Male Models*								
Business	23	29.1	25	31.2	78	24.8	226	21.7
Family	4	5.1	1	1.3	28	8.9	238	22.8
Social	13	16.4	25	31.2	103	32.8	269	25.8
Impersonal	39	49.4	29	36.3	105	33.5	310	29.7
	79	100.0	80	100.0	314	100.0	1043	100.0
Female Models**								
Business	13	27.7	9	18.8	36	17.6	137	14.0
Family	1	2.1	1	2.1	30	14.6	236	24.1
Social	13	27.6	23	48.0	50	24.4	245	25.0
Impersonal	20	42.6	15	31.1	89	43.3	362	36.9
	47	100.0	48	100.0	205	100.0	980	100.0

*Indicates a statistically significant difference in the distribution of racial groups across levels of perceived importance at $p < .001$.

**Indicates a statistically significant difference in the distribution of racial groups across levels of perceived importance at $p < .01$.

of financial services. The theme is underutilized in other product areas, as Eleanor N. Yu, president of AdLand, has pointed out. She devised a hypothetical scenario for a beer advertisement that might be more likely to foster Asian-American identification than a scene of men drinking in a bar. She suggests that if "two Asian men were drinking beer with their brothers at a picnic," it would be "a more familiar situation because of the Asian emphasis on family" (Weisendanger 1993, p. 101). Now that marketers of soft drinks, fast food, and airlines are seeking ways to enter the Asian-American market (Fisher 1994), they might consider featuring family and home instead of the workplace.

Tokenism

Such emphasis might also improve the centrality of Asian models in advertisements. Marketers have been advised to "include Asian-Americans in their advertising" (*Marketing Review* 1994, p. 16). At present, however, Asian-Americans are victims of tokenism, for they are the minority most likely to be depicted as anonymous figures in the background. Their presence as token faces in a crowd has negative consequences for both first-generation immigrants and the U.S.-born.

Joseph Lam of L3 Advertising points out that "immigrants always feel they are second-class citizens," (Weisendanger 1993, p. 101) and want to "assimilate as quickly and easily as possible." Yet they are often ignored by marketers who are "not interested in the Asian-American immigrants, but their children" (Paskowski 1986, p. 80). Nonetheless, the frequent depiction of Asian-Americans in general as peripheral in consumption scenes does not address younger Asian-Americans' desire to be "considered mainstream consumers" (*Marketing Review* 1994, p. 16). That market has been called "Generation A" (Sengupta 1996, p. 3) by Jeff Yang, the founder of a magazine of the same name. Yang notes that Generation A wants to see "positive, or at least interesting, Asian-American role models out there. . . . We want to pull the shroud off of people who have achieved . . ." (Sengupta 1996, p. 3). A decrease in tokenism may be a function of time, for other minority groups have progressed from low visibility in background roles to high visibility in major ones. Additionally, growth in the Asian-American market makes targeting that market increasingly feasible. The implication for advertisers is that the time has come to use Asian-Americans as central figures some of the time rather than to include one or two in the background more of the time.

Gender Asymmetry

Even though past tokenism has led Asian-American men to "perceive themselves as invisible" (*Marketing News* 1994, p. 16), it is Asian-American women who are the least visible, least important, and least multidimensional figures in television advertising. Asian-American women are seen less frequently than their male counterparts, and when seen, are rarely in nonbusiness settings. Such portrayal reverses the older advertising stereotype of women as housewives (Courtney and Whipple 1983), but has equally negative effects.

When Asian-American women do not see anyone like themselves associated with a product or a service, they are likely to feel neglected by marketers. Despite their "high purchasing power and disposable income, nobody talks to them. . . . It's a very lonely feeling" (Weisendanger 1993, p. 101). Inattention to what has been called the "silent minority" (Kan 1996, p. B-7) translates into a missed advertising opportunity. As Yu points out, "what makes an ad work is readers or viewers identifying themselves in the ad" (Weisendanger 1993, p. 101). Low visibility may send the signal that Asian-American women are overlooked by society, and although the message is probably unintentional, advertisers need to become aware of its consequences. The creation of innovative, nonstereotypical, breakthrough advertising would involve a return to depicting women in the home to balance a picture that is still askew.

STUDY LIMITATIONS AND FUTURE RESEARCH

Although our study findings corroborate those of previous studies of print media, they are not generalizable across all advertising. The most significant limitation of our study is that the sample of national ads was drawn from prime time network programming, which limits the findings to ads aimed at the large, heterogeneous U.S. population. If advertisers want to target Asian-Americans with television ads, they are less likely to use national network campaigns than to use local spots (perhaps on cable programming) in areas of high Asian-American concentration. Therefore, a study that investigates targeting of advertisements to Asian-Americans would require a different sample frame. In addition, the goal of cross-media generalizability necessitates study of direct mail, catalogues, and interactive appeals as well as traditional print and electronic media.

A second limitation is that our study did not distinguish among diverse Asian-American groups. Consequently, the influence of country-of-origin status on attitudes toward advertising models is not taken into account. Young American-born Asian consumers bitterly resent stereotyping on the grounds that it lumps disparate ethnic and national groups together (*Marketing Review* 1994, p. 16). They are sensitive to country-of-origin differences (Onishi 1996a, b), and research is needed to ascertain the influence of those differences on Asian-American consumers' attitudes toward ads.

A third limitation is that the study did not take age effects into account. Although the data were broken down by gender, research on the influence of interactions between age and gender is needed. As the literature on acculturation (e.g., Lee and Tse 1994) suggests that age is an important factor influencing consumption patterns, a study examining portrayals of older versus younger consumers would be worthwhile.

Finally, an inherent limitation of content analysis is that it measures only manifest content. Although our study provides considerable information about the actual nature of televised portrayals, the method does not permit measurement of consumer responses to different types of portrayals. We therefore advocate experimental studies that assess majority and minority consumer reactions to models varied by ethnicity/nationality. We also acknowledge the need for qualitative studies that probe more deeply into the underlying meanings conveyed by advertisements. We urge researchers to continue the study of Asian-Americans in the hope of contributing to effectively targeted advertising and fairer depictions of the richness that members of other cultures bring to our own.

APPENDIX 26.1. OPERATIONAL DEFINITIONS PERTAINING TO PERCEIVED IMPORTANCE OF CHARACTERS, SETTING, AND RELATIONSHIPS BETWEEN CHARACTERS

Perceived Importance of Minority Characters

Major role: A character who is very important to the advertising theme or layout, shown in the foreground or shown holding the product.

Minor role: A character who is of average importance to the advertising theme or layout. Generally, such characters are not spotlighted in the ad and do not hold the product, but are not difficult to find in the ad while casually looking at it.

Background role: A character who is difficult to find in an ad (i.e., not likely to be noticed by a reader glancing at the ad) and is not important to its theme or layout.

Setting

Business: Factories, sales or office rooms, and retail settings in which consumers are depicted inside stores.

Home, indoor or outdoor: Recognizable as a residence, room, or rooms, garage, yard, home or apartment driveway or parking space.

Outdoors/natural scenery: Includes forests, rivers, ocean, fields, or sky as well as streets, public roads, sidewalks, or pathways. Does not include outdoor settings at individuals' homes or outdoor social settings.

Social setting outside home: Includes public places such as auditoriums, restaurants, or movie theaters. Where people meet and congregate for social purposes.

Other: Includes artificial settings (stage or specially built props or backgrounds) and any other setting not listed above.

Relationship to Others in the Ad

Family context: Includes husband and wife and any relationship between relatives, including children as well as extended family such as aunts/uncles, grandparents, grandchildren, adopted children, foster children.

Social context: Includes friends or any other two people depicted in a social setting, with the exception of family members depicted in a social context.

Business context: The depiction of members of or workers in the same company, those who are employed by the same company. Also colleagues in the same profession or occupation even though they may be employed by different companies. Any relationship between employees or professionals who work together.

Impersonal context: More than one character appears in the ad, but there is no apparent relationship between the characters.

Nobody else in ad: Choose this option when only one model appears in the ad.

Other relationship: Any relationship other than those listed above.

Product Categorization Scheme

Food and beverages

Alcoholic beverages

Automobile/auto related

Over-the-counter drugs

Household/lawn and garden supplies

Electronic appliances

Cosmetics/personal care

Clothing/shoes/apparel

Furniture

Entertainment supplies

PCs/computer supplies

Sporting goods/toys

Publications

Retailers

Banking/financial services

Telecommunications services

Transportation services

Other products

Other services

REFERENCES

Ashmore, Richard D. and Frances K. Del Boca (1981), "Conceptual Approaches to Stereotypes and Stereotyping," in *Cognitive Processes in Stereotyping and Intergroup Behavior,* David L. Hamilton, ed., Hillsdale, NJ: Erlbaum, 1–35.

Bristor, Julia M., Renee Gravois Lee, and Michelle R. Hunt (1995), "African American Images in Television Advertising: Progress or Prejudice?" *Journal of Public Policy and Marketing,* 14 (Spring), 48–62.

Bureau of the Census (1996), *National Population Estimates,* Washington, DC: U.S. Department of Commerce.

Cheng, Wanla (1996), "An Interview with Wanla Cheng of Asia Link," *Marketing Review,* 51 (March), 12–13.

Cohen, Judy (1992), "White Consumer Response to Asian Models in Advertising," *Journal of Consumer Marketing,* 9 (Spring), 17–27.

Courtney, Alice E. and Thomas W. Whipple (1983), *Sex Stereotyping in Advertising,* Toronto: Lexington Books.

Dates, Jannette L. and William Barlow (1990), "Introduction: A War of Images," in *Split Image: African Americans in the Mass Media,* Jannette L. Dates and William Barlow, eds., Washington, DC: Howard University Press, 1–21.

Delener, Nejdet and James P. Neelankavil (1990), "Informational Sources and Media Usage: A Comparison Between Asian and Hispanic Subcultures," *Journal of Advertising Research,* 30 (June/July), 45–52.

Faber, Ronald J., Thomas C. O'Guinn, and Timothy P. Meyer (1987), "Televised Portrayals of Hispanics: A Comparison of Ethnic Perceptions," *International Journal of Intercultural Relations,* 11 (Spring), 155–169.

Fisher, Christy (1994), "Demographic Trends: Marketers Straddle Asia-America Curtain," *Advertising Age,* 65 (November 7), S-2, S-18, S-19.

Folkes, Valerie S. and Tina Kiesler (1990), "Social Cognition: Consumers' Inferences about the Self and Others," in *Handbook of Consumer Behavior,* Thomas S. Robertson and Harold H. Kassarjian, eds., Englewood Cliffs, NJ: Prentice Hall, 281–315.

Franke, George R. (1992), "Reliability and Generalizability in Coding the Information Content of Advertising," *Asian Journal of Marketing,* 1, 7–25.

Gerbner, George, Larry Gross, Michael Morgan, and Nancy Signorielli (1980), "The Mainstreaming of America: Violence Profile No. 11," *Journal of Communication,* 30 (Summer), 10–29.

Goffman, Erving (1979), *Gender Advertisements,* New York: Harper & Row.

Hughes, Marie Adele and Dennis E. Garrett (1990), "Intercoder Reliability Estimation—Approaches in Marketing: A Generalizability Theory Framework for Quantitative Data," *Journal of Marketing Research,* 27 (May), 185–195.

Jussim, Lee (1990), "Social Reality and Social Problems: The Role of Expectancies," *Journal of Social Issues,* 46 (Summer), 9–34.

Kan, Yue-Sai (1996), "Coty's Chinese Ally," *New York Times,* (June 4), B-7.

Kassarjian, Harold H. (1977), "Content Analysis in Consumer Research," *Journal of Consumer Research,* 4 (June), 8–18.

Kern, Richard (1988), "The Asian Market: Too Good to Be True?" *Sales & Marketing Management,* 141 (May), 38–40.

Kolbe, Richard and Melissa S. Burnett (1991), "Content Analysis Research: An Examination of Applications with Directives for Improving Research Reliability and Objectivity," *Journal of Consumer Research,* 18 (September), 243–250.

Krugman, Herbert (1965), "The Impact of Television Advertising: Learning Without Involvement," *Public Opinion Quarterly,* 29 (Fall), 349–356.

Lee, Felicia R. (1996), "Asian-American Men Use Art to Peel Away Stereotypes," *New York Times,* (April 7), 1, 32.

Lee, Wei-Na and David K. Tse (1994), "Acculturation Patterns Among Hong Kong Immigrants to Canada," *Journal of Advertising,* 23 (March), 57–70.

Marketing Review (1994), 50 (December), 6–18, 22–25.

Onishi, Norimitsu (1996a), "Affirmative Action: Choosing Sides," *New York Times: Education Life,* (March 31), 28–35.

———— (1996b), "New Sense of Race Arises Among Asian-Americans," *New York Times,* (May 30), A-1, B-6.

Paskowski, Marianne (1986), "Trailblazing in Asian America," *Marketing and Media Decisions,* 21 (October), 75–80.

Penaloza, Lisa (1994), "Atravesando Fronteras/Border Crossings: A Critical Ethnographic Exploration of the Consumer Acculturation of Mexican Immigrants," *Journal of Consumer Research,* 21 (June), 32–54.

Perreault, William D. and Laurence E. Leigh (1989), "Reliability of Nominal Data Based on Qualitative Judgments," *Journal of Marketing Research,* 26 (May), 135–148.

Pollay, Richard W. and Katherine Gallagher (1990), "Advertising and Cultural Values: Reflections in the Distorted Mirror," *International Journal of Advertising,* 9 (Winter), 359–372.

Rust, Roland and Bruce Cooil (1994), "Reliability Measures for Qualitative Data: Theory and Implications," *Journal of Marketing Research,* 31 (February), 1–14.

Schmid, Jill and Lawrence Bowen (1995), "Minority Presence and Portrayal in Magazine Advertising: An Update," in *Proceedings of the American Academy of Advertising,* Charles S. Madden, ed., Waco, TX: Baylor University, 12.

Sengupta, Somini (1996), "In Their Own Image," *New York Times: City Section,* (April 28), 3.

Signorielli, Nancy and Michael Morgan (1990), "Cultivation Analysis: Conceptualization and Methodology," in *Cultivation Analysis: New Directions in Media Effects Research,* Nancy Signorielli and Michael Morgan, eds., Newbury Park, CA: Sage, 13–34.

Statistical Abstract of the United States (1994), Washington, DC: U.S. Department of Commerce, 567–568.

Stevenson, Thomas H. and Patricia E. McIntyre (1995), "A Comparison of the Portrayal and Frequency of Hispanics and Whites in English Language Television Advertising," *Journal of Current Issues and Research in Advertising,* 17 (Spring), 65–74.

Taylor, Charles R. and Ju Yung Lee (1994), "Not in *Vogue:* Portrayals of Asian-Americans in U.S. Advertising," *Journal of Public Policy and Marketing,* 13 (Fall), 239–245.

———, ———, and Barbara B. Stern (1995), "Portrayals of African, Hispanic, and Asian-Americans in Magazine Advertising," *American Behavioral Scientist,* 38 (February), 508–621.

Weisendanger, Betsy (1993), "Asian-Americans: The Three Biggest Myths," *Sales & Marketing Management,* (September), 86–88, 101.

Wilkes, Robert E. and Humberto Valencia (1989), "Hispanics and Blacks in Television Commercials," *Journal of Advertising,* 18 (1), 19–25.

Yim, Yong Soon (1989), "American Perceptions of Korean Americans," *Korea and World Affairs,* 13 (3), 519–542.

Zinkhan, George M., William J. Qualls, and A. Biswas (1990), "The Use of Blacks in Magazines and Television," *Journalism Quarterly,* 67 (3), 547–553.

PART 5

APPENDIX

Useful Resources for Consumers and Advertisers in a Consumer Culture

Part 5 includes a variety of resources, such as trade association codes of ethics, government standards and guidelines for particular types of advertising, and information about self-regulatory organizations. Each source is briefly described with a corresponding Web site address in a table. The purpose of the appendix is not to provide every possible resource related to advertising, but to publish some of the most helpful materials and to make readers aware of the existence of others that might be slightly less well known. Whereas the first four sections of this book are composed of journal articles and book excerpts, Part 5 contains relatively short informational materials published by trade and regulatory organizations and descriptions of relevant associations and their Web sites. As acknowledged in the introduction, no readings book is ever complete. The inclusion of this appendix cannot compensate for all that we would have liked to add to this collection, but we are hopeful that it will make the book more complete than it would have been otherwise.

ADVERTISING RESOURCES: GOVERNMENTAL (U.S. AND INTERNATIONAL), TRADE, AND ACADEMIC

Nature of Web site	Web Address
1. U.S. and Foreign Government Organizations that Control Advertising	
Federal Trade Commission—standards, guidelines for consumers, advertisers and businesses	http://www.ftc.gov
Federal Communications Commission—standards, guidelines for consumers, advertisers and businesses regarding electronic media	http://www.fcc.gov
Food & Drug Administration—biological products, food, drugs, medical devices, cosmetics, non-alcoholic beverages	http://www.fda.gov/
Federal Communications Commission—aspects of advertisements aired on radio, TV, cable and related electronic media; indirectly through licensure of above stations and networks	http://www.fcc.gov/
United States Postal Service–regulations of advertisements sent via U.S. mail	http://www.usps.com/
Department of Treasury—regulation of imported goods and, through its Bureau of Alcohol, Tobacco & Firearms (ATF), alcohol, tobacco and firearms	http://www.atf.gov/
Library of Congress—Use and protection of copyrighted material. The oldest federal cultural institution and the research office of Congress	http://www.loc.gov/index.html
Regulation of Advertising Aimed at Children in European Union Member States	http://www.obs.coe.int/online_publication/reports/childadv.pdf.fr
Australian Broadcasting Authority	http://www.aba.gov.au/tv/content/requirements/advertising.shtml
Mediaknowall—review of advertising regulation around the globe	http://www.mediaknowall.com/Advertising/ad-standards.html
2. Sources of Advertising Self-Regulation and Industry Trade Associations	
The American Advertising Federation's Advertising Principles of American Business	http://www.aaf.org/about/principles.html
Council of Better Business Bureau's National Advertising Review Council	http://www.narcpartners.org
Advertising self-regulation through the Better Business Bureau	http://www.bbb.org/advertising.asp
Better Business Bureau Guidelines for Marketing to Children	http://www.caru.org/
Advertising regulation news from the Arent Fox law firm	http://www.arentfox.com/quickGuide/businessLines/advert/advertisingLaw/advertisinglaw.html
FindLaw—free access to court cases at multiple levels	http://www.findlaw.com
National Association of Broadcasters Statement of Principles	http://www.nab.org/newsroom/Issues/NAB%20Statement%200f%20Principles.html
Public Relations Society of America Code of Ethics	http://www.prsa.org
Magazine Publishers Association Guidelines for Special Advertising Sections	http://www.magazine.org
American Association of Advertising Agencies	http://www.aaaa.org/eweb/startpage.aspx
Advertising Self-Regulation in the UK	http://www.adassoc.org.uk/briefs/self-regulation.html

Nature of Website	Web Address
3. Assorted Resources	
Adbusters Magazine Web site	http://www.adbusters.org/home/
About-Face Web site devoted to images of women	http://www.about-face.org/
United States Bureau of the Census	http://www.census.gov
Advertising Age Magazine—Ad Age Magazine's links to collections of ads	http://www.adage.com/
	http://advertisementave.com/
The National Urban League's home page for information on local chapters, and regular reports on the state of Black America	http://www.nul.org/
Covers topics in international advertising	http://www.bgsu.edu/departments/tcom/faculty/ ha/intlad1.html
The Ad*Access Project, funded by the Duke Endowment "Library 2000" Fund, presents images and database information for over 7,000 advertisements printed in U.S. and Canadian newspapers and magazines between 1911 and 1955	http://scriptorium.lib.duke.edu/adaccess/
Monthly online newsletter about crisis communication within the Public Relations industry	http://www.anvilpub.com/crisis_counselor.htm
Advertising sources from The University of Texas Web site	http://advertising.utexas.edu/world/index.asp (links to various advertising)
Video of children saying why they want to go into advertising	http://www.geck09.com/whenigrowup.html
Advertising Intellectual Archives (award-winning ads, design, media)	http://www.ihaveanidea.org
Information about the ad industry	http://advertising.about.com/
4. Selected Academic Journals	
International Journal of Advertising	http://store.warc.com/productinfo/30.asp
Journal of Mass Media Ethics	http://www.jmme.org/
Journal of Consumer Culture	http://joc.sagepub.com/
Journal of Advertising	http://www.mesharpe.com/mall/ results1.asp?acr=jo
Journal of Marketing	http://www.marketingpower.com/ content1054.php
Journal of Marketing and Public Policy	http://bear.cba.ufl.edu/centers/jppm/
Advertising & Society Review	http://aef.com
Sex Roles: A Journal of Research	http://springerlink.metapress.com/content/ 1573–2762/
Journal of Consumer Psychology	http://www.journalofconsumerpsychology.com/
Journal of Public Relations Research	http://www.leaonline.com/loi/jprr?cookieSet=1
Journal of Communication Inquiry	http://jci.sagepub.com/
Journal of Advertising Research	http://journals.cambridge.org/action/ displayJournal?jid=JAR
Journal of Consumer Affairs	http://www.blackwellpublishing.com/ journal.asp?ref=0022–0078&site=1

Note: All the Web addresses herein were current as this book went to press. If you come up empty, please consult your favorite search engine.

INDEX

Italic page references indicate photographs, illustrations, boxed text, and tables.

ABOUT THE EDITORS

Roxanne Hovland (PhD, University of Illinois at Urbana) is a Professor in the School of Advertising and Public Relations at the University of Tennessee in Knoxville. Dr. Hovland served for three years as the Associate Dean for Undergraduate Studies in the College of Communication and Information at the University of Tennessee. Her 1989 book, *Advertising and Society* (co-edited with Gary B. Wilcox), was named as one of the field's most influential books in a survey of readers of the *Journal of Advertising*. Her scholarly work has been published in *Sex Roles: A Journal of Research, Communications and the Law, Alcoholism Treatment Quarterly, Research in Marketing, Journalism and Mass Communication Quarterly, Journalism Educator,* and *The Journal of Macromarketing.*

Joyce M. Wolburg (PhD, University of Tennessee, Knoxville) is the Associate Dean for Graduate Studies and Research in the J. William and Mary Diederich College of Communication at Marquette University and an Associate Professor in the Department of Advertising and Public Relations. Her early research examined the way advertising constructs and reflects cultural values in domestic and international ad campaigns. More recent research interests have included college students' responses to anti-smoking messages, the ritual meaning of binge drinking among college students, alcohol advertising and alcoholics, the lack of protection afforded to small U.S. businesses through anti-trust laws, risk communication strategies, and the unethical stereotyping of Native Americans in mascots for sports teams.

Eric Haley (PhD, University of Georgia) is a Professor in the University of Tennessee's School of Advertising and Public Relations. His academic interests include various topics related to advertising and societal issues, including advertising's impact on media content, advertising regulation, and the social construction of advertising. Additionally, he is an expert on paradigmatically qualitative research. His work has appeared in journals such as the *Journal of Advertising,* the *Journal of Current Issues and Research in Advertising,* the *Journal of Advertising Research,* and *Mass Media and Society.*

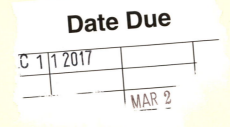